HUMAN RESOURCE MANAGEMENT

The Public Service Perspective

W. David Patton
Boise State University

Stephanie L. Witt
Boise State University

Nicholas P. Lovrich
Washington State University

Patricia J. Fredericksen
Boise State University

Houghton Mifflin Company   Boston   New York

Sponsoring Editor: Mary Dougherty
Development Editor: Katherine Meisenheimer
Associate Project Editor: Elisabeth Kehrer
Editorial Assistant: Christine Skeete
Associate Production/Design Coordinator: Christine Gervais
Manufacturing Manager: Florence Cadran
Marketing Manager: Jay Hu

Cover image: Harold Burch, NYC

Credits
Chapter 1: Reading: Sally Kraus Marshall and Marylou Whelan, "Changing Roles for Human Resources Professionals," 25 Years from *The Bureaucrat* to *The Public Manager,* Winter 1996–1997, 1996, pp. 27–29. Reprinted by permission of The Bureaucrat, Inc.

All other credits appear on page 448, which constitutes an extension of the copyright page.

Printed in the U.S.A.

Library of Congress Control Number: 2001131542

ISBN: 0-395-91814-6

3456789-DOC-05

Contents

1 New Roles, Directions, and Issues in Public Human Resource Management   1

2 The Changing Work Environment   14

15   New Roles and Competencies for Human Resource Management   391

Case Appendix   409

Topical Table of Contents

Table of Readings

Preface

After many years of teaching courses in Human Resource Management (HRM) for present and prospective public sector managers, it has become clear that a text was needed that addressed several important needs. Like most other teachers of HRM, we found ourselves searching for three or four books that could address all of the components of the course. First, we needed a textbook to discuss the functions performed in public HRM. Second, we selected a reader to introduce students to important documents and scholarly literature. Then we would add another book to address current issues of importance to the profession, and finally we would adopt a case/exercise book to provide examples and to apply the principles and practices learned to real-life settings.

OBJECTIVES

With these needs in mind, we established the following objectives for the text:

Objective 1.   Introduce the important purposes of public HRM (such as staffing the organization and protecting merit principles); the techniques used to accomplish those purposes; the applicable laws; and the values inherent in public service decisions (such as equity, responsiveness, and efficiency). Consider carefully the overall purposes of HRM to ensure that the goal of service to the public is not sacrificed to process and procedures, leading to a "triumph of technique over purpose."

Objective 2.   Provide exercises that will give students the opportunity to practice their skills after being introduced to both the core concepts and main techniques of public HRM.

Objective 3.   Facilitate instruction of the material by introducing important topics and issues with readings from the professional literature. We believe that the perspective of several important authors in the field can augment the experience and perspective of the student and the instructor.

Objective 4.   Provide information and examples that demonstrate the interrelatedness of many of the topics encountered in public sector HRM and the trends that have emerged in the field recently. We have highlighted three main themes throughout the text: diversity, ethics, and technology. We have also integrated several emerging contemporary issues, including service to the organization, the changing workforce, ongoing personnel reform efforts, service delivery through nongovernmental actors, and job relatedness.

Objective 5.   Demonstrate and describe the differences among HRM practices and values in public, for-profit, and nonprofit organizations. The public sector's increased reliance on nonprofit organizations for service delivery requires some discussion of

HRM practice in the nonprofit environment. We also know that a significant number of students who take this course will work in the nonprofit sector, so we have included specific information and numerous illustrative examples that will be helpful to them.

THE DESIGN OF THE BOOK

To accomplish these objectives, we have organized this textbook to provide a number of useful tools for teaching students about the issues, purposes, and techniques of public HRM and for enabling them to perform the functions of the profession. We have combined the following tools into a single text so that all the components useful for learning about public sector HRM would be available in a single source. Thus, each chapter includes:

- One or more selected readings intended to introduce major topical areas in public HRM
- Substantial discussion of the concepts and practices of each important subject
- A discussion of three important themes (diversity, ethics, and technology) throughout the book
- Examples drawn from actual HRM offices in state, local, and federal government agencies
- A listing of key terms used in the readings and chapter discussion
- Study questions designed to provoke thought and lively discussion in each topical area
- Applied exercises that allow students to practice the skills utilized in public HRM
- Case studies to help students consider important principles and apply them to realistic professional settings

As we noted above, each chapter includes one or more notable readings that illuminate the subject of the chapter. These readings are drawn from the academic and professional literature, and they present issues or problems in HRM and introduce the subject for further discussion in the text. (See the Table of Readings on p. xiii.)

Each chapter also provides a thorough discussion of the subject matter with extensive references to relevant literature. The principles and practices of HRM are presented using a practical approach, with emphasis on helping students understand both the how and the why of HRM activities.

We have included many examples of actual forms and processes to help students see what is being described in the chapter and to expose them to typical documents, systems, and procedures that they will encounter on the job. In addition, current issues and trends in HRM are included in chapter discussions to help students consider the problems confronted by modern HRM professionals. (See the Topical Table of Contents on p. xi.)

At the end of each chapter, we have included several tools to promote thoughtful discussion and a better understanding of the chapter material. Key terms, study questions, and exercises are included so that students can review the terminology used in public sector HRM, study the concepts presented in the chapter, and practice the methods and techniques described. Case studies are also provided, highlighting actual situations found in public and nonprofit organizations across the country. These cases are located in an appendix at the end of the text (see the Table of Cases and Relevant Chapters located on p. 409 of the Appendix), and guidelines for their use are provided at the end of each chapter.

The textbook is organized into fifteen chapters. The first group of chapters discusses the environment of public sector HRM. Public managers exist in a dynamic, political, and legalistic environment. Chapter One introduces the student to the potentially conflicting roles of HRM in organizations today and describes important public service, demographic, and technological trends that are affecting the function of HRM in the public workplace. Chapter Two examines dramatic changes in public service delivery, workforce demographics, and technology occurring in the public work environment. Chapter Three describes the important differences between HRM in the public, for-profit, and nonprofit sectors and guides the student through the evolution of the civil service system in the United States. Chapter Four discusses the web of public employee rights and restrictions that are granted as a result of the laws that apply to the public workplace. Chapter Five addresses the unique aspects of public sector labor-management relations and the trends and important steps involved in labor negotiations.

The second group of chapters deals with the techniques of human resource management necessary for employing a competent workforce. Chapter Six discusses the need for strategic planning to meet the HRM needs of public organizations as they encounter changes in their service missions, diversity in their workforce, and the aging of their workers. Chapter Seven discusses job analysis and classification as the basis of most HRM functions. Chapter Eight illustrates the design, analysis, and classification of jobs by describing how organizations recruit and select qualified candidates to fill needed jobs. Chapter Nine addresses employee compensation and the underlying principles used to develop a fair and competitive compensation plan. Chapter Ten continues with a presentation of mandatory and voluntary benefits commonly used in the public sector and a discussion of the administration of public benefit plans.

The third group of chapters addresses the development of public human resources into a high performing workforce. Chapter Eleven responds to the heightened call for improved productivity and performance of public sector employees through a discussion of technical issues in performance appraisal and the implications for organization-wide assessment in performance management systems. Training and development is the subject of Chapter Twelve. As government agencies become more responsive and flexible, human resource development (HRD) will become an increasingly important function of HRM professionals. Chapter Thirteen extends the discussion of performance management and employee development with a survey of issues and practices relating to employee discipline and termination. Chapter Fourteen discusses the need for and use of policies and procedures in the public workplace. Many policies and procedures are established through a centralized HRM department, but small public jurisdictions and nonprofit organizations may find this chapter to be of particular use. The concluding chapter addresses the competencies needed to understand how the HRM system works in the organization and to be successful in the field.

ACKNOWLEDGMENTS

We would like to acknowledge the wonderful working relationship experienced among the authors, Dave, Steph, Nick, and Patti, and with the publisher as we progressed on the text. Special thanks go to Katherine Meisenheimer and Elisabeth Kehrer at Houghton Mifflin. We are grateful as well for the support rendered to the authors by Boise State University and Washington State University in the form of timely sabbatical leaves and administrative support. We are particularly grateful to our loved ones for their patience, support, and professed interest during the writing and editing of this text, especially Wendy Patton and Andy Giacomazzi.

We are also grateful to the many people who read drafts of this book and provided us with suggestions for improving it: J. Norman Baldwin, University of Alabama; Peter J. Bergerson, Southeast Missouri State University; William Chappell, Columbus State University; Dennis M. Daley, North Carolina State University; Kathryn G. Denhardt, University of Delaware; Steven W. Hays, University of South Carolina; Florence Heffron, University of Idaho; Patricia Ingraham, Syracuse University; Douglas Ihrke, University of Wisconsin-Milwaukee; Donna R. Kemp, California State University, Chico; Renford Reese, California State Polytechnic University, Pomona; Sally Coleman Selden, Syracuse University; Ronald D. Sylvia, San Jose State University; and Edward M. Wheat, University of Southern Mississippi.

CHAPTER 1

New Roles, Directions, and Issues in Public Human Resource Management

Personnelists as we have known them are becoming obsolete.[1]

What's in a name? Why is this book titled *Human Resource Management: The Public Service Perspective* rather than, say, *Public Personnel Management?* The change in focus from personnel to human resource management (HRM) points to the broadening role that **personnel specialists** play in an organization. HRM is no longer confined to the narrow set of techniques associated with the old personnel function. As our opening reading by Sally Kraus Marshall and Mary Lou Whelan points out, the HRM function is taking on a consultative role to management within organizations, and many established personnel procedures are being abandoned to increase organizational flexibility and provide greater agency-level responsiveness to both internal and external clientele needs. This chapter discusses the *internal* changes occurring within the HRM profession. The next chapter focuses on the *external* changes in the work environment that affect HRM. Contemporary public sector managers need to understand these developments to make proper use of the new dynamism and innovative thinking that characterize this field.

INTRODUCTION TO READING

Our reading for this section discusses the change in role of public personnel from "system police" to a decidedly more consultative role. Personnel

specialists (or "personnelists") have long been considered outside the important functions of the organization. A study conducted by the National Academy of Public Administration in 1983 found that executives and line managers felt "almost totally divorced from what should be one of their most important systems."[2] The same study also confirmed that personnelists spent the bulk of their time on mechanical procedures and paperwork rather than on consulting with line managers or employees on positive personnel activities.[3] Steve Hays notes that "by enforcing torrents of picky rules and regulations, personnelists drove a wedge between the staffing function and line managers. Personnel offices came to be viewed as impediments to be overcome rather than allies in the pursuit of effective management."[4]

As you read the following selection by Marshall and Whelan, consider the following questions:

- Why do the authors say that "personnelists are becoming obsolete"?
- What will the shift from "people issues" to "people-related issues" mean for the role of HR managers in organizations?
- Do you think that the changes that Marshall and Whelan discuss will change the common perception of personnel offices as "impediments to be overcome"?

READING

Changing Roles for Human Resources Professionals

SALLY KRAUS MARSHALL AND MARYLOU WHELAN

> Personnel or human resources office: No matter what it is called, it must change. Personnelists as we have known them are becoming obsolete.

Federal human resources (HR) professionals must prepare to meet the challenges and assume the roles that are required for them to become strategic players in the management of federal human resources—people. While it is clear that HR programs, systems, and laws need to be reformed, these changes alone will not accomplish the needed transformation. Nor can the HR community afford to wait for Congress, new technology, or other influences to force change. Only by empowering the people who are providing HR services will the transformation occur in time to have an impact on the greater organizational evolution of government reinvention.

There is a growing concern in the business community about the purpose and value of the traditional personnel office and the question is equally appropriate in the federal government. A key component of the reinvention movement has been to question the added value of HR resources and staff in accomplishing agency missions and objectives. Examining the current and future roles and contributions of the personnel or the HR office provides a framework for defining and, as needed, changing the occupation and its work.

THE NEED TO CHANGE

Personnelists as we have known them are becoming obsolete. Their roles are changing and their numbers are shrinking. There is an almost overwhelming perception among federal managers and employees that the personnel office and its occupants are over-specialized, unresponsive, and/or inefficient.

Many personnelists feel like they are working in a monolith that needs to be modernized but they are unable to decide how or where to begin the re-building process. Others are wearing blinders and ignoring the signs of change. A few are redefining themselves and their roles to become human resources consultants, advisors and leaders. Unfortunately the odds of their succeeding are not high without a collective HR community shift in attitude.

Federal HR professionals have become increasingly aware of their vulnerability by the elimination of the *Federal Personnel Manual* and the National Performance Review's (NPR) identification of HR programs as in need of reinvention. Their traditional sense of security has been broken. As agencies deal with shrinking resources, line managers are more likely to seek and support only those services that add value to their programs.

Within this framework, HR programs and the roles, tasks, and responsibilities of HR staffs are receiving a great deal of attention. The 1993 NPR report on *Reinventing Human Resource Management* labels HR staffs as "the system's police" when they ought to be considered as part of an agency's management team. Similar findings come from a Merit Systems Protection Board study, *Federal Personnel Offices: Time for Change?* Comments from line managers reflect their concerns about their servicing HR organizations.

To change its focus and image, the HR community needs to identify the roles and characteristics, or competencies, that will transform HR professionals into business partners. These roles and competencies, once identified and defined, can then be used to develop a working model for staffing federal HR organizations. Professionals who have acquired and

Source: *Public Manager* (Winter 1996–1997).

mastered the competencies identified for success will effectively use their knowledges, skills, abilities, and other characteristics to contribute to mission accomplishment.

STRATEGY FOR CHANGE

This article outlines a strategy for change in the nature of HR work and how it is delivered and includes a model for achieving change. The model concentrates on the *new* compentencies needed in the work environment of a reinvented government organization. It also lays a foundation for applying the model. The article is based on a report, *A Competency Model for Human Resources Professionals,* published in 1996 by the National Academy of Public Administration (NAPA).

The purposes of developing a new competency model are to:

- Redefine the role of the HR organization and staff in federal agencies;
- Define the knowledges, skills, abilities, and other traits, that is, the competencies, needed by the HR professional;
- Establish the framework for building a performance-oriented and mission-driven HR organization;
- Design an approach to transform the federal human resources management program, HR leadership, and agency HR staffs;
- Identify and incorporate the best practices from private and public sector HR organizations into the design;
- Provide a tool for hiring, developing, and assessing the performance of HR staff members;
- Establish a framework for internal strategic and workforce planning for HR; and
- Define variances in competencies for different organizations, positions, and roles.

HR COMPETENCY MODEL: A DRIVER FOR CHANGE

The competency model developed for the federal HR community emulates a jigsaw puzzle. Each piece is critical—its shape, size, and placement determined by the level, task orientation, and role of the position in the serviced organization's mission and culture. The model can be rearranged as agency customer and organizational needs warrant.

Competency Model for HR Professionals

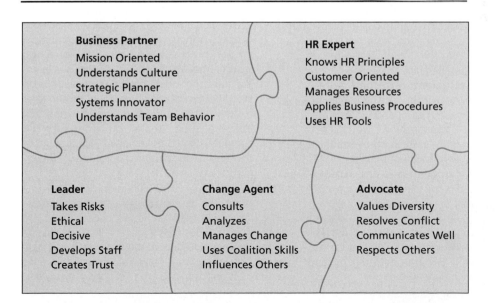

Business Partner
Mission Oriented
Understands Culture
Strategic Planner
Systems Innovator
Understands Team Behavior

HR Expert
Knows HR Principles
Customer Oriented
Manages Resources
Applies Business Procedures
Uses HR Tools

Leader
Takes Risks
Ethical
Decisive
Develops Staff
Creates Trust

Change Agent
Consults
Analyzes
Manages Change
Uses Coalition Skills
Influences Others

Advocate
Values Diversity
Resolves Conflict
Communicates Well
Respects Others

The model identifies five roles for the "new" HR professional. It can be tailored to fit the work culture and requirements of the organizations serviced. Each role is identified by its competencies, selected from a menu of competencies which has been compiled into a dictionary. The competencies in the model are not static; which ones define which role may vary with the agency and its needs.

NAPA's competency model is a roadmap for developing the HR professional of the future. The model is intended to be flexible, subject to modification and refinement as experience and customer needs warrant. The HR community can also use it as a tool to begin the self-examination process necessary for making effective change in *who* they are and *how* they do business.

STRATEGY FOR IMPLEMENTATION

A literature review and an examination of federal and private sector models identified seven essential steps that are needed to transform HR programs and develop new staff roles and competencies. All seven of these steps are critical and appear in some form in organizations that have successfully used a competency model. The seven-step strategy follows.

1. **Agree on the *need* to transform.** The need may be driven by budget cuts and downsizing threats, staff desire for new roles, customer demands for service, or application of new information and systems technology. The need to change may be directed from the top of the organization or self-identified by HR staff leadership or membership.

2. **Develop a statement reflecting agreement on the new role.** The role may be defined in a mission, vision, and values statement for the HR organization. The role certainly must integrate with the organizational mission, vision, and values statement.

3. **Identify roles, competencies, and accountability.** Covered in the identification are articulated customer needs, including those of line executives and managers, and assessment of the organization and its culture. Results should be validated by interviews with high performing HR staff, customers, and managers. Benchmarking data with other HR organizations may also be of value. It is im-

portant to build or adapt a competency model for *your* HR organization.

4. **Communicate roles and competencies throughout the organization.** This communication should occur not only within the HR community, but with customers/stakeholders as well. The model should be applied in recruiting, promoting, training, and rewarding all employees. It should be used to assign accountability and to evaluate staff performance.

5. **Establish the process to gain the competencies.** The process must include training and career development opportunities. It is important to clarify employee responsibility and accountability for gaining proficiency in the required competencies. Reinforcing mechanisms, in the form of rewards and recognition for achieving desired results and identification of the consequences for failure to change, should be provided. It may also be necessary to develop transition strategies for employees who are unable or unwilling to gain new competencies.

6. **Measure results of the HR staff's impact on mission.** Linkage to the Government Performance and Results Act (GPRA) and its organizational performance measures will aid in insuring results. Each HR professional's individual performance planning and evaluation process must be tied to and measured in the performance management process.

7. **Correct, adjust, and improve the transformation process based on experience and results obtained.** Establish continuous learning and continuous change as a way of life in the HR organization. Competencies and roles will not remain static over time. It is important to maintain an HR staff profile of skills and competencies compatible with fluctuations in the mission and business objectives of the organizations serviced.

Together, the model and the strategy illustrate how to manage the shift from "people issues" to "people-related business issues" so that the change process will produce an organization staffed by high performers who in turn make valuable contributions to the high performance organizations they support and service.

Once the agency has made the decision to start the change process as described in the first step and clearly spelled out its mission as described in step two, it must also verify that the competency model fits the organization. The purposes for using the model, the priority of the competencies sought, and the clarity and ease with which the competencies can be identified and measured are just a few of the considerations which must be accounted for in adopting and/or adapting the model to a specific HR staff and work environment.

Implementing a competency model effectively requires that the HR organization start the process using a business planning approach such as that described above. The implementation effort must also be specific to the needs of the customer organization's culture, mission, workload priorities, and performance requirements and measures. HR leaders and senior managers have a potential opportunity to test the usefulness and practicality of a strategic partnership when they are developing the agency's GPRA performance plan.

NEXT STEPS

A plan and a curriculum to develop the new competencies in HR professionals and to train them in their use are key to applying the model. Such efforts will require continuous learning experiences. Experiences will differ depending on the size, mission, and resources of the customer the HR staffer supports. The HR director of a large agency would find the report a starting place for action in terms of strategic workforce planning three to five years out. While the director of a small agency will also be doing strategic planning, it is more likely to be shorter range planning about outsourcing, cross-servicing, and other alternatives for coping with current workload. Development of training curricula, customizing the model to meet agency-specific needs, and refining the competency process to revitalize and motivate the federal HR workforce are part of the *next steps* to be considered in using this model as a tool for change.

TRENDS IN HUMAN RESOURCE MANAGEMENT

A recent study by the Long-Range Strategic Planning Committee of the International Personnel Management Association identified the major trends affecting HRM.[5] These trends reinforce the changing role of HR within the organization discussed in the HRM competency model set out in the reading. Following are these top HR trends and how we integrate them in this book:

1. Information technology: electronic commerce and communication (addressed throughout the book)
2. New role for HR as business partner/internal consultant (Chapter 1)
3. Globalization of HR (throughout the book)
4. New partnerships, particularly in the labor management relations area (Chapter 5)
5. Worklife issues: humanizing the workplace, family leave, flextime, telecommuting (Chapters 7 and 10)
6. Shifting demographics: diversity, labor pool shortages, shorter tenure of workers (Chapter 2)
7. Leadership development: employee development, retraining, need for continuous learning (Chapters 11 and 12)
8. Compensation packages: alternate reward packages, new practices in benefits packages (Chapter 10)
9. Selection process and new values: shift from knowledge, skills, and abilities (KSAs) to behaviors (Chapter 8)
10. Decentralization: shifting decision making closer to the customer (Chapter 2)
11. Managing change: downsizing, accountability, increased politicization, privatization, flexibility in systems, increased deregulation of HR authority (Chapters 1, 2, 3, 6)

Each of these trends represents a challenge to HR professionals and established practices in personnel management in the public sector. Many of them will require HR professionals to develop new skills and perspectives while working more closely with line managers. In addition, line managers must acquire the skills and knowledge about HRM in the public sector that had been previously shifted to a centralized HR department. We emphasize the importance of these skills throughout the book and develop them in particular detail in Chapter 15.

PUBLIC AND NONPROFIT SECTOR DIFFERENCES

Human resource management in the public sector differs from personnel management in the for-profit sector in several important ways. There are in particular two noteworthy constraints present in public sector management practices that are not encountered in the private sector.

Absence of a bottom line. For-profit organizations normally can judge their success or failure by the presence or absence of a profit or the proportion of market share. There is no such bottom line in the public or nonprofit sector. The public sector must be responsive to many values in addition to efficiency and effectiveness—such as inclusiveness, equal treatment, advance public notification, and public involvement—which may slow program activities or make them inefficient in financial terms. Budgets in the public sector are set by elected officials who may increase or decrease budget levels in response to political pressure that may have little connection to considerations of actual efficiency or effectiveness. As in the public sector, nonprofit organizations may have little control over revenue generated or the demand for services in particular communities at different times.

The role of citizens, elected officials, and the media. Citizens in a democratic society generally expect that government actions will be open to scrutiny by the public (or the press acting as public watchdog). As a consequence, HRM in the public sector is answerable to many more constituencies than HRM staff in the for-profit or nonprofit sectors. Nonprofit organizations may have a bit more discretion over management ac-

tivities within the organization and potentially less legal responsibility to disclose decisions publicly. However, staffing decisions in the nonprofit sector may also be subject to scrutiny by constituents and decisions made by an oversight board rather than individual managers. Civil service protections simply do not exist in the nonprofit sector. In the nonprofit sector, as in the for-profit sector, due process tends to be a lower priority than the maintenance of managerial discretion. In the public sector, due process is a deeply held value and constitutes a foundational element of the structure of democratic government in the United States.

VALUES IN PUBLIC HRM

In the midst of all this change, what are the key values that ought to inform the practice of human resource management in the public sector? Scholars have recommended many values as guides for the profession of HRM in general. One prominent study called for renewed attention to issues of accountability, diversity, justice, and culture.[6] We largely concur with this judgment, and set out here the key elements of each of these areas of core values considerations.

Accountability

With management discretion and flexibility should come strict **accountability.** Public managers are accountable to a variety of people and institutions, but unless that accountability is defined as both hierarchical and democratic, public managers run the risk of not being as responsive to the citizenry as they should be.[7]

In the hierarchy of agencies, public managers are directly accountable to their superiors. This reporting relationship is typically formalized in written and verbal reporting mechanisms, and is expressed ultimately in a performance appraisal system.[8] In the larger picture, however, public managers are accountable to the public through their elected representatives in the executive and legislative branches of government. In many cases, public managers have considerable discretion over the use of their authority and resources, and they must make decisions based on their own perception of the public good. In these instances, the law and professional codes of ethics provide some guidance to managers. Empirical evidence would seem to indicate that individuals with discretion tend to focus their work on where they believe they will be held accountable.[9] A student who knows she will be tested on the names of South American countries, for example, is likely to study Latin America diligently. The same is true with public sector managers and human resource professionals. Establishing clear lines of accountability in HRM will help to reconcile the benefits of flexible and responsive public administration with the necessary goals of due process and equity.

Diversity

Most attention to issues of **diversity** has centered on race, gender, and ethnicity. Often these issues have come to public attention because of exclusionary practices and longstanding disparities in employment patterns, promotional opportunities, and occupational representation. Significant effort has been made to address these issues of diversity, but work in this area is far from complete. We may find a more faithful reflection of society in public workplaces generally than in the past, but this is not yet the case at some levels of management and in many professional positions.

Beyond the familiar issues of gender, race, and ethnic diversity we must consider the broader question of comprehensive diversity in the public workplace. Is it important to have individuals in public service who represent the various races and ethnicities found in American society? Should diversity in staffing encompass a broader definition of a diverse workforce: range of experience, type of training or academic discipline, religion, culture, or physical ability, for example? In a democratic society, are there proper reasons to seek a diverse workforce other than satisfying the hope of reflecting the characteristics of jurisdiction being served?

One premise behind workplace diversity policies is that the variety of experiences and perspectives that employees have combine to benefit the organization in ways that are not possible with a homogeneous workforce. This hypothesis has an intuitive appeal consistent with the American tradition of open arms to the world's peoples, but it has remained largely untested.

Many factors enter into the effects of diversity on organizations, including social climate dynamics and the interplay of cultural values of people of differing backgrounds. With the variety of influences present in diverse groups, it is difficult to separate the causes and effects of organizational dynamics. The nature of diversity itself promotes new ways of looking at issues and occasions the consideration of various cultural perspectives in thinking through workplace problems. On the other hand, work group cohesiveness tends to be stronger in homogeneous work groups.[10] The implications of diversity for HRM have many dimensions; consequently, the subject is discussed throughout this book.

Justice and Equity

Human resource managers are the guardians of deeply held values in public organizations, including the core values of justice and **equity.** In HRM, justice is often thought of in terms of comparability with other employees or other similar organizations. It is important that employees perceive that their work is rewarded fairly as they compare their compensation and their responsibilities with other employees doing similar or comparable work. This comparison is a measure of *internal equity* from the perspective of the employee. Similarly, employees will look at comparable organizations to determine if salaries, benefits, and working conditions are at parity (*external equity*). (The use of equity in developing compensation systems is discussed in considerable depth in Chapter 9.) For example, we often hear about the differences among the public, for-profit, and nonprofit sectors in working conditions and compensation. These perceptions and the implications for HRM are addressed throughout this book.

The term organizational justice, however, entails more than simply comparing levels of compensation. Human resource managers are responsible to uphold the principles of justice and equity in several aspects of an employee's interaction with the organization. Beginning with the functions of recruitment and selection, human resource managers should be increasingly aware of the need to maintain equity and justice for all applicants, candidates, and newly hired employees with respect to employee development decisions, promotions, and the use of discipline. Employees expect the organization to be fair and just in all of its dealings with them, from the hiring process to providing opportunity for grievance against an action by management.[11] Human resource managers must also be aware of citizen perceptions of organizational equity and justice. Ideally, the public perceives their public agencies to be fair to their employees and equitable to all citizens who would approach this aspect of government for assistance of services. In some cases, the public perception of equity and justice is out of the hands of HRM, such as in the case of public hearings or scheduled deliberations of the legislative body; HRM can, however, set the standard for providing appropriate processes for equity and justice in public organizations.

Organizational Culture

Human resource managers are in a unique position to influence the beliefs and values of public organizations, that is, to help mold their **organizational cultures.**[12] Many of the recommendations for change in public organizations involve structural reorganization and alterations in management practices intended to decentralize decision making and enhance the participation of employees and citizens. Such restructuring and administrative methods work best in environments where the organizational culture is receptive, that is,

open to change and experimentation. For example, implementing a program of management flexibility in an environment of tight organizational control is largely self-defeating. The human resource manager can facilitate the communication of organizational values to employees and the public through its delegation of traditional HRM functions and the symbolic demonstration of the values held within the organization. An organization whose hiring practices consistently follow legitimate procedures, for example, sends a message about how it operates and adheres to publicly stated policy. Hiring that is done surreptitiously to circumvent the rules conveys the message that rules are not important and that managers are on their own when it comes to employment practices. With the role of HRM extending from rules enforcement to a more facilitative partnership with line supervisors, human resource managers need to be aware of the message they are sending through the symbols and values they portray.

Ethics

Every rule was devised for a reason. As we discuss in some depth in Chapter 3, civil service rules have been the source of much management frustration and the repeated target of reform. We should remember, however, that these rules were put into place for what were considered legitimate reasons at the time. We have whistle-blowing rules because people had been fired for pointing out internal corruption. There are rules to guide how an organization undergoes a reduction in force because somewhere, at some time in the past, someone had to decide how to lay off workers in the midst of a financial crisis. The rules can become cumbersome, but they are there to ensure an important principle. Similarly, rules were established for hiring procedures so that all applicants have a fair opportunity to fill public jobs. The most onerous (say many public managers) are the rules created for disciplining or firing public employees. Procedures for disciplinary action or termination were put into place to protect competent employees from the political strong-arm tactics of elected officials. Unfortunately, these rules have become intricate and cumbersome over time, severely limiting public managers in their ability to achieve higher productivity in the workplace. As reform efforts expand managerial discretion, we must maintain the balance between the values of flexibility and latitude and the strength of due process rules protecting the values of fairness and consistency. These are key elements of justice in any organization.

This need for balance does not diminish the importance of reform efforts. Ongoing improvement and innovation, particularly in the area of HRM practice, are critical. Legitimate reform efforts should always be seriously evaluated for the benefits they can provide in accomplishing the mission and objectives of public service. For example, reform efforts in public human resource management have centered on streamlining hiring and testing procedures, and developing effective performance management systems. Each of these recent reforms is discussed in the relevant chapter of this book.

THE ROLE OF HUMAN RESOURCE MANAGEMENT IN ORGANIZATIONS

The Difference Between Line and Staff Positions

It has been traditional to distinguish between line and staff positions in an organization. Personnel, or human resource management, has traditionally been considered a staff function. **Line positions** are in "the direct chain of command that [are] responsible for the achievement of an organization's goals."[13] **Staff positions,** in contrast, provide "expertise, advice, and support for line positions."[14] Line and staff positions often exercise different kinds of authority. Line positions are part of the organization's hierarchy and possess the authority that comes with the chain of command. Staff positions, however, may have only advisory authority (that is, to offer advice), or they may have limited functional authority, "which is formal or

legitimate authority over activities related [only] to the staff member's specialty."[15]

HRM is a classic example of a staff function. Although in many cases it has functional authority over types of selection processes and procedures for compliance with equal employment opportunity law, HRM's authority in regard to strategic planning and other employee-related issues typically is exclusively advisory. As a consequence, there is often tension between line and staff positions; line managers frequently perceive HRM staff as a threat to their own authority.[16] In many cases, there are also demographic differences between the two groups. "Line managers tend to be older, to be less well-educated, and to have risen through the ranks of the organization."[17] Staff specialists generally are younger, better educated, and more likely to have been hired directly into upper-level staff positions. These line-staff tensions contribute to the feeling among many managers that HRM exists outside the mainstream of the organization.

The successful reintegration of HRM into the larger organization would solve a longstanding problem linked to the dual roles that the public personnel function has played in the United States. It has a positive role to play—for example, in helping management to select qualified employees. At the same time, however, HRM also plays the role of guardian of the merit system,[18] a function frequently viewed negatively by line managers. The role of guardian of the merit system has dominated HRM, leading to Sayre's critique that public personnel administration too often represents "a triumph of technique over purpose."[19] Managers often do not find HRM helpful in getting their work done, and in fact they tend to share the view that the HRM office presents an obstacle course of rules and regulations that too often need to be circumvented for the public sector manager to be successful.

The Competency Model

The **competency model of HRM,** discussed in the chapter reading selection, illustrates a more comprehensive role for HRM in the organization. The literature refers to this new role as "strategic human resource management."[20] It is argued that the HR function is strategic in three specific ways.[21]

First, HRM contributes to the organization's overall performance. Technological and financial differences between organizations tend to equalize over time, but the quality and motivation of the human resources commanded by an organization can allow an organization to maintain a competitive edge over other organizations. This is particularly important with for-profit or nonprofit firms that are seeking competitive advantage, but is also important for public agencies faced with competition from privatization, nonprofit service providers, or neighboring jurisdictions and state or federal agencies. HRM officials can advocate best practices that will be most beneficial to the organization's performance.[22] Some of these practices are:[23]

- Recruiting with intensity
- Making timely selection
- Employing an enriched job design process
- Gaining broad access to training
- Making use of development-oriented performance appraisal
- Employing incentive compensation
- Developing clear criteria for promotion
- Providing fair grievance procedures
- Engaging in broad information sharing
- Conducting periodic workforce attitude assessments
- Encouraging collaborative labor-management participation

The HRM professionals who convince their managers to adopt these best practices are contributing greatly to their organization's success.

The second strategic role of HRM is to link HRM practices and processes to specific strategies that the organization adopts. The failure to link HRM practices with organizational strategies may account for much of the friction between line managers and HRM officials.[24] For example, when an organization is seeking to improve its

competitive position in research, HRM must find high-quality researchers and provide appropriate compensation and training programs to retain them. This type of cooperation between HRM and management has not been the norm in public agencies; too frequently agency managers have sought to recruit and hire employees with particular critical skills who would help them achieve policy goals, while HRM resisted exceptions to established selection criteria in the name of upholding merit rules. The need for compatibility between managerial needs and the dictates of equitable treatment of applicants requires HRM systems that are at once flexible and principled.

The third strategic HRM role is to align HRM policies and practices with the structure and culture of the organization.[25] When HRM practices do not fit well within their organizational context, the overall effectiveness of the organization suffers.[26] A number of personnel practices depend on the compatibility of the organization. For example, a complex benefit plan may be inappropriate for a fast-food restaurant, or a classic bureaucratic pyramid structure may not be conducive to participatory management practices. Similarly, experience has shown that cooperative labor-management relations are difficult to implement in organizations with long histories of labor-management conflict.

Not only are HR professionals to be HR experts—that is, acting in the traditional role of merit system protector—but they are also increasingly expected to be strategic managers as well. Part of being a strategic manager entails becoming a leader in developing staff. Hays and Kearney's study of personnelists indicated that this function, which includes a priority focus on training and employee development activities, would be the primary concern and most central activity of HRM by the year 2008.[27] As the competency model diagram in the Marshall and Whelan reading indicates, the role of change agent is based on a consultative approach to HRM operations. Taken together, these changes require a deemphasizing of the distinction between line and staff, with HRM becoming a key part of an effective management team in common pursuit of a strategic plan of action.[28] We extend this discussion in Chapter 6 with an overview of human resource management in the context of strategic planning.

One feature of this transformation from traditional personnel to strategic human resource management is that line managers acquire much more power over personnel decisions. This change creates a critical training and development need for supervisory and management personnel because few line managers have had any formal training in recruitment, selection, and retention practices. The International Personnel Management Association has developed a guide for HR offices to make available to line managers, which is intended to help administrators understand the range of their HR responsibilities.[29] Hays notes that meeting this need in a time when many public sector HR offices have been downsized will be difficult.[30]

ORGANIZATIONAL LOCATION OF THE HUMAN RESOURCES FUNCTION

The HRM function can be located in several alternative places within an organization. Many governmental jurisdictions have a **central HR agency;** the North Carolina Office of State Personnel and the City of Atlanta Department of Personnel and Human Resources represent such centralized offices. Other jurisdictions place the human resource function within an administrative agency, such as the Human Resource Services Division in the Oregon Department of Administrative Services. In a small jurisdiction, the city clerk or city manager's office is likely to carry out the HR function. Many large functional agencies also include HR functionaries. For example, a large state department of transportation or health and welfare may have its own HR office within the agency.

When a central HR agency is used, cooperation with operating agency line managers may be more challenging because the HR staff may be unfamiliar with the work of the agency. On the other hand, when HRM is handled by each operating agency without a central HR agency, it is more difficult to coordinate (or control) HR activities across the various agencies of the jurisdiction. For an organization to have line and staff positions, it does need to be sizable. Many nonprofit organizations and some very small public jurisdictions may have no such distinction.

A 1998 study conducted by the International Personnel Management Association and the National Association of State Personnel Executives featured a survey of human resource practices among the members of these organizations. The study found that most respondents (66 percent) maintain a centralized personnel agency.[31] The central HR agency was most likely to be responsible for the following types of activities:

- Recruiting (83 percent)
- Compensation administration (81 percent)
- HR planning (75 percent)
- Benefits administration (74 percent)
- Establishing lists of qualified candidates (75 percent)
- Labor-employee relations (73 percent)
- Applicant testing (73 percent)
- Certifying qualified candidates (70 percent)
- Position control (66 percent)

The same study found that operating agency line managers were most likely to be responsible for the following activities:

- Interviewing (67 percent)
- Hiring (52 percent)
- Training (48 percent)[32]

Changing the role of HRM within the organization, as the chapter reading described, will require a new look at these responsibilities and who is responsible for them.

■ CONCLUSION

The consultative role that the competency model of HRM presents entails broadening the role of HRM within the organization and making public sector managers more responsible for understanding HRM policies and practices. HRM is changing its role from that of system police to that of helping line managers accomplish the recruitment, selection, retention, training, and compensation tasks required to maintain a high-quality workforce. There are many new initiatives in human resource management, each addressing current issues in specific functions of HRM, such as issues of gender equity in employee compensation and employee rights when promoting the policy of a drug-free workplace. Probably the greatest demands for reform come as a result of important changes occurring in the public workplace. The face of government reflects changes in our society, gradually changing in age and racial and ethnic composition as the workforce becomes more diversified. There are more women and minorities in the workforce than ever before, and the average age of workers is increasing. Public agencies are becoming more accepting of employees with disabilities and learning how to deal professionally with female and minority coworkers and managers. Citizens are asking for better services and are demanding that public spending be restrained.

The next chapter addresses these demographic changes and changes in public expectations and how public agencies are responding with alternative employment arrangements and service delivery methods. Other chapters discuss important issues dealing with fundamental alterations in civil service systems, questions of employee and employer rights, and innovations in HRM tech-niques that seek to improve the services delivered by HRM professionals. Human resource management is a dynamic field with increasing demands to be responsive, effective, and efficient.

■ MANAGER'S VOCABULARY

personnel specialists
accountability
diversity
equity
organizational cultures
line positions
staff positions
competency model of HRM
central HR agency

■ STUDY QUESTIONS

1. What are some of the key differences between HRM in public or private and nonprofit organizations? How do these differences affect the practice of HRM in these different types of organizations?

2. What are the pros and cons of having a centralized versus decentralized HR office?

3. What are the different perspectives of line and staff managers? How can HRM improve its overall relationship with line managers?

■ EXPERIENTIAL EXERCISES

1. What are some of the key training needs for line managers in an organization moving to decentralized HRM? Develop a list of new skills that these line managers might need to take over with regard to HRM functions.

2. In your own city or county government, how many of the "best practices" of HRM are being used now? How would you determine their use? To whom would you talk?

■ CASE APPLICABLE TO THIS CHAPTER

"The Scheduling Software Case"

■ NOTES

[1] Sally Kraus Marshall and Marylou Whelan. "Changing Roles for Human Resources Professionals," *Public Manager* (Winter 1996–1997): 27.

[2] National Academy of Public Administration (NAPA), "New Concepts for Personnel Management," in Frank J. Thompson, ed., *Classics of Public Personnel Policy,* 2nd ed. (Pacific Grove, CA: Brooks Cole, 1991).

[3] Ibid., p. 169.

[4] Steven W. Hays, "The State of the Discipline in Public Personnel Administration," *Public Administration Quarterly* (Fall 1996): 285.

[5] "Top HR Trends," *IPMA News* (September 1999): 1.

[6] Gerald R. Ferris, Wayne A. Hochwarter, M. Ronald Buckley, Gloria Harrell-Cook, and Dwight D. Frink, "Human Resources Management: Some New Directions," *Journal of Management* 25:3 (1999): 400–405.

[7] Cheryl Simrell King and Camilla Stivers, "Strategies for an Anti-Government Era," in their *Government Is Us* (Thousand Oaks, CA: Sage, 1998), pp. 196–198.

[8] Neal P. Mero and Stephan J. Motowidlo, "Effects of Rater Accountability on the Accuracy and the Favorability of Performance Ratings," *Journal of Applied Psychology* 80:4 (1995): 517–525.

[9] Philip E. Tetlock, "The Impact of Accountability on Judgment and Choice: Toward a Social Contingency Model," in Mark P. Zanna, ed., *Advances in Experimental Social Psychology* (New York: Academic Press, 1992), pp. 331–377.

[10] Warren E. Watson, Kamalesh Kumar, and Larry K. Michaelson, "Cultural Diversity's Impact on Interaction Process and Performance: Comparing Homogeneous and Diverse Task Groups," *Academy of Management Journal* 36 (1993): 590–602.

[11] Robert Folger and Russell Cropanzano, *Organizational Justice and Human Resource Management* (Thousand Oaks, CA: Sage, 1998).

[12] Robert L. Dipboye, "Structured and Unstructured Selection Interviews: Beyond the Job-Fit Model," in Gerald R. Ferris, ed., *Research in Personnel and Human Resource Management,* vol. 12 (Greenwich, CT: JAI Press, 1994), pp. 79–123.

[13] Ricky W. Griffin, *Management* (Boston: Houghton Mifflin, 1984), p. 293.

[14] Ibid.

[15] Ibid., p. 294.

[16] Ibid., p. 295.

[17] Ibid., p. 294.

[18] Jay M. Shafritz, "Position Classification: A Behavioral Analysis for the Public Service," in Thompson, ed., *Classics of Public Personnel Policy.*

[19] Wallace S. Sayre, "The Triumph of Techniques over Purpose," in Thompson, ed., *Classics of Public Personnel Policy.*

[20] Ferris et al., "Human Resources Management," pp. 385–415.

[21] Clint Chadwick and Peter Cappelli, "Alternatives to Generic Strategy Typologies in Strategic Human Resource Management," in Patrick M. Wright, Lee D. Dyer, John W. Boudreau, George T. Milkovich, eds., *Research in Personnel and Human Resources Management, Supplement 4, Strategic Human Resources Management in the 21st Century* (Greenwich, CT: JAI Press, 1999), pp. 11–29.

[22] Mark A. Huselid, "The Impact of Human Resource Management Practices on Turnover, Productivity, and Corporate Financial Performance," *Academy of Management Journal* 38 (1995): 635–672.

[23] Ibid.

[24] Randall S. Schuler, "Strategic Human Resource Management and Industrial Relations," *Human Relations* 42 (1989): 157–184.

[25] Susan E. Jackson and Randall S. Schuler, "Understanding Human Resource Management in the Context of Organizations and Their Environments," *Annual Review of Psychology* 46 (1995): 237–264.

[26] Patrick M. Wright and Scott A. Snell, "Toward a Unifying Theory for Exploring Fit and Flexibility in Strategic Human Resource Management," *Academy of Management Review* 23 (1998): 756–772.

[27] Steven W. Hays and Richard C. Kearney, "The Transformation of Public Sector Human Resource Management," University of South Carolina, Substitute of Public Affairs, working paper, 1999, p. 11.

[28] Marshall and Whelan, "Changing Roles," p. 28.

[29] "Practical Pointers: Interview Guide," *IPMA News* (November 1998): 32.

[30] Hays, "State of the Discipline," p. 289.

[31] International Personnel Management Association (IPMA), *1998 IPMA/NASPE Pilot Human Resource Benchmarking Summary Report* (Alexandria, VA: IPMA, 1998), p. 8.

[32] Ibid., p. 9.

CHAPTER 2

The Changing Work Environment

The previous chapter discussed changes within the profession of HRM—that is, internal changes. This chapter examines changes in the external HRM environment.

Successful human resource management must anticipate and cope with a rapidly changing work environment. This chapter discusses several major trends relevant to HRM: (1) the move away from traditional civil service systems and the increased use in the public sector of nontraditional service delivery mechanisms such as privatization (formal service delivery arrangements through non-governmental actors) and alternative employment arrangements such as contract workers; (2) the use of downsizing, or reductions in force, to decrease the size of the workforce; (3) changes in the demographic makeup of the workforce, including increased numbers of women and minorities; and (4) the impact of technology on HRM and the workplace generally. Each of the trends in question can affect the ability of an organization to recruit, retain, and manage its employees effectively. The readings for this chapter highlight the first three trends just noted.

INTRODUCTION TO READING

The first selection, by Donald E. Klingner and Dahlia Bradshaw Lynn, describes alternative mechanisms for delivering public services such as privatization and contracting and draws out their impact on the HRM function. As the authors note, the traditional civil service model of employment is increasingly being replaced by these alternative work relationships. HRM managers now work within a variety of personnel systems and employment arrangements. Knowledge of these alternative systems and their impact on the public personnel system will become increasingly important for human resource specialists and the managers with whom they work.

The second reading is from a General Accounting Office study that examined downsizing practices and their organizational impacts in several for-profit sector and governmental settings. The selection highlights the need for thoughtful planning and identifies some of the unintended organizational consequences that can result from poorly planned downsizing efforts.

The third reading is the executive summary to *Workforce 2000,* a study of demographic changes that will bear on the makeup of the workforce. The report documents the increased numbers of women and minorities in the workforce and the increased percentages of aging workers as well. Each of these changes represents a considerable challenge to recruiting, training, and benefits management for HRM.

As you read these selections, consider the following questions:

- How does "reinventing" an organization affect the HR processes in that organization?
- Are there any limitations to the effectiveness of private sector HRM techniques in public sector agencies?
- How can organizations best plan to cope with downsizing?
- Will an increasingly diverse workforce affect the way that HR is practiced?

▒▒▒▒ READINGS

Beyond Civil Service: The Changing Face of Public Personnel Management

DONALD E. KLINGNER AND DAHLIA BRADSHAW LYNN

Contemporary public personnel management differs from the past because it is characterized by two emergent alternatives to traditional civil service systems for delivering public services: alternative mechanisms and flexible employment relationships. These alternatives are not new, but they are more commonplace than before. And when new public programs are designed, these alternatives have largely supplanted traditional public program delivery by "permanent" civil service employees hired through appropriated funds.[1]

ALTERNATIVES TO CIVIL SERVICE

Historically, it was taken for granted that public services would be delivered by a staff of career civil service employees, working within the structure of centralized public agencies budgeted with appropriated funds. Today, none of these is true—public programs are more than likely performed by alternative organizations or mechanisms rather than by public agencies;[2] and when public agencies are used, they are more likely to be staffed by contingent workers hired through flexible employment mechanisms rather than permanent employees protected by civil service regulations and collective bargaining agreements.[3]

Alternative Mechanisms for Delivering Public Services

Purchase-of-service agreements with other governmental agencies and non-governmental organizations (NGOs) have become commonplace. For example, Metropolitan Dade County, FL, now provides fire and rescue services to almost every small- and medium-sized municipality in Dade County (the exceptions are the cities of Hialeah, Miami Beach, and Miami). These arrangements were negotiated because they offer persuasive advantages for Dade County and municipalities. For Dade County, there is the opportunity to expand services within a given

geographic area using economies of scale. For municipalities, the arrangement offers the opportunity to reduce capital costs, personnel costs, and legal liability risks. In addition, because fire fighters are heavily unionized, it offers the opportunity to avoid the immediate political and economic costs associated with collective bargaining.

As another example, many local governments contract with individual consultants or private businesses to conduct personnel services such as employee development and training.

The use of outside consultants and businesses (hired under fee-for-service arrangements on an "as needed" basis) increases available expertise and managerial flexibility by reducing the range of qualified technical and professional employees that the agency must otherwise hire to provide training. The costs of service purchase agreements may actually be lower than the same function performed by in-house personnel, in that the government agency pays no personnel costs or associated employment taxes and reduces its own legal liability risks.

Privatization is the performance of a formerly public function by a private contractor. It differs from service purchase agreements primarily in philosophy and scope. While service purchase agreements contract for delivery of a particular service to a public agency, privatization means abolition of the entire public agency, replacing the infrastructure with an outside contractor who then provides all services formerly provided by the public agency. Pri-

Source: Public Personnel Management 26 (Summer 1997).

vatization has become commonplace over the past 15 years because it offers all the advantages of service purchase agreements, but on a larger scale. Privatization has become commonplace in areas such as solid waste disposal, where there is an easily identifiable "benchmark" (standard cost and service comparison with the private sector), and where public agency costs tend to be higher because of higher pay and benefits.[4] But privatization is spreading rapidly in other areas that have previously been almost entirely the prerogative of the public sector: schools and prisons.

In 1994, the school board of a working-class Pittsburgh suburb was facing desperate problems. It had the highest tax rate in the county; only one of 40 students who took the Scholastic Achievement Test in the year from June 1993 to June 1994 scored above the national average of 950 on math and verbal test results; and the number of high school graduates plummeted from 225 in 1978 to 60 in 1994. It sent layoff notices to teachers at one of four schools and hired a Tennessee company to pick its own teachers and run the school. Not surprisingly, it made this decision over strong opposition from unionized teachers and school administrators, who intimated that the purpose was union-busting rather than educational reform. A state court issued an injunction forbidding the contact; the district is considering an appeal.[5]

In 1990 a record of over one million people were incarcerated in federal and state prisons. Despite heavy increases in prison construction, most states have been at capacity for the past five years. Privatization is one option for increasing government performance while attempting to hold down costs. During the past five years, a number of private corporations have gotten into the business of managing prisons, halfway houses, boot camps, and detention facilities. These organizations offer elected officials an alternative to public construction and management of prison facilities, which is a soaring cost for most state governments.[6]

Franchise Agreements often allow private business to monopolize a previously public function within a geographic area, charge competitive rates for it, and then pay the appropriate government a fee for the privilege. Examples are private shuttle bus companies in many major cities using vans instead of buses. The vans frequently duplicate public transportation services by "skimming" riders off of popular bus routes; but municipalities often encourage the procedure because it reduces their own costs, provides some revenue in return, and results in a continuation of a desirable public service.

Subsidy Arrangements enable private businesses to perform public services, funded either by user fees to clients or cost reimbursement from public agencies. Examples include airport security operations (provided by private contractors and paid for both by passengers and airlines), some types of hospital care (for example, emergency medical services provided by private hospitals and reimbursed by public health systems), and some higher education programs. For example, a state may choose to subsidize a private university by paying it to operate a specialized program, rather than to assign responsibility and resources for it to a public institution. It is because of subsidy arrangements that the University of Miami, a private institution with a prestigious (and expensive) medical center, receives more appropriated funds from the state of Florida than does Florida International University, the state university in Miami.

Or, local housing authorities may choose to subsidize rent in public housing projects based on tenant income to encourage occupancy by low-income residents.

Vouchers enable individual recipients of public goods or services to purchase them from competing providers on the open market. Recent public opinion has focused on educational vouchers as a possible alternative to public school monopolies. Under this system, parents receive a voucher that could be applied to the cost of education for their child at a number of competing instutitions—public schools, private schools, etc. Another variant is housing vouchers as a substitute for publicly constructed and managed housing. These vouchers allow public housing recipients to purchase the best possible housing on a competitive basis from available private landlords.

Volunteers are widely used by a range of public agencies to provide services that might otherwise be performed by paid employees. These include community crime watch programs, which work in cooperation with local police departments. Volunteer teachers' aides provide tutoring and individual assistance in many public schools.

Self-Help is common in community development programs and correctional facilities. Community development programs frequently use residents on a volunteer basis to provide recreation, counseling, and other support services for a community. Frequently, such contributions are required to "leverage" a federal or state grant of appropriated funds. Contrary to the popular image of prisons as vacation resorts, prison inmates are usually responsible for laundry, food service and facilities maintenance.

Regulatory and Tax Incentives are typically used to encourage the private sector to perform functions that might otherwise be performed by public agencies with appropriated funds. The Job Training Partnership Act (JTPA), for example, was a tax incentive-based national system for manpower training that replaced CETA. CETA (the Comprehensive Education and Training Act) was a federally-funded program that passed money through to state and local governments for assessment, training and job placement activities. Its successor, [. . .] offered income tax deductions for corporations that hired, trained and retained disadvantaged employees. The intended effect—human resource development and employment—was the same as with CETA, only the mechanism was different.

Regulatory incentives include the zoning variances granted to condominium associations. Frequently, construction requires variances for roads, parking, waste collection and disposal. In return for these variances, the condominium association agrees to provide many services normally performed by local government. These include security (if the condominium has a gated entrance), waste disposal, public works (maintenance of common areas), etc. This may seem an unfair arrangement to the residents, who pay both maintenance fees to the condominium association and local property taxes for the same services (which are not provided by the municipality). But it does explain the increasing popularity among builders and residents of condominiums—their lower unit cost often makes them the only low or moderate housing available; and they would not be approved by local planning councils or zoning boards unless the contractor agreed in advance to require the condominium association to be responsible for services that otherwise would be the municipality's responsibility.

Flexible Employment Relationships for the Remaining Public Employees

All of these mechanisms are used for providing public services without using public employees, and in many cases through other funding sources besides appropriated funds. Yet even in those cases where public services continue to be provided by public employees working in public agencies funded by appropriations, massive changes have occurred in employment practices. Chief among these are increased use of temporary, part-time, and seasonal employment; and increased hiring of exempt employees (those outside the classified civil service) through employment contracts. These two devices, along with the increased use of outside contractors, have markedly changed the face of the public work force.[7]

Increasingly, employers reduce costs and enhance flexibility by meeting minimal staffing requirements through "permanent" employees, and by hiring "contingent" (temporary, part-time or seasonal) workers to meet peak workload demands. These positions usually offer lower salaries and benefits than career positions. And employees can be hired and fired "at will" (without reference to due process entitlements of civil service employees, or collective bargaining agreements). Skill requirements of these jobs are reduced by job-redesign or work simplification. Where commitment and high skills are required on a temporary basis, employers may seek to save money or maintain flexibility by using contract or leased employees to positions exempt from civil service protections.

Exempt positions are classified, in that positions must be created and funded before they can be filled. But they are not classified within civil service systems, so their incumbents are not "permanent" (at least, not in the sense of having a property interest in their positions). Instead, the terms and conditions of these positions are specified through performance contracts specifying pay and benefits, and limiting the term of employment. While contracts may be routinely renewed with the approval of the employee and the employer, employees may also be discharged "at will" in the event of a personality conflict, a change in managerial objectives, or a budget shortfall. Frequently, once employees become exempt, they lose their "bumping rights" back into a classified position in the event of a reduction in force (RIF). Increasingly, managerial and technical employees are hired into these types of contracts. They increase the salary and benefits that can be offered to highly qualified employees, and they enhance managerial flexibility to trim personnel costs quickly, should this be necessary, without having to resort to the bureaucratic chaos precipitated by the exercise of "bumping rights" during an RIF situation.

The impact of these two devices is accelerated by retirement "buyouts," which offer employees close to retirement age an incentive to retire early within a limited period of eligibility ("window"). In a typical example, employees with 17–20 years of service (in a jurisdiction with a 20-year eligibility requirement for retirement) may be offered, for a limited time period of two months, the opportunity to resign and receive retirement benefits equal to those they would have received with three additional years' service. And the employer may even "sweeten the pot" by offering to pay its share of the cost of employee and family health benefits during the early retirement period (before the employee is eligible for Medicare). If the plan is designed properly so that enough employees retire to save substantially, but enough stay to provide for organizational continuity and skills, both employer and employee benefit. The employee gets an option to retire early at close to current salary; the employer gets to fill the vacant position with an entry-level employee at a much lower salary. The major drawback for the municipality is unexpectedly large lump-sum payments for accrued annual leave or sick leave. For example, the City of Miami estimates that it will need to find $10 million to compensate 339 employees who elected early retirement. The highest payout is $87,000; the average is $20,000.[8]

IMPACT ON THE ROLE OF THE PUBLIC PERSONNEL MANAGER

The emergence of alternative personnel systems has meant changes in the role of the public personnel manager, and the comparative importance of personnel functions. First, historical traditions emphasize the technical side of personnel management, with less emphasis on policy-related analytical work, relationships with outside organizations and conflicting values. In addition, both employees and line management are seen as clients, and are perceived as being served through the merit system. The tradi-

tional department's work includes record keeping and the processing of personnel transactions, especially in smaller government agencies or units.

A more contemporary view emphasizes different activities and relationships. While the traditional functions continue to be important, they are relatively less important than the "brokering" or mediating of conflicts among competing personnel systems. For example, the modern personnel director might be called upon to prepare cost-benefit analyses of alternative pay and benefit proposals related to collective bargaining with employees in the solid waste department. At the same time, he or she might also be asked to evaluate the comparative feasibility, productivity and cost of privatizing or contracting this entire function out (thus making the collective bargaining analysis obsolete). Or, since the majority of employees in the department are minorities, the director might be asked to assess the impact of contracting out on the city's overall level of affirmative action compliance. Modern personnel directors do not work in isolation; rather, they work closely with other officials within their own agency (budget directors, attorneys, collective bargaining negotiators, affirmative action compliance officers, and supervisors) and outside it (legislative staff, union officials, affirmative action agencies, civil service boards, health and life insurance benefit representatives, pension boards, ethics commissions, and employee assistance programs dealing with substance abuse and other personal problems).[9]

NOTES

[1] The authors wish to express their appreciation for the cooperation of the Institute of Government at Florida International University, which organized the training seminar on "Alternatives to Civil Service" from which the focus group participants' responses and reactions were gathered.

[2] International City Management Association (1989). Service Delivery in the 90s: Alternative Approaches for Local Governments, Washington, DC: ICMA.

[3] Kilborn, Peter T. (1995). "Take this job: Up from Welfare: It's Harder and Harder." The New York Times (April 15), Section 4:1, 4.

[4] Mahtesian, Charles (1994). "Taking Chicago Private." Governing (April), 26–31.

[5] Applebome, Peter (1995). "Private Enterprise Enters the Public Schools," The New York Times (April 9), Y-10.

[6] Sullivan, John, and Matthew Purdy (1995). "In Corrections Business, Shrewdness Pays," The New York Times (July 23), A-1, 13.

[7] U.S. Merit Systems Protection Board (1994). Temporary Federal Employment: In Search of Flexibility and Fairness. Washington, D.C.

[8] Cavanaugh, Joanne (1995). Where (unused) time is money." The Miami Herald (August 27), A-1.

[9] Klingner, Donald and John Nalbandian (1993). Public Personnel Management: Contexts and Strategies, 3rd. Englewood Cliffs, NJ: Prentice-Hall.

Workforce Reductions—Downsizing Strategies Used in Selected Organizations: Report to Congressional Committees

U.S. GENERAL ACCOUNTING OFFICE

The March 31, 1994, enactment of the Federal Workforce Restructuring Act of 1994 presents significant human resource management challenges to federal agencies as they formulate strategies for complying with the statute's requirements that federal employment levels be reduced by 272,900 full-time equivalent positions during fiscal years 1994 through 1999. The statute was enacted in response to a recommendation by the National Performance Review—endorsed by the President—that federal employment levels be reduced. Other administration actions were announced in early 1995 that are aimed at additional staff reductions.

This report provides information on how 17 private companies, 5 states, and 3 foreign governments planned for and carried out their downsizings. The employers were generally selected because they were reputed to have downsized successfully. The information should be helpful to congressional and executive branch decisionmakers in determining how to implement the mandated reductions in federal employment.

We are addressing this report to you in your capacities as Chairmen and Ranking Minority Members of committees that have jurisdiction over federal employment matters. We are also sending copies of this report to the heads of all departments and agencies of the federal government and other interested parties.

The major contributors to this report are listed in the appendix. Please contact me on (202) 512-5074 if you have questions concerning this report.

Nancy Kingsbury
Director, Federal Human Resource
  Management Issues

EXECUTIVE SUMMARY

Purpose

During fiscal years 1994 through 1999, federal agencies must reduce employment levels by 272,900 full-time equivalent positions, or approxi-

mately 12 percent of the civilian nonpostal executive branch workforce. This requirement was incorporated into law by the Federal Workforce Restructuring Act of 1994 [P.L. 103-226, 108 Stat. 111 (1994)].

How can agencies ensure that they will be able to accomplish their missions with significantly fewer employees? What strategies will best accomplish the statute's objectives? How can employment levels be reduced in a manner that will effectively deal with employees who remain, as well as those who

Source: General Accounting Office. *Federal Downsizing: Better Workforce and Strategic Planning Could Have Made Buyouts More Effective.* 8/22/96 GAO/GGD 96–62.

leave? Finding answers to these and other questions may be a daunting challenge for congressional and executive decisionmakers as the downsizing progresses.

To obtain information that might be of value in carrying out federal downsizing, GAO contacted 17 private companies, 5 states, and 3 foreign governments, which had downsized in recent years. This report presents a compendium of the approaches these employers used, as described by management officials: the planning involved, the methods used to reduce their workforces, and the human resources aspects of the downsizing activities.

Background

President Clinton came into office with a pledge to reduce the federal workforce by 100,000 employees. Subsequently, the National Performance Review (NPR) recommended that the federal workforce be reduced by 252,000 positions, primarily in supervisory, auditing, accounting, budgeting, personnel, and procurement functions. In accepting the President's proposal that the workforce reductions recommended by the NPR be implemented, Congress increased the reduction to 272,900 positions and authorized agencies to offer separation incentives of up to $25,000 to federal employees who agreed to resign or retire. Other administration actions were announced in early 1995 that are aimed at additional staff reductions.

Many organizations in the private and public sectors have considerable experience with downsizing, and the governments of a number of foreign countries have reduced their workforces as well. Some of these employment reductions amounted to as much as 40 to 50 percent, often spread over a number of years. However, employment reductions of the magnitude contemplated are unusual in the federal government.

Results in Brief

In general, the private companies in GAO's [General Accounting Office] review said their decisions to downsize were the result of corporate restructuring actions designed to make work processes more efficient and/or eliminate less profitable and unnecessary functions. Reducing employment was seldom the initial objective. Rather, it was a consequence of eliminating unnecessary work. Officials of many of the companies stressed the importance of identifying needed structural changes and other revisions to traditional methods of operation. In contrast, downsizings by the states in GAO's review were generally undertaken as cost-cutting measures without consideration of work requirements. Although GAO did not identify detailed reasons for the downsizings in the countries it reviewed, their downsizings were generally characterized as the result of desires to streamline government and make the public sector more efficient.

Once their decisions to downsize had been made, 15 of the 25 organizations said they found it important to plan how the reductions would be carried out to retain a viable workforce when the reductions were completed. Those organizations that said they did not properly plan their downsizings acknowledged that they cut needed employees, suffered skills imbalances, and were often forced to rehire or replace employees who had been separated.

The organizations said they generally found that attrition and hiring freezes, while useful tools, were not always effective ways to achieve significant short-term reductions in the workforce. Thus, most of the organizations used monetary incentives to encourage "at risk" employees to resign or retire if they could not be redeployed to other jobs. Many offered separation incentives more generous than the incentives included in the federal government's "buyout" legislation, including early retirement without penalties, credit of additional years of service in retirement benefit determinations, and lump-sum severance payments of up to a year's salary. However, the organizations that had downsized several times over the years tended to reduce the separation incentives offered in successive downsizings. The organizations generally resorted to involuntary separations only after other tools such as attrition, hiring freezes, redeployments, and separation incentive programs did not achieve their employment reduction goals. Where possible, involuntary separations were managed by using various criteria to target specifically those parts of the workforce that were in keeping with the efficiency, profitability, span of control, or other restructuring goals of the organizations.

A concern GAO found among the organizations was the need to assist employees—both those at risk of losing their jobs and those who were ultimately retained—in coping with the personal disruptions caused by workforce reductions. The organizations found that frequent and open communications with their employees on all aspects of the downsizing were essential, along with programs to help affected employees through counseling, outplacement assistance, and retraining.

GAO'S ANALYSIS

Importance of Planning in Downsizing Decisionmaking

While not all of the organizations claimed to have done so, most (11 companies, 3 states, and 1 country) said that planning before initiating or carrying out downsizing activities was essential. The private companies said that decisions to downsize were the result of company restructurings based on strategic planning designed to shape and guide the companies' future directions. Most of the companies said they examined their functions and work processes to see if they should be revised or continued. Thirteen organizations also emphasized the importance of workforce planning procedures to determine the types and numbers of employees they would need in the restructured organization. An official in one company pointed out that simply reducing staff does not make the work they were doing go away, but with proper planning downsizing can be targeted to specific skills the organization no longer needs in its revised structure.

Restructuring based on strategic planning was generally not the impetus for the downsizings in the government organizations GAO visited. The state downsizings resulted primarily from budgetary considerations. For example, officials of one state said that it downsized because it had to fund retroactive salary increases ordered in a court decision. Another state reduced the number of employees after passage of a referendum limiting property taxes. An official of this state said the downsizing meant the state ended up doing less with less. Documentation from the three countries generally characterized the countries' downsizings as the result of declining economic conditions and changing attitudes toward government services.

Regardless of the reasons for their downsizings, the organizations generally believed workforce planning to be essential in identifying positions to be eliminated and pinpointing specific employees for potential separation. For example, one company believed work that added value to the organization was the ultimate test of an employee's worth and

evaluated the cost and value added to the final product of all its positions in determining whether employees in the positions would be retained or separated. Another company identified excess employees by reviewing work functions that appeared to be redundant or unnecessary for future operations.

In organizations where officials said planning did not occur or was not effectively implemented, difficulties arose in the downsizings. Officials in one company told GAO they recognized the importance of workforce planning in downsizing decisions when the company lost needed staff because it did not plan for skills retention. An official in another company observed that if an organization simply reduces the number of its employees without changing its work processes, staffing growth will recur eventually.

A number of factors may place constraints on organizations' downsizing strategies. This was particularly true for the governmental organizations, which were constrained by public sentiment, budget limitations, legislative mandates to maintain certain programs, and personnel laws.

Approaches to Reducing Workforce Size

Few of the organizations said they relied solely on attrition and/or hiring freezes to achieve significant workforce reductions. As officials in one organization explained, attrition is often not sufficient to reduce employment levels in the short term. Moreover, using attrition as a sole downsizing tool can result in skills imbalances in an organization's workforce because the employees who leave are not necessarily those the organization determined to be excess.

Once the organizations had identified the employees who were to be separated, they used a variety of approaches to accomplish their downsizing plans. Officials of about half of the organizations—including private companies, states, and countries—said they sought to redeploy affected employees to fill needed positions in other parts of the organization. Often, these organizations encouraged redeployment to other locations by paying travel and relocation costs and other allowances. In some cases, the organizations found that retraining at-risk employees for other positions was an effective means of avoiding employee separations and cost-effective for the organization.

Most of the organizations offered affected employees monetary incentives to leave voluntarily. Seventeen of the 25 organizations allowed employees to retire early. In some of these organizations, officials said early retirement penalties were waived, and the organizations often credited employees with additional years of service and/or added years to their ages so they could either qualify for retirement or receive enhanced benefit amounts, or both. Officials of three organizations said they supplemented early retirees' pensions until they were eligible for social security.

Lump-sum cash payments were often a feature of separation incentive programs. The amounts were usually based on the organizations' severance pay formulas—generally 1 or 2 weeks' pay for each year of service to a maximum of a year's salary. These payments were available to employees who resigned or retired.

Other, but less common, separation incentives included continuation of insurance benefits for specified periods, paid college tuition and other training programs, and new business start-up assistance. . . .

When redeployment and voluntary separation programs did not achieve the employment reductions needed to meet efficiency, profitability, span of control, or other restructuring goals, the organizations said they instituted, or planned to institute, involuntary separations as a final downsizing tool. Various criteria, including key skills and expertise, tenure, and/or performance, were used to determine which employees would be involuntarily separated.

Consideration of Employees' Personal Concerns in Downsizings

Officials of 21 of the organizations GAO reviewed said part of their restructuring and downsizing activities emphasized the "people issues" involved. They said they recognized that employees are apprehensive and concerned about how they will be affected when their employers restructure or cut employment levels.

Many of these officials emphasized the importance of communicating with employees during downsizing. Among the communication methods the various organizations used were staff meetings, employee newsletters, video presentations, and face-to-face discussions between employees and management. Officials in one company pointed out that a primary benefit of open communication between management and employees was helping to avoid distrust and morale problems. They said they made every effort not to appear as if they were withholding any information from employees.

Officials of these 21 organizations said they devised programs to assist employees who lost their jobs during downsizing. They provided, for example, employee and family counseling, job placement services, relocation assistance, and training for other careers. They also said they often found it important to address the morale and productivity of the "survivors" of downsizing by helping them deal with concerns brought about by the workplace changes.

Workforce 2000 Executive Summary

✷ WILLIAM B. JOHNSTON AND ARNOLD C. PACKER

The year 2000 will mark the end of what has been called the American century. Since 1900, the United States has become wealthy and powerful by exploit-

Source: "Executive Summary," in *Workforce 2000: Work and Workers for the Twenty-first Century.* Executive Summary by Johnston, William B. Copyright © 1987 by Hudson Institute Inc. Reproduced with permission of Hudson Institute Inc. in the format Textbook via Copyright Clearance Center.

ing the rapid changes taking place in technology, world trade, and the international political order. The last years of this century are certain to bring new developments in technology, international competition, demography, and other factors that will alter the nation's economic and social landscape. By the end of the next decade, the changes under way will produce an America that is in some ways unrecognizable from the one that existed only a few years ago.

Four key trends will shape the last years of the twentieth century:

- *The American economy should grow at [a] relatively healthy pace,* boosted by a rebound in U.S. exports, renewed productivity growth, and a strong world economy.
- Despite its international comeback, *U.S. manufacturing will be a much smaller share of the economy in the year 2000* than it is today. Service industries will create all of the new jobs, and most of the new wealth, over the next 13 years.
- *The workforce will grow slowly, becoming older, more female, and more disadvantaged.* Only 15 percent of the new entrants to the labor force over the next 13 years will be native white males, compared to 47 percent in that category today.
- *The new jobs in service industries will demand much higher skill levels* than the jobs of today. Very few new jobs will be created for those who cannot read, follow directions, and use mathematics. Ironically, the demographic trends in the workforce, coupled with the higher skill requirements of the economy, will lead to both higher and lower unemployment: more joblessness among the least-skilled and less among the most educationally advantaged.

These trends raise a number of important policy issues. If the United States is to continue to prosper—if the year 2000 is to mark the end of the *first* American century—policymakers must find ways to:

- *Stimulate Balanced World Growth:* To grow rapidly, the U.S. must pay less attention to its share of world trade and more to the growth of the economies of the other nations of the world, including those nations in Europe, Latin America, and Asia with whom the U.S. competes.
- *Accelerate Productivity Increases in Service Industries:* Prosperity will depend much more on how fast output per worker increases in health care, education, retailing, government, and other services than on gains in manufacturing.
- *Maintain the Dynamism of an Aging Workforce:* As the average age of American workers climbs toward 40, the nation must insure that its workforce and its institutions do not lose their adaptability and willingness to learn.

- *Reconcile the Conflicting Needs of Women, Work, and Families:* Three-fifths of all women over age 16 will be at work in the year 2000. Yet most current policies and institutions covering pay, fringe benefits, time away from work, pensions, welfare, and other issues were designed for a society in which men worked and women stayed home.
- *Integrate Black and Hispanic Workers Fully into the Economy:* The shrinking numbers of young people, the rapid pace of industrial change, and the ever-rising skill requirements of the emerging economy make the task of fully utilizing minority workers particularly urgent between now and 2000. Both cultural changes and education and training investments will be needed to create real equal employment opportunity.
- *Improve the Educational Preparation of All Workers:* As the economy grows more complex and more dependent on human capital, the standards set by the American education system must be raised. . . .

WORKERS AND JOBS IN THE YEAR 2000

Changes in the economy will be matched by changes in the workforce and the jobs it will perform. Five demographic facts will be most important:

- *The population and the workforce will grow more slowly than at any time since the 1930s:* Population growth, which was climbing at almost 1.9 percent per year in the 1950s, will slump to only 0.7 percent per year by 2000; the labor force, which exploded by 2.9 percent per year in the 1970s, will be expanding by only 1 percent annually in the 1990s. These slow growth rates will tend to slow down the nation's economic expansion and will shift the economy more toward income-sensitive products and services (e.g., luxury goods and convenience services). It may also tighten labor markets and force employers to use more capital-intensive production systems.
- *The average age of the population and the workforce will rise, and the pool of young workers entering the labor market will shrink:* As the baby boom ages, and the baby bust

enters the workforce, the average age of the workforce will climb from 36 today to 39 by the year 2000. The number of young workers age 16–24 will drop by almost 2 million, or 8 percent. This decline in young people in the labor force will have both positive and negative impacts. On the one hand, the older workforce will be more experienced, stable, and reliable. The reverse side of this stability will be a lower level of adaptability. Older workers, for example, are less likely to move, to change occupations, or to undertake retraining than younger workers. Companies that have grown by adding large numbers of flexible, lower-paid young workers will find such workers in short supply in the 1990s.

- *More women will enter the workforce:* Almost two-thirds of the new entrants into the workforce between now and the year 2000 will be women, and 61 percent of all women of working age are expected to have jobs by the year 2000. Women will still be concentrated in jobs that pay less than men's jobs, but they will be rapidly entering many higher-paying professional and technical fields. In response to the continued feminization of work, the convenience industries will boom, with "instant" products and "delivered-to-the-door" service becoming common throughout the economy. Demands for day care and for more time off from work for pregnancy leave and child-rearing duties will certainly increase, as will interest in part-time, flexible, and stay-at-home jobs.

- *Minorities will be a larger share of new entrants into the labor force:* Non-whites will make up 29 percent of the new entrants into the labor force between now and the year 2000, twice their current share of the workforce. Although this large share of a more slowly growing workforce might be expected to improve the opportunities for these workers, the concentration of blacks in declining central cities and slowly growing occupations makes this sanguine outlook doubtful.

- *Immigrants will represent the largest share of the increase in the population and the workforce since the First World War:* Even with the new immigration law, approximately 600,000 legal and illegal immigrants are projected to

enter the United States annually throughout the balance of the century. Two-thirds or more of immigrants of working age are likely to join the labor force. In the South and West where these workers are concentrated, they are likely to reshape local economies dramatically, promoting faster economic growth and labor surpluses.

In combination, these demographic changes will mean that the new workers entering the workforce between now and the year 2000 will be much different from those who people it today. Non-whites, women, and immigrants will make up more than five-sixths of the net additions to the workforce between now and the year 2000, though they make up only about half of it today:

	1985 Labor Force	*Net New Workers, 1985–2000*
Total	115,461,000	25,000,000
Native White Men	47%	15%
Native White Women	36%	42%
Native Non-white Men	5%	7%
Native Non-white Women	5%	13%
Immigrant Men	4%	13%
Immigrant Women	3%	9%

Source: Hudson Institute.

Juxtaposed with these changes in the composition of the workforce will be rapid changes in the nature of the job market. The fastest-growing jobs will be in professional, technical, and sales fields requiring the highest education and skill levels. Of the fastest-growing job categories, all but one, service occupations, require more than the median level of education for all jobs. Of those growing more slowly than average, not one requires more than the median education.

Ranking jobs according to skills, rather than education, illustrates the rising requirements even more dramatically. When jobs are given numerical ratings according to the math, language, and reasoning skills they require, only twenty-seven percent of all new jobs fall into the lowest two skill categories, while 40 percent of current jobs require these limited skills. By contrast, 41 percent of new jobs are in the three highest skill groups, compared to only 24 percent of current jobs. The changes ahead in the job market will affect different groups in the society in different ways. While young whites may find their job prospects improving, for black men and Hispanics the job market will be particularly difficult. In contrast to their rising share of the new entrants into the labor force, black men will hold a declining fraction of all jobs if they simply retain existing shares of various occupations. Black women, on the other hand, will hold a rising fraction of all jobs, but this increase will be less than needed to offset their growing share of the workforce.

REINVENTION, ALTERNATIVE SERVICE DELIVERY, AND THE HRM FUNCTION

In the first reading, Klingner and Lynn identify several important recent changes in public personnel systems as these systems move away from the traditional civil service model.[1] Public sector agencies are increasingly looking to alternative mechanisms for delivering public services.[2] These alternative delivery systems will change the role and duties of human resource management in public organizations. There are two chief characteristics of these alternative service delivery systems. First, a private sector or nonprofit organization may provide a service rather than permanent government employees. Second, when the service is provided by an actual public agency, the workers might be contracted, part-time, or seasonal employees as opposed to permanent civil servants.[3]

The increasing preference for these alternative mechanisms reflects the goal of achieving increasing flexibility in the delivery of public services. For example, it might take an agency two months to fill an open position within a traditional merit system;[4] using **contract** or temporary employees instead allows a public organization to hire much more quickly and to let the employees go when the demand for work decreases.[5] Also, **temporary or seasonal** and **part-time employees** are "cheaper" for the organization because they are generally paid less, have fewer benefits than permanent employees, are not entitled to the due process rights of civil service employees, and are seldom part of any collective bargaining agreement.[6] Exempt employees, meaning those who are exempt from civil service classification systems, have similar advantages to the public sector organization in terms of flexibility. They are generally hired through employment contracts that specify their pay and benefits, as well as their term of employment. An added advantage is that exempt employees may be discharged at will (without the need to show cause), or much more easily than would be the case with traditional civil service employees.[7] (The evolution of civil service systems in the United States is described in more detail in Chapter 3.) Nonprofit organizations are often selected to implement public services for three important reasons.[8] First, they are often capable of rapid implementation compared to the public sector because personnel startup activities are less cumbersome and the organizations tend to be smaller and able to respond to opportunities rapidly. Second, the nonprofit organizations can tailor programs in response to community conditions and needs. Third, nonprofit organizations may be able to deliver "confidential" services to individuals (such as unwed teen mothers or drug-abusing adults using contaminated needles) who might not be accessible through direct public administration channels.

Reinventing Government

Much of the organizational change taking place in public agencies has been done under the slogan of **"reinventing government,"**[9] although the authors of this movement disclaim many of the actions taken under this label. In Table 2.1, David Osborne and Peter Plastrik explain what reinventing government is and is *not*.

In describing their recommendations to reinvent government, Osborne and Plastrik introduce the

Table 2.1 What Reinventing Government Is and Is Not

Reinventing Government Is *NOT*	Reinventing Government *IS*
Reinvention does not mean changing the political system, such as campaign finance reform, legislative reform, or term limits and the like.	Reinvention means the fundamental transformation of public systems and organizations to create dramatic increases in their effectiveness, efficiency, adaptability, and capacity to innovate.
Reinvention does not mean reorganization.	Reinvention is restructuring public organizations and systems by changing their purposes, incentives, accountability, distribution of power, and cultures.
Reinvention does not mean cutting waste, fraud, or abuse or conducting one-time efficiency reviews.	Reinvention is constantly looking for ways to become more efficient.
Reinvention is not synonymous with downsizing government.	Reinvention is finding the size that maximizes performance; form should follow function, and size should follow strategy.
Reinvention is not synonymous with privatization.	Reinvention is competition and customer choice to force improvement; shifting from a public monopoly to a private monopoly seldom leads to a happy ending.
Reinvention is not making government more efficient.	Reinvention is making government more effective. Do you want cheaper schools or better schools? Cheaper police forces or lower crime rates?
Reinvention is not a synonym for total quality management or business process reengineering.	The goal is transformation; business management tools are not enough. Public organizations have multiple missions and multiple customers, low competition, few consequences for poor performance, no bottom line, and limited accountability. These systemic realities and related incentives must change before performance will improve.

term *entrepreneurial government.* This is an unfortunate use of words because it has contributed to what he laments as a "loss of clarity" and is one of the reasons that "'reinventing government' has been used so often by so many people to describe so many agendas that it has lost its meaning."[10] Reinvention is about replacing bureaucratic systems with what Osborne calls entrepreneurial systems. It is about creating public organizations and systems that habitually innovate and continually improve their quality without having to be pushed from outside. It is about creating a public sector that has a built-in drive to improve—what some call a "self-renewing system."[11]

Some states have attempted to increase the flexibility of their human resource systems by making widespread changes in the way their civil service systems work. Georgia is attempting to eliminate its civil service system altogether, and several others, such as Minnesota, Oklahoma, and South Carolina, are making large-scale reforms.[12] Many states have tried to reduce the number of job classifications used in their personnel systems "because the greater the number of classes, the narrower the focus of the individual job titles and the less flexibility managers have to give adequate raises or shift employees around where they are needed."[13] Increased flexibility has been sought by reducing the requirements for testing for civil service jobs in Wisconsin.[14] This makes it easier to attract and successfully hire good employees in a tight labor market, as well as dramatically reduces the amount of time needed to hire a new employee. Another example of increased flexibility is allowing managers to select potential employees from a list of the top ten candidates rather than only the top three candidates (the so-called "rule-of-three"). (Changes in recruitment and selection techniques are discussed in more detail in Chapter 8.) In addition, most states now use some type of pay for performance, or merit pay, in an attempt to reward high-performance employees and increase flexibility in civil service compensation systems.[15] (Innovations in compensation systems are described in Chapter 9.)

For-Profit Sector Management Techniques

One recurring call for government reform is the demand to "run government like a business." There are indeed many aspects of business that can be used in government for improved efficiency and effectiveness, and vice versa. For example, strategic planning, first used in the military, has proven effective for business and governmental settings alike. Many public agencies are finding the effort involved is a highly rewarding inclusive process of clarifying their mission, core purposes, and most essential goals (all key elements of strategic planning), and matching those to an analysis of the organizational environnment and current assets. Some important modifications, however, must be made to accommodate the values of democratic government (such as missions established by law, an environment dominated by the public interest, and strategic partnerships with a variety of groups that have a voice in the functions of government). This model of using the tools of business management adapted to the needs and values of government runs across virtually all business methods, from accounting and budgeting to organizing and staffing. The tools are useful, but the objectives and values may be entirely different in public and private sector settings. It is imperative that the values of democratic government (such as justice, fairness, limitation of power, and constitutional protections) not be lost in our enthusiasm to adopt the latest business practice. As one city manager, Tom Cort-

ney, put it at an Idaho local government conference in February 2000, citizens want us to "run government like a business—-but don't treat us like you were a business."

Focus on Privatization

It is important to consider **privatization** and its impacts, because it is an increasingly popular way for governments to attempt to streamline their operations and reduce both operating and capital costs. The federal government has a longstanding commitment to privatization. An Office of Management and Budget directive (**Circular A-76**) says in part, "The federal government will not start or carry on any commercial activity to provide a service or product for its own use if such service can be procured from for-profit enterprise through ordinary business channels."[16] State and local governments have made heavy use of privatization. Nearly every state, for example, contracts some mental health services with the for-profit or nonprofit sectors.[17]

Privatization is seen as a way to improve service delivery quality or reduce costs (or both). The cost savings are achieved mainly through the reduced salaries and benefits that the for-profit sector provides to the entry-level employees typically involved in privatization.[18] An employer in the for-profit or nonprofit sectors can more easily add or remove employees during peak and off periods of work than can a civil service system. Privatization also frees the public agency from dealing with various personnel concerns such as employee grievances, complaints, and appeals.[19] Selection and termination of employees may be delegated to the employer altogether, or the public jurisdiction may retain some control over those personnel decisions. Retention of control over selection and termination is especially important if the service includes specialized personnel who would be difficult to replace or whose replacement with lesser-qualified staff would reduce the quality of service provided.[20] Arguably privatization is a means to increase or maintain the level of service provided by the public sector without (at least in appearance) a commensurate increase in staffing.

Collective bargaining units have usually resisted privatization out of concern for decreased memberships, wages, benefits, and job security. Employee resistance to privatization has been decreased somewhat in many jurisdictions by allowing current employees to participate in the bidding process against for-profit or nonprofit providers, and by making arrangements with the private sector employer to use as many of the displaced public employees as possible.[21] (The role of collective bargaining units in HRM is discussed in Chapter 5.)

Public organizations considering privatization need to consider the legal constraints on HRM in their particular jurisdiction. State or local statutes, for example, may protect public employee pensions. Privatization efforts that affect the pension status of privatized employees may lead to a lawsuit. Ravitch and Lawther suggest that this can be avoided by having the request for proposal for the privatization decision require that the potential for-profit or nonprofit employer provide comparable pension benefits to any privatized employees.[22]

Managing personnel and services in a privatized environment requires HRM professionals to develop and maintain new sets of skills. Ewoh suggests that personnelists need training in the following areas: "(1) the public-private environment of many public programs, (2) the difficulties of setting performance standards in such a setting, (3) measuring performance in these arrangements, and (4) auditing expenditures and maintaining control in privatized areas of activity."[23] Reliance on the use of nonprofit organizations to deliver services has come under criticism in terms of tracking accountability and legal responsibility for program delivery and service provision to clientele.[24]

DOWNSIZING

Downsizing refers to the intentional reduction in the number of employees in an organization's workforce. It is also sometimes called a **reduc-**tion in force (RIF) or, simply, a workforce reduction. Downsizing has become prevalent across job sectors, as corporations adjust to the competitive global marketplace and governments adapt to periodically tight budgets.

Downsizing is often seen as an end in itself in the public sector, since many believe that a smaller government is better by definition. Politicians who are anxious to demonstrate to voters that they have cut the size and cost of government often point to smaller numbers of employees to prove their case. Public sector downsizing may be the result of sometimes hostile taxpayers who have passed tax limitation measures, refused to pass bond elections for public facilities, and voted for candidates promising to "cut the fat" from bloated bureaucracies. Although the evidence indicates that the results of organizational downsizing are generally negative or at best mixed,[25] reducing the size of government seems to sell well in political campaigns. Some of the most detrimental effects of downsizing have been witnessed on the employees who remain in the downsized organization and are asked to "do more with less."[26] Now that there are fewer employees who have to meet heightened demands for services, it is often the HRM professional who is asked to improve morale and make the diminished organization work.

The federal government has experienced a large reduction in force in recent years. Based on Vice President Al Gore's **National Performance Review,** which attempted to apply concepts from Osborne and Gaebler's *Reinventing Government,* Congress mandated a civilian workforce reduction of 272,900 positions, to be completed between 1992 and 1999.[27] Including Department of Defense workers, the federal workforce was reduced by approximately 336,500 positions as of the end of the Clinton-Gore administration.[28] Many state and local governments have downsized their workforces in response to budget shortfalls. As we shall see later, however, there is seldom a corresponding reduction in the work to be done by governments during downsizing, leaving fewer workers to shoulder greater responsibility (note this theme in the second reading). In contrast, a survey of downsizing practices by the General Accounting Office found that corporations seldom reduced their workforce for the sake of having fewer employees. Although the increase in short-term stock values may have played a role, it appears that for-profit firms downsized to make work more efficient by restructuring or eliminating unnecessary functions.[29]

For many nonprofit organizations, reduction in force is a way of life. Because many nonprofit organizations are heavily dependent on contracts and grants from government, corporate sponsors, or larger nonprofit organizations such as The United Way or other philanthropic foundations, rapid staffing changes are common. Nonprofit organizations hire in response to a new grant or contract to inaugurate a new program or enhance existing services. Nonprofits also lay off these employees if funding is not sustainable.

There are many methods by which an organization can reduce its workforce —-for example:[30]

Attrition: Reduction in numbers due to resignations, retirements, or death

Hiring freezes: Prohibition on filling vacant positions

Early retirement incentives: Reduction in numbers by offering access to full pension benefits, severance pay, or other monetary reward to encourage early retirement

Job reengineering: Reduction in numbers through elimination of functions and organizational processes

Redeployment and retraining: Reduction in numbers by shifting employees to positions elsewhere in the organization

Part-time employment: Reduction in numbers achieved by converting full-time positions to part-time positions

Involuntary separations: Reduction in numbers through layoffs and firings

Many of these methods are short-term solutions to reducing the overall number of employees in the workforce (for example, attrition and hiring freezes). Other techniques are aimed more at a work redesign strategy and involve the elimination of functions, hierarchical levels in the organization, or products.[31] This type of workforce reduction takes more time but may be more beneficial to the organization in the long run. The procedures used for reductions in force in nonprofit organizations vary, but in small organizations it is usually limited to a statement of this sort: "The grant/contract with [insert name of contract or granting organization] was not renewed. We have funding for your positions through [date]."

Reductions in Force in a Civil Service Setting

Civil service systems often have specific procedures for reductions in force that specify the order in which employees will be laid off from the organization.[32] The layoffs typically begin with temporary employees, then provisional, then probationary, and finally permanent employees. The order of layoffs of permanent employees is typically determined by a point system comprising a combination of years of service and performance indicators. It is common for war veterans to receive additional preference points. The employees are then listed in order of points, and those with the fewest points are the first to be laid off. Employees may choose to be demoted to a lower classification voluntarily rather than being laid off. This is referred to as **bumping** and allows an employee to stay with the organization, albeit in a lower-ranking position than in the past. Employees choosing a voluntary demotion are typically granted first rights on reapplication should their previous position become open. Bumping is often allowed across work groups and causes serious disruption to the organization as a chain reaction of bumped employees moves from position to position.

Lessons from Downsizing

Although downsizing may bring some short-term cost savings to an organization, studies assessing the effectiveness of downsizing have found that many organizations suffer losses in productivity and employee morale as a result.[33] Based on these analyses, two lessons about downsizing can be derived.

Downsizing and organizational planning   The first lesson is that downsizing must be coordinated with the long-term strategic planning efforts of the organization.[34] (The importance of strategic planning to an organization is discussed in Chapter 6.) Short-term reductions in force done without consideration of the critical knowledge, skills, and abilities required can be harmful. A properly planned downsizing begins with an assessment of what types of people (and skills) and how many people the organization needs to end up with after the downsizing is over.[35] Attrition, hiring freezes, and nontargeted early retirement incentives, for example, can result in critical skill shortages. These techniques do not allow the HRM professional to know whom the organization will be left with after the reduction in force. Managers may find that all the employees with knowledge of a critical process or procedure have left. Many organizations that have experienced this loss of expertise have found that they had to rehire or replace the employees who had just been separated from the organization.[36] Often these employees are rehired as consultants at a much higher cost to the organization than when they were permanent employees. Organizational memory—that is, an understading of how the organization has done things in the past—and expertise can also be lost.[37] These problems can be partially minimized by targeting the separation to particular employees, but collective bargaining agreements and civil service laws and regulations relevant in most public jurisdictions may limit the ability of governmental organizations to target reductions in force. A further possible step may be to ensure that critical skills are backed up by more than one person.[38] Linking downsizing to the organizational planning process can help with this.

While organizations may seek to reduce the cost of their personnel by reducing the number of employees, there is often no reduction in the work of the organization. A reduction in force thus leaves fewer employees to do more work. As noted above, many of the surviving employees may not have the skills to match the new work they are assigned. Organizations will need to plan for the training and the skills-development required to bring the skills of the remaining employees in line with the work.

Ethics and downsizing   The second lesson derived from studies of effective downsizing, the importance of communication, points to the ethical dimension in how downsizing is accomplished. A reduction in force can be traumatic not only to the employees released from the organization but to those who remain as well. Open communication between management and employees about the downsizing process can reduce the fear and mistrust often generated by a reduction in force.[39] There is also some evidence that organizations that involved employees in the development of and communication about the downsizing process retained higher levels of productivity than those organizations that did not communicate with employees about the reduction in force.[40]

Loss of morale, and consequently productivity, among employees who survive a downsizing has been reported in several studies.[41] Communication with these employees about the purposes of the reduction in force, its progress, and when it is completed can help alleviate the anxiety that survivors experience. The use of outplacement and training programs to help employees find new placements assists those who have been separated from the organization in their transition and have been shown to improve the morale and productivity of those who remain.[42]

While it is certainly legal to proceed with downsizing without communication or outplacement efforts, public sector organizations need to consider their ethical responsibility to treat their employees with respect. The payback will be in the continued productivity and loyalty of the employees who remain with the organization.

CHANGING DEMOGRAPHICS

The environment of the HRM professional is greatly shaped by the changing demographics and characteristics of the workforce. As the makeup of the workforce changes, all aspects of HRM must change as well. Good information about future trends is needed for human resource planning. Recruitment efforts may need to adapt to new pools of workers and their expectations. Training needs change as the qualifications of new and continuing workers change, and benefits and compensation packages will need to evolve to meet the changing needs of workers. Several important changes in the workforce will be important to the environment of the human resource specialists and the managers with whom they work in the near future.

Increased Numbers of Women in the Workforce

The number of women working outside the home has increased steadily over the past several decades. From March 1975 to March 1996, the "labor force participation rate of women rose from 46 percent to nearly 59 percent."[43] Seventy percent of women with children under age eighteen now participate in the workforce.[44] This development has obvious implications for work-life programs and the need for flexible work schedules and for options to deal with child care responsibilities. (See Chapter 11 for a discussion of these benefits.) In fact, one study found that 56 percent of women with children aged five and under said that locating affordable child care was a serious problem for them.[45] (Benefits programs to meet these needs are described in more detail in Chapter 11.)

Although women have entered the workforce in increasing numbers, the proportion of women in top management positions has not increased as rapidly. A landmark 1992 study by the Merit Systems Protection Board noted that while there were nearly as many women as men in federal white-collar jobs, they comprise only one out of four managers and one out of ten executives.[46] Sometimes referred to as the **glass ceiling,** women reach this career plateau for a number of reasons, including breaks in career taken for childbirth and child care, lack of experience in traditional male-dominated career paths necessary for promotion, and outright gender discrimination.[47]

Increasing Numbers of Minority Workers

Minorities comprised 25.5 percent of the nation's civilian workforce and 28.7 percent of the federal government's civilian workforce in September 1996.[48] This can be further broken down by black or African American (10.8 percent of the civilian labor force, or CLF), Hispanic (10.5 percent of the CLF), Asian Pacific Islanders (3.4 percent of the CLF), and American Indian/Alaska Natives (0.8 percent of CLF). While the percentage of blacks in the labor force is expected to remain steady, the percentages of Hispanics and the grouping of Asian Pacific Islander/American Indians and Alaska Natives are expected to increase to 11 percent and 5 percent, respectively.[49] Several states, such as California, Florida, and Texas, have such rapidly increasing percentages of minority workers that soon there will be no majority group in those states. The human resource professional should work to encourage tolerance for ethnic, racial, and cultural differences in the workplace. Guy and Newman point out that this is more than a legal compliance issue. Astute human resource managers recognize that a tolerant workplace can best use the multitude of talents brought by a diverse workforce.[50]

The Aging Workforce

The percentage of the U.S. population comprising middle-aged individuals will grow as the baby boom generation ages. The median age of the population reached thirty-six in the year 2000; that is, half of the population was older than thirty-six and half was younger. This is the oldest median age in the history of the United States.[51]

The well-known baby boom generation (1946—1964) will begin to reach retirement age in approximately 2008. The Bureau of the Census estimates that in 2020, the ratio of individuals over age sixty-five to the working-age adult population (eighteen to sixty-five years old) will increase 32 percent, to 27.7 per 100, from 1996 numbers.[52] As we approach 2010, the workforce will be made up increasingly of older workers who will have different needs and benefits preferences from their younger counterparts; for example, there may be an increased focus on retirement planning. A related challenge to human resource management arising from the aging of the workforce is the increased need for elder care benefits. Employees confronting difficult choices about health and long-term care for aging parents may need benefits structured to provide elder care options.

Generation X

The children of the baby boom generation have been referred to as **Generation X.** Generation X comprises approximately 52 million people born between 1965 and 1977. Members of Generation X are currently about a third of the workforce.[53] These workers began entering the workforce in approximately 1992 and will introduce continued pressures for change over the next twenty years.

Much has been made of the different experiences that Generation Xers bring to the employment marketplace.[54] Having watched firsthand the frequent downsizings of the 1980s and 1990s negatively affect their parents, these workers are thought to have lower expectations of staying with one employer for a prolonged period and are said to prefer team-based work environments rather than top-down organizations.[55] A recent study found that Generation Xers were more likely than baby boomers to value challenges and the ability to learn from a job over pay. Furthermore, Generation Xers are said to have lower levels of trust in established institutions and are believed to be more interested in maintaining a balance between work and family life than are boomers.[56]

Traditional recruitment techniques may not mesh with Generation Xers, who may ask, "Why should I work for your organization?" and who expect to work for any one employer only as long as it meets their personal growth goals. There is some evidence that older workers are resistant to the new attitudes toward work held by many Generation Xers. A study of older small business owners found that 21 percent said Generation Xers had a poor work ethic, 47 percent said that Generation Xers are less competent than workers from previous generations, 27 percent said that Generation Xers lacked motivation, and 26 percent said that Generation Xers are lazy.[57]

HR professionals will need to adapt to the differing values of these younger workers, especially as the number of qualified applicants in the workforce goes down and employers compete for employees. HRM specialists will need to help overcome the resistance of older managers who may hold negative opinions about Generation Xers.

Education Gap

The jobs of the future are likely to require increasing levels of technical skills and competencies. Employers are turning to remedial education programs to make up for the deficits new employees have in skills and abilities.[58] Implications for human resource management include difficulties in finding adequately qualified individuals for jobs and increased training needs for new and existing employees.

THE IMPACT OF TECHNOLOGY

A final external force on the work environment that must be anticipated by human resource professionals is the impact of technology. We believe that technology is such an important force in today's work environment that we devote attention to it in each chapter. It is featured in this chapter because it is clearly a part of the changing work environment.

Technology changes the nature of work itself and the nature of the relationship between worker and employer. There is now a computer-based application for nearly every human resource function described in this book. The pace of change in technology will continue to challenge HRM professionals to keep current. Not only will HRM applications come and go, but also the nature of the work described in classification and compensation systems will change rapidly, challenging traditional HRM processes to stay current.

An example is that advances in technology have allowed line managers to operate outside central personnel offices by advertising widely over the Internet. There are numerous sites listing available jobs in cities (see the City of Seattle Web site at **http://www.ci.seattle.wa.us/jobs/,** for example), counties, and state governments (such as the state of California at **http://www. spb.ca.gov/jobsrd.tm**). The federal government lists jobs on the Internet as well; for example, Gov Spot (**http://www.govspot.com**) and USAJOBS (**http://usajobs.opm.gov/**) list federal government jobs. General job listing sites such as Monster. com (**http://www.monster.com**) and America's Job Bank (**http://www.ajb.dni.us/**) list for-profit and nonprofit sector jobs as well as public sector jobs. Many public sector professionals belong to listservs where all members share e-mail messages. These are frequently used to advertise jobs specific to that profession. Professional associations also publish their newsletters and job announcements on their official Web page.

■ CONCLUSION

Organizational change for public agencies has become the norm rather than the exception. The causes of change have been enumerated here and in other publications, each documenting the rapid rate of technological innovations, experiments in organizational structure, and the changing nature of the workforce. Human resource managers are being asked to assist public officials in implement-ing change in the public workplace. Successfully implementing the competency model of human resource management described in Chapter 1 will require that HRM professionals anticipate and manage the changing external workplace.

■ MANAGER'S VOCABULARY

contract employees
temporary or seasonal employees
part-time employees
reinventing government
privatization
circular A-76
downsizing
reduction in force (RIF)
National Performance Review
attrition
hiring freezes
early retirement incentives
job reengineering
redeployment and retraining
part-time employment
involuntary separation
bumping
glass ceiling
Generation X

■ STUDY QUESTIONS

1. What are the HRM pros and cons of privatizing a governmental function?

2. What are some of the unintended impacts of a poorly planned downsizing effort?

3. How will HRM functions such as recruitment and benefits administration change with the increasingly diverse workforce?

■ EXPERIENTIAL EXERCISES

1. You are the new assistant to the HRM director for your city. The city is considering contracting out its garbage collection services to a for-profit company. The employees from the garbage collection services are very nervous about what might happen to them if the change goes through. The city council is hopeful that this move will save money. The HRM director has asked you to sketch out the possible impacts on HRM from such a move for the next city council meeting. What sorts of issues will you address in your briefing?

2. You are the assistant director and Dave Smith is one of your supervisors in the city public works department. He has been with the city twenty-five years. Dave comes to you to complain about Shane, a recently hired college graduate under his supervision. Although Shane's work is competently done, Dave notes that Shane does not seem interested in getting ahead. Dave is also worried that Shane's casual dress, earrings, and what he refers to as his "unusual" music at his workstation may be alienating the other engineers in the department. What do you recommend to Dave?

■ CASES APPLICABLE TO THIS CHAPTER

"Governor Pat Ronage's Hiring Freeze" and "Downsizing at the ACHD."

■ NOTES

1. Donald E. Klingner and Dahlia Bradshaw Lynn, "Beyond Civil Service: The Changing Face of Public Personnel Management," *Public Personnel Management* 26 (Summer 1997): 157–162.
2. See David Osborne and Ted Gaebler, *Reinventing Government—How the Entrepreneurial Spirit is Transforming the Public Sector* (Reading MA: Addison-Wesley, 1992).
3. Klingner and Lynn, "Beyond Civil Service," p. 161.
4. International Personnel Management Association (IPMA), *1998 IPMA/NASPE Pilot Human Resource Benchmarking Summary Report* (Alexandria, VA: IPMA, 1998), p. 15.
5. Klingner and Lynn, "Beyond Civil Service," p. 161.
6. Ibid.; see also L. B. Elam, "Reinventing Government Privatization Style—Avoiding the Legal Pitfalls of Replacing Civil Servants and Contract Providers," *Public Personnel Management* 26 (Spring 1997): 29.
7. Klingner and Lynn, "Beyond Civil Service," p. 162.
8. Judith R. Saidel, "Dimensions of Interdependence: The State and Voluntary-Sector Relationship," *Nonprofit and Voluntary Sector Quarterly* 18:4 (1989): 340.
9. Osborne and Gaebler, *Reinventing Government.*
10. David Osborne and Peter Plastrik, *Banishing Bureaucracy: The Five Strategies for Reinventing Government* (Reading, MA: Addison-Wesley, 1997), p. 10.
11. Ibid., p. 14.
12. "Human Resources," *Governing* (February 1999): 24.
13. Ibid., p. 25.
14. Ibid.
15. Steven W. Hays, "The State of the Discipline in Public Personnel Administration," *Public Administration Quarterly* (Fall 1996): 292.
16. Quoted in Andrew I. E. Ewoh, "An Inquiry into the Role of Public Employers and Managers in Privatization," *Review of Public Personnel Administration* 19 (Winter 1999): 10.
17. Ibid., p. 11.
18. Elam, "Reinventing Government Privatization Style," p. 29.
19. Wendell C. Lawther, "The Role of Public Employees in the Privatization Process: Personnel and Transition Issues," *Review of Public Personnel Administration* 19 (Winter 1999): 31.
20. Ibid., p. 30.
21. Ewoh, "An Inquiry," 9.
22. Frank S. Ravitch and Wendell C. Lawther, "Privatization and Public Employee Pension Rights: Treading in Unexplored Territory," *Review of Public Personnel Administration* 19 (Winter 1999): 53.
23. Ewoh, "An Inquiry," 22.
24. Robert S. Gilmour and Laura S. Jensen, "Reinventing Government Accountability: Public Functions, Privatization, and the Meaning of 'State Action'," *Public Administration Review* 58:3 (1998): 247–258. National Center for Nonprofit Boards, "Scandals, " *Board Member* 5:5 (1996): 2–15.

25 William McKinley, Carol M. Sanchez, and Allen Schick, "Organizational Downsizing: Constraining, Cloning, Learning," *Academy of Management Executive* 9 (August 1995): 2.

26 Kim S. Cameron, "Strategies for Successful Organizational Downsizing," *Human Resource Management* 33:2 (Summer 1994): 198.

27 General Accounting Office (GAO), *Federal Downsizing: Better Workforce and Strategic Planning Could Have Made Buyouts More Effective* (GAO/GGD 96–62) (Washington, D.C.: U.S. Government Printing Office, 1996).

28 James B. King, "The Government of the Future: A Personnel Perspective," *Public Manager* (Summer 1997): 21.

29 GAO, *Federal Downsizing: Better Workforce,* p. 0:3.

30 Adapted from Cynthia D. Fisher, Lyle F. Schoenfeldt, and James B. Shaw, *Human Resource Management,* 2nd ed. (Boston: Houghton Mifflin, 1993), p. 735; GAO, *Federal Downsizing,* p. 0:3.

31 Kim S. Cameron, "Strategies for Successful Organizational Downsizing," *Human Resource Management* 33 (Summer 1994): 198.

32 The following description of a reduction in force policy is taken from the State of Idaho, *Department of Administration Personnel Procedure Manual* (Boise: State of Idaho, January 2000), chap. 4, available at **http://ww2.state.id.us/adm/humanresource/index.htm.**

33 Cameron, "Strategies," p. 189.

34 GAO, *Federal Downsizing: Better Workforce*; General Accounting Office, *Federal Downsizing: Agency Officials' Views on Maintaining Performance During Downsizing at Selected Agencies* (letter report)(GAO/GGD 98–46) (Washington, D.C.: U.S. Government Printing Office, 1998).

35 GAO, *Federal Downsizing: Better Workforce*, p. 0:4.1.

36 Ibid., p. 0:3.

37 Cameron, "Strategies," p. 198.

38 GAO, *Federal Downsizing: Agency Officials' Views;* General Accounting Office, *Federal Downsizing: Better Workforce and Strategic Planning Could Have Made Buyouts More Effective* (GAO/GGD-96–62). Available at: **http://www.access.gpo.gov/su_docs/aces160.shtml.**

39 GAO 1998, *Federal Downsizing: Agency Officials' Views.*

40 Cameron, "Strategies," p. 202.

41 See, for example, GAO, *Federal Downsizing: Better Workforce,* p. 0:4.3.

42 Fisher, Schoenfeldt, and Shaw, *Human Resource Management,* p. 740.

43 Howard Hayghe, "Development in Women's Labor Force Participation," *Monthly Labor Review* (September 1997): 41.

44 Ibid., p. 42.

45 U.S. Department of Labor Women's Bureau, *Working Women Count: A Report to the Nation* (Washington, D.C.: U.S. Government Printing Office, 1994).

46 U.S. Merit Systems Protection Board, *A Question of Equity: Women and the Glass Ceiling in the Federal Government* (Washington, D.C.: U.S. Merit Systems Protection Board, October 1992).

47 See, for example, Stephen Barr, "Up Against the Glass," *Management Review* (September 1996): 12–17.

48 Office of Personnel Management, *Annual Report to Congress on the Federal Equal Opportunity Recruitment Program* (Washington, D.C.: U.S. Government Printing Office, 1996).

49 Quoted in Mary E. Guy and Meredith A. Newman, "Toward Diversity in the Workplace, " in Stephen E. Condrey, ed., *Handbook of Human Resource Management in Government* (San Francisco: Jossey-Bass, 1997), p. 77.

50 Ibid., p. 76.

51 William B. Johnston and Arnold C. Packer, *Workforce 2000: Work and Workers for the Twenty-first Century* (Indianapolis: Hudson Institute, June 1987), p. 79.

52 ICMA, *21st Century Workplace Trends.* Available at: **http:icma.org.**

53 Rick Mauer, "Don't Resist Generation X: Understand and Learn to Manage Them," *IPMA News* (November 1998): 19.

54 See B. Tulgan, *Managing Generation X* (Santa Monica, CA: Merritt Press, 1995).

55 Guy and Newman, "Toward Diversity," p. 78; ICMA, *21st Century.*

56 Mauer, "Don't Resist," p. 19.

57 Cited in ibid.

58 Claire J. Anderson and Betty Roper Ricks, "Illiteracy—The Neglected Enemy in Public Service," *Public Personnel Management* 22 (Spring 1993): 137–152.

CHAPTER 3

Development of Civil Service Systems in the United States

What doesn't work and you can't fire it?
An MX missile? A NASA rocket?
No. A civil service employee.[1]

Few other occupations have been the objects of as much ridicule as the federal civil servant. The stereotype of a swollen federal agency populated by an abundance of feckless, listless, and uncaring civil servants is so common it hardly requires illustration. The very word *bureaucrat* has become an epithet in common parlance.

How much truth is there to the offensive stereotype, and how did it develop? To approach an understanding of these questions, we must examine the evolution of public sector merit systems within the broader political context of American government. This chapter first describes the political environment of public personnel administration in the United States and then examines the historical development of our civil service system. Along the way, we will discover that important parts of the widely shared civil servant stereotype are quite undeserved.

INTRODUCTION TO READING

The reading for this chapter is taken from the work of Paul Van Riper and originally appeared as a chapter in his seminal treatise, *History of the United States Civil Service System,* published in 1958. The selection reprinted here details the legislative history of the Pendleton Act, the federal legislation that created the merit-based civil service system of the U.S. government in 1883. Substantial parts of that original system are still in place today. Prior to passage of the Pendleton Act, government jobs were generally awarded on the basis of political loyalty, or patronage. The civil service system was intended to remove the corruption often associated with patronage and to increase the efficiency and effectiveness of government operations.

The title of the reading, "Americanizing a Foreign Invention," refers to the fact that the Pendleton Act derives substantial inspiration from the British civil service system. The British system was much admired for its emphasis on merit-based testing and its perceived advantages of neutral service and independent expertise over our own patronage-based system of public employment. Congress, however, resisted importing many aspects of the British system, especially those that reinforced the class distinctions prevalent in British and European society generally at that time. The resulting legislation created a hybrid system, with political appointees preserved at the top levels of our agencies and civil service employees below.

As the civil service system became more complex, public sector managers became frustrated with its rule-driven nature. Calls for reforms to introduce management flexibility and do away with the practice of surreptitious evasion of the civil service system became constant themes in the literature of public personnel administration. Calls for change and reform of public personnel systems have been constant since personnel systems were first put into place. In commenting on a new public personnel textbook in 1948, Wallace S. Sayre criticized public personnel administration in a now-famous review:

> Personnel administration, then, has tended to become characterized more by procedure, rule and technique than by purpose or results. In the public field, especially, quantitative devices have overshadowed qualitative. Standardization and uniformity have been enshrined as major virtues. Universal (and therefore arbitrary) methods have been preferred to experiment and variety. From the perspective of the clientele (the public, the managers, and the employees), these traits increasingly connote rigidity, bureaucracy, institutionalism; and they are now beginning to evoke a reciprocal system of formal and informal techniques of evasion. Among personnel people there is an accompanying growth of frustration and a loss of satisfying participation in the real work of the organization.[2]

In 1973, E. S. Savas and Sigmund Ginsburg wrote this of New York City's civil service system:

> In trying to prevent itself from doing the wrong things of nepotism, patronage, prejudice, favoritism, corruption—the civil service system has been warped and distorted to the point where it can do hardly anything at all. In an attempt to protect against past abuses, the "merit system" has been perverted and transformed into a closed and meritless seniority system. A true merit system must be constructed anew; one that provides the opportunity for any qualified citizen to gain access nonpolitically, to be recognized and rewarded for satisfactory performance, and even to be replaced for unsatisfactory service.[3]

The complaints and calls for reform of HRM in the public sector have not changed greatly since 1948. Hays and Kearney point out that various studies, including the Volker Commission (1989), the Winter Commission (1989), and the National Performance Review (1993), all emphasize the importance of being responsive to the needs of those who depend on human resource services in public organizations.[4]

In a recent review of the literature, Hays and Kearney identify four major recommendations for HRM that echo throughout several recent reform proposals:

1. Enhancing management discretion in personnel management
2. Increasing the flexibility and responsiveness of public personnel systems
3. Improving public sector performance
4. Adopting private sector personnel management techniques

Each of these recommendations is related; together they are a call for human resource staff to be supportive of the mission of the public agency and contributive to agency productivity, efficiency, and effectiveness. Managers want their human resource staff to help them bring in qualified and competent people to do the work of the agency and help maintain a productive, reasonably satisfied workforce. They do not want rigid rules and extended processes interfering with the effective performance of the public's business.

In response to both the recommendations of high-level commissions and the stark necessities of a rapidly changing environment, a number of initiatives and reform efforts are gradually changing the face of human resource management in the public sector. Although some of these efforts have been dubbed with trendy names, such as "reinventing government" and "self-directed work teams," the effects of these ideas will continue to influence HRM for many years to come.

The challenge of finding the way to maximize the fairness and efficiency of operation of personnel management systems in government continues to this day. As you read the following selection, keep the following questions in mind:

- What attributes of European administrative systems were the writers of the Pendleton Act hoping to instill in the U.S. civil service system?
- In what ways is our system a hybrid of those European and American practices?

READING

Americanizing a Foreign Invention: The Pendleton Act of 1883

PAUL P. VAN RIPER

There seems to be a general impression both at home and abroad that the civil service in the United States has, as Americans sometimes put it, "just growed" without much conscious direction. To a limited extent this is true. Certainly civil service reform was not adopted as fully in as short a period of time as was the case in Great Britain.

However, a fairly complete and firm legislative foundation for the development of a civil service based on examinations and merit in the English manner has existed in the United States since the passage of the Pendleton Act of 1883.[1] It is important, therefore, that we consider this fundamental piece of legislation in some detail, not only because it was the first legislation of its kind in this country, but also because it today enjoys the unusual distinction of remaining on the statute books without fundamental change since its passage three-quarters of a century ago. Essentially a modification of a British political invention in terms of the constitutional and administrative inclinations of this country, the Pendleton Act becomes even more intriguing as a case study in cross-cultural adaptation, a topic of increasing interest and concern in the modern political world.

What kind of law, then, was this new civil service reform act of 1883, passed so precipitately by a Republican Congress hitherto apathetic at best toward governmental reform of any sort?

THE LEGISLATIVE DEBATE

The legislative debate which preceded the passage of the Pendleton Act was limited almost exclusively to the Senate. When the bill came before the House nearly all attempts to discuss it were literally shouted down, and it was overwhelmingly approved. The most likely explanation for the difference in legislative attitude lies in the fact that the members of the House knew they would be affected by the next election far more than the members of the Senate. The House was taking no chances. Reform was too important an issue at this time.

Fortunately for any analysis of congressional intent, the Senate debate was detailed and exhaustive.[2] Nearly all the major problems involved in the legislation were discussed at length. A sizable number of amendments—with only a few deliberately obstructionist—were considered and many adopted. The likely effects of the proposed legislation upon the constitutional position of the President and Congress, upon the party system, upon the civil service, and upon the public in general were thoroughly explored. Political assessments, the corruption of the previous twenty years, and the history of the reform before 1883 both in the United States and Great Britain were presented in detail. All in all the debate fills nearly 200 pages in the *Congressional Record*. That the argument frequently revolved around a strictly partisan quarrel over responsibility for the system which was to be reformed is quite true. But the major portion of the debate, occupying by far the greater part of the Senate's time for two weeks, was to the point.

This debate, plus the reports of two Senate committees, together with a consideration of the implications of certain events of the preceding twenty years or so, make possible a fairly clear analysis of the thinking involved in the new legislation.[3] An analysis of the voting shows that the later claims of both parties for credit for passage of the act are not entirely justified.[4] The Democrats by no means fully supported Senator Pendleton. If anything, the law must be considered primarily a Republican measure, spurred somewhat by the assassination of Garfield.

Source: Chapter 5 in *History of the United States Civil Service* by Paul P. Van Riper. Copyright © 1958 by Harper & Row, Publishers, Inc. by permission of the publisher.

However, this event has been overrated as an immediate cause of the enactment of the Pendleton Act. After all, Garfield had been shot a year and a half before its passage. More important as a motivating force for Republican action in late 1883 were the Republican reverses in the election of 1882. The Republicans were apprehensive about the 1884 election, while the Democrats were hopeful. Nevertheless, the sponsor of the new law was a prominent Democrat and the legislation profited from the careful attention of representatives of both parties.

FUNDAMENTALS OF THE ACT

The Pendleton bill as reported to the Senate provided, basically, for the adoption of the British civil service system in the United States. A commission was to administer competitive examinations; entrance into the public service would be possible only at the bottom; a full-scale career service was implied; and the offices were not to be used for political purposes. Throughout the Senate debate, reference was constantly made to European experience, and especially that of the British. However, the act as finally approved followed the British reform pattern only in a very general way.

In America, as in England, the central concept was that of *competitive examinations* for entrance into the public service. The Senate Committee on Civil Service and Retrenchment, in reporting the Pendleton measure, said:

> The single, simple, fundamental, pivotal idea of the whole bill is, that whenever, hereafter, a new appointment or a promotion shall be made in the subordinate civil service in the departments or larger offices, such appointment or promotion shall be given to the man who is best fitted to discharge the duties of the position, and that such fitness shall be ascertained by open, fair, honest, impartial, competitive examination.[5]

Though the old idea of pass-examinations was occasionally referred to in the Senate committee reports and the debate to follow, Congress showed no inclination to challenge the fundamental idea of entrance into the public service via a really serious competition.

Congress also accepted the idea of relative *security of tenure* for employees entering the service through the examination system. The whole idea of entrance by examination meant, in itself, a considerable guarantee of tenure, because it tended to eliminate the incentive for removals. Beyond this, under the new law appointing officers could not discharge classified employees[6] for refusal to be politically active. To be sure, this prohibition was not reinforced by any criminal penalty and its execution was entirely up to the pleasure of the executive branch of the government. There was little the Civil Service Commission could do by itself about political removals, other than investigate and publicize the facts. But as long as Congress favored the elimination of politics from the competitive service, President Arthur's support was assured.[7]

The final concept for which any debt is owed to the British is that of the *neutrality* of the civil service. Congress forbade any employees covered by the new act" to coerce the political action of any person," and the new Commission was directed to prepare rules to implement this prohibition as well as that directed against political removals of competitive employees. Further, the Senate amended the act to provide substantial penalties for political assessments of or by competitive employees, or by any other federal officials.[8] However, only in the case of assessments was any criminal penalty attached to the provisions designed to insure neutrality. Again, the constitutional authority as well as the inclination of the chief executive was to be relied upon. It would take a President Cleveland and a President Theodore Roosevelt to turn this possibility of developing a nonpartisan civil service into something approaching reality. In effect, the Pendleton Act *demanded* nonpartisanship in initial selection procedures (for a limited number of positions) but only *encouraged* nonpartisanship in other matters.

We can conclude, then, that the American legislation of 1883 stimulated the development in the United States of a *merit system* founded on British precedents: that is, a system of civil service recruitment and organization based on (1) competitive examinations, (2) relative security of tenure, and (3) political neutrality. On the other hand, the new act also reflected peculiarly American patterns of thought and action. If we appropriated the main outlines of the foreign device, we were anything but abject copyists. We thoroughly adapted it to the American political and social climate.

As early as December 6, 1881, President Arthur has referred to the Pendleton bill, even then before the Senate, in his first message to Congress and had noted its "conformity with the existing civil-service system of Great Britain." But he had also noted with prophetic insight that "there are certain features of the English system which have not generally been received with favor in this country, even among the foremost advocates of civil-service reform."[9] The problem was to reconcile British ideas with American experience and inclination.

THE POWER TO HIRE

First of all, the American conception of a proper competitive examination for public office differed radically from that of the British. Even the relatively down-to-earth examinations used by the Grant Commission had been criticized as too theoretical. Therefore, the Senate, by an amendment to the original legislation, instructed the new commission to make its tests "practical in character" and related to the duties that would be performed. The Senate and the public were averse to the academic essay-type of civil service testing then—and frequently still—current in Great Britain. Ever since 1883 testing development in this country has consistently reflected this basic American idea of the desirability of the "practical."

Many senators were especially incensed over the proposal of the Pendleton bill to permit entrance into the public service *only* "at the lowest grade." Finally, Senator Pendleton himself proposed an amendment to strike out the offending provision. It was overwhelmingly accepted without even the formality of a roll call. Another amendment opened up promotional examinations to more general competition than had been originally envisioned. We had no desire to develop an entirely ingrown civil establishment.

While the British civil service was normally closed to outsiders except at the bottom, the American federal service was to continue to be infiltrated by new talents at all levels. From 1883 to this day, one may enter the American public service at almost any level and at almost any age. Indeed, the adoption of age and other restrictions tending to prevent this mobility have been on many occasions, and often still are, bitterly attacked as "undemocratic."

Throughout the entire history of the public service the federal offices have never been permitted to form any kind of closed bureaucratic system on the European pattern. Such a mobile system, approaching the mobility of private employment, is unique among modern national public services. Its foundation was firmly embedded in the legislation of 1883. It has been responsible for the continuance of the representative type of bureaucracy which the Jacksonian Democrats had first declared to be a fundamental requisite of the democratic state.

In details of recruitment procedure the act also paid its respects to the Jacksonian theories of democracy in public office, and especially to the idea of rotation in office. No more than two members of the same family were declared to be eligible for public office. The majority of the clerical offices in the city of Washington were to be filled according to an "apportionment" of offices among the states, based upon population. Later in 1883, this last provision was interpreted to mean "as nearly as may be practicable." Its inclusion in the act undoubtedly secured much political support for the reform which otherwise might have been withheld. The authors of the legislation of 1883 and their political supporters, knowingly or unknowingly, were taking as few chances as possible that the American civil service might not be representative of the nation as a whole, in terms of geography, mobility, ideals, and outlook.

THE POWER TO FIRE

Americans also refused to accept the almost absolute security of tenure that has often been guaranteed to European civil servants, and which reflects the veneration by Europeans of the mechanisms of the state. Both the original civil service reformers and many subsequent American legislators have consistently fought against an overly absolute tenure as undesirable and unnecessary for civil service reform. Life tenure in office had been repudiated in 1829 and there was no desire to revive the idea in 1883. Besides, the removal power was a potent political tool which could not be lightly discarded.

Since 1829, the principal American controversy about tenure had been over whether the power to remove should be left primarily in the hands of the President or in the hands of Congress. That the removal power of the President was left largely untouched was the outstanding difference between pre–Civil War attempts at reform and the Act of 1883. Under the new legislation there was no bar to opening the so-called "back-door" to the classified service, as long as removals were not for partisan reasons. Undoubtedly the failure of the principal effort to limit the executive removal power, the attempted impeachment of President Johnson, helped force political minds to think in other terms. Senator George F. Hoar, a Massachusetts Republican, represented a fairly typical opinion when, during the course of the Senate debate on the Pendleton Act, he said:

> The measure commends itself to me also because. . . . It does not assert any disputed legislative control over the tenure of office. The great debate as to the President's power of removal, . . . which began in the first Congress, . . . does not in the least become important under the skillful and admirable provisions of this bill.
>
> It does not even . . . deal directly with the question of removals, but it takes away every possible temptation to improper removals.[10]

Nonetheless, a portion of the credit for this innovation must be given to the reformers, who consistently emphasized that, if the *front-door* were properly tended, the *back-door* would take care of itself. The supervision of the one would remove the incentive for the abuse of the other. George William Curtis, for instance, felt in 1876 that any system of "removal by lawsuit" would completely demoralize the service:

> Having annulled all reason for the improper exercise of the power of dismissal, we hold that it is better to take the risk of occasional injustice from passion and prejudice, which no law or regulation can control, than to seal up incompetency, negligence, insubordination, insolence, and every other mischief in the service, by requiring a virtual trial at law before an unfit or incapable clerk can be removed.[11]

Senator Pendleton accepted the reformers' view of the proper way to regulate dismissals, and it was not successfully challenged in the debates that followed. The Act of 1883 left the President in control of his own household as far as the power to fire was concerned. Once more the "decision of 1789" was reaffirmed.

ADMINISTRATIVE DETAILS

From an administrative point of view, the act was based firmly upon the experience gained from the ill-fated Grant Commission of 1871–75. In fact, the new law provided that the President should have all the powers of the 1871 legislation not inconsistent with the Pendleton Act. Similarly, the simple clerical classification acts of the 1850s and an already existing military preference statute of a mild, exhortatory character were specifically integrated into the bill. Senator Pendleton, in answering the first question put to him after concluding his initial speech in favor of the bill, replied:

> . . . this system is not entirely new, but . . . to a very large extent in certain offices in New York, in Philadelphia, and in Boston it has been put into practical operation under the heads of the offices there, and . . . they have devised, with the assistance of the commission originally appointed by General Grant, but largely upon their own motion, a system which I suppose would, to some extent, be followed under this bill.[12]

The careful statement of a careful legislator, his remarks indicate where indebtedness was due.

The agent of the executive branch in the establishment of the new personnel system was to be a bipartisan Civil Service Commission of three full-time members appointed for indefinite terms by the President with the advice and consent of the Senate.[13] The administration of the system was to be directed by a chief examiner.[14] He was to coordinate the work of the local examination boards, composed of government employees in local areas. The members of these local boards remained attached to their departments and were only to be loaned to the Commission for examination purposes. Just a very few permanent employees were expected to work full-time for the Commission itself. As the work became more and more complex and less a part-time operation, the dependence upon other departments for "details" of working personnel, full-time as well as part-time, caused the Commission many headaches. Full-time details ended in the 1920s, but the "local board system" still remains very much alive today. However, it now supplements the activity of a greatly expanded body of full-time Commission employees numbering more than 4,000 since 1950.

The new agency was required to keep the necessary records, conduct investigations, and make reports to Congress through the President. As soon as possible, it was to publish its rules implementing the act, subject of course to the approval of the President. For housekeeping purposes the Secretary of the Interior was designated to provide quarters and essential supplies for the new organization. He had, however, no other jurisdiction over the Commission. This arrangement was not entirely satisfactory and was completely terminated by 1925.

Turning to minor details, the act provided for a probationary period of six months. Applicants were forbidden to present recommendations from senators and representatives which referred to matters other than character and residence. Drunkards were made ineligible for governmental positions. Appointments were to be made from "among those graded highest." This latter phrase was then used for institutional rather than administrative reasons as a result of an important opinion of the Attorney General, discussed in detail shortly. In effect, this provided that the regulations must offer some discretion for the appointing officer. That the "rule of three" (a rule of "four" was adopted from 1883 to 1888), followed still today, was originally based upon constitutional necessity, rather than upon administrative desirability or upon any occult power of the word "three," is often forgotten. The act also provided that any commissioner or other public employee who might be found guilty of any collusion or corruption in the administration of the examinations should be open to punishment by a fine of up to $1,000 or imprisonment up to a year or both.

CONSTITUTIONAL QUESTIONS

In yet another important respect the Pendleton Act reflected the peculiarities of the American Constitution as well as those of the political tendencies of the times. The new legislation, for the most part, was *permissive* rather than mandatory. The act itself placed only slightly over 10 percent of the positions in the federal public service—mainly clerical positions in Washington and in post offices and custom houses employing fifty or more persons—under the merit system to form the *classified civil service.* The remainder of the civil service was left *unclassified,* to be brought under the new regulations by Executive Order when and if the President saw fit. The only public officials exempted from the authority of the President under the act were laborers and those whose appointments were subject to the advice and consent of the Senate. These exemptions accounted for roughly 20 to 30 percent of the federal civil service, which in the 1880s averaged over 140,000.

The permissive nature of the act—a relatively unusual characteristic in American legislation—stemmed from two somewhat different but temporarily compatible sets of circumstances. It was both politically and administratively impossible in 1883 to apply the merit system to the entire federal civil service. Administratively, the Civil Service Commission simply was not ready to do a complete job as yet. It takes time to develop examinations, to organize boards to administer the examinations, and to obtain the cooperation of the departmental agencies and the general public.[15] Permissiveness also had its political advantages. The politicians were able to announce that they had accomplished the desired reform—the rest being up to the President—knowing full well that they would not be hurt through a too sudden or drastic curtailing of their patronage. If the act permitted an orderly retreat of parties from their prerogatives of plunder, it made possible as well the gradual administrative development of the merit system.[16] Had the merit system been forced to wait for precise formulation and expansion by successive Congresses, no one knows what the result might have been. Under the law of 1883, the President was free to move as fast or as slowly as political circumstances might permit, under the broad, general rules laid down by Congress. The permissive feature was thus a recognition of practical political as well as administrative realities.

It probably was also necessary from a constitutional point of view. From the very beginning of the civil service reform movement, a large number of congressmen and politicians questioned the constitutionality of the new political device. Lionel Murphy, in his history of the first Civil Service Commission appointed by President Grant, has described how the new plan for centralized control of public personnel administration in the hands of a commission was attacked as an unconstitutional invasion of the powers both of Congress and of the President over personnel matters. The members of this Commission felt they had to defer any plans for a merit system until they first received an opinion by Attorney General Akerman on the constitutionality of the proposed arrangement.[17]

Akerman's opinion, however, did not fully resolve the conflict. One cannot join what is deliberately put asunder. He insisted that it was not constitutional for Congress by law to give to the Commission power which the Constitution places in the President, the department heads, and the courts of law. Congress "has no power to vest appointments elsewhere, directly or indirectly." However, in support of the Commission, Akerman went about as far as he could go. He concluded that:

> The test of a competitive examination may be resorted to in order to inform the conscience of the appointing power, but cannot be made legally conclusive upon that power against its own judgment and will. . . . Though the appointing power alone can designate an individual for an office, either Congress, by direct legislation, or the President, by authority derived from Congress, can prescribe qualifications, and require that the designation shall be made out of a class of persons ascertained by proper tests to have those qualifications.[18]

The ultimate constitutional dilemma involved in the regulation of the powers of appointment and removal within the American framework of government is well put in the unusually forthright conclusion to Akerman's opinion:

> The act under which the present civil-service commission has been organized gives the President authority "to prescribe such rules and regulations for the admission of persons into the civil service of the United States as will best promote the efficiency thereof," and this very ample authority will certainly embrace the right to require that the person admitted into the service shall have been found qualified by competent examiners.
>
> It has been argued that a right in Congress to limit in the least the field of selection, implies a right to carry on the contracting process to the designation of a particular individual. But I do not think this a fair conclusion. Congress could require that officers shall be of American citizenship of a certain age, that judges should be of the legal profession and of a certain standing in the profession, and still leave room to the appointing power for the exercise of its own judgment and will; and I am not prepared to affirm that to go further, and require that the selection shall be made from persons found by an examining board to be qualified in such particulars as diligence, scholarship, integrity, good manners, and attachment to the Government, would impose an unconstitutional limitation on the appointing power. It would still have a reasonable scope for its

own judgment and will. But it may be asked, at what point must the contracting process stop? I confess my inability to answer. But the difficulty of drawing a line between such limitations as are, and such as are not, allowed by the Constitution, is no proof that both classes do not exist. In constitutional and legal inquiries, right or wrong is often a question of degree. Yet it is impossible to tell precisely where in the scale right ceases and wrong begins. Questions of excessive bail, cruel punishments, excessive damages, and reasonable doubts are familiar instances. In the matter now in question, it is not supposable that Congress or the President would require of candidates for office qualifications unattainable by a sufficient number to afford ample room for choice. . . .[19]

There was little else that Akerman could say under our existing constitutional arrangement, and the principles of his opinion still govern today. No wonder Oliver Field, nearly seventy years later, considered the legal basis of our federal merit system to be somewhat uncertain and concluded that in the states, all of which also operate under the separation-of-powers doctrine, as well as in the federal government:

> The theory upon which civil service laws have been upheld as constitutional, in so far as they affect the appointing power itself, is that the officer to whom the appointing power is given retains that discretion which it was intended he should exercise in making appointments, but that as an aid to his exercise of the power, another body may be given the power to determine the qualifications necessary for the position under consideration.[20]

After Akerman's opinion and much discussion of the problem, Congress did not feel that it should—it is questionable if it legally could—go too far in making the provisions of the Pendleton Act mandatory upon the President. Indicative of current thinking on the subject was the testimony of George William Curtis before the Senate Committee on Civil Service and Retrenchment on February 26, 1882. Curtis was speaking here of two bills then before the Committee—that of Pendleton and another temporarily proposed by Senator Henry L. Dawes of Massachusetts—and in reply to questions by two senators concerning the effect of the bills upon the relationship of the President to the proposed Commission:

. . . Of course the bills in no sense change the President's constitutional power. The Pendleton bill simply recognizes that the President appoints, and substantially they both provide for the same exercise of power, so far as that is concerned, although the exercise is different in its details. If the President chose to disregard it, he would take no action, and there would be no remedy except in public opinion. *The whole thing presupposes a friendly President.*[21]

During the entire legislative debate and in the two major committee reports there was no attempt to change the presidential relationship described by Curtis.

There were, however, those like Senator Charles H. Van Wyck of Nebraska and Senator Wilkinson Call of Florida, who felt that the Pendleton bill—because it affected the power of the President so little—was unnecessary in light of the legislation of 1871. If the bill only outlined what the President already had authority to do, then why bother? But in 1882 the Senate accepted the proposition that, without congressional approval and encouragement, it was impossible for the executive branch to carry out the reform alone. Moreover, the portions of the bill which provided for criminal sanctions for several types of offenses were clearly beyond the power of the executive branch acting alone.

As a result, the act—and others like it, such as the more recent Ramspeck Act of 1940—for the most part merely authorizes, but does not require, the President to place offices in the classified civil service and under the merit system. This means that the great bulk of the federal employees under the merit system are there by Executive Order. Thus it would probably be legal for the President today to return to the processes of spoils politics a great many of the public offices now under the merit system. All the President needs do to accomplish this is to issue another executive order. Actually several presidents have returned positions to the unclassified service, McKinley, for instance, returning several thousand during his first term in office.

To put the whole problem another way: the constitutional realities of a separation of powers made it impossible for the American Congress to make the competitive system mandatory in the way that it had been made mandatory in Great Britain. From a superficial examination it might seem as if both coun-

tries had faced a similar problem, one to be solved in a similar fashion. British constitutional opinion, like American, agreed that the executive branch could be advised, but not directed, in its selection of personnel.

But the similarity ends there. The British Crown is not, nor was it in mid-nineteenth century, an executive comparable to the American Presidency. The one is shadow; the other is real. There has never been any great conflict in modern England arising from the separation of powers. That the British competitive system was the result of a series of Orders in Council is well known, but those Orders in Council actually represented the Cabinet which in turn represented the legislative branch of the government. British reform was therefore the result of legislative requirement and legislative mandate.

In the United States the legislative branch had attempted to coerce the executive branch in a similar fashion in the 1860s and failed. The Pendleton Act recognized that failure and attempted to avoid another such impasse. American constitutional realities simply are not British constitutional realities and the American version of British civil service reform has reflected, and will continue to reflect, such fundamental differences in governmental systems.

SAFEGUARDS

Since the Pendleton Act left the President's power to hire and fire relatively unimpeded, what safeguards were planned by a Congress which had not long before threatened a president with impeachment in an effort to control his relationship to public office-holders?

In the first place, the development of the merit system was considered as effective a check against the President as against Congress. Further, no more than two members of the agency administering the new law were to represent the same political party. Finally, the Civil Service Commission was to be outside the traditional administrative hierarchy. The new agency was to be as nonpolitical as possible and as free from interference from either the executive or the legislative branches as feasible under the American Constitution.[22] The Civil Service Commission thus became the first of the separate commissions, devised to remove controversial issues from the hands of the usual administrative and political channels and thus to avoid some of the most acrimonious of the presidential-congressional conflicts. The emergence of a new[23] administrative pattern on the federal scene was undoubtedly related to a perception by Congress—whether consciously verbalized or merely sensed does not matter—that the relatively novel idea of political neutrality in civil service selection methods deserved a relatively novel administrative solution if it was to survive.

Nevertheless, the Civil Service Commission differs in several important respects from later regulatory boards such as the Interstate Commerce Commission. The members of the Civil Service Commission may be removed by the President without restriction. While it is their duty to advise the President on matters of policy affecting the public service, the Pendleton Act specifies that the regulations made by them derive their authority from and will be promulgated by the President. Hence, the Commission cannot properly be classed as an *independent* commission, though it represents a political innovation of some importance.

THE END OF TWO ERAS

Just as 1829 marked the end of the bureaucracy of the Founding Fathers, 1883 marked the first great inroad into the spoils system of the mid-nineteenth century. Twice within a hundred years the American public service had been "reformed." What fundamental contrasts can be drawn between the two movements?

The Jacksonian movement can best be described as a class bursting bonds. As the new democracy received the ballot—its ticket of admission to participation in government—it insisted on a show to its pleasure. And the cast of characters was adjusted accordingly. American democracy moved by the logic implicit in its premises to recognition—practical this time, not theoretical—of the implications of both liberty and equality. Public office was to become almost a perquisite of citizenship and "rotation" the watchword. The spoils system provided a system of recruitment for public office very little at odds with the individualism of the day. May the best man win! The whole mechanism reflected the ideals and attitudes of American nineteenth century agrarian democracy.

In the decades immediately after the Civil War, however, individualism seemed to be producing inequality. The "best" men were winning by more of a margin than many people liked to see. And not a few questioned whether those who were winning were actually the "best." What had once been intended as an opening up of public office to the mass of citizens had all the earmarks of becoming the opening up of office to plundering by the politically privileged.

In 1883, contrasted to 1829, there was no new class to turn to, nor any particular desire to turn the clock back to 1829. If democracy was not satisfied with its own product, then it would have to reform itself. There was no one else to do it.

The invention of the merit system of recruitment for public office by examination made possible a new reformation of a different sort. Essentially a foreign idea, imported from a Europe which had faced similar problems earlier, civil service reform, suitably modified to conform to American ideas of a mobile, classless society, was a scheme brilliantly devised to meet the needs of our version of the modern democratic state.

First, the Civil Service Commission could distribute offices more systematically and rationally than the spoils system had ever been able to do. While the new scheme did not guarantee a partisan apportionment of offices to the party in power, it certainly did not guarantee offices to the opposition. If a compromise had to be reached, political neutrality in the distribution of public office was reasonably acceptable to all concerned.

Second, the merit system provided a remedy for those who objected to the obvious corruption and the oligarchical tendencies of the combination of business and politics into which the spoils system had developed. Civil service reform did again open up many of the public offices to all on a new kind of equal basis;[24] and it provided through a new measure of merit, the examination system, the rewards for individual effort so prized in American life.

Finally, the new reform laid the foundation for the development of that technical expertise crucial to the operation of the modern state. And it reached this goal without offending the democratic sensibilities of the great mass of American citizens. Posing no overt threat to the overpowering individualism of the day, it nevertheless gave implicit promise of other reforms to come. Once again a form of latent antagonism between liberty and equality—potentially so explosive in a democracy—was temporarily pacified.

NOTES

[1] We may even push this back to 1871, in terms of precedent though not of effective action, if we consider the short-lived Grant Commission.

[2] Carl Fish describes the debate as "entirely unworthy of the occasion, hardly touching any of the serious considerations involved." *The Civil Service and the Patronage* (New York: Longmans, Green and Co., 1905), p. 218. The writer does not accept this judgment for the reasons indicated in the text.

[3] For the debate see the *Congressional Record,* which records almost daily discussion in the Senate from December 12, 1882, through December 27, 1882, the date of the passage of the bill by the Senate. For the only important hearings on the legislation see U.S. Congress, Senate, *The Regulation and Improvement of the Civil Service,* 46th Cong., 3d Sess., Senate Report 872, 1881 (Washington: Government Printing Office, 1881); and U.S. Congress, Senate, *Report of the Committee on Civil Service and Retrenchment,* 47th Cong., 1st Sess., Senate Report 576, 1882 (Washington: Government Printing Office, 1882). In the House there were no committee reports of even minor importance. The House approved the bill on January 4, 1883), and President Arthur signed it on January 16. For a more detailed chronology, see USCSC, *Civil Service Act: Legislative History,* a currently updated copy of which is maintained in the Commission's library. For another type of analysis of the Act of 1883, done more in terms of a chronological consideration of amendments and counter-amendments, see A. Bower Sageser's important study of *The First Two Decades of the Pendleton Act* (Lincoln: University of Nebraska, 1935), ch. ii.

[4] As tabulated by Sageser, as cited in footnote 3, pp. 57 and 59, the final votes in the two houses were as follows: In the Senate the bill was passed by 38 to 5, with 33 absent. The affirmative vote included 23 Republicans, 14 Democrats, and 1 Independent; the negative vote, 5 Democrats; and those absent, 14 Republicans, 18 Democrats, and 1 Readjuster (Independent). In the House the bill was approved by a vote of 155 to 47, with 87 not voting. The affirmative vote was cast by 102 Republicans, 49 Democrats, and 4 Nationals (Independents); the negative vote, by 7 Republicans, 39 Democrats, and 1 National, with those not voting, 39 Republicans, 41 Democrats, and 7 Nationals. In its partial criss-cross of party lines, the vote was fairly typical of our national legislative practice.

[5] U.S. Congress, Senate Report 576, as cited in footnote 3, pp. IX-X.

[6] The term "classified service" has always been interpreted to cover positions where political removal is forbidden. Until about 1895 the terms "classified service," "classified employees," "competitive employees," "po-

sitions under the merit system," and "permanent service," while not exactly synonymous, were reasonably interchangeable; and they have been so used through this chapter and the next two to follow. However, after this date, the term "classified service" became sufficiently ambiguous, for reasons explained in the supplementary notes to ch. viii, that it has been used with much more care in the chapters covering the period from McKinley's administration to the present.

[7] See President Arthur's messages to Congress on December 6, 1881, and December 4, 1882. Moreover, everyone understood that the trouble was with the legislative rather than the executive branch. The former, not the latter, had forced the dissolution of the competitive system as first established under President Grant.

[8] The inclusion of other federal officials was designed to preclude a repetition of the Hubbell case, mentioned in the previous chapter. The law of 1876 against assessments was substantially reinforced.

[9] James D. Richardson (ed.), *Messages and Papers of the Presidents* (New York: Bureau of National Literature and Art, 1905), VIII, 60.

[10] *Congressional Record,* 47th Cong., 2nd Sess., 1882, XIV, Part I, 274.

[11] As quoted in Ruth M. Berens, "Blueprint for Reform: Curtis, Eaton, and Schurz" (unpublished Master's thesis, Department of Political Science, University of Chicago, 1943), p. 50. As we have become more security minded with respect to employment, both public and private, recent legislation and custom have tended to close the back door; but, compared to European practice, it is still ajar.

[12] *Congressional Record,* 47th Cong., 2nd Sess., 1882, XIV, Part I, 207. The New York, Philadelphia, and Boston references were to experimental postal and custom house competitive examination systems established in these cities under the authority of the rider of 1871 and continued, with some success, until they were incorporated in the larger program fostered by the Pendleton Act.

[13] In 1883 it was anticipated that the commissioners would serve perhaps indefinitely. However, within a decade or so it became customary for the commissioners to offer their resignations on the occasion of a change in administration. To provide more continuity, Congress directed in 1956 that the commissioners serve for six-year, staggered terms. They may be reappointed. Most commissioners have served for less than six years, and this new legislation could in fact provide more continuity than that of 1883. However, the 1956 law did not place any barrier in the way of removal by the President other than that suggested by the six-year term; and the resignation custom may, of course, still continue.

[14] In the nineteen thirties the "Chief Examiner" was retitled "Executive Director and Chief Examiner," and in the late nineteen forties "Executive Director," Under Reor-

ganization Plan No. 5 of 1949, effective in August of that year, the administrative direction of the work of the Commission was placed officially under the authority of the Chairman (formerly known as the "President") of the Commission. There is, however, still an Executive Director who is in fact the day-by-day chief administrative officer.

[15] In testifying before the Senate Select Committee to Examine the various Branches of the Civil Service on January 13, 1881, concerning the Pendleton proposal, Dorman B. Eaton said, "Another observation I want to make is, that I think no law should be passed which would require the application of this system of examinations to the whole civil service of the government at once, or even to all that part to which it is legitimately applicable, as I have defined it. It would be too large altogether. . . . We have got to create the machinery. . . . In bringing new men together and entering for the first time upon a new system, you would be utterly overslaughed and broken down if you were to be required to carry it all on at once." U.S. Congress, Senate Report 872, as cited in footnote 3, pp. 19-20.

[16] In his study of civil service law, Oliver P. Field regards this permissiveness as a defect in the federal personnel legislation. *Civil Service Law* (Minneapolis: University of Minnesota Press, 1939), p. 4.

[17] Op. Att. Gen. 516 (31 Aug. 1871). This was well before the Curtis case of 1882 . . . in which the Supreme Court implied the constitutionality of civil service reform.

[18] For this and the quotations above, *Ibid.*, pp. 521 and 524.

[19] *Ibid.*, pp. 524–25.

[20] As cited in footnote 16, p. 13.

[21] U.S. Congress, Senate Report 576, as cited in footnote 3, p. 178. The italics are added.

[22] The Senate Committee on Civil Service and Retrenchment, on reporting the Pendleton bill in 1882, said: "Such a board is necessary to secure the coherence, the authority, the uniformity, the assurance of freedom from partiality or influence which are vital to the system." U.S. Congress, Senate Report 576, as cited in footnote 3, p. X. Earlier, in reporting the same bill to a previous Congress, the Senate Select Committee on the Civil Service also concluded, "The commission needs a firm tenure, and should be as far as practicable removed from partisan influences. It needs to have knowledge of the practical methods of the departments, without falling under mere official control." U.S. Congress, Senate Report 872, as cited in footnote 3, p. 12.

[23] The word "new" is justified in so far as the Civil Service Commission was the first federal agency of considerable importance and permanence to be organized as a semi-independent, bipartisan agency for what, in the days of its formation, was considered a kind of policing function.

[24] As Dorman B. Eaton said in testifying before the Senate Committee considering the Pendleton Bill, "This bill assumes that every citizen has an equal claim to be appointed if he has equal capacity." U.S. Congress, Senate Report 576, as cited in footnote 3, p. 6.

THE CONTEXT OF PUBLIC PERSONNEL IN THE UNITED STATES

Understanding human resource management in the public sector is impossible without an understanding of the governmental context within which the human resource function is embedded. The governmental context includes not only the structures and legal powers of government, but features a wide variety of shapes, sizes, and missions of governments within the American governmental scene. A common misperception is that most people who work for government are federal civil servants. In reality, there are a whole host of governments and there are many types of government employees. Richard Stillman describes five distinct categories of public employees:

- Political appointees, who serve without tenure and are appointed based on party ties
- Professional careerists who have "specialized expertise in specific fields . . . usually based on advanced professional training"
- General civil service administrators and workers
- Unionized workers
- Contractual employees[5]

This same pattern of different types of public employees applies across all levels of government: federal, state, county, municipal, and special district.

Public employees work not only for the federal government, but also for each of our fifty states and more than 83,000 local and special district governments.[6] In fact, by a very large margin, most people who work in the public sector do *not* work for the federal government. Through the 1990s, there were approximately 2.7 million full-time federal employees, 3.9 million state employees, and 9.6 million local employees.[7] It is also noteworthy that state and local government ranks have grown much more quickly than those of the federal government over the past thirty years. The net growth in federal civilian employment was 15 percent between 1962 and 1995, contrasted with a rate of growth of 150 percent for state and local employment.[8]

A second important part of the context of human resource management in the public sector is that most federal employees do *not* work in Washington, D.C. In fact, only 12 percent of federal employees work in the Washington, D.C., metropolitan area; 88 percent are spread throughout the United States and, to a limited extent, abroad.[9]

Another important characteristic of the public sector workforce is that contract employees who are employed by private sector companies or nonprofit organizations now do an increasing amount of the government's public service work. Some federal agencies employ as many (or more) contract employees as they do permanent employees.[10] As we will discuss later, this noteworthy development presents a whole host of new challenges for human resource management in government.

A final important characteristic of the public sector workforce is that the much-maligned civil service system covers increasingly smaller percentages of the total government workforce. The civil service system, for example, currently covers only 56 percent of all federal employees.[11] There is also evidence that state governments increasingly use routes other than their respective civil service systems to hire and manage employees.[12] Increasing numbers of civil service jobs are being changed to "exempt-status (political) discretionary appointments. The United States uses a higher proportion of discretionary positions and political appointees than any other Western nation.[13]

In summary, the common perception that most public sector employees are federal civil servants is grossly incorrect. Most government employees work for levels of government other than the federal government, and there is a wide variety of employment systems present in the American public sector setting. The developments and frustrations that lead to the increasing use of non–civil service avenues to hire new employees is detailed below.

THE U.S. POLITICAL SYSTEM AND HUMAN RESOURCE MANAGEMENT

The political system determines how many positions there will be in government, how much these employees will be paid, and how people for those positions will be selected. Therefore, an understanding of that system and how it affects human resource management is important. The separation of powers, federalism, political parties, a tradition of strong individual rights, and the ubiquitous presence of interest groups all deserve special attention in this regard. These features of the American political setting work together to make for a highly politicized environment for public personnel administration.

Separation of Powers

The **separation of powers** between the executive and legislative branches means that the president and Congress share responsibility for the management of the federal civil service and most of its public agencies. The same can be said of governors and legislatures in the fifty states.

Power struggles between the executive and legislative branches can have a major impact on the structure and funding of executive branch personnel systems. Chief executives and members of the legislative branch often disagree on the proper scope of government action in particular areas, especially when they are from different political parties (an increasingly frequent occurrence in our political system). Public employees often find themselves in the middle of heated political battles and need to follow the shifting winds of politics to do their jobs effectively. How public personnel systems work in practice and human resource management is developed in the American public sector are often a reflection of the operating codes and practices of our political system.

Federalism

Federalism, or the division of governmental powers by state and substate levels, is one of the most important features of the U.S. political system that produces an impact on human resource management. The U.S. Constitution enumerates certain powers for the national government and reserves all other powers to the states and the people. In practice, the states and the federal government share responsibility for most major government programs. Many public employees work closely with their counterparts at other levels of government. The state and local governments are critical partners in most areas of public policy.

From time to time, the federal government places personnel-related requirements on state and local governments (such as affirmative action programs, workplace health and safety measures, and wage rates for government contractors). Changes in the nature of government programs, such as when the federal government changed how federal participation in the welfare system would occur, can have far-reaching effects on the human resource systems of state and local governments. Particular positions may have to be created, eliminated, or changed. Additional training may have to be provided for existing employees, and appropriate technology will often have to be purchased to help employees do their jobs well.

Human resource management is affected by changes in the intergovernmental system in many important ways. American federalism is changing over time to provide a larger role for state and local governments during an era of devolution of governmental responsibilities. The human resource management systems of state and local government are experiencing the challenges of recruiting and maintaining effective workforces able to make use of high-tech skills required for service provision and public policy problem solving in this decentralized environment.

Political Parties

Political parties, which have longstanding ties to public sector human resource management, are another feature of our political system. The practice of **patronage,** or the giving of government jobs based on membership or loyalty to a political party, has been a part of human resource management in the United States since the first days of our history as a political community. (The development of the patronage system and its eventual partial replacement by our civil service system are described below.)

Political parties can have an important impact on human resource management when different parties control the executive and legislative branches of government, a situation termed *divided government.* The inevitable differences between the two parties on which government programs should be enlarged, reduced in scale, or eliminated can result in uncertainty among government employees. In some settings this results in the need for the administration of cutback management (a planned reduction in force by not replacing vacancies, encouraging relocation and early retirement, and so forth) for human resource managers. (The prevalence of downsizing and its impacts on the public sector was described in Chapter 2.)

Constitutional Protections

The U.S. Constitution provides for the protection of individual rights and liberties against government action. These protections are contained in the **Bill of Rights,** the first ten amendments to the Constitution. These rights and protections extend to public employees inasmuch as their employers are engaging in state action, and therefore public entities are substantially more highly constrained by constitutional limits on government action than are private employers with respect to what latitude they have in the management of employees. Many decisions by the U.S. Supreme Court have outlined specific public sector personnel practices that are permitted and that are forbidden (such as random drug testing of public employees), and these decisions and derivative adjudication have greatly shaped the practice of public sector human resource management. (Some of these important decisions, and the legal rights of public employees derived from them, are described in Chapter 4.)

Interest Groups

A final characteristic of our political system relevant to human resource management in the public sector is the presence of a diverse universe of active **interest groups.** Americans are organized into every conceivable grouping, and many interest groups are concerned with pressuring government for policies that will benefit their particular group. Among the many interest groups seeking influence over public sector personnel policies and practices are public employee unions and their lobbying organizations. Although their presence and power vary from state to state, public sector unions and the interest group advocates that represent them are an important part of the political system. (The role of unions in public personnel policy development and personnel system operations in the United States is described in Chapter 5.)

THE EVOLUTION OF THE FEDERAL CIVIL SERVICE SYSTEM

It is important to understand the evolution of the federal civil service system because many of the characteristics of public sector employment described above are either precedents to or reactions against the federal civil service system. Most state public personnel systems are modeled after the major aspects of the federal civil service system. Many of the special characteristics and limitations of public sector employment are rooted in the evolution of the federal civil service system as well. Patricia Wallace Ingraham correctly notes that civil service systems have three principal purposes. First, they permit governments to recruit qualified personnel and, second, to reward and de-

velop the skills and abilities of that workforce. Third, "the civil service system provides guidelines and rules for organizing that workforce for public objectives."[14] Without employees, properly selected and managed, the government cannot accomplish its work, which is why a well-functioning public service HRM operation is critical to effective governance in any jurisdiction.

Ingraham also identifies three "key tensions" present within our public service system:[15]

- *Patronage versus merit.* Should jobs be awarded based on loyalty to political parties, or on the basis of competency and skills tests?
- *Neutrality versus responsiveness.* If civil servants are politically neutral, how can we be assured that they will be responsive to the elected chief executive or legislative authorities?
- *Efficiency versus effectiveness.* Public agencies have many goals other than efficiency; for example, a commitment to democratic process may cause public sector agencies to appear to be slow and inefficient. How do we manage demands for efficiency against other worthy goals? How do we measure whether public sector programs are effective while staying within the bounds of permissible, humane, and ethical means?

Ingraham points out that these tensions are the result of the interplay of our politics, our legal system and Constitution, our society, and our economy.[16] The evolution of our public personnel system is rooted in these tensions, and these tensions among conflicting values provide a useful framework for understanding the historical development and current conditions of public sector employment systems.

Historical Phases in the Development of the U.S. Civil Service System

Frederick C. Mosher identified six distinct phases in the development of the public service in the United States:[17]

Government by Gentlemen (1789–1829): The earliest presidents appointed men to the federal public service on the basis of "fitness of character," determined mostly by family background, education, honor and esteem, and loyalty to the new government. Another name for this phase is *government by aristocrats.* Tenure in office was assumed for middle- and lower-level officials.

Government by the Common Man (1829–1883): The beginning of the spoils system, or patronage system, is usually attached to the election of Andrew Jackson in 1829. Selection of public service workers was done on the basis of party loyalty, and government workers turned over with the election of a different political party.

Government by the Good (1883–1906): The **Progressive Movement** advocated eliminating corruption in government and instituting merit as the basis of selection for members of the public service.

Government by the Efficient (1906–1937): Scientific management swept into industry and government service on the heels of Progressive era reforms. Its emphasis on efficiency, rationality, and "one best way" to do things still influences the public service.

Government by Managers (1937–): As part of the New Deal and the building of federal government agencies, the emphasis shifted to the question of general administrative skills. Responsiveness to executives leadership was emphasized as a prerequisite of effective governance.

Government by Professionals (1945–): Increasing numbers of professionals are employed throughout the public service. Professions are characterized by their desire to control their own members and resist control from outside agencies such as civil service commissions or elected executives.

Each of these phases has contributed to our current understanding of merit, and portions of each phase remain prevalent in our system. It is important to look at these phases because our current federal, state, and local public service human resource management systems are reflections of all of the historical phases that constitute the legacy of public personnel administration. Mosher's description of the historical phases in the development of the U.S. Civil Service system was written in 1982. To describe today's public service comprising government, private, and non-profit contract workers, we suggest the use of Kettl's term, *Government by Proxy,* to describe the period since approximately 1980:[18]

Government by Proxy (1980–): Increasingly nonprofit and private sector workers are contracted to carry out the work of government. This phase is also referred to as the "Hollow State" or "Third Party Government" because of its reliance on nongovernmental agencies to provide public services.[19]

Patronage System

The patronage system became prevalent in the United States in the mid-1800s. Patronage refers to the practice of selecting government workers based on their ties to the political party currently in control of the executive branch of the jurisdiction (that is, the president, governor, or mayor). A person seeking a public sector job needed a patron within the party to recommend him or her for the position in question. The party that secured the presidency (or the governorship or mayorship at the state and local level) enjoyed the privilege of appointing people to many public sector jobs. (The patronage system was sometimes referred to as the spoils system, as in the common phrase, "To the winner go the spoils.") Although patronage was initially used to place members of the elite into positions of public trust, its use spread as political parties extended participation to wider segments of the population as a consequence of the democratization of American political institutions during Jackson's presidency.[20] The political parties came to rely heavily on the disbursement of public jobs to secure loyalty from party members.

Large and internally cohesive partisan political organizations, known as *machines,* built their power with patronage. They rose to prominence in many large urban areas and controlled many state and local governments across the country. As George Washington Plunkitt, a leader of the political machine in New York State, put it, "How are you goin' to interest our young men in their country if you have no office to give them when they work for their party?"[21]

Patronage was effective at ensuring party loyalty; however, it was less effective at placing competent employees in positions of public service. As the scope of government widened and the work of public agencies became more complex, the need for government employees to have strong skills related to their particular jobs became increasingly apparent. This is evidenced in Woodrow Wilson's broadly quoted statement, "It's getting harder to run a constitution than to frame one."[22] In addition to issues of competence and effective operation, the patronage system tended to be corrupt as well. Wilson wrote, "Not much impartial scientific method is to be discerned in our administrative practices. The poisonous atmosphere of city government, the crooked secrets of state administration, the confusion, sinecurism, and corruption ever and again discovered in the bureaus at Washington forbid us to believe that any clear conceptions are as yet very widely current in the United States."[23]

By the late 1800s, pressure began to build among groups interested in reforming this ineffective and often corrupt system. This coalition of reform-oriented groups active at the end of the nineteenth century is referred to as the Progressive Movement. Among other things, the Progressives were interested in how the newly developing science of administration could bring efficiency and competence to government.[24] A chief mechanism for improving government was held to be the removal of "politics" and corrupt politicians from administration.[25] Reforms advocated by the Progressives, such as nonpartisan elections and the council-manager form of local government, were intended to reduce the role of political parties in the administration of local government. The institution of the primary election, a uniquely American institution, was another powerful weapon that the Progressives developed to permit party rank-and-file members to control the choice of candidates for the party rather than allowing party bosses to control partisan candidacy. This mechanism allowed Progressives such as Woodrow Wilson and Theodore Roosevelt and their followers to gain prominent positions in the Democratic and Republican parties, respectively, despite the opposition of the party bosses of their day. The Progressive movement reform most directly relevant to public personnel administration was the institution of the civil service system.

The Civil Service System

The Pendleton Act The first significant experience with civil service in the United States began with the passage of the **Pendleton Act of 1883** (see Appendix). The enactment of this legislation was prompted in large part by the assassination of President Garfield several years earlier by a disappointed office seeker.[26]

Progressive reformers and public administration scholars admired the competency and professionalism of merit-based public personnel systems in Great Britain and on the continent of Europe. They favored a strong executive able to coordinate and manage the personnel function using a system of merit examination for selection and promotion of a politically neutral and loyal workforce competent to serve the public trust as determined by political superiors.[27] By importing portions of these foreign systems, Progressive reformers such as Woodrow Wilson and Theodore Roosevelt believed that the American system would become at once less corrupt, more professional, and more capable of achieving America's great democratic destiny. Advocates for change clearly recognized, however, that the European systems would have to be adapted to America's distinctly egalitarian political institutions and culture.[28] A particular concern of reformers was the class-based nature of European civil service systems in which only the privileged classes had access to the higher administrative ranks in government.[29]

The reading for this chapter highlights the course of the legislative battle fought over the Pendleton Act. In it Paul Van Riper examines how the statute combines elements of the European model of civil service with important concessions made to American sensibilities. Several forces combined to force Congress to accept a public policy that legislators knew would in time take away a powerful tool for reelection they had enjoyed since the days of Andrew Jackson (1830s): the pressure of a press "muckraking" for stories on political corruption, a substantial presence of Progressive sentiment within both the Republican and Democratic parties at the time, and the dramatic event of a presidential assassination at the hands of a disappointed patronage seeker.

The Pendleton Act originally applied to only 10 percent of all federal jobs, but provisions of the statute empowered the president to broaden the protections of the civil service by extension to new areas of coverage on the authority of presidential directives.[30] The Pendleton Act provided the following requirements:

- Competitive exams that were practical in content
- Tenure in office
- Political neutrality
- The creation of the U.S. Civil Service Commission[31]

The Pendleton Act established competitive exams for those lower-level administrative jobs in the federal government that were originally covered by the act. The American statute, as opposed to the equivalent legislation in European

governments, however, required that the competitive exams would be job specific rather than test general intelligence and command of language and culture reflective of formal education.[32] This reflection of the American egalitarian spirit led to the American emphasis on **rank in position,** that is, one's rank is based on the particular job held. In contrast, **rank in person** systems (such as in the military) follow a practice whereby a title stays with a person regardless of the specific duties he or she performs. Managers filling a position were allowed to select from among the top three scorers on the practical, job-specific exam (the **rule-of-three**).[33]

The Pendleton Act also features security of tenure in office and political neutrality for government workers, both of which represent ideas adopted from European systems.[34] Unlike the British and continental European civil service systems, however, which required new administrative personnel to enter at the bottom of governmental organizations, the Pendleton Act reflected the egalitarian ethos of American political life by allowing lateral entry into the civil service at all levels.[35] In an effort to make the Pendleton Act more palatable to the existing strong party organizations, the scope of civil service positions covered was restricted to the entry- and middle-level jobs of federal agencies. The top jobs would remain to be filled by partisan political appointees.

The American civil service system thus began as a hybrid of American and European approaches to public personnel systems.[36] This historically based situation leads to the continuing tension between patronage and merit present in the American civil service systems. The interests of political appointees, who are responsible to the president and sensitive to congressional political currents, and the civil servants, who are politically neutral and enjoy permanent status, are often at variance. These differences in basic orientation toward the public interest can make management of the executive agencies in federal, state, and local government difficult; indeed, observers from abroad are inclined to remark that American public sector administrative practices are far more complex than their own.[37] Much of the drama associated with the operation of the civil service in the federal government has application to the way in which the civil service systems of state and local governments work in relation to elected officials and the executive and legislative branches.

The bipartisan **Civil Service Commission** created by the Pendleton Act was composed of three full-time members who were to be appointed for indefinite terms by the president.[38] The model of independent regulatory commission, much favored by the Progressives as a means of taking some areas of public policy out of the political arena and making them administrative matters, was being applied to personnel practices by the U.S. Civil Service Commission. The commission became responsible for developing the rules necessary for implementing the new merit system, as well as for investigating any abuses of the merit system that were brought to the members' attention. These potentially incompatible responsibilities proved troublesome throughout the history of the commission.

The Pendleton Act "became the classic model for 'good personnel practices' throughout the nation."[39] A number of state and local governments adopted merit systems voluntarily, especially where the Progressives were strong. Many others, however, adopted them only after federal regulations such as the social security statutes and Intergovernmental Personnel Act of 1970 required them to do so. The U.S. Supreme Court began striking down patronage practices beginning in the 1970s to hasten the demise of patronage politics in state and local government (see *Elrod v. Burns,* 1976, or *Branti v. Finkel,* 1980).[40] Reflecting the fragmentation inherent in federalism, each state's civil service system is unique, featuring varying levels of civil service sophistication and continuing elements of patronage.

Technology and the civil service Technological change has played an important part in the development of the civil service throughout its history. When the United States first formed under the provisions of the U.S. Constitution, most government jobs were rather uncomplicated and finding employees capable of performing the tasks required was not difficult. The rapid growth of the country in its first one hundred years and the rising complexity of the tasks that government assumed, however, led to calls for more careful selection methods. Among those who advocated reform such that the selection of public sector workers would be based on merit was Woodrow Wilson. Wilson sought to apply the rigor of science to the study of administration. As he noted, "There is scarcely a single duty of government which was once simple which is not now complex."[41]

The science ("scientific management") that Wilson and other early scholars of public administration sought to apply to administration was rooted in the notion that there was "one best way"—the most efficient way—to do any particular job.[42] **Scientific management** (also known as *Taylorism*) brought the technology of the day to bear on the "time and motion" analysis of specific jobs in an attempt to make them more efficient and businesslike. The assumption that there was one best way to do nearly all things in the production process led naturally to a centralization of control over the human resource management process and its organization within the public sector environment. The standardization of bureaucratic practices is in part the enduring legacy of scientific management in the American public service.

The impact of technology in today's workplace often has the opposite effect of Taylorism. Rather than centralizing control and emphasizing one best way to do things, the diffusion of technology—for example, a personal computer on virtually every desk and access to all the information that the Internet supplies—encourages the decentralization of control. The rapid pace of change in today's technology and the associated diversification of professional competencies and areas of expertise have led modern scholars of public administration to recommend a decentralized approach to administration featuring a high degree of flexibility in job assignment and problem-solving activities. The "one best way" days of scientific management are largely gone from most public sector agency settings.

Development of the classification system The need to organize in a systematic way the many jobs that were progressively attached to civil service coverage by succeeding presidents became apparent early in the twentieth century. The **Classification Act of 1923** applied the logic of Frederick Taylor's scientific management approach to management to the federal civil service system by standardizing the classification and grading of civil service positions according to duties in ascending order of responsibilities.[43] The intent was to ensure that all employees in the classified ranks were being compensated on the basis of their work regardless of what agency (favored or disfavored) or what manager (friendly or unfriendly) they worked for in the public service. The result was a strict hierarchical system with narrow job descriptions and strict boundaries between jobs within which every classified service position had to be fit.[44] The five compensation schedules (or services) specified in the 1923 act were later collapsed into two broad categories in changes in legislation in 1949. Each of the two services was subdivided into grades, and uniform compensation schedules were enacted into law for each grade. Hence, "GS" (**General Service rank**) refers to federal government jobs.[45]

The **1949 Classification Act,** developed in response to criticisms of the centralized and complex 1923 system, also returned "extensive classification authority from the Civil Service Commission to the agencies" and "created the first 'supergrade' system at the top of the classified service hierarchy."[46] The agencies still had to comply with the strict, cumbersome personnel rules and procedures that were perceived to tie the hands of managers and make the removal of poorly performing employees difficult, if not impossible.[47] *The Triumph of Techniques over Purpose,* the title of a classic book review about public personnel by Wallace Sayre in 1948, sums up the great frustration of federal managers with the rule-bound classification system.[48]

The classification system in question still exists in the federal government, and it has first cousins in most state and local government jurisdictions. (It is discussed further in Chapter 8, which covers recruitment and selection in public personnel systems.) As presidents and federal agency managers became more frustrated with the rigidity of the established classification system, they developed alternative ways to hire federal employees. These are commonly referred to as **special hiring authorities,** and they represent exceptions to normal procedures that allow agencies to hire employees outside the classification system's normal testing procedures.[49] The increasing use of these special hiring authorities in part accounts for the fact that the civil service classification system currently applies to only 56 percent of federal employees.[50] Presidents, governors, mayors, and city managers all quite naturally want executive agencies to be responsive to their own policy priorities. In most cases, the inflexibility of the classification system makes the civil service less responsive to political executives than they would like. This situation reflects the inherent tension between neutrality and responsiveness described above by Patricia Ingraham.

Ethics and civil service systems Ethics is a part of most public personnel processes. Because we are talking about public employees (as opposed to private sector personnel), it is important to remember that expectations are higher for the public sector. As Carol Lewis puts it, "Facing up to the ethical demands on public managers starts with biting the bullet: public service ethics is different from ethics in private life. The reason [for this indifference] is that democracy is sustained by public trust, a link forged by stringent ethical standards."[51] Being ethical in the public sector is more than being legal. (It is, after all, possible to be legal but unethical.) That is part of the extra burden placed on public sector employees; the appearance of impropriety or harm to the public interest is enough to cast an ethical cloud over a public agency.

The inflexibility of the "one best way"-premised classification systems developed at the height of the scientific management movement's efforts to standardize civil service positions has led many managers to seek to get around cumbersome personnel procedures. Managers use temporary employees to avoid long civil service testing processes, and then they coach the temporary employees so they do well on the tests required for normal hiring decisions. Sometimes managers seek to write job descriptions to match only the one person they would like to fill a job opening. These practices are so common that scholars have described an "underground merit system" in which managers strive to get around the existing merit system using such surreptitious practices. An ethical dilemma arises for the conscientious public service manager: is it wrong for public administrators who say they are "just trying to get the work done" to find a quicker and possibly more efficient way to select employees? Which is the greater good: to obey the spirit and letter of the law or to achieve what may appear to be a greater good for the public by getting the job done expeditiously?

Civil Service Reform Act of 1978 Calls for modifying the civil service practices created with the Pendleton Act of 1883 have been nearly constant since its passage. Several prominent blue-ribbon commissions were convened by serveral U.S. presidents to study the civil service system and recommend changes for greater executive management direction of personnel practices. The Roosevelt administration's President's Committee on Administrative Management of 1937 (commonly called the Brownlow Commission) and the First and Second Hoover Commissions of 1949 and 1955, respectively, were the most noteworthy early efforts of this kind.[52] Although the federal civil service system had undergone some important changes before 1978 (for example, the addition of veterans' preference and the implementation of equal employment opportunity laws), it had not been thoroughly overhauled until 1978. The "Reorganization Plan No. 2 of 1978," that is,

the operational section of the **Civil Service Reform Act of 1978,** contained the following important changes:[53]

- Division of the Civil Service Commission's responsibilities between two new agencies: the **Office of Personnel Management** and the **Merit Systems Protection Board.**
- Creation of the **Federal Labor Relations Authority.**
- Creation of the **Senior Executive Service (SES).**
- Development of a **merit pay** system.

The Office of Personnel Management (OPM) is the "federal government's human resource agency. It administers the federal merit system to recruit, examine and promote employees."[54] It also prepares guidance on labor management relations and administers the federal retirement system and federal employee health insurance program.

The Merit Systems Protection Board (MSPB) is an independent, quasi-judicial agency in the Executive Branch that serves as guardian of federal merit systems. The MSPB assumed all employee appeal functions of the Civil Service Commission. It hears and decides "appeals from Federal employees of removals and other major personnel actions."[55] It also "reviews significant actions and regulations of Office of Personnel Management and conducts studies of merit systems."[56] The MSPB originally included the Office of Special Counsel that "investigates allegations of prohibited personnel practices."[57] This office became independent of the MSPB in 1989.

The Federal Labor Relations Authority (FLRA) "represents the federal government's consolidated approach to labor-management relations. It is 'three agencies consolidated in one.'. . . The Authority, a quasi-judicial body that adjudicates disputes concerning the labor relations statute or unfair labor practices, the Office of the General Counsel who investigates unfair labor practice complaints, and the Federal Service Impasses Panel that resolves impasses in negotiation between federal agencies and unions."[58]

The reorganization was intended to solve the

problem of the conflicting roles given to the old Civil Service Commission. In his testimony before Congress about the 1978 Civil Service Reform Act, Alan Campbell, a prominent public administration scholar and longtime member of the U.S. Civil Service Commission, noted that

> the Civil Service Commission currently has so many conflicting roles that it is unable to perform all of them adequately. At one and the same time it is expected to serve the President in providing managerial leadership for the positive personnel functions in the Executive Branch—that is, establishing personnel policies and advising and assisting agencies on personnel management functions—while also serving as a 'watchdog' over the integrity of the merit system, protecting employee rights, and performing a variety of adjudicatory functions.[59]

The OPM was intended to give the president the "personnel management staff arm" that he needed.[60] The president was given the power to appoint the director of the OPM. Ingraham notes that OPM's creation "marked a turning away from the 'policing' function of the Civil Service Commission to a more proactive planning and support function."[61] The OPM, however, never fully lived up to its promise in this regard. As presidents exercised more control over OPM and increasingly relied on political appointees in the executive branch generally, the OPM's effectiveness has continually decreased.[62]

The creation of the Senior Executive Service (SES) was intended to boost the president's power to coordinate and guide the management of the federal executive agencies. The SES comprises the top ranks (GS-16, 17, and 18 and Executive Ranks IV and V) in the General Service system.[63] Members of the SES were envisioned to be available to the president to move across agencies as their expertise was needed. Merit pay was also enacted to reward these top managers on the basis of performance rather than longevity. Initially, over 90 percent of all the eligible civil servants opted to

be part of the SES merit pay system, but by 1983 more than 40 percent of those executives had left government service.[64] Twelve states have adopted a version of the SES in an attempt to give their governors more flexibility in managing the state's workforce.[65] Stillman reports that, similar to the federal system, few of these state systems have been successful in their efforts to create a flexible and adaptive senior management corps responsive to executive leadership.[66]

The FLRA was intended to centralize the federal government's dealings with collective bargaining, which had been handled by several separate agencies. (Collective bargaining and the FLRA are discussed in considerable detail in Chapter 5.)

Diversity and civil service systems Diversity can be understood in many ways. One way that diversity is present in civil service systems is in the variety of personnel systems that exist among the tens of thousands of local governments. As the discussion of the historical phases in the development of civil service systems noted, each phase has added to the diversity of the American public service, and vestiges of each period remain in existing personnel systems. Scholars of public personnel have identified the existence of several different **personnel cultures or systems,** which embody "the laws, policies, rules, regulations, and practices through which personnel functions are fulfilled," in use in the United States.[67] Freyss, for example, empirically demonstrated three distinct cultural systems in her 1995 work:[68]

> *Merit system culture:* Emphasizes competence, political neutrality, and efficient and equitable service to the public. This culture is associated with rule-driven management and substantial difficulty in getting rid of employees because of strongly protected employee rights. These local governments (municipalities, counties, and special districts) use information-based management practices such as performance appraisals and

merit pay, and have adopted innovations such as flexible benefits and employee assistance programs.

Collective bargaining culture: Personnel matters are determined bilaterally with unions and the government in question, with an emphasis on protecting employee rights and public sector jobs. Recruitment is done by means of public notices and the use of minimum scores. The culture affects termination, discipline, and retirement policies, all of which tend to be highly formalized processes that permit employee groups to represent the interests of employees collectively and individually.

Affirmative action culture: Influences hiring processes with special consideration to race or ethnicity in screening job applicants and promotion. Strong attention is given to having the public workforce mirror the racial, ethnic, and cultural characteristics of the population being served.

Freyss notes that there is also a regional distribution to these personnel systems. The collective bargaining and affirmative action cultural systems are found more frequently in the northeastern and north-central states, while the merit system culture is more likely to be found in the West and the cities in the industrial states.

Human resource management in the public sector in the United States reflects the variety of experiences, political structures, and interest groups present throughout the country. There is tremendous diversity in the way in which public sector HRM is practiced. Each state and local government will reflect its own unique development and at the same time endeavor to keep pace with national trends and developments as they become evident.

■ CONCLUSION

Several primary forces have combined to lead chief executives and public agency administrators to find ways of getting around the civil service system. First, the nature of work in today's fast-paced global environment is ill suited for the rigid, slow, and legalistic civil service testing and classification system.[69] Hiring employees outside the civil service system can allow a manager greater flexibility in job design and in compensation.

Second, the political neutrality and tenure in office of civil service employees give presidents, governors, county and special district commissions, and mayors the impression (sometimes correctly) that civil servants are not particuarly responsive to their political goals. The extended use of political appointees and other special hiring authorities is one way by which chief executives and their appointed managers can hire those whom they trust to meet their political agendas.

Third, harsh budget realities have pressed many policymakers to look for the cheapest way to continue to provide government services. Private sector companies and nonprofit organizations increasingly are perceived to be a viable alternative to service provision by means of reliance on government employees. This economic reality, combined with a general political preference in the United States for smaller government, has led to an increased use of contract employees in public sector operations; naturally, these employees are not part of the civil service system.

■ MANAGER'S VOCABULARY

separation of powers
federalism
political parties
patronage
Bill of Rights
interest groups
Progressive Movement
Pendleton Act of 1883
rank in position
rank in person
rule-of-three
Civil Service Commission

scientific management
Classification Act of 1923, 1949
General Service (GS) rank
special hiring authorities
Civil Service Reform Act of 1978
Office of Personnel Management
Merit Systems Protection Board
Federal Labor Relations Authority
Senior Executive Service (SES)
merit pay
personnel cultures or systems

■ STUDY QUESTIONS

1. Why do some managers seek to get around the rules of civil service systems?

2. What are the key tensions inherent in our public service system that Ingraham identified?

3. What are the pros and cons of using patronage to fill government positions?

4. What were the key elements of the 1978 Civil Service Reform Act?

■ EXPERIENTIAL EXERCISES

1. This exercise is derived from interviews reported in Jorgenson, Fairless, and Patton's 1996 study.[70] You are the recently hired consultant asked to comment on the soundness of the state personnel system. You have interviewed agency heads and personnel directors at a variety of agencies, taking care to include small, medium, and large agencies into consideration, as well as inquiring about a wide variety of job classifications. Your results indicate that although managers say they are generally supportive of the merit system, widespread dissatisfaction with the state's personnel commission and an increasing willingness by managers to circumvent the system altogether are in evidence.

   Among your findings are the following results:

   • The average time for the personnel commission to conduct a test and compile a register of qualified employees is four months.

   • More than 50 percent of existing classified employees were originally hired as temporary employees outside the merit-based testing system.

   • Newspapers in the state capital have documented managers' refusing to hire one of the top five candidates from the register when the temporary employee currently in the job did not make the top five. Instead, the managers reopened the search, giving the temporary employee another chance at the test.

   • Five of the state's largest agencies have begun hiring their own personnel "consultants" in order to evaluate positions and help recruit for openings more quickly. The state personnel commission continues to duplicate the work of these consultants to ensure compliance with the commission's procedures.

   • Tests are often outdated and irrelevant to the jobs. For example, secretaries are being tested on electric typewriters when knowledge of word processing software is really required.

   • The number of state employees has increased by 26 percent in the past ten years, while the number of employees at the state personnel commission has remained constant.

Answer the following questions:

a. What would your recommendations be to the state personnel commission to improve the state's human resource system?

b. Line managers in the agencies complain bitterly about the quality of the civil service tests and the length of time required to assemble a register of candidates. Is your responsibility as a human resource professional to insist on compliance to civil service regulations, or is it to help the managers get the best personnel possible as quickly as possible to get the work of government done?

c. A systematic analysis of the performance reviews of employees serving as temporary workers and of those who entered the system of temporary workers indicates that they perform at or above the level of workers who entered the civil service through open, competitive testing. Consequently, is there any problem with the increasing use of temporary employees?

d. The governor's chief of staff has suggested that one solution to the widespread complaints heard about the state's civil service system is to eliminate many positions from the civil service altogether and replace them with political appointees. What are the relative merits and disadvantages to this solution?

2. Research the personnel culture prevalent in a city or state government with which you are familiar. Are appointments made on the basis of merit? Is there a strong collective bargaining culture? To what extent is there evidence of an affirmative action culture?

■ CASE APPLICABLE TO THIS CHAPTER

"Governor Pat Ronage's Hiring Freeze"

■ NOTES

[1] From Arthur L. Finkle, "Can a Manager Discipline a Public Employee?" *Review of Public Personnel Administration* 4 (Summer 1984): 83–87.

[2] Wallace S. Sayre, "The Triumph of Techniques over Purpose," in Frank J. Thompson, ed., *Classics of Public Personnel Policy,* 2nd ed. (Pacific Grove, CA: Brooks Cole, 1991), p. 155.

[3] E. S. Savas and Sigmund G. Ginsburg, "The Civil Service: A Meritless System?" in Thompson, ed., *Classics of Public Personnel Policy,* p. 165.

[4] Steven W. Hays and Richard C. Kearney, "The Transformation of Public Sector Human Resource Management," University of South Carolina, Institute of Public Affairs, working paper, 1999.

[5] Richard J. Stillman, "Inside Public Bureaucracy," in Richard J. Stillman, ed., *Public Administration Cases and Concepts,* 5th ed. (Boston: Houghton Mifflin 1996), p. 187.

[6] U.S. Census Bureau, *Statistical Abstract of the United States, 1993* (Washington, D.C.: U.S. Government Printing Office, 1993).

[7] Ibid.

[8] John D. Donahue, *Disunited States* (New York: Basic Books, 1997), p. 15.

[9] Information from the Office of Personnel Management Web page at **http://www.opm.gov,** Monthly Report of Federal Civilian Employment (SF 113-A), Office of Workforce Information, Office of Personnel Management (Washington, D.C., 1998).

[10] Donald F. Kettl, Patricia W. Ingraham, Ronald P. Sanders, and Constance Horner, *Civil Service Reform: Building a Government That Works* (Washington, D.C.: Brookings, 1996), p. 14.

[11] Ibid., p. 17.

[12] Lorna Jorgensen, Kelli Fairless, and W. David Patton, "Underground Merit Systems and the Balance Between Service and Compliance," *Review of Public Personnel Administration* 16 (Spring 1996): 5–20.

[13] Patricia W. Ingraham, *The Foundation of Merit: Public Service in American Democracy* (Baltimore: Johns Hopkins University Press, 1995), p. xix.

[14] Ibid., p. xv.

[15] Ibid., pp. viii–xxi.

16 Ibid., pp. vii.

17 Frederick C. Mosher, *Democracy and the Public Service,* 2nd ed. (New York: Oxford University Press, 1982), p. 52. The following section is drawn from Mosher's description of the phases of development of the civil service.

18 Donald F. Kettl, *Government by Proxy* (Washington, D.C.: Congressional Quarterly Press, 1988).

19 See H. Brinton Milward, Keith G. Provan, and Barbara A. Else, "What Does the 'Hollow State' Look Like?" in Barry Bozeman, ed., *Public Management: The State of the Art* (San Francisco: Jossey-Bass, 1993), pp. 309–322. See also Lester M. Salamon, "Rethinking Public Management: Third-Party Government and the Changing Forms of Government Action," *Public Policy* 29:3 (1981): 255 257.

20 Ingraham, *The Foundation of Merit,* p. viii.

21 William L. Riordon, *Plunkitt of Tammany Hall* (New York: Dutton, 1963), p. 11.

22 Woodrow Wilson, "The Study of Administration," in Jay M. Shafritz and Albert C. Hyde, eds., *Classics of Public Administration,* 4th ed. (Fort Worth, TX: Harcourt Brace, 1997), p. 15.

23 Wilson, "The Study of Administration," p. 16.

24 Samuel P. Hays, "The Politics of Reform in Municipal Government in the Progressive Era," *Pacific Northwest Quarterly* 55 (1964): 157–169.

25 Wilson, "The Study of Administration," p. 20.

26 Stillman, "Inside Public Bureaucracy," p. 198.

27 Wilson, "The Study of Administration," p. 16.

28 Ibid.

29 Paul P. Van Riper, *History of the United States Civil Service* (Evanston, IL: Row, Peterson and Company, 1958), p. 4.

30 Ingraham, *The Foundation of Merit,* p. 27.

31 "An Act to Regulate and Improve the Civil Service at the United States," 22 Stat. 27 (1883).

32 Mark W. Huddleston and William W. Boyer, *The Higher Civil Service in the U.S.: Quest for Reform* (Pittsburgh, PA: University of Pittsburgh Press, 1996), p. 17.

33 Ingraham, *The Foundation of Merit,* p. 27.

34 Huddleston and Boyer, *The Higher Civil Service,* p. 17.

35 Ibid., p. 18.

36 Ingraham, *The Foundation of Merit,* p. xix.

37 Ibid.

38 Van Riper, *History,* p. 103.

39 Stillman, "Inside Public Bureaucracy," p. 198.

40 See Stillman, p. 199. In both of these cases the U.S. Supreme Court acted to greatly restrict the use of patronage in government to those positions that exercise significant policy decision-making authority relevant to a politically responsible official. Lacking such authority, public employees enjoy the right of employment absent a sharing of the case of dismissal—even if the employee in question was originally appointed to a patronage position.

41 Wilson, "The Study of Administration," p. 15.

42 Jay M. Shafritz and Albert C. Hyde, eds., *Classics of Public Administration,* 4th ed. (Fort Worth, TX: Harcourt Brace, 1997), p. 5.

43 Ingraham, *The Foundation of Merit,* p. 39.

44 Ibid.

45 Huddleston and Boyer, *The Higher Civil Service,* p. 28.

46 Ingraham, *The Foundation of Merit,* p. 40.

47 Van Riper, *History,* p. 458.

48 Wallace S. Sayre, "The Triumph of Techniques over Purpose," *Public Administration Review* 8 (Spring 1948): 134.

49 Ingraham, *The Foundation of Merit,* p. 4.

50 Kettl et al., *Civil Service Reform,* p. 17.

51 Carol W. Lewis, *The Ethics Challenge in Public Service* (San Francisco: Jossey-Bass, 1991), p. 17.

52 See Van Riper, *History,* for a description of these commissions and their reports.

53 Alan K. Campbell, "Testimony on Civil Service Reform and Organization," in Thompson, ed., *Classics of Public Personnel Policy,* p. 85.

54 OPM **http://www.opm.gov/html/mission.htm.**

55 USMSPB **http://www.mspb.gov/.**

56 USMPB **http://www.mspb.gov/aboutus/aboutus.html.**

57 USMSPB **http://www.mspb.gov/aboutus/aboutus.html.**

58 FLRA **http://www.flra.gov/10.html.**

59 Campbell, "Testimony," p. 85.

60 Ibid., p. 87.

61 Ingraham, *The Foundation of Merit,* p. 77.

62 Ibid., p. 89.

63 Stillman, *Inside Public Bureaucracy,* p. 190.

64 Huddleston and Boyer, *The Higher Civil Service,* pp. 109, 112.

65 Stillman, "Inside Public Bureaucracy," p. 191.

66 Ibid.

67 Donald E. Klingner and John Nalbandian, *Public Personnel Management: Contexts and Strategies,* 4th ed. (Englewood Cliffs, NJ: Prentice-Hall, 1998).

68 Siegrun Fox Freyss, "Municipal Government Personnel Systems: A Test of Two Archetypical Models," *Review of Public Personnel Administration* 15 (Fall 1995): 69–93. The following section draws heavily from this work.

69 Kettl et al., *Civil Service Reform,* p. 16.

70 See Jorgenson, Fairless, and Patton, "Underground Merit Systems and the Balance Between Service and Compliance."

CHAPTER 4

Rights, Restrictions, and Laws of the Public Workplace

One of the most significant differences between public, for-profit, and nonprofit sector employment is the legal status of public employees under state and federal laws and the Constitution. Because of the unique legal protections of public employees, public sector managers must be careful how they work with employees, and they must remain aware of employees' legal rights and protections. Often these protections frustrate public managers because they seem to be barriers to effective management practices. Nevertheless, public managers must learn to work within these protections to accomplish the goals of their public agencies and effectively manage public employees. Public managers should understand the purposes of constitutional protections and how they apply to the public employees they manage to achieve the results needed in the public service and to avoid being subject to legal action.

INTRODUCTION TO READING

The following reading by David H. Rosenbloom discusses the evolution of judicial interpretation of public employee rights. For most of the history of the civil service in the United States, government managed its employees under the **doctrine of privilege,** which held that to work for the government was a privilege granted by the employer; hence, public employees had no legal rights to their jobs and could be hired or dismissed at will. In the famous words of Justice Oliver Wendell Holmes, a public employee "may have a constitutional right to talk politics, but he has no constitutional right to be a policeman."[1] This disposition toward public employees reflected the **doctrine of sovereignty,** whereby elected officials exercised the authority of the sovereign (the people) to manage the affairs of government unfettered by any consideration of employee rights other than those that the sovereign wished to bestow. Over time, however, U.S. courts recognized the claim of public employees to constitutional protections against violation of due process and inequitable treatment in "state actions," and American jurisprudence adopted a more balanced approach that now prevails as a guide to decide cases related to the violation of the statutory and constitutional rights of public employees. The balancing of management prerogatives versus employee rights requires courts to weigh equally the rights of the public employee against the interests of the government in its ability to operate efficiently and in the public's interest in the effective operation of government.[2]

Public employees do possess numerous rights in the public workplace under the Constitution, but these rights are not exclusive, and they cannot unduly interfere with the necessary operations of government. The first consideration in the process of the balance of interests is the range of constitutional protections accorded to public employees by the Bill of Rights. These rights are balanced by the government's interest as an employer and the provider of public services—in the words of the Supreme Court, "A balance between the interests of the employee, as a citizen, in commenting upon matters of public concern and the interest of the State, as an employer, in promoting the efficiency of the public services it performs through its employees."[3] This balancing of interests requires substantial interpretation of the interests of each party by the courts, and as a result this broad standard of law can lead to some apparent inconsistency. Fortunately, a body of common law legal precedents (that is, judge-made law) has developed giving a substantial amount of direction to public sector managers.

As you read the following selection, keep the following questions in mind:

- How has the Supreme Court's approach to defining public employee rights evolved?
- What interests does the Court balance when considering cases involving public employee rights?
- What legitimate needs do governments as employers have that could outweigh employee rights?
- Why do public employees have greater protections in speech, drug testing, and due process than for-profit or nonprofit sector employees?

<hr>

READING

What Every Public Personnel Manager Should Know About the Constitution

DAVID H. ROSENBLOOM

Until the 1950s, American public personnel managers needed to know very little about the Constitution. For the most part it was not viewed as a constraint upon the treatment of public employees. Since then, however, the courts have played a far larger role in public personnel administration and have left their stamp upon it (Rosenbloom, 1971, 1977). Consequently, nowadays public personnel managers can be oblivious to constitutional considerations only at the risk of having important aspects of their programs, including examination, hiring, and disciplinary procedures, overturned in court. This [selection] investigates the evolution of consti-

tutional doctrines affecting the rights of public employees and reviews the leading cases in areas of major concern to contemporary public personnel administration. Its purpose is to familiarize public personnel managers with constitutional concepts and to provide an up-to-date survey of the relevant constitutional law.

CONSTITUTIONAL DOCTRINES

Until the 1950s, the rights of public employees were governed by what has become known as the "doctrine of privilege." This approach relied on the premise that public employment was a privilege rather than a right or coerced obligation such as military service. Consequently, it was thought that it could be withheld for any reason that the governmental employer saw fit, however arbitrary. Not having a right to a position in the public service, the employee, upon dismissal, lost nothing to which he or she was entitled. As Justice Oliver Wendell Holmes

Source: David H. Rosenbloom, "What Every Public Personnel Manager Should Know About the Constitution," in Steven W. Hayes and Richard C. Kearney, eds., *Public Personnel Administration: Problems and Prospects* (Englewood Cliffs, NJ: Prentice Hall, 1990), pp. 39–56.

once expressed it, "The petitioner may have a constitutional right to talk politics, but he has no constitutional right to be a policeman" (*McAuliffe* v. *New Bedford,* 1892: 220). The precise nature of this doctrine was identified by Dotson (1955: 77), as follows:

> Its central tenet is that office is held at the pleasure of the government. Its general effect is that the government may impose upon the public employee any requirement it sees fit as conditional to employment. From the point of view of the state, public employment is maintained as an indulgence; from the position of the citizen, his job is a grant concerning which he has no independent rights.

While the doctrine of privilege contained a certain logic, it also ignored the realities of citizens' interactions with government in the administrative state. If a public employee could be denied his or her job for virtually any reason without violating the individual's constitutional rights, would not the same principle apply to other kinds of privileges, such as welfare benefits, government contracts, passports, and licenses? Could these be denied, as public employment was, for such reasons as the individual favored racial integration, read Tom Paine, or even the *New York Times,* failed to attend church services, or engaged in a host of nonconformist and unconventional activities (Rosenbloom, 1971: 160–168)? Obviously, to the extent that big government creates a dependency between the people and government services (privileges), strict adherence to the doctrine of privilege could easily lead to tyrannical circumvention of the Bill of Rights.

By the 1960s, the Supreme Court disregarded the long-standing distinction between rights and privileges (Van Alstyne, 1968), in substantial part on the grounds that it was no longer viable public policy. Thus, in *Sherbert* v. *Verner* (1963: 404), the Supreme Court proclaimed that "It is too late in the day to doubt that the liberties of religion and expression may be infringed by the denial of or placing of conditions upon a benefit or privilege." Although the demise of the distinction between rights and privileges has been uneven, by the early 1970s the Court left no doubt that in the realm of public employment (which by that time encompassed about 20 percent of the work force), it had "fully and finally rejected the wooden distinction between 'rights' and

'privileges' that once seemed to govern the applicability of procedural due process rights" (*Board of Regents* v. *Roth,* 1972: 571), and it "rejected the concept that constitutional rights turn upon whether a governmental benefit is characterized as a 'right' or as a 'privilege'" (*Sugarman* v. *Dougall,* 1973: 644).

Yet rejecting the doctrine of privilege has been easier than replacing it with a coherent alternative approach. An initial successor was the "doctrine of substantial interest," which held that "whenever there is a substantial interest, other than employment by the state, involved in the discharge of a public employee, he can be removed neither on arbitrary grounds nor without a procedure calculated to determine whether legitimate grounds do exist" (*Birnbaum* v. *Trussell,* 1966: 678). This doctrine had the effect of "constitutionalizing" public employment and forcing public personnel managers to be cognizant of the constitutional rights of employees and applicants in a wide variety of personnel activities. It also led to an increase in the number of public employment cases reaching the Supreme Court and posed difficult questions concerning the definition of "substantial interest."

Indeed, so complex were the issues involved that the Court was unable to formulate a general approach to the application of the concept. Instead, it was compelled to treat each case individually on the specifics of its own merits. This circumstance was exacerbated by the Court's changing membership and marked ideological divisions (the *New York Times,* 1974: 10). The resulting doctrinal change, which has been referred to as the "idiographic approach" (Rosenbloom, 1975), required that, in applying general personnel regulations and principles to individual employees, public employers address the specific sets of facts and circumstances involved. Thus, a large measure of individualized treatment of public employees was necessary constitutionally in terms of such questions as mandatory maternity leaves, assignment of personnel by race, the exclusion of aliens from specific positions, and the applicability of procedural due process.

The major limitations of the idiographic approach were that by stressing individualized treatment rather than broad definitions of rights, it led inevitably to an ever-increasing amount of litigation. Yet it provided little guidance on the nature of the constitutional aspects of the public employment relationship, thereby making public personnel management more difficult. By the mid-1970s, these drawbacks had become clear, but the Supreme Court has nevertheless been unable to develop a clear doctrinal replacement for case-by-case adjudication. In some instances, it seemed to favor "deconstitutionalization" of the public employment relationship. For example, in *Bishop* v. *Wood* (1976: 349–350), the Court reasoned that,

> The federal court is not the appropriate forum in which to review the multitude of personnel decisions that are made daily by public agencies. We must accept the harsh fact that numerous individual mistakes are inevitable in the day-to-day administration of our affairs. The United States Constitution can not feasibly be construed to require federal judicial reviews for every such error.

However, in *Elrod* v. *Burns,* decided the same year, it held that public employees have constitutional protections against patronage dismissals. As Justice Powell pointed out in dissent, the Court thereby "constitutionalized" an aspect of public personnel practice in a way that violated a venerable tradition.

During the 1980s, the Supreme Court continued to be beset by major divisions and to develop the law through case-by-case analysis rather than by the development of broad doctrines. Nevertheless, its main direction has been toward further constitutionalization of the public employment relationship. Thus, the Constitution remains very relevant to public personnel management.

FREEDOM OF SPEECH

Under prevailing constitutional interpretations, the public employee's right to freedom of speech is broadly protected, except where its exercise is in conjunction with a partisan political activity. In *Pickering* v. *Board of Education* (1968: 573), the Supreme Court held that the special duties and obligations of public employees notwithstanding, the proper test for the regulations of their speech is whether the government's interest in limiting their "opportunities to contribute to public debate is . . . significantly greater than its interest in limiting a similar contribution by any member of the general public." Its interest would be presumptively greater when

- There was a need for maintaining discipline and harmony in the work force.

- There was a need for confidentiality.
- The employee's statements would be hard to counter due to his or her presumed greater access to factual information.
- The employee's statements impeded the proper performance of work.
- The employee's statements were so unfounded that his or her competence was called into question.
- The employee's remarks jeopardized a close and personal loyalty or confidence.

The *Pickering* decision was significantly augmented by two Supreme Court decisions during the 1980s. In *Connick* v. *Myers* (1983: 147) the Court emphasized that the threshold requirement is that the employee's speech be on a matter of *public concern* rather than one of personal interest only, such as the failure to be promoted. Once the threshold test is met, it becomes necessary to strike the appropriate balance determining whether the speech is constitutionally protected. *Connick* laid down some broad guidelines. First, "When close working relationships are essential to fulfilling public responsibilities, a wide degree of deference to the employer's judgment is appropriate" (*Connick* v. *Myers,* 1983: 151–152). It is not necessary for the employer to wait until an office is disrupted or working relationships are destroyed before taking action. Second, "When employee speech concerning office policy arises from an employment dispute concerning the very application of [a] policy to the speaker, additional weight must be given to the supervisor's view that the employee has threatened the authority of the employer to run the office" (*Connick* v. *Myers,* 1983: 153). Finally, the degree of deference accorded to the employer might be inversely related to the extent to which the employee's speech involves matters of public concern.

If *Connick* seemed to presage a narrower range of free speech for public employees, *Rankin* v. *McPherson* (1987: 331), may carve "out a new and very large class of employees—i.e., those in 'non-policymaking' positions—who . . . can never be disciplined for statements that fall within the Court's . . . definition of public concern. Upon hearing of an assassination attempt on President Ronald Reagan, McPherson, a probationary employee in a constable's office, said, "If they go for him again, I hope they get him" (*Rankin* v. *McPherson,* 1987: 321). Her statement was made privately to a fellow employee, who was her boyfriend, and in the context of a discussion about Reagan's policies. But it was overheard by a fellow employee and she was subsequently dismissed. Eventually McPherson brought her case to the Supreme Court, which held that her remark was constitutionally protected. In the Court's view, it was on a matter of public concern, and

> . . . in weighing the State's interest in discharging an employee based on any claim that the content of a statement made by the employee somehow undermines the mission of the public employer, some attention must be paid to the responsibilities of the employee within the agency. The burden of caution employees bear with respect to the words they speak will vary with the extent of authority and public accountability the employee's role entails. Where, as here, an employee serves no confidential, policymaking, or public contact role, the danger to the agency's successful function from that employee's private speech is minimal (*Rankin* v. *McPherson,* 1987: 328).

It is obvious that the Supreme Court has given public administrators much to think about regarding the scope of public employee's constitutionally protected speech. At the very least, the following must be considered: whether the remarks in question involve a matter of public concern; the context in which they are uttered; the nature of the employee's position with reference to confidentiality, policymaking, and public contact; and the remarks' disruptive quality. To these concerns must be added others from earlier case law, including whether the speech involves prohibited political partisanship, is so without foundation that the employee's basic competence is properly at issue, or evinces disloyalty to the United States. Under such circumstances, it is not really surprising that the *Rankin* case was "considered five separate times by three different federal courts" (*Rankin* v. *McPherson,* 1987: 330), or that the Supreme Court itself has admitted that "competent decisionmakers may reasonably disagree about the merits of [a public employee's] First Amendment claim" (*Bush* v. *Lucas,* 1983: note 7). On the other hand, in *Rankin* five members of the Court could agree on the principle that "a purely private statement on a matter of public concern will rarely, if ever, justify discharge of a public employee" (*Rankin* v. *McPherson,* 1987: 327, note 13).

The growth of public employee' free speech protections has created a constitutional right to "whistleblow.' In *Pickering* (1968: 571–572), the Supreme Court reasoned that "free and open debate is vital to informed decision-making by the electorate. Teachers are, as a class, the members of the community most likely to have informed and definite opinions as to how funds allotted to the operation of the schools should be spent. Accordingly, it is essential that they be able to speak out freely on such questions without fear of retaliatory dismissal."

But what is true of teachers in the realm of education is also true of other public employees in other areas of public policy. Consequently, even in the absence of specific protections for "whistleblowers," such as those contained in the 1978 Federal Civil Service Reform Act, public employees who expose inefficiencies, fraud, or other shortcomings of their agencies or co-workers are generally protected by the Constitution from retaliatory adverse actions.

Public employees' constitutionally protected expression does not extend to the area of partisan speech and activity. In the early 1970s, there was sound reason to speculate that the Supreme Court would hold that regulations for political neutrality in the public service, such as those contained in the Hatch Acts, were unconstitutional. While these were upheld originally by a 4-to-3 margin in *United Public Workers* v. *Mitchell* (1947), both the scope of public employment and the content of constitutional law had changed sufficiently to cast great doubt upon the continuing validity of that decision. In *National Association of Letter Carriers* v. *Civil Service Commission* (1972), a federal district court held that past decisions "coupled with changes in the size and complexity of public service, place *Mitchell* among other decisions outmoded by passage of time" (585). On appeal, however, the Supreme Court reversed this decision in no uncertain terms (*Civil Service Commission* v. *National Association of Letter Carriers,* 1973: 556):

> We unhesitatingly reaffirm the *Mitchell* holding that Congress had, and has, the power to prevent [federal employees] from holding a party office, working at the polls and acting as party paymaster for other party workers. An Act of Congress going no further would, in our view, unquestionably be valid. So would it be if, in plain and understandable language, the statute forbade activities such as organ-

izing a political party or club; actively participating in fund-raising activities for a partisan candidate or political party; becoming a partisan candidate for, or campaigning for, an elective public office; actively managing the campaign of a partisan candidate for public office; initiating or circulating a partisan nominating petition or soliciting votes for a partisan candidate for public office; or serving as a delegate, alternate, or proxy to a public party convention.

In *Broadrick* v. *Oklahoma* (1973), a companion case, the Court was even willing to uphold political neutrality regulations that were worded so ambiguously that they might inhibit speech unrelated to the objective of maintaining a nonpartisan public service. Hence, restrictions on the partisan activities of public employees, unless drawn very poorly or implemented in some discriminatory fashion, are constitutional.

Can "whistleblowing" and related political speech always be distinguished from partisan expression? While the answer is patently "No," the Supreme Court has yet to be confronted with the need to create a distinction between them. In terms of public personnel management, therefore, some uncertainty remains in this area, especially during electoral campaign periods.

FREEDOM OF ASSOCIATION

Contemporary constitutional law regarding public employees' freedom of association is also of great importance to public personnel managers. Here again, however, the law is divided and perplexing questions remain. Although public employees' rights to join organizations voluntarily (including political parties, labor unions, and even subversive groups) is [sic] now well established (*AFSCME* v. *Woodward,* 1969); *Elfbrandt* v. *Russell,* 1966; *Shelton* v. *Tucker,* 1960), their right to refrain from associating with or supporting organizations has sharply divided the Supreme Court.

In *Elrod* v. *Burns* (1976), the Court held that patronage dismissals constitute an unconstitutional infringement on public employees' freedom of belief and association. However, it was unable to develop a majority opinion on the issue. Justice Brennan, joined by Justices White and Marshall, reasoned that (355): "The cost of the practice of patronage is the restraint it places on freedoms of belief and association" because it forces them to join or support a political party. Brennan concluded that such dismissals

were "not the least restrictive means for fostering" legitimate governmental ends, such as the promotion of efficiency and effectiveness, and, consequently, were unconstitutional (372).

Justice Stewart, joined by Justice Blackman, concurred, although he viewed the case in a more restrictive light (375): "The single substantive question involved in this case is whether a nonpolicymaking, nonconfidential government employee can be discharged from a job that he is satisfactorily performing upon the sole ground of his political beliefs. I agree with the Court that he cannot." Thus, while a majority of the Court considered the patronage dismissals of the employees in question to be unconstitutional, there was no majority consensus on precisely why. The issue was clarified further in *Branti* v. *Finkel* (1980).

Branti involved the patronage dismissal of two county assistant public defenders. In holding that their dismissals were unconstitutional, the Supreme Court established the principle that "the ultimate inequity is not whether the label 'policymaker' or 'confidential' fits a particular position; rather, the question is whether the hiring authority can demonstrate that party affiliation is an appropriate requirement for the effective performance of the public office involved" (1980: 518). It is evident that, under this standard, patronage dismissals in the public service will be extremely limited.

Elrod v. *Burns* and *Branti* v. *Finkel* protect most public employees from demands that they join or support political parties. But what about demands that they support labor unions through agency shop or fair share agreements? Most recently, the Supreme Court tackled this issue in *Chicago Teachers Union* v. *Hudson* (1986). Previously, in *Abood* v. *Detroit Board of Education* (1977), the Supreme Court "rejected the claim that it was unconstitutional for a public employer to designate a union as the exclusive collective-bargaining representative of its employees, and to require nonunion employees, as a condition of employment, to pay a fair share of the union's cost of negotiating and administering a collective bargaining agreement" (*Chicago Teachers Union* v. *Hudson,* 1986: 243–244). But the Court also held that "nonunion employees do have a constitutional right to 'prevent the Union's spending a part of their required service fees to contribute to political candidates and to express political views unrelated to its duties as exclusive bargaining representative'" (*Chicago Teachers Union* v. *Hudson,* 1986: 244). IN the *Hudson* case, a unanimous Court (with a concurring opinion) considerably strengthened the latter right. It held that unions must follow certain procedures to enable nonmembers to challenge the amount of the assessed fees: "We hold . . . that the constitutional requirements for the Union's collection of agency fees include an adequate explanation of the basis for the fee, a reasonably prompt opportunity to challenge the amount of the fee before an impartial decision maker, and an escrow for the amounts reasonably in dispute while such challenges are pending" (*Chicago Teachers Union* v. *Hudson,* 1986: 249).

From an historical perspective, it is striking that public employment now includes constitutional protection against patronage dismissals and the improper assessment of agency shop fees. *Branti* and *Hudson* represent considerable extensions of public employees' constitutional rights. *Hudson*'s requirement that an impartial decision maker be available to rule on the propriety of fees also introduces, on a constitutional basis, an additional adjudicatory function into public personnel administration.

PRIVACY

During the 1980s, the Supreme Court brought the Fourth Amendment to bear squarely upon public employment. Although the Court was unable to formulate a majority opinion in *O'Connor* v. *Ortega* (1987), all its members appeared to agree with the general proposition that public employees retain Fourth Amendment protections within the context of their employment. The case originated when O'Connor, the Executive Director of a state hospital, became aware of alleged improprieties in Dr. Ortega's management of the hospital's resident training program. While Ortega was placed on leave, hospital staff searched his office and "seized several items from Dr. Ortega's desk and file cabinets, including a Valentine's card, a photograph, and a book of poetry all sent to Dr. Ortega by a former resident physician" (*O'Connor* v. *Ortega,* 1987). The purpose of the search and seizure was unclear and the investigators found it impossible to separate all of Ortega's personal property from state property. Instead, everything was boxed-up together. No formal inventory of the property was ever made. Sub-

sequently, Ortega was dismissed, though the search appears to have had no significant bearing on the charges against him.

Justice O'Connor announced the Court's judgment to remand the case for trial at the district court level. Her plurality opinion was joined by Chief Justice Rehnquist, Justice White, and Justice Powell. She reasoned that "Individuals do not lose Fourth Amendment rights merely because they work for the government instead of a private employer" (*O'Connor* v. *Ortega,* 1987: 723). But the scope of those rights depended upon two considerations. First, whether the employee had a reasonable expectation of privacy in the workplace. In O'Connor's view, this matter required an idiographic, if not adjudicatory determination: "Given the great variety of work environments in the public sector, the question of whether an employee has a reasonable expectation of privacy must be addressed on a case-by-case basis" (723). Second, even if the employee did have such an expectation, his or her rights would not be violated if the government could show that "both the inception and the scope of the intrusion . . . [were] reasonable" (728). The latter standard was more appropriate than requiring warrants or probable cause, she argued, because "public employees are entrusted with tremendous responsibility, and the consequences of their misconduct or incompetence to both the agency and the public interest can be severe" (727).

Justice Scalia concurred separately in the Court's judgment. He argued that "the offices of government employees, and *a fortiori* the drawers and files within those offices, are covered by Fourth Amendment protections as a general matter" (*O'Connor* v. *Ortega,* 1987: 732). But in his view, as a rule, "searches to retrieve work-related materials or to investigate violations of workplace rules—searches of the sort that are regarded as reasonable and normal in the private-employer context—do not violate the Fourth Amendment" (732–733).

Justice Blackman's dissent, joined by Justices Brennan, Marshall, and Stevens, agreed that "[i]ndividuals do not lose Fourth Amendment rights merely because they work for the Government instead of a private employer" (*O'Connor* v. *Ortega,* 1987: 736). He also agreed that "Given . . . the number and types of workplace searches by public employers that can be imagined—ranging all the way from the employer's routine entry for retrieval of a file to a planned investigatory search into an employee's suspected criminal misdeeds—development of a jurisprudence in this area might well require a case-by-case approach" (733, note 2). However, he argued that the plurality was too quick to substitute a reasonableness standard for the more traditional Fourth Amendment requirements involving warrants or probable cause.

The Fourth Amendment rights of public employees are virtually certain to be clarified as the judiciary faces the progeny of *O'Connor* v. *Ortega* and cases involving drug testing. In the meantime, however, many public personnel administrators lack adequate guidance concerning searches of their own and their co-workers' offices. When is an expectation of privacy reasonable? When is a search reasonable in its inception and scope? These are the questions with which administrators contemplating searches in the workplace should now be preoccupied.

LIBERTY

The broad issue of public employees' "liberty" has also been the subject of substantial litigation. Over the years, public employees have been exposed to various types of coercion by their employers. For instance, in the 1960s, Senator Samuel Ervin found that public employees had been requested "to lobby in local city councils for fair housing ordinances, to go out and make speeches on any number of subjects, to supply flower and grass seed for beautification projects and to paint other people's houses" (U.S. Senate, 1967: 9). Among the important contemporary areas of restriction of public employees' liberty are mandatory maternity leaves, grooming standards, and residency.

Cleveland Board of Education v. *La Fleur* (1974) and *Cohen* v. *Chesterfield County School Board* (1974), which were argued and decided together, involved issues posed by mandatory maternity leaves. The regulations being challenged forced teachers to leave their jobs, without pay, several months before the expected date of birth of their children. The Supreme Court, per Justice Stewart, elected to decide the case on the basis of "liberty" rather than equal protection. The Court held that "by acting to penalize the pregnant teacher for deciding to bear a child overly restrictive maternity leave regulations can constitute a heavy burden on the exercise of . . .

protected freedoms" (640). The regulations were found unconstitutional because they infringed on the teacher's free choice in matters of marriage and family life without advancing any valid state interest: "the provisions amount to a conclusive presumption that every pregnant teacher who reaches the fifth or sixth month of pregnancy is physically incapable of continuing. There is no individualized determination . . . to any particular teacher's ability to continue at her job" (644). For such general regulations to be constitutionally valid, they must not require leave in the absence of an individual physical examination except very late in the normal term of a pregnancy. Similarly, a regulation barring a teacher from returning to work within three months after the birth of her child was held unconstitutional.

In the Court's view, the liberty to bear children must remain free of undue or purposeless governmental interference. Other liberties, however, have been considered less fundamental. Thus, in *Kelly* v. *Johnson* (1976), the Court found no constitutional barrier to grooming regulations applying to male police officers. Although a lower court held that "choice of personal appearance is an ingredient of an individual's personal liberty" (241), the Supreme Court reasoned that the burden of proof should be on the employee challenging the regulation to "demonstrate that there is no rational connection between the regulation . . . and the promotion of safety of persons and property" (247). Since the Court thought that such regulations might enhance the public's ability to identify police officers and contribute to an *esprit de corps* within the police department, it found the challenge to the grooming standards inadequate. In view of the fact that these justifications were exceedingly weak—after all, police wear uniforms to facilitate identification and at least some of these were opposed to the regulations enough to support the suit—it is unlikely that the Supreme Court will overturn similar kinds of restrictions unless they are utterly arbitrary, capricious, or unfairly enforced. This conclusion may be strengthened somewhat by the Court's holding in *Goldman* v. *Weinberger* (1986), that the Air Force could legitimately discipline an officer for violating its dress code by wearing a religious skullcap (*kipah*).

Finally, in *McCarthy* v. *Philadelphia Civil Service Commission* (1976), the Supreme Court upheld the constitutionality of a residency requirement for firefighters. However, it did so without much discussion of the issues involved, and, therefore, it remains unclear whether there are constitutional limits to a public employer's ability to require that its employees live within its jurisdictional boundaries.

EQUAL PROTECTION

The Supreme Court's decisions concerning grooming and residency indicate that public employers have substantial leeway in dealing with aspects of their employees' lives. Its decisions concerning equal protection of the laws also serve to reduce the likelihood that public personnel administrative actions will infringe unconstitutionally upon fundamental rights. Thus, the Court firmly established the principle that public personnel practices having a harsh or disparate racial or gender impact will nevertheless be upheld constitutionally unless they manifest a discriminatory *purpose.*

This line of constitutional interpretation was developed first in *Washington* v. *Davis* (1976). The case involved a challenge to the constitutionality of a written qualifying examination given to applicants for positions as police trainees in the District of Columbia. The exam had a disproportionately harsh racial impact by disqualifying four times as many blacks as whites. Several lower court decisions held that such a disparity required the governmental employer to demonstrate that the exam in question served a compelling state interest. This generally entailed a demonstration of the test's validity (Rosenbloom and Obuchowski, 1977). However, the Supreme Court rejected this approach in favor of one requiring that "an invidious discriminatory purpose" (*Washington* v. *Davis,* 1976: 242) be shown to overturn a public personnel practice on the grounds that it violates the Equal Protection Clause (241–242):

> This is not to say that the necessary discriminatory racial purpose must be express or appear on the face of the statute, or that a law's disproportionate impact is irrelevant in cases involving Constitution-based claims of racial discrimination. . . .
>
> Necessarily, an invidious discriminatory purpose may often be inferred from the totality of the relevant facts, including the fact, if it is true, that the law bears more heavily on one race than another.

At the time it was decided, it appeared that the impact of *Washington* v. *Davis* on public personnel

management would be limited because identical issues can be litigated under federal equal employment opportunity statutes that, unlike the Constitution, do not require that a discriminatory purpose be shown to invalidate a public personnel practice having a harsh racial impact. However, the significance of the *Washington* v. *Davis* decision was made evident in *Personnel Administrator* v. *Feeny* (1979), which involved a challenge to the constitutionality of Massachusetts' veterans preference law on the grounds that it violated the equal protection clause by disproportionately excluding women from public employment. The Equal Employment Opportunity Act of 1972 foreclosed the possibility of challenging such regulations on statutory grounds by providing that "nothing contained in this title [VII] shall be construed to repeal or modify any Federal, State, territorial, or local law creating special rights or preference for veterans." (EEO Act, 1972: Sec. 712). The Supreme Court agreed with the challengers that the impact of the Massachusetts law on the "public employment opportunities of women has . . . been severe" (*Personnel Administrator* v. *Feeny,* 1979: 271). Nevertheless, it upheld the constitutionality of the "absolute" preferential scheme on the basis that not impact, but rather "purposeful discrimination is the condition that offends the Constitution" (274).

Washington v. *Davis* did not address the constitutionality of affirmative action, which is purposeful differential treatment based on race, sex, and/or ethnicity. In several cases during the 1980s, the Supreme Court sought to negotiate the tensions between equal protection and affirmative action. Specifically, the Court addressed the constitutionality of affirmative action that is imposed as a remedy for admitted or proven past illegal discrimination, unconstitutional discrimination, or both. It also suggested, but did not actually rule upon, the conditions under which affirmative action that is voluntarily adopted by a public employer to redress social imbalances in its work force might be constitutional. For the sake of legal and constitutional analysis, it is important to distinguish between "voluntary" and "remedial" affirmative action. Voluntary affirmative action may seek to overcome the effects of past discrimination, but it is not a "remedy" in the legal sense because it is not based on a legal finding or admission of past unconstitutional practices, illegal practices, or both.

United States v. *Paradise* (1987) is the Supreme Court's most recent wide-ranging effort to deal with the constitutionality of remedial affirmative action. It grew out of a federal district court decision in 1972, holding that Alabama had unconstitutionally excluded blacks from its force of state troopers for almost four decades. The district court issued an order requiring the Department of Public Safety to refrain from discriminating and it imposed a quota hiring system as a remedy for past discrimination. Although blacks had been hired pursuant to the order, by 1979 there were still no blacks in the department's upper ranks. In that year, the department entered into a consent decree requiring it to promote blacks. By 1981, however, no black troopers had been promoted. A second consent decree was then approved by the district court. It specified that a promotion exam would be administered to applicants and that the results would be reviewed to determine whether there was an adverse impact on blacks. The test had such an impact and, in 1983, the district court ordered the department to submit a plan to promote at least 15 qualified candidates in a manner that would not adversely affect black troopers seeking promotions. The department proposed that four blacks be among the 15 troopers promoted. The district court rejected this plan and ordered that, "for a period of time," at least 50 percent of those promoted to the rank of corporal be black, if qualified black candidates are available. It also imposed a 50 percent promotional requirement in the other upper ranks, but only on the conditions that (1) there were qualified black candidates, (2) in the ranks covered, less than 25 percent of the work force was black, and (3) the department failed to establish a promotion plan for the rank involved that did not have an adverse impact on blacks (*U.S.* v. *Paradise,* 1987: 204). The district court also ordered the department to submit a realistic schedule for developing promotional procedures for all its ranks. The department proceeded to promote eight blacks and eight whites under the district court's order. The United States, that is, the Solicitor General, appealed the district court's order on the grounds that it violated the Equal Protection Clause. The Court of Appeals affirmed and subsequently the Supreme Court took the case on writ of certiorari.

The high court upheld the order, but it failed to formulate a majority opinion. Justice Brennan announced its judgment in a plurality opinion joined by Justices Marshall, Blackman, and Powell. Brennan reasoned that although "It is now well established

that government bodies, including courts, may constitutionally employ racial classifications essential to remedy unlawful treatment of racial or ethnic groups subject to discrimination" (*U.S.* v. *Paradise,* 1987: 220), two issues remained. First, was the plan sufficiently "narrowly tailored"? Brennan responded affirmatively because it was "temporary and flexible" and applied "only if qualified blacks are available, only if the Department has an objective need to make promotions, and only if the Department fails to implement a promotion procedure that does not have an adverse impact on blacks" (*U.S.* v. *Paradise,* 1987: 232).

Second, was the district court's order realistically related to the percentage of blacks in the relevant work force? Brennan noted that the 50 percent promotional quota was intended to fulfill a goal the district court had established earlier of having 25 percent black representation in the department's entire personnel complement. Thus, "the 50 percent figure is not itself the goal; rather it represents the speed at which the goal of 25 percent will be achieved" (*U.S.* v. *Paradise,* 1987: 229). Since the 25 percent figure was realistic, the district court's order was deemed satisfactory.

Justice Sevens concurred in the Court's judgment, but he objected to Brennan's concern with narrow tailoring: "the record discloses an egregious violation of the Equal Protection Clause. It follows, therefore, that the District Court had broad and flexible authority to remedy the wrongs resulting from this violation" (*U.S.* v. *Paradise,* 1987: 235).

Justice O'Connor dissented in an opinion joined by Chief Justice Rehnquist and Justice Scalia. She argued that the plurality had inappropriately adopted "a standardless view of 'narrowly tailored' far less stringent than that required . . ." (*U.S.* v. *Paradise,* 1987: 240) Justice White dissented separately on the basis that the district court had exceeded its equitable powers. Justice Powell joined in the plurality's opinion, but also concurred separately. He emphasized that the district court's order was narrowly drawn and properly scrutinized by the plurality.

In *Paradise,* the burden imposed on (or the advantage taken away from) nonminority troopers involved the opportunity for promotion. In other cases the burdens may be heavier or the advantages more costly to forfeit. This may affect the legality of affirmative action plans. For instance, in *Wygant* v. *Jackson* (1986), which involved voluntary affirmative action, the Supreme Court reached the judgment that a collective bargaining agreement providing for layoffs based on a racial classification that favored minorities was in violation of the Equal Protection Clause. In *Firefighters Local* v. *Stotts* (1984), the Court overturned a district court's injunction against laying off black employees as a means of preserving the intent of a consent decree formulated to remedy past discrimination in hiring and promotional practices.

Paradise did not address the constitutional issues posed by voluntary affirmative action. *Johnson* v. *Transportation Agency* (1987) established that such affirmative action, intended to redress sexual imbalances in a public employer's work force, can be *legal*. Presumably, this conclusion holds for imbalances involving racial, ethnic, and religious minorities as well. *Johnson* also strongly suggests, but does not hold, that voluntary affirmative action can be constitutional. Due to the way the case was argued, "no constitutional issue was either raised or addressed . . ." (*Johnson* v. *Transportation Agency,* 1987: 623, note 2). However, if the Court's decision in *City of Richmond* v. *Croson* (1989), which dealt with public sector contracting set-asides for minority business enterprises, can be used as a guide, such voluntary affirmative action will be subject to strict judicial scrutiny and will have to be narrowly tailored if it is to be constitutional.

PROCEDURAL DUE PROCESS

The Constitution protects citizens against governmental denial of their life, liberty, or property, without due process of law (Fifth and Fourteenth Amendments). Although perplexing to define in a technical sense, due process generally refers to fundamental fairness (*Hannah* v. *Larche,* 1960). In the realm of public employment it raises the issues of when an adverse action constitutionally requires that a hearing be held and what form such a hearing must take.

In *Board of Regents* v. *Roth* (1972), the Court addressed the applicability of the Constitution in adverse actions in the public sector. It identified four situations in which public employees would have a constitutional right to a hearing in dismissal actions: (1) where the dismissal was in retaliation for the exercise of protected rights, such as freedom of speech; (2) "where a person's good name, reputation, honor or integrity is at stake because of what

the government is doing to him, notice and an opportunity to be heard are essential" (573); (3) where a dismissal diminished a public employee's future employability; and (4) where the employee has a property right or interest in a position, such as tenure or a contract.

Later in the 1970s, the Court handed down some decisions that seemed to indicate that it would take a limited view of the applicability of due process (*Arnett* v. *Kennedy,* 1974; *Bishop* v. *Wood,* 1976; *Codd* v. *Velger,* 1977). However, in *Cleveland Board of Education* v. *Loudermill,* decided in 1985, the Court was unequivocal in holding that procedural due process will often govern dismissals from the public service. The case concerned the dismissal of a security guard by the Cleveland Board of Education on the grounds that he lied on his job application in stating that he was never convicted of a felony. Under Ohio law, Loudermill was a "classified civil servant," who could be fired only for cause and was entitled to an administrative review of any such discharge.

The Supreme Court, per Justice White, held that Loudermill's due process rights depended on whether the Ohio civil service statute gave him a property interest in his job. Upon finding that the law did so, White argued that deprivation of the interest was controlled by the Constitution, rather than by the *statute's* provisions for dismissals:

> The point is straightforward. . . . The right to due process "is conferred, not by legislative grace, but by constitutional guarantee. While the legislature may elect not to confer a property interest in [public] [sic] employment, it may not constitutionally authorize the deprivation of such an interest, once conferred, without appropriate procedural safeguards" (*Cleveland Board of Education* v. *Loudermill,* 1985: 541).

Having established that Loudermill's due process rights were governed by the Constitution, the Court next found he was constitutionally entitled to a pretermination hearing. Though such a procedure was necessary, it "need not definitively resolve the propriety of the discharge. It should be an initial check against mistaken decisions—essentially, a determination of whether there are reasonable grounds to believe that the charges against the employee are true and support the proposed action" (*Cleveland Board of Education* v. *Loudermill,* 1985: 545–546).

Justice White noted, however, that the extent of due process required prior to dismissal in this case was related to the opportunity for a more elaborate posttermination hearing under Ohio's law.

Additionally, public personnelists should be aware that if an adverse action is taken against an employee who has engaged in constitutionally protected conduct, such as free speech, then the employer may have to show "by a preponderance of the evidence that it would have reached the same decision . . . even in the absence of the protected conduct" (*Mt. Healthy City School District Board of Education* v. *Doyle,* 1977: 287).

LIABILITY

It is important to stress that, for the public personnel manager, knowledge of the constitutional rights of public employees is anything but academic. As a result of several Supreme Court decisions over the past two decades, such knowledge has become a positive job requirement. Today, the public personnel manager is likely to be *personally* liable for infringing upon the constitutional rights of public employees and applicants if he or she violates "clearly established statutory or constitutional rights of which a reasonable person would have known" (*Harlow* v. *Fitzgerald,* 1982: 818).

An exception to personal liability exists for federal personnelists in some cases where the individual whose rights have been violated is able to obtain a remedy in another way, such as through appeal to the Merit Systems Protection Board (*Bush* v. *Lucas,* 1983). Damages awarded against public employees may be punitive as well as compensatory (*Smith* v. *Wade,* 1983). Punitive damages are intended to punish the offending official and to deter others from violating protected rights. Compensatory damages, such as back pay, seek to make the aggrieved party whole. In some instances, the government jurisdiction may indemnify a personnelist against whom damages have been accessed. Liability may be attached to agencies when their policies are the source of illegal or unconstitutional abridgments of individuals' protected rights (*Monell* v. *New York City Department of Social Services,* 1978; *Pembaur* v. *Cincinnati,* 1986).

Finally, it should be noted that a nascent right to disobey unconstitutional orders has grown out of public employees' potential liabilities for violating individuals' constitutional rights (*Harley* v. *Schuylkill County,* 1979). As Robert Vaughn (1984: 16–13) notes, "the court reasoned that since [officials' liability] protected the constitutional rights of a person subjected to governmental action, it must, as a corollary, protect the rights of public employees who refuse to obey orders depriving third persons of their constitutional rights."

CONCLUSION

Discussions of the constitutional rights of individuals often have an air of unreality about them. There is no doubt that attempting to vindicate one's rights through a lawsuit that turns on matters of constitutional interpretation is an arduous process. It is time consuming, expensive, and psychologically burdensome. Thus, it would come as no surprise if there were a substantial gap between the constitutional rights of public employees in theory and practice. Nevertheless, the public personnel manager should always remain watchful of judicial decisions.

Citizens enjoy considerable constitutional rights while in public employment, including those in the realm of nonpartisan speech, association, liberty, privacy, and protection from intentional discrimination based on unconstitutional factors such as race or religion. They also have extensive rights to due process. Regardless of the overall trend of judicial decisions, some of these rights will be expanded over the next decade. Given public personnel managers' liability for breaches of constitutional rights that they may inflict, personnelists must always remain cognizant and up to date regarding such legal developments.

It should be noted with emphasis that judicial decisions concerning the public employment relationship generally seek to establish a balance between the constitutional rights of public employees and the needs of public employers. Their efforts can provide public personnel managers with guidance as to how public personnel policy can create a greater harmony between the needs of the administrative state for productive, efficient employees and those of constitutional democracy for free citizens.

In sum, the constitutional status of public employees is likely to remain a problematic area for public personnel managers and one that will present public personnel administration with great challenges and opportunities in the years to come.

REFERENCES

Abood v. *Detroit Board of Education.* 1977.   431 U.S. 209.

AFSCME v. *Woodward.* 1969.   406 F.2d 137.

Arnett v. *Kennedy.* 1974.   416 U.S. 134.

Birnbaum v. *Trussell.* 1966.   371 F.2d 672.

Bishop v. *Wood.* 1976.   426 U.S. 341.

Board of Regents v. *Roth.* 1972.   408 U.S. 564.

Branti v. *Finkel.* 1980.   445 U.S. 507.

Broadrick v. *Oklahoma.* 1973.   413 U.S. 601.

Bush v. *Lucas.* 1983.   462 U.S. 367.

Chicago Teachers Union v. *Hudson.* 1986.   89.1.Ed.2d 232.

City of Richmond v. *Croson.* 1989.   57.L.W. 4132.

Civil Service Commission v. *National Association of Letter Carriers.* 1973.   413 U.S. 548.

Cleveland Board of Education v. *La Fleur.* 1974.   414 U.S. 632.

Cleveland Board of Education v. *Landermill.* 1985.   470 U.S. 532.

Codd v. *Velger.* 1977.   429 U.S. 624.

Cohen v. *Chesterfield County School Board.* 1974.   414 U.S. 632.

Connick v. *Myers.* 1983.   461 U.S. 138.

Dotson, A. 1955. "The Emerging Doctrine of Privilege in Public Employment." *Public Administration Review* 15 (Spring): 77–88.

Elfbrandt v. *Russell.* 1966.   384 U.S. 11.

Elrod v. *Burns.* 1976.   427 U.S. 347.

Equal Employment Opportunity Act. 1972.   86 Stat. 103, March 24.

Firefighters Local v. *Stotts.* 1984.   467 U.S. 561.

Goldman v. *Weinberger.* 1986.   475 U.S. 503.

Hannah v. *Larche.* 1960.   363 U.S. 420.

Harley v. *Schuylkill County.* 1979.   476 F. Supp. 191.

Harlow v. *Fitzgerald.* 1982.   457 U.S. 800.

Johnson v. *Transportation Agency.* 1987.   94 L.Ed.2d 615.

Kelly v. *Johnson.* 1976.   425 U.S. 238.

McAuliffe v. *New Bedford.* 1892.   155 Mass. 216.

McCarthy v. *Philadelphia CSC.* 1976.   424 U.S. 645.

Monell v. *New York City Department of Social Services.* 1978.   436 U.S. 658.

Mount Healthy City School District Board of Education v. *Doyle.* 1977.   429 U.S. 274.

National Association of Letter Carriers v. *Civil Service Commission.* 1972.   346 F. Supp. 578.

New York Times. 1974.   July 1, p. 10.

O'Connor v. *Ortega.* 1987.   94 L.Ed.2d 714.

Pembaur v. *Cincinnati.* 1986.   475 U.S. 469.

Personnel Administrator v. *Feeny.* 1979.   422 U.S. 256.

Pickering v. *Board of Education.* 1968.   391 U.S. 563.

Rankin v. *McPherson.* 1987.   97 L.Ed.2d 315.

Rosenbloom, D. 1971.   *Federal Service and the Constitution.* Ithaca, N.Y.: Cornell University Press.

———. 1975.   "Public Personnel Administration and the Constitution." *Public Administration Review* 35 (January–February): 52–60.

———. 1977.   "The Public Employee in Court." In C. Levine, ed., *Managing Human Resources.* Beverly Hills, Calif.: Sage.

Rosenbloom, D., and C. Obuchowski. 1977.   "Public Personnel Examinations and the Constitution." *Public Administration Review* 37 (January–February): 9–18.

Shelton v. *Tucker.* 1960.   364 U.S. 479.

Sherbert v. *Verner.* 1963.   374 U.S. 398.

Smith v. *Wade.* 1983.   461 U.S. 30.

Sugarman v. *Dougall.* 1973.   413 U.S. 634.

United Public Workers v. *Mitchell.* 1947.   330 U.S. 75.

United States v. *Paradise.* 1987.   94 L.Ed.2d 203.

U.S. Senate. 1967.   "Protecting Privacy and the Rights of Federal Employees." Report 519. 90th Cong. 1st sess. Washington, D.C.: August 21.

Van Alstyne, W. 1968.   "The Demise of the Right-Privilege Distinction in Constitutional Law." *Harvard Law Review* 81: 1439–1464.

Vaughn, Robert. 1984.   *The Merit Systems Protection Board.* New York: Law Journal Seminars Press.

Washington v. *Davis.* 1976.   426 U.S. 229.

Wygant v. *Jackson.* 1986.   476 U.S. 267.

CONSTITUTIONAL RIGHTS IN PUBLIC EMPLOYMENT

The Constitution of the United States, and more specifically the Bill of Rights, was designed to protect citizens from arbitrary or malicious actions of government. Thomas Jefferson expressed his dissatisfaction with an early draft of the Constitution in a letter to James Madison because that draft did not include an enumeration of specific rights: "A bill of rights is what the people are entitled to against every government on earth, general or particular, and which no government should refuse, or rest on inference."[4]

In the public employment setting, the employer is the government; as a consequence, any and all units of American government are restricted by the Constitution in dealings with their employees. Common employment practices performed in the nonprofit and for-profit sectors (such as random drug testing or searches of work areas) under most circumstances are unconstitutional when done by public managers. The most obvious example of a major constraint on public sector managers is the contrast with the ability of managers in the for-profit or nonprofit sectors to fire employees for almost any reason—or no reason at all—so long as they are not firing the employee for specifically illegal reasons, such as discrimination. Public managers are required in most cases to have a justifiable reason to dismiss an employee and must allow the employee the right to *due process* in challenging a dismissal as guaranteed in the Fifth and Fourteenth amendments.

Public managers act as agents of the government employer in a wide variety of employment practices. Almost every aspect of public personnel administration is affected by constitutional considerations. In the hiring, recruitment, and testing and selection processes, the practices of public sector agencies are influenced by requirements for equal protection. Provisions of the Fifth and Fourteenth amendments cover employee development practices such as training and promotion. Union activities and collective bargaining are covered by the freedom of association guaranteed under the First Amendment. Employee discipline and termination are covered by the requirement for due process, giving employees the right to grievance procedures and challenging adverse personnel actions. These constitutional protections may make it more difficult to hire the applicant a manager wants to hire, promote a promising young employee, or fire someone broadly considered to be unproductive or "dead wood." These restrictions also prevent government managers from hiring individuals for political reasons; from discriminating on the basis of race, sex, or national origin; or from taking away the livelihood of government workers for arbitrary or political motivations. To illustrate how specific provisions of Jefferson's beloved Bill of Rights came into play in public sector HRM, several provisions of the listing of enumerated rights of citizens are considered next.

Freedom of Speech and Assembly

[First Amendment] Congress shall make no law . . . abridging the freedom of speech, or of the press; or the right of the people peaceably to assemble.

Freedom of speech Is it legal for a public employer to dismiss an employee for speaking out against the employer or other government such as the state or federal government? In one case, a nineteen-year-old black female probationary clerical employee of a county law enforcement agency was overheard having a conversation about the attempted assassination of President Reagan in 1981. She was heard saying, "If they go after him again, I hope they get him." When the sheriff fired her, she sued the county for violating her right to free speech. The Supreme Court weighed the competing interests of the employee's right to comment on matters of public interest and the employer's need to operate the government agency efficiently. In the balancing process, the Court considered whether the employee's comment was a matter of public concern and the manner, time, and place of the employee's statement and the context in which the statement was made. It found that the employee was "commenting upon matters of public concern" and that the county produced "no evidence that it interfered with the efficient functioning of the office."[5] The right to free speech can be limited only when statements adversely affect the efficient operation of government services, or when it is reasonable to infer that speech might become disruptive.

In two recent cases of particular note with the increase in the contracting out of government services to private and nonprofit providers, the Supreme Court has ruled that freedom of speech extends to independent contractors as well as public employees.[6] In one case, the contract of a government contractor was terminated after the contractor publicly criticized county policies and criticized the sitting Board of County Commissioners. The contractor sued for breach of contract, and the Courts ruled that the government could not place conditions on someone's rights under the Constitution and reinstated the compensation owed the contractor.[7] In another case, a towing company was removed from the list of contractors that a city used repeatedly because the company refused to make a political contribution to the mayor's campaign and ended up supporting the mayor's opponent. The Court ruled that the city violated the contractor's First Amendment rights if it terminated the contract for political reasons.[8]

Political activity   The Federal Employees' Political Activities Act of 1939 (**Hatch Act** of 1939) was intended to prevent "pernicious political activities" and ensure the political neutrality of government workers. The statute had four objectives that it sought to achieve by making partisan political activity by federal and other government workers illegal. The act was intended to restrict partisan elected officials from using government employees for political purposes and to prevent the public employee's loyalty going to the political party of a public official. The Hatch Act was also intended to protect public employees from politically motivated job actions, and to limit the potential political power of the bureaucracy.

The Hatch Act prohibited federal government employees, as well as state and local government employees who receive loans or grants from the federal government, from engaging in partisan political activity. Nonpartisan political activities were permitted, and the act did not apply to federal department heads, their assistant heads, anyone working in the president's office, or anyone appointed by the president. The act prohibited those many public employees covered by its provisions from engaging in partisan political management or partisan political campaigning in any way, although the right to vote was specifically reserved. The Supreme Court upheld the 1939 Hatch Act, saying,

> If, in [the] judgment [of Congress and the president], efficiency may be best obtained by prohibiting active participation by classified employees in politics as party officers or workers, we see no constitutional objection. . . . Congress may regulate the political conduct of government employees "within reasonable limits," even though the regulation trenches to some extent upon unfettered political action.[9]

The Court heard arguments against the Hatch Act again in 1973 and once more narrowly upheld the precedent established in its initial ruling of using the rationale of the need for

> a balance between the interest of the [employee], as a citizen, in commenting upon matters of public concern and the interest of the [government], as an employer, in promoting the efficiency of the public services it performs through its employees. Although Congress is free to strike a different balance than it has, if it so chooses, we think the balance it has so far struck is sustainable.[10]

After several attempts, Congress finally passed a major revision to the Hatch Act in 1993. The Federal Employees' Political Activities Act of 1993 gave federal government workers expanded rights to engage in political activity. The revision generally allows federal and U.S. Postal Service employees to engage in partisan political activity as long as they do so on their own time and not on the job. Federal workers are permitted to run for partisan political office without taking a leave of absence, unless running for office would interfere with the performance of their job. They are still prohibited from using their official authority or public offices to interfere with or affect the result of an election. They still may not knowingly solicit or discourage political participation from a person who has applied for a government grant, contract, or other government business from their agency. Government employees are still prohibited from giving political contributions to their superiors or from soliciting contributions from subordinates.[11]

The U.S. Office of Special Counsel has published a list of do's and don'ts and a number of advisory opinions regarding participation in political activities under the current Hatch Act (see Box 4.1).

Box 4.1   Do's and Don'ts for Federal Employees Who May Engage in Partisan Political Activity

Do's	Don'ts
Be candidates for public office in nonpartisan elections; register and vote as they choose	Use official authority or influence to interfere with an election
Assist in voter registration drives	Solicit or discourage political activity of anyone with business before their agency
Express opinions about candidates and issues	Solicit or receive political contributions (may be done in certain limited situations by federal labor or other employee organizations)
Contribute money to political organizations	Be candidates for public office in partisan elections
Attend political fund-raising functions	Engage in political activity while on duty, in a government office, wearing an official uniform, or using a government vehicle
Join and be an active member of a political party or club	Wear partisan political buttons on duty
Sign nominating petitions	
Campaign for or against referendum questions, constitutional amendments, or municipal ordinances	
Campaign for or against candidates in partisan elections	
Make campaign speeches for candidates in partisan elections	
Distribute campaign literature in partisan elections	
Hold office in political clubs or parties	

Source: U.S. Office of Special Counsel Political Activity (Hatch Act), **http://www.osc.gov/hatch1.htm,** January 17, 1999.

The 1993 statute applies to federal employees and to certain state and local government employees who are working in programs funded in whole or in substantial part by federal loans or grants. Most states have passed "mini—Hatch Acts" that limit political activity in these states along pretty much the same lines as the federal law (see Box 4.2).

Most states have passed legislation similar to the original federal Hatch Acts prohibiting partisan political activity among state and local government workers. Although the federal statute applied to many state and local government workers, these state laws outlaw most political activities for all government employees. With the passage of the amended Hatch Act of 1993 at the national level, most states have acted to loosen political restrictions on public employees.

Nonprofit sector employees are not specifically subject to Hatch provisions, but their activities within the context of the nonprofit are limited for certain organizations exempt under Internal Revenue Service regulations. As a rule, 501c(3) organizations (nonprofits organized for charitable and religious purposes) may jeopardize their tax-

Box 4.2   Do's and Don'ts for State and Local Government Employees Who May Engage in Partisan Political Activity

Do's	Don'ts
Run for office in nonpartisan elections	Be candidates for public office in a partisan election
Campaign for and hold office in political clubs and organizations	Use official authority or influence to interfere with or affect the results of an election or nomination
Actively campaign for candidates for public office in partisan and nonpartisan elections	Directly or indirectly coerce contributions from subordinates in support of a political party or candidate
Contribute money to political organizations and attend political fund-raising functions	

Source: U.S. Office of Special Counsel, Political Activity (Hatch Act), **http://www.osc.gov/hatch1.htm,** January 17, 1999.

exempt status if the "substantial part of the activities of such organization consists of carrying on propaganda, or otherwise attempting to influence legislation."[12] In fact, nonprofits receiving federal funds (and some states require this as well) are asked to sign compliance forms indicating that they limit information dissemination to policymakers to an amount below some set proportion of their funding and do not use public funding in this regard.

Political patronage   The freedom of speech guaranteed under the First Amendment also applies to the freedom of individuals to express their political views and not be punished through the withholding of employment opportunities as a result of the expression of these views. The historical practice of **political patronage** was considered by many to interfere with this freedom by precluding otherwise qualified individuals from gaining employment in public agencies because they belonged to the political party that happened to be out of power at the time, or because they supported the losing candidate in the last election. The beginning of the coming to an end of political patronage in the United States came in 1883 with the passage

of the Pendleton Act, which resulted in part from the assassination of President Garfield by a disgruntled office seeker who felt entitled to a government job after helping in the presidential campaign (see Chapter 2 for a description of the Pendleton Act). The last few nails in the patronage coffin were hammered in a series of decisions by the Supreme Court in 1976,[13] 1980,[14] and 1990.[15] In the 1990 decision in ***Rutan v. Republican Party of Illinois,*** the Court directed that government agencies may not hire, promote, transfer, recall, or dismiss public employees solely on the basis of their political affiliation or activity unless party affiliation is a *legitimate requirement for the job* (a rare condition in public service):

> The First Amendment forbids government officials to discharge or threaten to discharge public employees solely for not being supporters of the political party in power, unless party affiliation is an appropriate requirement for the position involved. Today we are asked to decide the constitutionality of several related political patronage practices—whether promotion, transfer, recall and hiring decisions involving low-level public employees may be constitutionally

based on party affiliation and support. *We hold that they may not* [emphasis added].

Freedom of assembly Can a government employer restrict its employees from joining groups for political or union-related activities? One case dealing with this issue involves a state law that required all teachers in a state-supported educational institution to list every organization they belonged to in an effort to find teachers who were communist sympathizers. The Supreme Court ruled that such an employment requirement impaired "that teacher's right of free association" and deprived teachers of "their rights to personal, associational, and academic liberty, protected by the Due Process Clause of the Fourteenth Amendment from invasion by state action."[16] In another case, the court ruled that a state could not refuse to hire individuals, even as correctional officers, who were members of the Ku Klux Klan.[17]

In a number of cases, public employers have tried to prohibit or disqualify some of their employees from joining unions. Congress passed the Lloyd-La Follette Act in 1912 giving federal employees (specifically postal workers) the right to organize and join unions so long as the union prohibited strikes against the federal government. In the case of *Atkins v. City of Charlotte,* the state of North Carolina had passed legislation prohibiting any employee "engaged full-time in law enforcement or fire protection activity from being or becoming a member of any labor organization."[18] The U.S. District Court declared this broad prohibition unconstitutional under the First and Fourteenth amendments. In an earlier case, the Supreme Court had stated,

It is beyond debate that freedom to engage in association for the advancement of beliefs and ideas is an inseparable aspect of the "liberty" assured by the Due Process Clause of the Fourteenth Amendment, which embraces freedom of speech. Of course, it is immaterial whether the beliefs sought to be advanced by association pertain to political, economic, religious or cultural matters, and state action which may have the effect of curtailing the freedom to associate is subject to the closest scrutiny.[19]

Protection from Unreasonable Search and Seizure

[Fourth Amendment] The right of the people to be secure in their persons, houses, papers, and effects, against unreasonable searches and seizures, shall not be violated, and no warrants shall issue, but upon probable cause, supported by Oath or affirmation, and particularly describing the place to be searched, and the persons or things to be seized.

The most controversial issue related to searches and seizures in public employment is the question of drug testing. Here the difference among the employment sectors (public, nonprofit, and for profit) is very important indeed. For-profit and nonprofit sector employers are not bound by the limitations of the Fourth Amendment. The prohibition against violating the people's right to be secure in their persons applies to actions taken by the government. In the case of drug testing, the government is severely limited in its ability to test for drug use by its employees. There must be *a prevailing public service interest* to override the individual's protection of privacy.

In a 1989 case, the U.S. Supreme Court sought to outline the limits of a public service interest in ruling that the U.S. Customs Service could require a urinalysis test for employees actively involved in drug interdiction or those who were required to wear firearms, but did not allow drug testing on other employees without probable cause or reasonable suspicion.[20] The Court stated that "the Fourth Amendment protects individuals from unreasonable searches conducted by the Government, even when the Government acts as an employer." The Court intended to "balance the individual's privacy expectations against the Government's interests to determine whether it is impractical to require a warrant or some level of individualized suspicion in the particular context."

The compelling government interest need not include suspicion of individual misconduct if other public interests, such as public safety, outweigh an individual's expectation of privacy:

> Government's need to discover such latent or hidden conditions, or to prevent their development, is sufficiently compelling to justify the intrusion on privacy entailed by conducting such searches without any measure of individualized suspicion. We think Government's need to conduct the suspicionless searches required by the Customs program outweighs the privacy interests of employees engaged directly in drug interdiction, and those who otherwise are required to carry firearms.[21]

Courts have generally sustained the power of government employers to require persons in safety-sensitive positions (police officers,[22] firefighters,[23] prison employees,[24] and public health workers[25]) to submit to urinalysis where there is a reasonable basis to suspect drug use. Random testing of nonsafety employees has normally not been permitted.[26]

Another privacy or illegal search issue is the government's ability to search employee offices and desks. In an important case, the Supreme Court decided that a public employer could search an employee's office, files, or desk without resorting to obtaining a warrant. The justices held that in some cases, public employee offices are so open to other employees or the public that there is no reasonable employee expectation of privacy. Other public employees may have a reasonable expectation of privacy when they are able to lock their doors or cabinets. Even when there is a reasonable expectation of privacy, the Court said there must be a balance between "the invasion of the employees' legitimate expectations of privacy against the government's need for supervision, control and the efficient operation of the workplace."[27] Such searches must meet the reasonableness standard, but could be done to find a needed item in an employee's office (such as a client file) or when there is reasonable suspicion of evidence of work-related misconduct in the employee's office or files.

Technology and Privacy in the Public Workplace

The prevalence of personal computers and the availability of e-mail have created new dilemmas regarding privacy in the public workplace. Technology allows us to send letters to large numbers of people across the globe. We are able to converse with colleagues and friends and exchange all sorts of information that may be directly related to our work, or it may be entirely personal in nature. Moreover, the Internet offers virtually every kind of information, including web sites about different public jurisdictions, professional associations, merchandise auctions, product sales, as well as the darker side of entertainment such as computer games, chat rooms, and pornography.

According to some researchers, American employees spend an average of 1.2 hours per day at work on e-mail.[28] Employees can spend several hours each day surfing the Internet, many in sites not related to their work. In the light of the expanded use of the Internet, how much of our use of computers is private? Does a government employer have the right to read employee e-mail without permission if it is generated or received on computers owned by the government? Can a public employer review the sites that employees visit on the Internet while working on their government jobs?

To maintain business efficiency and check on the performance of their employees, many businesses are monitoring employee e-mail. The American Civil Liberties Union estimates that 20 to 25 million workers have their workplace e-mail files monitored. In some industries, such as insurance and banking, the figure may be as high as 80 percent. Software is available to allow employers to track web sites visited by employees in their system, as well as to monitor e-mail.[29] The courts have generally ruled in favor of the employer's right to search employee messages, saying there is no reasonable expectation of privacy in e-mail communications.[30] The rationale of not having a reasonable expectation of privacy is consistent with other court rulings allowing an employer to search through office desks and files if the search is done for the purpose of efficient and proper operation of the workplace. Although public employers are more restricted by the Fourth Amendment, the courts generally have permitted public employers the right to search if the purpose is to satisfy the government's interest in operating efficiently or for proper supervision of its employees.[31]

Due Process of Law

[Fifth Amendment] No person shall be . . . deprived of life, liberty or property, without due process of law.

[Fourteenth Amendment] No State shall make or enforce any law which shall abridge the privileges or immunities of citizens of the United States; nor shall any State deprive any person of life, liberty, or property, without due process of law.

A public agency may not take away a person's liberty or property without **due process of law**. The Supreme Court has heard numerous cases related to employee claims of being deprived of property rights when they have lost public employment. The Lloyd-La Follette Act of 1912 gave federal employees the right to petition the government for redress of employment-related grievances, implying a property interest in their jobs. For public employees, the granting of tenure or "permanent status," a formal contract, or clearly implied promises of continued employment are all sufficient to establish a *property interest*. Property interests are not limited to formal agreements, but may be established through existing rules or understandings between employer and employee. "Classified" or "permanent" employee status or the completion of probationary status may be all that is needed to show a property interest.

Federal and state laws and administrative rules provide for, while the Fifth and Fourteenth Amendments to the U.S. Constitution guarantee, substantive due process. The concept of due process can be summarized as the government's attempt to be fair:

Due Process of Law—The idea of "fair play" in the government's application of law to its citizens, guaranteed by the Fifth and Fourteenth Amendments. Substantive due process is just plain *fairness,* and procedural due process is accorded when the government utilizes adequate procedural safeguards for the protection of an individual's liberty or property interests.[32]

Due process of law requires that an action that would constitute a loss of a property interest "be preceded by notice and opportunity for hearing appropriate to the nature of the case."[33] Employees who have a property interest in their employment must be given an opportunity to present reasons that the proposed action should not be taken before action is taken against that employee.[34] The courts have stated that such hearing need not be elaborate; "something less than a full evidentiary hearing is sufficient prior to adverse administrative action."[35] (See Figure 4.1 on p. 82.)

Equal Protection Under the Law

[Fourteenth Amendment] No State shall make or enforce any law which shall abridge the privileges or immunities of citizens of the United States . . . nor deny to any person within its jurisdiction the equal protection of the laws.

The most frequently noted constitutional protection is the **equal protection** provision of the Fourteenth Amendment. Although the wording of the equal protection clause would appear to be straightforward, the interpretation of this legal doctrine has led to significant controversy related to **equal employment opportunity (EEO)** laws and affirmative action (AA). Court rulings have not been entirely consistent when deciding cases dealing with these matters, but there do appear to be meaningful trends in evidence.

Equal protection under the law has been defined in several acts, specifically in the Civil Rights Act of 1964 (CRA) and later amendments. Title VII of this law prohibits discrimination or harassment in all personnel actions on the basis of

**Figure 4.1   Example of Procedural Due Process:
Steps Required to Fire a Poor Performer**

Agencies operating under Chapter 75 of the US Code (5 U.S.C. 7512 and 5 C.F.R. 752.404, must give the employee:

Step One
Notice in writing, 30 days in advance, of the specific reasons removal
is being proposed.

Step Two
A chance to review the supporting material relied on by the agency.

Step Three
A reasonable amount of official time to review that material and prepare an answer,
including time to obtain affidavits to attach to the answer.

Step Four
An opportunity (at least 7 days after the notice) for the employee to respond both
orally and in writing to the charges.

Step Five
The opportunity to be represented by an attorney or other representative.

Step Six
A written decision giving specific reasons for the decision.

Source: U.S. Merit Systems Protection Board, Office of Policy and Evaluation, *Removing Poor Performers in the Federal Service,* issue paper (September 1995), p. 13.

race, color, religion, sex, or national origin. Other laws protecting specific classes of individuals have followed the CRA and provide protection against discrimination for groups not included in the CRA. Persons over forty years of age are protected under the 1967 Age Discrimination in Employment Act (ADEA); any maximum age for protection under the act was removed in 1987. However, the Supreme Court ruled in 2000 that the ADEA's abrogation of state immunity under the Eleventh Amendment exceeded Congress's authority, adding that "age is not a suspect classification under the Equal Protection Clause."[36] From this it appears that age is not provided the same protection as other protected classes such as race, color, sex, and national origin, and that the indi-

vidual states may permit age-based classification if the age is rationally related to a legitimate state interest.[37] Those with disabilities are protected under the Rehabilitation Act (1973) and the Americans with Disabilities Act (ADA, 1990). All public employees are protected from employers' paying less than minimum wage, not adequately compensating for overtime, and requiring employees to work unreasonable hours by the Fair Labor Standards Act (1938), which has been judged to apply to state and local governments as well as for-profit and nonprofit employers.[38] Employees are also permitted to take up to twelve weeks of uncompensated leave without penalty to care for themselves or family members according to the Family and Medical Leave Act (1993).

EQUAL OPPORTUNITY, AFFIRMATIVE ACTION, AND DIVERSITY IN THE PUBLIC WORKPLACE

The term *discrimination* should not always carry the connotation of unfairness and injustice. In reality, it is a necessary part of managing any organization. Managers must discriminate among job applicants who are qualified and those who are not. Discrimination is required when someone is selected for promotion over other candidates. Every time a performance appraisal is done, the manager must discriminate regarding the quality of an employee's work performance. *Illegal* discrimination happens in the workplace when people discriminate against individuals in a *protected class* based on factors that are not related to the job. Civil rights laws have identified specific groups as protected classes based on a characteristic of that group, such as their age, race, color, religion, sex, national origin, disability, or veteran status.

The issue of equal rights and equal opportunity has been highly divisive. This issue has often focused on the workplace, where individuals from a wide variety of ethnic, religious, and racial groups have been discriminated against because of their ancestry or beliefs rather than being judged on the basis of their qualifications. From the beginning of American history, immigrants from all parts of the world have suffered the prejudice of the majority and have been denied the right to work and live on an equal basis with others in society. Religious groups have been persecuted, women have often not enjoyed equal status in the workplace, and racial minorities have been denied basic privileges guaranteed by the Constitution.

In response to these historical inequities, which played a major role in the causes and effects of the Civil War, the government acted to make gender, racial, and ethnic prejudice-based discrimination illegal. These amendments and civil rights statutes guaranteed to women and minorities fundamental rights as citizens. However, other overt forms of discrimination persisted throughout the country, such as the disparity between salaries paid to men and women for the same work and the deliberate discrimination against minorities and women in hiring, promotion, and pay. A second wave of civil rights activity gained momentum in the early 1960s, resulting in the passage of far reaching laws guaranteeing civil rights. Box 4.3 on page 84 lists chief provisions of the major civil rights enactments in the United States.

Equal Employment Opportunity

Civil Rights Act of 1964 **Title VII of the Civil Rights Act of 1964** deals specifically with employment discrimination. The law prohibits discrimination in the terms and conditions of employment (including recruitment, selection, promotion, training, pay, benefits, discipline, and termination), when it is based on race, color, religion, sex, or national origin. Title VII applies to virtually all nonprofit and for-profit (with fifteen or more employees) and public organizations including state and local governments (except elected officials and their staff), as of 1972. The law also includes the following stipulation:

> SEC. 703. (a) It shall be an unlawful employment practice for an employer—(1) to fail or refuse to hire or to discharge any individual, or otherwise to discriminate against any individual with respect to his compensation, terms, conditions, or privileges of employment, because of such individual's race, color, religion, sex, or national origin.

The Civil Rights Act of 1964 has been amended by the Equal Opportunity Employment Act of 1972, the Pregnancy Discrimination Act of 1978, and the Civil Rights Act of 1991 (discussed later in this chapter). The first statute established the Equal Employment Opportunity Commission (EEOC) to oversee compliance. Currently the EEOC administers Title VII of the Civil Rights Act, the Equal Pay Act of 1963, the Age Discrimination in Employment Act of 1967, the Rehabilitation Act of 1973, the Americans with Disabilities Act of 1990, and the Civil Rights Act of 1991.[39]

Box 4.3   Constitutional Amendments and Federal Laws Related to Employment

Thirteenth Amendment of 1865	Abolished slavery.
Fourteenth Amendment of 1868	Protects the rights of citizens from actions of the state and guarantees everyone equal protection of the laws.
Fifteenth Amendment of 1870	Gave all men the right to vote regardless of race, color, or previous condition of servitude.
Nineteenth Amendment of 1920	Gave women the right to vote.
Civil Rights Act of 1866	Affords all citizens the right to make contracts.
Civil Rights Act of 1871	Gave all citizens the right to sue if their constitutional rights are infringed.
Equal Pay Act of 1963	Prohibits discrimination in pay on the basis of sex for work of equal skill, effort, responsibility, and similar working conditions (not necessarily the same job).
Civil Rights Act of 1964	Prohibits discrimination on the basis of race, color, religion, sex, or national origin. This act is the fundamental law for civil rights legislation in the United States.
Age Discrimination in Employment Act of 1967	Establishes age as a protected class by prohibiting employment discrimination against applicants and employees who are forty years of age or over.
Older Workers Protection Act of 1990	Amended the Age Discrimination in Employment Act to include distinctions in employee benefits, when based on age, as prohibited age discrimination.
Vocational Rehabilitation Act of 1973	Requires employers with federal contracts to take affirmative action toward workers with disabilities by seeking out qualified applicants with disabilities and making reasonable accommodation to their needs in the workplace.
Pregnancy Discrimination Act of 1978	Amended the Civil Rights Act of 1964; requires that employers not discriminate in providing employee benefits by excluding pregnancy and childbirth in medical insurance and sick leave policies.
Immigration Reform and Control Act of 1986	Prohibits employers from knowingly hiring illegal aliens. Employers must determine the legal status of job applicants and complete the I-9 form required under this act.
Americans With Disabilities Act of 1990	Prohibits discrimination based on disabilities that substantially limit major life activities of qualified individuals.
Civil Rights Act of 1991	Prohibits discrimination on the basis of race, color, religion, sex, or national origin as even a contributing factor in employment actions; shifts the burden of proof to the employer in cases of "disparate impact" (statistical disparity in employment outcomes affecting protected classes) and allows for punitive damages when discrimination is intentional.
Family and Medical Leave Act of 1993	Permits employees to take up to twelve weeks of unpaid leave during any twelve-month period to tend to family needs.

Sexual harassment An important dimension of Title VII is the major issue of employment discrimination on the basis of sex and the related cases of **sexual harassment.** The courts have interpreted sexual harassment as illegal discrimination based on sex under Title VII of the Civil Rights Act of 1964.[40] Sexual harassment is defined as follows:

Unwelcome sexual advances, requests for sexual favors, and other verbal or physical conduct of a sexual nature constitutes sexual harassment when submission to or rejection of this conduct explicitly or implicitly affects an individual's employment, unreasonably interferes with an individual's work performance or creates an intimidating, hostile or offensive work environment.[41]

The Supreme Court has agreed with the EEOC in saying that sexual harassment is involved when sexual favors are required to receive employment or employment-related benefits, referred to as **quid pro quo sexual harassment.** The Court has also said that sexual harassment may occur when there is a **hostile or abusive work environment:**

> For sexual harassment to be actionable, it must be sufficiently severe or pervasive "to alter the conditions of [the victim's] employment and create an abusive working environment." Respondent's allegations in this case—which include not only pervasive harassment but also criminal conduct of the most serious nature—are plainly sufficient to state a claim for "hostile environment" sexual harassment.[42]

EEOC guidelines set out six criteria for determining whether a work environment is hostile:

1. Whether the conduct was verbal or physical, or both
2. How frequently it was repeated
3. Whether the conduct was hostile and patently offensive
4. Whether the alleged harasser was a co-worker or a supervisor
5. Whether others joined in perpetrating the harassment
6. Whether the harassment was directed at more than one individual

In determining whether unwelcome sexual conduct rises to the level of a "hostile environment" in violation of Title VII, the central inquiry is whether the conduct "unreasonably interfere[s] with an individual's work performance" or creates

"an intimidating, hostile, or offensive working environment."[43] Thus, sexual flirtation or innuendo, or even vulgar language that is trivial or merely annoying, would probably not be sufficient to establish a claim of suffering from a hostile environment.

In a series of recent decisions on sexual harassment, the Supreme Court has broadened the scope of who is protected from sexual harassment and defined when employers are liable for the discriminatory actions of their employees. In *Oncale v. Sundowner Offshore Services,*[44] the Court stated that acts of sexual discrimination between individuals of the same sex are illegal under Title VII. In two other cases, the Court described the liability of employers for sexual harassment on the job.

In *Burlington Industries, Inc. v. Ellerth*[45] and *Faragher v. City of Boca Raton,*[46] the Court found that the employer is liable for sexual harassment perpetrated by the organization's supervisors or managers. "An employer is subject to vicarious liability to a victimized employee for an actionable hostile environment created by a supervisor with immediate (or successively higher) authority over the employee."[47] Even if the victimized employee suffers no adverse, tangible consequence of the harassment, the employer is still liable unless he or she can produce an affirmative defense:

> When no tangible employment action is taken, a defending employer may raise an affirmative defense to liability or damages, subject to proof by a preponderance of the evidence. . . . The defense comprises two necessary elements:
> (a) that the employer exercised reasonable care to prevent and correct promptly any sexually harassing behavior, and
> (b) that the plaintiff employee unreasonably failed to take advantage of any preventive or corrective opportunities provided by the employer or to avoid harm otherwise.[48]

The employer is strictly liable if there is tangible harm to the victimized employee as a result of harassment by company (or agency) supervisors. "No affirmative defense is available, however, when the supervisor's harassment culminates in a tangible employment action, such as discharge, demotion, or undesirable reassignment."[49]

Americans with Disabilities Act of 1990 The **Americans with Disabilities Act (ADA),** which is administered by the EEOC, expands on the basic provisions of the Vocational Rehabilitation Act of 1973 by prohibiting discrimination based on an individual's disability for all firms and agencies employing fifteen or more personnel. The act covers disabilities that substantially limit major life activities of qualified individuals who can perform the essential functions of a job with or without reasonable accommodations. The general rule of the act is as follows:

> No covered entity shall discriminate against a qualified individual with a disability because of the disability of such individual in regard to job application procedures, the hiring, advancement, or discharge of employees, employee compensation, job training, and other terms, conditions, and privileges of employment.[50]

The terms ***disability,*** *qualified,* ***reasonable accommodation,*** and *undue hardship* are critical to complying with ADA and are defined in the act:

(2) **Disability.** The term "disability" means, with respect to an individual (A) a physical or mental impairment that substantially limits one or more of the major life activities of such individual; (B) a record of such an impairment; or (C) being regarded as having such an impairment [. . .]

(8) **Qualified individual with a disability.** The term "qualified individual with a disability" means an individual with a disability who, with or without reasonable accommodation, can perform the essential functions of the employment position that such individual holds or desires. For the purposes of this title, consideration shall be given to the employer's judgment as to what functions of a job are essential, and if an employer has prepared a written description before advertising or interviewing applicants for the job, this description shall be considered evidence of the essential functions of the job [. . .]

(9) **Reasonable accommodation.** The term "reasonable accommodation" may include (A) making existing facilities used by employees readily accessible to and usable by individuals with disabilities; and (B) job restructuring, part-time or modified work schedules, reassignment to a vacant position, acquisition or modification of equipment or devices, appropriate adjustment or modifications of examinations, training materials or policies, the provision of qualified readers or interpreters, and other similar accommodations for individuals with disabilities [. . .]

(10) **Undue hardship.** (A) In general, the term "undue hardship" means an action requiring significant difficulty or expense [. . .][51]

Civil Rights Act of 1991 In reaction to a series of Supreme Court decisions,[52] Congress passed the Civil Rights Act of 1991 to clarify a number of points:

- Employers have the burden of proving that a "disparate impact" was not due to illegal discrimination.
- Race norming, the practice of grouping test scores by race or otherwise adjusting scores to account for race or other factors, is illegal.
- It is unlawful for race, color, religion, sex, and national origin to be even one of several motivating factors in making employment decisions.
- Employee discharge cases were covered under civil rights legislation.
- In cases of intentional discrimination, the plaintiff may sue for compensatory and punitive damages.

- Civil rights laws apply to U.S. citizens working in foreign countries for American firms.

Family and Medical Leave Act of 1993 (FMLA)

This law permits employees to take up to twelve weeks of unpaid leave during any twelve-month period to tend to family needs. The employee is entitled to retain the position held before taking leave or be relocated to an equivalent position. Employees must give employers thirty days' notice whenever possible. Employees may take FMLA leave for any of the following purposes: the birth and care of a child, adoption or foster care placement of a child with the employee, caring for family members (spouse, child, or parents) with serious health problems, or taking care of the employee's own serious health problems.

Affirmative Action

Defining affirmative action President Kennedy issued Executive Order 10925 in 1961, just after taking office. This important document first used the term *affirmative action* in government. The order, directed toward employment in the federal government and its contractors, reads in part:

> The Contractor will not discriminate against any employee or applicant for employment because of race, creed, color, or national origin. The Contractor will take affirmative action to ensure that applicants are employed, and that employees are treated during employment, without regard to race, creed, color, or national origin.[53]

In 1965, Executive Order 11246, issued by President Lyndon Johnson, reinforced the use of the concept of affirmative action by reinforcing the requirement of the federal government's not contracting with any party (public or private) found to be discriminating on the basis of race, color, religion, or national origin in their personnel practices. Executive Order 11375, which President Johnson issued in 1967, added sex as a prohibited basis of discrimination. The amended version reads in part as follows:

> The contractor will not discriminate against any employee or applicant for employment because of race, color, religion, sex, or national origin. The contractor will take affirmative action to ensure that applicants are employed, and that employees are treated during employment, without regard to their race, color, religion, sex or national origin. Such action shall include, but not be limited to the following: employment, upgrading, demotion, or transfer; recruitment or recruitment advertising; layoff or termination; rates of pay or other forms of compensation; and selection for training, including apprenticeship. The contractor agrees to post in conspicuous places, available to employees and applicants for employment, notices to be provided by the contracting officer setting forth the provisions of this nondiscrimination clause.

President Johnson explained his ideas for affirmative action in his 1964 commencement speech at Howard University in the following terms:

> But freedom is not enough. You do not wipe away the scars of centuries by saying: Now you are free to go where you want, and do as you desire, and choose the leaders you please.
>
> You do not take a person who, for years, has been hobbled by chains and liberate him, bring him up to the starting line of a race and then say, "you are free to compete with all the others," and still justly believe that you have been completely fair.
>
> Thus it is not enough just to open the gates of opportunity. All our citizens must have the ability to walk through those gates.
>
> This is the next and the more profound stage of the battle for civil rights. We seek not just freedom but opportunity. We seek not just legal equity but human ability, not just equality as a right and a theory but equality as a fact and equality as a result.[54]

Affirmative action has been the subject of divisive debate in the United States, and in the process of public deliberation, its definition and purpose have become rather obscured. Affirmative action has come to mean what some groups want it to mean or fear it might mean. The Department of Labor describes what affirmative action is *not* and specifies what it is in the following words:

> Affirmative action is not preferential treatment. It does not mean that unqualified persons should be hired or promoted over other people. What affirmative action does mean is that positive steps must be taken to ensure equal employment opportunity for traditionally disadvantaged groups.[55]

Affirmative action means an organization can take positive steps to ensure that everyone, including members of disadvantaged groups, has the opportunity to apply, be interviewed, and be hired for public employment. Once hired, everyone has an equal opportunity to be considered for opportunities in the workplace, including promotions. Most of the debate concerning affirmative action occurs over what these positive steps should be. Most would agree that an organization could take steps that do not overly trammel the rights of those in nonprotected groups, such as those described in Box 4.4.

Affirmative action plans The courts have defined affirmative action through the cases they have heard and the decisions made in these cases. They have approved **affirmative action plans** that meet the standards of strict scrutiny:

1. The plan satisfies a compelling governmental interest, such as correcting the effects of past discrimination or a significant imbalance in specific job categories.
2. The plan is narrowly tailored to address the problem.

In some cases, these plans will call into question the tests and other employment practices used to make hiring, promotion, and other employment decisions. Affirmative action plans upset some traditional ways of conducting personnel actions. They can cause hiring authorities to think seriously about the opportunities given to qualified individuals in protected classes who may not have been given the same opportunities as others who have received jobs and promotions.

The U.S. Department of Labor requires that all organizations that have fifty or more employees or receive more than $50,000 in federal funds must have an affirmative action program (AAP).[56] The program must include four key elements:

- *Organizational commitment.* The AAP should include a description of organization policies, structure, and resources demonstrating the organization's commitment to equal employment opportunity and affirmative action. The program should identify who is responsible for the affirmative action program, any procedures used to guarantee equality, and the amount and type of resources that will be devoted to achieving equity in the workplace.
- *Self-evaluation.* The AAP should identify where the organization may be underutilizing women and minorities in its employment positions. It should identify any barriers or obstacles that act to prevent women and minorities from accessing employment at all levels of the organization. The organization should evaluate the positions held by minorities and women currently within the organization to determine if their skills and abilities are being fully used. The program should include a study of the number and percentage of females and minorities in every job classification compared to the number and percentage of qualified females and minorities in the appropriate job market.
- *Full utilization goals and timetables.* Using the information obtained in the self-study, the agency must establish realistic objectives to achieve full utilization of all human resources available to the organization. Ob-

---

Box 4.4   Some Common Affirmative Action Procedures

- Set employment targets based on proportion of qualified female or minority applicants.
- Change negative race and gender attitudes at all levels to create a more tolerant workplace.
- Staff positions responsible for promoting equal opportunity in the organization.
- Job recruitments must have clear job descriptions and specification of qualifications.
- Discontinue word-of-mouth recruiting.
- Undertake outreach efforts to encourage applications and to give advice on how to apply for a position.
- The recruitment process is monitored for fairness.
- Job advertisements are translated into other languages and placed in minority press outlets.
- Training in race, ethnicity and gender awareness for those involved in recruiting.
- Advertisements encourage applications from minorities, women and people with disabilities.
- All vacancies advertised externally as well as internally.
- "Race-proofing" application forms (requesting only job relevant information from job applicants).
- English as a second language training.
- The encouragement of minority support groups within the organization.
- Training and mentoring of female and ethnic staff by senior officers.
- Line and middle managers are trained in their equal employment opportunity responsibilities.
- Managers' performance appraisal includes items concerning their development and effort toward the achievement of equal opportunity goals.
- Pre-entry training courses for women and minorities.
- Promotion and pay are monitored for inequalities.
- Decisions to terminate minorities, women and persons with disabilities are given a second review by higher management.
- The organization develops a parental leave policy separate from the disability plan.

Source: Anthony R. Pratkanis and Marlene E. Turner, "The Proactive Removal of Discriminatory Barriers: Affirmative Action as Effective Help," *Journal of Social Issues* 52:4 (1996): 113.

---

jectives for the timely elimination of any barriers to women and minorities in the workplace should be identified. Goals and strategies (such as training programs) for the full utilization of current employees within the organization should be described. Goals, timetables, and strategies for the recruitment of women and minorities to achieve utilization comparable to the appropriate market should be identified.

- *Performance monitoring.* A plan should be included describing how the organization will track the progress made toward the achievement of AAP goals. The organization should determine how progress will be measured and what indicators will be used to determine whether the organization is successful in achieving its goals.

Judicial Interpretation

Although legislation and executive orders are important factors in defining affirmative action, probably the greatest influence on the meaning and impact of affirmative action has been that of the courts. Since 1971, the Supreme Court has made a number of decisions that have served to guide human resource professionals in the application of affirmative action steps taken in the workplace.

Griggs v. Duke Power Co. *Griggs* is an important case not only for its implications for equal opportunity and affirmative action, but also for its conclusions about employment testing.[57] The Supreme Court ruled that Title VII of the Civil Rights Act of 1964 requires "the removal of artificial, arbitrary, and unnecessary barriers to employment when the barriers operate invidiously to discriminate on the basis of racial or other impermissible classification."[58] The requirements of a high school diploma and passage of an intelligence test were not shown to have a "demonstrable relationship to successful performance," but instead acted as "built-in headwinds for minority groups and are unrelated to measuring job capability."[59]

In his decision in *Griggs,* Justice William Brennan emphasized that affirmative action does not mean that the less qualified should be hired over more qualified individuals of nonprotected groups. Rather, real qualifications should be the controlling factor. Race, sex, and other non-job-related characteristics should be "irrelevant" in employment decisions:

> Nothing in the Act [Civil Rights Act of 1964, Title VII] precludes the use of testing or measuring procedures; obviously they are useful. What Congress has forbidden is giving these devices and mechanisms controlling force unless they are demonstrably a reasonable measure of job performance. Congress has not commanded that the less qualified be preferred over the better qualified simply because of minority origins. Far from disparaging job qualifications as such, Congress has made such qualifications the controlling factor, so that race, religion, nationality, and sex become irrelevant. What Congress has commanded is that any tests used must measure the person for the job and not the person in the abstract.[60]

University of California Regents v. Bakke The Court held in *Bakke* that the University of California had established admission quotas and separate candidate pools for minority and nonminority candidates that served to exclude a white male applicant to the medical school at the University of California at Davis in favor of black and Mexican-American applicants who had lower grades and admission test scores.[61] This case established the concept of reverse discrimination as a consequence of adopted affirmative

action programs. The decision disallowed the use of separate candidate pools, but indicated that minority status could be taken into account in calculating admission scores if racial and ethnic diversity was believed to promote educational purposes.

Steelworkers v. Weber In *Steelworkers,* the Court upheld a voluntary affirmative action plan on the grounds that it was consistent with the intent of Title VII, to eliminate discrimination in employment based on race, color, religion, or national origin.[62] Kaiser Aluminum and Chemical Corp. had instituted an affirmative action plan that included reserving 50 percent of its craft training openings for black employees because its craftwork forces were almost exclusively white. The decision's rationale was that although the act provides that nothing contained in Title VII shall be interpreted to require any employer to grant preferential treatment, *it does not prohibit voluntary race-conscious affirmative action.* The affirmative action program in question was found to be acceptable because it was:

> structured to open employment opportunities for Negroes in occupations which have been traditionally closed to them. At the same time, the plan does not unnecessarily trammel the interests of white employees, neither requiring the discharge of white workers and their replacement with new black hires, nor creating an absolute bar to the advancement of white employees since half of those trained in the program will be white. Moreover, the plan is a temporary measure, not intended to maintain racial balance, but simply to eliminate a manifest racial imbalance.[63]

Firefighters Local Union 1784 v. Stotts The Supreme Court decided that a seniority-based layoff system (last hired, first fired) could take precedence over a voluntary affirmative action plan even though it had an adverse effect on recently hired black firefighters.[64] The priority assigned to bona fide employee benefit and collective bargaining-generated practices derives from the specific language of the Civil Rights Act of 1964.

Wygant v. Jackson Board of Education In *Wygant,* the Court established the principle that "strict scrutiny" should be applied to preferential consideration of minorities and women.[65] It cited an earlier case: "Any preference based on racial or ethnic criteria must necessarily receive a most searching examination to make sure that it does not conflict with constitutional guarantees."[66] Examination under the principle of strict scrutiny would include two focuses. First, any racial classification must be justified by a compelling governmental interest. Second, the means chosen by the state to effectuate its purpose must be narrowly tailored to the achievement of that goal.[67] The Court ruled that the affirmative action plan to retain minorities at the current percentage during a layoff did not meet either of the two criteria of a strict scrutiny test.

United States v. Paradise After finding that the Alabama Department of Public Safety had discriminated for forty years against hiring blacks as state troopers, the U.S. Federal District Court imposed hiring quotas on the department.[68] The court again stepped in when it was found that no blacks had been promoted to the upper ranks of the department in nine years. It then ordered that 50 percent of promotions be qualified black candidates, if available. The Supreme Court approved of this lower court order, noting there was a compelling governmental interest in eliminating persistent discrimination and that the remedy developed was narrowly tailored to address the deficiency in the upper ranks. Furthermore, the plan did not trammel the rights of white candidates since it was temporary, only postponing advancement of qualified white candidates.

Johnson v. Transportation Agency The Santa Clara County Transportation Agency established a voluntary affirmative action plan for hiring minorities and women that allowed for the consideration of race and sex as one factor in the qualification of applicants.[69] The plan was intended to improve the percentage of minorities and women working in the Transportation Agency in line with the percentage of these groups in the workforce. Of seven qualified candidates, the agency selected a woman for a position as a skilled craft worker (there were no women in the 238 positions falling within this classification), whereupon a male candidate filed suit saying sex was the determining factor in the decision. The Court upheld the hiring because the agency's plan reflected a moderate, flexible, case-by-case approach toward gradual improvement in a conspicuous imbalance in identified job categories and did not trammel the rights of male employees. There were no set-aside positions or quotas. The male had no claim on the job opening, and the plan was temporary in its application.

Richmond v. J. A. Croson Co. In the *Croson* case, Richmond, Virginia, required contractors to set aside at least 30 percent of their subcontract dollars for minority businesses.[70] The Court found that there was no compelling governmental interest justifying the set-aside plan since no past discrimination in the industry was found to exist for minorities affected by the plan. The plan was not narrowly tailored since any minority business from anywhere in the country could benefit from the plan, and there was no clear rationale for setting a quota at 30 percent.

Wards Cove Packing Co. v. Atonio The Supreme Court held that in order to show a *prima facie* case of disparate impact, the appropriate comparison between at-issue jobs and the qualified labor force population must be conducted.[71] Simple comparisons to the general population will not suffice. The Court also established that those who claim discrimination must not only show a disparate impact in hiring outcomes, but must also identify specific employment practices that have caused the disparate impact.

Adarand Constructors Inc. v. Pena   The Court established in *Adarand* that the Fifth and Fourteenth Amendments protect persons, not groups.[72] Any governmental action based on race should apply strict scrutiny to ensure the protection of individual rights. It reaffirms that affirmative action plans are constitutional: "When race-based action is necessary to further a compelling interest, such action is within constitutional constraints if it satisfies the 'narrow tailoring' test set out in this Court's previous cases."[73] *Adarand* placed the burden of proof on the government to show that the AAP in question serves a compelling government interest and is narrowly tailored to address identified problems of past discrimination.

Trends in Affirmative Action

New cases will continue to shed light on the view of the Supreme Court toward affirmative action plans. A 1996 case heard at the U.S. Court of Appeals for the Fifth Circuit resulted in a ruling that race could not be used as a factor in granting admissions or scholarships at state institutions of higher education in Texas.[74] The Supreme Court allowed this ruling to stand by deciding not to hear the case.

In 1998, the Supreme Court agreed to hear a case regarding the layoff of a white schoolteacher when a black schoolteacher, who was originally hired on the same day, was not laid off. The parties agreed to settle the issue before it reached the Court because of the concern that the Court would issue a decision harmful to affirmative action. A case in the U.S. Court of Appeals for the Third Circuit was decided against the Township of Piscataway, New Jersey, that had an affirmative action plan that was implemented to achieve the objective of "diversity" rather than serve as a means to rectify past discrimination.[75]

A possible new trend that may be beginning is the use of the citizen initiative to make laws relating to affirmative action. Reminiscent of the tax limitation initiatives that began in California in 1978, California passed a citizen initiative in 1996 known as Proposition 209 that effectively prohib-

ited affirmative action in state and local government. The substantive part of the initiative reads as follows:

(a) The state shall not discriminate against, or grant preferential treatment to, any individual or group on the basis of race, sex, color, ethnicity, or national origin in the operation of public employment, public education, or public contracting.[76]

The initiative passed with 54 percent voting in favor. The Supreme Court decided not to hear arguments challenging the California law and therefore allowed the law to stand. Despite passage of Proposition 209, affirmative action has not disappeared in California. The initiative specifically exempted any affirmative action required by federal law. A law very similar to that passed in California was also established by initiative in Washington in 1998 (I-200); the Washington statute has had comparable effects to the California law whereby federally required affirmative action programs persist, but state and local government-initiated efforts are no longer permitted.

The direction of the courts has unquestionably changed over the years as the effects of Reagan and Bush judicial appointments on the federal bench have come into play. It is difficult to determine how future courts, and citizen initiatives, will decide on affirmative action laws. However, certain principles have been established over the lifetime of affirmative action:

- Affirmative action plans should be designed to address a "compelling governmental interest," such as to eliminate past unlawful discrimination in the workplace or address a "manifest imbalance" between the number of women and minorities in a job classification and the number of qualified women and minorities in the appropriate job market.
- AAPs should be narrowly tailored to address the problem identified, and if race based, they should be the only way to address the problem after all other remedies have been considered. The remedy should not unnec-

essarily trammel the rights of unprotected individuals by preventing their hiring or advancement.

- The plan should be temporary, existing only until the time that the problem has been corrected.
- Quotas are not acceptable, but goals are allowed. Quotas are considered specific numbers that are inflexible requirements that an organization must meet. Goals are targets that the organization should work toward in a good-faith effort.
- The courts favor voluntary, flexible plans that do not establish strict guidelines but instead consider situations on a case-by-case basis.
- Employment decisions made solely on the basis of sex or race alone are not acceptable; individuals should be qualified for the positions they are hired or promoted to perform.

The criticism and defense of affirmative action depend on the values held by those taking a position. The side against affirmative action typically emphasizes individual liberty in their comments, believing that the rights guaranteed in the Constitution are individual rights, while affirmative action addresses group rights. Although there is precedent for protecting group rights (the Fourteenth Amendment), most of the liberties and rights we enjoy are individual protections. Those against affirmative action do not believe that discrimination can be justified as a remedy for past discrimination. One student referred to this kind of action as being similar to a "make-up call" in a sporting event. If the first decision was in error, deliberately making a second wrong decision to make up for the first call does not make things equal. Those defending affirmative action emphasize equality, arguing that discrimination has been based on group characteristics, not individual abilities; therefore, the remedy has to be directed toward the affected group. There may be a need to take positive steps to ensure that all individuals have an equal opportunity to compete for jobs or promotions. One

author has listed several of the arguments used to criticize affirmative action and proposes his own arguments to counter these (see Box 4.5 on the following page).

Full-Spectrum Diversity

There is a growing argument that the affirmative action approach has focused too narrowly on just a few groups that have never been fully accepted due to tradition, prejudice, and ignorance. It is not common to see an affirmative action plan addressing a "manifest imbalance" in the number of Muslims employed in an organization compared to the number of qualified Muslims in the local workforce. Similarly, AAPs do not single out individuals whose national origin might be Sweden or those who are over age forty. The argument for a more diverse workplace calls for having the workforce "reflect proactively the gender, cultural and ethnic complexity of each local community as well as the American society."[77]

Where affirmative action was mainly motivated by laws to promote equality in the workplace, diversity can be motivated by economics. A more diverse workforce can revitalize the organization by providing it with resources capable of enhanced creativity and improved problem solving.[78] The benefit of **full-spectrum diversity** is that employees from a broad range of backgrounds, ancestry, genetic heritage, and beliefs can contribute to a fuller dialogue on how an agency can better satisfy the needs of clients or customers. To achieve full-spectrum diversity, managers must consider what is best for their organizations in the modern workplace. In a diverse society, it is a distinct advantage to bring qualified professionals into an organization hailing from a variety of backgrounds; they can collectively bring a wider range of experiences and insights to bear on issues arising in response to citizen needs than any single, homogeneous group of professionals could muster. Full-spectrum diversity is different from, but not at odds with, traditional affirmative

Box 4.5   Ten Myths About Affirmative Action

Myths Against Affirmative Action	Responses in Favor of Affirmative Action
The only way to create a color-blind society is to adopt color-blind policies.	Color-blind policies reinforce existing advantages. Preexisting inequities have to be corrected first.
Affirmative action has not succeeded in increasing female and minority representation.	Several studies have concluded that affirmative action has been successful in achieving improvements in racial and gender equity.
Affirmative action may have been necessary 30 years ago, but the playing field is fairly level today.	Women continue to earn 72 percent of male wages, Blacks have twice the unemployment rate of Whites, minorities and women hold fewer upper management jobs than white males in most organizations.
The public doesn't support affirmative action anymore.	Polls show that most people want to continue affirmative action programs at some level. The public opposes quotas, set-asides, and "reverse discrimination."
A large percentage of White workers will lose out if affirmative action is continued.	Affirmative action applies only to qualified candidates—the actual percentage of affected Whites would be less than 1 percent.
If Jewish people and Asian Americans can rapidly advance economically, African Americans should be able to do the same.	Historical and social reality has been very different for each of these groups, allowing for integration into the White majority by some and not by other racial and ethnic groups.
You can't cure discrimination with discrimination.	Prejudice and exclusion is not the same as making special efforts at inclusion.
Affirmative action tends to undermine the self-esteem of women and racial minorities.	Research shows this to be a problem in some cases, but they are rather rare. Recent polls suggest 90 percent of employed Blacks and employed women do not feel affirmative action affected their self-esteem.
Affirmative action is nothing more than an attempt at social engineering by liberal Democrats.	Various forms of affirmative action have been supported by Republican as well as Democrat administrations.
Support for affirmative action means support for preferential selection procedures that favor unqualified candidates over qualified candidates.	Selection of unqualified candidates over qualified candidates is not legal affirmative action. Most people support the selection of a female or minority candidate when the choices are from equally or comparably qualified candidates.

Source: Scott Plous, "Ten Myths About Affirmative Action," *Journal of Social Issues* 52:4 (1996): 25–31.

action programs. Some of these differences are illustrated in Box 4.6.

ETHICAL CONSIDERATIONS AND GAY RIGHTS

The principle of equal rights for homosexuals has been hotly debated because gays do not fall within any of the protected classes addressed hitherto. Some have argued that adding homosexuals to the list of protected classes adds to the burden of hiring authorities by proliferating the list of those who can file suit against employers for illegal discrimination. This brings into question whether it was wise to begin a list of those who could not be discriminated against in areas such as employment, school admission, or housing. It may have been better to make a categorical statement that no one could be discriminated against in the work environment for reasons other than those related to performance on the job or legitimate business or government purpose. The courts have ruled on government employers' taking adverse actions against homosexuals. In one case, the Supreme Court ruled that the FBI could fire an employee who announced her homosexuality.

The Court used the following reasoning:

> The FBI, as the Bureau points out, is a national law enforcement agency whose agents must be able to work in all the states of the nation. To have agents who engage in conduct criminalized in roughly one-half of the states would undermine the law enforcement credibility of the Bureau. Perhaps more important . . . criminalization of homosexual conduct coupled with the general public opprobrium toward homosexuality exposes many homosexuals, even "open" homosexuals, to the risk of possible blackmail to protect their partners, if not themselves.[79]

The Court cautioned that any discrimination against homosexuals would not necessarily be acceptable to the Court. In the *Padula* dicta, they warn,

> That does not mean, however, that any kind of negative state action against homosexuals would be constitutionally authorized. Laws or government practices must still, if challenged, pass the rational basis test of the equal protection clause. A governmental agency

---

Box 4.6   Differences Between Full-Spectrum Diversity and Affirmative Action

Full-Spectrum Diversity Proactive	Affirmative Action Reactive
• Concern about all groups in the community, including members of underutilized groups	• Concern for members of underutilized groups
• Recognition of diversity within the individual	• Simplification and stereotyping
• Value of merit and the value of diversity: competitive	• Value of merit and the value of diversity: noncompetitive
• Internally driven factors	• Externally driven factors

Source: James D. Slack, "From Affirmative Action to Full Spectrum Diversity in the American Workplace," *Review of Public Personnel Administration* 17:4 (1997): 82. Reprinted by permission of the publisher, Institute of Public Affairs, University of South Carolina.

that discriminates against homosexuals must justify that discrimination in terms of some government purpose.

In an earlier case the Court ruled that NASA had acted illegally when it terminated a budget analyst for making a homosexual advance to another employee. The Court ruled there had been no connection made between the conduct and the efficiency of the government service.[80] Although there are no federal statutes specifically protecting homosexuals in the workplace, the Constitution does give homosexuals, like everyone else, equal protection of the laws, and any attempt to discriminate against individuals within this group in public employment must be justified by a prevailing government purpose.

■ CONCLUSION

Times have changed dramatically when considering the rights and restrictions of public employees. No longer are public employees considered privileged to be fortunate enough to work for government and therefore work at the will and whim of elected officials. Today public employees receive unique protections due to their being employees of the government, and they have a right to protections from government (state) action against citizens found in the Constitution. Although much of the employment law detailed in this chapter applies to private and nonprofit sector employees, public sector employees enjoy some unique protections. Personnel managers must keep pace with new laws that are being passed regularly, giving special rights to additional groups or new benefits to employees. They must be aware of the meaning of court decisions on employment law as it applies to the employees under their jurisdictions. This may be an onerous task without sound legal advice. Lawyers who specialize in employment law make their living keeping up with changes in the law, administrative regulations, and court decisions. Unfortunately, the complexity of employment law and the rapidity with which it can change

make personnel practice particularly challenging for small nonprofit organizations and public jurisdictions without ready access to specialists. Federal offices, such as the Office of Special Counsel, Equal Employment Opportunity Commission, and the Wage and Hour Division of the Department of Labor have responsibility to enforce some of these laws and assist public organizations in complying with the requirements of the law. State and local governments also have specialists (such as attorney general offices, city attorneys, state departments of labor, or personnel offices) assigned to enforce and advise public agencies as to their responsibilities under these laws. Their services may be able to keep public organizations from experiencing contentious and costly lawsuits by helping HRM specialists and their managers keep policies and practices up to date when it comes to employee rights and limitations.

■ MANAGER'S VOCABULARY

doctrine of privilege
doctrine of sovereignty
Hatch Act
political patronage
Rutan v. Republican Party of Illinois
due process of law
equal protection
equal employment opportunity
Title VII of the Civil Rights Act of 1964
sexual harassment
quid pro quo sexual harassment
hostile or abusive work environment
Americans with Disabilities Act of 1990
disability
reasonable accommodation
affirmative action
affirmative action plan
full-spectrum diversity

■ STUDY QUESTIONS

1. How are public employees viewed as different from private employees under the Constitution? Is the gap between the perceived rights of public and employees in the nonprofit and for-profit sectors widening or narrowing?

2. Do you think there is sufficient justification to support the idea that public employees should be limited in their right to participate in political activity?

3. Should modern public personnel systems allow some degree of patronage? What are the advantages and the disadvantages of patronage?

4. Why do public managers need to be particularly careful about employee rights when they are contemplating a drug testing program? What principles should they follow in developing a drug testing program?

5. What is the responsibility of the public manager to ensure that the workplace is free of sexual harassment?

6. What would be reasonable accommodation for an employee who admits to being an alcoholic?

7. What do you think should be done when it is determined that a manifest imbalance in the number of minorities exists between workers employed in your agency and those available in the appropriate market?

■ EXPERIENTIAL EXERCISES

1. *You Rule! McMillan v. Northern Minnesota State University*

Bill McMillan was excited about starting his career in the Department of Political Science at Northern Minnesota State University and quickly accepted a one-year appointment as a non–tenure track lecturer. The semester was not easy. In addition to having to prepare and teach three classes, he was negotiating with publishers to get his dissertation published. He made some comments to his friends in the department that he thought the administration could do a better job at allocating teaching loads and that faculty salaries were really not on par with the other public universities in the state. Bill thought things were going well until he received official word on January 23 that his contract would not be renewed for the next academic year. No explanation was given. Disappointed and angry (and having just taught a course on the Constitution and Bill of Rights), Bill sued the university saying the administration had infringed on his First Amendment right to free speech and his Fourteenth Amendment rights to due process because the university failed to give him any reason for not renewing his contract and had not provided an opportunity for a hearing.

a. If you were the judge hearing this case, how would you rule?

b. What rights does an untenured professor have to employment with the state?

c. Is there any reason to believe that the university violated Bill's right to free speech?

d. Is the university obligated to provide procedural due process to Bill?

(This case was based on *Board of Regents v. Roth,* 408 U.S. 564, 92 S. Ct. 2701, 33 L. Ed. 2d 548 [1972].)

2. *You Rule! U.S. Customs Service v. Mary Whanah*

After careful study of the validity and reliability of drug testing techniques, the commissioner of the U.S. Customs Service announced a new drug testing program using urine sampling. Any applicant for or incumbent of specific positions that meet one or more of the following criteria would be tested: (1) the position involves drug interdiction or enforcement; (2) the employee is required to carry a firearm; or (3) the employee handles classified material. Customs employees who test positive for drugs and can make no satisfactory explanation are subject to dismissal. The union agrees that there is a legitimate government interest in a drug-free workplace, but argues that this drug testing program was overly intrusive and violated the employees' right to privacy, and it lacked any stipulation of probable cause or reasonable suspicion.

   a. Does requiring a urine sample constitute a search?

   b. Are such searches warranted in the case of U.S. Customs agents?

   c. Should each of the employees in all three categories listed be subject to the drug testing program?

(This case was based on *National Treasury Employees Union v. von Raab,* 489 U.S. 656, 109 S. Ct. 1384, 103 L. Ed. 2d 685 [1989].)

3. *Prepare an Affirmative Action Plan*

As the assistant city manager over human resources, you have been asked by the city manager to prepare an affirmative action program for police officers that the city council will review. You work in Equitable, Wisconsin, a small city outside Milwaukee, and complaints have been made that the police force does not adequately reflect the African American or female composition of the community. You have collected the following statistics for use in your report:

Current Utilization	Number	Percent
Police officers in Equitable	**36**	**100%**
Male	28	77.8
Female	8	22.2
White	25	69.4
White male	22	88.0
White female	3	12.0
Black	6	16.7
Black male	2	33.3
Black female	4	66.7
Hispanic	2	5.6
Hispanic male	2	100.0
Hispanic female	0	0

Asian	0	0
Asian male	0	0
Asian female	0	0
American Indian	3	8.3
American Indian male	2	66.7
American Indian female	1	33.3
Population in Equitable	**908,000**	
White	610,000	67.2
Black	218,000	24.0
Hispanic	54,000	5.9
Asian	19,000	2.1
American Indian	7,000	0.7
Total qualified individuals in recruiting area	**90,908**	
Male	63,635	70.0
Female	27,273	30.0
White male	42,806	47.0
White female	18,346	20.2
Black male	15,288	16.8
Black female	6,552	7.2
Hispanic male	3,758	4.1
Hispanic female	1,611	1.8
Asian male	1,337	1.5
Asian female	573	0.6
American Indian male	446	0.5
American Indian female	191	0.02

a. Write a statement that you would recommend to be used as a policy statement regarding equal employment opportunity and affirmative action for the Equitable Police Department (EPD). Also describe who should be responsible for coordinating EEO/AA programs and what you would recommend they do in this responsibility.

b. Consider the number of women and minorities serving as police officers, and determine if there is full utilization of these groups in the EPD. Identify barriers that the department might look for that may be interfering with full utilization.

c. Recommend goals and timetables for full utilization.

d. Describe what measures you would recommend for the EPD to monitor the achievement of these goals.

■ CASES APPLICABLE TO THIS CHAPTER

"Governor Pat Ronage's Hiring Freeze"

■ NOTES

[1] *McAuliffe v. Mayor of New Bedford,* 155 Mass. 216, 220, 29 N.E. 517 (1892).

[2] *Connick v. Myers,* 461 U.S. 138 (1983).

[3] *Pickering v. Board of Education,* 391 U.S. 563, 568 (1968).

[4] Thomas Jefferson to James Madison, December 20, 1787, reprinted in Richard B. Bernstein and Jerome Agel, *Amending America* (New York: Times Books, 1993), p. 36.

[5] *Rankin v. McPherson,* 483 U.S. 378, 107 S. Ct. 2891, 97 L. Ed. 2d 315 (1987).

[6] Heidi Koenig, "Free Speech: Government Employees and Government Contractors," *Public Administration Review* 57:1 (1997): 1–3.

[7] *Board of County Commissioners, Wabaunsee County, Kansas v. Umbehr,* 116 S. Ct. 2342 (1996).

[8] *O'Hare Truck Service, Inc. v. City of Northlake,* 116 S. Ct. 2353 (1996).

[9] *United Public Workers of America v. Michell,* 330 U.S. 75, 67 S. Ct. 556, 91 L. Ed. 754 (1947).

[10] *United States Civil Service Commission v. National Association of Letter Carriers,* 413 U.S. 548, 93 S. Ct. 2889, 37 L. Ed. 2d 796 (1973).

[11] "The Week in Congress," *Congressional Index,* March 5, 1993.

[12] 26 U.S.C. sec. 501c, as qualified by subsec. h.

[13] *Elrod v. Burns,* 427 U.S. 347 (1976).

[14] *Branti v. Finkel,* 445 U.S. 507 (1980).

[15] *Rutan v. Republican Party of Illinois,* 497 U.S. 62 (1990).

[16] *Shelton v. Tucker,* 364 U.S. 62 (1960).

[17] *Curle v. Ward,* 46 N.Y.2d 1049, 389 N.E.2d 1070 (1979).

[18] *Atkins v. City of Charlotte,* 296 F. Supp. 1068 (W.D.N.C. 1969).

[19] *NAACP v. Alabama ex rel. Patterson,* 357 U.S. 449, 460–461 (1958).

[20] *National Treasury Employees Union v. von Raab,* 489 U.S. 656, 109 S. Ct. 1384, 103 L. Ed. 2d 685 (1989).

[21] Ibid., p. 1384.

[22] *Copeland v. Philadelphia Police Department,* 840 F.2d 1139 (3d Cir. 1988).

[23] *Seelig v. Koehler,* 76 N.Y.2d 87, 556 N.E.2d 125 (1990).

[24] *McDonell v. Hunter,* 809 F.2d 1302 (8th Cir. 1987).

[25] *AFGE v. Skinner,* 885 F.2d 884 (D.C. Cir. 1989).

[26] *NTEU v. Yeutter,* 918 F.2d 968 (D.C. Cir. 1990).

[27] *O'Connor v. Ortega,* 480 U.S. 709 (1987).

[28] Mark S. Dichter and Michael S. Burkhardt, "Electronic Interaction in the Workplace: Monitoring, Retrieving and Storing Employee Communications in the Internet Age" (paper presented at the American Employment Law Council, Fourth Annual Conference, October 1996). Available at: **http://www.mlb.com/speech1.htm.**

[29] Ibid., p. 3.

[30] *Smyth v. The Pillsbury Co.,* 914 F. Supp. 97 (1996); *Bourke v. Nissan Motor Corp.,* No. BO68705 (Cal. Ct. App. 1993).

[31] *O'Conner v. Ortega,* 480 U.S. 709 (1987).

[32] Data Research, *United States Supreme Court Employment Cases,* 4th ed. (Rosemount, MN: Data Research, 1998), pp. 319–320.

[33] *Mullane v. Central Hanover Bank & Trust Co.,* 339 U.S. 306, 313 (1950); *Boddie v. Connecticut,* 401 U.S. 371, 379 (1971); *Board of Regents v. Roth,* 408 U.S. 564 (1972).

[34] *Cleveland Board of Education v. Loudermill,* 470 U.S. 532, 105 S. Ct. 1487, 84 L. Ed. 2d 494 (1985).

[35] *Mathews v. Eldridge,* 424 U.S. 319 (1976).

[36] *Kimel et al. v. Florida Board of Regents et al.,* No. 98–791, sec. IV.C.1 January 11, 2000.

[37] Ibid., sec. IV.C.2

[38] *Christensen et al. v. Harris County et al.,* no. 98–1167, decided May 1, 2000, that allows public employers to require the use of compensatory time.

[39] Laws Enforced by the EEOC, available at: **http://www. eeoc.gov/laws.html.**

[40] *Barnes v. Costle* 561 F.2d (1977); *Meritor Savings Bank v. Vinson* 477 U.S. 57 (1986); *Harris v. Forklift Systems* No. 92–1168, November 9, 1993.

[41] EEOC Facts About Sexual Harassment, available at: **http://www.eeoc.gov/facts/fs-sex.html,** January 15, 1997.

[42] *Meritor Savings Bank v. Vinson,* 477 U.S. 57 (1986).

[43] 29 C.F.R. sec. 1604.11(a)(3), July 1, 2000.

[44] *Joseph Oncale v. Sundowner Offshore Services, Incorporated,* U.S. S. CT. No. 96–568, March 4, 1998.

[45] *Burlington Industries, Inc. v. Kimberly B. Ellerth,* U.S. S. CT. No. 97–569, June 26, 1998.

[46] *Beth Ann Faragher v. City of Boca Raton,* U.S. S. CT. No. 97–282, June 26, 1998.

[47] *Burlington Industries, Inc. v. Kimberly B. Ellerth,* pp. 20–21.

[48] Ibid.

[49] Ibid.

[50] Americans with Disabilities Act, U.S. Code Title 42, Chapter 126, Sec. 12102 Definitions (1990).

[51] Ibid.

[52] See the following cases: *Wards Cove Packing Co. v. Atonio,* 490 U.S. 642 (1989); *Richmond v. J. A. Croson Co.,* 488 U.S. 469 (1988); *Price Waterhouse v. Hopkins,* 490 U.S. 288 (1989); *Martin v. Wilkes,* 490 U.S. 755 (1989); *Patterson v. McLean Credit Union,* 485 U.S. 617 (1988).

[53] John F. Kennedy Executive Order 10925 (1961).

[54] Lyndon B. Johnson, Howard University commencement speech, 1964.

[55] Employment Standards Administration, Office of Federal Contract Compliance Programs Fact Sheet E.O. 11246, available at: **http://ww.dol.gov/dol/esa/public/regs/compliance/ofccp/fs1,** July 13, 2000.

56 Ibid.

57 *Griggs v. Duke Power Co.,* 401 U.S. 424 (1971).

58 Ibid., pp. 429–433.

59 Ibid., p. 429.

60 Justice Brennan in ibid.

61 *University of California Regents v. Bakke,* 438 U.S. 265 (1978).

62 *Steelworkers v. Weber,* 443 U.S. 193 (1979).

63 Ibid., pp. 208–209.

64 *Firefighters Local Union 1784 v. Stotts,* 467 U.S. 561 (1984).

65 *Wygant v. Jackson Board of Education,* 476 U.S. 267 (1986).

66 *Fullilove v. Klutznick,* 448 U.S. 448 (1980).

67 *Wygant v. Jackson Board of Education,* p. 273.

68 *United States v. Paradise,* 480 U.S. 149 (1987).

69 *Johnson v. Transportation Agency,* 480 U.S. 616 (1987).

70 *Richmond v. J. A. Croson Co.,* p. 469.

71 *Wards Cove Packing Co. v. Atonio,* 490 U.S. 642 (1989).

72 *Adarand Constructors, Inc. v. Pena* (1995).

73 Ibid., p. 36.

74 *Hopwood v. State of Texas,* 78 F.3d 932 (5th Cir., 1996).

75 *Sharon Taxman v. Board of Education of the Township of Piscataway,* U.S. Court of Appeals for the Third Circuit No. 94–5090 August 8, 1996.

76 California state Proposition 209, "Prohibition Against Discrimination or Preferential Treatment by State and Other Public Entities. Initiative Constitutional Amendment," available at: **http://vote96.ss.ca.gov/Vote96/html/BP/209.htm.**

77 James D. Slack, "From Affirmative Action to Full Spectrum Diversity in the American Workplace," *Review of Public Personnel Administration* 17:4 (1997): 76.

78 Taylor H. Cox and Stacy Blake, "Managing Cultural Diversity: Implications for Organizational Competitiveness," *Academy of Management Executive* 5:3 (1991): 45–56.

79 *Padula v. Webster,* 822 F.2d 97 (D.C. Cir. 1987).

80 *Norton v. Macy,* 417 F.2d 1161 (D.C. Cir. 1969).

CHAPTER 5

Labor-Management Relations in the Public Sector

Most people would describe labor relations as confrontational, adversarial, and basically unpleasant. We can conjure up visions of smoke-filled rooms where angry people are seated across a table taking unreasonable positions or saying some very disagreeable things about the other's parentage. Unions have been successful in developing the image that they are difficult to work with and that they make taking any kind of managerial action to discipline employees or to attempt to improve productivity almost impossible. Managers on too many occasions have also proven to be everything the unions want to fight, for example, by taking unilateral actions, showing favoritism, and otherwise being arbitrary or unfair in their treatment of employees. The result of these circumstances is that labor and management too often take on the roles of bitter enemies battling for control of employees and influence over the work of the organization. As most of us believe, warfare is usually unproductive, destructive, and certainly inefficient (at least in the short term). To improve matters, there has been a broad call across the country to improve labor-management relations through cooperation instead of conflict.

report of my death was an exaggeration."[1] For the past several years membership in labor unions has declined considerably, and some commentators have predicted the virtual end of organized labor.[2] The reality is that a multitude of employee groups continue to organize and seek representation in their dealings with employers. The traditional reasons of improving salaries and working conditions remain a major impetus for employees to organize into unions. In this era of reinventing government and organizational downsizing, employees are looking for a voice in the changes happening in their jobs and for job security in a rapidly changing workplace. Public employees feel the need to add their voice to the many competing interests that are lobbying state legislatures and local government officials for public funding. Still, one of the most basic reasons for employees to organize is protection from unjust or malicious decisions by management. As much as we would like to believe that all managers are well trained and competent, too many managers continue to operate outside the rules or with poor judgment. As long as there are conflicting interests between workers and management, unions will continue to exist.

IS THERE STILL A NEED FOR LABOR UNIONS?

Discussions about the need for labor unions remind us of the words of Mark Twain when he said, "The

THE RISE AND FALL OF UNION MEMBERSHIP

Probably the most significant contribution to the decline in union membership has been the change in the structure of the U.S. economy.[3] When large manufacturing plants dominated the economies of large cities, organizing large groups of employees in one location was relatively easy. Factories were dangerous, inhospitable places, and labor was simply viewed as a cost of production. These employees commonly felt a need for someone to represent them to their employers, who often appeared arbitrary and uncaring about employee problems. More often than not, the employees were poorly educated and unskilled, and they lacked the mobility to find other work. Today, many of these conditions have changed as the result of previous union activity, as well as a consequence of government regulation of the workplace.[4]

Demands for better wages and working conditions were once the battle cry of the union movement. Today many of these demands have been met and are guaranteed by the government. In many ways, the government, through labor laws and employer regulations, has become a substitute for unions. Wages and hours have improved and become standardized through federal law such as the Fair Labor Standards Act. Safety and health concerns have been significantly reduced through improvements in the workplace and enforcement by federal, state, and local government regulators. The economy has shifted in the direction of the growth of service-oriented and information-intensive jobs. Workers tend to be more dispersed

and difficult to organize. A feeling of union solidarity, or a common belief in a union cause, is almost nonexistent in the contemporary setting. Jobs paying wages sufficient to maintain a middle-class lifestyle require more education and employment-related skills. Unions are simply not as popular with the general public as they were in the 1940s and 1950s. Two reasons for the decline of unions are an increase in employer resistance to unionization resulting from heightened market competitiveness and the fact that workers are more satisfied with their jobs and believe that unions would not significantly improve their working conditions.[5] Undoubtedly news stories about union corruption and the involvement of union money in political campaigns have negatively affected public perceptions of union activity.

Union membership has been falling in the private sector (both nonprofit and for-profit organizations should be considered the private sector for the purposes of discussion in this chapter) due in large part to changes in the economy, but union membership in the public sector has consistently increased over the past several decades (see Figure 5.1). As of 1997, 37.2 percent of public employees belonged to labor organizations, while only 9.8 percent of employees in private, nonagricultural employment belonged to unions. The percentage of union membership in the public sector may have peaked in 1994, when 38.7 percent of

Figure 5.1   Labor Union Membership, by Sector: 1985–1997

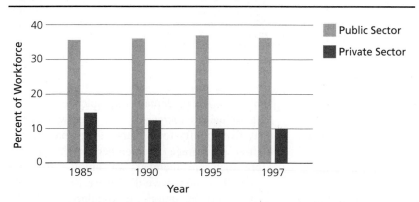

Source: Bureau of Labor Statistics (BLS), Union Members Summary, **http://stats.bls.gov/newsrels.htm.**

Table 5.1   Percentage of Union Members by Selected Characteristics, 1997

Characteristic	Percentage of Total Number with This Characteristic Who Are Union Members
Age	
16–24	5.2
25–34	11.7
35–44	15.9
45–54	20.5
55–64	19.2
Sex	
Women	11.6
Men	16.3
Race	
Hispanic	11.8
White	13.6
Black	17.9
Job status	
Part-time workers	7.0
Full-time workers	15.6
Occupational category	
Farming, Forestry, Fishing	4.6
Technical/Sales/Administrative Support	9.1
Managerial/Professional	13.2
Services	13.2
Operators, Fabricators, Laborers	21.5
Precision, Production, Craft, Repair	22.6
Government	37.2

Source: U.S. Department of Commerce, Bureau of the Census, Economics and Statistics Administration, *Statistical Abstract of the United States, 1998, Labor Force, Employment, and Earnings* (Washington, D.C.: U.S. Government Printing Office, 1999), Table 713, p. 444.

the public workforce were members of unions. The highest percentage of union membership in the public sector is found in local government, where 43.4 percent of city, county, and special district employees belong to a labor organization.[6]

A number of factors influence union membership; age, gender, race, and type of job all play a role in the decision whether to join unions (see Table 5.1). The percentage of employees who belong to unions increases with age, with those forty-five to fifty-four years of age having the highest percentage of membership in unions. More men are members of unions than are women. Hispanics have the lowest percentage of membership in unions (particularly Hispanic women, at 10.6 percent), and black men had the greatest percentage of union membership (20.2 percent). The occupational category of farming, forestry, and fishing had the lowest percentage of union members of any other characteristic, followed by the technical/sales and managerial/professional categories. Government employees had the highest percentage of union membership. The reasons behind union membership in each category deserve further research attention. It seems apparent that there may be connections between categories; for example, women were less likely to be members of unions and are also more dominant in occupations that had a lower percentage of union membership.

WHY EMPLOYEES JOIN UNIONS

Employees weigh the cost of joining unions with the benefits. The greatest benefit for most employees are **economic benefits**: the prospect of higher salaries, improved fringe benefits, and greater safety provisions in the workplace through collective bargaining.[7] Unions also offer employees greater **job security benefits** through bargaining for grievance procedures, which allow employees to have a voice in actions taken against them and professional representation during these procedures.[8] Some people enjoy the **social benefits** of joining with others and working to improve the working conditions of all members of the group and participating in other social activities with the group. Unions offer employees the opportunity to participate in a social organization at many levels, possibly rising through the union hierarchy itself. Finally, public employees are attracted to unions by **political benefits,** with the opportunity to influence the political environment in which they work.[9]

Public unions often form political action arms or political action committees (PACs) to influence the political process and have a voice in determining their political leadership after the next election. Unions employ lobbyists who work with Congress, the state legislatures, and local government officials to argue for legislation in the union membership's interest. Many large unions provide research and information on employment conditions and methods for improving working conditions. Another way public unions may influence public policy is by organizing in cooperation with specialized client groups, such as female employees seeking day-care facilities or Native Americans, that are served by government agencies.[10] There is also the opportunity to exercise political power within the organization. Unions usually conduct collective bargaining with employers, working for improved wages, benefits, and working conditions. Some employees enjoy the power of helping to determine the policies and procedures of the organization or the terms and conditions of employment.

In contrast, there are also costs associated with union membership. The greatest cost on the minds of most employees is economic: the amount of union dues. Union dues for some public employees amount to over $1,000 per year. Union members might also pay dues to the national, state, and local organizations. In addition to dues, members may be asked to pay into a PAC for making contributions to political campaigns. Another economic consideration is the cost to each employee if a dispute arises between management and labor. Picketing can involve extra time, contract impasses can postpone wage increases, and even entail work stoppages (and paycheck stoppage). Union membership also comes with social and political costs. Employees may feel they lose their personal identity when joining unions. Some people prefer to handle their employment relationship between their employer and themselves individually, solving grievances, salary, and promotion situations themselves. But employees are required to let the union bargain on their behalf when a union is elected as an exclusive representative of their bargaining unit. In many states employees are required to pay union dues (or a service charge to the union) even if they do not wish to belong to a union.

Employers often deal with their employees differently when a union is involved. Relationships can become strained, and an atmosphere of conflict and adversarialism sometimes pervades the unionized workplace.

A SHORT HISTORY OF LABOR RELATIONS

The work environment is changing in ways that make public sector unions' goals and objectives more difficult to attain than in the past. Employers, employees, and their representatives are facing a shift away from manufacturing toward services, information exchange, and technology-intensive enterprises. Increased competition from all over the world and heightened consumer expectations are requiring higher quality and lower costs in governmental enterprises. The workforce is more diverse, including more minorities and women, and the average age of American workers is gradually increasing. Many workers are better educated than was the case in the past, and better educated employees desire more input into management decisions. Employee representatives and employers alike have been somewhat slow to adjust to these changes, and for the most part they continue to conduct labor relations under the model established over sixty years ago.

These changes in the work environment are not limited to the private sector. Citizens are demanding more services for their tax dollars and at the same time endorsing legislation and public referenda to lower the taxes they pay to governments. Government organizations are increasingly privatizing public services and choosing intergovernmental competition to respond to citizen demands for lower taxes and more services. Government officials often act unilaterally to address these problems, leaving those with the greatest knowledge about public services—those doing the work—largely out of the discussion. Management and labor still tend to look at each other with suspicion and mistrust, as if the other side were an enemy. This adversarial model may have appeared to work while the United States was undergoing its industrial revolution and later when it dominated the global economy in the 1950s and 1960s. Now, adversarial employee relations may be particularly counterproductive and self-defeating as employers and employees in both the public and private sectors face the chal-

lenges of the global economy and the modern high-tech workplace.[11]

As early as the 1860s, national organizations of labor began to coalesce in the United States; the first major coalition, the Knights of Labor, was established in 1869.[12] This coalition emphasized political action, education, and arbitration to replace increasingly common strikes. The Knights of Labor was a collection of many different, often-competing trades and occupations, a fact that led to its ultimate decline in the 1890s.

The American Federation of Labor (AFL) was organized by a group of craft unions in 1886 and used the practice of **collective bargaining** to improve the working conditions of its membership of skilled workers. Rapid industrialization in the United States created large numbers of workers who possessed limited transferable skills. In 1938, unions composed of these blue-collar workers formed the Congress of Industrial Organizations (CIO).

As the American economy grew after the end of World War II, unionism reached a peak, with over one-third of the nonagricultural American workforce belonging to unions. Competition between the two major labor organizations, the AFL and the CIO, was harmful to the union movement as a whole, and ultimately the AFL-CIO was created in 1955 to overcome this problem.[13] Since the merger, the percentage of employees belonging to unions has steadily declined from a peak of 35.5 percent in 1945 to only 14.1 percent in 1997, falling almost one-half of 1 percent each year.[14]

THE LEGAL ENVIRONMENT OF UNIONS

The legal environment has had the greatest influence on the success of union organization and the growth of organized labor.[15] From the earliest days, laws and court rulings suppressed union organizing. Employers used the **conspiracy doctrine,** which held that cooperation among employees to challenge an employer constituted an illegal restraint of trade, to stop employees from striking. Collective action that harmed the economic interests of others was considered unlawful under prevailing business practice laws, and the courts generally prohibited strikes on these grounds.[16] By the middle of the nineteenth century, the conspiracy doctrine began to give way to a different set of legal arguments as judges ruled that the objectives of the collective activity had to be illegal for an action to be considered a conspiracy. In *Commonwealth v. Hunt* (1842), the Massachusetts Supreme Court ruled in favor of shoemakers who had struck over the hiring of nonunion shoemakers, holding that the strike had no illegal purpose and was therefore not a conspiracy.[17] Adopting an **antitrust approach** to thwarting unions, the U.S. Supreme Court agreed with business owners in the famous Danbury Hatters (1908) case, deciding that unions were a "combination" that sought to "obstruct the free flow of commerce."[18]

During this time period, organized labor had no legal protection, and many businesses enforced union-busting practices to keep employees from organizing. With industrial relations weighing so heavily on the side of the employer, labor unrest increased as the nation moved into the new century. Federal and state legislatures began to look at the balance of power between labor and employer and nervously watched labor-supported social movements grow more extreme worldwide. The Great Depression brought further labor unrest, along with national calls for legislation to limit the power of businesses to restrict employee organization.

By the early twentieth century, the legal environment was shifting significantly in favor of organized labor. A series of congressional acts altered the labor-management relationship substantially and opened the door to a rapid increase in organized labor. In 1912, Congress passed the Lloyd–La Follette Act that allowed federal workers (specifically U.S. postal workers) the right to form and join unions, with the provision that the union would not strike against the federal government. The Railway Labor Act (1926) gave railway workers the right to organize into unions, engage

in collective bargaining, and, in the case negotiations broke down, to strike. The Norris–La Guardia Act (1932) limited employers' ability to stop collective labor actions by court injunctions and prohibited employers from entering into agreements with employees whereby employees agree not to join a union (known as *yellow dog contracts*).

The most important piece of labor legislation in the history of the United States was a key New Deal enactment entitled the National Labor Relations Act (NLRA) (1935), popularly known as the **Wagner Act,** named after its primary congressional sponsor, New York Senator Robert F. Wagner. The NLRA gave all private sector, nonagricultural employees the right to organize, engage in collective bargaining, and strike. Although the act did not apply to public employees, many of its provisions have been adopted in state labor laws, and the decisions of the National Labor Relations Board (NLRB), established to administer the provisions of the act, are often used as precedent in public sector labor relations.

Wagner Act

The NLRB defined employees as nonsupervisory or managerial workers, prohibited unfair labor practices for management, and established the scope of bargaining as "wages, hours of employment, or other conditions of employment." It also set guidelines for the determination of employee bargaining units within an organization and the election of exclusive employee representatives for bargaining units. The act described the rules of collective bargaining, establishing the following as **unfair labor practices** for management:

- Interfering with employees' right to organize, bargain collectively, or engage in other collective action
- Interfering with any labor organization or influencing employees to join or not join a particular labor union
- Refusing to **bargain in good faith** with the elected representative of each bargaining unit

- Discriminating against any employee because of any union-related action taken under the provisions of the NLRA

The Wagner Act shifted the balance of power away from management and reinforced the bargaining position of labor. The result was an increase in labor organizing and collective bargaining. In 1946, 50,000 collective bargaining agreements were in place across the nation. The act was successful in decreasing the number of organizational strikes, but most likely had the effect of increasing strikes over wages, hours, and working conditions.[19]

Taft-Hartley Act

As a result of the increase in strikes and the fear that labor unrest could harm the national economy (and even endanger national security), Congress passed the Labor Management Relations Act (1947), popularly known as the **Taft-Hartley Act.** Taft-Hartley was intended to bring balance once again to labor-management relations by prohibiting certain unfair labor practices by *unions,* protecting the rights of employees and employers regarding unions, and setting guidelines for the peaceful resolution of strikes, particularly those involving national security.[20] Regarding unfair labor practices, labor unions were prohibited from the following acts:

- Restraining or coercing employees in the exercise of their collective bargaining rights
- Causing an employer to discriminate against an employee to affect union membership
- Not bargaining in good faith with employers if they were elected as the exclusive bargaining representative
- Calling some types of strikes or boycotts if the purpose of the job action was to force an employer to join a labor or employer organization or stop dealings with another employer (referred to as a secondary boycott); compel recognition as the exclusive bargaining agent without NLRB certification; or

compel an employer to designate particular work assignments
- Charging excessive or discriminatory union dues
- Attempting to cause an employer to pay for services not actually rendered by the union (referred to as featherbedding)

The Taft-Hartley Act protected the rights of employees by prohibiting **closed shops,** where all workers have to be union members at the time they are hired. It allowed states to pass labor laws related to **union security** known as **right-to-work laws** that prevented **union shop** provisions in labor contracts, requiring employees to be members of the union in order to keep their jobs. The act also permitted **dues checkoff,** whereby the employer deducts union dues from the employee paycheck only if the employee authorizes the deduction in writing. Employees were also given the right to present grievances directly to the employer without the union's deciding on the merit of the grievance.

Taft-Hartley allowed employers to give their opinions and views regarding union representation to their employees so long as they did not attempt to interfere with union representation elections by threatening reprisals or promising benefits. Employers could also call for representation elections, refuse to bargain with supervisors' unions, and file unfair labor practices complaints against unions with the NLRB.

Taft-Harley was designed as well to protect national security. If the president of the United States determines that a strike seriously threatens national health or safety, he may take action to restrain the strike for up to eighty days. This **cooling-off period** is designed to protect the public and allow for the time needed to mediate a settlement. The act also established the Federal Mediation and Conciliation Service to help employers and unions resolve disputes without resorting to strikes, and it established steps to keep industries operating when strikes created national emergencies.[21]

PUBLIC SECTOR LABOR RELATIONS

Public employees were excluded from the two important labor relations statutes enacted into law in the 1930s and 1940s.[22] The reasons for their exclusion were primarily legal. In the early decades of the twentieth century, the federal government believed it was severely limited in its power to regulate activities occurring in the states (Tenth Amendment), and the courts ruled that public employees could be prohibited from joining unions under the **doctrine of sovereignty.** The argument went something like this: despite the right of employees to associate freely, there was no constitutional right to government employment, and the government's need (or the public interest) to maintain public services without interference outweighed the employees' right to associate.[23]

Calvin Coolidge was propelled into the national spotlight in 1919 when he took a strong stand as governor of Massachusetts against striking Boston police, stating, "There is no right to strike against the public safety by anybody, anywhere, anytime."[24] It was generally believed that public sector unions would interfere with the sovereign right of governments to represent the people in formulating and implementing public policy. Collective action by public unions could place undue pressure on public policy decisions, leaving citizens with relatively little voice. Public employees were perceived by the public to enjoy the "privilege" of working for government as public servants and had no property rights to their jobs. They were also thought of as having lifetime job security and had no need of bargaining rights. Furthermore, public employees were involved in police and fire protection activities; any strike by public employees could directly endanger the public safety of all citizens.

Clearly, however, the government in its sovereign power can allow for discussions with its employees over working conditions and bargain collectively with employee representatives. In no way is the government compelled to agree to union demands or forced to take any actions as a result of collective bargaining. The governing body must always approve agreements made through the bargaining process. Today the sovereignty doctrine is no longer used as a prohibition against union organizing in the public sector, and most states have their own version of the Wagner Act governing public employee organizations, mediation and arbitration services, and protections of employees and employers involved in employment disputes.

No nationwide labor relations law governs the union activities of public sector unions. For most of the twentieth century, labor organizing activities were not protected by law, and they are still prohibited in a few areas of the country. President Kennedy issued the first executive order to allow federal workers limited rights to organize and bargain. This was followed by additional related executive orders from Presidents Nixon and Ford. In 1978, Congress passed the Civil Service Reform Act, which replaced these executive orders and established a limited right to organize and collectively bargain for federal workers as a matter of statutory law. Federal unions are restricted in their **scope of bargaining,** being prohibited from bargaining over wages and benefits, however, and they are prohibited from engaging in strikes. Labor disputes are settled with the help of the Federal Mediation and Conciliation Service or the Federal Impasse Panel.

State and local government workers face an uncoordinated and confusing mixture of labor relations laws that vary by state.[25] Only thirty-one states require state and local governments to bargain with legitimate employee representatives. Thirty-nine states continue to prohibit strikes. Some states allow some employees to bargain collectively (teachers and firefighters), but outlaw other public workers from exercising the same rights. Table 5.2 on page 110 shows the states that allow collective bargaining (or in some cases "meet and confer" arrangements) for public employees and those that limit the right of public workers to bargain collectively.

The public sector labor relations model has

Table 5.2   State Collective Bargaining Practices

States Allowing Some Form of Bargaining for State Employees	States Allowing Some Form of Bargaining for Local Government Employees	States Allowing Some Form of Bargaining for Police (P), Firefighters (F), or Teachers (T)	States Not Allowing Public Sector Bargaining
Alaska	Alaska	Alabama (F)	Arizona
California	California	Alaska (P, F, T)	Arkansas
Connecticut	Connecticut	California (P, F, T)	Colorado
Delaware	Delaware	Connecticut (P, F, T)	Louisiana
Florida	Hawaii	Delaware (P, F, T)	Mississippi
Hawaii	Iowa	Florida (P, F, T)	North Carolina
Illinois	Kansas	Georgia (F)	South Carolina
Iowa	Maine	Hawaii (P, F, T)	Utah
Kansas	Maryland	Idaho (F, T)	Virginia
Maine	Massachusetts	Illinois (P, F, T)	
Massachusetts	Michigan	Indiana (T)	
Michigan	Minnesota	Iowa (P, F, T)	
Minnesota	Missouri	Kansas (P, F, T)	
Missouri	Montana	Kentucky (P, F)	
Montana	Nebraska	Maine (P, F, T)	
Nebraska	Nevada	Maryland (T)	
New Hampshire	New Hampshire	Massachusetts (P, F, T)	
New Jersey	New Jersey	Michigan (P, F, T)	
New Mexico	New Mexico	Minnesota (P, F, T)	
New York	New York	Missouri (F)	
North Dakota	North Dakota	Montana (P, F, T)	
Ohio	Ohio	Nebraska (P, F, T)	
Oregon	Oklahoma	Nevada (P, F, T)	
Pennsylvania	Oregon	New Hampshire (P ,F, T)	
Rhode Island	Pennsylvania	New Jersey (P, F, T)	
South Dakota	Rhode Island	New Mexico (P, F, T)	
Vermont	South Dakota	New York (P, F, T)	
Washington	Vermont	North Dakota (P, F, T)	
West Virginia	Washington	Ohio (P, F, T)	
Wisconsin	West Virginia	Oklahoma (P, F, T)	
	Wisconsin	Oregon (P, F, T)	
		Pennsylvania (P, F, T)	
		Rhode Island (P, F, T)	
		South Dakota (P, F, T)	
		Tennessee (T)	
		Vermont (P, F, T)	
		Washington (P, F, T)	
		West Virginia (P, F, T)	
		Wisconsin (P, F, T)	
		Wyoming (F)	

Source: Reprinted from Richard C. Kearney, *Labor Relations in the Public Sector,* 2nd ed. (New York: Marcel Dekker, 1992), pp. 27–34. Courtesy of Marcel Dekker, Inc.

closely followed the private sector model, although there are some important economic, legal, and political differences between the two. Shafritz describes four important features of private sector labor relations that differ from the public sector:

1. The parties to collective bargaining are more or less equal in the private sector.
2. Private companies and unions are constrained by market forces, while public sector labor relations are dominated by politics.
3. Economic issues are distributive in the private sector. In other words, wages, capital, and profits all come from the firm's earnings, and the issue is how these earnings are distributed. A gain by the union usually means a reduction in the amount distributed to investment or profits.
4. In the private sector, economic disputes can be settled by strikes, lockouts, and other job actions, which are illegal under most circumstances in the public sector.[26]

These differences bring into question the appropriateness and effectiveness of traditional approaches to collective bargaining in the public sector.

Most public sector labor laws place management and labor in unequal positions. The government is not neutral in its decisions about public sector labor relations; it is the employer in the public sector and defines its own provisions for labor relations. Government defines the scope of bargaining, identifies management rights, and determines the methods of dispute resolution employed. It can outlaw strikes and specify what it considers to be unfair labor practices. Government can define its labor relations policy by law. In the federal government, unions cannot bargain over wages, hours, budgets, or management rights to operate. State and local labor relations laws often restrict the right of public employees to exercise bargaining rights commonly found in the private sector. These laws limit which public employees have the right to bargain; in some cases, firefighters may bargain, but police cannot, or public school teachers are given the right to bar-

gain, but public university professors are denied that right. These laws can limit what issues may be discussed and what recourse may or may not be taken in the event of an impasse (most states prohibit strikes by public employees).

The second difference is also significant; the government is not as susceptible to market forces as is the private sector.[27] The economic power derived from employees organizing for collective action is not as significant in the public sector as it is in the private marketplace. In most cases, the absence of the right to strike removes the strongest economic weapon from public unions. Boycotts are seldom effective because governments provide essential services and operate as monopolies over public services. Picketing is sometimes done in the public sector, but its impact is not economic, as is the case in the private market; instead, it can only be used for public relations and citizen information dissemination purposes.

The public sector depends on tax dollars and voter support, not company earnings. When public officials must consider union demands, the decision is not whether to direct more of the company's earnings to employee pay or benefits; instead, the decision may be whether to reduce the level of a government service or increase taxes. In difficult times, public employers have had to make the determination to reduce the number of public employees (often police or firefighters, who make up the largest group of local government employees) in order to give raises to the remaining employees. When citizens already think they are paying too much in taxes (especially property tax), the decision to raise taxes to pay for employee raises is less of an option for elected officials. As one author aptly described the difference between public and private labor relations, "Collective bargaining in the private sector is about economics; in government, it is about politics."[28]

The ultimate weapon of private sector unions, the strike, is not an option for most public employees. In some cases, such as teacher unions, public officials have allowed a strike even if it were technically illegal to promote labor peace, but this is no guarantee that illegal strikes will continue to go unpunished. The famous Professional Air Traffic Controllers Organization (PATCO) strike in 1981 and the summary firing of the air traffic controllers by President Reagan taught a lasting lesson to public employees attempting to use the strike as a tool of labor.

The dilemma in public labor relations is how unions have any power or leverage in collective bargaining if they are denied the right to strike, and what substitute for a strike can be used to compel a sovereign government to action on employee workplace issues. A final answer to these questions has not yet been discovered, but some alternate methods of dispute resolution are being used in public sector applications.

Discrimination in Labor Relations

Most of us are aware that civil rights legislation has focused on the employment practices of public and private employers. Interestingly, the Civil Rights Act of 1964 and other laws have also targeted labor unions in their efforts to eliminate discriminatory practices in the workplace. Here is what that Civil Rights Act has to say:

> (c) It shall be an unlawful employment practice for a labor organization—(1) to exclude or to expel from its membership, or otherwise to discriminate against, any individual because of his race, color, religion, sex, or national origin; (2) to limit, segregate, or classify its membership or applicants for membership, or to classify or fail or refuse to refer for employment any individual, in any way which would deprive or tend to deprive any individual of employment opportunities, or would limit such employment opportunities or otherwise adversely affect his status as an employee or as an applicant for employment, because of such individual's race, color, religion, sex, or national origin; or (3) to cause or attempt to cause an employer to discriminate against an individual in violation of this section.

These prohibitions against discrimination by labor unions illustrate the close linkage between labor unions and the workplace. Labor organizations cannot discriminate against their members or applicants for membership because of race, color, religion, sex, or national origin. They are proscribed from classifying their membership by these criteria and may not limit employment opportunities on the basis of these protected classes. These restrictions apply to all union practices, including negotiations and representation. In collective negotiations, unions cannot classify one of the protected groups for different benefits. Similarly, in the case of grievance or other form of representation, a labor organization cannot fail to represent a member because of that person's race, color, religion, sex, or national origin.

Public Labor Organizations

Dozens of public sector labor organizations represent public employees at all levels of government, ranging from the National Association of Aeronautical Examiners to the West Point Elementary School Teachers Association.[29] Most of these unions are affiliated with the AFL-CIO, the largest being the **American Federation of Government Employees,** representing 546,468 employees in 1997. Other large unions are the National Treasury Employees Union (133,680) and the National Federation of Federal Employees (118,285).[30] The most active unions in organizing public sector workers, particularly in state and local governments, are the following:

American Federation of State, County and Municipal Employees (AFSCME)

National Education Association (NEA)

International Brotherhood of Teamsters (IBT)

Fraternal Order of Police (FOP)

International Association of Fire Fighters (IAFF)

Service Employees International Union (SEIU)

American Federation of Teachers (AFT)

Communications Workers of America (CWA)[31]

Union Certification and Recognition in the Public Sector

Most public jurisdictions have modeled their labor relations laws after the major national labor laws, the Wagner and Taft-Hartley acts. Public labor laws or implementation policies usually contain guidelines or procedures for **union certification** (official legal standing as a trustee of employees' rights and interests) and representation of the employee bargaining unit. When a group of employees is convinced they would like to have a union to represent them to management, they must complete the certification process, which typically entails an election process, before representation can take place.

The certification process formally begins when authorization cards are distributed to all employees in the proposed bargaining unit. These signature cards authorize a specific union to be the exclusive bargaining agent for that employee, but do not by themselves constitute an election for a union. Typically at least 30 percent of the affected employees must sign the authorization cards before a recognition election can take place. If an employee organization is authorized, employees petition the government body for a recognition election; that agency then designates the extent of the bargaining unit (that is, who are the elegible employees) and conducts an election. A **bargaining unit** is generally determined by commonality of interests and groupings by wages, skills, and working conditions. An election can be held with one or more employee organizations competing for representation, along with the option for no union representation being made available to employees. The choice receiving the majority of votes wins the election. If no single choice available receives a majority vote, a runoff election is held, with the majority electing the winner. In the event a union (or guild, association, brotherhood, etc.) is elected by a majority of employees in the bargaining unit, that employee organization becomes the **exclusive bargaining agent,** and management must bargain in good faith with that entity—and only that organization. Historically,

the percentage of elections resulting in employees selecting a union is just under 50 percent, and often such elections are decided by fewer than ten votes.[32]

Like the National Labor Relations Act, state and local labor laws prohibit unfair labor practices by management and unions during an election campaign, and these laws typically restrict other activities related to certification elections. Both employees and employers are allowed to express their views and opinions regarding the election so long as there are no threats of retribution or promises of reward offered for voting a certain way in the election. Employers can inform employees of their opinion of the benefits offered by unions, and employees can advertise the expected benefits of union membership. Employers may restrict union organizers from contacting employees at the workplace so long as there is reasonable access to employees through advertisement or meetings away from the workplace, and equal treatment of other nonemployees who may also desire access to employees at the work location or facility is provided. Employees may campaign at the workplace, but are restricted to times when they and other employees are not working and in locations away from work areas.

In the same way that certification elections take place, employees may petition the National Labor Relations Board to hold a **decertification** election. In these cases, employees may seek to discontinue having a particular union or employee organization represent them in negotiations with management. Decertification elections have increased in frequency in recent years, and unions have lost most of these elections. [33]

COLLECTIVE BARGAINING

Good-Faith Bargaining

Under most state labor laws, the employer has a duty to bargain in good faith exclusively with a legally elected employee representative. The duty to bargain in good faith "requires active participation in negotiations with a sincere effort to reach an agreement."[34] Good-faith bargaining means conducting negotiations under rules of fairness, usually including these elements:

- A time frame for beginning and conducting negotiations
- Making information available that is relevant to negotiations
- Not bypassing the official bargaining representatives by discussing bargaining issues with the other side rather than through the bargaining team
- Not making unilateral changes in working conditions while negotiations are being conducted
- Not engaging in a strike during negotiations (if allowed by law) and following formal procedures for **impasse resolution**
- A willingness to put a negotiated agreement in writing and execute the agreement
- Not engaging in insincere bargaining as demonstrated by delaying the bargaining process, failing to offer legitimate proposals or counterproposals, or refusing to make concessions on any issue[35]

The exclusive bargaining representative has the right to negotiate a contract with management for employees in the bargaining unit over specific issues referred to as the *scope of bargaining*: rates of pay, wages, hours of employment, or other conditions or benefits of employment. Collective bargaining does not have to be the traditional across-the-table, confrontational, and stressful process, but it must be approached in an organized, documented, and professional way.

Collective Bargaining Process

The cycle of labor negotiations has at least eleven commonly noted phases or processes:

1. Initiation
2. Preparation
3. Internal negotiations
4. Informal discussions
5. Preliminary negotiations
6. Issue identification
7. Problem solving
8. Impasse resolution
9. Settlement
10. Ratification
11. Contract management

Step 1: Initiation In most public jurisdictions, the legislation authorizing collective bargaining requires either party to a labor contract to notify the other party of its desire to open negotiations within a specific number of days prior to the expiration of the labor contract. For example, a city labor relations ordinance may require the union and city officials to notify each other within sixty days prior to the expiration of the existing contract if they intend to renegotiate the contract. This timeframe allows the two bargaining sides sufficient time to prepare for negotiations.

Step 2: Preparation As with most other complex efforts, failing to prepare for negotiations is the surest way of not succeeding in protecting one's own interests and being subject to those who are better prepared. The organization's long-term goals are the first consideration in negotiations, and negotiations should always be aimed toward satisfying them.

Tactical planning is the determination of how negotiations will be conducted, what specific issues are to be introduced in negotiations, and what the desired objectives are for each issue. Box 5.1 lists questions to ask in this phase. Caution should be taken at this phase of planning because of the natural tendency to succumb to "groupthink" when working in a setting of us-versus-them negotiations. It is often helpful to have one or two people involved in tactical planning who can offer genuine insight into how the other bargaining team and their constituents will react to issues and actions proposed for negotiations before face-to-face bargaining begins and a number of strategic decisions have to be made.

Each issue is defined in terms of the interest it serves or the underlying goal desired by introduc-

---

Box 5.1   Questions to Ask in Preparation for Negotiations

Administrative Arrangements

- What is the commitment of upper-level management to the bargaining process?
- How united is the governing body in supporting the bargaining effort?
- What human and time resources will be committed to the bargaining process?
- What style of bargaining is to be used? When would this style change during negotiations?
- Who will lead the negotiations?
- What personnel will be assigned to act as the bargaining team and advisers to the team?
- What is the reporting relationship to the governing bodies involved in making administrative decisions during the bargaining time period?
- How will tactical decisions be made throughout the bargaining period?
- What will be done in the event of job actions during negotiations or at impasse?
- Who should work with the media, and what should be said?

Issue Analysis

- What are the specific issues to be proposed for negotiation?
- What is the priority ranking for each issue?
- What are the current trends in the industry regarding this issue?
- What is the history of this issue in previous negotiations?
- What is the range of acceptable solutions for each issue?
- What are the costs and benefits across the range of acceptable solutions?
- Can contract language be prepared reflecting acceptable solutions to important issues?
- What are the acceptable and expected outcomes of negotiations for each issue?
- What is the alternative to negotiated settlement on each issue? Is it acceptable?

Understanding the Opposite Bargaining Team

- Who will be on the negotiating team?
- Who will be the team's chief spokesperson?
- What are the political interests and needs of the negotiating team?
- What is their expected negotiating style?
- What are the expected issues from the other group?
- What are their individual interests regarding bargaining issues?
- What are their likely goals for settlement?
- What level of support do they have from their constituents?
- What decision-making authority do they have?

---

ing this issue. During the process of negotiations, it is likely that solutions will be found that satisfy a team's interests, although the team did not previously consider them. A negotiating position should not interfere with a legitimate solution. Objectives are established for each issue anticipated to be addressed in negotiations. For example, the issue may be to revise the grievance procedure, which commonly drags on too long and needs to be shortened. The objective would be to reduce the number of procedural steps from five to three.

Procedural planning is used to identify the negotiation assignments for members of the bargaining team, including assignments for chief spokesperson, personnel policy adviser, budget adviser, legal adviser, and issues related to the specific bargaining unit. Decisions on how the bargaining team will report to its administrative oversight group and preferences for bargaining ground rules are often discussed at this stage.

Step 3: Internal negotiations. Sometimes the most difficult part of collective bargaining is **internal negotiations,** that is, the negotiating process within the organization. It is easy to assume that the conflict over interests will begin once the two sides meet at the bargaining table, but in fact a variety of interests, frequently interests that conflict with others, can exist within the administrative organization. Public agencies can have a conflict between the members and interests of political parties, political ambition can create conflict between elected officials, and department heads may disagree about bargaining strategies to be employed as a result of prior competition between departments. In many cases, personality conflicts may carry over to the planning and conduct of collective bargaining. Union organizations also experience similar internal conflict. There is often a conflict between factions within the union who are vying for leadership and control of the union. Sometimes there is a conflict between the interests of the new employees, who tend to be more interested in increasing wages, and those more experienced employees who are inclined to be more interested in job security and health and retirement benefits. The negotiating team may have representatives of many of these factions and interests, and it should be prepared to deal with each of these during the course of negotiations.

Step 4: Informal discussions Experienced negotiators frequently contact the leader of the opposite team prior to formal negotiations and at critical points throughout the bargaining process to discuss the ground rules and expectations and explain actions that will take place or have already happened at the bargaining table. It is somewhat dangerous to develop solutions to specific issues during these informal sessions, but they can be used to establish the framework for discussions and reduce tensions. In the later stages of negotiations, informal discussions (or sidebars) can help create a plan for resolving the remaining issues.

Step 5: Preliminary negotiations Before grappling with the issues to be discussed and negotiated in the formal bargaining sessions, it is important to establish the rules under which negotiations will take place. **Ground rules** are usually agreed to in the first sessions. After the groups have introduced themselves, rules such as the following are often agreed to by both parties:

- Schedule for negotiating sessions, including dates and times
- Location for sessions
- Who will be invited to attend negotiating sessions
- What will be the roles and functions of those attending
- Who will act as chief spokesperson
- Method of recording sessions
- What information will be available to both groups during negotiations
- How negotiating teams will handle the media during negotiations
- The number of proposals to be considered by each side
- The procedure for presenting proposals (the order of presenting proposals)
- When new issues will no longer be accepted for negotiation
- How caucuses (recesses for the party delegations to meet apart from the opposing side) are to be called, how long caucuses will take, and a private place to hold caucuses
- Whether agreements will be made issue-by-issue (tentative agreements) or as a total package

Step 6: Issue identification During the process of issue identification, the bargaining teams present their issues, proposals, or demands to the other side. This is often done briefly, presenting the topic to be discussed without going into much detail at first until all the individual issues are on the table. Once both sides have heard all the issues to be discussed in negotiations, they may retire, or **caucus,** to discuss how they will approach each issue. Some subjects are mandatory subjects of bargaining, others are permissible, and still others may be impermissable (illegal). The issues to be discussed are referred to as the scope of bargaining and fall within legal restrictions of what may and may not be discussed in collective bargaining according to statutes governing the labor-management process.

Virtually all legislation authorizing collective bargaining specifies what types of issues can be discussed during labor negotiations. **Mandatory issues** must be negotiated by both parties in good faith if either side desires to bring up such an issue. However, this does not mean that either party must agree or settle the issue. Mandatory issues usually include wages, hours, and conditions of employment. These three categories often encompass fringe benefits, overtime hours, pay scales, management rights provisions, union security and union rights provisions, grievance procedures, safety, and other conditions of employment. **Permissive issues** are those that can be negotiated if both parties agree to discuss them, but neither party is required to bargain over these issues. Examples are management or union operations such as budgeting procedures or service levels and can include items not normally covered by a contract such as benefits for retired employees. If both parties agree to negotiate permissive issues but cannot reach an agreement on them, it is illegal to pursue the issue to the point of impasse. Neither labor nor management can bring illegal issues to the bargaining table. Illegal issues are those that contemplate breaking the law—for example, illegal discrimination in hiring and promotion, management financial support for the union, or salary increases in return for political contributions.

Wages are the most familiar issue brought to the bargaining table. Unions typically negotiate for higher average wages to keep pace with inflation in the region or to bring salaries and wages up to the level of comparable public entities. They may negotiate for higher wages than paid in surrounding communities if they feel their work requires a higher standard. Unions also commonly negotiate for predictable incremental wage increases, usually to compensate for an employee's seniority rather than performance or productivity that is subject to management discretion. Man-

agement in many jurisdictions is moving toward more open pay scales, with increases in salaries and wages awarded on the basis of individual performance. During negotiations, the parties may decide to defer compensation or put potential wage increases into better benefits. Deferred compensation plans are becoming increasingly popular with baby boomer–aged employees, who are interested in improved retirement benefits. Unions often face competing demands from their constituents when they make demands for better fringe benefits. Younger employees tend to favor improvements to medical and dental insurance plans, while older workers are more interested in pension plan improvements.

Contract negotiations often include issues dealing with job security, work rules, and grievance procedures. Most contracts also include a statement of management and union rights. Negotiations may encompass issues that seek to establish rules in the event of layoffs and grievance procedures for ensuring due process in cases of employee discipline or dismissal. With the increased attention being given to contracting out and privatization, negotiations frequently examine issues related to subcontracting. Management often prefers to state its rights in regard to areas such as organizational operations, decision making, service levels, and implicitly all other rights not specifically granted to the union as a part of the contract. Unions also may desire a statement of their rights under the contract and bring issues into negotiations to amend this statement.

Union security issues are often negotiated where the union is compensated for by all employees in the bargaining unit, whether covered employees are members of the union or not. There are several options for union security arrangements. The least controversial and most common union security provision is dues checkoff: that is, the employer deducts dues automatically from the employee's pay until the employee specifically requests in writing that payments be stopped. A union shop requires all employees covered in the bargaining unit to join the union within a specific number of days after they are hired. An agency shop does not require membership in the union, but all nonmembers must pay a representational fee to the union for services rendered as the exclusive bargaining agent of the bargaining unit. This fee is usually equal to or only slightly less than the dues paid by members of the union. The closed shop is illegal under the National Labor Relations Act and all other public labor laws. A closed shop requires membership in the union before consideration to be hired to a position within the bargaining unit. A number of states have passed right-to-work legislation to outlaw all forms of union security provisions except dues checkoff. These states are located in the South and Rocky Mountain West regions of the United States.

The next time the teams meet, they may want to clarify each issue by asking what purpose or interest is behind the issue and what rationale, documentation, or other evidence supports the need to address the issue.

Step 7: Problem solving Once the issues have been identified, the negotiating teams can begin working on solving the problems presented to them. During this phase, the two sides develop ideas, proposals, and counterproposals with the objective of resolving the issues at hand. It is sometimes helpful to create subcommittees to work on specific issues and come up with a suggested resolution to the problem. Special guests with relevant information (for example, an expert on workplace ergonomics) can be called to testify or explain specific issues.

Step 8: Impasse resolution If a settlement is not reached through the course of negotiations, often guidelines in the relevant labor law require specific impasse resolution steps. The National Labor Relations Act, for example, requires notification of the Federal Mediation and Conciliation Service if negotiations have not reached an agreement within thirty days of the initial notification of intent to renegotiate the contract. Most public jurisdictions have incorporated similar provisions in public labor laws. If both parties in negotiations

are making progress, they may extend the contract even after its expiration date. If there is no progress and settlement does not appear to be forthcoming, the parties are at an impasse and may need to seek outside assistance or apply extraordinary pressure to settle the contract.

The private sector and some public jurisdictions allow employees to strike or employers to lock out employees after the expiration of the contract. These actions place tremendous strain on the employer and employees alike. The employer may not be able to continue producing products or services, and the employees lose their paychecks. Strikes and lockouts represent an open conflict, with the outcome usually determined by the side that can afford to suffer longer. Strikes receive a great deal of media attention but occur in relatively few negotiations, and their incidence is steadily declining over time. Of all the labor contracts negotiated in the United States in 1970, there were 381 strikes or lockouts. In 1993, there were 35 work stoppages. One of the reasons for the decreasing rate of strike activity is that mechanisms for impasse resolution have improved.

Management and labor use a number of methods to assist in the settlement of labor disputes that have reached impasse. In order of their level of assertiveness, these are mediation, fact finding, mediation-arbitration, conventional arbitration, and final offer arbitration.

In **mediation** a third-party such as an employee of the Federal Mediation and Conciliation Service or other neutral party assists the union and management negotiators in reaching an agreement. A mediator has no binding authority, but rather facilitates agreement by working between the two parties to keep communication channels open, carry proposals from one party to the other, suggest ideas, give each party a realistic or an outside view of the proposals, and generally keep the talks going by summarizing discussions and bringing proposals to a conclusion. Mediators are often skilled at interest-based negotiations, keeping interests in the forefront of discussions while encouraging the negotiating parties to postpone taking hardened positions.

Fact finding is more formal than mediation and can consist of one neutral third party or a panel of individuals, with one selected by the union, a second selected by management, and a third selected by the first two. As the name implies, fact finders use formal hearings, call witnesses, research pertinent documents, and often consult similar settlements from outside the organization to determine the facts relevant to negotiations. The fact finders then prepare a report that can make a recommendation for settlement. The report is not binding, but does place additional pressure on the negotiating parties to reach a settlement.

Arbitration is a much more formal process, and the settlement decided by the arbitrator is binding on both parties. The arbitrator is usually a professionally trained attorney, retired judge, or labor relations professor who holds formal hearings to hear the facts of the negotiation. The parties to the negotiation present their arguments to the arbitrator, who then prepares a written decision. In *conventional arbitration* the arbitrator uses the evidence and the positions presented during the hearings to craft whatever settlement is most fair in the judgment of the arbitrator. A different form of arbitration, called *final offer arbitration,* has fewer negative consequences than conventional arbitration. In final offer arbitration, the two parties to the negotiation present their final offers to the arbitrator, who then selects one offer or the other. Depending on the type of arbitration described in the particular labor laws, final offers may be in the form of an entire package, including all the outstanding issues in negotiations, or final offers by each separate issue, where the arbitrator selects the final offer issue by issue.

Mediation-arbitration, or med-arb, is a combination of these two forms of impasse resolution. A third party is called in to mediate negotiations for a limited time period. If settlement is not reached during that specified time, the mediator switches roles to an arbitrator and imposes a settlement for all remaining issues. Med-arb is a simplified version of impasse resolution, reducing the possible number of people involved and the time taken in settling the dispute. Participants view med-arb view more as arbitration and position themselves in much the same way as they would as if going before a formal arbitration hearing.

Arbitration has a number of advantages and a number of disadvantages. Like other forms of impasse resolution, arbitration is conducted by a neutral third party. The outside perspective is useful in calming emotions and getting to the facts in dispute. The primary goal of arbitration is to prevent labor conflict in the form of a strike by imposing a fair settlement. In situations where a strike may be illegal and endanger the public safety of citizens, arbitration gives the union an alternative, where its arguments can be given a fair hearing and they will not be entirely subject to the will of management. There is even an advantage for the employer, since arbitration can be the political safety valve for elected officials. Elected officials can say they were strong and took a hard-line approach during negotiations, but have to abide by the decision of the arbitrator.

The first problem with arbitration is the chilling effect it has on the conduct of normal negotiations. At times, negotiators bargain toward arbitration instead of toward settlement.[36] In other words, the parties position themselves to look good before an arbitrator instead of working together to reach an agreement. The second problem, related to the first, is that arbitration can become habit-forming; that is, management and union negotiators can lose their ability to work out solutions for themselves and instead always go to arbitration. It is also a natural tendency for arbitrators to find something for both sides of the conflict, and they will often split the differences between the two parties. This may have worked for the biblical Solomon, but it discourages meaningful bargaining since both sides know they should take a somewhat extreme position during negotiations. A settlement bringing both sides to the middle will be much higher if one side positions itself at an extremely high level going into arbitration. Finally, and particularly important for politically elected public officials, arbitration turns decision-making authority over to an unelected and practically unaccountable third party.

Arbitrators make decisions directly affecting public policy and public funds, but they are neither elected nor are they there to oversee the implementation of their decisions.

Final offer arbitration reduces some of the negative aspects of conventional arbitration. Negotiators must seriously bargain before the case goes to the arbitrator so their final offers will be most acceptable. Negotiators often reach a settlement when getting to their final offers, thereby promoting problem solving rather than deferring it. Arbitrators cannot split the difference between management and labor positions, and there are no incentives for taking extreme positions. Finally, the settlement comes from the final offers as determined by the negotiating parties, not a settlement imposed by a third party. At least one of these represents the elected government.

Step 9: Settlement As negotiations reach a conclusion, either by resolving the issues identified or as the expiration of the previous contract approaches, the teams must decide if a settlement is likely; if it is not, they must decide what their next steps should be. A third party, such as a mediator, fact finder, or arbitrator, may be required by the applicable legislation, or a mediator may be requested to assist the negotiating teams in reaching a settlement.

Step 10: Ratification Once the two negotiating teams have reached an agreement on the issues, the package must be presented to the members of the bargaining unit for ratification. A negotiated agreement is not permanent or legal until ratified by the union membership and the governing body of the public jurisdiction.

After the key elements of the agreement are voted on and approved by the governing bodies of both the union and employer, they must be incorporated into a new contract. The process of preparing language for inclusion in the contract can be almost as painstaking as the actual negotiation. Typically the specific implementation language for each issue is negotiated during the bargaining process, but there is often a need to change language in other parts of the contract that were influenced by changes made as a result of negotiations.

The lead negotiators and their legal representatives meet to finalize the contract language before it goes for final approval. In state and local governments, the agreement and subsequent contract must be passed by legislative action by the elected legislative body. Contracts are usually ratified because the leadership of the union and the public agency's negotiating team typically argue in favor of ratification because they have negotiated the best agreement they feel they were able to reach. When the agreement is not approved by the members of the governing body, the negotiating teams must reconvene to find a new solution to the issues still in contention.

Step 11: Contract management Collective bargaining is usually an open and helpful exchange between management and labor. Unfortunately, it can become acrimonious and leave deep emotional scars on the parties involved. It is helpful to maintain a good relationship throughout negotiations for two important reasons: the interested parties will come together again when the new contract expires, and they must meet together often to clarify contract language and resolve contract disputes that arise during the term of the contract.

As soon as the new contract is ratified and formal negotiations have ended, the process of contract management begins. Throughout the life of the contract, issues arise that are either not covered in the contract or the contract is not specific enough to resolve clearly. In these cases, informal discussions between management and labor can resolve the majority of questions. Some questions must be left for resolution at the bargaining table when the contract expires, and some interpretations of contract language or disputes about performance under the contract must be resolved through a quasi-legal process called the **grievance procedure.**

The grievance procedure is a process incorporated into most contracts to resolve disputes arising from the interpretation of the contract or a claim that the rights of an employee under the contract have been violated. There are usually three or four steps in the grievance procedure, beginning with the immediate supervisor and ending with the chief executive or a neutral arbitrator. The objective of the grievance procedure is to resolve the dispute at the lowest possible level before involving upper management or resolution through a third-party arbitrator. The vast majority of grievances are settled before going to the final steps of the process.

The first step in the grievance procedure in most contracts is for an employee to take a complaint to the immediate supervisor. This is usually done informally, with the employee, possibly accompanied by a union representative, and the supervisor meeting to discuss the problem. According to the grievance procedure, the supervisor has a limited amount of time to respond to the issue. If the response is unsatisfactory to the employee, the grievance may be handled directly by the union and is put in writing and submitted to the next level of management for resolution. This level may be a division or department manager or an individual in human resource management. Within the specified period of time, the manager must submit a response to the grievance. If the response is unsatisfactory, the grievance can be appealed to the next level, usually to upper management or the chief executive. In some cases, the response of the chief executive is the final step in the procedure. Many contracts, however, allow for binding arbitration as the final step in the grievance procedure.

In most cases where grievance arbitration is allowed, the contract specifies how the arbitrator will be selected. The Federal Mediation and Conciliation Service or the American Arbitration Association can provide a list of qualified arbitrators and their work histories for selection by the union and management. Usually both parties share the cost of the arbitrator.

BARGAINING STYLE

Over the course of time, the conflict of interests between management and employees has produced an adversarial relationship and has resulted in the development of a contentious bargaining style that has become almost synonymous with labor relations. With the increase in worldwide competition in the private sector and the advent of significant pressure to economize and privatize in the public sector, the designated representatives of both management and labor have found it in their interest to work together to improve their competitive position. The increasing realization of common interests in many governmental jurisdictions has encouraged the development of a cooperative bargaining style, particularly when both sides can see the advantages of working together to improve the conditions of both management and labor.

Distributive (Adversarial) Bargaining Style

The inherent conflict between labor and management has bred a **distributive (adversarial) bargaining** style sometimes similar to haggling at a street bazaar, at other times akin to courtroom theatrics, and at yet other times more like open warfare. The reason for the open animosity and lack of trust in many labor-management relationships is the perspective of the parties that bargaining is a zero-sum game; for employees to receive more money in their paychecks, employers must give up some of their income or assets. Many of the strategies and tactics of collective bargaining, as described in Box 5.2, are designed within the conventional winner-loser distributive framework.

Some economists and other social scientists have used the analytical ideas employed in game theory to explain the strategies most commonly used in collective bargaining. Game theory is used to understand how people make decisions when their strategy is contingent on the decisions or actions of other people. One of the classic "games" used in game theory is the **Prisoner's**

Box 5.2   Tactics for Competitive Negotiations

- Press and push (subtly) attitude—continually asking for a decision
- Obscuring–Br'er Rabbit—pretending an important issue is of no importance or vice versa
- Taking unilateral action
- Setting strict limits; stating only the bottom line
- Boulwareism—making one "best" offer, then refusing to negotiate
- Good cop/bad cop—a quick settlement with friendly negotiator and avoiding dealing with difficult negotiator
- Set-up and silence—waiting for the opposite side to make a move or give a concession
- Argument
- Strong positioning
- Belly-up—pretending they are powerless and the decision is out of their hands
- Threats

- Maximum plausible position
- Never saying yes to first offer
- Flinch, shock, surprise
- Reluctant buyer/seller
- Vice—you'll have to do better than that
- Don't split the difference
- Cool and aloof attitude
- Patience—set pace, control deal
- Delay—defense against pressure
- Apathy
- Walking out
- Nibbling—asking for a new item to close the deal
- Limited authority
- Passive-aggressive
- Auction—throwing out several alternatives in rapid succession

---

Source: Adapted from Roy J. Lewicki, David M. Saunders, and John W. Minton, *Negotiation,* 3rd ed. (New York: McGraw-Hill, 1999), sec. 3.

Dilemma. This situation describes how two individuals make separate, logical decisions that make both worse off than if they were to make the decision without consideration of the other's action. It describes how collective bargaining often works as each side considers the motives and decisions of the other side.

Ethics and Negotiation Tactics

The Prisoner's Dilemma originated with Albert Tucker, who described the problem facing two prisoners who must decide whether to confess to a crime or remain silent. In the Prisoner's Dilemma, each prisoner is placed in a separate room and given a choice. If Capone confesses and Dillinger remains silent, the charges against Capone will be dropped and Dillinger will do hard time. If Capone remains silent and Dillinger confesses,

Capone will go to jail. If both Capone and Dillinger confess, the prosecutor will go easy on both. If both remain silent, the prosecutor can get convictions only on minor charges. The matrix in Figure 5.2 sets out the dilemma.

This game captures a problem of self-interest versus cooperation. If Capone and Dillinger cooperate by both staying silent, both win, but they must trust that the other will not confess. If one sings, he hurts the other, but is better off still, but must believe the other will keep quiet.

The Prisoner's Dilemma is an ethical problem as well and is frequently found in labor negotiations. For example, the union negotiators may personally be better off by agreeing to a two-tiered wage increase (with senior employees given a larger wage increase than new hires), but the union might suffer overall. This "game" is frequently demonstrated using successive rounds

Figure 5.2   Prisoner's Dilemma Matrix

	Capone Confesses	**Capone Remains Silent**
Dillinger Confesses	Both go to jail.	Capone does hard time. Dillinger goes free.
Dillinger Remains Silent	Dillinger does hard time. Capone goes free.	Both get off with minor charges.

where each side must decide to cooperate or compete. The outcome is calculated so cooperation is rewarded and competition punished, but if one side strategically chooses to compete on any round when the other is cooperating, they can get more points. Both will receive less-than-optimal points, however, if neither cooperate.

The newest practice in labor relations negotiations is based on the development of capacity for cooperation and trust. Management and union negotiators are instructed to bargain over interests as opposed to positions. At every step of negotiations, cooperation builds and each side opens its range of needs to the other to reach mutually beneficial agreements, or win-win solutions. There are times when it might be more beneficial for one side to "defect" or intentionally harm the other side, so trust frequently can be fragile. Either side stands ready to revert to traditional, adversarial bargaining if they sense that the other side can no longer be trusted.

Power in Negotiations

Another theory of bargaining is based on the relative power of each party to the negotiation. In the context of bargaining, power can be understood as the ability to withstand the costs involved in negotiations.[37] Costs may be inflicted on one side by the other, or costs may be incurred by one side as a result of the decisions they make. The typical economic costs to management are job actions by union members such as a strike, work slowdown, or boycott. In the public sector, several of the traditional economic costs found in private sector

settings do not exist, but there are political costs to consider such as adverse media reporting, loss of support in public opinion, loss of votes in the next election, or diminished public services or increased taxes if union demands are met. The union representatives also face costs, including lost or delayed wages, a possible loss of jobs due to layoffs, and the dissatisfaction of members resulting in loss of membership or the possibility of losing the next union leadership election.

Power in bargaining is also realized when one party has more options to bargaining than does the other side.[38] Some of these options for public employee unions include lobbying public decision makers at all levels of government where public labor relations policy is made. Unions are also heavily involved in election campaigns, raising campaign funds and mobilizing members to work in political campaigns and get-out-the vote efforts. Unions and management may see some dispute resolution mechanisms as alternatives to bargaining. When the issues of negotiation will eventually go to an arbitrator for a decision on their merits, bargaining may be reduced to formalities while the real attempt at settlement is delayed until the arbitration.

Integrative (Cooperative) Bargaining Style

There is an emerging trend in labor relations to bargain in a less confrontational style, under conditions where both sides seek to understand each other's genuine interests and needs and cooperate in finding acceptable solutions to these interests.

Box 5.3   Tactics for Collaborative Negotiations

- Simple and direct attitude
- Identify issues/interests
- Compromise/concession
- Third-party participation
- Empathy
- Initiative
- Question assumptions
- Cooperate
- Integrate interests
- Inquiry: Why? What do you think about. . . ?
- Brainstorm; be flexible on ideas, firm on principles
- Joint problem solving

- Trial balloons
- Share information
- Propose drafts
- Effective listening
- Observe nonverbal communication
- Ensure mutual understanding of goals, interests, and solutions
- Justification
- Deadlines
- Separate the people from problem
- Focus on interests not positions
- Invent options for mutual gain
- Insist on objective criteria

Source: Adapted from Lewicki, Saunders, and Minton, *Negotiation,* sec. 4.

In reality, negotiations have always used problem solving as part the bargaining process when it has been in the interest of both parties to work together. The process of this style of bargaining, referred to as **integrative (cooperative) bargaining,** has been popularized by Fisher, Ury, and Patton in their book, *Getting to Yes* and subsequent books.[39] The basic ideas are to:

1. Separate the people from the problem.
2. Focus on interests, not positions.
3. Invent options for mutual gain.
4. Insist on using objective criteria.[40]

Although integrative bargaining has helped negotiations become more congenial in some cases, it does not provide answers to all bargaining situations. In areas where mutual gain is a possibility and the interests of both sides can be served, "principled" or "interest-based" bargaining has been used successfully. When the interests of the bargaining parties are diametrically opposed, negotiations often revert to traditional, adversarial bargaining.

INTRODUCTION TO READING

The following reading is the executive summary from a report by the Task Force on Excellence in State and Local Government Through Labor-Management Cooperation of the Department of Labor entitled *Working Together for the Public Service.* The selection describes the need for better labor-management cooperation, citing its advantages over adversarial relations, and recommends some concrete steps that contribute toward implementing cooperative relations. In consideration of the changing demands on governments for improved services, the report claims that "traditional methods of service delivery, traditional personnel and administrative systems, traditional styles of supervision and workplace communication, and *traditional approaches to collective bargaining* will not be sufficient" (italics added). Quoting from the reading, the task force found that labor-management cooperation which engaged employees in decisions around service planning and implementation typically resulted in "improved labor-management relations, less conflict, faster conflict resolution, more flexible contracts, and emphasis on mutual responsibilities for service improvement."

Labor-management cooperation may be the only way to survive in our increasingly dynamic and demanding world, but is it not rather naive to think that cooperation will replace adversarialism? One of the problems with labor-management cooperation is the successful transference of cooperation to the negotiating table. It seems that cooperation through interest-based bargaining works fairly well when discussing policy or procedural issues. When the questions turn to economic matters, where it is more difficult to find a win-win solution, the negotiation tends to revert to distributive or competitive bargaining. A serious question to ask is whether cooperation means ultimate capitulation by one side of the negotiations or the other. Some midlevel managers and some union leaders believe they are the ones who will lose when labor relations turn to win-win solutions arrived at by union leaders and government negotiators.

As you read the following selection, keep the following questions in mind:

- Is it naive to think that cooperation between labor and management will replace adversarialism?
- Does cooperation ultimately mean capitulation by one side of the negotiations in order to reach agreement?
- Are distributive or adversarial labor negotiations unproductive? Should they be replaced by cooperative negotiations?
- Are there real (tangible) advantages to integrative (cooperative) labor management relations?

▓▓▓▓ READING

Working Together for Public Service: Executive Summary

The economic success of our nation and the social well-being of its citizens depend, in large measure, on the essential services and infrastructure provided by state and local governments. We rely upon those employed within the public sector to teach our children, to protect us from crime and fire, to maintain roads, bridges and sanitation systems, to provide necessary social services, and to safeguard the environment.

"In this era of reinventing government, our nation's citizens need and deserve high-quality, cost-effective state and local government services," observed US Secretary of Labor Robert B. Reich when he formed this Task Force to examine labor-

Source: U.S. Secretary of Labor's Task Force on Excellence in State and Local Government Through Labor-Management Cooperation, *Working Together for Public Service* (Washington, D.C.: U.S. Department of Labor, 1996).

management cooperation in state and local governments. "Further, the imperative to compete in an increasingly worldwide economy and to respond to increasing societal demands requires that governments at all levels perform in a timely and cost-effective manner.

"I am relying on this Task Force to chart a clear path toward that goal through labor-management cooperation."

To this end, the Task Force's research included five regional visits across the United States, seven Washington, D.C. hearings and approximately 55 detailed responses to a Task Force survey. During the regional visits, the Task Force carefully examined and analyzed nearly 50 examples of cooperative approaches to labor-management relationships that were instrumental in creating service-oriented environments. The examples came from state, county and city governments, schools, transit and other special services. First-hand observations were further supported by reports of other impressive service improvements from jurisdictions the Task Force was unable to visit.

KEY FINDINGS

The findings in this report are the unanimous conclusions of a 14 member Task Force on Excellence in State and Local Government through Labor-Management Cooperation, whose members were drawn from the ranks of labor, management, elected officials, neutrals and academics.

The findings include the following:

- To meet their obligations, state and local governments must transform the way services are planned and delivered, the way the public workplace is managed and how public worker knowledge is engaged in the process.
- In most places, the public workplace of the future will have to be different than it is today in order to meet the challenges it will face. Traditional methods of service delivery, traditional personnel and administrative systems, traditional styles of supervision and workplace communication, and traditional approaches to collective bargaining will not be sufficient.
- In order to meet these challenges, many state and local governments have begun to move away from traditional ways of doing business. Like many successful private sector companies, they are depending upon the participation of employees. When successful, this strategy leads to continuous improvement, not merely one-time changes.
- Service improvement through workplace cooperation requires that the confrontational rhetoric be lowered and that elected officials, union leaders and workers focus on their common tasks. To do so, they will need new tools. Those tools are in use in many places now.
- A focus on service with employee participation can also be a doorway to reducing confrontation in collective bargaining relationships that have had a history of conflict.
- The possibilities appear to be greater than recognized for labor-management cooperation in the public sector to contribute to service improvement and provide avenues for employee

participation, and perhaps greater than in the private sector.
- Looking across the dozens of examples that it examined, the Task Force found that labor-management cooperation which engaged employees in decisions around service planning and implementation typically resulted in:
  - *Better Service.* Services frequently became faster; often new or expanded services were offered, and all were more responsive to citizens.
  - *More Cost-Effectiveness.* Money was saved and money better spent.
  - *Better Quality of Work Life.* Employees experienced far more involvement and greater opportunities to contribute, learn skills. They gained greater job security and found increased respect.
  - *Improved Labor-Management Relations.* Less conflict, faster conflict resolution, more flexible contracts, and emphasis on mutual responsibilities for service improvement.

CHALLENGE TO LABOR AND MANAGEMENT

In view of these and other findings summarized below and the need for transformation in the way public services are delivered, the Task Force challenges labor and management leaders, both locally and nationally, to follow the lead of the examples in this report, to break some molds, forge new ground and seek a new approach.

SOME QUICK EXAMPLES

Here is a sample of what was observed

- A labor-management committee in Connecticut's Department of Mental Retardation with District 1199/New England Health Care Employees Union (SEIU) tackled the issue of how to improve employee safety. In one year, the committee's recommendations produced a 40 percent reduction in injuries and a 23 percent reduction—or nearly $5 million—in what had been an annual $25 million workers' compensation expenditure.
- In Peoria, Illinois, health care was becoming a yearly budget-buster. Costs were climbing annually at 9 percent to 14 percent, while total city revenues were going down. With cooper-

ation of all city unions, Peoria took health care off the bargaining table in 1993 and placed it in its own Joint Labor-Management Committee to Control Health Care Costs. The result was 1994 health care costs of $1.2 million less than the expected $6 million. In sharp contrast to past experience, when virtually every health care decision was fought over and bitterly arbitrated, no health care decisions have been arbitrated since the plan was implemented.

- In Madison, Wisconsin, as part of a city-wide quality initiative, labor-management cooperation dramatically improved a contentious relationship between city building inspectors, represented by AFSCME Local 60, and private electrical contractors. Management, employees and their union worked together with contractors to develop a compliance effort that emphasizes education instead of punishment. It led to a program that now enhances electrical safety, conserves resources, focuses inspection efforts on safety outcomes instead of inspection processes, and improves customer relations. Inspectors happily report they now receive compliments instead of complaints.

- Spurred by a severe, city-wide budget crunch, the Los Angeles Bureau of Standards formed a joint labor-management committee with SEIU Local 47 in 1994 with the twin goals of trimming costs and improving service delivery. Thanks to the work of this committee, the Bureau increased truck availability from 75 percent to 94 percent, largely by improving cooperation between drivers and mechanics and their respective departments; and reduced overtime by 54 percent due to increased truck availability. Over the ensuing three years, it expects a 25 percent departmental cost reduction without lay-offs.

- At the Foshay School in south-central Los Angeles, scholastic records were among the lowest in the state before the new principal and the leadership of United Teachers of Los Angeles introduced a Leadership Council, which brings together administrators, teachers, parents and community members to work together to improve the education of the largely minority student body. Student drop-outs have fallen from 21 percent of the student body to 3.5 percent; suspensions have dropped from 400 cases to 40, and student scores on a comprehensive test of basic skills in math, reading and language have improved to near the state average.

- In Phoenix, Arizona, a new fire chief and new president of Firefighters Local 493 took office in 1978. They decided it was time to work together and end nearly 40 years of contentious and adversarial relations. They initiated annual planning retreats during which labor and management jointly develop annual plans for addressing problems and seeking improvement. Arbitration has not been used in Phoenix for 10 years.

Similar stories sprinkled through this report are found in activities that cover a spectrum of services, in jurisdictions large and small, and in all regions of the country. They tell of improvements that citizens, workers, managers, elected officials and union leaders everywhere would be happy to see occur within their own communities.

The experiences of these jurisdictions and programs provide compelling evidence that engaging employees in workplace decision-making—a model with parallels to similar efforts in the private sector—can be a powerful tool to achieve tangible improvements in service, cost savings, quality of work life and labor-management relations.

These examples, and several others in richer texture, make up Chapter One, "Typical Results." Six examples, called "Snapshots," are presented in considerable detail following each chapter, and dozens of others are used to illuminate the principles in Chapter Four. (The Appendix includes a full listing of examples visited and submitted.)

PRESSURES AND CHALLENGES TO CHANGE

Chapter Two, reviewing pressures on state and local government, and Chapter Three, on trends that define and affect state and local government employment, describe some of the important forces that compel or offer opportunities for change:

- More pressure to take up tasks formerly or currently done by the Federal government
- Increasing challenges as communities grow more complex and more diverse, as environmental pressures grow and as technology

changes the way people live, work and communicate

- Growing awareness of and demand for quality services
- Financial pressures requiring more cost effectiveness, better ways of delivering service
- Growing awareness of the need to handle pension funds responsibly
- Decades of using procedures for budgeting, personnel, and labor relations which don't easily permit a focus on service delivery, stemming from traditions and practices developed in a different era
- Trend towards joining unions, reflecting partially a desire to better bring problems and ideas to the attention of employers
- A highly educated public workforce, which shows a strong interest in participating in workplace decisions
- A desire among workers for more cooperative ways of dealing with employers
- Pressures to perform better, forcing labor and management to examine relationships that have traditionally been conflictual
- Public employee unions active nationally and locally, that support workplace innovation and service improvement
- Generally, a less adversarial labor-management climate than in the private sector
- Despite rhetoric to the contrary, willingness among many elected officials and managers to work with the workforce and with union leaders
- A growing realization that labor and management are in the same boat. They must work together and contribute their respective influence, knowledge and skills to improve public service
- Increased interest in contracting out as an alternative for cost reduction or service improvement has created a variety of pressures and responses, many of which vary from common perceptions on the subject. (See Chapters Two and Three for discussions of issues and trends in contracting out.)

Overall, there is a confluence of pressures, interests and opportunities for change in the way public services are delivered, and the opportunity to use participative workplace principles, particularly labor-management cooperation, as a primary means to do so.

HOW TO IMPLEMENT BROADER USE OF WORKPLACE PARTNERSHIPS THAT IMPROVE SERVICE

Chapters Four ("Nuts and Bolts") and Five ("Everyone Has a Role to Play") describe barriers and ingredients to developing workplace partnerships.

Typical Barriers to Establishing Workplace Partnerships

- Mistrust, often arising from a history of difficult workplace relationships, recent campaigns, impasses, or other conflicts
- Lack of skills for carrying on participative relationships. Parties otherwise fall back on skills common to hierarchical management or traditional labor-management relationships
- Failure to recognize that the partnership program must be developed in concert with all affected parties. It rarely works if it is only the idea of one group
- Continued reliance on formal aspects of personnel/labor relations, such as refusal to try new approaches, or reluctance to discuss issues necessary to service improvement
- Fear of job loss makes employees and some managers reluctant to join in problem-solving
- Union leaders, unwilling to support the effort if a participative program ignores their role and is seen as an attempt to bust the union
- Mid-level managers or union officials who may feel their traditional roles or status threatened by the team-oriented and participative arrangements

How to Begin

- *Start Small.* Typically, the effort starts small, in one part of the jurisdiction or agency, takes time to develop, take root, and spread. Some begin with a broader scale attempt to alter the work culture. Most start with one of the following:
  - A service improvement project—usually one that has posed challenges
  - Desire to reduce conflict, usually grievances
  - Desire to improve a difficult collective bargaining relationship

- *It's a Circle.* Whether the participative effort begins with a service project, or any of the others, the same skills, people and relationships are involved. These factors, and the trust that builds, can transfer from one area or project to another.
- *Where You Start Depends on Where You Begin.* Every place has its own history and possibilities. Therefore, the choice of where to begin must be a local decision by the parties.
- *Leadership Commitment.* Success requires leadership commitment, on both sides, to start and overcome mistrust, to keep people focused in the early going, overcome early barriers and resistance, and put the effort and relationship on track after inevitable mistakes.
- *Break with Past Habits.* It is too easy to revert to old habits and ways of doing business. To move into these new ways of planning and delivering services, there must be no more business as usual.
  - *Training.* Usually, there was some degree of training to help the parties get started. When training is connected to beginning and sustaining new ways of managing and of involving workers, it's likely to be a good investment. The most effective and accepted training is jointly developed and sponsored. Necessary are development of new skills:
    - in conflict resolution and group problem solving
    - in order to perform jobs in new ways
    - for analyzing and changing work processes
  - *Neutral Assistance.* Most new relationships had the benefit of a skilled neutral to assist and often to train the parties.
  - *Conflict Resolution.* Ensure that efforts and mechanisms to resolve conflicts are in place. Unnecessary conflict can breed mistrust that interferes with cooperation and participation. Make use of alternative dispute resolution practices that fit the issues.
- *Employment Security.* It may seem counter intuitive, but although layoffs are often a favorite method of seeking cost savings, examples show the opposite to hold more promise:
  - Job "safety net" programs, including in some instances no-layoff guarantees, were common practice in workplaces that have achieved significant cost savings and service improvements.
  - This doesn't mean there are no layoffs, but when there are, it is done under a plan that shows commitment to employee welfare.
  - The security assurances allow employees to focus on innovation without undue fear of job loss. They also allow union leaders to focus on service improvement rather than spending time seeking ways to save jobs one at a time.
- *Respecting the Role of the Union.* Similarly, when the legitimacy and role of the union is not challenged, union leaders can focus their efforts on service improvement. Mutual respect of labor and management leadership is critical to success.
- *Flexibility on Both Sides.* A willingness to try new approaches as well as new processes for decision-making are necessities for finding innovative service solutions.
- *Increased Cohesion Within Each Side.*
  - Legislative and executive branches, and the various management functions, must be in sufficient harmony; otherwise one or the other of the factions can upset the relationship by acting in the old ways or being otherwise unaware.
  - By the same token, unions involved normally form a coalition. Among other things, such coalitions facilitate resolution of jurisdictional problems interfering with service.
- *Changed Roles for Labor and Management in Collective Bargaining Relationships.*
  - In successful cooperative arrangements, management operates in less hierarchical ways and agrees, through joint and team structures established, to share decision-making authority where it has not traditionally done so.
  - The counterpart phenomenon is that union leaders share power in a responsible fashion while still vigorously defending worker interests. Normally there is less necessity to defend in the old ways, since many problems are resolved through joint problem-solving over service issues before they become contentious.
  - In these successful ventures, union leaders often take on, and execute well, significant

responsibility for service delivery improvement and cost control.

- *Success Can Come from Even the Poorest of Histories.* Some of the most impressive successes come from relationships that had been extremely contentious.

Spreading and Sustaining Successful Cooperative Relationships

- *Spreading the Innovation and Expanding the Participation.* Even successful experiments struggle with how to spread the use of a successful cooperative effort to another service or department. It is important that the same leaders have influence in the new area, and that there are leadership and training resources applied to the germination. Also, the new effort must come to be owned by those newly involved, which implies that they have a role in forming it.

- *Leadership Turnover.* Perhaps the largest challenge is sustaining useful changes in the face of the common phenomenon of leadership turnover. Unlike many private sector leadership changes, in public life, there seems to be a more common penchant for declaring "ineffective" everything that came before. Campaigns are often run and won this way. Particularly with the frequent occurrence of blaming problems on public employees, a return to confrontation is often a danger in a period of turnover. A number of methods seem to contribute to sustaining the grains of a cooperative relationship following a transition— some formal, some informal:
  - Among the more formal is the presence in a labor contract of the main features of the system, including a joint committee, training and other features.
  - Less formal is the involvement of a broad sample of front line workers committed to the system.
  - In non-bargaining situations, a major factor seems to be the tenure of a long serving chief executive committed to employee involvement.

- *Improvements in Administrative Systems.* Improvements that make administrative systems more responsive to service needs accompany most of the successful examples. Front line workers and union leaders have demonstrated they have a lot to contribute in identifying system blockages and proposing practical reform:
  - Personnel systems were changed to allow more responsiveness to service.
    - classification systems were revised to have fewer titles, some reduced by more than 50 percent, and ranges broadened to allow more flexible deployment in the face of changed service delivery methods and efficiencies
    - advent of gainsharing
    - much greater use of team, rather than individual, recognition
    - improved accountability and coaching for workers
    - more use of peer evaluation and scrutiny to ensure everyone is carrying his or her share of the load
    - better management development and selection to improve accountability and management style in a non-hierarchical setting
  - Changes in accounting, budgeting, and purchasing practices to better measure and support service improvement.
  - Improved cost and quality measures, to allow examination of inputs to services, and make more accurate comparisons with privately offered services
  - Simpler procurement and other internal systems

Many of these systems have for years been targets of generalized reform. Examples from this effort suggest reform may come more easily and have more community and political support if the change is more targeted, and explicitly related to service and cost improvement. Labor and management often go together to the appropriate authorities to seek changes that, in past years, they might have fought over.

- *Service-Oriented Relationships and Collective Bargaining Structures.* Employees have shown a strong interest in, and ability to contribute to, workplace decisions affecting service quality if the requisite structure is in place for them to do so. In specific ways outlined in the report, the Task Force found that the structure and roles in a formal labor-management relationship, when carried out using cooperative principles, are extremely supportive of quality improvement efforts and outcomes in public services.

Public employees have shown in the large majority of the instances where they have the opportunity, an interest in being collectively represented. There is reluctance among managers and elected officials in many places to afford employees the right of representation by unions. Unfortunately, not all labor-management relationships are productive and some are overly conflictual.

However, the application of a cooperative, service-focused model of labor-management relationships, as the Task Force has seen, is capable of producing superior service results and cost effectiveness as key products of the relationship. Although adversarial aspects of the workplace relationship necessarily remain, a far different climate and result pertain when the relationship is based on cooperative and service-oriented principles.

Task Force members support the right of individuals to choose whether or not they wish to have collective representation. Where public employees choose to be represented, their collective bargaining rights should be exercised in a framework where: the focus is on service delivery; conflicts can be effectively resolved; and where the relationship, structure and roles are defined and developed to support service improvement, effective workplace participation and partnerships, and constructive conflict resolution.

Jurisdictions contemplating the establishment of collective bargaining relationships should develop their laws with these cooperative, service-oriented principles in mind. In doing so, the laws should be drawn in a way that the parties can realistically address service problems. On the other hand, in making these arrangements, care should be taken not to unduly interfere with the overall mission of an agency or program and the responsibilities of public officials.

Where an established bargaining relationship has been conflictual, the parties should move towards the cooperative model. The possibility of doing so—even out of historically difficult relationships—has been clearly demonstrated in the work of the Task Force. This report contains guidance on how to begin or how to transform labor-management relationships into mutually productive vehicles for quality service and more satisfying work.

Whether or not employees are collectively represented, the examples in bargaining and non-bargaining settings examined by the Task Force make it clear that employees, managers, elected officials and citizens benefit from employee participation and involvement in determining how best to provide public services.

Organizational Structures That Support Participation

- *Flatter Organizations.* Rather than rely on hierarchy, common organizational changes in successful service partnerships include fewer supervisory layers and the use of teams. These often cross departmental lines and include a greater proportion of employees in line service positions. Teams make, or continue to make, key decisions that were previously the preserve of a supervisor. Often heard were phrases like "None of us is smarter than all of us."
- *Joint Labor-Management Committees.* Perhaps the most common organizational and communications device in successful partnerships is the establishment of a top level labor management committee, usually in a department, but sometimes in the overall jurisdiction. This group typically sets the agenda and the pace for partnership initiatives, and has representation from union leadership and program management. Personnel and labor professionals are most productive in this setting when their role becomes facilitative rather than advocacy; a role transformation, and one they report as very satisfying. Such a committee meets regularly and identifies agreed upon areas for activity and then engages appropriate talent and resources in specific projects.
- *Project Teams.* Typically, project teams are formed, often receiving their mandate from the joint committee. Project teams, or teams for an ongoing activity, are one of the primary engines in workplace participation. They bring together workers and managers from different parts and levels of the organization to resolve problems and make improvements.

- *Team and Committee Selection.* Even in non-bargaining states where the Task Force saw examples, employees involved, not chosen by their peers, found that their standing and capacity to act within the committees or teams would have been enhanced if they had been chosen by their co-workers rather than by management. Thus, in either case, it is important for effective labor-management cooperation that employee representatives be selected by their co-workers. When employees have an opportunity to choose representatives to reflect their own viewpoints and represent their interests on joint labor-management committees and project teams, the results of participative committees and similar activities have a greater likelihood of being trusted, accepted and implemented by the rank and file.
- *Meetings are better.* Without the need to observe hierarchy, with new skills for group problem solving and a mandate to solve problems, be flexible, and try new things, there is greatly improved communication, participation and problem-solving efficiency in workplace meetings.

CHANGES IN LABOR-MANAGEMENT RELATIONS

In addition to what has already been discussed, important improvements in collective bargaining relationships accompany service-oriented workplace partnerships:

- Greater mutual focus on service delivery within and around the bargaining relationship
- Reduction in conflict; reduced reliance on legalistic, formal means of resolution; many fewer formal grievances
- Faster contract settlements, sometimes in weeks; reduction in resort to arbitration
- Predominance of "win-win" and "collaborative bargaining" rather than traditional bargaining, but parties are still effective advocates for their constituency's interests
- Contract preambles describing mutual service responsibilities and mutual respect
- More flexible contracts, allowing easier adjustments to service needs
- More focus in contracts on how problems will be resolved

- Labor relations professionals on both sides to concentrate on the service impact of the relationship
- More candid mutual acknowledgment of electoral and constituency issues faced by both management and labor leaders
- Parties willing and able to discuss all issues affecting service delivery without invoking formal constraints and fear of precedent

INSTITUTIONAL SUPPORT

Successful parties are not alone. New skills are necessary, and so is peer support. It's difficult for a labor or management leader to step out and take the risks inherent in breaking with the past. (Chapter Five discusses some of these support needs, and efforts already underway.)

- *Labor Organizations.* National and international unions are increasingly active in support of these workplace innovations.
  - Many have already invested in activities to develop local leadership abilities to participate in cooperative workplace partnerships. Support of national and regional leaders and institutions provide peer support as does training and consulting resources made available by national organizations.
  - Also, service to individual members concerning their own professional development is growing, as for example in education, in which there are major national initiatives.
  - Many of these service activities and the support of union leadership would be surprising to some observers, yet they support what surveys cited in Chapter Two describe as employee interest in participation and adding to the quality of the service.
- *Management Institutions.* Management organizations that help elected and appointed officials get acclimated to new roles are in a pivotal position to help them gain immediate perspective on how to engage in the more complex, but ultimately productive, dialogue with the workforce and its representatives; to show newly elected officials and their key advisers this positive tool for resolving service and cost issues for which they are accountable and jointly responsible.

- *Finance and Personnel Professionals.* National organizations supporting finance, personnel and other key professions can assist and are already pursuing system changes that will better support services, and can develop more service-oriented principles to guide administrative systems.
- *Universities and Training Centers.* These institutions can also expand their efforts and offerings to support labor and management leadership development that displays these more effective approaches. For almost everyone involved in workplace relationships and public service systems, new roles and approaches are necessary and the places where individuals receive their professional training, information and guidance will have to adapt to the needs of the public sector workplace.
- *Neutral Agencies.* Also helpful are many neutral agencies, none more than the Federal Mediation and Conciliation Service, with its technical assistance to parties, and particularly well-regarded workplace cooperation grants and conferences program supporting cooperative labor-management relationships. Many of the state public employment relations boards have begun, and others are beginning, to expand their preventative training and technical assistance activities.

Without the support of national labor and management organizations, and other institutions affecting the process, the local parties will not have the resources, the knowledge or the backing to make the necessary changes.

FOOD FOR THOUGHT

A number of issues require further observation in order to assist the success of participation and cooperative labor-management relations in promoting service delivery improvement. (A number of these, although by no means a comprehensive list, are presented in Chapter Six.) For example:

- Determining how to spread the new approaches from one project to broader application
- Assessing and gaining leadership commitment and involvement
- Connecting quality efforts and collective bargaining

- Developing better cost and quality measures
- Identifying the most important skills for effective worker and management participation
- Identifying resistance of mid-level supervisors and union officials
- Examining effects of unit composition and scope of bargaining
- Defining changed roles of key players in the process
- Studying impacts and efficacy of contracting out
- Assessing use of ADR [alternative dispute resolution] for resolving disputes over workplace rights

Without question, the challenges facing state and local government can get an important assist from the application of significant employee participation and cooperative labor-management relationships. Large scale service improvement, major cost savings, more loyal, creative and satisfied employees, and better labor-management relations are the result. Elected officials and managers, as the following examples show, are as gratified by the results as are employees and union leaders. Many elected officials, who were skeptical of public workers' ability to meet service and cost goals, later became convinced of the value of the participative approach and of doing so within a labor-management partnership. In some instances where contracting out was the preferred strategy during an election campaign, cooperation became the dominant strategy after some experience with both.

While the practice of contracting out takes place in some jurisdictions as part of an overall service-improvement strategy, the degree and simplicity of contracting out does not appear to be as substantial or on the rise to the extent portrayed in popular discussion. Within a cooperative workplace partnership, for most core services, reforms that emerge from employee participation usually produce equal or better quality and cost results than contracting out.

There are identifiable ingredients to begin and support cooperative, service oriented workplace relationships. Some are directly part of the workplace relationship, others involve other systems and institutions that affect service delivery. Almost all can be affected through a labor-management partnership.

The Task Force, composed of elected officials, managers, neutrals, academics and labor leaders, is unanimous in its view that this cooperative and participative approach represents a significant opportunity to respond to the pressures and demands on public officials and public workers. It can help turn confrontative labor-management relations into a productive interaction that enhances service improvement and cost consciousness and is representative of the way in which the public workplace must be transformed to respond to the forces that are already upon us.

Not every jurisdiction or workplace can do this. Some histories are too bitter; some leaders lack the ability. But many more than are currently engaged can do so, given the knowledge, resources and peer support becoming available. The Task Force urges them to try. Many painful histories have been plowed under as a result of successful cooperation.

The Task Force has had an opportunity through its regional visits and hearings to get a glimpse at the future of the state and local government workplace. Elected officials, administrative professionals, managers, union leaders and the organizations that support each of them, and which prepare them for and chronicle their interactions, all have an obligation to each other and to citizens to take up the unanimous challenge of this Task Force: to break the traditional habits of hierarchy, bureaucracy, confrontation, and over-reliance on formalities, and begin now—even while protecting their capacity to exercise their responsibilities—to develop the cooperative and participative patterns in the public workplace and in labor-management relations that support innovation and mutual focus on excellence in public service.

■ CONCLUSION

Labor-management relations in the public sector have evolved considerably over the past few decades. For most of the history of this nation, unions were considered a devious conspiracy of workers who posed a threat to sovereign government. Since public employees were paid from tax dollars and worked for the general public, holding a government job was considered a privilege. The threat of a strike by public employees was almost considered treasonous, since the employer, in essence, was the general public. Some of this reasoning regarding public unions was probably related to the practice of political patronage, whereby public employees often obtained their jobs in return for their support of and assistance to elected officials. The thought of employees' needing to bargain collectively about wages, benefits, and conditions of employment seemed inconsistent for jobs that were a privilege to possess. As merit systems spread throughout all levels of government and public sector jobs became more professional, employees began to voice their concerns about how they were treated in the workplace, and concerning discrepancies between private and public sector workers (sometimes performing essentially the same job) became apparent.

Labor relations in the public sector began to take on many of the same characteristics as were seen in union-management relations in the private sector. Public employees started holding elections for union representation, pressing for collective bargaining, and either ratifying contracts or taking job actions. The adversarial form of public sector negotiations took on the same form as that created for private companies and their employees.[41] However, the nature of labor relations is quite different in the public sector, and new methods of negotiating and settling disputes have been developed in recent years. Labor relations—and specifically, collective bargaining—are evolving toward a more mature, cooperative style of negotiation. The traditional, adversarial style will persist in conditions where trust has not developed between labor and management, but more and more public agencies are discovering the benefits of working together to solve common issues.

■ MANAGER'S VOCABULARY

economic benefits
job security benefits
social benefits

political benefits
collective bargaining
conspiracy doctrine
antitrust approach
Wagner Act (National Labor Relations Act)
unfair labor practices
good-faith bargaining
Taft-Hartley Act (Labor Management Relations Act)
closed shop
union security
right-to-work laws
union shop
dues checkoff
cooling-off period
doctrine of sovereignty
scope of bargaining
American Federation of Government Employees
American Federation of State, County and Municipal Employees
National Education Association
union certification
bargaining unit
exclusive bargaining agent
decertification
impasse resolution
internal negotiations
ground rules
caucus
mandatory issues
permissive issues
mediation
arbitration
grievance procedure
distributive (adversarial) bargaining
Prisoner's Dilemma
integrative (cooperative) bargaining

■ STUDY QUESTIONS

1. What are the advantages and disadvantages to adversarial labor negotiations? Is it to the advantage of management and labor to adopt a cooperative approach to negotiations?

2. What are the barriers to establishing labor-management cooperation?

3. Has the government replaced labor unions as the protector of employee rights and workplace safety?

4. Should there be a national labor relations law for all public employees similar to the provisions of the Wagner Act? What would be the advantages and disadvantages of such a law? What obstacles prevent such legislation?

5. Do the political strategies available to public sector unions offset their restrictions to strike?

6. Should public employees be allowed to strike? Is there a difference between the kinds of employees (for example, public safety versus technical/clerical) regarding their right to strike?

7. When would a distributive negotiation style be preferable to an integrative negotiation style? When would an integrative style be preferable?

8. Would mediation be a useful strategy during negotiations as well as a dispute resolution technique? How should such mediation be conducted?

9. How would arbitration as an impasse resolution strategy cause a "chilling effect" on the conduct of negotiations? How could this problem be overcome?

■ EXPERIENTIAL EXERCISES

1. *Bargaining in Good Faith*

As the bargaining agent for your school board, you have been asked to prepare a defense against a complaint filed by the local teachers' union that you have been bargaining in bad faith. Your state bargaining law requires the board to "confer in good faith with respect to salaries and other conditions of employment, or the negotiation of an agreement, or any question arising thereunder and the execution of a written contract incorporating any agreement reached if requested by either party, but such obligation shall not compel either party to agree to a proposal or require the making of a concession."[42] The complaint states that on the issues of class size, teacher load, assignment, and compensation for extracurricular activities and submission of grievances to binding arbitration, you have (1) not made counterproposals and (2) have taken the position that these issues are the unilateral prerogatives of the board. Prepare a defense of the board's positions.

2. *Organizing a Graduate Assistant Bargaining Unit*

Assuming that collective bargaining for university personnel is permitted in your state, prepare a campaign for organizing graduate assistants (graduate teaching and research assistants). Consider what union might be the best fit for graduate assistants, address the benefits of being organized for graduate assistants, and decide on a strategy for organizing.

3. *Preparation for Negotiations*

Analyze any current negotiation situation: local or national labor negotiations, political negotiations in your legislature or Congress, or international negotiation in business or foreign relations. Describe the preparations required for these negotiations and whether you believe the parties to negotiations were ready to negotiate.

4. *Negotiations Between Students and Faculty*

Consider the possibility of negotiations between students of your program and the faculty of that program to consider course offerings, schedules, and the type of assignments given. What ground rules would you ask for before discussions on the issues actually begin?

5. *Integrative versus Positional Bargaining*

In negotiations with the International Fire Fighters Association (IFFA), the Fire Department has delivered a list of its positions on the issues. As the negotiator for the city's employee relations office, how would you present these issues to IFFA if you are trying to change negotiations from being adversarial to integrative or collaborative negotiations? Convert the following list of positions for presentation in collaborative negotiations:

   a. Hold wages to a total 2 percent increase over last year's budget.

   b. No increase in the pension contribution.

   c. The number of firefighters assigned to equipment is a management prerogative.

d. The grievance procedure will remain three steps: from supervisor, to commanding officer, and finally chief for the final decision.

e. In the event of an impasse to negotiations, the City Council will conduct fact finding and make a recommendation.

6. *Bargaining Style*

Contact a public sector labor union in your area, and discuss with its leaders the style of bargaining they use in negotiations and the reasons that they use traditional distributive bargaining (adversarial model) or interest-based (integrative) negotiations, or a combination of both.

■ CASES APPLICABLE TO THIS CHAPTER

"City of Franklin versus AFME: A Collective Bargaining Role Play," "Negotiator's Dilemma," and "Three Strikes and You're Out!"

■ NOTES

[1] Note to London correspondent of the *New York Journal,* June 1, 1897.

[2] Robert P. Engvall, "Public-Sector Unionization in 1995 or It Appears the Lion King Has Eaten Robin Hood," *Journal of Collective Negotiations in the Public Sector* 24:3 (1995): 255.

[3] Thomas A. Kochan, Harry C. Katz, and Robert B. McKersie, T*he Transformation of American Industrial Relations* (New York: Basic Books, 1986).

[4] Daniel Nelson, *Shifting Fortunes: The Rise and Decline of American labor (1820s to Present)* (Chicago: Ivan R. Dee, 1997).

[5] Henry S. Farber, "The Decline of Unionization in the United States: What Can Be Learned from Recent Experience?" *Journal of Labor Economics* 8:1 (1990): S75–105.

[6] Bureau of Labor Statistics (BLS), Union Members Summary, available at: **http://stats.bls.gov/newsrels.htm.**

[7] John A. Fossum, *Labor Relations: Development, Structure, and Process,* 5th ed.(Homewood, IL: Irwin, 1991).

[8] Sidney Webb and Beatrice Webb, *Industrial Democracy* (New York: Kelly, 1965).

[9] Mancur Olson, *The Logic of Collective Action: Public Goods and the Theory of Groups* (Cambridge, MA: Harvard University Press, 1971), p. 68.

[10] Paul Johnston, *Success While Others Fail: Social Movement Unionism and the Public Workplace* (Ithaca, NY: ILR Press, 1994), p. 28; Victor G. Devinatz and Wayne Kennedy, "AFGE Local 2816 and 'Community Unionism': A New Conception of Public Sector Unionism," *Journal of Collective Negotiation* 24:2 (1995): 121–132.

[11] W. David Patton, "Teaching Labor Relations: A Choice Between Paleontological and Contemporary Approaches," *Review of Public Personnel Administration* 14:4 (1994): 52–65.

[12] W. David Patton, "Labor Unions," in Joseph M. Bessette, ed., *Ready Reference: American Justice* (Pasadena, CA: Salem Press, 1996).

[13] Adrian A. Paradis and Grace D. Paradis, *The Labor Almanac* (Littleton, CO: Libraries Unlimited, 1983).

[14] BLS, Union Members Summary.

[15] John F. Burton Jr. and Terry Thomason, "The Extent of Collective Bargaining in the Public Sector," 1988, in Benjamin Aaron, Joyce M. Najita, and James L. Stern, eds., *Public Sector Bargaining,* 2nd ed. (Washington D.C.: Bureau of National Affairs), pp. 1–51; Benjamin J. Taylor and Fred Whitney, *Labor Relations Law,* 4th ed. (Englewood Cliffs, NJ: Prentice-Hall, 1983), p. 9.

[16] W. David Patton, "Labor Law," in Timothy L. Hall, ed., *Magill's Legal Guide* (Pasadena, CA: Salem Press, 1998)

[17] *Commonwealth of Massachusetts v. Hunt,* 4 Met. 3 (1842).

[18] *Loewe v. Lawlor (Danbury Hatters),* 208 U.S. 274 (1908).

[19] Taylor and Whitney, *Labor Relations Law,* pp. 209–211.

[20] Ibid., pp. 229–235.

[21] Ibid., p. 236.

[22] James W. Hunt, *The Law of the Workplace: Rights of Employers and Employees,* 2nd ed. (Washington, DC: Bureau of National Affairs, 1988), p. 117.

[23] Kurt L. Hanslowe, "The Emerging Law of Labor Relations in Public Employment," in Harry T. Edwards, R. Theodore Clark, Jr., and Charles B. Craver, *Labor Relations Law in the Public Sector,* 4th ed. (Charlottesville, VA: Michie, 1985), pp. 33–35.

[24] Sherry S. Dickerson and N. Joseph Cayer, "The Environmental Context of Public Labor Relations," in Jack Rabin, Thomas Vocino, W. Bartley Hildreth, and Gerald J. Miller, *Handbook of Public Sector Labor Relations* (New York: Marcel Dekker, 1994), p. 3.

[25] Richard C. Kearney, *Labor Relations in the Public Sector,* 2nd ed. (New York: Marcel Dekker, 1992), pp. 27–34.

[26] Jay M. Shafritz, Norma M. Riccucci, David H. Rosenbloom, and Albert C. Hyde, *Personnel Management in*

Government: Politics and Process, 4th ed. (New York: Marcel Dekker, 1992), p. 322.

[27] Ibid., pp. 327–333.

[28] Kearney, *Labor Relations in the Public Sector,* p. 134.

[29] Center for Partnership and Labor-Management Relations, *Union Recognition in the Federal Government* (Washington, D.C.: U.S. Office of Personnel Management, June 1997), pp. 10–14.

[30] Ibid., p. 26.

[31] Kate Bronfenbrenner and Tom Juravich, *Union Organizing in the Public Sector* (Ithaca, NY: ILR Press, 1995), pp. 20, 26; Kearney, *Labor Relations in the Public Sector,* p. 34.

[32] Bronfenbrenner, p. 39.

[33] Bronfenbrenner and Juravich, p.7.

[34] Kearney, *Labor Relations in the Public Sector,* p. 137.

[35] Joel A. D'Alba, "The Nature of the Duty to Bargain in Good Faith," in Muriel K. Gibbons et al., eds., *Portrait of a Process* (Fort Washington, PA: Labor Relations Press, 1979), pp. 149–172.

[36] Joseph B. Rose and Christine Manuel, "Attitudes Toward Collective Bargaining and Compulsory Arbitration," *Journal of Collective Negotiations* 25:4 (1996): 303.

[37] Neil W. Chamberlain and James W. Kuhn, *Collective Bargaining,* 2nd ed. (New York: McGraw-Hill, 1965).

[38] Samuel B. Bacharach and Edward J. Lawler, *Bargaining Power, Tactics, and Outcomes* (San Francisco: Jossey-Bass, 1981).

[39] Roger Fisher, William Ury, and Bruce Patton, *Getting to Yes,* 2nd ed. (Boston: Houghton Mifflin, 1991); William Ury, *Getting Past No* (Boston: Houghton Mifflin, 1991).

[40] Fisher, William Ury, and Patton, *Getting to Yes*.

[41] Patton, "Teaching Labor Relations."

[42] *West Hartford Education Association v. Decoury,* 162 Conn. 566, 295 A.2d 526 (1972).

CHAPTER 6

Strategic Planning for Human Resources

Human resource departments are responsible for both control and support operations. Consideration of human resources in planning activities sometimes occurs only when the human resource department is asked to forecast staffing needs (regarding retirements or turnover, for example) or to conduct skill inventories to identify employee deficits. Often discussions about planning in human resource textbooks tend to focus on various models of forecasting or anticipated problems to consider. In earlier chapters, we discussed the context of human resource activities for public and nonprofit organizations. Obviously, in the contemporary context of public and nonprofit organizations staffing considerations are highly important. However, it is the very turbulence of this environment that warrants a discussion of **strategic planning** here.

Increasingly, the human resource function is viewed as the pivotal arena for strategic planning and action. This planning requires more than formulaic workforce calculations; it requires the integration of human resources to achieve organizational objectives. This may mean that centralized human resource departments are fully aligned with executive-level decisions. Conversely, if human resource responsibilities are decentralized to line managers and supervisors, then in planning activities human resource issues are weighted with the same level of importance as any other area of operation such as finance, operations, capital budgeting, and so forth.

In this chapter we focus on planning and strategy and explore the implications these concepts have for human resource management. We begin with a review of some basic definitions of planning, with attention to both traditional workforce planning and strategic planning. After a brief exploration of strategic planning initiatives in state governments, we discuss difficulties associated with strategic planning in public and nonprofit organizations and address the limitations of an uncritical application of private sector planning templates to the public sector. Next, we outline a general strategic planning script. Although the outline of strategic planning will serve as a review for students familiar with planning processes, the brief discussion of the strategic planning script illustrates the challenges associated with recommending the "one best way" strategic planning process in public and nonprofit organizations. Finally, we consider strategic human resource management—human resource professional as partner versus adviser or compliance officer—in the development of organizational strategy.

INTRODUCTION TO READING

Planning as a simple forecast of staffing levels for production or succession is no longer adequate for many contemporary public and nonprofit sector organizations. In the following reading, James Perry discusses the pivotal role that human resource management holds in public service at the federal level. Although some issues (e.g., the nuances of the federal civil service) may not be of direct concern in all jurisdictions or to nonprofit organizations, the implications for leveraging organizational effort warrant serious consideration. Perry considers the potential of efforts to invigorate and sustain the public sector through an emphasis on strategy-driven human resource activities. He also cautions us about the managerial and structural impediments that could hinder successful integration.

As you read the selection, keep the following questions in mind:

- How are human resource activities characterized within an organization in terms of very tangible components such as organizational structure and formal responsibilities for support of agency operations?
- How might ambiguous notions such as discretion, responsibility, and accountability be variously defined or affected in planning efforts?
- How might Perry's observations be reframed for state or local government?
- What additional issues may be of concern in nonprofit organizations?
- How would strategy-driven human resource management be handled in a patronage-based jurisdiction versus one with a well-established civil service system?

READING

Strategic Human Resource Management

JAMES L. PERRY

Human capital, the knowledge, skills and experience possessed by individuals, has become pivotal for the successful performance of the federal government's missions (McGregor, 1988). Because human resource management focuses largely on the acquisition and utilization of human capital, it too has attained new significance for federal organizations. In fact, many management scholars argue that human resource management is now an important, perhaps the most important, determinant of organizational effectiveness (Devanna, Fombrun, and Tichy, 1984; Schuler, 1990).

As human resource management has acquired greater importance, the research and professional literature has increasingly distinguished between conventional human resource management practice and strategic human resource management (see Lengnick-Hall and Lengnick-Hall, 1988 for a com-

prehensive review of this literature; McGregor, 1988, 1991). The distinction is intended to differentiate between conceptions of human resource management as functionally or administratively-oriented activities as opposed to integrated or strategy-driven activities. One idea associated with strategic human resource management is that the style of human resource management is consistent with the strategy of the organization and that human resource practices are adjusted, accepted, and used by line managers and employees as part of their everyday work (Schuler, 1992). Dyer and Holder (1987) suggest that a strategic perspective requires focusing first on organizational goals in defining the role of human resource management. "To manage strategically means that traditional HR objectives such as turnover or performance are superseded by organization-wide goals designed to complement a specific business strategy" (Dyer and Holder, 1987: 1).

The changing role of human resource management is part of a larger set of organizational changes involving strategy, structure and control systems. Or-

Source: James L. Perry, "Strategic Human Resource Management," *Review of Public Personnel Administration* 13:4 (1993): 59–71. Reprinted by permission of the publisher, Institute of Public Affairs, University of South Carolina.

ganizations are increasingly giving subunits autonomy and holding them accountable for specific results (Barzelay, 1992; Osborne and Gaebler, 1992).
They also rely increasingly on *adhocracies,* groups
of experts temporarily brought together for specific
projects (Reich, 1987; Peters, 1987; Peters and Waterman, 1982). Coordination often occurs through
mutual adjustment across groups whose members
overlap (Mintzberg, 1983). Jobs are vertically and
horizontally broader in scope and less likely to require direct supervision. The expansion of job scope
creates greater autonomy and entrepreneurship. This
approach to empowering organizational members is
readily extended to customers (Osborne and Gaebler, 1992). Organizations are also becoming more
attentive to the costs of internal rules, striving to ensure that rules add value to goods or services.

How does human resource management in the
federal government measure up to the visions of
strategic human resource management articulated in
the literature? Can federal human resource management become more strategic, i.e., integral to strategy making, adaptive, and useful to line managers
and employees in their daily activities? This [read-
ing] addresses these questions. It argues that federal
human resource management can become more
strategic, but for this to occur, new organizational
designs must be used. The presentation proceeds in
two stages. It begins by summarizing criticisms of the
federal civil service, and then presents alternatives
for improving human resource management.

CRITICISMS OF FEDERAL HUMAN RESOURCE MANAGEMENT

Criticisms of federal human resource management
typically involve at least three arguments. The most
common is that federal personnel activities are overregulated and too constraining (Colvard, 1988;
Cooley, 1987; Horner, 1988; MSPB, 1993). Federal
human resource management is perceived to be
heavily constrained by statutory requirements and
regulations directed toward preventing failures.
Managers and their agencies thus feel limited in
their ability to tailor personnel policy to their own
goals and missions. One Office of Personnel Management (OPM) Director (Horner, 1988; 35) explained her view of the consequences:

Each of the rules, regulations, and requirements of
the U.S. Civil Service is well intentioned and designed

to preclude unfairness or error. Together they have
led to an administratively moribund system that disal-
lows the exercise of human judgment and discretion.

A closely related criticism is that the system is, in
the words of an OPM Associate Director, "complex
and undecipherable to the unanointed" (Cooley,
1987: 1). Complexity is, in part, a product of the
sheer volume of regulations. For example, even a
Director of OPM (Horner, 1988: 35) found the
74 pages of rules on how much to pay a secretary excessive. The technical character of federal personnel
administration also makes for complexity. The tendency of the personnel system to focus on technical
issues such as number of rating levels and detailed
classification standards has led to a situation where
"rather than an integral part of the management
process, the personnel system has become a separate and somewhat alien process" (Cooley, 1987: 1).

A third criticism is that the federal personnel system does not meet the needs of line managers. This
problem is partly a result of the gulf between cultures—that is, between line managers and personnel
professionals—that produces adversarial relationships. Line managers perceive personnel professionals
as obstructionists. For their part, personnel professionals perceive line managers as uncooperative and
either disinterested or, worse, antagonistic to merit
principles. The two cultures are indeed separate and
alien, limiting the prospects for making personnel an
integral part of the management process.

The latter criticism is also a reflection of the inability of agencies and managers to tailor the system
to meet their goals and missions. According to Associate OPM Director Claudia Cooley: "When managers look to the personnel system to meet their
human resource needs, too often they get 'correct'
answers which don't solve their problems" (1987:
1). King and Bishop (1991) attributed a high failure
rate of new personnel programs to the disparity between personnel professionals' and line managers'
perceptions of the criteria for human resource effectiveness. They concluded:

Eighty (80) percent of proposed personnel project/
program improvements are dropped or modified,
formally or informally, within three years following
implementation. The latter findings indicate that
most failures result from difficulties in matching functional criteria to line managers' needs rather than
from managers' reluctance to pursue corporate

human resource goals. Clearly, HR professionals have good ideas which may be accepted, but these good ideas are not aligned to major business priorities.

TOWARD STRATEGIC HUMAN RESOURCE MANAGEMENT

The criticisms indicate clear impediments to strategic human resource management in the federal government. A structure for effective management of human resources must:

1. Give agencies latitude to design human resource policy to match organizational strategies and missions.
2. Accord managers a high degree of responsibility for human resources.
3. Create clear accountability.
4. Establish appropriate support activities.

What changes would increase human resource management's integration with organizational strategy, its flexibility, and its utility to organizational members? The proposals below provide the design for more strategic human resource management.

The OPM-Department Relationship

How might the relationship between OPM and cabinet departments and agencies be structured to allow agencies to design human resource policy that fits their organizational strategies? One way would be for OPM to develop broad performance contracts with departments for a fixed time span, for example, five years. These contracts would permit the department to articulate the goals for human resource management, identify objectives, and measure progress using appropriate indicators such as productivity levels, employee satisfaction, and skill development. During the course of the performance contract, departments would report progress against their goals. OPM would monitor progress and evaluate performance at the conclusion of the period prior to authorization of a new contract.

The performance contracting approach has several advantages. First, it allocates a high degree of autonomy to departments and agencies, which gives them the flexibility to tailor their human resource management systems to their own mission and goals. For example, an agency such as EPA [Environmental Protection Agency] might be given the latitude to eliminate individual appraisals and rewards for its professional staff and instead use

group appraisal and incentives exclusively to meet the needs of a highly technical, research-oriented work force.[1] The flexibility of the performance contracting approach would eliminate the "one size fits all" nature of the present system and maintain meaningful oversight.

A second advantage is that performance contracting shifts attention from compliance with rules to showing results. The central question confronting OPM and the departments becomes: What results do we want to achieve and how do we achieve them? The propensity of performance contracting to increase the focus on results complements the recommendations of GAO [General Accounting Office] (1992) and MSPB [Merit Systems Protection Board] (1992) in recent reviews of OPM's personnel management evaluation system. In calling for better indicators of personnel management effectiveness, MSPB (1992a: vi) recommended: "Such indicators should seek to establish and reinforce the link between mission accomplishment capability and various personnel management practices, policies, and procedures."

Performance contracts can be written to protect the merit system. Verification of prohibited personnel practices would be the basis for withdrawing agency autonomy and tightening OPM regulation. The system would continue to be anchored in merit principles, but it would not involve nearly as much red tape.

The shift to performance contracts as an oversight instrument does not necessarily mean immediate or radical change. Agencies would be free to develop new tools at their own pace. What this more flexible arrangement would mean is a shift in responsibility for human resources and new criteria by which agency activities would be assessed.

An idea similar to agency-level performance contracts is already being tested in Great Britain (Corby, 1991). In 1988, *The Next Steps* report found that the civil service was too big and diverse to be managed centrally under common rules. By 1991, responsibility had been transferred to 34 agencies, and actions involving another 28 agencies were pending. Initial indications are quite positive for this experiment.

Despite granting increased autonomy to departments and independent agencies, coordination among federal organizations can be maintained with a minimum of rules. What are some of the characteristics of the new architecture for coordination? One is the use of ad hoc arrangements (Mintzberg, 1983). OPM has been moving slowly toward adhocracies in testing, classification, and training. Several features will be hallmarks of the adhocracies. One feature is that a variety of people from throughout government, both line and staff, will contribute their expertise, leadership, and vision. OPM will often play a supporting role. Another feature is that the adhocracies will permit choices about sources for internal services. A third feature is that they will be funded by revolving funds or similar mechanisms, much like many training services are presently supported (Agresta, 1993; OPM, 1992b). Interagency task forces could also provide important forums for exchange of information. Some of these mechanisms are already being used by the Clinton Administration to tackle major public problems such as health care and welfare reform (Pearlstein, 1993).

Another mechanism for linking loosely coupled units is information systems that support flexibility, communication, and oversight (Gerstein, 1992). The design and operation of most personnel information systems is presently driven by the regulatory needs of personnel offices. These systems are less management information systems than they are personnel record keeping systems. Newell (1992: 42) provides an example of the present gap between data availability and useable management information:

> In short, OPM collects 57 types of demographic, occupational and salary information from more than three million civilian workers, generating more than 400 reports a year. But attempting to use the data to help managers manage better would be like trying to explain what makes the space shuttle fly by looking at a list of its parts.

Flexible, comprehensive information systems that permit data aggregation in a variety of ways can encourage interactions between line managers and personnel support units and move the personnel function toward a consultative orientation. Such information systems must be available on distributed networks while, at the same time, providing appropriate privacy protections.

The Roles of OPM and the Departments

Changing the relationship between OPM and the departments affects their respective roles. As the relationship becomes less adversarial and more collaborative, OPM will need to increase its capacity to produce useful information and the departments will need to become more proactive in developing personnel policy.

- **OPM's role.**[2] When it was created in 1978, the OPM was conceived to be "the right arm of the president as leader of the federal public service" (Zuck, 1989: 21). The Civil Service Reform Act of 1978 (CSRA) intended that OPM provide broad policy guidance to agencies, conduct research and development, and oversee implementation of merit system principles (Lane, 1992). From the perspective of several oversight bodies (National Academy of Public Administration, 1983; GAO 1989; MSPB, 1989; National Commission on the Public Service, 1989), OPM's performance has fallen short of expectations. OPM acknowledged the need for change in its 1990 strategic plan (OPM, 1990): "OPM's emerging leadership style, while retaining guidance, assistance and oversight, relies increasingly on communication, research, flexibility and involvement."

The changes in the OPM-department relationship will require OPM to revise its mission[3] to allow for a larger role for research and development activities. In today's highly complex and rapidly changing world, OPM can wield far more *positive* influence over the merit system via the knowledge it develops and disseminates than the rules it writes. However, OPM has almost no research and development capacity. The agency now spends only .01 percent of the civilian payroll on research and development (Newell, 1992).

Greater research and development capacity would permit quicker and more effective responses to the types of problems that have beset federal human resource management in recent years in the areas of pay, performance management (Milkovich and Wigdor, 1991), labor relations (U.S. GAO, 1991), and automation. Reported inadequacies in many human resource programs admittedly are caused by factors beyond OPM's control, but the problems are exacerbated by its inability to generate ideas to deal with them quickly and effectively (GAO, 1989 and MSPB, 1992b).

- **Departments' role.** As OPM becomes a more research oriented, knowledge-based enterprise, departments and agencies would assume responsibility for policy making and programming to meet organizational mission requirements. Allocating policy-making responsibility to departments and agencies is the first step in locating accountability for human resource management where it used by program units and line managers. As a manager at an agency exempted from title 5 U.S.C. observed at a 1990 National Academy of Public Administration symposium: "We know we can never be on automatic pilot. We're responsible for managing our people well; if something isn't going well we can't blame some 'regulations' someone else issued. It's up to us to fix it." One means for creating line management's commitment to human resource management is to integrate it more effectively with agency mission. The most direct way of doing so is to give greater latitude to departments and agencies for policy development.

Turning over policy development to departments and agencies is a step toward decentralization and internal deregulation, but it does not assure optimal human resource management. Departments often retain authority that is better delegated to subordinate levels (U.S. OPM, 1992a). In its oversight and leadership role, OPM could develop means for facilitating decentralization within agencies. Futhermore, once a greater policy role is delegated to departments and a new course is set for relationships among organizations, bureaus and other subordinate units may seek greater autonomy for human resource management.

Integration of Functional Activities

The changes in the roles of OPM and the departments will begin to break down traditional barriers between specialized personnel functions, but restructuring must be reinforced throughout government. The existing functional bias of human resource organization must be dealt with explicitly. Among the mechanisms for doing so are modification of career paths for managers and specialists, and carefully rethinking the internal organization of personnel departments.

• **Reorganizing human resource units.** Baird and Meshoulam (1988) argue that efforts to produce integration and flexibility in the human resource function require that it be structured around core points of integration, not based on subfunctions such as classification and pay. They suggest this requires organization around client groups or integrative activities such as planning, research, and information systems. Miles and Snow (1984) suggest that organizations using ad hoc, flexible, loosely coupled structures are likely to stress services such as career and human resource planning, job rotation, organization development and team building.

• **Developing generalists.** A variety of well-known job rotation strategies (Hall, 1976), which have been little utilized in federal organizations, could contribute to integration. Rotating line managers through human resource functions and human resource specialists through line positions as part of career development programs would help to reduce existing organizational barriers. There is some research which indicates that there is a better linkage between strategy making and human resources in firms requiring senior human resources executives to have substantial line experience (Baird and Meshoulam, 1988; Buller, 1988). The higher integration can be explained in two ways: (1) broadly experienced human resource executives have a good knowledge of the organization and its human resources and are thus in a good position to integrate the two; and (2) because of their line experience, functional managers are perceived as credible by top managers and thus are given a fuller role in the planning process.

Another step toward integration would be to redefine the job of personnel specialists. When personnel specialists at each level of federal organization dominate policy making about particular issues, such as classification or pay, it is difficult to distribute ownership for human resource management. The role of the personnel specialist must become broader. These jobs must be enlarged and enriched as a means of integrating functional activities. For example, the Bureau of Labor Statistics has experimented successfully with customer-focused teams of personnel generalists as a way of broadening personnel positions (Coffee, 1992).

A third means for increasing integration would be through manager training. For example, the research and professional literature indicate the value of managers being trained in career counseling and job design skills (Hall, 1976). To the extent that line managers have such skills, they will be better able to manage human resources effectively. At the same time, devolving such responsibilities to the line manager facilitates development of a leaner and more consultative role for the personnel department.

Leadership

Although many of the current problems of federal human resource management involve organizational design issues, the impetus to bring about fundamental change requires political leadership. The

President and the director of OPM must commit to bringing about the organizational changes that will facilitate substantive responses to the needs of federal organizations. Executive leadership must begin with a perspective that recognizes the dynamic relationships among strategy, structure, human resource management, and performance (Senge, 1990). A vision that is sensitive to the needs of all stakeholders is vital for effective human resource management (National Academy of Public Administration, 1993).

Executive leadership must be manifest in more than the vision for federal human resource management. As the short history of the Office of Personnel Management reflects (Lane, 1992), a president's choice for director of the Office of Personnel Management has considerable influence on the performance of the agency. The OPM director establishes a course for the agency, makes important decisions about staff that affect agency capacity, and creates a climate for congressional and interagency relations. Each of these activities is essential to the long-term effectiveness of federal human resource management.

Given the size and scope of the federal government, transformational leadership must diffuse well beyond the Executive Office of the President and OPM. Cabinet members, assistant secretaries, and personnel directors must work to ensure that authority and responsibility for human resource management is delegated to the lowest possible levels in their organizations. This process would be facilitated by opportunities for cabinet members to develop close working relationships with the OPM director.

Another leadership issue is congressional-executive relations. The authorization and long-term implementation of the changes outlined above will require development of constructive, trusting relationships between Congress and the executive branch. Such relationships are the mutual responsibility of Congress and the executive branch. However, steps by the President and the director of the Office of Personnel Management can go a long way toward encouraging a mutually satisfactory response from Congress.

CONCLUSION

One test of the effectiveness of our public administration institutions is whether they can adjust to new circumstances and yet retain the core values that make them so important to our society. One public administration institution, the federal civil service,

has endured for over a century because of its ability to adapt. In recent years, powerful environmental forces—a soaring federal deficit, global economic competition, information technology—have created new challenges for the federal civil service.

This [selection] offered several ideas for responding to the new challenges. It proposed restructuring federal civil service to align it more closely with developing strategic, structural, and control systems. Among the proposed changes were using performance contracting as a mechanism for setting direction and assessing results, shifting OPM's mission toward more research and development to improve its capacity for guiding federal human resource management, and giving greater autonomy to departments and agencies to tailor policies to their missions. The proposed changes would decrease the regulatory character of current systems and diffuse ownership for human resource management more widely. More important, such changes would renew the capacity for the federal civil service to pursue meritocratic values.

NOTES

[1]Statutory changes would be needed to facilitate the flexibility envisioned by this proposal. OPM has some discretion to authorize alternative systems for title 5 agencies. For example, the Federal Employees Pay Comparability Act of 1990 (FEPCA) allows OPM to use title 38 for some health care occupations currently covered under title 5 (U.S. MSPB, 1991). This type of statutory discretion would need to be broadened. One way might be to permit OPM to authorize the use of any existing legislation for agencies that can demonstrate its appropriateness. Another would be to allow the use of demonstration provisions that are proven useful in a five-year-trial. This approach would encourage more rapid diffusion of innovations and avoid the need to show their government-wide applicability, which has been a stumbling block to benefits from Title VI of CSRA (see Ban, 1992).

[2]In addition to its core mission of providing strategic direction for federal human resource management, OPM has operational responsibility for investigations and federal employee retirement systems. This article addresses only OPM's core mission.

[3]For another proposal for radical redefinition of OPM's mission to align it with new organizational realities, see Abramson (1988). The present analysis ignores the issue of OPM's location in the federal administrative structure. For example, some have proposed that OPM and OMB be merged. Although changing OPM's organizational

location may have merit, the proposals do not deal directly with the systemic problems of overregulation and lack of line manager ownership. For a history and analysis of the OPM/OMB relationship see Radin (1992).

REFERENCES

Abramson, M. A. (1988). "Statement before the House Committee on Post Office and Civil Service." Mimeo, March 24.

Agresta, R. J. (1993). "The Service Marketplace: Building Choice into Line-Staff Relationships." *The Public Manager* 22 (Spring): 47–50.

Ban, C. (1992). "Research and Demonstrations Under CSRA," pp. 217–235 in P. Ingraham and D. Rosenbloom (eds.) *The Promise and Paradox of Civil Service Reform.* Pittsburgh, PA: University of Pittsburgh Press.

Barzelay, M. (1992). *Breaking Through Bureaucracy.* Berkeley, CA: University of California Press.

Baird, L., and I. Meshoulam (1988). "Managing the Two Fits for Strategic Human Resource Management." *Academy of Management Review* 13: 116–128.

Buller, P. (1988). "Successful Partnerships: Human Resources and Strategic Planning at Eight Top Firms." *Organizational Dynamics* 17 (Autumn): 27–43.

Coffee, J. (1992). Transcript of a presentation by Joe Coffee, Personnel Chief, Alcohol, Tobacco, and Firearms, to a Jerry Collins Conference on Organizing and Managing Personnel in a Decentralized System, Florida State University, School of Public Policy and Administration, January 30.

Colvard, J. E. (1988). "Reflections on the Personnel Business." *The Bureaucrat* 17 (Spring): 3–5.

Cooley, C. (1987). "OPM Initiatives: Simplify, Delegate, Increase Flexibility." *Classifiers Column* 18 (January): 1–3.

Corby, S. (1991). "Civil Service Decentralization: Reality or Rhetoric?" *Personnel Management* 23 (February): 38–42.

Devanna, M. A., C. Fombrun, and N. Tichy (1984). "A Framework for Strategic Human Resource Management," in C. Fombrun, N. Tichy, and M. A. Devanna, (eds.) *Strategic Human Resource Management.* New York: John Wiley.

Dyer, L. and G. Holder (1988). "A Strategic Perspective of Human Resource Management," in L. Dyer and C. Holder (eds.) *Human Resource Management: Evolving Roles and Responsibilities.* Washington, D.C.: Bureau of National Affairs.

Gerstein, M. S. (1992). "From Machine Bureaucracies to Networked Organizations: An Architectural Journey," pp. 11–38 in D. A. Nadler, M. S. Gerstein, R. B. Shaw (eds.) *Organizational Architecture: Designs for Changing Organizations.* San Francisco: Jossey-Bass.

Hall, D. (1976). *Careers in Organizations.* Santa Monica, CA: Goodyear.

Horner, C. (1988). "Beyond Mr. Gradgrind: The Case for Deregulating the Public Sector." *Policy Review* (Spring): 34–38.

King, A. S. and T. R. Bishop (1991). "Functional Requisites of Human Resources: Personnel Professionals' and Line Managers' Criteria for Effectiveness." *Public Personnel Management* 20: 285–298.

Lane, L. E. (1992). "The Office of Personnel Management," pp. 97–119 in P. Ingraham and D. Rosenbloom (eds.) *The Promise and Paradox of Civil Service Reform.* Pittsburgh, PA: University of Pittsburgh Press.

Lengnick-Hall, C. A. and Lengnick-Hall, M. A. (1988). "Strategic Human Resource Management: A Review of the Literature and a Proposed Typology." *Academy of Management Review* 13, 3: 454–470.

McGregor, E. B., Jr. (1988). "The Public Sector Human Resource Puzzle: Strategic Management of a Strategic Resource." *Public Administration Review* 48 (November/December): 941–950.

McGregor, E. B., Jr. (1991). *Strategic Management of Human Knowledge, Skills, and Abilities.* San Francisco, CA: Jossey-Bass.

Miles, R. E. and Snow, C. C. (1984): "Designing Strategic Human Resources Systems." *Organizational Dynamics* 12 (Summer): 36–51.

Milkovich, G. T. and A. K. Wigdor (eds.) 1991. *Pay for Performance: Evaluating Performance Appraisal and Merit Pay.* Washington, D.C.: National Academy of Sciences, National Academy Press.

Mintzberg, H. (1983). *Structure in Fives: Designing Effective Organizations.* Englewood Cliffs, N.J.: Prentice-Hall.

National Academy of Public Administration (1993). *Leading People in Change: Empowerment, Commitment, and Accountability.* Washington, D.C.: National Academy of Public Administration.

National Academy of Public Administration (1983). *Revitalizing Federal Management: Managers and their Overburdened Systems.* Washington, D.C.: National Academy of Public Administration.

National Commission on the Public Service (1989). *Leadership for America: Rebuilding the Public Service.* Washington, D.C.: The National Commission on the Public Service.

Newell, T. (1992). "Our Endangered Human Resources Investment." *Government Executive* 24 (January): 42–43.

Osborne, D. and T. Gaebler (1992). *Reinventing Government: How the Entrepreneurial Spirit is Transforming the Public Sector.* Reading, Massachusetts: Addison-Wesley.

Pearlstein, S. (1993). "Can Clinton Use the 'Adhocracy' Approach to Retool Government?" *Washington Post* January 31: H1.

Peters, T. (1987). *Thriving on Chaos: Handbook for a Management Revolution.* New York: Harper & Row.

Peters, T. J. and R. H. Waterman, Jr. (1982). *In Search of Excellence.* New York: Warner Books.

Radin, B. A. (1992). "The Search for the M: Federal Management and Personal Policy," pp. 37–62 in P. Ingraham and D. Rosenbloom (eds.) *The Promise and Paradox of*

Civil Service Reform." Pittsburgh, PA. University of Pittsburgh Press.

Reich, R. (1987). "The Entrepreneur as Hero." *Harvard Business Review* 65 (May/June): 71–83.

Schuler, R. S. (1990). "Repositioning the Human Resource Function: Transformation or Demise?" *Academy of Management Executive* 4, 3: 49–60.

Schuler, R. S. (1992). "Strategic Human Resource Management: Linking the People with the Strategic Needs of the Business." *Organizational Dynamics* 21, 1: 18–32.

Senge, P. *The Fifth Discipline: The Art and Practice of the Learning Organization.* New York: Doubleday Currency.

U.S. General Accounting Office (1991). *Federal Labor Relations: A Program in Need of Reform* (GAO/GGD-91-101). Washington, D.C.: US GAO (July).

U.S. General Accounting Office (1989). *Managing Human Resources: Greater OPM Leadership Needed to Address Critical Challenges* (GAO/GGD-89–19) Washington, D.C.: U.S. GAO (January).

U.S. General Accounting Office (1992). *OPM Reliance on Agency Oversight of Personnel System Not Fully Justified* (GAO/GGD-93-24) Washington, D.C.: U.S. GAO (December).

U.S. Merit Systems Protection Board (1992a). *Civil Service Evaluation: The Role of the U.S. Office of Personnel Management.* Washington, D.C.: MSPB.

U.S. Merit Systems Protection Board (1989). *Delegation and Decentralization: Personnel Management Simplification Efforts in the Federal Government* Washington DC: MSPB (October).

U.S. Merit Systems Protection Board (1993). *Federal Personnel Offices: Time for Change?* Washington, D.C.: MSPB.

U.S. Merit Systems Protection Board (1992b). *Federal Personnel Research Programs and Demonstration Projects.* Washington, D.C.: MSPB.

U.S. Merit Systems Protection Board (1991). *The Title 38 Personnel System in the Department of Veterans Affairs: An Alternative Approach.* Washington, D.C.: MSPB.

U.S. Office of Personnel Management (1990). *Strategic Plan for Federal Human Resources Management* Washington, D.C.: OPM (November).

U.S. Office of Personnel Management (1992a). *Delegation of Personnel Management Authority.* Washington, D.C.: OPM (January).

U.S. Office of Personnel Management (1992b). *Human Resources Development Initiatives.* Washington, D.C.: OPM.

Zuck, A. M. (1989). "The Future Role of OPM." *The Bureaucrat* 18, Spring: 20–22.

INTRODUCTION TO PLANNING

The word *plan* serves as both a noun and a verb. As a noun, it denotes "a method of doing or proceeding with something formulated beforehand" or "a project or definite purpose."[1] As a verb, to *plan* suggests both foresight and intention. Simply, planning is the nexus of knowledge and intention.

People plan every day. On a basic level, when we decide what to prepare for a meal or how to study for an exam, we are engaged in planning. We develop sequences of activities that occur in response to certain stimuli. Sometimes our plans become a matter of habit, no longer requiring conscious thought or decision. For example, when you leave your home or office each day to attend class, you probably follow an established routine. You may check to be certain that you have gathered your reading materials and any assignments that are due. If you drive to your class site, you will likely engage in a series of steps to start your vehicle and select a route to bring you to the class. Whether you bike, walk, or travel by train or bus,

you will develop a sequence of actions. You may have thought about the eventual goal (arriving fully prepared to class). You may be aware of the series of objectives that you must also address in order to achieve the main goal (e.g., review the assigned material, access transportation, assign sufficient time to travel). You may have even given thought to the small tasks necessary to address each of the objectives (perhaps you adjusted your seat and mirrors, purchased your token, or secured your helmet).

In most cases, we do all of these things without a great deal of consideration. However, if we begin to select among multiple courses of action using some criteria (say, speed versus safety or most direct route versus most scenic route of travel) in order to develop different responses to different situations, then we engage in a more complex level of planning. In response to new information or the appearance of an unexpected opportunity or threat, we may begin to apply more information to our situation and consider different combinations of actions and resources. For example, you may add a quick errand prior to arriving at class to save yourself time later, or you might consider the possibility of roadwork on your usual route and adjust your timing or selection of avenues accordingly.

Workforce and Succession Planning

For many years, textbooks in personnel administration identified planning as a centralized forecasting function maintained in a personnel department.[2] In traditional **workforce planning**, human resource analysts examined the levels of staff, considered the number and types of positions that might be added, noted the projections for retirement, and applied past turnover rates to develop a formula that would project future staffing level needs. Projected staffing levels would prompt responses from other functions in personnel and eventually from other organizational departments. Although we will discuss some of the nuances of the specific functions of human resource management in later chapters, in theory workforce forecasts would drive all subsequent human resource activities. For example, if analysts determined that the agency would need additional engineers because of retirements or pending projects, specialists in job analysis and classification would identify the responsibilities for potential new employees and assign them to a classification level commensurate with the required knowledge, skills, and abilities (KSAs). The classification level would shape the compensation package. Recruiting specialists would use the resulting position descriptions and compensation package to seek applicants. Selection of the final candidate would occur in response to a sufficient pool and in consideration of criteria generated by job analysis and classification.

Succession in organizations was often a matter of identifying upcoming retirements and considering possible successors from among the eager entry-level and midlevel managers. In many cases, senior management may have identified certain individuals as being likely candidates and steered them onto particular promotional tracks to provide the necessary experiences. Although the

hierarchy in an organization suggests some path to promotion (e.g., from an assistant director to associate director to the director), much of the logic of succession and promotion appeared to be linked to informal organizational culture and legend. Some career paths were more likely than others to lead to higher management positions; for example, fiscal and production types of activities were more often the path to the top than "softer" managerial activities such as human resources.

These informal approaches are no longer adequate (or even legal) as organizations seek to manage rapid changes in the knowledge and skills required for different positions. The workforce has become diverse, with the single-organization, career-oriented "organizational man" of the 1950s who sacrificed his personal life for total allegiance to the organization being replaced by employees who are more mobile in their careers, less invested in their current employer's organizational culture, and are trying to balance the competing demands of their professional and personal lives.[3] Traditional succession planning also presumes long-term alliances between organizations and employees. As discussed in Chapter 2, employees may not be planning on a twenty- or thirty-year commitment to the organization. No longer can succession planning be premised on the assumption that employees uniformly seek to work their way up through the organizational hierarchy. (The issues related to employee development, retention, and performance management are addressed in greater detail in Chapters 11 and 12.) Although simple staff forecasting influences activities throughout the organization, more sophisticated human resource planning efforts have extended to the maintenance of an inventory of the skills possessed by the current workforce. As we discuss in Chapter 12, identifying gaps in skills for promotion or new projects may prompt training in deficiencies.

Strategic Planning

Use of the term *strategic* in combination with the word *plan* is somewhat like saying "planned planning." However, in application, strategic planning has come to denote a process for orchestrating organizational direction through individual action after a careful evaluation of an organization's external environment and internal capacity.[4]

"Strategic planning helps an organization match its goals and capabilities to the anticipated demands of the environment to produce a plan of action that will assure achievement of goals."[5] Essentially, planning in an organization suggests developing guidelines to accomplish organizational goals. The guidelines could range from a relatively simple statement of goals and organizational direction to a complex document with a hierarchy of goals, objectives, tasks linked to time lines, and detailed evaluation criteria. Whether simple or complex, the process of strategic planning and the preparation for a planning effort require an awareness of how different decisions, structures, goals, and values can influence organizational efforts. As Figure 6.1 illustrates, strategic planning and management transcend a categorization of needs/demands in operation versus the workforce. Instead, strategic planning and management require an integration of all aspects of the organization in context with their internal and external environments.

Strategic planning is distinguished from other more general planning activities in three principal ways: an emphasis on **implementation** (that is, actual application in practice, as opposed to theoretical design of intended plan), a detailed assessment of the organization's internal and external environments, and some degree of stakeholder participation.[6] Each organization has a distinctive environment. The particular characteristics of this **organizational environment**

Figure 6.1   Traditional Planning and Management versus Strategic Planning and Management

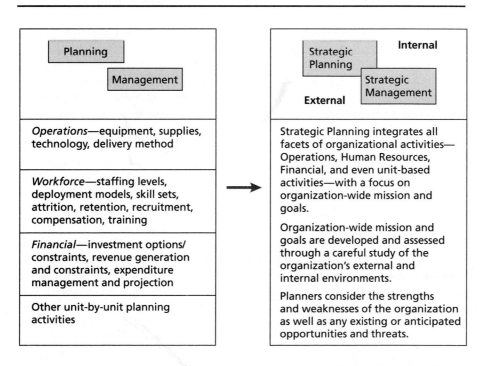

could be categorized as social/demographic, political/legal, geographic, and economic/technological.[7] These categorizations are a bit artificial, and there may be some overlap. For example, demographic considerations such as the aging of a population could prompt economic concerns (about a retiring workforce) or be linked with geography (aging populations may be more concentrated in certain sunbelt regions). Environmental changes require special attention from managers as a means to improve organizational performance.[8] Strategic planning implies that organizations will be mission driven, with goals, objectives, and eventual actions identified through a careful analysis of the organization's environment. Later in this chapter we examine a general script for strategic planning.

The organizational context coupled with the impetus for the initiation of strategic planning determine the best methods to employ.[9] For example, planning may occur in response to anticipated change. In this case, organization members may have greater control over process and outcome than if they are reacting to a particular event. However, organization members may plan in response to some pivotal incident. Depending on the nature of the event, organization members may be required to change direction and organizational activities very quickly in response to community demands. In the public and nonprofit sectors, catalytic events can trigger community concern that the organization is not responding effectively to a problem. Strategic planning in this venue is quite reactive and challenging as organization members combat a natural defensiveness that may arise in response to community critique. Strategic planning requires organizationwide cooperation and commitment to the planning process. Unfortunately, employees in these organizations may be feeling neither cooperative nor committed.

Finally, organization members may not be driven by anticipated threats in their environments or by some specific event, but rather plan in response to opportunities.

Strategic Planning in the Public or Nonprofit Sector

Planning in times of certainty, with full knowledge about the implications of different options, can occur comfortably with small shifts from the current situation in response to new conditions.[10] However, for employees in public and nonprofit organizations uncertainty appears to be one of the most certain aspects of their work. Managers in organizations attempt to manage uncertainty by assembling an image of an environment derived from a composite of organizational functions, the medium or domain within which the organization operates, and the organization's clientele.[11] The external environment for nonprofit and public sector organizations is generally quite turbulent, reflecting changing expectations from clientele and other stakeholders, fluctuating resource levels, and increasingly blended roles for public, private, and nonprofit organizations.[12] Calls for reform, new approaches to delivering public goods, shifting workforce demographics, and evolving technology all require organizations to prepare for change. Within those organizations, managers and line supervisors, either with primary human resource responsibility or working in conjunction with a human resource department, can instigate and manage necessary adaptation through the efforts of skilled, effective employees and carefully calibrated employment practices.

Since effective strategic planning reflects the source of authority for an organization, these efforts vary by organization and sector. For public sector organizations, the citizenry, through their designated legislative body, must play a critical role in strategic planning. For nonprofit organizations, the service constituency and directing board must contribute in planning. Effective strategic planning in public and nonprofit organizations is highly participatory in nature with staff and client participation and insight from multiple levels and functional areas within the organizations.[13] In organizations that are expected to be community based, such as government agencies and nonprofit organizations, strategic planning must involve many individuals at many levels. Effective change in organizational practices or policy direction is most readily accomplished by involving anyone who will be affected by the change. This means including outside stakeholders, the service providers who will work directly with these stakeholders, and the internal staff who will be supporting organizational efforts. A renewed emphasis on the citizenry in the delivery of public goods and services underlies the premise of a democratized public administration.[14] Democratic administration requires working with, rather than administering over, citizens and necessitates changing established procedures that hamper this collaborative effort.

Ethical issues Ethical considerations in strategic planning for public and nonprofit organizations parallel other issues raised throughout this book. As planners examine the organizational environment in which their agency or unit of government operates and anticipate social trends, they should be aware of how their personal values may shape their analysis and perceptions. Stereotypes that are used to support prejudicial assessments of the capacity or interests of others can detract from the integrity of planning and the proper inclusion of all stakeholders. In addition, planning for the sake of generating a plan in response to some legislative or board mandate may backfire, especially when agencies engage in a strategic planning process as a matter of form or give only superficial attention to an invitation to participate. Staff who do provide their sincere input expect that it will at least be considered, and they will resent efforts that simply collect data, opinions, and attitudes without any genuine assessment of those data in developing organizational direction. Community members will resent agencies that invite them to participate in a process, only to witness community recommendations being ignored. Agencies may not implement all community recommendations, but issues raised through a public process warrant due consideration and sincere re-

spect for the stakeholders and citizens who donated their time to participate.

How common is strategic planning in government? It is somewhat difficult to assess the extent, effectiveness, and administration of strategic planning efforts in government. At the federal level, strategic planning was mandated for all federal agencies by the Government Performance and Results Act of 1993.[15] Some research on state-level planning efforts suggests that many state agencies are engaged in some type of strategic planning effort. Berry and Wechsler found that approximately 60 percent of responding agencies indicated the use of some type of strategic planning exercise.[16] Typically the planning efforts undertaken were prompted by agency leadership rather than imposed by legislative or executive mandate.[17] Conversely Selden, Ingraham, and Jacobson looked at states generally and found that central human resource departments from more than thirty states reported either no planning or only a limited degree of basic workforce planning, and only five states had integrated workforce planning with overall strategic planning.[18] Local governments continue to draw on the resources offered through the International City/County Management Association.[19]

Perceived barriers to strategic planning Wolch suggests three major barriers to planning in nonprofit organizations that may echo difficulties with public sector strategic planning: the skill level of managers charged with planning, the diversity of agendas for the various stakeholders, and concerns about the rigidity of formal plans.[20]

First, staff may be relatively unskilled in planning and management techniques.[21] Just as traditional workforce planning efforts were often relegated to centralized human resource departments, other planning efforts might be compartmentalized, delegated as the domain of a particular department in an agency or retained at a certain level of organizational decision making. Under these circumstances, little active participation would be required from line supervisors. However, with strategic planning, workforce planning is integrated with all other aspects of operations and in consideration of other environmental factors. This means that line managers as well as human resource specialists need to be familiar with strategic planning generally, and with the issues attendant to traditional workforce planning. Training is necessary in the techniques of planning and environmental assessment methods. Even if employees (and outside participants) are familiar with the general concepts of strategic planning, the complexity of the data to be considered may be overwhelming. The addition of complex modeling programs to manage all of the detail about the organization's environment, staffing levels and characteristics, range of project types, varying time lines, and diverse benchmarking criteria could hinder active participation by those who are unfamiliar with or intimidated by statistical analysis.

Second, the diversity of goals, values, and interests of the people associated with the organization makes planning difficult.[22] For example, bringing out the perspectives of clients, donors (taxpayers), volunteers, staff, and board members (political decision makers) can be difficult enough. Meshing these views may require some vagueness in goals and objectives to limit internal conflict between organization stakeholders. Unfortunately, ambiguity in goals and objectives makes it difficult to develop a tangible series of actions as a result. The very nature of ownership in the public and nonprofit sectors can complicate an already complex process. In the private sector, ownership and direction are a bit easier to ascertain for planning purposes. For the public sector, agencies are responsive to citizens indirectly, as citizens select the representatives comprising the legislative bodies that authorize and fund the agency, and directly, when the citizens are members of the constituency served by the agency's mission. For nonprofit organizations, ownership can be just as complex, with a directing board, clientele, donors, contracting agencies, and granting foundations, each claiming a piece of the nonprofit activity. For both public and nonprofit

organizations, the only certainty is that demand will exceed resources.

A third problem is that in nonprofit sector organizations, staff members and volunteers may resist planning because it seems a bit too corporate or businesslike rather than client responsive.[23] They echo concerns frequently expressed by public sector administrators that formal plans have the potential of limiting flexibility of action or, alternatively, imposing "bureaucracy" on adaptive or innovative activities.[24] Within public agencies or nonprofit organizations, line managers and personnelists must respond to their own professional expertise in substantive policy areas or to the legal constraints of civil service systems. If the plan does not consider these perspectives, then it will not work.

Additional problems with strategic planning may stem from previous efforts. Unfortunately, it is not unusual for public managers to find themselves buffeted by "flavor of the week" management trends.[25] Strategic planning has often been treated as one such faddish effort. Suddenly an agency is asked to develop a plan by a legislative body or executive branch official; consultants are hired and committees are formed, and day-long work sessions are scheduled. Midlevel managers are thrown together with a sprinkle of line-level supervisors to develop a mission statement, goals, and objectives in an eight-hour retreat. The comments are scribbled on large pieces of paper for the group to see and then carefully transferred to a document that will become *The Strategic Plan of Agency X*. Copies of this document are distributed to managers throughout the agency and made available to appropriate political decision makers.

This rapid-fire approach to strategic planning is fairly common—and typically results in considerable difficulty in implementation.[26] Often the haste of plan development precludes a careful assessment of organizational resources and environmental concerns or opportunities. Even if managers attempt to implement some objectives within the plan, ill-considered issues frequently stymie their efforts. In addition, if participation in plan development is limited, then the important perceptions of other employees and the organization's external stakeholders may not be represented. The practical disadvantages that this entails parallel the ethical considerations raised earlier. The buy-in, or commitment, by employees and stakeholders is diminished. Most employees and many citizens, if asked, will offer input and their commitment to planning and organizational change. However, if the employees make an investment in a planning activity and see no effort to implement or believe that their input was not valued, then they will become increasingly cynical and detached from these efforts.

Another problem that may frequent planning efforts is overplanning. The highly detailed scheduling of implementation efforts or the development of overly structured plans can often impede organizational responsiveness. Some individuals do tend to invest heavily in the written plan and limit their efforts exclusively to those activities that are specifically detailed, thereby limiting innovation and adaptability. The organization's environment will still be fluid even after a plan is in place, so a general focus on goals and a willingness to let the organization respond to environmental cues is important.[27] Managers should have the latitude to respond to shifts and be comfortable with change and variety while recognizing that even small decisions can lead to larger outcomes for good or ill.[28]

STRATEGIC PLANNING SCRIPT

Although failing to plan certainly can have serious consequences, sloppy planning efforts may be even more threatening because they lull managers into a false sense of security. A plan that is thrown together without adequate research and analysis will seldom be implemented successfully. A plan that is developed without representation from all key organization personnel likewise is unlikely to be implemented successfully, nor will a plan to integrate community members or policy constituents be successfully implemented unless representatives from those groups have the genuine opportunity to participate. Strategic planning in a public or nonprofit sector organization serves as a mediating activity, blending people, information, and organizational direction into a collective effort of coordinated activities. The general template that we offer for planning has three main steps—preparation, data collection and analysis, and development of the plan, as illustrated in Figure 6.2.

Nevertheless, it is important to note the limitations of any strategic planning template. In planning, there is no magic formula, nor does one format work for every organization. Organizations differ greatly in terms of their legal or social mandates. For example, a police department may be expected to protect and serve the public by apprehending offenders; a nonprofit organization dedicated to youth advocacy may have an entirely different mandate and working relationship with juvenile offenders. Both mandates are compelling and binding in terms of the employees and stakeholders for those organizations, and both mandates ultimately will guide individual and organizational action. Organizations differ in terms of their history, as well as in their prior actions. Relationships with other agencies also vary widely. Finally, the people in an organization differ in terms of their aptitude and skills. These differences should be considered as critical resource issues in the design of strategic planning efforts.

Stage 1: Preparation

Organization members should prepare to plan, following the steps set out in Box 6.1. It is common, though not critical in many cases, to bring an outside facilitator into an organization to assist

---

Box 6.1   Steps in the Preparation Phase

1. Identify the organizational leadership.
2. Train the organizational leadership.
3. Identify the planning team.
4. Train the planning team.
5. Identify participating organizational members.
6. Identify participating community members.

Figure 6.2   Strategic Planning Stages

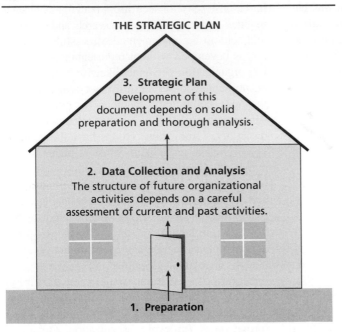

THE STRATEGIC PLAN

3. Strategic Plan
Development of this
document depends on solid
preparation and thorough analysis.

2. Data Collection and Analysis
The structure of future organizational
activities depends on a careful
assessment of current and past activities.

1. Preparation

with initial planning efforts. The facilitator can work with organizational leadership to adapt the planning effort to the needs of the organization. Core managers who will lead planning efforts should be identified and trained in all major aspects of planning. These planning leaders then identify a list of employees to comprise the planning team.

The planning team members may be managers and representatives from all facets of the organization. These individuals may hold formal leadership or managerial roles in the organization, but would definitely demonstrate informal leadership. The employees who are often sought for advice and counsel by others may be the ideal members for a planning team. The planning team should draw on expertise from all facets within the organization. Technical specialists with knowledge about human resource management issues and financial management, for example, are critical. There should also be plenty of opportunity for participation by community mem-

bers and representatives of other appropriate agencies and organizations. The planning team may have members from the community or outside organizations, but will also serve to identify others (community and interorganizational) who should hold an advisory role as the planning process unfolds.

Stage 2: Data Collection and Analysis

In the second stage of planning, depicted in Box 6.2, organizational members begin to identify and gather data. One of the primary steps in strategic planning is an assessment of the organization's environment in terms of strengths, weaknesses, opportunities, and threats, commonly known as the **SWOT analysis.** Environmental data can be categorized in a number of ways. Categorizing data in terms of source (internal or external) can offer a simple preliminary picture of the organization. Box 6.3 provides a sample of questions that can generate useful information in considering

Figure 6.3   Organizational Environments

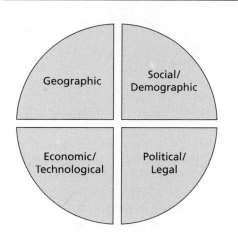

the internal environment of the organization.[29] For example, careful analysis of the organizational structure is quite useful to identify organizational culture or to note access points for citizens. The degree of formalization present in policies, procedures, and communication lines is also important to assess. Another important dimension of the organization has to do with the internal distribution of personnel, programs, and responsibility.

Data can also be sorted into the broad categories identified in Figure 6.3 (social/demographic, political/legal, economic/technological,

and geographic). We tend to think of these categories as depicting the external environment for an organization; however, SWOTs that are identified as part of the external environment usually are reflected internally.

Social/demographic environment   The unique **social/demographic environment** for a particular community and the diversity of cultures within that community shape the community and employee preferences for the direction that an organization will take. The extent to which there is a great deal of agreement or disagreement on community priorities and methods of addressing those priorities also shapes the tensions in the planning process.

Political/legal environment   The **political/legal environment** can be defined in terms of the process used to distribute resources or public goods, or as the end result or policy established to address the distribution of resources or goods in society. For example, if we define public safety as a social good, then political decision making in terms of how much a community may wish to spend for a particular level of public safety is a highly relevant concern in strategic planning. Also, the means or process by which a community is willing to achieve a certain level of public safety is an important political issue with great import for the planning process.

Box 6.2   Steps in the Data Collection Phase

---

1. Identify and gather relevant data.
   - Assess organizational capacity (internal documents, employee focus groups, surveys, and so forth).
   - Assess the organization's environment (SWOT analysis, community documents, surveys, focus groups, and so forth).
   - Develop a summary report and supporting documentation for the planning process.
2. Review the data.
   - Identify issues.
   - Consider alternatives.
3. Develop a summary of the issues and key findings.

Box 6.3   Sample Questions for the Internal Assessment

Power and Decision Making

- Is power decentralized or centralized?
- Who holds responsibility in the organization?
- Who makes decisions?

Policies and Procedures

- How important and detailed are policies and procedures in daily operations?
- Who determines policy?
- How important are traditions or informal policies?
- How is important information communicated?
- How reliable or important is the organizational grapevine?

Structure and Program Distribution

- Is the organization relatively flat, or are there many levels of management?
- Are there multiple departments?
- Are people organized into small work groups or into large, multijurisdictional arrangements?
- How is responsibility for different programs distributed?
- Is responsibility distributed to a work unit or to teams drawn from different units or departments?
- How is performance measured, and by whom?

Formal parameters defined through law will serve to institutionalize the types of issues raised in the political arena. Community values and priorities are often defined in terms of legal versus illegal actions. For example, one community may consider graffiti to be the pinnacle of evil, while another community is preoccupied with drug use among teenagers.

Economic/technological environment   **Economic/technological environment** issues range from the types of jobs and development issues that a community faces to the ability of a region to address fiscal issues drawn from growth and infrastructure demands. Planning efforts must consider the fiscal resources that are required to sustain a given level of public safety and recognize the link between other infrastructure demands in a community, such as schools, recreation facilities, and educational programs.

What technology is available for use to achieve the mission of the nonprofit or public agency? Do we rely on sophisticated computer systems, or can we do our work without being wired? What type of communication system supports our efforts? What science informs our efforts? What expectations do citizens, legislators, directing boards, or clients have about the use of technology? Recently one of us was shocked to discover that the only way to contact a city council member was by calling the person at home. The city had no web site, no e-mail system, and no voice mail for anyone other than department directors. A citizen who wanted information about city services had to use the telephone or drive to city hall.

Geographic environment   According to the old adage in real estate, whether buying or selling you must think "location, location, location!" Location is also important in planning. The **geographic environment** of a particular community in terms of natural lines of demarcation that may exist (hills and waterways) as well as climate and proximity to various natural resources will affect much public decision making. For example, if a community wishes to decentralize the police department and establish a geo-based service provision structure, then it is important to consider the layout of the city and the location of critical areas in making that determination.

Technology and data analysis in planning In addition to the considerations of technology for organizational activities and mission, we must also examine the implications of technology for strategic planning and management. The explosion of data that can now be compiled with even the most basic of computer applications offers both opportunity and challenge.[30] Potentially managers could track a great deal of data—for example, training backgrounds of employees, their preferred career paths, education levels, and other demographic characteristics. This information could be employed with modeling software to predict skill needs for particular projects or time lines or even to manage a work team from afar; an entire work team could telecommute.[31] Along with the greater access to information come some predictable frustrations. As planning group members proceed with their aggregation and analysis of data, they should consider a few precautionary notes.

First, as we employ more data and rely heavily on automation to gather and compute them, we do raise the specter of inaccuracy. As Ripley cautions us:

> Don't forget that every number the system produces, except for today's actual data is a guess—a very good guess; perhaps, but still only that. Also, the further out the projection, the more the data degrade. Building an automated system that defines future gaps or surpluses in very specific detail implies a degree of precision that simply doesn't exist.[32]

Second, as we consider more variables in planning, we are also expected to employ those data to develop contingency responses to imagined scenarios. This raises the possibility that data could impede rather than enhance planning. How do managers sift through a cascade of noise to determine what is relevant? Managers are increasingly frustrated by their inability to manage information, and the volume of information and speed of technical change are intimidating to many employees. As sophisticated modeling techniques become available in strategic planning to address workforce forecasting, there is a propensity to defer analysis to those comfortable with those programs; too often critical evaluation by line managers does not occur. Decision making about staffing may become increasingly disconnected from assessment by line managers because of the medium of the information. In some ways the potential for specialization of planning with technology echoes Sayre's dour pronouncement: a "triumph of technique over purpose."[33]

Implications for diversity in analysis and planning Diversity in an organization may bring a wealth of viewpoints and interpretations that can be brought to bear on some bit of data. Contending analysis and alternative solutions drawn from different perspectives are considered to be among the advantages of a diverse organization. However, it is important to note as well that contending viewpoints may also spark unresolved conflict, and the resulting frustrations in the workplace could impede strategic planning efforts. This can be particularly dysfunctional when the contending views become crystallized as an "us-versus-them" dispute. Cox and Finley note that diversity in an organization does not rest simply with characteristics such as gender or ethnicity, but may also rest with differences derived from functional roles in the organization and professions.[34] For this reason, most general strategic planning processes encourage comprehensive representation (across departments and decision-making levels and from inside and outside the organization) to ensure broad participation and representation of different functional perspectives in the development of the plan.

Stage 3: Development of the Plan

Once the planning team has finished generating and assessing data, it is time to begin a draft of the plan. Sometimes organizations rush to this step at the expense of the preplanning and data collection phases. However, this phase benefits from a careful selection of planning participants and careful and thorough data collection and analysis. This document usually includes a mission statement, goals, objectives, and action steps. It is important to continue to consult advisory members of the organization and the community as the document is developed and strategies for implementation are derived. The general procedural activities are outlined in Box 6.4. Although there are many different approaches to capturing the perspectives emerging from the data collection and assessment phase, generally the following components should be addressed: a mission statement; goals, objectives, and action steps; operations integration; contingency planning; implementation; and evaluation.

Mission statement A **mission statement** offers direction. It is quite common for mission statements to include a lengthy list of missives complete with elaborate statements about organizational values and trendy words like *empower,* *collaborate,* and *commit.* Too often employees in the organization either have no idea what the formal mission statement says, or they point to a framed document on a wall, the meaning of which they would be hard-pressed to explain. Like constitutions and charters of government, mission statements (and strategic plans generally) should be simple, brief, and clear, and should summarize the general caveat for the organization—that is, who belongs to the organization and what the organization does. For mission statements, less really is more. The mission statement in a public sector or nonprofit agency should convey a common purpose that can inspire commitment on the part of all employees.

Goals, objectives, and action steps A **goal** is a general statement of intent. Attaining goals relies on attaining the subcategories for each goal, which are the more detailed objectives and tasks. For each goal, **objectives** identify more specific activities, often by organizational unit, that will contribute to goal attainment and some criteria for assessment. For each objective, **action steps** are specific segments of activity assigned to an identified organizational unit to implement some action within a specified time frame. Action steps could also be characterized as specific tasks with deadlines and an assignment of responsibility.

Box 6.4   Steps in Developing the Plan

1. Write the mission statement
2. Develop goals, objectives, and action steps.
3. Integrate the plan into ongoing operations.
   - Identify unit responsibility, and designate communication lines.
   - Identify performance expectations, and document contingency conditions.
4. Do contingency planning: What happens if . . . ?
5. Implement the plan.
6. Evaluate the plan.
   - Evaluating process: Examine the planning process using the criteria established during preplanning activities.
   - Evaluating outcome: Assess the resulting performance of the organization using the criteria established through the mission, goals, and objectives.

Operations integration Once the basic outline of the plan is drafted, planning team members should work with others in the organization to identify appropriate unit responsibilities for different activities and establish performance expectations. This reflects the implementation responsibilities and guidelines for the identified activities and, in theory, the objectives and goals.

Contingency planning No organization can ever be entirely certain of the environment that it faces, so it is useful for planning team members to address **contingency planning**, that is, what actions would be taken if critical assumptions about the environment must be revised.

Evaluation Unfortunately, in the excitement over finally completing the planning document, team members often do not consider the importance of revisiting their efforts to be certain that the organization is proceeding appropriately. It is very important to consider the expectations that are established in planning in terms of performance and responsibilities and build an **evaluation** component into the strategic plan.

Evaluation requires the organizational leadership and planning group to identify some criteria for each objective and action to assess whether the overall goals, and thus achievement of the organization mission, were met. In addition, evaluation may require a constant assessment of the availability of resources, environmental change, and whether the completion of an action really did contribute to goal attainment. Evaluation requires both quantitative and qualitative assessment.

STRATEGIC HUMAN RESOURCE MANAGEMENT

Thorough strategic planning efforts incorporate the specific actions that will be taken to bring organizational goals to life, drawing guidance from a detailed assessment of the organization's internal and external environments and the participation of interested parties from the organization

and its community. Bryson echoes other theorists in arguing that public and nonprofit organizations face uniquely turbulent environments necessitating coordinated action.[35] Organizational leadership must think in terms of internal operations and external environments to translate potential organizational responses into goals that are coordinated and serve to mesh organizational efforts with environmental demands. Leadership must extend this effort beyond general goals to action, necessitating an assessment of organizational capacity and concern with the ability of the organization to respond to environmental cues.[36] The rationale for the importance of strategic planning in public and nonprofit organizations grows as we note that the distinctions among different arenas of authority—public, private, and nonprofit—have become increasingly vague.[37] Particular actions may no longer be routinely considered to be the exclusive domain of the public sector in an era of privatization and public-private partnerships.

Strategic human resource management requires that human resource departments move beyond the conventional, limited roles of facilitator or adviser to an integration of human resource management activities into strategic planning, management, and action. Strategic human resource management is "the pattern of planned human resource deployments and activities intended to enable an organization to achieve its goals."[38] It occurs when the human resource unit recasts itself as part of the decision-making team rather than viewing itself as an agent of internal accountability and control. Considering human resource efforts in the context of organizationwide strategic planning reflects the acknowledgment of the key role that employees play in organizational success. The link between human resource practices and strategic management to accomplish organizational objectives requires close coordination of human resource practices with organizational mission.[39] Strategic human resource management becomes relevant for other organizational actors when it is intimately linked to the enhancement of organizational capacity; lacking such a close linkage, line managers are unlikely to accord much priority to human resource development initiatives or supportive services.[40]

Unfortunately, if human resource activities are not integrated into organizational strategy or if strategic planning is simply left to human resource departments as one more management fad to be borne, then decisions made in the human resource department or by other agency departments could be ill considered. Ospina offers the example of how short-run problem solving can lead to a larger organizational problem.[41] What might occur if staffing became ad hoc, with managers adding people in response to a perceived shortage without regard to civil service procedures? Potentially such actions could disrupt salary levels and raise thorny equity issues. Career ladders may become quite convoluted, leading to employee morale and motivation concerns. Employees may leave for organizations with more consistency and predictability in questions regarding career path progress or expectations about responsibilities, thereby raising problems with employee retention. "Quick fix solutions to human resource problems that arise in the normal course of work will often have unanticipated and negative consequences that are costly to the agency."[42]

CONCLUSION

Performance in the public sector and in nonprofit organizations that deliver public goods and services hinges on the effective management of people to accomplish organizational goals. In this regard, traditional views of human resource planning and the role that human resource departments play in organizations are inadequate for meeting the challenges of contemporary public sector management. Strategic human resource management and planning in the public sector cannot be accomplished with a linear focus on each traditional human resource function as distinct from the realities of line management and public service delivery systems. Instead, agency planning efforts must incorporate human resource

specialists along with line managers as integral partners in strategic management, and such efforts must draw on a variety of sources and perspectives, including the evolving public expectations of public service. Without this level of organizationwide planning, adaptation to changing expectations by citizens, different means of evaluating performance, or different demands for service delivery from new and nontraditional clientele (e.g., minority racial, ethnic, and cultural groups) will be difficult. Strategic human resource management may offer a means to increase productivity and organizational capacity as the various resources available to the department are identified to respond to more clearly etched expectations from clientele and political decision makers.

■ MANAGER'S VOCABULARY

strategic planning
workforce planning
implementation
organizational environment
SWOT analysis
social/demographic environment
political/legal environment
economic/technological environment
geographic environment
mission statement
goal
objectives
action steps
contingency planning
evaluation
strategic human resource management

■ STUDY QUESTIONS

1. How might traditional workforce planning differ from strategic planning?

2. In what ways might planning activities differ among public, private, and nonprofit sector organizations?

3. What factors would be likely characteristics of the external environment for a nonprofit organization? For a public sector organization?

4. How should we evaluate planning efforts in public sector organizations? In nonprofit organizations?

■ EXPERIENTIAL EXERCISES

1. Assume that your class is an organization. You have some structure of authority (formal and informal) and some shared activities that will result in accomplishing a collective purpose. Divide into two or three equally sized groups. Each group will decide how to proceed to fulfill the following charges:

   a. Conduct a brief SWOT analysis to generate two each of the strengths, weaknesses, opportunities, and threats facing the class.

   b. Generate a brief summary of the environment of the class/organization.

   c. Based on the assessment of the organizational environment, develop a mission statement for the class, and outline three broad goals.

   After each group completes its mini-plan, the class regroups as a whole for a presentation of the plans and to consider the following discussion questions:

   • What decision-making process did each group employ to develop its plan?

   • How committed were group members to their group's mini-plan?

   • How different are the missions and goals that the groups devised?

   • Would the class as a whole approve or disapprove of the different missions? Goals?

2. Select a public or nonprofit sector organization for discussion. As you consider this organization today, address the following questions:

   • What is its mission?

   • What are the organization's strengths? Weaknesses?

   • What opportunities are available to the organization?

   • What threats must it endure?

   Now jump forward ten years:

   • What may change?

   • What may stay the same?

   • How do you know?

3. Think about the high school that you attended, and consider the following questions as you develop a basic model depicting the staffing and activities of that school:

   • What kinds of employees were necessary to keep that school in operation?

   • What levels of education were necessary to perform the different jobs?

- Select three or four employee types. What did they do?

- How might employees have been selected?

- How long did the different employees stay with your high school?

- Who was served by the school?

- Who volunteered at the school?

- What did the volunteers do?

- What kinds of things did you do as a student in your high school?

Now, consider a high school today:

- What has changed in terms of community expectations about schools?

- What do lawmakers expect?

- What activities occur in high schools?

- Have the types of jobs changed since you were in school? How?

- What should decision makers consider in terms of staffing? Job structure? Employee skills?

■ CASES APPLICABLE TO THIS CHAPTER

"Liberty Police Department" (Task 1) and "Helping Hands" (Task 1).

■ NOTES

[1] Definitions are drawn from *The Random House Dictionary* (New York: Random House, 1980), p. 670.

[2] Coleman noted the importance of the personnel department for what he referred to as manpower planning between 1950 and 1973. Despite calls for more sophisticated comprehensive plans throughout states, comparatively few have been developed. See Charles J. Coleman, "Personnel: The Changing Function," *Public Personnel Management* (May–June 1973).

[3] William Whyte, Jr., *The Organization Man* (Garden City, NY: Doubleday, 1956).

[4] Many excellent books are devoted to strategic planning. In this chapter, we rely heavily on John Bryson, *Strategic Planning for Public and Nonprofit Organizations* (San Francisco: Jossey-Bass, 1995), and Robert Denhardt's treatment of strategic planning in the public sector in *Public Administration: An Action Orientation* (Belmont, CA: Brooks/Cole, 1991).

[5] Denhardt, *Public Administration,* p. 235.

[6] Bryson, *Strategic Planning for Public and Nonprofit Organizations,* p. 1; Denhardt, *Public Administration,* pp. 235–236.

[7] A variety of categorizations are in use. Bryson (*Strategic Planning,* p. 87) considers PESTs (political, economic, social, and technological), but this adaptation is sufficiently detailed to demonstrate our point.

[8] Jean M. McEnery and Mark L. Lifter, "Demands for Change: Interfacing Environmental Pressures and the Personnel Process," *Public Personnel Management* 16:1 (1987): 62–63.

[9] Bryson, *Strategic Planning,* pp. 18–19, 104–129.

[10] Charles E. Lindblom, *The Policy Making Process,* 2nd ed. (Englewood Cliffs, NJ: Prentice Hall, 1980), p. 38; Charles E. Lindblom, "The Science of 'Muddling Through,'" in Jay M. Shafritz and Albert C. Hyde, eds., *Classics of Public Administration,* 3rd ed. (Pacific Grove, CA: Brooks/Cole, 1992), pp. 233–234.

[11] James Thompson, *Organizations in Action* (New York: McGraw-Hill, 1967), p. 27.

[12] McCann and Selsky offer an interesting discussion of organizational response to what they term "hyperturbulence" as organizations face demands from their environments that overwhelm their ability to respond. Joseph E. McCann and John Selsky, "Hyperturbulence and the Emergence of Type 5 Environments," *Academy of Management Review* 9:3 (1984): 460–470.

13 Denhardt, *Public Administration,* p. 237; Bryson, *Strategic Planning.*

14 Cheryl Simrell King and Camilla Stivers, eds., *Government Is Us* (Thousand Oaks, CA: Sage, 1998), pp. 195–202.

15 Government Performance and Results Act of 1993.

16 Frances Stokes Berry and Barton Wechsler, "State Agencies' Experience with Strategic Planning: Findings from a National Survey," *Public Administration Review* 55:2 (1995): 160.

17 Ibid., p. 60.

18 Sally Coleman Selden, Pat Ingraham, and Willow Jacobson, "Human Resource Practices in State Governments: Findings from a National Survey" (paper presented at the National Conference of the American Society for Public Administration, Orlando, FL, April 10–14, 1999), pp. 12–13; cited with permission.

19 The web site for the International City/County Management Association is a good place for local governments and small nonprofit organizations to begin: **www.icma.org**.

20 Jennifer R. Wolch, *The Shadow State: Government and Voluntary Sector in Transition* (New York: Foundation Center, 1990), pp. 222–223.

21 Ibid., p. 222.

22 Ibid., p. 223.

23 Ibid.

24 Rosabeth Moss Kanter and David V. Summers, "Doing Well While Doing Good: Dilemmas of Performance Measurement in Nonprofit Organizations and the Need for a Multiple-Constituency Approach," in Walter W. Powell, ed., *The Nonprofit Sector* (New Haven, CT: Yale University Press, 1987).

25 H. George Frederickson, "Painting Bull's-Eyes Around Bullet Holes," *Governing* 6 (October 1992): 13.

26 Douglas H. Vinzant and Janet C. Vinzant, "Strategy and Organizational Capacity: Finding a Fit," *Public Productivity and Management Review* 20:2 (1996): 139–157.

27 Jason Stilwell, "Managing Chaos," *Public Management* 78:9 (1996): 6–8.

28 Ibid., p. 8.

29 See Bryson, *Strategic Planning,* Chap. 5, for a detailed description of the internal and external environmental assessments.

30 David E. Ripley, "How to Determine Future Workforce Needs," *Personnel Journal* (January 1995): 83–89.

31 Ibid., p. 84.

32 Ibid., p. 89.

33 Wallace S. Sayre, "The Triumph of Techniques over Purpose," in Frank J. Thompson, ed., *Classics of Public Personnel Policy,* 2nd ed. (Pacific Grove, CA: Brooks/Cole, 1991).

34 Taylor H. Cox, Jr., and Joycelyn A. Finley, "An Analysis of Work Specialization and Organization Level as Dimensions of Workforce Diversity," in Martin M. Chemers, Stuart Oskamp, and Mark A. Costanzo, eds., *Diversity in Organizations* (Thousand Oaks, CA: Sage, 1995).

35 Bryson, *Strategic Planning,* p. 1.

36 Ibid.; Vinzant and Vinzant, "Strategy and Organizational Capacity"; McCann and Selsky "Hyperturbulence."

37 Bryson, *Strategic Planning,* pp. 3–4.

38 Patrick M. Wright and Gary C. McMahan, "Theoretical Perspectives for Strategic Human Resource Management," *Journal of Management* 18:2 (1992): 298.

39 Wright and McMahan, "Theoretical Perspectives," p. 298.

40 Sonia Ospina, "When Managers Don't Plan: Consequences of Nonstrategic Public Personnel Management," *Review of Public Personnel Administration* 12:1 (1992): 53.

41 Ibid., p. 62.

42 Ibid., p. 64.

CHAPTER 7

Job Design, Analysis, and Classification

In a strategic management paradigm, decisions about positions in an organization, the requisite skills and knowledge needed by employees, and the structure of work should be consistent with the organization's mission and goals. Anyone who has worked with a large organization probably has seen an outline of what they are responsible to do in their position or inspected a schedule of salary ranges to identify what they were being paid. These small snapshots of an organization may or may not make very much sense in the context of organizational goals. For example, if we use a construction analogy, we might view planning activities as the blueprint for structure. However, the foundation on which this building would rest is composed of the design, analysis, and classification of positions. Much of what we discuss in later chapters on recruitment and selection, compensation, and performance management hinges on the analysis, classification, and evaluation of work performed in particular positions. **Job analysis**—and the resultant **job classification** and **job evaluation** of organizational positions—is simple in concept but tends to be quite complicated in application.

The dependence on classification systems in the public sector and in larger nonprofit organizations is an important factor in any schism that exists between line supervisors or managers and HRM support staff. Many managers express frustration as they try to hire an additional employee to respond to demands on their work unit or attempt to reclassify an existing member of their work team. The personnel need that managers try to articulate to human resource staff often has to be translated into a large, rigid system that is based on formulas and task definitions. In addition, job evaluation and classification decisions for a particular jurisdiction are constrained by merit system practice, labor law, and the usual public sector due process expectations. Complete books devoted to job analysis and classification cannot capture the nuances of all the various approaches in use. In this chapter, we introduce job analysis, evaluation, classification, and design and offer an overview of common practices, terms, and issues.

Let us assume that a job is a collection of tasks and duties associated with a particular activity in an organization. The intent behind job analysis is to identify exactly what those tasks are, the ramifications to the organization (or work group) of performing those tasks, and the skills and knowledge needed to perform the identified tasks competently. Once these tasks are identified, it is possible to specify the relative importance, difficulty, and scale of contribution of the competently performed job to the overall organizational effort. After specifying the tasks and the implications of those tasks to the organization, the analyst next considers the skills or knowledge necessary to perform the tasks and fulfill the duties of the position in question. From job analysis, position descriptions are developed that typically identify the overall rationale and objective for the position, list the specific tasks that are required, and identify the requisite skills or knowledge that the employee must possess. The evaluation of jobs allows them to be grouped in classes and be assigned their relative worth. Classification is the process of grouping similar jobs together, usually for the purpose of developing uniform compensation levels and establishing appropriate recruitment strategies. The logic of job analysis in an organization presumes that it is possible to identify clearly and completely the tasks and duties associated with a particular position.

Analysis, evaluation, and classification comprise a complex and time-consuming process intended to ensure equity and consistency in practice. Because of the expertise required and resources consumed in this exercise, detailed job analysis is more common in very large organizations. Although these analytical activities are advantageous from a legal and economic perspective, small, nonprofit organizations or local government public sector jurisdictions may dispense with many of those outlined in this chapter. Instead, such organizations may consider position descriptions (without the preliminary stages of analysis and evaluation) to be adequate for their purpose. In very small organizations, it is common to find that employees work without any formal position definitions or written job parameters.

INTRODUCTION TO READING

Because job analysis is a basic first step in recruitment and selection, performance management, and compensation packaging, it is very important that positions are examined accurately, without either deliberate error or unintentional bias. In the following reading, Jonathan Tompkins considers the evaluation phase of these activities. In his review, Tompkins examines job analysis and the design of the instrument for job evaluation. Recognizing that job analysis (the identification of tasks) is closely linked to job evaluation (the valuation of that cluster of tasks), he discusses the potential for measurement error that may exist in the judgment of the relative worth of different positions.

As you read the selection, keep the following questions in mind:

- Who pays attention to job analysis activities in an organization?
- What proportion of employees understand what this process means?
- What assumptions might employees make about the accuracy of position analysis, evaluation, and classification?
- What types of errors may exist in an assessment of the merits of one job over another?
- Why might some jobs be considered more important than others in achieving organizational goals?
- What does the potential for measurement error and bias in job analysis and evaluation have for discussions about workplace diversity?

███████   **READING**

Sources of Measurement Error and Gender Bias in Job Evaluation

JONATHAN TOMPKINS

INTRODUCTION

Concern over pay equity has occasioned new interest in the study of job evaluation both because job evaluation plans are said to contain gender biases and because they remain the principal means for establishing the comparability of jobs. Before gender biases can be removed from existing job evaluation plans, or before new "bias-free" plans can be developed, research is needed to determine whether identified sources of bias are actually producing gender-specific effects on job evaluation scores. The purpose of this [reading] is to facilitate research by identifying in the job evaluation literature those sources of measurement error that may reduce the reliability of evaluation judgments and the validity of evaluation results. Special attention is given to those sources of systematic error that may result in the undervaluation of female-dominated jobs.

As Remick (1983) notes, the search for a "bias-free" job evaluation system does not imply the search for a value-free one. Values are necessarily reflected in the factors, factor weights, and factor scales used to determine job worth. In addition, the search for a "bias-free" system does not assume that all biases can be removed. The goal of a bias-free job evaluation plan is to design a system that is as free of measurement error and gender as possible.

Figure 1, derived in part from Madigan (1982), presents potential sources of measurement error identified in the job evaluation literature and arranges them according to whether they manifest themselves in the design of the job evaluation instrument or in the process of evaluation itself. While much has been written on job evaluation design, and a separate literature is now emerging on gender bias in job evaluation processes, Figure 1 provides a single, comprehensive framework for identifying measurement error in both design and process. Persons interested in identifying and correcting measurement errors in existing evaluation plans, and those interested in developing new, bias-free plans, cannot accomplish their tasks if they focus on one to the exclusion of the other. Each potential source of error is discussed in turn below.

Figure 1   Potential Sources of Measurement Error in Job Evaluation

Design of the Job Evaluation Instrument
1. Choice of Factors
   a. factor independence
   b. factor comprehensiveness
2. Choice of Degree Level Definitions
   a. definition discriminability
   b. definition inclusiveness
3. Choice of Weights
   a. marketing contamination
   b. subjective judgments
   c. factor variability

The Evaluation Process
1. Job Analysis and Data Formatting
   a. instrument deficiencies
   b. analyst bias/inconsistency
   c. formatting deficiencies
2. Job Rating
   a. instrument deficiencies
   b. rater bias/inconsistency

Source: Jonathan Tompkins, "Sources of Measurement Error and Gender Bias in Job Evaluation," *Review of Public Personnel Administration* 9:1 (1988): 1–16. Reprinted by permission of the publisher, Institute of Public Affairs, University of South Carolina.

DESIGN OF THE JOB EVALUATION INSTRUMENT

The analysis that follows focuses on the traditional point-factor method of job evaluation because of its increasing popularity and its frequent use in comparable worth analysis. Traditional point-factor job evaluation plans are designed to measure variations in job content in order to determine the relative value of jobs in a given workforce. For job evaluation scores to be valid (i.e., reflect true variations in job content as, for example, determined through criterion-related or construct validity), the job evaluation instrument must be content valid (Tompkins, 1987). Content validity (or face validity) requires designing the measurement instrument in such a way that the content measured objects are clearly represented in the content of the instrument itself. In the context of job evaluation, establishing the plan's content validity requires selecting factors and factor degree level definitions that will allow accurate measurement of variations in the jobs to be evaluated.

Choice of Factors

Factors and their weights represent judgments regarding which dimensions of job content should be measured to establish internal job alignment, and what their relative importance should be. For job evaluation to measure the variations in the content of jobs in a given workforce validly, the factors selected must satisfy two requirements. First, factors should be relatively *independent* of each other. If factors actually measure the same dimension of job content, then that dimension will contribute more to the overall assessment of job worth than the designers of the system intended. Where such duplication exists, many jobs may be overevaluated.

Second, factors should be *comprehensive*, i.e., represent all major job content dimensions found in varying degrees in a majority of jobs. Failure to include an important factor may lead to undervaluation of certain jobs relative to others. As a practical matter, job evaluation designers seek a balance in the number of factors selected. If too few factors are included, adequate differentiation between jobs may not be possible. If too many factors are chosen, duplication may occur and differentiations may be too fine to be meaningful. Plans typically designate five to nine factors (Henderson,

1979). Research (Lawshe, 1945; Lawshe and Maleski, 1946) indicates that relatively few factors are necessary to adequately differentiate between jobs, provided that the important, "universal" factors have been identified.

Failure to select factors that are independent and comprehensive will not only reduce the validity of evaluation results generally, but may also produce biases that are gender specific. Systematic gender biases may be introduced where factors are *inappropriate* to the work being evaluated, and where important factors have been *omitted* from the plan. Factors, for example, originally selected to evaluate male-dominated, blue-collar jobs may not be as appropriate for evaluating female-dominated, clerical jobs. Where this is the case, female-dominated jobs may be undervalued.

Concern about the "inappropriateness" of factors has probably been overstated. It is not a problem in itself if physical strength has no relevance to clerical jobs, for example, as long as physical strength has been determined to be an important factor for evaluating at least a majority of the jobs covered by the evaluation plan. A more serious problem occurs when all important factors have *not* been identified and included. In contemporary practice, missing factors may well result in the undervaluation of jobs held predominantly by women. Gold (1983) suggests, as an example, that compensable factors chosen for the job of hod carrier would likely include physical effort but exclude ability to function well under time pressures. If the hod carrier's job evaluation plan were applied to a word processor in an executive office, the latter's job would likely be incorrectly evaluated.

Biases in favor of categories of jobs held predominantly by men have occurred in part because many factors were originally selected for evaluating predominantly male, blue-collar occupations. One possible corrective may be factor balancing, i.e., adding or eliminating factors to assure that male- and female-dominated jobs are fairly and completely evaluated. For example, if a plan includes a physical strength factor, it should perhaps include a manual dexterity factor. If a plan includes a physical stress factor, it should perhaps include a mental stress factor. This factor balancing should not, however, be carried to ridiculous extremes in which endless factors are developed to reward every major category of work. It would be a mistake to pursue pay equity either by adding new factors simply to assure more points for female-dominated jobs or by eliminating those factors that tend to legitimately benefit male-dominated jobs.

Factors identified in the literature (Remick, 1979, 1984b; Steinberg, 1984; Treiman, 1979) as awarding points principally to male-dominated jobs at the expense of female-dominated jobs include: (1) physical demands, (2) physical danger, (3) responsibility for property, (4) fiscal responsibility, (5) level of decisionmaking, (6) level of schooling required, and (7) supervision given. Factors identified as major components of female-dominated jobs that are often missing from job evaluation plans include: (1) speed and fine motor skills, (2) visual scanning skills, (3) responsibility for care of people, and (4) amount of interruption and simultaneous processing.

Comparable worth advocates argue that such factor imbalances reflect not only traditional ways of designing job evaluation plans for blue-collar occupations, but also underlying, deeply-rooted cultural values. Remick, (1984a: 97), for example, argues that "virtually all women's work suffers from the cultural perceptions that its main purpose is to help, not to do, and that there need to be men around to tell women what to do." To the extent that such cultural biases are operating, certain factors may be ignored or overlooked because we do not think to include them (Steinberg, 1984).

While it is clear that employers should be sensitive to the existence of gender-specific cultural stereotypes, and should exercise care in selecting factors that are not as a whole biased in favor of either gender, there is little research to guide their efforts. A study by Doverspike and Barrett (1984) supports the expectation that factor scales measuring interaction with people will favor female sex-typed jobs, while scales measuring interactions with things will favor male sex-typed jobs. However, one cannot conclude that the job evaluation plan studied by Doverspike and Barrett was inappropriately biased toward a particular gender. Factor scale "biases" may reflect legitimate variations in job content. Before bias-free plans can be developed, much more must be learned regarding the actual gender-specific effects produced by the factors employed.

Degree Level Definitions

In point-factor evaluation plans, jobs are differentiated by determining which factor degree levels best describe their content or demands made of their incumbents. Stated differently, degree levels for each factor comprise ordinal scales by which variations in job content are measured. Certain requirements must be met if measurement results are to be valid. First, degree levels must allow evaluators to *discriminate* between distinct gradations of the factor being measured. Second, the operational indicators contained in the degree level descriptions must be *inclusive* to assure that all relevant job elements are measured.

The first requirement involves the number of degree levels necessary to define the underlying job content dimension of each factor adequately and the ease with which they allow evaluators to differentiate between jobs. There must be enough levels to describe the complete range of differences, yet not so many that evaluators cannot easily differentiate between levels. Henderson (1979) suggests that a range of six to eight degrees is generally appropriate, although the number will vary with the nature of the factor or subfactor and the operational indicators employed. Failure to describe distinct degree levels poses a threat to the reliability of rater judgments, and hence to the validity of evaluation results.

The second requirement is that operational indicators must allow job content dimensions to be measured in a comprehensive fashion. Indicators must be *inclusive* enough to allow measurement of all relevant job content characteristics being evaluated. If the choice of operational indicators, for example, permits more differentiation among predominantly male jobs than among predominantly female jobs, then female-dominated jobs are likely to be undervalued (Treiman, 1979).

Operational indicators identified in the comparable worth literature as potential sources of gender bias (Eyde, 1983; Madigan, 1982; Remick, 1979, 1984a, 1984b; Steinberg, 1984; Treiman, 1979) include: (1) measuring skill requirements more in terms of experience than formal education; (2) measuring physical effort in terms of maximum periodic force applied rather than cumulative impact on the employee (fatigue); (3) measuring manual skill factors in terms of ability to handle tools but not in terms of speed or manual dexterity; (4) measuring interpersonal skills more in terms of negotiating than counseling and conciliating; (5) measuring responsibility in terms of supervisory or budgetary control but not in terms of organizing; (6) measuring responsibility in terms of money, materials, and safety of co-workers but not in terms of quality of health or safety of clients, customers, or citizens; (7) measuring adverse working conditions in terms of physical hardship (e.g., dampness, dirtiness) but not in terms of noise of office machines, strain of word processors, or restricted body movement; (8) measuring stress in terms of physical stress but not in terms of emotional/psychological stress or stress from constant interruption and simultaneous processing; and (9) measuring physical danger in terms of heights and use of machinery but not in terms of such things as exposure to disease or psychotic patients.

In addition, Remick and Steinberg (1984) have identified inconsistencies regarding the aspects of job content to which the operational measures are applied. For example, the content of a firefighter's job is typically evaluated according to work performed in rare emergency situations. The job is not devalued to reflect the content of most of the work routine. The work of jail matrons in the *Gunther* (1980) case, by contrast, was devalued because they were engaged in routine, clerical work when not tending to prisoners. Inconsistent evaluation of duties and responsibilities according to their frequency represents another potential source of gender bias.

When it is understood that men and women tend to do different kinds of work (Eyde, 1983), it becomes apparent why it is important to employ operational indicators that allow measurement of all relevant job content characteristics. Correcting for possible gender biases requires evaluating the operational indicators currently in use and analyzing how to operationalize factors differently. Remick (1979) suggests, as examples, giving points according to total weight lifted during a day or for total caloric output in lifting objects and both for full body movement and repeated and confined use of only a few muscles. Remick also would expand negative working conditions to include confinement to small spaces, restricted body movements, use of magnifying equipment, and noise from office machines measured for both average and peak levels.

While it seems likely that job evaluation validity is threatened by gender biases contained in operational measures, little systematic evidence exists regarding which operational definitions produce gender biases and what the magnitude of those bi-

ases might be. In the absence of such knowledge, there is little to guide those wishing to remove biases contained in operational measures. Practical difficulties arise as well. Although there may be compelling reasons for measuring mental and physical stress, for example, those factors are very difficult to operationalize because stress tends to vary with the incumbent as well as with the position. Extended outdoor activity, for example, may be viewed by some incumbents as physically stressful and by others as a source of welcomed exercise. In addition, there may be a danger of "correcting" biases in inappropriate ways. Berger (1984: 71) argues, for example, that it would be a mistake to attach more value to educational credentials just because more women than men attend college; the result would be to create a "blatant antiworking class and antiblue-collar bias . . . introduced under the disguise of justice and equity."

Choice of Weights
The organization's understanding of job worth is embodied in the choice of job content factors and in decisions regarding their relative importance. Those factors that the organization feels contribute the most to defining the relative value of jobs are assigned higher weights. Assuming that the requirement of factor independence has been met, changing the weights assigned to the various factors may substantially alter the organization's internal job alignment (Treiman, 1984). For those concerned about pay equity, the weights selected by the organization may represent an important source of systematic gender bias. It is entirely possible, for example, that final job evaluation results may accurately reflect the organization's understanding of which factors are most important for establishing relative worth, and yet be invalid in the sense that systematic biases have been introduced.

Systematic gender biases may be introduced through *market contamination* or as the result of *subjective judgments.* Because job evaluation plans often select factor weights that will maximize the relationship between internal job alignments and existing pay rates, weights will incorporate effects of any discrimination existing in the marketplace. Such biases may reflect historical undervaluation of female-dominated jobs based on stereotypes regarding the value of work; the traditionally weaker union power of women; the location of jobs in the competitive economic sector; purposeful gender discrimination; and other determinants of compensation not associated with job content, such as seniority and supply and demand.

From a pay equity perspective, the problem is not that market considerations are allowed to influence final wage determinations *per se,* but that those market influences may contain gender biases. The difficult yet essential task for compensation specialists today is to find ways of setting wages consistent with prevailing market rates without incorporating biases that unfairly result in the underpayment of female-dominated jobs. More attention is now being directed to this problem. Remick (1983), for example, suggests clustering female-dominated job titles with similar male-dominated job titles, using the latter as key classes in wage surveys, and setting pay rates for both accordingly. Another approach used increasingly (e.g., San Jose, Colorado Springs) is to estimate the amount of undervaluation related to the sex composition of job categories and to adjust the pay rates of female-dominated jobs by that factor.

Some organizations establish factor weights through group consensus. *Subjectivity of judgments* by those involved constitutes a second potential source of gender bias. A consensus may be reached, for example, that physical effort should be weighted more than interpersonal skills without those involved being fully aware that a potential bias has been created in favor of male-dominated, blue-collar jobs. Such biases may reflect traditional ways of designing job evaluation plans as well as underlying cultural stereotypes regarding which aspects of work should be valued most highly (Hartmann, Roos, and Treiman, 1985). Since there is no ultimate criterion for validating factor weights, employers wishing to avoid gender-specific biases have little to guide them. A study by Treiman (1984) suggests the kind of gender- and race-specific effects that might be expected from varying factor weights, but much more research is needed.

A third kind of bias results from the amount of job content variability found in specific workforces. If jobs tend to cluster around the same point on a point-factor scale, then the actual weight of that factor in differentiating between jobs may be small in comparison with its stated weight. "Ties" in total scores between jobs will be broken by those factors on which jobs are broadly distributed across factor scales. These factors will have an impact on final rankings out of proportion to what was intended by their assigned weights. Fox (1962: 435) provides an example:

> A simple example of this effect may be given by assuming that *all* jobs receive a rating of "60" on Factor "A" (consequently, no variability), whereas they are rated from 20 to 100 on Factor "B." It is apparent that the job's *final relative* value will depend *entirely* upon Factor "B" ratings regardless of how Factor "A" has been "intentionally" weighted relative to Factor "B." Admittedly, this is an extreme case, but the same thing holds true to some extent where there are differences in variability of ratings for the different factors. These factors will automatically weight themselves on the basis of the variability of their distributions.

This variability effect does not necessarily produce systematic gender bias. Factor variability may, however, negatively affect female-dominated jobs if those factors having the greatest actual weight are ones already biased in favor of rewarding male-dominated jobs (e.g., physical demands), particularly where these factors have a low "intended" weight.

THE EVALUATION PROCESS

When job evaluation procedures are examined for possible sources of random error or systematic bias, analysis tends to center on questions of reliability. In the context of job evaluation, reliability involves the ability of the measurement instrument to produce relatively consistent job evaluation scores across multiple evaluators and on different occasions.

Although measurement error can be traced to inadequate job information or ambiguous factor scales (instrument considerations), most of the reliability research focuses on random error attributable to the individual raters. Problems of reliability arise because job description and evaluation involve difficult and complex judgmental tasks that challenge the ability of raters to make accurate, unbiased judgments. The analysis that follows focuses on the judgmental tasks related to job analysis, data formatting, and job rating.

Job Analysis and Data Formatting
Instrument Deficiencies   Job analysis involves identifying and describing the work content of each job

in terms of the *nature* of the work (e.g., duties and responsibilities) and the *level* of the work (e.g., levels of skill, effort, responsibility, and working conditions). When deciding upon the means for conducting job analysis, the principal concern is to choose that method or combination of methods that facilitates the job rating process by providing information that is complete, accurate, and unbiased. Commonly used procedures for collecting job information include interviews, work observations, questionnaires, logs, and task inventory checklists. Each procedure is characterized by limitations that threaten the reliability of job information.

Each method of job analysis, for example, tends to be subject to an *availability bias*, i.e., a bias toward those pieces of information that are most readily available or come most easily to mind. The reliability of the interview method, for example, depends on the ability of the person being interviewed to recall all relevant job activities. As McArthur (1985) notes, there is a tendency to recall those activities done most frequently, done most recently, or that are most perceptually salient. An example of the latter arises, for example, when supervisors identify typing as the principal activity of secretaries because the noise of typing is what is most salient to them.

Similarly, the reliability of the observation method depends on the ability of observers to witness the full range of activities characteristic of a particular job. It is likely, for example, that tasks performed only periodically will escape observation. The reliability of the log method depends on the willingness or ability of incumbents to record all pertinent information, and it is probably a rare individual that is so disciplined. Questionnaires are also subject to measurement error. If open-ended questions are employed, the resulting data are difficult to compare and will vary greatly in terms of completeness. In addition, the amount and quality of data provided may vary more with the thoroughness and writing skills of the person completing the questionnaire than with the content of the job itself. Conversely, where questions are highly structured (as with checklist methods), the information may be accurate but the kind and amount of information may not be sufficient for purposes of job rating.

In theory, incomplete or inaccurate job content information poses a threat to the validity of evaluation scores for male- and female-dominated jobs alike. In actual practice, however, it is possible that this source of measurement error is producing gender-specific effects on job evaluation scores. Unfortunately, very little is yet known about the effects of job analysis techniques and job information quality on job evaluation scores.

Job Analyst Bias/Inconsistency   Related to the issue of which procedure(s) to employ is the issue of who will be asked to supply job information. Even when a combination of techniques is employed to enhance the quality of job information, those involved in gathering data may introduce their personal biases. Biases or inconsistencies in judgment may be related to the institutional position of those supplying job information, the amount of their training or job knowledge, culturally-engendered attitudes, or some other set of personal characteristics.

Research designed to determine the amount of agreement among institutional actors regarding job requirements has produced mixed results. Relatively high agreement in rating required job abilities has been found among incumbents (Fischer and Sobkow, 1979), among supervisors (Desmond and Weiss, 1973), and among trained analysts (Mosel, Fine, and Boling, 1960). Further, Smith and Hakel (1979) found similar, moderately high, mean reliability coefficients for supervisors, incumbents, personal specialists and students analyzing the same set of 25 jobs using the Position Analysis Questionnaire (PAQ). Except for the fact that supervisors and incumbents were found to be more lenient in evaluating jobs than personnel specialists, results of this study suggest that it makes little practical difference who conducts job analysis, at least when using the PAQ.

Other studies, however, have produced markedly different results. Meyer (1959) found fairly low agreement between foremen and general foremen regarding the responsibilities of the foremen. In only 58% of the cases was there agreement as to whether the foreman had "complete," "partial," or "no" responsibility for a given task. Similarly, O'Reilly (1973) found that incumbents and supervisors disagreed in 67.2% of cases regarding the level of skill/knowledge required to perform given jobs. Finally, Jenkins, Douglas, Nadler, and Lawler (1975) found moderate agreement using a structured observation technique, with agreement varying widely by factor. Why these studies should produce different results is not clear. Differences in job knowledge, the nature of the job studied, characteristics of the measuring instruments, or some combination of these factors may well have contributed to the results.

Those involved in gathering job information, whether incumbents, supervisors, or personnel specialists, may be subject to several kinds of personal biases. A *halo bias,* for example, is introduced where the job information recorded is influenced by knowledge of a job's prestige, its assumed salary, or its association with a particular gender. A related bias, an *expectancy bias,* is introduced where judgments about the characteristics of people or jobs tend to be overly influenced by information that confirms what they expect, e.g., a tendency to describe a job with whatever characteristics are culturally expected for that job. Widespread stereotypes concerning differences in ability and personality between men and women may bias job descriptions. For example, if women are viewed as less independent, competitive, or ambitious than men (Broverman, Vogel, Broverman, Clarkson, and Rosenkrantz, 1972), then such stereotypes may create assumptions regarding what abilities are needed for jobs typically held by women. Gender-based expectancy biases are difficult to eliminate because men and women tend to share the same stereotyped views of sex roles (Broverman et al., 1972) and because it is difficult to conceal from the job analyst knowledge of a job's prestige, salary, or gender composition.

The potential biases described above would not be problematic if the same constant error existed for all jobs. There is concern, however, that a portion of the error is gender-specific. As McArthur (1985: 66–67) notes,

> The halo bias will overestimate the worth of work that is relatively prestigious and well paid—men's work. The expectancy bias will overestimate the skills, leadership, training, and effort that are required by work that is culturally expected to require such qualities—men's work. And the availability bias will reinforce this tendency, inasmuch as it will overestimate the frequency of familiar—i.e., expected—job activities, in addition to those that are recent or perceptually salient.

The extent to which these biases are actually affecting job evaluation scores, however, is not yet known.

Formatting Deficiencies   Data supplied through job analysis are generally aggregated into standardized job descriptions. Where job evaluation is based on existing job descriptions that have not been recently audited and updated, the information contained in them is likely to be inaccurate and evaluation results not fully valid.

The traditional narrative job description presents problems for job evaluation even when accurate. Because it is seldom formatted along specific job content dimensions, not all relevant information is supplied. As a result, attention is selectively directed toward existing information, thereby creating an availability bias. In addition, because job evaluation requires the translation of descriptive information into comparable data, the absence of standardized formats makes the comparison of jobs difficult. In short, the job description valid for hiring purposes may not be equally valid for job evaluation purposes. These problems can be addressed in part by preparing structured job descriptions in which information is supplied on dimensions reflecting the factors on which jobs will be evaluated, and by using quantitative data where possible.

Even where data are provided in standardized formats, significant variations may exist in the descriptive language employed. Because job descriptions are not all written by the same person, and because it is difficult to standardize the language used, introduction of gender bias is possible. Remick (1979) notes that linguists have found patterns in the wording used in men's and women's job descriptions. Position descriptions written by women tend to use "weaker" verbs. For example, men may "manage" and women "supervise"; men may "interpret" and women "use."

As noted above, assuring the validity of job evaluation results requires making the job analysis process as reliable as possible. While much research is yet needed, some tentative conclusions can be drawn from the literature regarding how to enhance the reliability of job analysis techniques and procedures. First, alerting analysts to potential biases may help them avoid biases. Second, using a combination of job analysis techniques, such as questionnaires followed by interview/observation audits, may minimize the inherent shortcomings of any particular technique. A recent study by Schwab and Grams (1985) suggests that this is the current practice in many organizations. Third, using questionnaires that explicitly require information pertinent to job content factors will help assure that appropriate and necessary data are obtained. Finally, analysis should be done independently by more than one person, including incumbents and supervisors as well as trained analysts.

Job Rating

Judgments involved in job rating may be as problematic as those involved in job analysis. Where raters fail to produce similar ratings, or where the same rater fails to make consistent judgments over time, the validity of evaluation results will be reduced. The fault may lie with deficiencies in the instrument or with rater biases or inconsistencies.

Instrument Deficiencies   Even assuming that factors and operational measures are relatively unbiased and that data supplied by job analysis are accurate, biases can be introduced as the result of lack of clarity or discriminability in the measurement scales. Where this is the case, inconsistencies of judgment are likely among raters, regardless of their intended objectivity. Research (e.g., Doverspike and Barrett, 1983; Fraser, Cronshaw, and Alexander, 1984; Lawshe and Wilson, 1947) consistently shows lower reliability coefficients for individual factors than for overall scores. The results of such studies provide guidance in redesigning those scales which produce the lowest reliabilities. Unfortunately, very few studies have examined reliability of factor scales by type, e.g., qualitative versus quantitative scales, grid versus graphic presentations, or scales varying by number and range of degree levels (Madigan, 1982).

Although inconsistencies will threaten validity even where they do not produce systematic biases, they also increase the chances of gender bias by creating an ambiguous judgment environment in which individual biases may become the basis for judgment, either intentionally or unintentionally. Because factors often represent abstract constructs, achieving clear definitions and unambiguous scales is difficult as it is necessary.

Rater Bias/Inconsistency   Job raters, as well as job analysts, may be influenced by biases related to their institutional position, amount of training or job knowledge, culturally-engendered attitudes, or some other set of personal characteristics. Some of these

factors may result in random measurement errors, while others may produce systematic biases. Studies generally have found high interrater agreement (e.g., Ash, 1948; Chesler, 1948; Doverspike and Barrett, 1984; Lawshe and Farbo, 1949; Lawshe and Wilson, 1947). In addition, similarly high reliability coefficients have been found between incumbents and supervisors (Satter, 1949) and between incumbents and managers (Chambliss, 1950).

A possible source of bias is the amount of job familiarity each rater possesses. In one of the very few studies on the subject, Madden (1962) found that Air Force officers consistently gave higher ratings to those job specialties with which they had the greatest familiarity. Much more research is needed regarding the effects of raters' job familiarity, training, and experience on evaluation scores.

As noted above, a consistent finding in the research on sex roles is that males and females are evaluated differently (Shepela and Viviano, 1984; Broverman et al., 1972). A concern expressed in the comparable worth literature is that job raters may intentionally or unintentionally undervalue jobs performed predominantly by women. Judgments, for example, may vary as a result of the gender of the evaluator, perceptions of the gender composition of the job, and perceptions of the salary level or prestige of the job.

It might be hypothesized, for example, that males evaluate female-dominated jobs less favorably than females evaluate them. Although the effects of sex-stereotyping have been investigated in the areas of personnel selection and performance appraisal, very little research has been conducted regarding the effects of sex-stereotyping on evaluation scores. Preliminary evidence (Arvey, Passino, and Lounsbury, 1977; Doverspike, Carlisi, Barrett, and Alexander, 1983; Schwab and Grams, 1985) suggests that judgments do not vary significantly as a function of the gender of the rater.

Although judgments may not vary with the gender of the rater, it is possible nonetheless that raters are influenced by shared biases. Male and female raters, alike, for example, may be influenced by knowledge of the job's gender composition, prestige, or salary. Unfortunately, very few studies have addressed these questions. Studies by Grams and Schwab (1985) and Schwab and Grams (1985) found little or no evidence that evaluators were influenced by the gender composition of jobs. Their findings, however, must be treated as preliminary since only three jobs were evaluated and only one of these was manipulated in terms of gender composition.

A recent study by Mount and Ellis (1987), in which two jobs were manipulated in terms of gender composition, found evidence of a marginally significant gender effect. A job was rated more highly when given a female job title (nurse aide or YWCA director) than when given a male title (orderly or YMCA director), suggesting a pro-female bias. While the explanation of this effect is not known, it is likely that the evaluators, who had been trained to participate in a comparable worth study, had been sensitized to issues of pay equity. As a result, evaluators may have overcompensated in evaluating female-dominated jobs. While these studies provide interesting findings, the evidence remains very limited. Research is needed on a greater range of jobs, particularly on those such as nurses and secretaries thought to be most susceptible to sex-stereotyping, and in more "real world" settings.

Although little evidence of direct bias was found, these studies did find evidence of indirect bias. College students (Grams and Schwab), compensation professionals (Schwab and Grams), and trained job analysts (Mount and Ellis) appeared to be influenced by knowledge of the salary of the job. Those raters who were told the job received a specific salary scored the job lower than those raters who were told the job received a higher salary. The pay effect in the study by Mount and Ellis, however, was much weaker than that reported in Schwab and Grams, explaining 1% of the variance as compared with 12%. This preliminary evidence suggests that where female-dominated jobs are currently receiving wages that are unjustifiably low in terms of their job content, knowledge of their wages may produce a systematic gender bias on job evaluation scores.

RESEARCH ISSUES

Eliminating gender bias does not mean removing all factors, factor weights, or factor definitions that result in female-dominated jobs being awarded fewer points than male-dominated jobs. After all, points awarded to male-dominated jobs may legitimately reflect characteristics of the work, and the principal source of pay inequalities may lie in the fact that women have had restricted access to correctly eval-

uated male-dominated jobs. Thus, eliminating gender bias from job evaluation plans involves identifying and removing those unjustified biases that work to the disadvantage of either gender.

Before bias-free plans can be developed much more research must be conducted. This [reading] has identified reputed sources of bias which can serve as points of departure for future research efforts. [. . .]

REFERENCES

Arvey, R. D., E. M. Passino, and J. W. Lounsbury (1977). "Job Analysis Results as Influenced by Sex of Incumbent and Sex of Analyst." *Journal of Applied Psychology* 62: 411–416.

Ash, P. (1948). "The Reliability of Job Evaluation Rankings." *Journal of Applied Psychology* 32: 313–320.

Berger, B. (1984). "Comparable Worth at Odds with American Realities," pp. 65–71 in U. S. Commission on Civil Rights, *Comparable Worth: Issues for the 80s.*

Broverman, I. K., S. R. Vogel, D. M. Broverman, F. E. Clarkson, and P. S. Rosenkrantz (1972). "Sex-role Stereotypes and Clinical Judgements of Mental Health." *Journal of Social Issues* 28: 59–78.

Chambliss, L. A. (1950). "Our Employees Evaluate Their Own Jobs." *Personnel Journal* 29: 141–142.

Chesler, D. J. (1948). "Reliability and Comparability of Different Job Evaluation Systems." *Journal of Applied Psychology* 32: 465–475.

County of Washington v. *Gunther* (1980). 101 S Ct. S. C. 352.

Desmond, R. E. and D. J. Weiss (1973). "Supervisor Estimation of Abilities Required in Jobs." *Journal of Vocational Behavior* 3: 181–194.

Doverspike, D. and G. V. Barrett (1984). "An Internal Bias Analysis of a Job Evaluation Instrument." *Journal of Applied Psychology* 69: 648–662.

Doverspike, D., A. M. Carlisi, G. V. Barrett, and R. A. Alexander (1983). "Generalizability Analysis of a Point-method Job Evaluation Instrument." *Journal of Applied Psychology* 68: 476–483.

Eyde, L. D. (1983). "Evaluating Job Evaluation: Emerging Research Issues for Comparable Worth Analysis." *Public Personnel Management* 12: 418–424.

Fischer, D. G. and J. Sobkow (1979). "Workers' Estimation of Ability Requirements of Their Jobs." *Perceptual and Motor Skills* 48: 519–531.

Fox, W. M. (1962). "Purpose and Validity in Job Evaluation." *Personal Journal* 41: 432–437.

Fraser, S. L., S. F. Cronshaw, and R. A. Alexander (1984). "Generalizability Analysis of a Point Method Job Evaluation Instrument: A Field Study." *Journal of Applied Psychology* 69: 643–647.

Gold, M. E. (1983). *A Dialogue on Comparable Worth.* Ithaca, NY: Industrial and Labor Relations Press.

Grams, R. and D. P. Schwab (1985). "An Investigation of Systematic Gender-Related Error in Job Evaluation." *Academy of Management Journal* 28: 279–290.

Hartmann, H. I. (ed.). (1985). *Comparable Worth: New Directions for Research*. Washington, D.C.: National Academy Press.

Hartmann, H. I., P. A. Roos, and D. J. Treiman (1985). "An Agenda for Basic Research on Comparable Worth," pp. 3–33 in H. I. Hartmann (ed.) *Comparable Worth: New Directions for Research*.

Henderson, R. I. (1979). *Compensation Management: Rewarding Performance*. Reston, VA: Reston Publishing Company.

Jenkins, G. D., D. A. Nadler, E. E. Lawler III, and C. Cammann (1975). "Standardized Observations: An Approach to Measuring the Nature of Jobs." *Journal of Applied Psychology* 60: 171–181.

Lawshe, C. H., Jr., (1945). "The Adequacy of Abbreviated Point Ratings for Hourly-paid Jobs in Three Industrial Plants." *Journal of Applied Psychology* 29: 177–184.

Lawshe, C. H., Jr. and P. C. Farbo (1949). "The Reliability of an Abbreviated Job Evaluation System." *Journal of Applied Psychology* 33: 158–166.

Lawshe, C. H., Jr. and A. A. Maleski (1946). "An Analysis of Point Ratings for Salary-paid Jobs in an Industrial Plant." *Journal of Applied Psychology* 30: 117–128.

Lawshe, C. H., Jr. and R. F. Wilson (1947). "The Reliability of Two Point Rating Systems." *Journal of Applied Psychology* 31: 355–365.

McArthur, L. Z. (1985). "Social Judgment Biases in Comparable Worth Analysis," pp. 53–70 in H. I. Hartmann (ed.) *Comparable Worth: New Directions for Research*.

Madden, J. M. (1962). "The Effect of Varying the Degree of Rater Familiarity in Job Evaluation." *Personnel Administrator* 25: 42–46.

Madigan, R. M. (1982). *Job Evaluation as a Determinant of Job Worth: A Conceptual and Comparative Analysis*. Ph.D. dissertation, Michigan State University.

Meyer, H. H. (1959). "A Comparison of Foreman and General Foreman Conceptions of the Foreman's Job Responsibilities." *Personnel Psychology* 12: 445–452.

Mosel, J. N., S. A. Fine and J. Boling (1960). "The Scalability of Estimated Worker Requirements." *Journal of Applied Psychology* 44: 156–160.

Mount, M. K. and R. A. Ellis (1987). "Investigation of Bias in Job Evaluation Ratings of Comparable Worth Study Participants." *Personnel Psychology* 40: 85–96.

O'Reilly, A. P. (1973). "Skill Requirements: Supervisor-Subordinate Conflict." *Personnel Psychology* 26: 75–80.

Remick, H. (1979). "Strategies for Creating Sound Bias-free Job Evaluation Plans," in *Job Evaluation and EEO: The Emerging Issues*. NY: Industrial Relations Counsellors, Inc.

Remick, H. (1983). "The Comparable Worth Controversy." *Public Personnel Management Journal* 12: 371–382.

Remick, H. (1984a). "Dilemmas of Implementation: The Case of Nursing," pp. 90–98 in H. Remick (ed.) *Comparable Worth and Wage Discrimination: Technical Possibilities and Political Realities*. Philadelphia: Temple University Press.

Remick, H. (1984b). "Major Issues in a priori Applications," pp. 99–117 in H. Remick (ed.) *Comparable Worth and Wage Discrimination*.

Remick, H. and R. J. Steinberg (1984). "Technical Possibilities and Political Realities: Concluding Remarks," pp. 285–302 in H. Remick (ed.) *Comparable Worth and Wage Discrimination*.

Satter, G. A. (1949). "Method of Paired Comparisons and a Specification Scoring Key in the Evaluation of Jobs." *Journal of Applied Psychology* 33: 212–221.

Schwab, D. P. and R. Grams (1985). "Sex-related Errors in Job Evaluation: A "Real-world Test." *Journal of Applied Psychology* 70: 533–539.

Shepela, S. T. and A. T. Viviano (1984). "Some Psychological Factors Affecting Job Segregation and Wages," pp. 47–58 in H. Remick (ed.) *Comparable Worth and Wage Discrimination*.

Smith, J. E. and M. D. Hakel (1979). "Convergence Among Data Sources, Response Bias, and Reliability and Validity of a Structured Job Analysis Questionnaire." *Personnel Psychology* 32: 677–692.

Steinberg, R. J. (1984). "Identifying Wage Discrimination and Implementing Pay Equity Adjustments," pp. 99–116 in U. S. Commission on Civil Rights, *Comparable Worth: Issues for the 80's*.

Tompkins, Jonathan (1987). "Comparable Worth and Job Evaluation Validity." *Public Administration Review* 47 (May–June): 254–258.

Treiman, D. J. (1979). *Job Evaluation: An Analytic Review*. Washington, D.C.: National Academy of Sciences.

Treiman, D. J. (1984). "Effects of Choice of Factors and Factor Weights in Job Evaluation," pp. 79–89 in H. Remick (ed) *Comparable Worth and Wage Discrimination*.

Treiman, D. J. and H. I. Hartmann (ed.) (1981). *Women, Work, and Wages: Equal Pay for Jobs of Equal Value*. Washington, D.C.: National Academy Press.

U.S. Commission on Civil Rights (1984). *Comparable Worth: Issues for the 80's*. Washington, D.C.: U.S. Government Printing Office.

ANALYSIS AND CLASSIFICATION IN CONTEXT

Much of contemporary job analysis and classification is founded in Progressive era calls for neutral, competent public servants. Because the Pendleton Act calls for a civil service predicated on competence rather than patronage, there must be some means to identify what competencies are necessary for the different positions in government. As Figure 7.1 illustrates, a variety of forces shape contemporary analysis, description, evaluation, and classification. Civil service reform and the notion of equity in compensation provide fertile ground for contemporary analysis, description, evaluation, and classification. These personnel activities ensure that patronage is on the decline because jobs are specifically defined in terms of necessary competencies rather than political ties.

Paralleling concerns in the political arena about neutrality and competence in government, a collection of early twentieth-century organization theorists studied the implications of organization structure and procedure for productivity; these practice-oriented scholars are often collectively referred to as the *classical school of organization theory.* This school is predicated on the belief that it is necessary to control the irrationality of humans to improve organizational effort.[1] Two major approaches are associated with classical organization theory. The **science of administration** approach holds that human beings can be controlled to improve organizational outcomes through the development of appropriate authority structures. **Scientific management,** in contrast, focuses concern on control over behavior exercised through the structure of tasks associated with the positions within organizations.

Structuring the Organization for Efficiency

Max Weber's depiction of the ideal structure of **bureaucracy** is the cornerstone to the science of administration movement.[2] Weber, a German sociologist, believed that a particular organizational structure could improve the rationality of the col-

Figure 7.1   Analysis and Classification: Context and Development

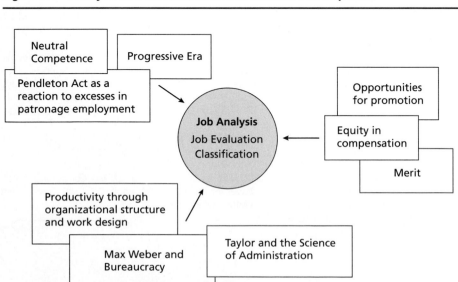

Figure 7.2   Bureaucracy

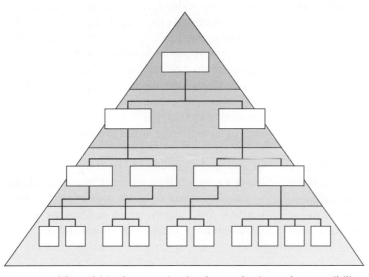

A position within the organization has authority and responsibility bounded by the scope of activities for that position.

lective efforts of human beings, reducing the likelihood of arbitrary and capricious action.[3] This structure—the bureaucracy—hinges on the division of labor and hierarchical authority relationships that is explicitly detailed in organizational policies and rules. Adam Smith, in his monumental tome *The Wealth of Nations,* published in 1776, noted the importance of the division of labor to the efficient use of resources and the generation of wealth; Max Weber counted on the craft and professional specializations that would emerge in industrializing countries to argue that organizational productivity required a high degree of division of labor giving structure to uniform work processes and outcomes.[4] The division of responsibility for particular tasks presumes a clear distribution of authority and a limited span of control to ensure direct supervision of subordinates (see Figure 7.2). Authority should be commensurate with the narrow responsibilities associated with a particular job, and so it tends to be centralized and reflective of a monocratic hierarchy. In bureaucratic models, individuals hold positions in the structure and are selected according to their ability to perform the defined job. Authority rests with the position and remains fixed to the location of the position in the hierarchy. Authority does not rest with individuals, and jobs do not belong to people. Employees can move in and out of different positions with no discernible effect on the organization. In this sense, all employees are by design and intention interchangeable and replaceable.

Structuring the Job for Efficiency

For scientific management theorists such as Frederick Taylor, the work associated with position (rather than the organizational authority structure) can be structured to improve organizational productivity. In this regard, jobs can be reduced to a collection of small tasks. Productivity can be improved by identifying the most efficient way to perform each of these tasks. Taylor believed there was "one best way" to complete every meaningful task and that people, properly motivated with the right incentive, would work to optimum.[5] The tenets of scientific management emphasize technical efficiency to enhance organizational activity.

ANALYSIS AND CLASSIFICATION IN HUMAN RESOURCE MANAGEMENT

The practice of administration, as prescribed through classical organization theory, means that some method is required to allow the positions in organizations to be studied and categorized. If the goal is to improve efficiency for the organization and to deal with employees on the basis of merit, then decisions should hinge on competence in task

rather than on personal characteristics. Contemporary job analysis, evaluation, and classification emerged to address concerns about subjectivity, equity, merit, and efficiency. Today these functions are fundamental to established personnel systems in the public, private for-profit, and not-for-profit sectors alike. The structural linkages among the very technical activities of analysis, evaluation, and classification and other personnel functions are detailed in Figure 7.3. Analysis, evaluation, and classification are linked to the overall compensation package offered to employees. In theory, salaries and wages should be commensurate with the tasks or services provided by the employee.

Employees are recruited and selected using a **position description,** which outlines the general responsibilities, duties, and requisite qualifications

Figure 7.3   Analysis, Evaluation, and Classification in Human Resource Management

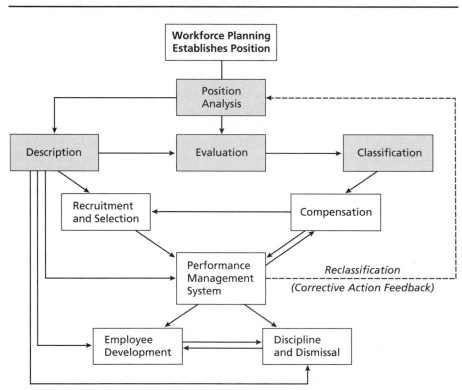

of the job. In a performance management system, the position description suggests baseline performance expectations for an employee's expected performance. In combination, job analysis, evaluation, and classification activities support employee development activities. Employees can assess their skills and knowledge and their responsibilities in terms of the expectations for a related position or a position to which they aspire. Training needs and opportunities for advancement can be identified through job analysis. Finally, the position description outlines the appropriate scope of a position for an employee. The responsibilities and duties outlined in the job description provide some guidance to an employee and the employer as to the minimum expectations about performance for a position. Disciplinary action must be consistent with guidelines established about employee responsibilities and behavior.

A component of the organization's strategic planning effort should be to identify the types of activities that an organization is performing currently, as well as those that may be necessary in the short-term and more long-term future. Obviously we need to determine what types of jobs we will have in an organization, what jobs we will need in the future, and what kinds of people we will need to find to fill those jobs. We have to make these decisions in the context of a budget, as well as the political demands on our organization for action. How much of the budget can we allocate to hire people to perform certain activities? How much will we have to pay to acquire the people with the knowledge and skills that we need, or alternatively, how much should we invest in the training and development of employees to acquire needed knowledge and skills?

In addition to budgetary and political considerations, the nature of work is changing along with people's expectations about their jobs, as we discovered in earlier chapters. The skills associated with different positions have changed rapidly even within the past few years. The use of technology, communication skills, language versatility, equity and access, and even the physical environment of work affect employee attitudes toward different positions. The dynamics of organization effort and the evolving scope of many traditional jobs affect the expectations that employers have about minimum qualifications and performance levels for different jobs.

JOB ANALYSIS

The premise behind job or position analysis is relatively simple. Job analysis identifies the tasks necessary for a competent performance of a particular activity. The person who holds the job under scrutiny is usually called the **job incumbent**. To develop a complete picture of what a particular job may entail, the analyst may interview the job incumbent, his or her supervisor, and often others with whom this person works. The analysis must focus on the tasks and duties affiliated with a particular position, not on the person in the position or any unique contribution he or she brings to their work.

A job analyst determines the specific duties associated with a position and identifies the amount of time associated with each major duty. It is customary to identify the tangential positions associated with a particular job. What levels of supervision occur, and what kinds of decisions does the job incumbent have authority to make? Does the job incumbent have to perform the work in conjunction with others, such as a supervisor or peer? For each task, the job analyst needs to identify the knowledge, skills, or abilities (**KSAs**) that may be required. **Knowledge** required for a position suggests that a person is informed about the body of procedures and techniques associated with a particular area of activity. *Skills* and *abilities* are somewhat similar in meaning. An **ability** suggests the potential or capacity to perform, while a **skill** may be a specific mastery of a technique or tool. Next, the job analyst would need to identify any formal training or education that may be necessary to certify those elements of knowledge, skill and ability. For example, what is necessary to manage a particular computer-related task—an engineering degree or select courses in a software application?

It is very important, as we will see in later chapters, that the tasks specified be logically linked to a particular job and the qualifications (e.g., education or training) be related to the tasks. Tasks should be legitimately associated with a position, and the qualifications should be commensurate with the required KSAs. In addition to training or education, there may be qualifications necessary for a particular position. Are there legal requirements for licensure, as in the medical profession? Does the job incumbent need to operate machinery that may require licensure or a particular permit? What are the physical and operational parameters of the positions? Does it require that the job incumbent work evening shifts? Does the job incumbent work outside or in an office?

Strategic job analysis requires a consideration of the demands or requirements of a position over time rather than through a static assessment of the tasks at one point in time.[6] Managers seeking a new position or a reclassification of an existing slot need to consider carefully the position in context: over time, in comparison to similar positions in different units, and with regard to organizational goals. For analysts, the focus is often on how the job may evolve in the future in response to the work environment, changing technology, or different mandates specified for public sector organizations. Both managers and human resource specialists must recognize the practical, legal, and political constraints facing the organization in terms of an existing structure or personnel system if the political will necessary to revise an existing classification system does not exist.

Technical considerations in job analysis also warrant attention. Two procedures are most commonly used to conduct job analyses: the *Task Inventory Procedure* and the *Position Analysis Questionnaire*. There are various permutations of these two general methods, and substantial research time has been devoted to developing these procedures. Job analysis can be a very complicated specialty within human resource management.

Task Inventory Procedure

Although there are variations in the **Task Inventory Procedure,** generally the job incumbent identifies the list of tasks he or she performs.[7] The incumbent is then asked to assess the relative difficulty of each task and then to indicate how often the task is performed.[8] Job incumbents may also be asked to assess the difficulty of learning a particular task relative to other job-related activities. Incumbents may be asked to assess the importance of the task in terms of their other activities, as well as to the organization as a whole. In some cases, supervisors are asked to assess the difficulty, frequency, and importance levels that employees assign.[9] Job incumbents tend to rate as higher in importance those tasks that are difficult to learn and difficult to perform rather than those that are relatively more time intensive or associated with greater responsibility.[10] There appears to be an acceptable level of inter-rater validity: incumbents tend to be fairly consistent in how they assess different tasks for many of the difficulty, frequency, and centrality scales.[11] Interestingly, researchers who found evidence of some variability in the assessment of different tasks attributed the variation to personal characteristics of the incumbent rather than actual variations between positions. "Such idiosyncratic perceptions of job tasks might in turn be moderated by differing degrees of job experience or educational level or perhaps by true differences in the manner in which jobs are performed."[12]

A sample of task dimensions is outlined in Box 7.1. Note in this sample that tasks are differentiated in terms of difficulty and relative significance to the organization. Difficulty and significance may be established from multiple perspectives; for example, significance could be time spent, task criticality, or task importance. A simple list of tasks does not capture the relational aspects of the position, such as responsibilities to coordinate information or prioritize correspondence and reaction to queries from other organizational units or from outside the organization. The task list

Box 7.1   Sample Dimensions of Task

Task Dimension	In Application . . .
Time spent	The amount of time spent by the job incumbent on a task relative to other tasks in a job
Task difficulty	The difficulty in performing the task that is perceived by the incumbent relative to other tasks in the job
Task criticality	The degree to which incorrect performance of the task by the incumbent would result in negative consequences relative to other tasks in a job
Difficulty of learning the task	The amount of time and effort that the incumbent believes he or she exerted to learn the task relative to all other tasks in a job
Task responsibility	The degree of responsibility that the incumbent holds for completing a task without supervision, relative to all other tasks in a job
Overall task importance	The overall importance that the incumbent perceives the task to hold relative to all other tasks in a job

Source: The task dimensions are drawn from Juan I. Sanchez and Edward L. Levine, "Determining Important Tasks Within Jobs: A Policy Capturing Approach," *Journal of Applied Psychology* 74:2 (1989): 337.

similarly does not establish job context; the level of authority, noise levels, or frequency of interruptions are not captured.

Position Analysis Questionnaire

The **Position Analysis Questionnaire** (PAQ), developed by Ernest McCormick and his associates over the course of several years, presumes that a job can be broken down into "discrete job variables," which can then be "identified and quantified as they relate to individual jobs."[13] McCormick distinguishes between job variables that are technical kinds of skills, such as may be identified in task inventories, and those that relate to the interpersonal and behavioral nature of work.[14] The PAQ contains questions designed to generate data for differentiating positions according to the general categories of information input,

mediation processes, work output, interpersonal activities, work situation, job context, and a catch-all category for miscellaneous aspects.[15] Box 7.2 on page 182 contains a list of these categories, along with sample job elements for the PAQ. The job elements normally would be assessed according to the frequency of occurrence or perhaps the level of importance of the job element to the overall position. The PAQ attempts to identify the range of behaviors necessary to complete a particular task rather than identify the discrete task.

Limitations of Job Analysis

Both the Task Inventory Procedure and PAQ are used to analyze jobs in preparation for subsequent personnel activities. The procedures identify slightly different types of information. The Task Inventory Approach focuses on the aggregation

Box 7.2   Position Analysis Questionnaire

General Categories	Subdivisions of Activity	Job Element
Information input	Sources of job information Discrimination and perceptional activities	Use of written materials Estimating speed of moving objects
Mediation processes	Decision making and reasoning Information processing Use of stored information	Reasoning in problem solving Encoding and decoding Using mathematics
Work output	Use of physical devices Integrative manual activities General body activities	Keyboard Handling objects Climbing
Interpersonal activities	Communications Interpersonal relationships Supervision and coordination	Instructing Coaching Level of supervision received
Work situation and job context	Physical working conditions Psychological and sociological aspects	Low temperature Civic obligation
Miscellaneous aspects	Work schedule Job demands Responsibility	Irregular hours Specified/controlled work pace Responsible for the safety of others

Source: The PAQ is drawn almost directly, though certain job elements were adapted for clarity, from Ernest McCormick, Paul R. Jeanneret, and Robert C. Mecham, "A Study of Job Characteristics and Job Dimensions as Based on the Position Analysis Questionnaire (PAQ)," *Journal of Applied Psychology* 56:4 (1972): 337.

of tasks necessary for a job, while the PAQ includes behavioral and interpersonal activities. The choice of job analysis method could result in a different snapshot of the same position, with implications for other personnel activities within an organization. James Clifford found great differences between the results of a job analysis that employed both methods to examine the same jobs during a similar point in time.[16] "Of the total universe of work that was studied by both approaches to job analysis, the Position Classification Questionnaire approach organized that work into sixteen unique classifications. The Task Inventory approach organized that work into 28 unique classifications."[17]

As a means to illustrate the potential for problems associated with a focus on tasks, let us consider a familiar position: the position of secretary, one of the most critical and demanding jobs in any organization. Secretaries often serve a central co-

ordinating function in work units and quite commonly are responsible for the overall flow of administrative operations. If we developed an inventory of tasks performed by someone in this position, we would identify several activities, including word processing, scheduling, photocopying, transcription, and dictation, among other things. Consider first how these tasks may have evolved in the last five years.

Applications in technology and software have changed simply typing to word processing. Scheduling may require the mastery of complex software and an ability to link multiple operating sites. Documents have become graphic masterpieces using basic word processing software. In the past, document development of this nature was the bailiwick of a graphic arts or printing specialist rather than a department secretary. Photocopying now presents a dizzying array of choices: paper size; color scale; and whether to collate, staple, or duplex. Dictation may be obsolete with the latest in voice recognition software. Some scanners can translate handwritten documents. Clearly the position of secretary is driven, shaped, and constrained by technology as we enter the first decade of the next century. What might we expect in the next five years?

Now consider the categorization of activities and elements in the PAQ depicted in Box 7.2. In addition to the problems introduced with task identification, we must also consider that work behaviors and relational aspects in the workplace are changing rapidly. As responsibilities evolve and people develop new sets of skills, their relationships with others and interpersonal demands will also change. In addition, as we discuss later in this chapter and revisit in Chapter 11, the structure of organizations and the location in which people will do their work is in flux. Assessing behaviors and interpersonal activities becomes even more complex when we are studying a position that may interact with a work team that is fluid in composition, drawn from across departments and composed of some members who are physically present and others who are located in a different office, city, state, or even country.

Traditional job analysis focuses on a snapshot of the tasks or work behaviors at the moment of study. For this reason, the rapid changes in the work environment and in the character of work make it difficult to maintain up-to-date job analysis data. Strategic job analysis requires a consideration of the demands or requirements of a position in the future rather than a static assessment of the tasks performed today.[18] Managers are concerned with how a job may evolve in the future in response to the work environment, changing technology, or different mandates for public sector and non-profit organizations. This must be the focus that analysts in a strategically adaptive organization share.

POSITION DESCRIPTION

A position description is drawn from the job content analysis. Thus, any limitations or errors that have been introduced in job analysis will be transferred to the job description. A position description should offer a summary of the general responsibilities and feature a listing of the specific duties associated with a particular position in an organization. Most job descriptions are meant to be somewhat generic to describe a type of position rather than being tailored to a unique type of job or set of professional characteristics possessed by an individual. Since these descriptions are quite time-consuming to develop, they tend to outlive the contemporary realities of the work in a position. Position descriptions usually include a general statement about the objectives of the position. In addition, there may be a general summary of the environment and overall obligations of the position. The essential job duties are usually listed specifically, a requirement of the Americans with Disabilities Act. Finally, most position descriptions include a section identifying the specific KSAs required for the position. Position descriptions usually identify the means by which a person can demonstrate that he or she has the appropriate knowledge; a specific degree or training program or a specified amount of related job experience is often stipulated.

Let us look at the principal components of a position description by continuing our focus on the secretarial position. In Box 7.3, the position description for a secretary for the State of California is broken down according to the components for a position description. Compare this characterization of duties for a similar position in Texas denoted as Secretary I in Box 7.4. What responsibilities receive emphasis? Does the list of duties differ between the two position descriptions? What might be missing? Do the qualifications seem reasonable given the expectations outlined? Both of the positions are at similar pay levels in their respective states. What does this suggest about performance expectations and employee qualifications? Sometimes position descriptions and the data generated from the job analysis reflect social norms in a particular community, and they can even reflect social biases, as we saw with the Tompkins reading selected

Box 7.3   Sample Position Description: Secretary for the State of California

General Statement: This is the journeyperson level. Under general direction and following general procedures, incumbents in a secretarial capacity receive and screen telephone calls and visitors, use considerable judgment in providing factual information in response to numerous inquiries; establish and maintain confidential and administrative files and prepare summaries of data pertinent to the work of the supervisor or the office. The work typically requires a detailed knowledge of the programs, policies, and activities of the employing unit.

Job Environment: Office setting, variable hours, generally 8–5 P.M., light to medium physical labor

Duties: Incumbents screen incoming correspondence, refer to appropriate staff member for reply, and follow up to insure that deadlines are met; arrange correspondence for administrator's personal reply in order of priority with appropriate background material attached for reference; independently or in accordance with general instructions, compose correspondence on a wide range of subjects requiring a thorough knowledge of the procedures and policies of the office; review outgoing correspondence prepared by other staff members for administrator's signature for consistency with administrative policy as well as for format, grammatical construction, and clerical error; gather and summarize data; brief reports and correspondence; attend meetings and conferences, take and/or summarize notes into minutes, and distribute minutes; screen a variety of visitors and telephone calls, and where appropriate, refer to other staff members or personally provide authoritative information on established agency programs and policies; arrange meetings for administrator, prepare agenda, and make adjustments as necessary in scheduled meeting times; relieve the administrator of routine office details; maintain confidential and administrative files.

Knowledge, Skills, and Abilities: Knowledge of: Modern office methods, supplies and equipment; business English and correspondence. Ability to: Read and write English at a level required for successful job performance; type at 40 words per minute; perform difficult clerical work; make clear and comprehensive reports and keep difficult records; prepare correspondence independently; communicate effectively; meet and deal tactfully with the public; and direct the work of others.

Qualifications:

Either I: In the California state service, one year of experience performing clerical duties at a level of responsibility not less than that of an Office Assistant, Range B.

Or II: Two years of experience in clerical work. [Academic education above the twelfth grade may be substituted for one year of the required general experience on the basis of either (a) one year of general education being equivalent to three months of experience; or (b) one year of education of a business or commercial nature being equivalent to six months of experience. Students who are enrolled in the last semester or its equivalent of course work, which upon completion will fulfill these requirements, will be admitted to the examination, but they must submit evidence of completion before they can be considered for appointment.]

SPECIAL PERSONAL CHARACTERISTICS—A demonstrated interest in assuming increasing responsibility; mature judgment; loyalty; poise; tact; and discretion.

ADDITIONAL DESIRABLE QUALIFICATIONS—Education equivalent to completion of the twelfth grade; ability to take dictation at 110 words per minute

Source: The position description is for a secretary, class code 1176, drawn from the Department of Personnel Administration, State of California, October 1, 1999, **http://www.dpa.ca.gov/.** We added the information for job environment to the position description; this was implied but not specifically identified in the document on the web site.

Box 7.4   Sample Position Description: Secretary I for the State of Texas

---

General Statement: Performs entry-level secretarial work. Work involves typing letters, memoranda, and reports; taking and transcribing dictation; opening and routing mail; receiving visitors; answering the telephone and taking messages; keeping records of appointments and due date controls; maintaining routine files; and assembling and organizing materials used by the supervisor in completing work assignments.

Job Environment: Office setting, variable hours, generally 8–5 P.M., light to medium physical labor [authors]

Works under close supervision with minimal latitude for the use of initiative and independent judgment [specified in the description]

Duties: Types correspondence, letters, memoranda, and reports; takes and transcribes dictation, articles, payrolls, manuals, legal documents, and minutes on general or technical subjects. Opens and distributes mail; assembles related material for use by supervisor in answering mail; answers routine inquiries not requiring interpretations of laws, rules, and regulations. Serves as receptionist; makes appointments; answers routine questions from the public about operations; assists individuals in completing forms and applications. May maintain files. May make routine mathematical computations and calculations and keep fiscal records. May check reports and records for completeness and accuracy in coding, classification, and mathematics. May operate electronic calculator, automated equipment, transcribing machine, and other office machines. Performs related work as assigned.

Knowledge, Skills, and Abilities: Knowledge, Skills, and Abilities: Knowledge of business terminology, office practices and procedures; of spelling, punctuation, grammar, basic arithmetic; and of the use of automated equipment and software. Skill in machine transcription, word processing, or shorthand. Ability to maintain clerical records and prepare routine reports; to make basic mathematical computations and tabulations; to compose routine letters and memoranda; and to operate automated equipment.

Qualifications:

Experience and Education: Familiarity with secretarial and/or clerical work. Graduation from a standard senior high school or equivalent is generally preferred. Education and experience may be substituted for one another.

Source: The position description is for a secretary, class code 0131, drawn from the Department of Human Resources, State of Texas, October 1, 1999, **http://www.hr.state.ex.** We added the information for job environment to the position description; this was implied but not specifically identified in the document on the web site.

---

for this chapter. Do these position descriptions evidence this concern?

Problems with position descriptions can occur as expectations change about different jobs and as the tools for performing the job change. When the tasks or tools change, the need to revise the requisite KSAs arises. If organizational mission changes, might this also be cause for a revision of position descriptions? Sometimes, to consider the various contingencies that will rise for different positions, the position description is written to be rather general and therefore apply to as many jobs as possible. Yet a very general position description may be almost as inappropriate as one that is too

specific. If we look to the position description to guide employees in what to do and to serve as the basis for job evaluation and classification activities, then descriptions that are either too general or too specific can be useless at best and dysfunctional at worst. Ideally, position descriptions should establish the parameters of the position, offer a link to performance management systems, and communicate standards for performance as well as priorities for activities.

The language used in a position description can have serious implications during the job evaluation stage. The valence of information (positive or negative) and its placement in the position description affect the later assessment of job worth.[19] "Positive information [sensitive information] placed at the beginning of a description tends to increase its evaluation, whereas negative information [routine matters] placed at the beginning tends to lower the evaluation."[20] The sensitivity of position description language serves as a warning that the "objectivity" of the classification system is at least somewhat tenuous.

JOB EVALUATION

After jobs are analyzed for content and a position description is generated, an evaluation is conducted of different jobs to assess their relative worth to the organization in question. Consistent with Weber's caution that authority rests with the position rather than the person, the worth of a position to an organization should be considered separate from the qualities of any person who might occupy the position under consideration. The job should be evaluated in terms of the value of a position when performed at a minimally competent level. After the relative value of a particular job to the organization is assessed, similar jobs are grouped or classed together and eventually assigned to a specific compensation level.

Job evaluation has important implications for subsequent personnel activities. As the job is evaluated in terms of the work environment and demands of the position, then recruitment and selection strategies will be driven by assumptions about the relative value of the skills necessary in a particular position as well as the characteristics of the job. Assumptions about the nature of a position and the relative hazards or expectations about minimum performance have implications for the performance management system in terms of motivation and supervision.

Employee Motivation and Job Evaluation

Two perspectives on motivation are important to consider before we look at the different methods that may be employed to assign worth to jobs. **Expectancy theory** suggests that an individual's motivation is linked to whether what he or she expects to occur in response to his or her effort actually does take place and whether the person is looking forward to that outcome.[21] **Equity theory** suggests that people pay close attention to the relationship between the effort they expend and the outcome realized, but they also consider the effort that others expend and the rewards that they receive.[22]

Job evaluation efforts should consider the motivational effects of different assessments. Internal equity suggests that the preparation required for the position (the knowledge, skills, and ability), the demands placed on the employee (physical, intellectual, or emotional), and the significance of the position in terms of organizational activities should be commensurate with the assessed worth of the job to organizational members. External equity would draw a similar analogy, except that jobs would be compared between organizations (the state of California versus the state of Texas) or job sectors (private, nonprofit, or public).

Point-Factor Evaluation

Job evaluation methods vary from a simple ranking of positions according to some set of criteria to complex weighted factors systems. One of the more common methods in current use is **point-factor evaluation.** (You will learn a bit more about one variation of point-factor evaluation, the Hay factor method, in application to compensation systems in Chapter 9.) The point-factor evaluation process relies heavily on an assessment of the content of jobs. Although point-factor approaches vary to some degree, most include the following essential steps. First, the evaluator gathers data about the jobs under scrutiny. Sometimes the evaluator categorizes jobs generally in terms of whether they are management or line positions. Next, the evaluator identifies the factors to be used in a study of the different jobs. The factors may be general variables such as knowledge, supervisory responsibility, or working conditions. Within each of these factors, the evaluator may

Box 7.5   Sample Point-Factor Instrument

Factors	Weight 100 pt scale	Definition of Factor
Accountability	17	Impact of decisions and errors
Job Scope	16	Standardization of duties and closeness of supervision received
Communication Exchange	14	Frequency, importance, and complexity of interpersonal communication
Job Preparation	13	Education, training, and/or experience required
Task Variety	12	Diversity of duties performed
Task Complexity	11	Technical complexity and uncertainty
Work Conditions	8	Work environment and conditions such as noise levels, temperature, lighting, required exertion
Job Pressure	9	Demands upon the incumbent including time pacing, deadlines, physical and emotional hazards

FACTOR 1: Accountability (17)

Degrees	Degree Points
Decisions/errors have a significant impact on the organization.	10
Decisions/errors have an impact on the work unit.	5
Decisions reflect limited authority. Errors are managed within a work group.	2
Decisions are not made. Errors would barely be noticeable in the context of operations.	0

Source: The factors were drawn from those studied in Kermit R. Davis, Jr., and William I. Sauser, Jr., "A Comparison of Factor Weighting Methods in Job Evaluation: Implications for Compensation Systems," *Public Personnel Management* 22:1 (1993): 95–96.

have different degrees to assess relative positioning within the factors. For example, how much knowledge is required? What type of information or experience is necessary? How many individuals are supervised? How much discretion do the subordinates exercise? Some percentage or point weights are assigned to each factor as a whole, with those points then being distributed to the degrees within the factors. The more critical factors warrant a higher weight, and within the factors higher degrees of knowledge or discretion warrant a greater value than others. Jobs are examined in terms of the factors used to develop a point total for each job. Similar jobs, in terms of the point total, can then be grouped for the purpose of compensation ranges or recruitment strategies. Evaluators assess the relative weight of the job factors and the points assigned to different degrees of applicability within the job factors.

In Box 7.5 on page 187, we illustrate the logic of a point-factor system with a sample instrument drawn from a study reported by Davis and Sauser.[23] For the purpose of this example, we assigned the weights and developed the degrees for accountability as a means to illustrate the logic of a point-factor evaluation. In this example, we are weighting the job factor "accountability" at 17 as having greater import in the organization than other job factors (e.g., job scope at 16, communication exchange at 14, and task complexity at 11). Note also that the degrees within the factor vary in value according to the manner in which this job factor applies to a particular position. Although every job is evaluated using accountability, in some positions "decisions/errors have a significant impact on the organization" and in others "decisions are not made" and in yet others "errors would be barely noticeable in the context of operations."

Suppose we examined a position and found that a person holding that position would make decisions that reflected limited authority and the consequence of errors was limited to the scope of the work group. In our evaluation of that job, we might assess the degree of accountability as 2. We would then multiply the weight for accountability (17) by the degree to which accountability was

evidenced in the position (2), for a score of 34. We would then continue assessing the job in terms of the remaining factors to develop an overall score for the job. In the case of the instrument in Box 7.5, the maximum score would be 1,000 and the minimum would be 0. Collectively, all positions would be scored, ranked, and value assigned.

Considerations in Job Evaluation

It is clear from the forgoing that what appears to be a rigorous quantitative process on the surface actually features quite a bit of room for subjectivity and value-based assessment throughout. Potentially, job evaluation is subject to bias in terms of the evaluator's assessment of job factors dealing with the capacity of the employee to perform certain tasks at an acceptable level.[24] For example, the relative merits of experience versus education have been hotly debated in many public sector hallways. Is speed more important than accuracy? How can we identify the necessary degree or experience that will capture some level of interpersonal skills? What are interpersonal skills? What are adverse working conditions—constant interruptions or the low thrum of a copy machine next to one's desk? How do we capture job factors related to physical threat or danger—proximity to certain machines or exposure to disease? What about the dangers a department secretary faces from desperate students who cannot find a professor for a signature? Tompkins tells us that even the valuation that we assign to job factors is problematic:

> Weights will incorporate effects of any discrimination existing in the marketplace. Such biases may reflect historical under valuation of female-dominated jobs based on stereotypes regarding the value of work; the traditionally weaker union power of women; the location of jobs in the competitive economic sector; purposeful gender discrimination; and other determinants of compensation not associated with job content, such as seniority and supply and demand.[25]

In a study of employees who evaluated a diverse set of jobs, Davis and Sauser found that the weights assigned to jobs varied when the employees believed that they were evaluating male-dominated jobs as opposed to female-dominated jobs.[26] Male-dominated jobs received a generally higher overall valuation.[27] Observers concerned with external equity suggest that job sector (public, private, nonprofit) or location may have more to do with an assessment of job worth than any type of objective analysis.[28] Treiman and Hartmann suggest that even the most technically pristine approach to job classification and evaluation is still predicated on the social valuation of certain types of work:[29]

> We make no judgments regarding the relative value of jobs to employers or to society or the appropriate relationships among the pay rates for various jobs. The concept of intrinsic job worth—whether there is a just wage—has been a matter of prolonged dispute. We do not believe the value—or worth—of jobs can be determined by scientific methods. The hierarchies of job worth are always, at least in part, socially constructed and a reflection of values.[30]

Other methods of assessing and categorizing jobs link to the skills and characteristics of the employees rather than the position. In **rank-in-person systems,** the unit of analysis is the person. Promotion and compensation are based on individual qualifications, not career classification patterns. This approach may be more common when there is a clear protocol for assessing the skills of interest. For example, rank-in-person is common in public sector settings where the rank is less a matter of placement in the hierarchy and more likely to be drawn from experience, education, or achievements—for example, in academic settings where the instructor's rank (assistant professor, associate professor, full professor) is a matter of the person's experience, level of education, publication record, or accomplishments in teaching or community service.

Ethical Considerations: Equity versus Efficiency

Job analysis and position description serve as the basis for affirmative action to control for bias and ensure that the selection of employees is based on their competence. The concern about the relative merits of one position or type of job over another is pressing. If, as Treiman and Hartman suggest,[31] prevailing social values place less importance on positions that are commonly held by women versus men, for example, then decisions about the weights of job factors that arise in evaluation are especially salient. Is it incumbent on public sector organizations to make a special effort to compensate for such social inequity? Should public sector organizations simply be bound by the market? Should we consider the possible gender bias implicit in job evaluation to be comparable with external equity issues generally? Does it matter if we are comparing similar positions but in different geographical areas, as illustrated in the case of the two secretarial positions in Texas and California? These are all questions that arise for every jurisdiction in government, and they require that human resource specialists frame these issues clearly and sensitively with respect to equity issues and that they place them before politically accountable authorities for their determination of policy.

JOB CLASSIFICATION

Federal legislation, such as the Federal Classification Act of 1923 and the Classification Act of 1949, served as pioneer activity in public sector job evaluation and classification. In response to provisions in the Pendleton Act, which established the federal civil service system, it became apparent that some means was necessary to establish accountability in the compensation of government employees. Classification presumes a collective of "formal job descriptions that organize all jobs in a given organization into classes on the basis of duties and responsibilities for the purpose of delineating authority, establishing chains of command, and providing equitable salary scales."[32] Positions were categorized—that is, classified—on the basis of duties, and salaries were established to correspond with classification.

Classification, as the mainstay to public sector human resource management, is definitely on the decline. According to Hays and Kearney, position classification may be increasingly less important in the next decades.[33] This erosion may be due to concerns that rigid classification systems impede the ability of management to respond to performance demands and do not fully apply to contemporary organizations. Shafritz argued for the obsolescence of classification systems in the public sector because they presume the accuracy of classical organization theory assumptions about workers and their roles in the organization.[34] In addition, classification systems in the public sector were established primarily as mechanisms to prevent patronage abuse, and consequently they may not be useful for managing employees.[35] Cipolla suggests that "classification has always been viewed as a 'personnel' program or system and will continue to be unless managers are put in control of work distribution and assignments without being restricted by artificial position controls and grade-level distinctions."[36] In some cases, the technical nature of analysis and classification may take precedence; the structure itself may serve to shape the behavior of employees rather than support their ability to perform their work.[37] Efforts to manage human resources despite the constraints of classification systems erode the rationale for their inception, rewarding merit without regard to personal characteristics or political affiliation. There may be incentives in the classification schema to reduce productivity and efficiency:[38]

> The informal practices that have evolved from the formal structure—the provisions of the charter and the civil service regulations—can hardly be considered constructive when they allow personnel favoritism to play a greater role in determining reallocations than any objective evaluations of merit.[39]

Calls for the reform of civil service often focus on the classification system. Because classification, analysis, and evaluation require a substantial concentration of time, effort, and technical skill, revision of these systems is no small matter. At times the complexity of reform efforts overwhelms jurisdictions, resulting in disjointed and episodic microadjustments of positions here and there. Unfortunately, piecemeal reclassification, while a means to remedy a problem in one area or work unit, results in even more inconsistencies. These attempts to restructure classification systems are confounded by political and economic constraints in many jurisdictions.

One alternative to highly detailed classification systems is **broadbanding**—that is, the collapsing of many related classifications into a smaller number of classes with substantially broader ranges of compensation within these classes. (Broadbanding will be discussed in greater detail in Chapter 10.) Although the number of states considering the use of broadbanding classification systems has increased, this sign of professional interest has not translated into widespread adoption.[40] The number of jobs subject to classification decreased in thirty states, but not everyone is engaging in broadbanding efforts; jobs subject to classification increased in fifteen states.[41] Broadbanding systems are showing a great deal of promise in compensation packaging schemes in the public sector, particularly in flatter, less hierarchical organizations. In some states administrators are responding to concerns over the lack of flexibility in classification systems by decentralizing authority for classification. In Georgia, each agency is responsible for its own classification process.[42] (Broadbanded systems and the role of classification systems in employee compensation packaging are explored in Chapter 9.)

IMPLICATIONS OF JOB ANALYSIS, EVALUATION, AND CLASSIFICATION

As we attended to each particular segment of this chapter—analysis, evaluation, and classification—

we have discussed some of the issues that may result from the techniques and practices in the public sector generally or in larger nonprofit organizations. Now we offer a discussion of broader concerns that may transcend the particulars of job analysis, classification, or evaluation.

Technology: Terror or Tool?

Only a few years ago, if we wanted to share a document with a colleague in another community, we mailed it and patiently waited for delivery and reply—without express (pony or otherwise) mail options. In due time, the fax became a new tool of the rapid transfer of printed information. Documents and draft materials were furiously pumped through telephone lines to be printed at the other end. Now such documents can be attached to e-mail and instantly deposited into a waiting computer. With advancements in workplace technology, the pace of work and the rapidity of communications has changed dramatically, as have

the tools and processes that must be mastered to take advantage of the power of technology. Box 7.6 summarizes reasons offered by Ganzel for the increasing stress that employees may face in response to technology.[43] This list is suggestive of the dramatic changes in the way that work is done today and posits that escalating demands will likely be placed on employees in the future as technology continues to speed up and complicate our workplace lives. Tasks, skills, and requisite knowledge change rapidly in response to evolving technology; the tools and practices of human resource management of necessity must keep up with those changes, or organizational effectiveness will suffer greatly. Certainly the increasing frustration that supervisors and managers report in their interaction with human resource specialists may also find root in advancement in technology. Computer software advances in data management and manipulation have made it possible to tabulate the responses for a job analysis instrument quickly and accurately. This approach

---

Box 7.6   Job Demands and Technology

Information is everywhere and it seems to be growing. Technology enables employees to receive an enormous amount of information every day. The challenge may lie in how and what people process.

The pace of work is increasing. The pace of work seems to be increasing with the speed of our electronic tools. People are slower than their electronic equipment. People do not process information as quickly as computers. People do not retain as much data as computers.

Computers exact a physical and mental price. We pay a physical price when we work at a computer for long periods of time. Eye strain, back strain, and reduced opportunities for exercise all affect employee health. Our reliance upon technology to communicate means that people are less likely to work face to face but keyboard to keyboard.

Sometimes technology does not work. In many tasks, we have come to rely upon technology to the extent that we cannot function if it is not working. Computers fail or come down with viruses. Servers go down. Documents may not translate between software packages. Printers go offline. Batteries fail in electronic organizers. Floppy and zip disks become corrupt. When these things occur, technology-driven tasks are affected. Frustration will rise. Productivity will drop.

Technology can be scary. Some jobs have changed dramatically leaving highly competent employees to continually try to keep up with the changes. Within a five year span, desks that had typewriters were transformed into computer work stations. Training may not keep up with technology for many organizations. Valuable employees who are not able to self-teach may be lost.

Source: Adapted from Rebecca Ganzel, "Feeling Squeezed by Technology," *Training* 35:4 (April 1998): 62–70.

to analysis becomes increasingly dependent on formulas that are derived and applied without a human assessment of each particular job. Furthermore, many of the tools used for human resource management work are becoming highly sophisticated and thus may serve as a barrier to individuals who do not have the requisite skills or equipment to use them.

Diversity: Assessing Difference

The practice of job analysis and the development of classification systems spring from the belief that there is an accurate and unbiased means to assess the tasks associated with a particular position without regard to the person holding that position. These objective assessments are intended to grant some security to individuals who worry about whether salary levels are being determined for reasons other than merit or whether job qualifications are genuinely essential or are established to exclude some people. If the position analysis is accurate and the resulting position description is unbiased, then individuals of differing personal qualities or backgrounds would not be held hostage by assumptions about what they can or cannot do.

In a different vein, Cox and Finley examined the role that organizational level and work specialization had on attitudes toward work and other indicators of workplace adaptation.[44] They anticipated that work specialization and organizational level shaped the experiences that employees had and the perceptions that employees held about their own work and their own role in the organization. The latter dimension is particularly of interest for employees who are minorities within their organization—that is, they are either in less common occupations or in demographic groups that are less well represented.[45] Cox and Finley found that gender, race, and age matter in terms of job performance, compensation satisfaction, and allegiance with organizational identity.[46] These findings were compounded by work specialization and hierarchy: "Different specializations or levels may represent different work cultures. . . . Differences in rates of promotion and in job performance ratings may be attributable to different opportunity structures and different performance expectations across groups."[47] Hierarchy and job classification can serve to alienate groups of workers to a similar degree that gender and race have been considered to categorize and limit opportunity inappropriately for people.[48] Consequently, one important task for HRM specialists and public service managers is the promotion of activities such as strategic planning to reinforce the realization that organizations reflect collective efforts to accomplish shared goals and those goals are most effectively approached by organizations in which inclusiveness, trust, and mutual support are broadly practiced norms of conduct.

JOB DESIGN

Job design reflects a slightly different focus in perspective than classic analysis, description, and evaluation. Recall our earlier discussion about organization theory and the structuring of the organization or the position to achieve efficiencies or a certain level of performance. By contrast, job design is a bit more organic, meaning adaptive and flexible in nature. Jobs are designed in consideration of the organization's goals and resources as well as the individual's goals and resources. The resulting job would be some composite reflecting the best fit for both the organization and the individual.

As organizational structure becomes flatter and work groups evolve and become project driven, the nature of jobs to be done has changed. In the area of job design, the analysis begins with what needs to be done (hence, the close connection between strategic planning and job analysis). After determining who will do the work (through recruitment and selection), it is necessary to determine the processes and the locations where work is to be accomplished. Job design entails the framing of work and tasks in the context of overall organizational goals and in concert with stakeholder interests in the organizational environment. The design of some aspects of the job may even be adapted to mesh with the characteristics or needs of the employees performing the work (for example, providing accommodation for employees with disabilities). As we noted in Chapter 2, the work environment has changed quite dramatically over the past two decades. For this reason, Hays and Kearney call for an increased focus on innovative approaches to job design in the coming decades, especially with regard to job sharing, job enlargement, and job rotation.[49]

Flex-design for jobs in terms of location (**telecommuting**) or scheduling (**flextime** or **job sharing**) has become increasingly common. Research evidence suggests that telecommuting can improve employee productivity in a wide range of settings.[50] Flexibility in scheduling can be a significant advantage of a particular job (as you will see in Chapter 10). Flex-design can also aid organizations as they accommodate employees who are differently abled. Job design strategies such as job enlargement can be used to encourage employees to develop additional skills. Job enlargement occurs when employees have the opportunity to take on tasks in tangential positions (**horizontal job enlargement**) or to learn tasks associated with positions holding a higher rank in the organization (**vertical job enlargement**).

■ CONCLUSION

Job analysis serves to frame almost all subsequent personnel activities. As you read about recruitment and selection in Chapter 8, you will understand how important a clear and accurate position description becomes in the search and selection of new employees. Certainly the proper valuation of the position as you attempt to recruit employees to critical positions in a seeker's market illustrates the importance of carefully assessing the necessary knowledge, skills, and abilities required and then offering appropriate compensation packages to those employees. In the chapters on compensation (Chapter 9) and benefits (Chapter 10), the use of a classification system in establishing pay ranges and grades is apparent. So too you will see

that if the job analysis is inaccurate, there may be serious implications related to equity and comparable worth for the workforce. The position description is a critical baseline document in any performance management system, as you will discover in Chapter 11. If employees are to learn what is expected of them in a given position and if they are to understand what they might need to know to be promoted, then appropriate job classification offers an important tool for human resource development (Chapter 12). Finally, the position description can serve as an outline for employees to identify the critical tasks and, if necessary, be used by managers to address performance problems, as you will see in Chapter 13. Job content analysis plays a pivotal basic role in contemporary personnel systems. Unfortunately, job analysis is complex and, as Tompkins notes, fraught with all of the same types of measurement biases that tend to exist whenever we endeavor to assess human activity. A thoughtful, objective, accurate assessment of the tasks associated with a particular position and the appropriate valuation of those tasks to an organization lie at the very heart of the legitimacy of a merit-based personnel management system.

The nature of the work done in and by government and the expectations held about public sector jobs are changing. As public goods and services increasingly are delivered through grant and contract arrangements by nongovernmental organizations, the nature of many public sector jobs and the means for assessing the worth of particular activities will change apace. Traditional approaches to job evaluation may prove to be inappropriate in the new setting of the "hollow state" environment discussed in our introductory chapter. Job analysis per se as a function of human resource management may become less important to an organization than the ability to outline the scope of a grant or contracted project, assess any required competencies or licensure requirements associated with service delivery, and set the compensation levels for the project team in terms of the prevailing market for similar activities. As the focus for organizational performance hinges on the outcome versus the detail of the task, the mechanism that we use to outline the scope of a person's responsibilities or to assess value to his or her efforts will change to reflect an emphasis on observed results.[51]

■ MANAGER'S VOCABULARY

job analysis
job classification
job evaluation
science of administration
scientific management
bureaucracy
position description
job incumbent
KSAs
knowledge
skills
abilities
strategic job analysis
Task Inventory Procedure
Position Analysis Questionnaire
expectancy theory
point-factor evaluation
equity theory
rank-in-person
broadbanding
job design
flex-design
telecommuting
flextime
job sharing
horizontal job enlargement
vertical job enlargement

■ STUDY QUESTIONS

1. How might changing technology influence how you study in the next year? In how you pursue your career over the course of the next decade?

2. What might organizations need to consider in designing alternative work arrangements for employees?

3. How might organization theories that address individual and group behavior influence job analysis and classification schemes?

■ EXPERIENTIAL EXERCISES

1. What Does a Student Do?

   Identifying the specific tasks associated with a particular position can be more difficult than it might first appear. To gain a better understanding of the amount of detail entailed in analysis and evaluation, consider what you do as a student enrolled in a human resource management course. Answer the following questions to develop a snapshot of your position as a student. Then develop a position description using the general categories suggested in the samples in Boxes 7.3 and 7.4.

   • What tasks do you have in your role as a student?

   • What do you do in class?

   • What do you do to prepare for class?

   • How do you prepare for examinations?

   • How do you develop and complete assigned papers?

- How often do you perform the tasks listed above?

- How important are different tasks to your performance as a student?

- How would you characterize the relative difficulty of each of the tasks that you identified?

- Who supervises your activities as a student?

- With whom do you work when you complete the various tasks?

- What knowledge, skills, or abilities must you have in order to complete each of the tasks?

- What qualifications should you have to be a student in this class?

2. Devolution and Descriptions

As a class, come up with two positions at your university (e.g., lecturer and groundskeeper, or director of alumni affairs and dean of faculty), and obtain the position descriptions, which are readily available through the central human resource office of the university or through a government web site such as the central personnel site for the state. Divide into teams of three to devolve the position descriptions in the context of the task inventory approach to job analysis discussed in this chapter.

a. Using the position description, identify the tasks that job incumbents perform. Identify only tasks that are readily discerned from the position description.

b. Are all the tasks that one might assume to be part of what the incumbent might do apparent from the position description? What might be missing?

c. Select five of the tasks that were clearly identifiable through the position description.

d. Develop a rank order of the five tasks performed by the job incumbent according to the level of difficulty (with 5 being most difficult and 1 the least difficult).

e. Develop a second rank order of the same five tasks according to the relative frequency with which the task is performed.

■ CASES APPLICABLE TO THIS CHAPTER

"Radicals in the Rank and File" and "Helping Hands" (Task 2).

■ NOTES

[1] Brian R. Fry, *Mastering Public Administration* (Chatham, NJ: Chatham House, 1989), pp. 3–5.

[2] Max Weber, "Bureaucracy," in Jay M. Shafritz and J. Steven Ott, eds., *Classics of Organization Theory,* 2nd ed. (Chicago: Dorsey Press, 1987), pp. 81–87.

[3] Ibid., pp. 81–83.

[4] Adam Smith, "Of the Division of Labour," in Shafritz and Ott, *Classics of Organization Theory,* pp. 30–35.

[5] Frederick Winslow Taylor "The Principles of Scientific Management," in Shafritz and Ott, *Classics of Organization Theory,* pp. 66–81.

[6] Benjamin Schneider and Andrea M. Konz, "Strategic Job Analysis," *Human Resource Management* 28:1 (1989): 51–63.

[7] Jimmy L. Mitchell and Walter Driskill, "Military Job Analysis: A Historical Perspective," *Military Psychologist* 8:3 (1996): 119–142.

[8] Juan I. Sanchez and Edward L. Levine, "Determining Important Tasks Within Jobs: A Policy Capturing Approach," *Journal of Applied Psychology* 74:2 (1989): 337.

[9] James P. Clifford, "Manage Work Better to Better Manage Human Resources: A Comparative Study of Two Approaches to Job Analysis," *Public Personnel Management* 25:1 (1996): 91.

[10] Sanchez and Levine, "Determining Important Tasks," p. 338.

[11] Juan I. Sanchez and Scott L. Fraser, "On the Choice of Scales for Task Analysis," *Journal of Applied Psychology* 77:4 (1993): 549–550.

[12] Ibid., p. 549.

[13] Ernest McCormick, Paul R. Jeanneret, and Robert C. Mecham, "A Study of Job Characteristics and Job Dimensions as Based on the Position Analysis Questionnaire (PAQ)," *Journal of Applied Psychology* 56:4 (1972): 348.

[14] Ernest McCormick, "The Development of Processes for Indirect or Synthetic Validity: Application of Job Analysis to Indirect Validity," *Personnel Psychology* 12 (1959): 402–413.

[15] McCormick, Jenneret, and Mecham, "A Study of Job Characteristics," p. 349.

[16] Clifford, "Manage Work Better," p. 98.

[17] Ibid.

[18] Schneider and Konz, "Strategic Job Analysis," pp. 51–63.

[19] Brian N. Smith, Jeffrey S. Hornsby, and Philip G. Benson, "The Effects of Job Description Content on Job Evaluation Judgments," *Journal of Applied Psychology* 25:3 (1990): 305.

[20] Ibid.

[21] Victor H. Vroom, *Work and Motivation* (New York: Wiley, 1964).

[22] J. Stacy Adams, "Inequity in Social Exchanges," in L. Berkowitz, ed., *Advances in Experimental Social Psychology* (New York: Academic Press, 1965), pp. 267–300.

[23] Kermit R. Davis, Jr., and William I. Sauser, Jr., "A Comparison of Factor Weighting Methods in Job Evaluation: Implications for Compensation Systems," *Public Personnel Management* 22:1 (1993).

[24] Jon Tompkins, "Sources of Measurement Error and Gender Bias in Job Evaluation," *Review of Public Personnel Administration* 9:1 (1988): 5.

[25] Ibid., p. 7.

[26] Davis and Sauser, "Comparison of Factor Weighting Methods in Job Evaluation," p. 99.

[27] Ibid.

[28] A. O. Bellak, M. W. Bates, and D. M. Glasner, "Job Evaluation: Its Role in the Comparable Worth Debate," *Public Personnel Management* 12:4 (1983): 418–424.

[29] Ibid., p. 422, references the following study: Donald J. Treiman and Heidi I. Hartmann, *Women, Work, and Wages: Equal Pay for Jobs of Equal Value* (Washington, D.C.: National Academy Press, 1981), p. 10.

[30] Treiman and Hartman, *Women, Work and Wages,* p. 10, as cited by Bellak, Bates, and Glasner, "Job Evaluation," p 422.

[31] Treiman and Hartman, *Women, Work and Wages,* p. 10, as cited by Bellak, Bates and Glasner, "Job Evaluation," p. 422.

[32] Jay M. Shafritz, "Position Classification: A Behavioral Analysis for the Public Service," in F. J. Thompson, ed., *Classics of Public Personnel Policy,* 2nd ed. (Pacific Grove, CA: Brooks/Cole, 1991), p. 175.

[33] Steven W. Hays and Richard C. Kearney, "Anticipated Changes in Human Resource Management: Surveying the Field" (paper presented at the National Conference of the American Society for Public Administration, Orlando, FL, April 10–14, 1999), p. 15, cited with permission.

[34] Shafritz "Position Classification," pp. 175–176.

[35] Ibid., p. 176.

[36] Frank P. Cipolla, "Human Resources Management in the Federal Government: A Retrospective," *The Public Manager* (1996): 18.

[37] Shafritz, "Position Classification," p. 177.

[38] Maurice Penner, "How Job-Based Classification Systems Promote Organizational Ineffectiveness," *Public Personnel Management* 12:3 (1983): 268–276.

[39] Shafritz, "Position Classification," p. 186.

[40] Sally Coleman Selden, Pat Ingraham, and Willow Jacobson, "Human Resource Practices in State Governments: Findings from a National Survey" (paper presented to the National Conference of the American Society for Public Administration, 1999 Orlando, FL, April 10–14), p. 19, cited with permission.

[41] Ibid., pp. 19–20.

[42] Ibid., p. 20.

[43] Rebecca Ganzel, "Feeling Squeezed by Technology," *Training* 35:4 (April 1998): 62–70.

[44] Taylor H. Cox, Jr., and Joycelyn A. Finley, "An Analysis of Work Specialization and Organization Level as Dimensions of Workforce Diversity," in Martin M. Chemers, Stuart Oskamp, and Mark A. Costanzo, eds., *Diversity in Organizations* (Thousand Oaks, CA: Sage, 1995), pp. 62–88.

[45] Ibid.

[46] Ibid., p. 83.

[47] Ibid.

[48] Ibid., p. 85.

[49] Hays and Kearney, "Anticipated Changes," p. 12.

[50] Marc Hequet "How Telecommuting Transforms Work," *Training* 31:11 (1994): 57–61.

[51] Jonathan Walters, *Measuring Up* (Washington, D.C.: Congressional Quarterly Books, 1998),and "Fad Mad," *Governing* 9:12 (1996): 48–52.

CHAPTER 8

Recruitment and Selection

Recruitment is the process of finding and attracting the best people to fill vacancies in new or existing jobs within any type of organization, including nonprofits and public agencies at every level of government. Recruitment can be done either internally, from existing employees, or externally. The nature of the job determines the extent of the search involved. There are three fundamental guidelines to recruitment that will be discussed in this chapter:

1. Know what you are looking for. Begin with an accurate, up-to-date job description.
2. Conduct the search process so as to find the best match between employee skills and the job.
3. Be aware of legal constraints and procedural guidelines to conducting recruitment activities.

Selection is an important process because of its long-term impact on the performance of the organization resulting from the employees selected in the hiring process. Nevertheless, surprisingly little attention is given to selection procedures, and in practice an overreliance on often illegal application forms and faulty interviews is rather commonplace. Some mistakes frequently made in the selection process include the following:

- Unclear job requirements
- Invalid or unreliable tests
- Untrained interviewers
- No reference check

Each of these topics is discussed in this chapter.

The recruitment and selection process in gov-ernment organizations is notorious for being inflexible and aggravatingly slow. Of course, this may not be true for all (or even most) public agencies; many government jurisdictions have enacted significant human resource management reforms to improve performance.[1] Moreover, states and local governments are using some innovative techniques such as skills assessment, job simulations, and video testing for selecting employees.[2] Still, the reputation of government personnel systems' being overly rigid and inefficient persists. In some organizations, it may still take up to six months for an applicant to be hired through the normal civil service system, and many of the best-qualified applicants are no longer available when called for further testing or interviews. Unyielding rules used in the recruitment and hiring process can place limits on the number of people a manager may interview or narrow the type of qualifications requested of the applicants so that appointing authorities feel they have sufficient information to make appointment decisions. As a result of the slowness of the system and the relative inflexibility of the rules associated with the hiring process, managers often complain that they are not able to find qualified people or that they must waste valuable time waiting to fill a job opening.

In contrast, the perception is that recruitment and selection activities in the for-profit and nonprofit sectors are rapid and effective processes. This may or may not be true depending on the position in question, the skills required, the job market, and the structure of the organization. For nonprofit organizations, fiscal uncertainty and the same planning constraints outlined in Chapter 6 may complicate the recruitment and selection process. It is not unusual to have a situation in which a nonprofit organization suddenly receives word that it has been awarded a grant and may face a very short period in which to recruit and hire personnel. Often nonprofit organizations also must hire employees as a provision of a particular contract or grant. As you will discover in this chapter, the extent of use of temporary employees is rising in all sectors. The public sector may face a unique environment in terms of recruitment and selection. Although much of the legal environment is consistent across job sectors (Chapter 4), most public sector jurisdictions must acquire employees within civil service systems.

INTRODUCTION TO READING

The chapter reading discusses the problems with traditional civil service systems and what managers are doing to circumvent established personnel processes. Carolyn Ban writes that the slowness and rigidity of traditional civil service systems are an unfortunate result of good intentions. The government's recruitment and selection processes were designed to ensure equal access on the part of citizen applicants and prevent favoritism or political patronage from affecting the process of hiring. But the rules established to prevent abuse have had an unfortunate unintended effect: public managers often find it difficult to hire with dispatch applicants whom they consider to be well qualified. As a result, some managers have found ways of thwarting the rules by entering a personnel netherworld of dubious practices.[3] In some cases, managers hire employees as temporary workers and later convert these employees to permanent status.[4] Similarly, employees may be hired as contract workers and are later brought under direct government employment. One method used frequently is to design a unique job that only a desired applicant is qualified to perform.[5] At

other times, a manager may coach an applicant so that this person places among the top candidates on the job register. Another practice is asking the top candidate to decline a job offer so a preferred candidate can be offered the position. In most cases, these practices are certainly unethical, if not illegal, but frustration leads to creative behavior on the part of line managers who are directly responsible for producing outcomes in the form of public goods or services. The result of the use of these nefarious circumventing practices can be harmful to an organization; these practices can lead to poor morale, the unwise proliferation of job titles, and the introduction of fundamental unfairness in the selection process.

In the reading that follows, Ban examines some of the public personnel reform efforts that have been designed to help managers speed up the recruitment and selection process, and identifies some of the measures taken to help find the most qualified persons for job vacancies. Some of the objectives of the several reform movements directed toward public sector selection processes include the following: improving access to employment by minorities and others who are not sufficiently informed of public service opportunities; decentralizing and streamlining the recruitment and selection processes; promoting public agency responsiveness; and giving managers more discretion in the hiring process to permit more effective team building at the operations unit level of public agencies.

As you read the selection, keep the following questions in mind:

- According to Ban, has the main focus of human resource officers been on serving line managers' personnel needs, or has it been the enforcement of complex personnel rules?
- How has the traditional focus of HRM specialists affected the relationship between themselves and line managers?
- How have the line managers of public agencies acted to circumvent human resource rules and regulations?

- What are the systemic consequences of line managers' circumventing merit system rules?

- What reforms does Ban recommend to improve public sector recruitment and selection procedures?

Hiring in the Public Sector: "Expediency Management" or Structural Reform?

CAROLYN BAN

It may seem, in the current fiscal environment, that governments at all levels are more preoccupied with cutting back than with hiring. But even in tight times governments must continue to hire, and, as work forces shrink, maintaining a high quality work force is more important than ever. Traditional civil service systems for hiring new employees have come under increasing criticism for being too slow and rigid and thus making it harder for managers to get good people on the job quickly. Indeed, personnel offices have come in for broad criticism for being more focused on enforcing complex rules than on serving their "customers," the line managers (U.S. MSPB, 1993). As Chapter 18 makes clear, even though personnel offices are often involved in training other departments on Total Quality Management (TQM), they have been slow to espouse this approach themselves.

Managers, faced with the problem of how to get people hired, often find ways around the system (Ban, 1991, 1995). This kind of informal manipulation may solve their short-term problem, but it can have unintended longer-term consequences, both

Source: Carolyn Ban, "Hiring in the Public Sector: 'Expediency Management' or Structural Reform?" in Carolyn Ban and Norma Riccucci, eds., *Public Personnel Management: Current Concerns, Future Challenges,* 2nd ed. (New York: Longman, 1997), pp. 189–203. Copyright © 1997, 1991 by Longman Publishers USA. Reprinted by permission of Pearson Education, Inc.

for the individual hired and for the legitimacy of the system as a whole. Over the past five years there has been increased recognition of the problems caused by an overregulated system (National Commission on the State and Local Public Service, 1993; National Performance Review, 1993) and attempts to address these problems at a systemic level, by improving and streamlining hiring methods. This [reading] begins with a look at the traditional system and at individual-level strategies for coping with it. It then turns to an examination of some of the systemic changes that have recently been implemented, both by state governments and by the federal government. In so doing, it raises some questions about the most effective routes to reform.

THE TRADITIONAL MODEL OF THE MERIT SYSTEM

The traditional merit system was based on several key assumptions. First, it assumed that an individual's future job performance could be predicted by his or her score on a written test. Certainly the elaborate efforts at documenting the validity of written tests have shown that in some cases this was true, although with what precision is debatable. But recent critics have raised troubling questions about the validity of written tests. Even supporters have noted that written tests cannot test for such critical personal characteristics as motivation or ability to work with other people (Rudner, 1992). Further, there is disturbing evidence that some tests, both written tests and physical agility tests for some jobs, are not clearly job-related and have adverse impact on some protected classes (Riccucci, 1991).

The second assumption on which the traditional system is based is that managers should be kept at arms' length from the process until the very end, when they are presented with a short list of finalists (often only three) from which they are required to select. It was assumed (1) that professional personnelists were more qualified than managers to review the qualifications of applicants and to rank them, and (2) that keeping the managers out of the process until the very end would reduce the potential for abuse—that is, for hiring political cronies or personal friends.

Personnel psychologists continue to defend some aspects of this traditional system, particularly the use of written tests, but even they admit that the tests cannot make such fine distinctions that one can conclude that someone who received a 97 will perform better than an individual who received a 96. Yet the traditional approach of ranking candidates and requiring managers to choose from the top three names often assumes just this. And critics now challenge both the necessity and the appropriateness of keeping managers at arms' length from the process (Palguta, 1993).

"Expediency Management": How Managers Cope with the Traditional Hiring System

Line managers have long been critical of the traditional hiring systems. They see them as too slow and as often providing candidates who do well on tests but who may lack the specific skills needed for the position. Further, the hands-off nature of the system makes life much harder for aggressive managers who actively recruit candidates to ensure that they can then hire the people they recruit (Ban, 1995). In response to these problems, some managers have turned to what Ospina calls "expediency management." As she explains it:

> When excessively rigid procedures threaten effective management practices, it may be necessary to circumvent the rules in the name of legitimate organizational goals. This argument is at the basis of what may be viewed as creative management in public organizations. According to the argument, under

highly bureaucratic constraints, public managers may choose to emphasize administrative expediency, ignoring rules and regulations to expedite the decision-making process. (Ospina, 1992: 405).

Making Use of Existing Flexibilities

In fact, this image of excessive rigidity is, at least in part, a straw man. Particularly at the federal level, there are already a number of hiring methods that have introduced considerable flexibility and management discretion into the system. Three of the most important are case examining, the outstanding scholars program, and direct hire. In case examining, an agency advertises a specific position, determines the needed qualifications (with input from the manager), and rates and ranks the candidates, based either on scores on a test or, more typically, on an assessment of the individual's training and experience. If the manager has a preferred candidate, he or she can "name request," that is, can request that if that person is qualified, his or her name be placed on the final list. This process may still take two to three months to meet the requirements of advertising the position and to complete the ranking of candidates, but it provides the agency and the individual manager considerable control over the process.

Two other hiring techniques enable the manager to hire virtually on the spot, without requiring the candidate to take a test or to compete with other candidates. First, for entry-level positions, if a candidate had a 3.5 undergraduate grade-point average or was in the top 10 percent of his or her class, the candidate can be hired immediately under the outstanding scholars program. This program was originally designed to make it easier to hire minority candidates. Second, the direct hire authority allows agencies that have shortage categories (i.e., positions they are having difficulty filling) to hire candidates who meet specified qualifications, such as professional training or licenses, on the spot without a competitive process. Both these approaches speed up the process drastically and give managers great leeway in identifying and selecting candidates.

Managers' Coping Strategies: Functional or Dysfunctional?

Given the flexible methods described above, savvy managers in the federal government don't necessarily need to find a way around the system; rather, they need to understand the range of methods available and how to use them. Indeed, it is clear that they are increasingly choosing to use the more flexible methods as opposed to the traditional hiring method via a civil service test and certificate listing the top three names (U.S. MSPB, 1994).

However, many state and local governments don't permit use of the approaches described above—their systems still fit the model of the traditional system. And even in the federal government these methods were, until recently, not always available. So managers have developed a variety of ways to game the system—some legal, some borderline, and some clearly illegal.

Strategies to Save Time First, managers have tried to get around the long delay in hiring by finding ways to bring people on immediately. One technique that has been used for years is to hire an entry-level professional first into a secretarial position and then move him or her into a professional position. Although this is legal, bringing a new employee in as a temporary while waiting for a permanent position to open up is a borderline method—technically legal but beyond the intent of civil service law. Further, it's far from fool-proof (Ban, 1995). Clearly over the line is getting a contractor working with the agency to hire the individual so that he or she can start work immediately while the manager is shepherding his or her application through the process. Indeed, some managers have faced sanctions because of this abuse of the process (Ban, 1995).

A different technique for speeding up the process, more common in state and local governments, involves hiring new employees as provisionals. Provisional employees can be hired noncompetitively, but they are supposed to occupy their positions only temporarily, usually until the time that the civil service department can conduct a formal test upon which a permanent appointment can be based. Of course, if the civil service department is overworked (as is often the case), it may be some time before the test is given. Managers in New York sometimes game the system further by reclassifying the position, creating a "unique" title, that is, a new job for which there is no existing test (Ban and Riccucci, 1994). They know that the overburdened civil service department will consider this a lower priority than testing for more common occupations, so their

provisional employee may in fact stay in the job for years.

Many strategies for beating the system may be functional on a short-term basis but have unfortunate system-level consequences. One dysfunctional result of the strategy discussed above in New York is the proliferation of titles, many with only one or two occupants (Ban and Riccucci, 1994; Ban and Riccucci, 1993). Ospina (1992) documents effectively the use of expediency management in a municipal agency in New York City, where most analysts are hired as provisionals and stay in that status throughout their careers. Although hiring in this way has short-term benefits for managers and employees, since it permits faster hiring and gives managers more flexibility to negotiate terms of employment, there are significant long-term costs, in particular the lack of a clear career progression and a pervasive sense of inequity that lead eventually to lowered morale and higher turnovers.

Strategies for Maximizing Managerial Discretion In addition to trying to speed up the process, managers use a variety of techniques to try to gain control of the process, so that they can hire the people they have recruited. Hiring employees provisionally may meet both goals. Similarly, moving a position from classified (i.e., competitive) to exempt is another, even more controversial, approach. Even when the position is competitive, managers can coach the desired applicant in how best to fill out the forms. More on the edge ethically is "tailoring," that is, fitting the job description for the opening to the specific skills of the individual the manager wants to hire. And clearly illegal is what is technically called "soliciting a declination," that is, talking people higher on the civil service list into withdrawing from consideration so as to reach a preferred candidate who is not among the top three candidates. They may be told that the position is undesirable, the work unpleasant, or the chances for promotion slim. Or they may be informed quite bluntly that if they say no to this position, they will be helped in the future.

Of course, not all managers use these techniques, even the legal ones. Some managers are quite content to take a relatively passive approach to the hiring process, simply turning in a request to the personnel office and waiting for a list of finalists to show up on their desk (U.S. MSPB, 1993; Ban,

1995). This passive approach is not a problem when applicants are plentiful, but some managers (and, in some agencies, most managers) have found that they need to play an active role in the recruitment process in order to attract high-caliber candidates. These are the managers most frustrated by the traditional system, since all too often the formal system makes it difficult or impossible to hire the promising candidates they have identified (Ban, 1995; U.S. MSPB, 1994). Thus these managers are more likely to try to find creative ways to circumvent the system in order to meet the laudable goals of hiring individuals they feel are most qualified in a reasonable period of time.

STRUCTURAL REFORM: EVOLUTIONARY OR REVOLUTIONARY?

Individual "gaming" of the system is, at best, a stop-gap solution to systemic problems. Increasingly there has been recognition of the need for system reform. In recent years, increased pressure to reform government personnel systems, including hiring, has come from a number of sources, starting with the 1983 report of the National Academy of Public Administration and including most prominently the National Commission on the Public Service (the Volcker Commission) and the National Commission on the State and Local Public Service (the Winter Commission). Although specific emphases varied, all raised concerns about the continued ability of government to attract top people, and all called for continued deregulation and decentralization of the recruiting and hiring process.

The approaches to reform have differed at the state and the federal levels. States have generally followed an incremental reform strategy, whereas the federal government has attempted to implement far-reaching, comprehensive changes flowing from the National Performance Review. The following section describes each process and discusses the pros and cons of these differing strategies.

State-Level Reforms: Evolutionary Change

State reforms have touched a number of areas in human resources management. Various states have introduced reforms in the hiring area, including the recruitment process, testing, and criteria for selection. Some themes that emerge from an examination of these changes are decentralization, opening up the process (including finding ways of bringing in different groups of people), streamlining the process, and increasing managerial discretion. Let us look at some examples of each.

Decentralization   California is one state that has moved from a centralized to a far more decentralized system. It has decentralized to individual departments the entire hiring process (from recruitment through test development and administration, to certification of eligibles) although the central agency, the State Personnel Board, still administers exams for many generalist entry-level positions (Harmon, 1992; Jensen, 1992). Other states that have maintained a more centralized system have increased agency involvement in test development. In these cases the assumption is that the use of tests is valid, but that agencies will be better served if they can perform these functions themselves or at least play an active role in the process.

Opening Up the Process   One of the biggest concerns of all levels of government is how to attract top-quality employees, given that salaries are often not competitive with those in the private sector and that they can no longer promise new employees job security. This has led to a variety of methods for opening up the process, both making access easier and actively recruiting from different groups than in the past. Efforts to open up the process include making access to civil service tests easier. For example, Illinois increased the number of testing sites around the state as well as the services available at those sites and also held job information workshops targeted at areas with minority populations. Illinois also established a Minority Management Training Program to attract potential management candidates and prepare them for administrative positions (Schnorf, 1994). Wisconsin took the bold step of moving to a walk-in testing process. Prospective employees are no longer required to sign up in advance (Wisconsin Department of Employee Relations, 1995; *PA Times,* 1995). Forms, like tests, can be daunting to applicants. Minnesota is exploring ways to make its application form more "user-friendly" (Minnesota Department of Employee Relations, 1994).

Changes in job requirements and testing procedures are also ways of opening up the process. California has abandoned a number of non-job-related requirements such as physical characteristics and educational levels. In addition, it has moved away from reliance on written tests and toward more alternative testing methods. One interesting effort in California was a demonstration project called the Limited Examination and Appointment Process (LEAP), designed to increase hiring of persons with disabilities through use of an alternative selection process that included a screening interview and an on-the-job trial period (Harmon, 1992).

Streamlining the Process   Civil service systems have often been faulted for their slowness and rigidity. Many of the attempts to streamline the process make use of new technologies both to open up the process and to speed it up. Wisconsin has done both by putting vacancy announcements on-line, both within state government and, via the Internet, nationwide (Wisconsin Department of Employment Relations, 1995).

New technology can also be used to streamline and to strengthen the testing process. Even though machine scoring of tests is not a new idea, some new approaches to testing are quite creative. For example, New York adapted the test for corrections sergeants to make it more "real-life" by showing videos of typical prison situations and then asking how the individual would respond (Ban and Riccucci, 1994).

Similarly, many jurisdictions now maintain lists and generate hiring certificates (i.e., lists of top-ranked candidates) via computer. But some states have gone even further. Illinois, for example, is trying to make it easier for agencies to determine if applicants really are a good "fit" for the specific position by using "imaging" technology to permit the "hiring agent" to review the actual application forms on-screen (Schnorf, 1994).

Increasing Managerial Discretion   As we saw above, the traditional civil service model intentionally limited managers' role in the hiring process to selecting from a small group of finalists, determined

by the personnel staff. Often this was formalized into a "rule of three," that is, a requirement that selection be made from among the top three people on a civil service list. States have taken two different approaches in moving away from a rule of three. Some have simply increased the number—to a rule of five or ten (Ban and Riccucci, 1993). Minnesota adopted an interesting variant: a rule of 10 for internal hires and of 20 for external hires, but with what they call "expanded certification" as an affirmative action tool. If groups are underrepresented in that job category, they will go down the list to ensure the inclusion of at least two people from each underrepresented group who passed the test (Minnesota Department of Employee Relations, 1991).

A different option is zone scoring. Essentially, all those whose scores fall within a band (e.g., from 100 to 90) receive the same score and are referred as a group. Zone scoring is in increasingly widespread use (Ban and Riccucci, 1993). Even New York, which still adheres in most cases to the rule of three, has experimented with zone scoring but with mixed success. One of the tough issues in zone scoring is where to place the cut-offs, that is, how large the zones should be. In one case, the state was successfully sued by the unions for creating a top zone so large that almost everyone who passed fell into it (Ban and Riccucci, 1994). Zones that were more narrowly constructed were later upheld.

In sum, although many states have attempted to reform their hiring practices, most have taken a gradualist, evolutionary approach. Contrasting the relatively modest innovations in the states with the more drastic changes now being implemented in the federal government allows us to examine the pros and cons of evolutionary versus revolutionary approaches to reform.

Hiring in the Federal Government: Revolutionary Changes?

The National Performance Review (NPR), chaired by Vice-President Gore, called for sweeping reform of the federal personnel system. [. . .] The NPR recommendations stressed four values: cutting red tape, reengineering to cut waste, putting customers first, and empowering employees to get results. All four themes bear directly on the hiring process. The overall NPR report called for decentralizing the personnel process, delegating authority down to line managers "at the lowest level practical in each agency" (NPR, 1993a: 22), and cutting the size of the personnel staffs.

These recommendations were expanded upon in the NPR report "Reinventing Human Resource Management." First on its list of priorities was the need to "create a flexible and responsive hiring system" (NPR, 1993b: 9). It faulted the system for being time consuming and unresponsive and singled out the requirement for Office of Personnel Management (OPM) testing as a serious problem:

> The issue is not merely convenience; more importantly, the public's perception of the federal government as a responsive employer suffers tremendously when agency managers are forced to send applicants to OPM for examination, with no guarantee that they will ever be within reach for positions at that agency on a centralized register. (NPR, 1993b: 11)

The NPR Human Resources report presented an image of an ideal system, which was decentralized, that empowered managers and held them "accountable for adherence to principles of merit and equal opportunity through a performance-based assessment of staffing outcomes" (NPR, 1993b: 12). The specific reforms called for by the NPR are discussed below.

Achieve Maximum Delegation of Examining
Based on the Civil Service Reform Act of 1978 (CSRA), agencies could be delegated the authority to do their own examining only for positions that were unique to that agency. For positions common to several agencies, OPM conducted examinations centrally, often maintaining standing registers (i.e., ranked lists of qualified candidates) and sending the top scorers remaining on the list to agencies that wished to hire. The NPR report called for "authoriz[ing] agencies to establish their own recruitment and examining programs [and] abolish[ing] central registers and standard application forms." In other words, the NPR model is an "agency-based, market-driven hiring system" (NPR, 1993b: 13), much closer to a private sector model than to the traditional civil service model.

Simplify the System and Reduce Red Tape   The traditional civil service system has long been faulted for its dependence on complex, rigid rules. The sym-

bol of this system was the Federal Personnel Manual, which was literally thousands of pages long. In the hiring area, there were over 300 separate hiring authorities. The NPR recommended a drastic reduction—to only three competitive service appointment types: permanent, temporary indefinite, and temporary not to exceed (one-year limit). Recommendations for reducing red tape and empowering managers included giving agencies the authority to decide when they had a recruitment shortage (i.e., were having trouble filling specific positions) and could thus use streamlined hiring methods, called "direct hire" authority, without coming to OPM for prior approval.

The federal government has already begun implementing those recommendations of the NPR that do not require legislative approval. It has also sent to Congress a bill that would make more drastic changes. [. . .] As we shall see below, the changes are quite dramatic in some areas, but there are other important issues that the NPR has avoided.

Decentralize   The federal government had already made considerable strides in decentralizing the hiring process. Historically, there have been pendulum swings between decentralization and recentralization of federal hiring (Ban and Marzotto, 1984). Since the Civil Service Reform Act of 1978, the general trend (with the exception of the early Reagan years) has been toward decentralization, with responsibility for recruiting and testing for many positions being delegated to the agencies. The tendency was accelerated when the standardized test used for entry-level hiring for over 100 job titles was abolished as a result of a consent decree settling a lawsuit charging the test with having adverse impact (i.e., with discriminating against minority applicants). For several years, agencies were free to recruit and hire individuals for these positions without going through OPM (Ban and Ingraham, 1988). But the final result of several lawsuits was the reintroduction of centralized testing by OPM, using six different tests under the broad label of Administrative Careers with America (ACWA). Applicants who were tested were placed on a standing register (i.e., a ranked list of those who passed the test), and the top three names on the list were referred to agencies.

Although this sounds like a straightforward approach, and although the tests apparently had reasonably high validity, from the point of view of managers trying to hire, they were a disaster. Managers found the process of getting names to be very slow, and often the people whose names were sent were, in fact, not interested in the position that was offered. Further, managers who actively recruited found it very difficult to "reach" the people they wanted to hire from the ACWA lists. As a result, managers most frequently used a variety of other hiring methods—including the outstanding scholars program discussed above—or internal promotion, and avoided using ACWA (Ban, 1995; U.S. GAO, 1994). As a result the number of names on the ACWA lists continued to grow, and the chances of entering government employment via ACWA continued to decrease.

The OPM's solution to this dilemma was drastic. It abolished the standing registers and allowed agencies to use the ACWA as a screening tool for candidates if they wished. Candidates now apply to a specific job, either directly through the agency or at OPM. They complete a questionnaire on their training and experience, which is quickly scored, and the hiring official is given a list of the top three scorers from which to select. The proposed legal changes would allow agencies to control the recruitment and testing process even for common occupations, such as secretaries, accountants, or policy analysts.

Open Up and Streamline the Process   The OPM has attempted to make it easier for people to apply for federal employment. First, the OPM abolished the mandatory use of a standard application form, known as SF-171, which was daunting and difficult to complete. New applicants can submit a resumé or use a new optional form (OF-612). The OPM has attempted to maintain central information about job openings in the agencies and to make this available to applicants through a 900-number phone service.

The federal government has also gone further than the states in using new technology. The questionnaires that applicants complete on their training and experience are scored by computer to speed up the process. And for some occupations, such as nurses, the applicant can actually complete the questionnaire by phone, pressing buttons on a touch-tone phone to key in responses.

Increase Managerial Discretion   It remains to be seen how much these reforms actually increase managers' freedom to participate actively in the process and to select the people they recruit. This will depend on the extent to which they play a role in designing the questionnaires used to screen applicants and on the extent to which they can name request (i.e., ask that if the person they wish to hire is eligible, his or her name would appear on the list). Just speeding up the process will make it easier for managers to hold on to good candidates who, in the past, might have grown tired of waiting for months for a decision and gone elsewhere.

Potential Problems
with Federal Reforms

Many of the reforms being made by the federal government are long overdue. They are a genuine attempt to open up and streamline what has been a cumbersome and slow hiring process. But the sweeping nature of the reforms, coupled with changes in the OPM's role, have prompted some experts in the field to raise troubling questions. Some feel the reforms have gone too far; others feel that in critical areas, they have not gone far enough.

First, some question the appropriateness of abolishing the ACWA and maintain that the rating schedules being used have no predictive validity. If this is indeed the case, then the quality of new hires may decline. Further, the functions of the "reinvented" OPM have changed in ways that have direct effects on the hiring process. As Lane and Marshall point out, "OPM would be converted from a central management agency, with an emphasis on direction and regulation, to a commercial-style entrepreneurial agency that would hawk its wares to potential customers in the rest of the executive branch" (1995: 4). That change is already reflected in the requirement that henceforth, OPM would assist agencies in developing tests only on a "cost-reimbursable" basis. That is, OPM would start charging for its services. Small agencies, or those with low budgets, won't be able either to hire their own staffing specialists or to make use of OPM's. This would exacerbate the problems created by moving away from formal written tests. As one expert told me, "If agencies start using 'seat of the pants' approaches because they don't have the money to do it right or to pay OPM, productivity will go down."

Another potential problem is OPM's virtual abdication of its oversight function. Traditionally, OPM has not only established regulations for proper hiring procedures but has exercised its oversight role by making occasional visits to agencies to monitor whether the rules are actually being followed. Both the massive budget cuts at OPM and its redefined role mean that very little, if any, active oversight will remain (Lane and Marshall, 1995). The merit system was originally established to protect against wholesale abuses of the "spoils system." Although the absence of effective oversight probably won't lead to widespread abuse, there is ample evidence that, at least at some agencies, both the hiring of people because of political contacts and the hiring of cronies is still a problem (Ban and Redd, 1990). Without adequate controls, with maximum delegation and increased managerial discretion, abuse or the appearance of abuse may become an increasing problem.

Ironically, even though the federal government has taken some reforms much farther than the states have, it has lagged behind the states in one critical area: the rule of three. The federal government is still required by statute to provide hiring officials with the names of only the top three scorers on an examination. That includes such "unassembled" examinations as ratings of training and experience. As we saw above, many states have given managers far more discretion by expanding the numbers of people on the list from which the manager can hire. The U.S. Department of Agriculture has been conducting a demonstration project using category rating (i.e., zone scoring). As one MSPB report notes, "The importance and meaning of small differences in scores is questionable. . . . [T]he category rating process of the USDA demonstration project may be fairer than using specific scores to determine the order of candidates" (U.S. MSPB 1995: 33 of draft).

Further, the rule of three is narrowly defined in the federal government to mean three names, not three scores. When individuals are tied, the personnel staff applies a "tie-breaker." The first tie-breaker, by law, is veterans preference. If the hiring official has "name requested" a specific individual, he or she would go on the list ahead of others with the same score. Finally, personnel officials use random numbers to break ties among individuals. In contrast, even some states that still use the rule of three interpret it to mean the top three scores, which can yield far more than three names, and which does not require any discrimination against individuals with identical scores (U.S. MSPB, 1995).

The problems created by the rule of three are exacerbated by the federal government's long-standing policy of veterans preference. Veterans preference actually dates to the Civil War era, and the current law was enacted in 1944 during World War II. As the law currently works, veterans, their widows or widowers, or the spouses of disabled veterans or mothers of individuals who lost their lives while serving in the armed forces are all eligible for veterans preference under certain circumstances. Eligibles have points added to a passing score on an examination; disabled veterans have 10 points added. Further, disabled veterans with service-related disabilities of 10 percent or more "float to the top," that is, they are listed first on registers or lists of eligibles (U.S. MSPB, 1995, Appendix 2).

Veterans preference is not popular with managers or personnel specialists. In responding to a survey from the General Accounting Office, both managers and OPM and agency personnel staff were often critical of veterans preference. Particularly in conjunction with the rule of three, it was seen as "decreas[ing] their ability to obtain a quality pool of candidates" and as slowing down the process (U.S. GAO, 1995: 30). In fact, the GAO found that it sometimes played a role in managers' decision to return a list of candidates without making a selection, or in the decision to use alternative hiring mechanisms, such as the outstanding scholars program, which do not require application of veterans preference (U.S. GAO, 1995).

The unwillingness on the part of the NPR authors to take on veterans preference is understandable. Previous attempts to limit it have failed (Ingraham and Ban, 1983). Although politicians today attack affirmative action as undermining the merit system, veterans preference (which gives much greater advantages) does not come in for similar criticism. And effective lobbying by veterans groups has meant that veterans preference remains politically untouchable.

In sum, even though the federal reforms are addressing many of the factors that make the hiring system unwieldy from the point of view of managers, they do not touch the politically sensitive issues of veterans preference and the rule of three. Further, the pendulum is swinging so far in the direction of decentralization that agencies will lose the advantages of reasonable economies of scale, thereby increasing duplication of effort and costs. The absence of effective oversight by OPM is also troubling.

CONCLUSIONS

This [reading] has explored the changing approaches to hiring in the federal and state governments. As we have seen, "expediency management"—that is, individual managers gaming the system—is still with us, but many jurisdictions have at least begun the effort of structural reform to address the underlying problems that make such gaming necessary in the eyes of managers.

If we compare the reforms recommended by the Winter Commission and the changes being implemented by some states with those called for by the NPR, we see two models: an evolutionary approach based on gradual reform, and revolutionary reform, that is, abrupt and drastic system changes (Palguta, 1993). Which approach to take will depend to a great extent on the diagnosis of the problem. If one thinks that civil service systems are basically sound but need technical fixes or moderate reforms to make them work better, then obviously the evolutionary approach will be seen as appropriate (Palguta, 1993). But if one concludes that the existing systems are causing serious problems, then one is more likely to agree with a former head of the New York State Civil Service Commission, who once said (probably only half in jest) that he had concluded that the system couldn't be reformed and that it should be blown up (Ban and Riccucci, 1994). The differences in approach at the federal and state levels may reflect different perceptions of the severity of the problem or different political environments providing different levels of support for radical change.

Whichever route to change is followed, there are several broad conclusions that can be drawn about the reform process. First, the process of change is usually slow. Formal change requires revising rules, passing new laws, and even amending the state constitution. Successful implementation also requires changing both the formal roles and the culture of the personnel office. It also requires a willingness on the part of managers to take on a broader responsibility in recruiting and selecting candidates (Ban, 1995). Without these changes, new systems may not work as expected.

Second we will always have to struggle to find the proper balance between the need for control to prevent abuses and the need to give managers enough discretion to do their jobs well. In the area of hiring, the assumption of the reformers is that the values of a merit system are firmly planted, and that giving managers more discretion will not lead to widespread abuse. But even those who share that assumption (the author among them) recognize the need to maintain effective oversight of a decentralized hiring process to make sure new discretions are not abused. We need to recognize the risk that abuses will undercut the legitimacy of the merit system in the public's eyes (Masden, 1995).

Finally, attempts to reform hiring point, once again, to the importance of the political environment in personnel policy. At the federal level, the creation of the National Performance Review provided an environment where quiet revolutionary change was possible. Both at the federal and state levels, fiscal austerity has created problems but also opportunities to find ways to streamline processes. The political environment also limits what reforms are attempted. This is particularly true for veterans preference.

REFERENCES

Ban, Carolyn. 1991. "The Realities of the Merit System," in Carolyn Ban and Norma M. Riccucci, eds., *Public Personnel Management: Current Concerns—Future Challenges.* New York: Longman.

———. 1995. *How Do Public Managers Manage? Bureaucratic Constraints, Organizational Culture, and the Potential for Reform.* San Francisco: Jossey-Bass.

Ban, Carolyn, and Patricia W. Ingraham. 1988. "Retaining Quality Federal Employees: Life after PACE." *Public Administration Review* 48, no. 3: 708–718.

Ban, Carolyn, and Toni Marzotto. 1984. "Delegations of Examining: Objectives and Implementation," in Patricia W. Ingraham and Carolyn Ban, eds., *Legislating Bureaucratic Change: The Civil Service Reform Act of 1978.* Albany: State University of New York Press.

Ban, Carolyn, and Harry Redd III. 1990. "The State of the Merit System. Perceptions of Abuse in the Federal Civil Service." *Review of Public Personnel Administration* 10, no. 3: 55–72.

Ban, Carolyn, and Norma Riccucci. 1993. "Personnel Systems and Labor Relations: Steps toward a Quiet Revitalization," in Frank Thompson, ed., *Revitalizing State and Local Public Service.* San Francisco: Jossey-Bass.

———. 1994. "New York State Civil Service Reform in a Complex Political Environment." *Review of Public Personnel Administration* 14, no. 2: 28–39.

Harmon, Gloria (Executive Officer, California State Personnel Board). 1992. "Remarks to the National Association [*sic*] on the State and Local Public Service."

Ingraham, Patricia W., and Carolyn Ban. 1984. *Legislating Bureaucratic Change: The Civil Service Reform Act of 1978*. Albany: State University of New York Press.

Jensen, Cristy. 1992. "Briefing Paper: California State Government." Prepared for the National Commission on the State and Local Public Service.

Lane, Larry M., and Gary Marshall. 1995. "Reinventing OPM: Adventurers, Issues, and Implications." Paper presented at ASPA Material Conference.

Lavigna, Robert (Administrator, Division of Merit Recruitment. Wisconsin Department of Employment Relations). 1995. Personal Interview.

Masden, Daniel. 1995. "Observations and Comments on Reinventing Government." *Public Personnel Management* 24, no. 1: 113–126.

Minnesota Department of Employee Relations. 1991. *Personnel Management and Affirmative Action; Management Development Care Program*. St. Paul: MDER.

———. 1994. *State of Minnesota Civil Service Pilot Projects*. St. Paul: MDER.

National Academy of Public Administration. 1983. *Revitalizing Federal Management: Managers and Their Overburdened Systems*. Washington, D.C.: National Academy of Public Administration.

National Commission on the Public Service [Volcker Commission]. 1990. *Leadership for America: Rebuilding the Public Service*. Lexington, Mass.: Lexington Books.

National Commission on the State and Local Public Service [Winter Commission]. 1993. *Hard Truths/Tough Choices: An Agenda for State and Local Reform*. Albany, N.Y.: Nelson A. Rockefeller Institute of Government.

National Performance Review. 1993a. *From Red Tape to Results: Creating a Government That Works Better and Costs Less*. Washington, D.C.: U.S. Government Printing Office.

———. 1993b. *Reinventing Human Resource Management*. Washington, D.C.: U.S. Government Printing Office.

Ospina, Sonia. 1992. "'Expediency Management' in Public Service: A Dead-End Search for Managerial Discretion." *Public Productivity and Management Review* 15, no 4: 405–421.

PA Times. 1995. "Personnel Department Eases Access to Best and Brightest." 18, no. 4 (April 1).

Palguta, John. 1993. "Federal Recruitment and Selection Methods: In Need of Evolution or Revolution?" Paper presented at the annual meeting of American Society for Public Administration.

Riccucci, Norma M. 1991. "Merit, Equity, and Test Validity: A New Look at an Old Problem." *Administration and Society* 23, no. 1: 74–93.

Rudner, Lawrence. M. 1992. "Pre-Employment Testing and Employee Productivity." *Public Personnel Management* 21, no. 2: 150.

Schnorf, Stephen (Director, Illinois Department of Central Management Services). 1994. Correspondence.

U.S. General Accounting Office. 1994. *Federal Hiring: Testing for Entry-Level Administrative Positions Falls Short of Expectations* (GAO/GGD-94-103). Washington, D.C.: USGAO.

———. 1995. *Federal Hiring: Reconciling Managerial Flexibility with Veterans' Preference* (GAO/GGD-95-102). Washington, D.C.: USGAO.

U.S. Merit Systems Protection Board. 1993. *Federal Personnel Offices: Time for Change?* Washington, D.C.: USMSPB.

———. 1994. *Entering Professional Positions in the Federal Government*. Washington, D.C.: USMSPB.

———. 1995. *The Rule of Three in Federal Hiring: Boon or Bane?* Washington, D.C.: USMSPB.

Wisconsin Department of Employment Relations. 1995. *Recruiting the Best and the Brightest: Reinventing Wisconsin's Civil Service Hiring System*. Madison: Wisconsin Department of Employment Relations.

OVERVIEW OF RECRUITMENT AND SELECTION

One of the most important activities that managers perform is the selection of skilled and capable employees. The quality of performance of any organization depends heavily on the skills, character, and level of commitment of its people. The most direct way of ensuring excellence in performance is to hire highly talented and enthusiastic employees. The first step in the hiring process is to attract the attention of such applicants, and the second step is to select the most qualified individual from among highly qualified candidates. Careful and thorough selection procedures can help managers avoid personnel problems in the future by weeding out candidates who are not capable or not motivated. The recruitment and selection process should be well planned and efficiently executed to find the best possible employee as quickly as possible. Managers should carefully plan the recruitment and selection process, using a clear and up-to-date job description of the duties and responsibilities of the position in question. Advertising should be effective and informative. Selection methods should be appropriate for the position, and the criteria used to evaluate candidates should be fair, comprehensive, and job-related.

A number of important objectives and principles can be followed to select the best candidates, but the overriding principle to be adhered to throughout the hiring process is to base all recruitment information, tests, and selection decisions on the specific requirements of the particular job to be done. Factors unrelated to the job—such as political affiliation, personal appearance, common school ties, or friendship—have no place in the process.

The recruitment process ends with the consummation of an employment contract and employee orientation. The purpose of both activities is to prevent misunderstandings between the employer and the employee about job-related expectations. Applicants not selected for this particular position should be promptly notified about their no-hire status and thanked for applying. These same people might also fit vacancies that arise and might indeed be the best candidates in other job searches. In the event of legal challenges, a critical part of the public sector recruitment and selection process is the need to document every significant step of that process, including the job description, all relevant announcements and advertising, all applications, the selection criteria employed, the selection methods used, and the evaluation results for each candidate.

RECRUITMENT

Recruitment is the process of finding and attracting the best people to fill vacancies in new or existing jobs within the jurisdiction. **Internal recruitment** is done among existing employees within the jurisdiction's workforce. **External re-** **cruitment** goes outside the workplace. The nature of the job determines the extent of the search process used. For positions where an intimate knowledge of current operations is highly desirable, an internal search is perhaps indicated; for positions in which a job skill is needed that no current employees command, an external search would be more likely.

Adequate recruitment efforts entail costs in the posting of announcements and advertising, require staff time in managing the recruitment process and evaluating candidates, and require substantial effort in interviewing (which may include travel expenses). The higher the level and the more professional the position, the higher the cost of recruiting and generally the longer it takes to fill open positions.

Who Is Responsible for Recruitment

In the absence of an HRM director or personnel department, in most cases the city manager, county executive, or the head of the department with the job opening in question handles recruitment. Whoever does the hiring should work closely with the direct supervisor of the position in question. The supervisor is one of the best sources of information about the knowledge, skills, and abilities (KSAs) needed to fill the vacancy. However, the supervisor's understanding of the open position should be based on a carefully researched job analysis.

The recruitment process encompasses several administrative tasks, such as developing and purchasing advertisements, compiling a set of recruitment files, and systematizing the files. The recruiting administrator needs to establish a secure place for the applicants' documents and to plan for the additional work the hiring process may require from him or her and from clerical support personnel.

If the administrator establishes a search committee to do the recruitment and hiring, that committee should include the direct supervisor of the open position. A search committee is indicated when a position entails working with two or more units of the organization and the job incumbent needs to be accepted by all significant administrators in those units. The search committee requires the same administrative support already noted: staff time, access to a telephone, and a secure place for the search materials generated by the search process to reside. It is necessary to develop a recruitment information system and single point of contact so candidates know where they stand in the selection process and whom to communicate with regarding the search process.

Regardless of who is in charge of the recruitment process, the equal employment opportunity (EEO)–affirmative action officer should be included in planning for the recruitment effort. If the city, county, or state agency does not have such a staff person, the legal counsel of the jurisdiction should review the recruitment process for compliance with legal requirements.

Using the Job Analysis

The best tool to begin the recruitment process is a recently completed job analysis (see Chapter 7), which identifies the KSAs required for the opening. It describes the nature of the work, lists the essential and secondary tasks the job incumbent must complete, specifies the experience and education required, and identifies the placement of the incumbent in the chain of command. When contemplating recruitment, the organization should determine whether an accurate and up-to-date job analysis exists for the position in question. The emergence of a vacancy in an established position normally provides a good opportunity to update an existing job analysis.

Job Announcement

An announcement of the particular job to be filled and the detailed job description is developed from the job analysis. Job analyses lead to the generation of documents that are much more complex than the job description; an effective job announcement relies on that documentation so that it will attract applicants with the needed KSAs.

The job announcement should specify the job duties, location, pay rate, and qualifications for the job.[6] It is important to ask for only those skills, education, and experience necessary for the successful performance of the job. For example, unless the agency can demonstrate that the duties of the job require a high school education, it would be unlawful to require a high school diploma from an applicant.[7] Basing the recruitment efforts on the job analysis—that is, linking it to the specific tasks, KSAs, and experience required by the job—avoids potential affirmative action/EEO problems later.

Determining the salary range of a new position should be based on the previous salary offered to the last occupant; the KSAs needed by the job and pay scales relevant to those KSAs in other similar jobs within the area; and the relevant external market (regional or national). Changes made to existing job descriptions during the recruitment phase may be of concern to union leadership.

Internal Versus External Recruitment

Once the job announcement has been developed, a decision has to be made about whether to recruit from inside or outside the organization. Both strategies have advantages and disadvantages, and some positions are better suited to one or the other. Using external recruitment methods may bring new ideas into an organization, while hiring from within signals a high degree of confidence in the workforce.

Internal recruitment Internal recruitment, which draws on existing employees to fill an open position, is less expensive and takes significantly less time than external recruiting does. It is most appropriately used for positions for which existing employees are likely to have the requisite skills. An added advantage is that the employees' strengths and weaknesses are known to the organization, and the employee applicants are likely to know the goals and objectives of the unit doing the hiring.

Filling positions from inside the organization,

however, may create a ripple effect as several people change jobs. Also, factions in the workforce may be aggravated when the internal promotion strengthens one faction and weakens another. Highly specialized or professional jobs may require the use of external recruiting in order to take advantage of a national labor market. Collective bargaining agreements often feature rules on bidding on open jobs, so that awareness of relevant features of labor agreements constitutes an essential aspect of the internal versus external recruitment decision.

In an internal recruitment effort, the job announcement is placed in newsletters, posted on workplace bulletin boards, announced via e-mail through Intranet messages, and distributed to the collective bargaining units if appropriate. Interested employees can apply directly for the opening. Providing feedback to employees who apply but are not selected reinforces the idea with applicants that the selection process is open and fair.[8]

Internal recruiting must comply with existing civil service procedures, collective bargaining agreements, and other personnel rules under which the jurisdiction may be operating. The collective bargaining agreement and personnel rules often prescribe the procedures to be used in filling many types of openings. Seniority can be an overriding principle in such agreements. In some cases, the rules of selection require that the employee with the most seniority has the first claim to an open position, even if that person is only minimally qualified. The administrator in charge of the hiring or the search team needs to consult these documents (and legal counsel) to make certain that the recruitment process adheres to all requirements stipulated in the personnel policy document and existing labor agreements.

External recruiting External recruiting draws on applications made from outside the organization. The administrator needs to determine the proper pool of candidates based on the type of job to be filled. For example, it would not be necessary to recruit nationally for a secretary-receptionist position. The local labor market is likely to have many applicants with the necessary KSAs for that job, and an advertisement in the local newspaper will probably generate an adequate number of qualified applicants. Other positions, however, such as engineer or city manager, require a regional or nationwide search. The jurisdiction should allow for the increased cost and time associated with a national search. Generally, the higher the salary is, the longer it takes to fill the position. Costs associated with external recruitment include advertising the position, long-distance telephone calls to check references, and travel expenses if candidates are invited for personal interviews. In some cases consulting firms are used to recruit and pre-screen applicants and collect background information for sensitive or high-profile positions.

Many resources can be used to assist in external recruiting. Technical assistance in conducting the search is often available through professional organizations, some of them described in this chapter. On-line services bring employers and job seekers together for many types of specializations. Employment services may also be available through state employment agencies and registries maintained by professional associations and accreditation agencies.

University internship programs may be another resource for finding paraprofessional or young professional workers. Internships are especially suited for short-term projects for which permanent staff is unavailable. However, interns require supervision and opportunities for learning more about the larger issues of management and operations facing the whole organization. Moreover, significant staff time needs to be set aside for their supervision and evaluation.

Management recruitment firms are available in a number of areas to assist in finding professional employees. In exchange for a fee, the human resource management consultant locates professionals meeting the job description. Local governments considering this option should investigate the cost carefully, as it is likely to be substantial; often it is based on a substantial (often up to one-third) percentage of the open position's salary. The cost of a recruiter may be justified by the fact that most public organizations underestimate the indirect costs incurred when staff members handle a search from beginning to end.[9] There is some evidence as well that external recruiters can complete a search more quickly than an internal committee can.[10] Care should be taken in choosing an external recruiter; however, the recruiter should have worked with public sector agencies before and must understand the jurisdiction's commitment to affirmative action, diversity, and any other relevant organizational priorities.

Advertising for the Job Opening

The decision about where and how to advertise should be based on the nature and size of the applicant pool. Placing an advertisement in a local or regional newspaper will suffice for many entry-level positions. The local state unemployment office also is an option. More specialized positions need to be advertised in national publications. Most professions have their own journals, newsletters, and on-line services. To find an appropriate pool of candidates, generally the more professional the position or the more elevated the status of the position, the more likely it is that a regional or national search for candidates will be necessary to signal that sufficient effort was expended to locate the most qualified person for a key organizational position.

There are also innovative methods to advertise a job opportunity, including sending direct mail to professional associations and schools, using outplacement firms, and contacting employers that have recently laid off large numbers of employees.

Targeting minorities and women An agency that is attempting to attract more minority applicants should consider placing advertisements in neighborhood weeklies based in ethnically diverse areas or contacting placement offices at colleges and universities with large ethnic and/or minority student populations, such as historically black colleges. Thinking creatively about new outlets for recruitment ads can increase the diversity of the applicant pool substantially.

The recruitment of women and minorities has been a challenge for many organizations across the country interested in diversifying their workforce. The federal Office of Personnel Management (OPM) has issued special guidance for federal agencies seeking women and minorities. OPM has authorized a lump-sum payment of up to 25 percent of base pay for recruitment or relocation bonuses if a position is difficult to fill. In addition, federal agencies may offer up to a 30 percent higher rate of pay for occupations that need to be paid above normal federal rates, and they may offer flexible work schedules.[11]

Content of the advertisement The advertisement should attract applicants with the right skills and deter applicants without the appropriate skills. It should be specific enough to attract interest, but not too specific (e.g., in regard to levels of compensation) so that it does not obligate the jurisdiction to contractual arrangements prematurely. The advertisement should have many of the same details as the job announcements for internal recruiting.

An effective advertisement should include the following components:

- Job title
- Education or experience required
- Skills, certifications, or licenses required
- The materials needed to apply (for example, diplomas, certificates of study, and college transcripts)
- Where to send the documents
- A statement of the jurisdiction's compliance with the Americans With Disabilities Act and EEO laws
- A deadline for application

There must be a good match between the KSAs needed for the job as described in the job analysis and the qualifications set forth in the advertisement. Advertisements placed in periodicals distributed outside the organization's geographic area may contain general information about the area jurisdiction, including the size, range of amenities, and other characteristics that might attract interested applicants.

All advertising (plus application, testing, and selection procedures) needs to be in compliance with affirmative action and EEO laws and other legal requirements. The advertisement should avoid any mention of gender, race, religion, age, ethnic origin, and physical capabilities, unless those characteristics are considered **bona-fide occupational qualifications** (BFOQ) for the job—that is, qualifications considered essential to the successful performance of the job. For example, it would probably be illegal to advertise for male lifeguards for a city swimming pool or for a female receptionist. Certain public safety jobs, such as police and firefighters, however, require physical testing that grants advantage to males as a part of the selection process. Ethnic origin may be a BFOQ in a case where an agency operates a program of outreach to an unassimilated immigrant ethnic group, or law enforcement is seeking to establish a closer working relationship with a specific ethnic or racial group in its jurisdiction.

All organizations must be prepared to make reasonable accommodations for applicants who may request them under the Americans with Disabilities Act (ADA). Title II of ADA requires compliance from local governments with more than fifteen employees. ADA requires personnel actions of local government to be unrelated to either the "existence or consequences of a disability."[12] Some advertisements notify potential applicants of specific selection procedures to be used (e.g., pen and paper testing, physical agility testing), so that applicants who wish to ask for reasonable accommodation under the ADA can request that accommodation in a timely manner.

SELECTION PROCESS

The primary goal of selection procedures is to find the individual who can be expected to per-

form most successfully in a specific position. An important principle to follow throughout the selection process is to base all tests and selection decisions on the specific requirements of the job to be done and the KSAs needed, not factors unrelated to the job such as political affiliation or friendship. Courts have determined that for selection criteria to be valid, they have to be job-related as documented by the job analysis. Hiring based on extraneous factors can often lead to employees who are not capable of doing the jobs they are hired to do, and, just as important, this practice can give rise to claims of illegal discrimination on the part of better-qualified applicants who were not hired.

In fact, the second objective of the selection process is to provide a fair opportunity for all applicants to be hired. The selection process should be open to anyone who feels qualified to apply, and any tests administered should provide each applicant who reaches that testing level the same opportunity to demonstrate his or her abilities. Whether the selection process is brief or lengthy, the process that every organization should follow to find the most qualified employees is as follows:

1. Determine who will make the hiring decision.
2. Analyze the job to define important duties and responsibilities.
3. Determine the level of KSAs needed to perform the job duties.
4. Establish the minimum qualifications of the position.
5. Design or acquire tests to measure and evaluate each candidate's KSAs.

Determining Who Makes the Hiring Decision

In most organizations a number of people are involved in the selection process. Clerical employees may receive and review applications for completeness; HR specialists may screen applications on the basis of minimum qualifications and prepare a list of qualified or eligible candidates;

and managers from each of the departments affected by the work done in the position will want to interview or test the candidates.

Although only one manager will usually have direct responsibility for the future employee, there are advantages to having more than one administrator participate in making a hiring decision. A variety of perspectives allows for several people to provide information about the job and supply their perceptions of each candidate's ability to perform in the position. Having several people on a hiring panel permits the discussion of the advantages and disadvantages of each candidate, and a decision can be made based on a consensus of needs instead of how a candidate fits the job requirements as perceived by a single manager. Finally, with the potential for claims of discrimination, it is a good idea to have several people involved in the selection process to help keep the questioning on track and job-related and to provide eyewitness testimony against false claims.

Determining the Knowledge, Skills, and Abilities of the Position

The first step in the hiring process is job analysis, which provides an understanding of the fundamental elements of the job. Then the level of KSAs needed to perform the duties of the position in question must be determined. For example, the job of police officer includes the enforcement of laws. To accomplish this responsibility, the officer must possess driving and weapons skills, the ability to handle difficult people and situations, and a working knowledge of criminal law. This set of KSAs is added to those from other responsibilities of the police officer position to establish what KSAs are needed to do the job successfully.

Determining Minimum Qualifications

Minimum qualifications describe the essential KSAs needed to perform the job; applicants who do not meet the minimum qualifications are removed from further consideration. Usually minimum qualifications include knowledge of the principles related to the work to be performed, experience doing similar work, and specific job skills needed to perform the job duties. Each qualification must be a valid indicator of performance. Nevertheless, quite often employers specify qualifications that are not clearly job-related. For example, many employers use a college degree as a minimum qualification for vacant positions without determining whether having earned a degree is directly related to the performance of a specific job. It may be that the knowledge needed to perform a job could be obtained through experience, or by means of a combination of education and experience.

In some cases, minimum qualifications have been established by law or public policy. Child labor laws apply to all government employment, and professional certifications are required to perform certain jobs. In some cases, residency requirements have been allowed as minimum qualifications in local governments. In addition to minimum qualifications, a list of preferred or desired qualifications can be prepared to identify those applicants who would be the best prepared to perform successfully in the position.

Testing

To accomplish the important task of hiring the right person for the job, most organizations use several selection tools in sequence, such as application forms, performance tests, personal interviews, and reference checks. Each of these selection instruments must be designed to measure an applicant's abilities as they relate to actual job requirements and should not disqualify candidates because of factors unrelated to the job.

Every step of the selection process, from the application form to the final interview, is considered a "test" in legal proceedings and should be viewed as such by those making the hiring decision. Each test in the hiring process must be job-related and equitably administered. To meet the first criterion, tests must measure factors related to specific requirements of the job the prospective employee is expected to perform. To meet the second criterion, tests must be applied consistently among applicants. At every step of the hiring process, the HR specialist and manager should be asking, "Is this question job-related? Am I being consistent with all candidates?"

Validity and reliability Validity refers to the adequacy of the test instrument—that is, whether it accurately measures those attributes of a job that it is intended to measure. To be a valid employment test means that a selection instrument or process must be proven to be job-related. There are three types of validity or ways to establish job-relatedness: content validity, criterion-related validity, and construct validity. **Content validity** means that test questions and processes (such as assessment center exercises) are directly related to the KSAs needed to perform the duties and responsibilities of a job. To be valid in its content, the test has to cover the whole domain of the job and not leave out important KSAs.

Criterion-related validity means that test results or scores have a strong relationship to required job behaviors and future performance. Criterion-related validity is demonstrated by means of archival records demonstrating that scores on a selection test or series of tests correlate (covary) with indicators of success in the job such as performance evaluations, rate of retention, rate of subsequent promotion, and record of follow-up training required.

Construct validity is the most abstract form of proof of job-relatedness in a selection test or process. Some characteristics being sought in an applicant cannot be directly observed, and it is necessary to rely on surrogate measures presumed to be indicative of the desired trait. For example, in the hiring of law enforcement officers it is important that persons armed with lethal weapons empowered to enforce the law be mentally stable and well adjusted. Although these character traits cannot be directly observed, several psychological inventories have sufficiently proven predictive power to permit a hiring authority to disqualify a candidate for having failed a psychological screening test.

Reliability means that a test produces the same measurement outcome over repeated use. For example, a reliable scale will read 180 lbs, ten out of ten times, weighing the same 180-lb object; an unreliable scale would produce a different (higher and lower) weight each time it was used to weigh the same object.

The U.S. Supreme Court has ruled that selection criteria that are not directly related to job performance are prohibited.[13] In 1978, the Uniform Guidelines on Employee Selection Procedures were issued by the U.S. Departments of Labor and Justice and the Equal Employment Opportunity Commission (EEOC). These guidelines provide generally accepted rules for selection procedures and standards for the validation of selection tests.

Selection tests often have **face validity,** meaning that they appear to measure specific KSAs required on a job, but under scrutiny they may not. Consequently, selection tests should be tested for validity. Local government administrators have several options in obtaining validated selection tests. Several public personnel organizations, including the International Personnel Management Association (IPMA) and the International City and County Management Association (ICMA), offer standardized validated tests for use in local governments. Consultants may be hired who specialize in the construction of valid selection tests. In addition, managers may design their own test validation procedures.

Concurrent validation and **predictive validation** represent two approaches to test assessment. Concurrent validation uses a sample of current employees who take the proposed selection test while evaluators simultaneously collect information on the job performance of these employees. The test in question is considered valid when the range of low to high performance parallels the range of low to high test scores. In predictive validation, the test results of job applicants are compared to actual performance after applicants have been hired and have been on the job for a period of time.

Administrators should always be careful to use tests that are considered valid by ensuring that questions on application forms, in interviews, and in all other tests are job-related. Selection test questions should measure only what is intended to be measured and should not lead to information in an area protected by discrimination laws bearing on race, ethnicity, religion, marital status, health status, age, and political preference.

Technological Considerations in Recruitment and Selection

Governments are using computer software to assist managers in a wide array of HRM functions, including recruitment, classification, performance evaluation, and grievance handling. The U.S. Office of Personnel Management has developed a computer-based information system called *Human Resource Manager* designed to assist managers in federal, state, and local governments develop position descriptions and compose selection processes. The Human Resource Manager contains tasks, competencies, and qualifications for 67 clerical and technical occupations and for 105 middle and upper managerial positions.

Probably the most frequently used technological resource for traditional human resource management functions is the access available on the Internet to jobs at all levels of government. Some examples include OPM's USA Jobs, which lists current job openings and features access to on-line application services. The Canadian federal government has its counterpart with Government Jobs Canada, which lists public service jobs in one location for the federal government, the provinces, and major Canadian cities. All states have web pages, and most of these list employment opportunities. For example, Texas's Governor's Job Bank lists state jobs by region, type of work, salary, and education level. The Commonwealth of Massachusetts provides a search engine for finding government job opportunities. Other agencies provide major job search capability for government jobs of all types and at all levels. America's Job Bank boasts more than 1.3 million available jobs and 1.3 million registered job seek-

ers (at the time of this writing). Public Sector Jobs, sponsored by the IPMA, provides job listings for job seekers and opportunities for public employers to list their job openings.

Selection Methods

After the KSAs and minimum qualifications are determined, a series of tests should be used to find those who rate the highest on the specific job qualifications. Because not all jobs are the same, selection methods differ somewhat from job to job. The following list shows a typical sequence of selection methods:

1. **Application forms** and resumés—to evaluate candidate training and experience
2. **Written tests**—to measure and evaluate knowledge or analytical skills
3. **Performance tests**—to measure and evaluate abilities and skills
4. **Oral examinations (interviews)**—to evaluate knowledge, communication skills, and lessons learned from experience
5. **Background investigations**—to evaluate past performance and behavior
6. **Probationary period** (on the job)—to measure and evaluate performance on the job

Tests that are applied to a large number of applicants are less expensive than those given on a one-to-one basis. The least costly method is the detailed application form, which can be administered to many applicants and used to identify the relatively few candidates who meet all the requirements of the job. The most expensive approaches are performance tests administered at assessment centers, skill demonstration tests, and interviews because of the time required of those conducting the interviews. These types of tests should be administered to the smallest number of candidates for critical positions to find those who are most qualified.

Application forms and resumés Application forms and resumés are usually the first in a series of selection methods. They are usually used to screen out applicants who do not meet the minimum qualifications and to gather information for personnel records. These selection devices can provide information on an applicant's basic qualifications such as level of education, employment experience, and job skills. They usually provide personal employment information as well, such as name, address, social security number, and telephone number.

The information requested on applications should be related directly to the job to be done by the prospective employee and must not ask questions that directly or indirectly lead to information about age, race, color, sex, religion, national origin, physical disability, or personal information that is unrelated to required employment information or potential job performance. For example, common questions found on application forms include age and marital status, but this information is usually irrelevant to the eventual performance on the job and could be used to make hiring decisions that arc legally impermissible. Such information may be needed for determining benefits, but should be collected only after an applicant has been hired.

Because most information on job applications is factual (places of employment, degrees earned, certifications, and so forth), the information can—and should—be verified. Managers should exercise extreme caution when reviewing application forms because the evidence is strong that nearly half of all applicants exaggerate their qualifications on application forms and resumés.[14] Managers should ask for supporting documentation (such as education transcripts, certificates, and degrees awarded) and contact former employers to confirm prior work experience.

Most organizations have a single application form for all jobs within the organization. In this case, there may be serious questions of job-relatedness, and the information may not be sufficient to determine minimum qualifications for the specific job that needs to be filled. A supplemental application form may be required for some jobs asking for information specific to the job in question.

Eligibility lists After reviewing application forms, many organizations establish an eligibility list, or a list of candidates who meet the minimum qualifications and are considered the most promising applicants for further evaluation. The most common number of candidates passed on for consideration to management is three, and the process of recommending a set of those best qualified applicants is referred to as the *rule of three.* Occasionally only one candidate is sent on for further testing and management interviews, but managers usually find a single candidate too limiting a choice. Recent trends show that eligibility lists have grown to between five and ten certified or eligible candidates for most job openings. Other ideas for certifying eligible candidates are to use a percentage of those who meet minimum qualifications or to establish categorical groupings such as satisfactory, good, and excellent, then allowing for further testing of everyone in the "excellent" category.

Many public organizations have a policy of awarding extra consideration in thc selection process to veterans (**veterans preference**). This is often done in the establishment of eligibility lists when veterans are given extra points and are moved further up on the list of eligible candidates.

Written tests Written tests are standardized methods applied to measure the knowledge or ability of individuals in specific job areas, predict future performance, and compare other applicants. Testing fell into disfavor with the courts and public employers in the 1960s and 1970s because many general tests used at that time (such as intelligence and mechanical comprehension tests) were not clearly tied to performance in a specific job and had an adverse impact on minorities. Tests that have been carefully constructed to measure indicators related to job performance increasingly are being used to help managers make informed hiring decisions. Even tests of intelligence and employee character are making a comeback in situations where strong criterion validity evidence is available.[15]

In many cases, standardized tests for specific jobs are available from firms specializing in constructing these tests. Other organizations such as the ICMA and IPMA have tests available for public agencies. Typically written tests are multiple choice, easy to construct, quickly scored, and require little interpretation. Written tests are easy to administer and can be given to large numbers of applicants with relatively little cost to the organization.

Performance tests Performance tests are often given to applicants to measure their ability or skill at performing some specific aspects of a job or assess their ability to be trained to do the work in question. These tests frequently simulate a major facet of the job. Usually they are used to evaluate skills for manual jobs, but are used as well for testing computational ability or computer skills. Since these tests are taken from an important function of the actual job, there is a strong relationship between the test and the job, and they are consequently considered content valid. These tests are expensive to administer to individual applicants, however.

Physical tests are often given to candidates who will be required to perform physical tasks in the performance of their jobs. These tests must accurately reflect the common physical requirements of the job and cannot eliminate candidates for the inability to perform extreme cases of the physical requirements. The ADA requires that written and physical tests allow for "reasonable accommodation" of applicants taking these tests. The ADA prohibits employers from discriminating against employees who cannot perform marginal physical requirements of the job—in other words, infrequent or nonessential physical tasks.

Interviews Aside from the application form, interviewing is the most commonly used selection device. The interview, however, may also be the least valid and least reliable method of selecting future employees.[16] Managers use the interview to determine a candidate's ability to communicate and interact effectively, and to ask probing questions about performance and behavior in circumstances similar to potential job situations. Because of the personal interaction in an interview, managers can explore interests or concerns in greater detail than written tests or application forms can, but this characteristic of the interview also opens the door to questions that are not job related and could lead to information that could be used to make discriminatory or unfair decisions.

The validity of an interview becomes questionable when it strays into areas of questioning unrelated to the job. Personal interaction and human nature can combine in the interview to produce error and even uncover subconscious bias. A number of common **interview errors** can cloud the interviewer's judgment:

Similarity error. One candidate may appear similar to the interviewers and therefore be inappropriately favored by the panel.

Comparison error. One candidate may stand above the rest of the applicants by comparison but still not meet the requirements of the job.

First impression error. One candidate may become a favorite of those interviewing due to some information on the application form or other communication, and gain an advantage before any interviewing actually takes place. Research on interviewing finds that managers make up their minds about how they will decide about a candidate being interviewed in an average of four minutes.

Halo and horns effect. One candidate may qualify in one aspect of a job that influences the remainder of the interview, or interviewers may overreact to one unfavorable response. Unfortunately for the job candidate, one bad impression tends to influence those conducting the interview more than the positive responses do.

Other factors that can influence the outcome of an interview inappropriately include nonverbal behaviors such as body language, accent, friendliness, posture, and enthusiasm. There is strong evidence that the clothing that candidates wear can inappropriately influence an interview. Research indicates that nonverbal behavior tends to have a greater influence on a hiring decision in an interview than verbal responses. And interviewer biases on the basis of age, race, and sex can also exercise an undue influence on decisions made as a result of an interview.

Finally, administrators may not be trained to conduct interviews properly and may have poor listening and communication skills. Much of the important information to be transmitted in an interview may never be heard, or it may be misinterpreted as a result of error and bias.

The reliability of interviews is typically poor. In most cases, interviews are conducted by more than one person to gain the advantages of multiple perspectives and to protect the interviewers from any false claims from disgruntled candidates. Although agreement among interviewers on the facts and overall evaluations of candidates tends to be fairly high, inter-rater reliability on subjective characteristics such as candidate leadership potential or honesty is often poor. Another aspect of interview process reliability is consistency, or how the interview is conducted for one candidate compared to others. It is common to have an established list of questions that are asked of each candidate, but it is also common to see the line of questioning diverge from the plan in the actual interview.

To avoid many of the pitfalls of employment interviews, administrators should plan their questions in advance, and each candidate should be asked these identical questions in the same way.

This does not mean that other questions cannot be asked of each candidate to follow up on partial answers or examine the candidate's response in greater detail.

Managers should ask anything they think is important to understanding how the candidate will perform on the job, but these questions must be limited to job-related issues. Many interviews consist of questions that offer little information about how a candidate will perform in the position being considered. Questions resulting in yes or no responses are useful for confirming factual details, but provide little information about the candidate. Many other general questions such as, "What is your greatest weakness?" contribute little to the information needed to make a rational hiring decision.

The best interview questions are those that provide the interview panel with information about the candidate's KSAs and attitudes necessary to perform successfully on the job. Questions that ask whether a candidate commands a given skill or is able to perform a specific task rely on the candidate's assessment of abilities. More thoughtful questions would ask what the candidates would do in a hypothetical situation (one that is related to the job to be performed) or, better yet, what they have actually done in another job similar to the one for which they are interviewing. Behavioral and situational questions have been found to be both valid and reliable, and good predictors of future performance.

Tips for successful interviewing The most common errors that administrators make in employment interviews is not knowing the specific duties and responsibilities of the job to be performed, not planning out their questions (related to job duties) in advance of the interview, and straying into areas during the interview that are either not job-related or unnecessary (and a waste of time).

Diversity considerations in recruitment and selection The asking of illegal questions leads to information that could be used to discriminate illegally against protected classes of applicants. In other cases, ill-considered questions about a person's background provide information that is irrelevant to a candidate's future performance on the job. In rare cases there is a real and important job requirement (the BFOQ) that may require interview questions related to otherwise illegal information. For example, a female guard may be required for a specific position (such as conducting body searches) in an all-female jail facility. But in most public sector job interviews, questions that call for unnecessary or illegal information must be carefully avoided. If necessary for personnel records or employment benefits, some questions can be asked *after* the hiring decision has been made.

In many cases there are ways of asking questions that provide the performance-related information needed to make a hiring decision but avoid introducing unneeded information. The examples in Box 8.1 set out the types of questions to avoid in the selection process, whether on the application form or in job interviews, and alternative questions that seek specific, job-related information that should be used instead.

Cone method of interviewing A popular technique of conducting employment interviews is known as the Cone method.[17] The interviewers first determine their objectives for the interview, then examine each selected topic by using broad questions first, followed by more specific questions related to that topic. For example, if one of the objectives for the interview is to determine the amount of supervisory experience the applicant has had, the cone for this topic may proceed as follows:

Assessment centers Some jobs, such as management positions, require an employee to perform a wide variety of tasks. Testing and interviews alone may assess only a few of the many tasks expected of these employees. **Assessment centers** have been developed as evaluation processes to appraise the abilities of candidates who are applying for managerial and other complex jobs.

Assessment centers are designed to measure several different aspects of a job using a variety of techniques. A common test used in assessment centers is an in-basket exercise, where candidates are given an in-basket full of letters, memos, and telephone messages and are asked to handle each item by determining the importance and urgency of each, then making decisions about how to take action on the information provided. Another test is the leaderless group problem. A small group of candidates is brought together and asked to solve a management problem. The solution is not as important as the process developed, and the candidates are observed and scored on their leadership traits and ability to work in groups.

Assessment centers also have interviews, with each candidate being asked questions about his or her behavior on some of the tests and any experience handling work situations similar to those expected to be performed on the job in question.

Assessment centers may also include job-specific tests measuring *personal characteristics* (such as leadership, personality, management style, and intelligence), *performance tests* (for example, writing memos, handling a problem employee, using listening skills, preparing and delivering a speech, and dealing with sexual harassment

Opening question	Describe your experience supervising employees.
More specific questions	What were your responsibilities as a supervisor?
	What problems did you experience as a supervisor?
Probing questions	How did you handle that problem?
	Did you seek advice in responding to the problem?
More specific questions	How did you improve the performance of your employees?
	What were the duties of the employees you supervised?

Box 8.1   Reframing Illegal Questions

Illegal Question	Alternative Wording
Race, Creed, and National Origin	
What is your race?	Are you legally able to work in the United States?
What organizations do you belong to?	Who would you like to be notified in the event of an emergency?
What country does your family come from?	
Where are you a citizen?	
What is your previous foreign address?	
What is your birthplace?	
What is the name of a relative to be notified in case of emergency?	
Have you acquired the ability to read, write, or speak a foreign language?	
What is your native language?	
Sex, Marital Status	
Are you male or female?	Do you have relevant work experience while using another name?
What is your maiden name?	
Have you changed your name?	
What is your sexual orientation?	
Are you married?	
Are you pregnant?	
How many children do you have?	
Do you have child care?	
Do you plan on having any more children?	
Age	
What is your age?	Information about age is almost always unnecessary.
What is your birthdate?	
Disability	
What are your height and weight?	Is there any reason you would not be able to perform the responsibilities and tasks of this position?
Do you have any disabilities?	
Have you had certain diseases?	
Religion	
What is your religion?	Would you be able to perform the required duties of this position?
What religious holidays do you celebrate?	
In what groups are you a member?	
Military Service	
Have you been dishonorably discharged from the military?	Do you have relevant work experience?
Criminal Record	
Have you ever been arrested?	Have you been convicted of a crime related to the duties and responsibilities of this position?
Have you been convicted of any crime?	

Sources: Paul Balbresky, "An Employment Related Lawsuit May Put Your Local Government at Risk," *Public Management* 75:11 (1993): 13–15; James A. Buford, Jr., *Personnel Management and Human Resources in Local Government* (Auburn, AL: Auburn University Press, 1991), pp. 170–171.

problems), *management exercises or games* (such as delegation, team building, conflict management, and performance evaluation), and *job simulations,* where a rather elaborate series of job-related situations is presented to a group of candidates who behave in roles assigned by the assessors. The simulation allows for multiple responses and has pre-planned steps for the candidates to act on as the simulation unfolds.

Typically a group of candidates for the same position is tested simultaneously in an assessment center. Many of the tests measure how the candidates work in groups, and the larger number of candidates gives the assessors an opportunity to compare the highest-rated candidates against each other after they have passed a series of preliminary tests. Assessment centers usually use a team of trained evaluators who conduct the tests and then discuss the results as a group. The group of assessors may include representatives from the departments or areas where the candidate is to be employed and thereby can offer a wide range of perspectives for determining the preferred candidate.

The most important advantage of assessment centers is that the tests can be designed to focus on very specific aspects of the job and can therefore be content valid. Assessment centers can also reliably test a number of candidates going through similar testing procedures. The biggest problem with assessment centers is their high cost. These candidate evaluation processes can run from one to five days in duration, and they occupy the time of numerous assessors and candidates. Because of the cost, assessment centers are usually conducted only for candidates applying for upper-level management or highly technical positions.

There is also a risk of bias in assessment centers related to measurement standards. The conventionally accepted characteristics of good managers or leaders are sometimes biased against women candidates, who often display management traits different from those of men. Women leaders may use a more participative or democratic style while men tend to use a more autocratic or directive style of mangement.[18] Successful managers may display these male-oriented management traits, but female-oriented traits may be equally valid predictors of good leadership and effective management.

Background investigations (reference checks)
The objectives of conducting background or reference checks, like any other selection method, should be determined before beginning the procedure. The simplest objective is to verify information obtained from candidates from the application form, testing, and interviews. Another valuable use of reference checks is to determine past performance. One of the best indicators of future performance is how the employee performed in similar situations in the past. Asking former employers and others familiar with the job candidate's work product about the performance of the prospective employee can provide important information about that person's work habits and abilities.

It is usually a good idea to inform the candidate that you will be asking former employers and others who are familiar with his or her work for confidential personnel information. A notification and checkoff on the application form or a separate signed release can be used to let the candidate know that reference checks will be conducted.

The list of references can come from the candidate, former employers and instructors, and others who are not listed by the candidate. Other references from those volunteered by the candidate can be obtained by asking the listed references for others who are familiar with the candidate's work history.

Reference checks are frequently conducted by telephone to save time and to gather spontaneous responses from those interviewed. It is useful to develop a set of job-related questions before beginning any reference interviews. Background checks by mail have advantages (the responses can be more thoughtful than spontaneous answers, and the sources will include clues to the real performance history of the candidate) and disadvantages (they are slow, and the responses can be carefully crafted and uninformative). Reference checks are also done in person on occasion, but typically only for high-ranking, security-sensitive positions.

Reference checks are useful for finding candidates who have given false or misleading information in the selection process and to uncover behavioral problems. Employers are obligated to find any problems related to the candidate's ability to perform the job before hiring, especially in the event of harm or injury to someone else. The employer can be liable for negligent hiring if the hired employee causes harm when a pattern of behavior in past employment indicated the presence of this danger. Conversely, former employers can be liable for negligent referral if they hold back information that could have prevented a person from causing harm to others in a future job situation. There are also liability questions surrounding those who give poor references to prospective employers. Everyone has heard of employers being sued by former employees for giving unflattering references. Because of this possibility, many organizations do not allow their managers to give any more information than the job description and dates of employment of the former employee.

Probationary period Obviously the most valid predictor of future performance is actual performance on the job. Most public organizations make use of a probationary period of three months to one year, when the employee is evaluated after working on the job for the designated period. The probationary period presents an opportunity for managers to evaluate the performance of a provisionally employed employee while working on the job. During probation, the employee is subject to termination at will and has fewer employment rights than permanent employees. The length of the probationary period is determined by the amount of time it takes to learn the responsibilities of the job and to accumulate a record that can be evaluated.

Often managers do not consider the probationary period as part of the employee selection process. Instead, it is used as a learning period for new employees. During the term of the probation-ary period, employees are trained, observed, counseled, and evaluated while performing the work they were hired to do.

Whatever the purpose of the probationary period, managers are responsible to train probationary employees properly and evaluate their performance accurately. These evaluations should be regular and frequent, and they should provide the employee with an assessment of performance and guidance on how to improve. At the end of the probationary period, a final evaluation should be scheduled with the employee to determine whether he or she has the potential to perform successfully on the job. If proper training and regular guidance have been conducted, the outcome of the final evaluation should come as no surprise to the employee.

Ethical Considerations in Recruitment and Selection: Drug Testing

There are some good reasons to test candidates for the use of illegal drugs. Research shows that drug and alcohol abuse is directly related to employee absenteeism and accidents on the job.[19] There may also be employer liability concerns when an employee who is under the influence of a drug causes an accident.

Extreme caution should be exercised when considering drug testing because public employers are by definition engaged in state action, and the state is held to a higher standard in respecting employee privacy than is the case for private sector employers. The U.S. Constitution limits the government from illegal searches and other privacy infringements (see Chapter 4). The courts have attempted to balance this right to privacy with the public interest (safety) and have usually allowed drug testing for applicants and current employees who are involved in dangerous occupations (fire, public works), jobs where harm may come to others (drivers), or where drug laws are enforced (police). If drug testing is adopted, special caution should be given to testing procedures. Drug testing is expensive, and evidence shows that most job candidates—whether drug users or not—say they are less likely to apply for jobs where drug testing is practiced.

COMPLETING THE PROCESS

Employment Contracts

Individual employment contracts are agreements between the agency and an employee that describe job responsibilities, reporting arrangements, the terms of employment, and separation provisions. These contracts are useful to attract key personnel by specifying salary, benefits, and incentives, and they can include protections against arbitrary firings.

Because employment contracts are legally binding on the agency and the employee for the term of the contract, great care should be taken in drafting these documents. Employment contracts are useful for managers in politically sensitive positions, such as city and county managers, because their employment can otherwise be terminated for reasons completely unrelated to work performance. Such contracts are not an advantage for a local government when offered to rank-and-file employees because case law protects these employees against arbitrary dismissal (see Chapter 4).

Employee Orientation

After the hiring decision has been made and the candidate has accepted it, the selected employee most likely has the requisite KSAs to do the work expected. However, in most cases, newly hired employees are not familiar with the specific requirements of the new job or the working environment. They need to understand their duties and the ins and outs of the organization in which they find themselves. Newly appointed employees often feel a great deal of anxiety in a new job as they look for acceptance from their new coworkers and seek an understanding of how things are done in the organization. Employee orientation training

introduces new employees to the requirements of the job and the general operation of the organization. The formal orientation can prevent misunderstandings and guard against informal orientation that may be inconsistent with official policies and practices and therefore misleading. Orientation training can also speed up the socialization process by introducing new employees to their coworkers, supervisors, and those who can help answer questions and make employees become comfortable in their new work environment.

All employees should be carefully prepared to perform their work assignments and be oriented to the organization and culture in which they will be working. They should be trained on organization rules and regulations, introduced to those who will either affect the work product or will receive the work of the employee, and trained so they fully understand the demands of the work expected of them. A separate orientation can be arranged for the new employee with supervisors, who can explain the work product needed, the supervisory arrangements in place, and how the work fits into the overall service of the government agency in question.

An orientation session should also be scheduled with HRM specialists to explain employee benefits and the method of pay distribution. Employees should understand the culture of the organization, including its history, the important people involved in the clientele community, and the way each department is integrated into the overall mission of the jurisdiction in question.

A small investment in time and orientation training materials can provide substantial benefits in employee productivity much sooner than if employees are left to their own devices to figure out their responsibilities and their connections to their coworkers. An employee orientation checklist can be very helpful to ensure that all the topics needed for the successful integration of the new employee are covered. Box 8.2 is an example of an employee orientation checklist.

Not everything about the job or the organization can be taught in a formal employee orientation

---

Box 8.2   Employee Orientation Checklist

General orientation to the organization—conducted by the organization head

- Mission and goals
- History
- Services provided
- Structure
- Who's who in the organization
- Culture, values, and ethical principles

Specific orientation to the organization's policies and procedures—conducted by a personnel officer

- Employee handbook
- Work hours
- Vacation and leave rules and procedures
- Provision of pay and description of benefits
- Discipline system
- System for complaints and suggestions

Specific orientation to the department—conducted by the department head

- Departmental goals
- Relationship to other units and departments
- Operational procedures
- Work flow
- Facilities
- Schedule
- Introduction to coworkers

Specific orientation to the job—conducted by the supervisor

- Goals and performance standards
- Job duties, responsibilities, and performance expectations
- Work station
- Computer system and capabilities
- Tools and equipment

Supervisory arrangements

- Where to find help
- On-the-job and other job training plans and schedule
- Performance appraisal schedule and content
- Promotion criteria
- Salary increase schedule and criteria
- Training plans

Source: Personnel Management, 3/e by Dessler, © 1984. Reprinted by permission of Prentice Hall, Inc., Upper Saddle River, NJ.

---

training session. The best source of information is often coworkers, who explain facts and situations in the context of the organization's way of doing things. Mentoring or arranging for the opportunity to meet with several coworkers informally, such as over lunch or after work, can help the new employee feel comfortable asking questions and provide an opportunity to learn many of the values, professional and ethical norms, and attitudes of important people within the organization.

■ CONCLUSION

Recruitment and selection describe methods that human resource officials use to attract and hire qualified candidates for service in the organization. It is very important to find and match people with the appropriate qualifications for vacancies in the organization. Failure to find the right matches of people to positions can result in performance and behavior problems that can plague an organization for years. Because of the need to make civil service systems more professional and equitable, public personnel systems have developed rules and regulations to open the system to all qualified applicants and theoretically eliminate the ability of public officials to hire or fire employees with either favoritism or malice. The result of these rules in some cases has been human resource systems that are slow and rigid. Reform has again been called for to decentralize human resource decisions and make the rules more flexible. Public agencies are now experimenting with innovative methods of recruitment and selection while attempting to maintain the objectives of merit and equity. This is a difficult balance that has more resembled the swinging of a pendulum than the balanced scales of justice.

A Sample of Internet Sites with Public Sector Job Listings

US Office of Personnel Management, USA Jobs: **http://www.usajobs.opm.gov/**

Government Jobs Canada: **http://www.pse-net. com/joblistings/joblistingCan.htm**

State and Local Government including links to individual states: **http://www.loc.gov/ global/state/stategov.html**

Texas Governor's Job Bank: **http://www.twc. state.tx.us/jobs/gvjb/gvjb.htm**

Massachusetts Jobs: **http://www.state.ma.us/ hrd/ceo**

America's Job Bank: **http://www.ajb.org**

International Personnel Management Association, Public Sector Jobs: **http://www. publicsectorjobs.com**

■ MANAGER'S VOCABULARY

internal recruitment
external recruitment
bona-fide occupational qualifications
content validity
criterion-related validity
construct validity
reliability
face validity
concurrect validation
predictive validation
application forms
written tests
performance tests
oral examination (interview)
background investigations
probationary period
veterans preference
interview error
assessment center

■ STUDY QUESTIONS

1. When managers find that the eligible candidates for a job do not meet the requirements of job openings, what steps should they take to find the best candidates?

2. What reforms to civil service systems would you recommend to help recruitment and selection processes be more efficient, meet managers' needs, and still maintain the principles of merit such as hiring qualified candidates, fairness, equal access, and protection from political abuse (such as patronage, cronyism, and political intimidation)?

3. What advantages to government employment would you emphasize when advertising for new employees?

4. What places or publications would be the most effective in finding qualified minorities and women candidates for government employment?

5. Are there specific types of jobs that are better recruited internally or externally? Explain your answer.

6. In what cases would it be appropriate to hire a recruiting firm to help find candidates for job openings in a public organization with which you are familiar?

7. What concerns would you have about validity in the interview process? How would you address these concerns?

8. Which selection method do you consider the best method for finding the most qualified candidate? Explain your answer.

■ EXPERIENTIAL EXERCISES

1. Select a job in a public agency near you, and interview the incumbent of that job to determine the knowledge, skills, and abilities needed to perform that job. Then prepare a recruitment plan for someone to fill that job.

2. Prepare an advertisement for the newspaper of the largest city near you for a transportation policy analyst in your state's Department of Transportation.

3. Develop a selection plan (including the tests to be administered to candidates) for a nurse in your local hospital.

4. Obtain a copy of an application form from a public agency near you, and analyze the questions. Are any of them discriminatory in nature?

5. Develop a list of questions to be used to interview five candidates who have been selected as the top applicants for a job teaching government and history in your local high school.

6. Describe the kinds of tests and exercises you would ask the candidates for teacher (from number 5 above) to perform as part of an assessment center.

■ CASE APPLICABLE TO THIS CHAPTER

"A Quandary Over Accepting the Job."

■ NOTES

1 Dennis L. Huett, Robert J. Lavigna, and Herbert G. Heneman III, "Recruiting the Best and the Brightest: Reinventing Wisconsin's Civil Service Hiring System" (paper presented at the National Conference of the American Society for Public Administration, June 1996).

2 Keon S. Chi, "State Civil Service Systems: A Review of Reform Efforts" (paper presented at the American Society for Public Administration Annual Conference, May 1998).

3 Jay Shafritz, "The Cancer Eroding Public Personnel Professionalism," *Public Personnel Management* (November–December 1974): 486–492.

4 Lorna Jorgensen, Kelli Fairless, and W. David Patton, "The Underground Merit System: A Look at Merit in the State System," *Review of Public Personnel Administration* 16:2 (1996): 5–21.

5 E. S. Savas and Sigmund G. Ginsburg, "The Civil Service: A Meritless System?" *Public Interest* 32 (Summer 1973): 70–85.

6 Cynthia D. Fisher, Lyle F. Schoenfeldt, and James B. Shaw, *Human Resource Management,* 2nd ed. (Boston: Houghton Mifflin, 1996), p. 240.

7 Paul Balbresky, "An Employment Related Lawsuit May Put Your Local Government at Risk," *Public Management* 75:11 (1993): 13–15.

[8] Fisher, Schoenfeldt, and Shaw, *Human Resource Management,* p. 232.

[9] Catherine Rush and Lizbeth Barclay, "Executive Search: Recruiting a Recruiter," *Public Management* 77:7 (1995): 20–22.

[10] Ibid., p. 21.

[11] U.S. Office of Personnel Management, *Employment Service, Women in the Federal Government: A Guide to Recruiting and Retaining* (Washington, D.C.: U.S. Government Printing Office, June 1998).

[12] Balbresky, "Employment Related Lawsuit," p. 14.

[13] *Griggs v. Duke Power Company,* 401 US 424 (1971); It was deemed that the requirement of a high school diploma or intelligence test was not related to job performance. *Wards Cove Packing v. Atonio,* 490 US 642 (1989). Decision based on selection criteria not being related to job performance: nepotism, a rehire preference, a lack of objective hiring criteria, seperate hiring channels for skilled and unskilled jobs, and a practice of not promoting from within.

[14] Selection based on Thomas E. Becker and Alan L. Colquit, "Potential Versus Actual Faking of a Biodata Form: An Analysis Along Several Dimensions of Item Type," *Personnel Psychology* 45:2 (1992): 389–408.

[15] Orlando Behling, "Employee Selection: Will Intelligence and Conscientiousness Do the Job?" *Academy of Management Executive* 12:1 (1988): 77–86.

[16] A. I. Huffcutt and W. Arthur, Jr., "Hunter and Hunter (1984) Revisited: Interview Validity for Entry-Level Jobs," *Journal of Applied Psychology* 79:2 (1994): 184–190.

[17] Thomas L. Moffatt, *Selection Interviewing for Managers* (New York: Harper and Row, 1979).

[18] Eagly, A and Johnson, "Gender and the Emergence of Leaders: A Meta-Analysis," *Psychological Bulletin* 108 (1990): 233–256.

[19] Edward F. Etzel, Christopher D. Lantz, and Catherine A. Yura, "Alcohol and Drug Use, and Sources of Stress: A Survey of University Faculty, Staff, and Administrators," *Employee Assistance Quarterly* 11:1 (1995): 51–58.

CHAPTER 9

Salary and Wage Management

Compensation, the principal means by which organizations attach value to the jobs established in their workforce, refers to the total package of salary and benefits paid to an employee. (See Figure 9.1 for an illustration of the total compensation package.) This total sum of remuneration includes base salary, short-term incentives such as bonuses, long-term incentives such as extra compensation for productivity improvements or cost reductions, as well as various cash and noncash benefits programs.[1] This chapter discusses salary and wage management, and the next chapter investigates benefits.

As you learned in Chapter 7, jobs typically are organized on the basis of the knowledge, skills, and abilities (KSAs) required; on the level of responsibility; and on the impact on the organization attached to each job category. When the content of a job changes, the appropriate level of pay changes as well—at least in principle. In organizations without job classification systems, compensation appears to be less systematically assigned and more a function of what the market or the organizational budget will bear.

INTRODUCTION TO READING

As Risher notes in the reading for this chapter, traditional public sector compensation systems are deeply rooted in the tradition of scientific management. The goals of such systems were guidance for and control over managers' use of resources, maintenance of employee motivation, and assurance of fair treatment of employees. As with the classification systems from which compensation plans are derived, they are most easily administered in hierarchically structured and relatively static jobs such as those frequently found in the manufacturing sector.

As human resource professionals have attempted to modify these rigid plans to fit the

Figure 9.1   The Total Compensation Package

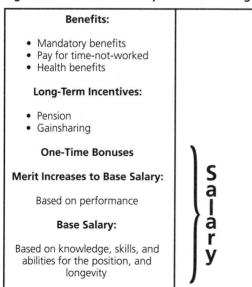

swiftly changing nature of today's knowledge-based organizations, they have suggested many possible changes that can be made in pay practices to provide for more effective outcomes for employees and organizations alike. Risher reviews the changing nature of salary and wage management in the public and private sectors, and he describes the likely shape of the next generation of public sector compensation programs.

As you read the selection, keep the following questions in mind:

- What is the "new pay" program that Risher describes?
- What are some of the challenges inherent in implementing the new pay program in public sector organizations?
- Will the new pay program "solve" the problems commonly associated with traditional compensation programs?

READING

Are Public Employers Ready for a "New Pay" Program?

HOWARD RISHER

Wage and salary management is at a cross-road. After following the same path for almost half a century, a growing number of corporations are moving in a new direction. They have largely abandoned the traditional program concepts and are building new programs around ideas that are still being refined. There is a high level of interest among public employers in moving in the same direction. But at least in the public sector those new concepts are not wholly compatible with the values and beliefs that have served as the foundation for public pay programs. That makes program planners hesitant to take the new path.

The hesitancy is not surprising. Public employers feel the pressure to change but, thus far, very few have implemented and lived with the new program model. Charlotte, NC seems to be the only example of a comprehensive "new pay" program in government. There may be few defenders of the traditional program model, but managers and employees alike are comfortable with that model. The transition from that model to the new one is not going to be easy.

As the leader of the IPMA/ACA workshop on broad banding, I have now had the opportunity to discuss the new pay model with human resource managers from all levels of government. The discussions evidence considerable interest in new ideas in the abstract, but there is also a realization that their organizations may not be ready for the new pay model. This article looks at some of the issues that go into that decision.

Source: Howard Risher, "Are Public Employers Ready for a 'New Pay' Program?" *Public Personnel Management* 28:3 (Fall 1999): 323–343.

WHAT'S CHANGED?

The traditional program model has lost much of its credibility. It was introduced roughly a half century ago and has gotten old. Managers and employees alike know that it can be "gamed" to achieve desired answers. Classification and compensation specialists are expected to defend traditional policies and practices with diminished resources and against mounting pressure to accommodate other organizational changes.

The origins of the traditional model go back to the principles of scientific management and the thinking of industrial engineering that served as the foundation for the management of work and workers in industrial America through most of the 20th century. Workers were an extension of a machine, and the goal was to make them as efficient and reliable as their machines. They were expected to do exactly what management told them to do. Their activities were documented in lengthy job descriptions.

In that early era supervisors had considerable latitude to hire, discipline, and fire workers for reasons that would be totally unacceptable today. Their dictatorial powers carried over to every aspect of the employer/employee relationship. The reactions of workers were predictable; they fought back and organized for self-protection. The early personnel functions were intended to bring labor peace and more harmonious working relations. Personnel specialists gained centralized control of the decisions affecting workers and developed rules that limited the decision making power of supervisors.

Wage and salary management thinking evolved in factory settings with union involvement or with a goal of avoiding unionization. The early pay systems were as structured and rigid as the work environment. Since workers rarely moved from one employer to another, it was natural to focus on internal considerations. The model for job evaluation was developed by industrial engineers. In that environment a worker's performance was dictated by the machine that he tended; as long as he obeyed the rules and performed adequately, he could expect the standard pay increase.

That era is effectively over. The manufacturing industries where that thinking dominated are now fighting to survive in this country. We have become a knowledge economy where success depends on creativity and responsiveness to customer needs. Workers who are able to think outside of the box and to solve problems are now valued more highly than those who resist change. Our thinking about how to organize and manage work is in a continuous state of flux. Every organization, private as well as public, is under pressure to improve performance.

In government the changes in the way work is organized and managed have come together with new priorities and with tightened budgets. Voters who are forced to live with increased pressures to perform at higher levels and "to do more with less" in their companies have made it very clear that they are no longer willing to support a traditional, bureaucratic government.

At the same time there have been significant changes in our work force. The generation that is now coming into the workforce has grown up in a period of prosperity. Job security is decidedly less important than it was to their parents. Women are no longer a new phenomenon in most occupations. Job opportunities are plentiful and people with knowledge or experience credentials can readily move to new jobs with higher pay. There is no reason to wait in that same tenure-based line for promotions and pay increases.

We also have come to appreciate that pay does in fact affect the way workers see their work situation and the way they perform their job. Opportunities to earn more money via incentives can trigger higher levels of performance, and many people want those opportunities. There has been a dramatic shift away from the old "don't pay them any more than we have to" to thinking about how we can use pay more effectively as a management tool to achieve organizational goals.

Most of our managers and employees have not fully acclimated their beliefs and values to the new paradigm. What satisfies a 25-year-old worker is very different from what a 55-year-old is looking for. If we were to design HR policies and programs to compete for "X generation" employees, their expectations would lead us in a different direction.

This new world has undermined the foundation of traditional pay programs. Realistically we are still searching for and experimenting with new ideas for managing employee compensation in a way that supports the new work paradigm. If the new ideas were proven and predictable, it would make it easier to gain acceptance for a new program model. The transition from the old to the new will be difficult for everyone.

PROBLEMS WITH TRADITIONAL PROGRAM CONCEPTS

The criticism of traditional program concepts is not new. That's the norm in every organization. Managers and employees alike are often dissatisfied with the way they are paid. Almost everyone would like to be paid more and are convinced they deserve a higher salary. Despite this, there was very little research or time spent developing new programs until the late 1970s when feminists starting arguing that female-dominated jobs were underpaid. Those concerns prompted the first creative thinking since the post–World War II period.

Over the next decade consulting firms invested in the development of computer-based job evaluation systems that used structured questionnaires to collect job information and multiple regression analysis to determine relative job value. Those systems met one of the basic concerns of the comparable worth advocates—the use of computers minimized evaluator bias. They also speeded up the decision process and made it more reliable.

Despite the advantages, however, the technology is not readily understood and employees come to view these systems as a "black box." Job evaluation decisions are more valid and reliable than is typical of more conventional systems, but that does not guarantee credibility. Since these systems are based on the conventional logic of point factor systems, they perpetuate all of the other problems with that approach.

Then, at the end of the decade, one of the most respected experts in the compensation field, Edward Lawler, head of the Center for Effective Organizations at USC and author of a number [of] books and articles on compensation, focused his writings on a number of inherent problems in the traditional model. The points he made are summarized in Table 1. It took a few years but a rapidly growing number of corporations and now public employers have acknowledged the problems and moved to new compensation models.

Lawler probably should be credited with triggering the shift away from traditional salary management concepts. At this point many human resource practitioners have gotten on that bandwagon. It is now almost impossible to find an article or conference presentation on traditional topics like job evaluation or merit pay. Those issues are no longer discussed.

It is important to appreciate how rapidly employers are moving away from the old model. Roughly six years ago the state of Georgia awarded a major contract to a consulting firm to develop a new computer-based job evaluation system. It

Table 1 Criticism of the Traditional Compensation Model

- Reinforces the importance of the job hierarchy at a time when organizations are trying to downplay their hierarchical differences to promote teamwork
- Overemphasizes salary grade changes and promotions as the basis for salary increases rather than focusing on the need to develop and enhance job competence
- Motivates "game playing" and dishonesty as the basis for justifying a higher salary grade
- Hinders organizational change and downsizing since all job changes have to be re-evaluated under traditional compensation programs
- Perpetuates overly rigid and inflexible rules governing compensation
- Creates a sense of entitlement if pay is increased across the board
- Takes too much time and costs too much to maintain the program
- Requires excessive time to prepare for and make administrative decisions
- Perpetuates bureaucratic management
- Establishes implicit limits on what employees are willing to do since their pay is based on the duties listed in their job descriptions
- Creates tension between line managers and the human resources staff who are required to defend the program principles and "police" the decision process

took four years to develop and install the system but in a discussion with the author a year or two ago, the former State Director of Personnel, B. J. Bennett, mentioned that if she had to make the same decision now, she "would go in a different direction."

BANDING—THE NEW FRAMEWORK FOR SALARY MANAGEMENT

The new framework is, of course, known as broad banding. Banding opens the door to a very different environment for salary management. It changes the organization, but then, that is commonly one of the goals. As the leader of the workshop on banding, it is clear that a lot of the interest in banding among public employers is attributable to pressure from line managers who argue, "That looks like an idea that we should consider."

The idea was conceived at a naval research organization in the San Diego area, often referred to as China Lake, where two labs were merging. The classifiers estimated that it would take three years to reclassify the jobs after the merger and the commanding officer decided that was unacceptable. They decided to develop a new salary program that resembled a faculty program (i.e., full professor, assistant professor, etc.). He took his direct reports into a room and said, "If you have any questions, now is the time to ask. Once we leave this room, you will support the new program and we will make it work." The leadership and the authority of the commanding officer are a key.

Banding has been a hot-button in industry now for most of this decade. There are sure to be anecdotal stories about companies that tried and abandoned banding. Johnson & Johnson is one of those firms. It is important, however, to appreciate that the number of companies adopting a banded structure is growing and those that decided it did not fit their needs have not gone back to a traditional salary structure. There are rumors that banding has fallen out of vogue but that is simply not true. Surveys show that the concept can work well in a corporate environment.

Despite the high level of interest, however, there are few public employers that have adopted a banded structure. Charlotte, NC, is the most prominent, and that program is very much a success. The Charlotte banded structure is illustrated in Figure 1. It is a very simple concept.

South Carolina has also adopted banding for state employees. Washington State has a banded structure for managers. Wisconsin recently adopted a separate banded structure for IT [information

Figure 1   Broad Banding Salary Structure—Charlotte, North Carolina

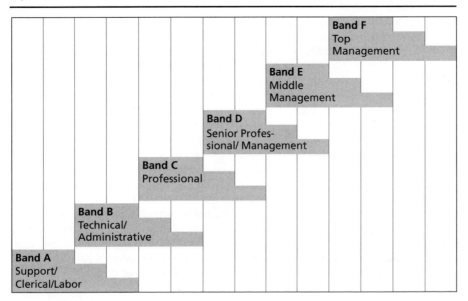

technology] specialists. Several small federal agencies have adopted it. There are other banded programs in government, but the total could be less than 20.

Banding opens the door to a very different way of managing salaries, and employers have to be ready for the changes in the way managers and employees view the program. The changes are more likely to be accepted in a corporate environment. The changes include:

- reducing the importance of personnel in salary management. It may lead to a reduction in the staff and resources needed for this purpose. Charlotte has one person who manages the city's compensation program.
- changing the role of managers and requiring them to make decisions that they may not have made before. There was turnover among managers at China Lake after banding was adopted.
- reducing the relevance of and possibly eliminating the need for job evaluation and job-to-job comparisons. The message is that all of the jobs assigned to a band are more-or-less equal, and the organization is no longer going to focus on minor differences.
- increasing flexibility prompts rethinking of general increases and step increases. Consider the number of steps in a 100% band!
- maintaining close, centralized control. That often prompts employers to worry about losing control of salary increase costs. (ACA surveys have found that this has not been a problem in corporations.)
- opening the door to the mismanagement of salaries if managers do not have adequate training and support. That can lead to legal problems such as gender discrimination.
- reducing the opportunities for promotions (although within-band promotions can certainly be permitted). At the same [time], it can open up opportunities for job growth and expanded duties since one of the goals is to encourage employees to broaden their roles.
- It reduces the organizational emphasis on job-to-job comparisons. If job evaluation is dropped (which is common in the private sector), there is no longer any way to determine if a job is more or less valuable than others in the same band.
- In de-emphasizing the job hierarchy, job incumbents will also feel a loss of status. That's not necessarily bad but it requires time to become comfortable with the change.

The design of a banded salary program revolves around natural groupings of jobs. Charlotte's program has six bands, defined to encompass career ladders. All of the clerical, labor, and support jobs are in a single band. The second band includes all technical and administrative jobs. That effectively obviates all of the arguments over which range these jobs are in. The jobs in these bands could have been assigned to three or more bands but that would have complicated the program's administration since it would have opened the door to people who want to question the band assignment. Every organization has to develop their own logic and rules for defining bands that fit the organization.

Banding changes the organization and should be managed as a change initiative. The organization will never be the same. In contrast to the work involved in designing a traditional program where there is heavy emphasis on number crunching, here the focus is properly on the softer, process issues. In a discussion of the technical design issues in one of the workshops, one participant said, "Is that all there is to it?"

In the typical corporation managers have always played a role in managing staff salaries. Merit pay is virtually universal and managers expect to make those decisions (within structured guidelines). The shift to banding is not traumatic and the expanded role is often welcomed by managers.

In government, however, for managers who have been shielded from compensation decisions, the redefinition of their role and their expanded responsibility can make them very uncomfortable. The organization should plan to support them with adequate training and to stand behind their decisions. It may make sense to gradually phase them into their new role.

Banding can in fact solve, or at least diminish, the problems listed in Figure 1. It reduces the organization's attention and resources needed for salary management. It is not, however, a panacea.

Actually the problems that emerge from banding

may not be apparent for several years. When a banded structure is first introduced, jobs and salaries are typically shifted without change to the new bands. But then future increase decisions are made to one degree or another by managers, and when those increases are compounded over time, the original pay relationships are redefined. Some jobs and some job families will go up faster than others.

It's fully possible that bias and discrimination will emerge. A major corporation that implemented banding made executives and managers wholly responsible for managing salaries. Female managers learned that males were granted larger increases and filed a discrimination claim. In reading the testimony of the human resource staff, it became obvious that they no longer felt responsibility for managing the salary program. It was now the managers' job! The company settled before it went to trial. At a minimum HR has to monitor decisions affecting individual salaries.

This is a very different environment for salary management in government. The primary control is actually the salary increase budget. When that pool of funds is fixed, managers have to learn to make tough decisions on how they are going to allocate their budget. Now they have to be ready to answer to their staff; they can no longer "blame it on personnel." They will learn quickly that they need to be able to explain and defend their decisions.

MARKET PRICING—THE NEW FOCUS ON EXTERNAL PAY LEVELS

The tight labor market has heightened virtually every employer's concern with market pricing, as that phase is used in compensation, and with the need to maintain competitive pay levels. This focus on external pay levels represents a significant philosophical and practical change from the traditional government concentration on internal salary relationships.

Corporations, in contrast, are accustomed to using multiple pay surveys to analyze competitive pay levels. There is an emerging trend to shift away from internal equity considerations and to adopt a completely market-based pay strategy. For example, Johnson & Johnson and Steelcase, an office furniture company, now develop separate salary ranges

for hundreds of benchmark jobs that are adjusted as necessary to maintain a planned market alignment. Clorox has adopted a different approach. They have established separate, market-based salary structures for each of nine job families.

More than a few government pay programs have been managed with little or no concern with how much employees are paid in other organizations. As a consultant to both private and public employers, the contrast in the attention to survey data has always been striking. Some public employers use survey data to adjust salary ranges, with the same across-the-board or general increase for all ranges. Many others, of course, rely on collective bargaining to determine the range adjustment. Some rely simply on cost-of-living adjustments.

When surveys have been used, it is common to rely on the average increase in market pay rates as the adjustment. To illustrate this point, if the market pay rates for two jobs increase 4% and 6%, the general increase might be 5%.

Now, however, it is fully possible that the market rate for a hot-skill IT job might have increased 20% from the date of the late annual survey while pay for a low skill clerk job increased only 2%. The average is 11% but that is clearly not the right answer for either job. It would significantly overpay the clerk but make it difficult to attract or retain the IT specialists.

When jobs are paid without regard to market rates, pay levels can get out of line with the market. New Jersey, for example, reportedly pays some of its secretaries $55,000 annually when the market rate is closer to $35,000.

The high pay may make the secretaries happy, but it represents a problem for the state. The example highlights the obvious fact that public budgets are constrained and that salary management is an allocation problem. Paying some employees well above market uses money that could be used for other purposes without accomplishing anything for the state.

For at least the next decade labor markets will be tighter than we have seen them for a long time. Some hot-skill markets will be much tighter than others, but the demand will exceed the supply for many jobs. That is driven by a healthy economy as well as demographic trends that follow an aging workforce. Inevitably pay rates go up more rapidly when demand exceeds supply. With higher increases and compounding, some specialists will steadily pull away from the pack.

This reality is the reason Wisconsin adopted a separate banded structure for its IT specialists. The new structure will help the state to maintain competitive salaries and to adjust salaries independent of the increases for other job families.

Significantly Wisconsin has increased the number of IT classes. That labor market pays significant premiums to new hot skills like Web Masters. Not all IT specialists have skills that warrant a premium. The state wanted the flexibility to pay premiums selectively.

From a different perspective, the trends in our labor markets raise serious questions about continued reliance on a one-size-fits-all salary structure. It's possible to accommodate modest differences in increase rates, but it would be unrealistic to live with differences of the magnitude that we are currently seeing in many labor markets. For example, the federal government pays all (except for engineers) of its white collar employees under the General Schedule, and a serious gap has opened in starting rates for new college graduates. Their starting rates are sometimes as much as $10,000 or more below the market for new graduates.

One of the advantages of broad banding is that it provides the flexibility needed to respond to differences in the pay increases dictated by the labor market. When market rates go up rapidly, the increases can be more readily managed within a band than in a traditional salary range. Charlotte, for example, provides a summary of salary survey data to managers and they are expected to manage staff salaries relative to market rates.

In light of the tight labor market, a practical answer is to adopt separate salary structures for hot-skill job families. The Wisconsin precedent could be the first of many separate pay structures for IT specialists. There is a long history of separate pay structures for police and fire, for teachers, and for physicians and nurses. The pressure to remain competitive over the next year or two may force employers to back away from the well-established practice of granting the same increases for the balance of the workforce.

Over the past decade or so, employers have become more sensitive to payroll costs and to the need to avoid unnecessary increases. In the typical company, payroll accounts for roughly half of all operating costs, and in government that percentage could reach 80% of budget. Moreover, government budgets are already tight; so anything more than a minimal increase in pay may mean a reduction in funds available for other purposes. It would be advantageous to decide simply that "we're not going to try to compete with private sector pay levels." But that will inevitably affect the caliber of employees hired or, at the extreme, mean that jobs go unfilled.

The shift from an internal focus to an external, market focus represents a significant change for many public employers. At a minimum it will require better knowledge of labor markets and the methods used in market pricing. More importantly, it will require new policies to govern pay adjustments. The process to develop needed policies should consider the following issues:

- Do we understand our labor markets? Are we competing with the private sector?
- Are we prepared to align the pay for all job families with market rates? Or are we going to be selective in switching to the new policy?
- For job families that are below market, are we prepared to raise pay to market levels?
- For those that are above market, how should we handle salaries?
- Are we prepared to guarantee market adjustments to all hot-skill employees? Can we identify those that do not warrant the full increase?
- How can we best explain the need for the new policy to employees in occupations where pay increases are below the average?
- Can we accommodate the need for special increases within our current salary structure?
- Do we know how our benefit package affects our ability to compete? Should we look closely at total compensation?
- What are the alternatives to matching market pay rates? If we experience problems hiring adequately skilled people, should we consider outsourcing of the hot-skills functions?

PAY-FOR-PERFORMANCE—
THE NEW FOCUS
ON EMPLOYEE CONTRIBUTION

Pay-for-performance has gotten increased attention at all levels of government. It is seen as important by a variety of individuals in both political parties. They expect to realize several benefits. First it represents a symbolic break from the entitlement culture that is all too common in government. Second it should send the message to both employees and taxpayers that performance is important. Third it should introduce incentives for improved performance.

These are not new ideas. Merit pay has been tried by many public employers, including the federal government. The track record is not a good one. In some public agencies, attempts to introduce merit pay can almost trigger an armed revolution.

Gain sharing, the phrase used to refer to a variety of group incentives, does not have the same negative reputation but it's a radical idea for government. Group and team incentives are mushrooming in the private sector so it may be inevitable for this trend to carry over to public employers. There are still many critics of government who would argue that it should not be necessary to pay bonuses.

The fact is that companies have a culture that makes merit pay and gain sharing a natural fit. The importance of performance is communicated in different ways throughout each day. Financial reports and accounting statements regularly inform employees of how well their company is doing. Performance is almost an obsession; they do not need to be reminded that performance is important.

Another difference is the powerful incentives provided to corporate executives to maintain solid performance. Companies assume that their executives will make good performance a priority for everyone.

Despite the past, merit pay and other pay-for-performance concepts are on the horizon for government. Vice President Gore recently announced that pay-for-performance will be on the agenda for reinventing the federal government. Several years earlier the then president of the American Federation of Government Employees, John Sturdivant, told me in an informal conversation that his union "has to learn to live with merit pay." He could see the direction in which government is moving. In the past few years states like New Jersey, Maryland, Colorado, and Georgia have all taken at least preliminary steps down this path.

This could be the bumpiest path of all. The culture issue is critically important. If performance is not seen as a priority, then pay-for-performance is not going to fit. The transition to a true performance culture will take time, an investment in training, and a commitment to make it successful. Human resources can play a behind-the-scenes role, but the initiative has to be led by the organization's leaders.

One of the reasons that merit pay has not been accepted in government is that it has been used as a reason to deny increases to poor performers. In contrast, in the corporate world the emphasis is on recognizing and rewarding the better performers with above average increases. That gives merit pay a much more positive image. A few employees are denied an increase but that is essentially ignored by corporate leaders and is rarely a topic for the employee grapevine.

Surveys show that employees would prefer merit pay—they want to have their value recognized. If it is ever to be accepted in government, the focus has to shift from denying increases to rewarding employees whose performance stands out as exemplary.

Two recently adopted merit pay policies are based on a concept that has merit in the government environment. One is the Colorado Peak Performance policy and the second is the merit policy recently adopted by the FAA [Federal Aviation Administration]. Interestingly the FAA chose not to use the phrase "merit pay," which was seen as too inflammatory. Both policies are based on a three-level rating scale. Employees can meet expectations, exceed expectations or fail to meet expectations. Everyone who meets or exceeds expectations is granted the basic increase—FAA calls this the "Organizational Success increase." Employees who exceed expectations also receive a "Superior Contribution Increase." The Colorado policy reflects the same thinking.

Organizations need to know who their outstanding people are. Policies based on two levels of performance—a pass/fail system—send the message that the minimum effort to meet threshold expectations is adequate. If that policy is continued for too long, the best performers will begin to think about moving to an organization where their efforts will be recognized.

The use of the three-level scale addresses one of the issues that was prominent in the writings of Dr. W. Edwards Deming. He made the point that performance rating scales are not valid because one supervisor might say an employee is a "3" while another supervisor might say the same employee is a "4." That is a valid criticism.

Research has shown that employees generally know and agree on which of their co-workers are outstanding, and they also agree on the few people whose performance is inadequate. The former group is typically 15 to 20% of the work force. Significantly the FAA has communicated that they expect 15% to warrant a Superior Contribution Increase. At the other end of the scale it would be rare to find more than 2 or 3% who fail to meet expectations. The fact that other employees are likely to agree on who deserves to be recognized in this way is a key to a successful merit policy.

The mechanics of a merit increase policy is the easy part to plan, the "softer" side represents perhaps 90% of the problem. There have been too many failed merit policies. For a new policy to succeed, it will be important to plan the design and implementation process.

- Can we articulate the reasons for moving to a merit policy? Have we communicated those reasons? There needs to be a credible purpose that will benefit the organization.
- Have we planned for the impact of the new policy on the organization? Have we anticipated how the policy will affect supervisor/subordinate relationships? Are we prepared to assist in ameliorating problems?
- How can we best support managers?
- Do we have top management's commitment to the policy? Will they provide leadership? They should be seen as the driving force for the change. It cannot be a personnel initiative.
- How will the planned changes affect the merit principles? What right will employees have under the new policy?
- Do we communicate the agency's progress in achieving its mission? Goals? Do we track progress in achieving operating goals? Do we track performance data?
- Have we provided training for both supervisors and employees on two-way communications? Have they had sufficient training on goal setting and performance planning? Those skills are essential.
- Do our plans include process steps to consider the views and concerns of stakeholders?
- Would it be feasible to adopt a pay-for-performance plan for managers? That will reinforce the importance of performance to them. The FAA adopted this strategy in its new program.
- Have we provided for feedback on the new policy? Are we ready to modify the policy as we gain experience? When it is clear change is needed, it is better to acknowledge it.

Gain sharing is an alternative pay-for-performance concept that promises to grow in importance in the public sector. In the private sector, these plans are referred to by several new phrases—goal sharing, results sharing, and success sharing are common—and they all reflect the philosophy that employees should share in the success of the organization. Gain sharing has become an umbrella concept that is applied to almost any group incentive plan.

Research by the American Compensation Association confirms that group incentives work—they contribute to improved performance. That research shows that companies have benefited by roughly $2.50 for every $1 paid to employees. Charlotte has a gain sharing program and their experience has been similar to this. Payouts there have been in the $400 to $600 range—which is low relative to the typical payout in the corporate world—but Ken Wallace, Charlotte's manager of compensation, says he is always surprised to see "how excited employees get when they receive their check."

In the public sector gain sharing payouts probably have to come from savings. That was true with the first plans in industry. Experience shows that employees always know where money can be saved. Charlotte, for example, has a savings goal for FY 1999 of $3 million and they have had similar goals in each year of the plan. When the payouts come from savings, it means the plan does not add to costs. In fact, since the typical arrangement shares only a portion of any savings, it means the organization ends up spending less for the year.

Even then, however, there may be a reluctance to pay lump sum awards. The old thinking was always, "That's part of their job and we're already paying them a decent salary to do their job. Why should we pay them more for something they should already be doing?" Industry has largely gotten over that hurdle. Realistically the savings would not have been realized if the gain sharing plan was not adopted.

Gain sharing changes the culture. It can only work if employees are empowered to solve problems. If their understanding is that management does not expect them to do anything beyond their normal job duties, that is not an environment where gain sharing is going to succeed.

The shift in culture is generally welcomed by employees—they have an opportunity to demonstrate their capabilities and earn more money—but it may be resisted by managers. As employees come up with better ways of operating, it highlights problems that managers presumably should have recognized and solved. Managers can effectively nullify the power of gain sharing.

WHAT ABOUT PAY EQUITY?

In the private sector pay equity is no longer a consideration. Legislative attempts to mandate pay equity never succeeded and it was forgotten in the economic slow down at the beginning of this decade. The Clinton Administration recently proposed amendments to the Equal Pay Act that would strengthen that statute but passage is unlikely.

Another factor is the now quiet revolution in the career choice process for young women. It has now been over two decades since pay equity and comparable worth first surfaced, and women have moved into many careers that were formerly dominated by men.

In today's tight labor market, when men and women work in the same job, it would be surprising to find an employer that does not pay them on the same basis. There are sure to be places where that is not true. I serve occasionally as an expert witness and I can confirm that a few employers have not learned how much they risk by allowing discrimina-

tion to continue. That appears to be limited to companies and industries where employment patterns are static.

We need to recognize, however, that the goals of the "new pay" model are not wholly consistent with pay equity goals. Broad banding masks and diminishes the emphasis on the job-to-job comparisons that have been central to pay equity. Organizations that move to banding often continue to use a job evaluation system but over time it becomes less important. Job evaluation is very definitely less important today than it was a decade or so ago, and anecdotal evidence suggests this trend will continue. Market-based pay decisions have always been seen as a problem by pay equity advocates. Merit pay opens the door to possible discrimination in granting increases.

Recently I have had occasions to work with a couple of the older job evaluation systems. In some key respects the words and phrases used to describe the compensable factors sound like a different era. The paradigm utilized to organize and manage work has changed in ways that are not always apparent until we try to work with management systems developed before we started rethinking the way government operates. For example, a manager's job should not, from my perspective, be evaluated on the basis of his or her budget responsibility or the number of subordinates.

The choice of compensable factors is always a key design consideration. It was shown two decades ago that factors can be defined to be gender neutral. That is routine in areas with pay equity legislation. The factors send a message to employees about what is valued or not valued. The older job evaluation systems were developed before we started thinking, for example, about the importance of satisfying customers.

Actually the Charlotte model makes all of the office and clerical support jobs "equal" to the hourly jobs. They are all assigned to the same band. That is an important message.

One of the advantages of banding is that it reduces the artificial barriers to career progression. In running the banding workshop for a federal union, they jumped on the fact that the overheads failed to highlight the new opportunities that become available when we no longer focus on salary grades and job descriptions. People who want to move to new career ladders in the same band find that it is easier to make the change.

The new emphasis on market pricing may be a problem. The gap between the average pay for men and women is gradually closing but it is still very real. In hot-skill jobs men and women are likely to be paid the same. Actually in government when men and women work in the same job family, they are likely to be paid on the same basis. But there are still many jobs that are sex segregated and those that are male-dominated are often higher paid. Employers that want to shift more toward a market pay strategy will have to be sensitive to those differences.

Overall the new pay model is neutral. It reflects somewhat different values, e.g., the reduced emphasis on internal job comparisons, but it does not in concept conflict with pay equity goals. The pay equity goals and those that prompt the interest in the new pay model can be accommodated.

SHIFTING COMPENSATION BELIEFS AND PROGRAM GOALS

The heart of the problem is the shift in the way people think about pay and in the beliefs that drive their decisions. That shift started a decade or so ago and probably could be traced to Deming. He more than anyone prompted us to rethink the traditional work paradigm and the low expectations we have had for front line workers. If organizations were still the same as they were when we entered the 1980s, there would be little reason to change pay programs.

A new set of underlying beliefs is emerging. It is established better on the beaches of the corporate world, but there is still resistance. Significantly those organizations where the frequent introduction and marketing of new products is essential to the business strategy have found it easier to adapt to the new beliefs. That's probably because those organizations are accustomed to change and to the flexible entrepreneurial culture needed to make new products successful.

There is no universal list of the beliefs that are key to the new pay model, but they probably include some or all of those listed in Table 2. This list is intended to be illustrative, not all-inclusive.

The traditional beliefs are still firmly entrenched in many corporations. They would find it just as dif-

ficult to accept and live with a new pay concept like banding as a public employer.

It is important to appreciate that people need to agree on the beliefs that underlie the pay program in their organization. For example, the shift to a market-based pay strategy violates the belief in the primacy of internal equity. If a key employee group is convinced internal equity is essential, they are less likely to resist the change. Managers and employees who want to oppose a change in policy may adopt different strategies but their goal is the same.

This makes it important to understand the beliefs and to address the need for a consensus in planning the change initiative. That could be the biggest hurdle. One of the earliest steps should be a series of focus groups to understand how people feel about the new concepts.

The new model also reflects new priorities and new program goals. Corporations are now placing much more emphasis on the use of pay as an incentive to improve performance. The public sector will have to decide how important that goal is. Corporations are also moving from the traditional focus on internal job value to a closer alignment with market pay rates. In a recent conversation the director of compensation in a prominent company said, "We've thrown out internal equity." Their goal was to become more competitive and to keep payroll costs in line with their competitors.

One overriding goal that has not received much attention is the increasing importance of the organization and its needs. Those needs are generally much more important than the needs and the satisfaction of employees. That enables corporations to justify program changes that might be unacceptable in government.

The specific corporate goals are of course not directly relevant to government employers. It is important to appreciate, however, that companies focus on those goals in planning new pay programs. When government starts with a different set of goals, it may mean that the corporate answers are not appropriate.

WHICH PATH IS THE FUTURE?

Somehow the path to the new pay model reminds me of the scene out of the movie *Raiders of the Lost Ark* when Harrison Ford is standing at the edge of a

Table 2   Shifting Compensation Beliefs

Traditional Beliefs	New Pay Beliefs
We have good relationships with our employees and try to be diligent in avoiding problems. We feel we have a good work force.	Every employee is expected to contribute. The compensation system was designed and is managed as an incentive for employees to use their capabilities to achieve our goals.
Compensation is an HR system. We look to the HR specialists to manage the program and payroll increases.	Compensation is seen as a management system, with HR serving as a consultant to help managers make pay decisions.
It is important to maintain consistency in salary management.	Management flexibility is an overarching program goal.
Employees need to know we are paying them fairly but we see no reason to involve them when we redesign our pay programs.	Whenever we redesign a pay program, we look to managers and employees in the business unit for their input to insure that the charges are accepted and meet their operational needs.
Pay increases are based primarily on job tenure.	Pay increases are based primarily on individual performance and competence.
We rely on a proven job evaluation system to insure that pay is equitable.	Pay levels reflect the value of the person as dictated by the labor market and individual capabilities.
Our base pay program is based on internal equity principles.	Our program is aligned with prevailing labor market pay rates.
Our program is consistent with widely used program design principles. A number of leading employers rely on the same salary management practices.	Our program is based on our business needs, our values, and the way work is organized and managed in each business unit. It was designed to fit our organization.
Virtually all of our employees are good people and earn their pay. Salary increases reward them for their continued efforts.	Our managers are expected to identify the best contributions and to make sure the pay differentials reflect their contribution.
Our salary increase budget depends on several factors but primarily what we can afford.	We rely on variable pay plans to tie rewards to the achievement of our organizational goals and to our ability to pay.

precipice but there is no visible bridge to where the Holy Grail is hidden. He throws a handful of dirt on the bridge and that makes it visible. If it was that easy to visualize a safe bridge to the new pay world, it would be a lot easier to take the initial step.

First we need to recognize that there is no Holy Grail in compensation management. Changing a pay program is potentially problematic. There is nothing that an organization does that triggers more employee interest and anxiety. Every employee will react to changes in the pay program. There is no approach or method that will always avoid problems when a new pay program is rolled out.

When I went to graduate school, an instructor taught us what he knew about job evaluation from a set of notes that were turning yellow from age. If you followed the steps listed in his notes, you could design a job evaluation system. The systems always looked alike, but until recently, that was the way compensation projects were planned.

The thinking fortunately has taken a new path. Now we understand that a new pay system has to "fit" the organization. It has to reflect the mission, organizational goals, shared values, and other considerations. That shifts the focus to the "softer" program planning issues. The numbers and the technical issues are still important but even technically sound programs can fail if the design and installation process hits a landmine. The technical considerations are the easy part.

Moving to a new pay model will change the organization and needs to be managed as a change initiative. Change is more likely to be successful when the initiative has a sponsor to lead it. There is a bandwagon pulling out and the leader has to get people to climb on. It will also help if there is agreement on why change is needed and agreement on the goals in moving to a new pay system. The latter involves the shaping of a vision and the desired outcomes. Once we know where we are trying to go, we can develop a game plan to get there.

The HR function needs to take a key role in developing the plan and in managing the process to get there. It is not realistic, however, for HR to define the goals without a lot of input from other organizational leaders and from stakeholders. They have to buy into the planned changes and the game plan. That is essential.

When I was involved as the managing consultant for federal pay reform, I learned how important the process issues are in rethinking public pay programs. I could handle the analysis and interpretation of local salary survey information but I was definitely out of my league when it came to the planning to secure congressional acceptance of the program changes. In those discussions I sat and listened. There are always a lot of people in government who have to accept or at least acquiesce to the changes. Planning the process is the key to success.

On a final note, public pay programs are not changed very often. Any changes today will hopefully stand the test of at least the next five years and quite possibly many more. For that reason it is important to look into the future to identify the changes that will affect the pay program. As an example, the large number of baby boomers will begin to retire over the next few years. Their replacements are likely to come from the X generation or the Y generation. That has implications for the pay program. Once we know all of this, we are in a position to decide what path to take.

TYPES OF PAY SYSTEMS

Several different approaches to salary and wage compensation systems are described in this chapter. We begin with traditional pay determination systems based on the job classification and job evaluation systems. Frustrations with this system have led to the development of several innovations in compensation systems, each linking pay to a different set of criteria. The alternative approaches are summarized in Table 9.1 and described in greater detail in the balance of the chapter.

THE IMPORTANCE OF COMPENSATION

Compensation policies and practices ideally should be linked to the larger human resource efforts of the organization, and they should help the organization achieve its mission and follow

Table 9.1   Types of Compensation Systems

Compensation System	Linkage to Pay Levels
Traditional compensation system	Pay linked to seniority and rank
Broadbanding	Pay linked to broad occupational categories
Merit pay	Pay linked to job performance
Skill based/competency pay	Pay linked to employee knowledge
Gainsharing (incentives for productivity and/or cost reduction)	Pay linked to group performance

through on its strategic plans. For example, compensation policy is critical to an organization's ability to recruit and retain the best employees, and it has an important impact on employee morale and workforce productivity. An understanding of how public sector compensation programs work in practice and a clear comprehension of their role in recruitment, retention, and sustaining productivity represent a critical part of public sector management generally and human resource management in particular.

SALARIES IN THE PUBLIC POLICY PROCESS

The use of complicated classification tables and salary ranges might suggest that the determination of salaries in the public sector is a precise scientific process; the reality is that salaries and wages are very much a key part of the political process. Public employee pay levels are determined as part of the budget-making process involving elected officials in both the executive and legislative branches. Budget makers must weigh the cost derived from the maintenance of competitive employee salaries and wages against other public needs. This political reality often means that public sector salaries do not share the market competition emphasis that private sector organizations' salaries and wages do.[2] In fact, as Risher notes, "The need to pay competitively is almost never the controlling factor in public wage decisions."[3]

Salaries for lower-level jobs tend to be higher for public sector workers than they are for private sector workers.[4] This may be due to the influence of public sector unions in negotiating on behalf of workers who tend to be concentrated at the low end of the organization's hierarchy, or it may be the result of classification systems' pulling lower salaries higher than the market due to value comparisons. According to Kearney, "Unions are associated with higher wages and benefits in state and local government," although their monetary impact on compensation is estimated to be lower than that of private sector unions.[5] In contrast,

management and professional workers consistently enjoy higher salaries in the private sector.[6] Particularly striking is the difference in pay between private sector chief executive officers and department heads and elected officials found in the public sector.[7]

Compensation in the nonprofit sector is very much a function of organization size. Little research has focused on nonprofit organizations in terms of compensation, probably due to the widespread assumption that heavy reliance is placed on volunteers in nonprofit organizations. However, Oster found that executive compensation varies widely within the nonprofit sector, depending on the fiscal resources of the nonprofit and the scope of activities (e.g., the arts or social services).[8] However, perceptions about the philanthropic and voluntary nature of nonprofit activities also serve to limit the salary ranges, as directing boards are concerned about the public perception that the nonprofit may be overspending.[9]

Recruiting and retaining employees when public sector wages are lagging behind private sector rates can be challenging, especially in key job categories such as computer network specialists and operations engineers. Many public sector organizations have established separate salary structures for these highly competitive job categories to avoid the inflexibility of the government's traditional General Service (GS) system. It is difficult to discern whether governmental reluctance to implement recommended salary increases is due to an inability to pay competitive salaries or a reluctance to tax the public at a level adequate for competitive salaries.[10]

TRADITIONAL SYSTEMS OF COMPENSATION

Pay Grades and Ranges

The heart of the compensation process is assigning a salary level for each job. Job classification tables are used to establish **pay grades** and **pay ranges** within each grade. Table 9.2 shows the compensation schedule for the State of Idaho for fiscal year 1999. The grades for classified jobs in the state system are analogous to the federal government's GS schedule. The table also displays the point value for each job derived from the Hay factor plan, as well as the corresponding minimum, **salary midpoint** (or **policy line**), and maximum annual salary in dollars.

The information in Table 9.2 is used to illustrate the structure of pay grades and ranges graphically in Figure 9.2. Pay grades are "groupings of a variety of positions of similar internal job ranking."[11] Each pay grade has a minimum (point *a* in Figure 9.2), midpoint (point *d*), and maximum (point *e*) salary range. The midpoint is used as a control point for the administration of pay, and the series of midpoints (*dgi*) represents the policy line of the organization.[12]

The pay grades and ranges can be developed using either of two methods.[13] The grades can be

Table 9.2   State of Idaho Compensation Schedule FY 2001 Annual Rates (5% Payline Move, Effective 6-11-2000)

Pay Grade	Minimum Points	Midpoint	Maximum Points	Minimum Annually	Policy	Maximum Annually
A		99	106	$12,607	$ 14,831	$ 18,539
B	107	114	122	$13,919	$ 16,376	$ 20,470
C	123	131	140	$15,407	$ 18,126	$ 22,658
D	141	151	161	$17,158	$ 20,185	$ 25,232
E	162	173	185	$19,083	$ 22,450	$ 28,063
F	186	200	213	$21,446	$ 25,230	$ 31,538
G	214	229	245	$23,984	$ 28,216	$ 35,270
H	246	263	281	$26,959	$ 31,717	$ 39,646
I	282	303	325	$29,334	$ 34,510	$ 43,138
J	326	349	374	$31,814	$ 37,429	$ 46,786
K	375	401	430	$34,618	$ 40,727	$ 50,909
L	431	461	492	$37,854	$ 44,534	$ 55,667
M	493	531	566	$41,628	$ 48,975	$ 61,218
N	567	610	655	$44,709	$ 52,599	$ 65,749
O	656	702	753	$47,930	$ 56,388	$ 70,485
P	754	807	867	$51,605	$ 60,712	$ 75,890
Q	868	928	997	$55,841	$ 65,696	$ 82,119
R	998	1067	1146	$60,559	$ 71,246	$ 89,057
S	1147	1227	1319	$64,581	$ 75,978	$ 94,973
T	1320	1412	1516	$69,232	$ 81,450	$101,812
U	1517	1623	1744	$74,537	$ 87,691	$109,614
V	1745	1867	2006	$80,672	$ 94,908	$118,635
W	2007	2147	2307	$87,711	$103,190	$128,987
X	2308	2469		$95,806	$112,713	$140,892

Source: Idaho State Government Division of Human Resources, available at: **http://www.dhr.state.id.us/cmpa01.htm.**

Figure 9.2   Typical Pay Structure Using State of Idaho Compensation Schedule Pay Rates

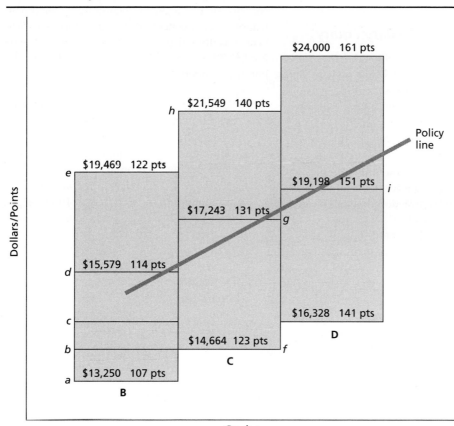

Source: Point values and dollar figures are taken from Table 9.2: State of Idaho Compensation Schedule. Adapted by the authors.

Table 9.3   Pay Grades Broken Down by Points

Points	Point Spread	Grade
Up to 49	50	1
50–99	50	2
100–149	50	3
150–225	75	4
226–300	75	5

Source: This example is from Thomas S. Roy, "Pricing and the Development of Salary Structures," in Milton L. Rock and Lance A. Berger, eds., *The Compensation Handbook,* 3rd ed. (New York: McGraw-Hill, 1991), p. 108.

assembled based on the internal ranking of the value of the job; for example, point values assigned by the Hay factor method can be used to align pay grades and ranges. Alternatively, grades can be separated by equal numbers of points or by a predetermined percentage of points between grades. Table 9.3 shows an example of this method.

Pay grades and ranges can also be developed using the salary midpoints to distinguish one grade from another—for example, having a 10 percent difference between one grade's salary midpoint to the next. The job evaluation and classification process assigns value to each job, and salary ranges should reflect that process of prioritizing.

Internal and External Salary Equity

Equity has to do with the perception that the organization's compensation schedule and policies are *fair.* Fairness in pay is often assessed in terms of its proportionality in the internal ranking of jobs (**internal equity**) and the comparability of the compensation schedule and policies relative to those of competing organizations (**external equity**). Research has demonstrated that employee reactions to perceived inequities in the compensation structure can influence decisions about accepting or rejecting job offers, whether to stay with an organization, or how hard to work at the job.[14] Analyzing jobs and ordering them within the classification system is a systematic way of assigning more value, and hence more pay, to the jobs that are more highly valued. This alignment of jobs according to intrinsic value ensures the internal equity of the organization's salary structure.[15]

In theory, minimally qualified new employees would start at the bottom of the range for their particular grade, and new employees with more experience and better skills would begin at a higher point in the range.[16] Ideally, the midpoint of each salary range should be tied to a competitive pay level in the relevant job market. Federal salaries have used private sector wage comparisons to ensure comparability between public and private civilian wages since the adoption of the Federal Pay Comparability Act of 1970.[17] Many state and local governments use some analogous type of comparability study when setting their salary rates.[18] A recent study found that 81 percent of local governments used salary surveys of other jurisdictions in their metropolitan area or state when setting salary ranges.[19] This process of assessing comparability in salaries ensures the approximation of external equity of the salary structure.

Salary surveys are useful for helping an organization to maintain its salary structure's external equity by comparing its own structure to that of a relevant competitive market.[20] Put more di-

rectly, a salary survey can help the organization avoid paying either too much or too little.[21] Salary surveys can be conducted internally by the organization or data generated by the government, private consulting firms, or trade associations can be used.[22] There are several common steps to the internally undertaken salary survey process:[23]

1. Select the jobs to be surveyed. This often includes "key jobs"—that is, a sample that reflects the organization as a whole.
2. Define the relevant labor markets. Is this a job for which the organization can recruit *locally* (e.g., secretary), *regionally* (e.g., accountant), *nationally* (e.g., professor), or *internationally* (e.g., trade and commerce manager)?
3. Select the comparison organizations. Choosing organizations of similar size is important.
4. Decide what information to ask for from the comparison organizations: base salaries, bonuses, benefits, and so forth.
5. Decide on a data collection technique; for example, telephone survey or mail survey.
6. Administer the survey.

There are also many external sources of data that can be used for salary survey purposes. The Bureau of Labor Statistics produces periodic area wage surveys and industry wage surveys. Other sources of external salary data are trade groups, professional associations, and private consulting firms specializing in compensation analysis.[24] An accurately conducted salary survey can help management make informed pay decisions, which is important not only in individual pay considerations but also in setting an effective larger compensation policy for the organization.

Impact of Compensation Equity on the Organization

Managing internal and external equity can be challenging for an organization because the goals of each can come into conflict. For example, keeping up with rapidly rising salary rates to maintain external equity may distort the internal equity of the compensation schedule by bringing in new employees at higher salaries than those who have been with the organization a longer time.[25] Problems with either kind of equity can affect employee behavior adversely. Failure to maintain external equity can hinder the organization's ability to recruit and retain high-quality employees; conversely, failure to maintain internal equity can poison employee morale and undermine the perceived legitimacy and fairness of management.

Problems with Traditional Systems

Inflexibility In a review of the federal government's compensation system, Wamsley identifies several problems worthy of attention. The first problem is with the classification system concept itself, which she describes as inefficient for a variety of reasons, including the fact that it is too complex a process to classify positions precisely in a mechanical way.[26] Moreover, rapid changes in technology and job content can make even the most carefully crafted job classifications obsolete in a short time.[27] The inflexibility of classification systems makes it difficult to respond to these changes in work, leading managers to seek out ways around the established classification system.[28] Similarly, training and development programs are frequently the first items to be cut in tight budget times so that the gap between the skills needed to perform jobs adequately and those held by job incumbents can widen. Wamsley also notes that there are problems with employees' automatically receiving wage increases for longevity. Over time, this practice will erode the principle of equal pay for equal work and disrupt the internal equity of the salary structure.[29]

Technology and compensation A key challenge facing public sector organizations is that of recruiting and retaining trained staff in information technology (IT) fields. Compensation is a critical part of this process. The scarcity of qualified IT applicants has resulted in the need to pay relatively high salaries to these employees as compared to other personnel of equivalent age and experience. Public and nonprofit agencies are finding that turnover among IT staff can average as much as 15 percent, with rates even higher among those with specialized technical skills.[30] In fact, one expert found that as many as 10 to 25 percent of governmental IT positions are unfilled at any given time.[31] In a recent survey undertaken by the International Personnel Management Association (IPMA), 48 percent of the respondents reported that they had a shortage of IT staff.[32]

Salaries that lag behind those in the private sector are a key problem for public sector organizations attempting to recruit or retain IT staff. Governments filling IT positions often find that the new employees can command salaries 15 to 35 percent higher than the employees they are replacing.[33] Forty-seven percent of the respondents in the IPMA survey reported that low base salaries were either major barriers or somewhat of a barrier to hiring IT professionals, and 43 percent indicated that low base salaries were either a major barrier or somewhat of a barrier to retaining IT professionals.[34]

Traditional compensation systems can make it difficult for public managers to offer competitive salaries, since changing salaries and benefits may require legislative approval. Some public jurisdictions have established differential salary schedules for professions whose market salaries are too high for the rest of the classification system—for example, engineers or physicians. Other jurisdictions focus on the flexibility in benefit packages possible in the public sector; for example, some jurisdictions allow telecommuting options as a form of employment benefit.

Diversity and compensation In spite of the equal pay laws described in Chapter 4 and the civil rights laws that prevent workplace discrimination based on race, sex, national origin, or ethnicity, a gap persists between the earnings of white men and those of women and minorities in the United States. In 1989, for example, black men earned 67 cents for every dollar earned by white men—a *decrease* from 71 cents on the dollar in 1979.[35] The average annual salary of women continues to lag behind that of white men as well. A recent survey of more than 4,500 managers conducted by the American Management Association, for example, found that the average female respondent's salary was 62.7 percent of the average male respondent's.[36]

Some of this aggregate difference in earnings can be attributed to occupational segregation; that is, white men tend to be concentrated in certain occupational categories with higher salaries than those that white women and male and female non-white workers tend to occupy. The higher salaries for some occupations versus others are a reflection of classification and compensation systems that placed a higher valuation on those particular occupations.

In the 1980s, many scholars and practitioners alike began to question the relative importance placed on certain knowledge, skills, and abilities as opposed to others that underlie the classification systems that result in this unequal pay structure. This questioning led to what is referred to as the **comparable worth** debate. For example, in one court case, clerical workers (predominantly women) at a community college challenged the classification system that paid janitorial staff (predominantly men) significantly higher wages than the clerical workers received. The unequal wages allocated to these jobs were the result of a point system that placed higher value on KSAs that happened to be concentrated in the mostly male occupations. There have been several court challenges to state and local classification systems based on the principle of comparable worth. Although some have successfully challenged established compensation systems, the implementation of remedies has usually met with resistance from legislatures unwilling to fund such systemic raises in public salaries as would be required to fully implement comparable worth.

Search for New Salary Models

Perhaps because of these problems with complexity, inflexibility, and lack of focus on or connection to performance, the credibility of traditional compensation systems is not high. One study found that 65 percent of personnel directors and classifiers felt the system was not fair and equitable.[37] It is in response to complaints such as these that changes to the compensation system have been proposed.

BROADBANDING: SIMPLIFYING PAY SCHEDULES

A broadbanded pay structure has four design features:

- Fewer grade levels and titles
- Alternative career tracks, especially for non-managers
- Wider salary ranges with no midpoints
- Two or more bands, preferably based in the relevant salary market[38]

Table 9.4 compares a traditional narrow grade system with a broadbanded alternative. LeBlanc notes that the number of appropriate pay bands will vary from organization to organization, but in general that there should be one band for each layer of management.[39] Each job family—for example, "technician"—would have up to three layers or bands. The salary ranges within each band are unhooked from midpoints, and they are wider than pay grades and ranges found in traditional compensation systems.[40]

Advantages to Broadbanding

Risher notes that broadbanding is a popular component of reformed compensation systems because it:

- Reduces the administrative costs of the salary program.
- Deemphasizes hierarchy and fine distinctions among similar jobs.

Table 9.4   Comparison of Traditional Compensation and Banded Compensation Structure

Traditional Compensation		Banded Structure	
Grade	Title	Band	Title
14	Senior budget analyst	6	Senior budget analyst
12	Budget analyst III		
10	Budget analyst II		
8	Budget analyst I	5	Budget analyst

- Facilitates the creation of effective teams.
- Provides more flexibility to reward individual contributions.
- Makes it easier to reorganize and redefine job responsibilities.
- Facilitates lateral career moves.
- Eliminates some difficulties with reductions in force.
- Reduces tension between human resources and the rest of the organization over job evaluation decisions.[41]

In spite of these advantages, a recent IPMA study found that only 8 percent of local governments were using broadbanding for any portion of their positions.[42]

Implementing Broadbanding

Broadbanding works best in organizations with flatter hierarchies that are already experimenting with team-based structures, cross training, and increasing employee involvement in agency decision making.[43] Employees in organizations with traditional hierarchies may resist a change to a system that eliminates some of the career markers such as job titles that will be consolidated under broadbanding.[44] Resistance to broadbanding may also arise because of the possibility of fixed-cost escalation if the move to bands is perceived as a way to push people to higher salaries in their range.[45] This possibility is heightened if salaries in the organization have fallen significantly behind market rates. Broadbanding may simplify the salary structure, but it will not eliminate the need for carefully developed job measurements or for adequate communication with employees about the salary structure.[46] Finally, while managers frequently say they want flexibility to pay people differentially, they often "back down once given the flexibility to do so." Broadbanding would provide just such an opportunity.[47]

Nicolai puts forth the following suggestions for making broadbanding work:

(1) Assess your current system to make sure broadbanding is warranted. What, if anything, is wrong with your current system, and will broadbanding fix it? (2) Involve employees to get their opinion on what a [properly] restructured compensation system would look like. (3) Involve top management in discussing what the compensation system should be doing [for the organization] and whether broadbanded or narrow classification works best for that [purpose]. (4) Conduct job analysis on each job to determine in which band they will belong. (5) Use job analysis to create a classification system that fits the organization's strategies. Don't automatically throw out all of the old system. (6) Make sure that management gets adequate training and information about the changes made.[48]

MERIT PAY: LINKING PAY TO PERFORMANCE

The most common reform to traditional compensation systems advocated in the HRM literature is **merit pay,** or pay for performance. Merit pay was instituted for the federal government's Senior Executive Service as part of the Civil Service Reform Act of 1978. It was extended to federal managers and supervisors in 1981.[49] Recent changes to the federal compensation system, however, have eliminated merit pay as an addition to base salary.[50] A 1994 study found that thirty state governments had adopted merit pay as part of their compensation methods.[51] An IPMA survey of local governments found that 54 percent used performance to determine some or all of their salary decisions.[52] Merit increases can be percentage increases to base salary or one-time bonuses. Adding to the base salary is more costly to the organization in the long run; however, fearing to appear too generous in the eyes of their constituents, policymakers often resist providing bonuses.

In traditional compensation systems, employees are often rewarded on the basis of seniority; as their tenure with the organization lengthens, so does their progression through the salary ranges. This practice has been criticized in the main because it features no direct link to employee performance. Barely adequate employees are rewarded equally with excellent employees. Merit pay has been instituted to try to provide that direct link to performance. In spite of the popularity of merit pay, however, empirical studies of its effectiveness point to several problems of effective implementation.

Problems with the Theory Underlying Merit Pay

Motivation Pay for performance is based on **expectancy theory**—that is, the individual believes that personal effort leads to desired levels of performance and that that performance results in desired outcomes (for example, higher salary).[53] Studies of what actually motivates employees, however, indicate that intrinsic factors such as feeling valued or serving the public interest may be as important in motivation as extrinsic factors such as salary.[54] A recent study of personnel managers in U.S. states found that only 39 percent thought that merit pay increased motivation among employees.[55] Merit pay seems to have been most effective at increasing productivity in routine, nonmanagerial jobs.[56]

Level of funding The amount of money provided as "merit" money is often not large enough to motivate employees adequately.[57] Most organizations try to combine cost-of-living increases with merit pay, thereby decreasing the amount of money tied to performance.[58] Ingraham's study of state implementation of pay for performance found that "a large majority of the states reported problems with inadequate, inconsistent, and in some cases *no* funding. Of the 21 states responding, only 4 reported funding every year of the program's life."[59] Seventy percent of the personnel directors in state agencies surveyed in Kellough and Selden's study indicated that lack of adequate funding made implementation of merit pay difficult.[60] Pressure to maintain the internal and external equity of the salary system can also lead to distortions in the amount of money allocated to merit pay.[61]

Performance appraisal process Pay-for-performance systems must have a performance appraisal process that is able to discriminate among employees correctly to separate the truly meritorious from the less meritorious.[62] There are two problems with the performance appraisal process relevant to merit pay. The first problem encountered is with the instrument itself. Performance appraisal applications that are not sufficiently valid (measuring what they intend to measure) or reliable (able to be replicated consistently) make it impossible to discriminate accurately between highly meritorious and less meritorious employees.

The second problem with the performance appraisal process relates to the unwillingness or inability of managers who must use performance appraisal systems to make meaningful distinctions among employees. The result is that most employees are rated above average.[63] In 1991, for example, 82 percent of those in the federal merit pay system were rated above average.[64] A review of state merit pay programs found several instances in which over 90 percent of state employees received a merit raise.[65] Dividing the amount of money allocated for merit among such high percentages of employees makes each employee's share very small. Naturally this near universal distribution of small pay increments decreases the ability of managers to motivate effectively with salary.

The inability or unwillingness of managers to determine which employees are worthy of merit pay and which are not may be related to a lack of adequate training and communication with managers.[66] A study of state pay-for-performance systems noted widespread dissatisfaction with the performance appraisal process. "One respondent noted that the problem was with trying to 'force managers to be more honest' in the appraisals, and another observed that her state was having problems attempting to make the appraisal process more 'legally defensible.'"[67] In the absence of standardized criteria for evaluating employees and assigning merit pay awards, overt bias (for example, against women) or incidental bias (for example, the halo effect) can enter the evaluation process.[68]

Ethics and compensation: Rating inflation The problems associated with merit pay and the performance evaluation process can present public managers with an ethical dilemma about the most equitable way to distribute merit increases. Is it ethical for managers to rely on performance evaluations they believe to be inaccurate? Is there an ethical responsibility to be honest in the perfor-

mance evaluation process? Is it an ethical problem that 82 percent of employees were rated above average by federal managers, or is it more ethical for a manager to attempt to advocate for higher salaries for employees they feel are already falling behind market salary rates? Perhaps managers should divide the merit increases equally, but would this be fair to the best employees to reward them equally with poor performers? The issue of ethics and compensation presents public managers with many vexing questions.

Persistence of Merit Pay

Given all the problems with merit pay and its implementation, it is fair to question why it remains so popular. One reason is that pay for performance is a private sector innovation, and a common assumption is that private sector techniques will improve public sector performance.[69] This stereotype persists in spite of numerous studies indicating that pay for performance has been less than an unqualified success in many private sector settings.[70] Another reason for merit pay's popularity is its role in the symbolic politics of keeping bureaucracy accountable.[71] Finally, there may be some reluctance to admit that a policy that has had such a large investment made in it is failing.[72]

Smith suggests that organizations contemplating merit pay should consider the following questions:

- Will pay for performance support the organization's mission and goals?
- Is there strong management support for a pay-for-performance plan?
- Are funds available to make distinctions among levels of performance?
- What are the standards to be measured, and how will they be measured? How are superior, average, and poor performance defined?
- Will the rewards provided serve as an incentive?
- Should individual or team performance (or both) be rewarded?[73]

SKILL-BASED AND COMPETENCY-BASED PAY: LINKING PAY TO KNOWLEDGE

Rewarding Skills as the Basis for Compensation

Another reform of traditional compensation programs that public sector organizations are considering is **skill-based pay** (also referred to as competency-based pay). In traditional compensation programs, employees are rewarded based on the job that they occupy. Jobs are ranked in classification systems according to the value and level of KSAs required for a particular job. The salary structure reflects that prioritizing, giving higher salaries to those with more demanding jobs according to the classification schedule. In skill-based pay, the unit of analysis is not the job the incumbent holds but rather the skills the employee possesses.[74] In other words, "they are paid for skills they are capable of using and not for the jobs they are performing at a particular point in time."[75] Consequently, it is possible that an employee's job might not change, but the certification that that employee has mastered a set of skills valued by the organization might result in a pay raise.

Implementing Skill-Based Pay

There are several ways to reward skills. Employees can be rewarded for knowing more than others about a specialized area (depth of skill); they can be rewarded for learning skills that are "upstream, downstream, or parallel" to their position in the production or service delivery phase (breadth of skill); or they can be rewarded for self-management skills such as scheduling of work, problem solving, or training (vertical skills).[76]

Among the advantages to skill-based pay are the increased flexibility to move employees who already have skills to new positions within the organization as is needed.[77] This type of flexibility can be especially helpful in a period of cutback management or downsizing.[78] Skill-based

pay systems are also important in improving employee satisfaction and promoting personal development.[79]

The ability to monitor and assess accurately the quantity and quality of skills that employees learn is critical to all skill-based pay systems, whether that assessment is done by certification testing or some alternative means.[80] The organization is well advised to make a sizable investment in training and assessment.[81] Skill-based pay systems are also likely to cost the organization more in total salary in the short run as employees accumulate more skills.[82] Similar to broadbanded pay systems, skill-based pay is most effectively administered in flatter organizations employing a team orientation.[83] It is also likely that important public sector stakeholders such as state legislatures, Congress, and the OPM might resist skill-based pay for its anticipated increased costs and challenge to traditional hierarchy.[84]

GAINSHARING AND TEAM-BASED PERFORMANCE PAY PROGRAMS

Gainsharing is a term used to describe various pay incentives designed to reward group performance in contrast to individual pay-for-performance programs. It is similar to other programs such as profit sharing. Although this type of incentive was developed for use primarily in the manufacturing sector, it is becoming more common in the public sector as well.[85] The goal of a gainsharing program is to encourage changes in employee behavior by rewarding improvements in productivity or cost savings (or both) financially.[86] For example, in Charlotte, North Carolina, department employees were rewarded for achieving targeted reductions in workers' compensation costs, vehicle accidents, and use of sick leave.[87] In another example, Baltimore County, Maryland, employees made cost reduction suggestions and were eligible to share in half of the actual money saved.[88]

Research indicates that group incentives "have a significant positive impact on performance."[89]

Risher notes an American Compensation Association study that found that employers tend to gain three to four dollars of benefit from employee effort for every dollar paid out to employees in gainsharing rewards.[90] The impact of group incentives on employee attitudes and morale is also important. Gainsharing has been found to increase the long-term identity of the employee with the organization and to improve employee morale generally.[91] These improvements are possible even with only modest gainsharing rewards.[92]

There are many ways to calculate the financial rewards used in gainsharing plans. They may be based on physical measures such as the number of units produced in a manufacturing situation, or they may be more broadly construed such as sharing a percentage of cost savings among employees.[93] Ross and Ross suggest that whatever measure is used to calculate rewards, they should have these characteristics:

- They must be perceived as fair by employees, management, and customers.
- They must meet management's objectives for performance improvement.
- They must be understandable.
- They must be easy to administer.

■ CONCLUSION

Compensation is critical to the success of human resource management generally. Pay is connected to the motivation, morale, and retention of valuable employees. Salary and wage systems that are not competitive can greatly hinder the successful

hiring of the best available applicants for public sector and nonprofit agency jobs. The compensation system that an organization chooses must fit its overall mission and culture, and it must link up with the organizational structure and management practices in place.

■ MANAGER'S VOCABULARY

pay grades
pay range
salary midpoint
policy line
internal equity
external equity
salary survey
comparable worth
broadbanding
merit pay
expectancy theory
skill-based pay
gainsharing

■ STUDY QUESTIONS

1. What are the types of compensation systems, and how is each one linked to pay levels?

2. What are some of the major problems with traditional compensation systems?

3. Is pay for performance effective? Why or why not?

4. Explain the benefits of broadbanded pay systems.

■ EXPERIENTIAL EXERCISES

1. Daley City is about to renegotiate its contract with the collective bargaining unit representing its local police force. The major issue up for negotiation is salary levels. The union is using a survey of cities of comparable size in Daley City's three-state region. The city council has decided to use comparison salaries only from organizations and corporations within a 100-mile radius, since nearly 100 percent of Daley City's existing police force comes from that area.

a. Design a salary survey process that Daley City should follow to determine equitable salary levels for its police department.

b. What are the pros and cons of the approaches that the city council and police union are taking?

2. The governor has asked you to investigate the advisability of moving your state's compensation system from a traditional system that increased salaries based on time in rank to either a pay-for-performance or broadbanded system. What do you recommend? What are the advantages and disadvantages of each approach?

■ CASES APPLICABLE TO THIS CHAPTER

"Salary Compression at State University" and "Negotiator's Dilemma."

■ NOTES

[1] Thomas S. Roy, "Pricing and the Development of Salary Structures," in Milton L. Rock and Lance A. Berger, eds., *The Compensation Handbook*, 3rd ed. (New York: McGraw-Hill, 1991), p. 105.

[2] Howard Risher and Charles H. Fay, "Rethinking Government Compensation Programs," in Howard Risher and Charles H. Fay, eds., *New Strategies for Public Pay* (San Francisco: Jossey-Bass, 1997), p. 11.

[3] Howard Risher, "The Emerging Model for Salary Management in the Private Sector: Is it Relevant to Government?" *Public Personnel Management* 23 (Winter 1994): 650.

[4] Risher and Fay, "Rethinking Government Compensation Programs," p. 12.

[5] Richard C. Kearney, *Labor Relations in the Public Sector,* 2nd ed. (New York: Marcel Dekker, 1992), p. 22.

[6] Risher and Fay, "Rethinking Government Compensation Programs," p. 12.

[7] Elder Witt, "Are Our Governments Paying What It Takes to Keep the Best and the Brightest?" *Governing* (December 1988): 30.

[8] Sharon M. Oster, "Executive Compensation in the Non-profit Sector," *Nonprofit Management and Leadership* 8:3 (1988): 207–219.

[9] Ibid., p. 219.

[10] Dale Belman and John S. Heywood, "The Structure of Compensation in the Public Sector," in David Belman, Morley Gunderson, and Douglas Hyatt, eds., *Public Sector Employment in a Time of Transition* (Madison, WI: Industrial Relations Research Association), p. 132.

[11] Roy, "Pricing," p. 108.

[12] Ibid., p. 109.

[13] See ibid., p. 108, for a description of these methods.

[14] Mark J. Wallace and Charles H. Fay, *Compensation Theory and Practice* (Boston: Kent Publishing, 1983), p. 19.

[15] Risher and Fay, "Rethinking Government Compensation Programs," p. 3.

[16] Howard Risher, "Salary Structures: The Framework for Salary Management," in Risher and Fay, eds., *New Strategies for Public Pay,* p. 40.

[17] Belman and Heywood, "Structure of Compensation," p. 128.

[18] Ibid., p. 129.

[19] Eleanor Trice, "Compensation Practices," *IPMA News* (November 1998): 27.

[20] Wallace and Fay, *Compensation Theory and Practice,* p. 111.

[21] D. Terence Lichty, "Compensation Surveys," in Rock and Berger, eds., *The Compensation Handbook,* p. 88.

[22] Wallace and Fay, *Compensation Theory and Practice,* p. 121.

[23] This section draws heavily from ibid., p. 112.

[24] Ibid., p. 121.

[25] Ibid., p. 22.

[26] Barbara S. Wamsley, "Are Current Programs Working? Views from the Trenches," in Risher and Fay, eds., *New Strategies for Public Pay,* p. 27.

[27] Ibid., p. 28.

[28] Ibid., p. 31.

[29] Ibid., p. 29.

[30] Wayne Hanson, "How to Attract and Retain Qualified IT Staff," in Howard R. Balanoff, ed., *Annual Editions Public Administration 99/00* (Guilford, CT: Dushkin/McGraw-Hill, 1999), p. 105.

[31] Ibid.

[32] IPMA/NASPE, "Information Technology (IT) Turnover," Human Resource Benchmarking Project, available at: **http://www.impa-hr.org/private/bench/it/itturnover.html.**

[33] Hanson, "How to Attract and Retain," p. 105.

[34] IPMA /NASPE, "Barriers to Recruiting and Retaining Information Technology (IT) Staff," available at: **http://www.impa-hr.org/private/bench/it/barit.html.**

[35] Lisa Saunders "Relative Earnings of Black Men to White Men by Region, Industry," *Monthly Labor Review* (April 1995): 69.

[36] American Management Association/Business and Professional Women, "Compensation and Benefits: A Focus on Gender," available at: **http://www.amanet.org.**

37 Noted in Wamsley, "Are Current Programs Working?" p. 30.

38 Peter V. LeBlanc, "Banding—The New Pay Structure for the Transformed Organization," *Perspectives in Compensation* 13 (March 1992): 1.

39 Ibid., p. 2.

40 Ibid., p. 4.

41 Risher, " The Emerging Model," p. 655.

42 Eleanor Trice, "Compensation Practices," *IPMA News* (November 1998): 25.

43 David Hofrichter, "Broadbanding: A Second Generation Approach," *Compensation and Benefits Review* 25 (September–October 1993): 53–58.

44 "Broadbanding's Claimed Benefits Hide Fatal Flaws for Many Organizations," *IPMA News* (January 1998): 17.

45 Ibid.

46 Ibid.; Hofrichter, "Broadbanding," pp. 53–58.

47 Anne Nicolai, "The Road to Riches," *Public HR*, February 26, 1999, p. 24.

48 This section is derived from ibid.

49 J. Edward Kellough and Haoran Lu, "The Paradox of Merit Pay in the Public Sector: Persistence of a Problematic Procedure," *Review of Public Personnel Administration* 13 (Spring 1993): 45.

50 J. Edward Kellough and Sally Coleman Selden, "Pay for Performance Systems in State Government," *Review of Public Personnel Administration* 25 (Winter 1997): 6.

51 Ibid.

52 "Broadbanding's Claimed Benefits," p. 27.

53 James L. Perry, "Merit Pay in the Public Sector: The Case for a Failure of Theory," *Review of Public Personnel Administration* 17 (Fall 1986): 57–69.

54 Kellough and Lu, "The Paradox of Merit Pay," p. 54; Herbert H. Meyer, "The Pay for Performance Dilemma," *Organization Dynamics* 3 (Winter 1975): 40; Nicholas Lovrich, "Merit Pay and Motivation in the Public Workforce: Beyond Concerns of Technique," *Review of Public Personnel Administration* 7 (Spring 1987): 54.

55 Kellough and Selden, "Pay for Performance Systems," 11.

56 See, Perry, "Merit Pay in the Public Sector," p. 199.

57 Kellough and Lu, "The Paradox of Merit Pay," p. 52; Brigitte W. Schay, "Paying for Performance: Lessons Learned in Fifteen Years of Federal Demonstration Projects," in Risher and Fay, eds., *New Strategies for Public Pay,* p. 254.

58 Witt, "Are Our Governments Paying," p. 33.

59 Patricia W. Ingraham, "Of Pigs in Pokes and Policy Diffusion: Another Look at Pay-for-Performance," *Public Administration Review* 53 (July–August 1993): 353.

60 Kellough and Selden, "Pay for Performance Systems," p. 15.

61 Kellough and Lu, "The Paradox of Merit Pay," p. 52.

62 Witt, "Are Our Governments Paying," p. 31; Kellough and Lu, "The Paradox of Merit Pay," p. 49; Schay, "Paying for Performance," p. 254.

63 Kellough and Lu, "The Paradox of Merit Pay," p. 49.

64 Schay, "Pay for Performance," p. 266.

65 Wendell C. Lawther, H. John Bernadin, Earle Traynhan, and Kenneth Jennings, "Implications of Salary Structure and Merit Pay in the Fifty American States," *Review of Public Personnel Administration* 19 (Spring 1989): 8.

66 Witt, "Are Our Governments Paying," p. 32.

67 Ingraham, "Of Pigs in Pokes," p. 353.

68 Kellough and Lu, "The Paradox of Merit Pay," p. 51.

69 Ingraham, "Of Pigs in Pokes," p. 348.

70 See ibid., p. 350, for a description of these studies.

71 Kellough and Lu, "The Paradox of Merit Pay," p. 55.

72 Ibid., p. 56.

73 Maureen Smith, "Pay for Performance: Rewarding Employees for a Job Well Done," *IPMA News* (February 1999): 13.

74 Nina Gupta, "Rewarding Skills in the Public Sector," in Risher and Fay, eds., *New Strategies for Public Pay*, p. 128.

75 Reginald Shareef, "Skill Based Pay in the Public Sector: An Innovative Idea," *Review of Public Personnel Administration* 14 (Summer 1994): 61.

76 Summarized in ibid.

77 Ibid., p. 66.

78 Ibid.

79 Gupta, "Rewarding Skills," p. 135.

80 Ibid., p. 128; Shareef, "Skill Based Pay," p. 64.

81 Shareef, "Skill Based Pay," p. 64.

82 Ibid., p. 134.

83 Ibid., p. 133.

84 Ibid., p. 132.

85 Howard Risher, "Can Gainsharing Help to Reinvent Government?" in Balanoff, ed., *Annual Editions Public Administration 99/00*, p. 146.

86 Timothy L. Ross and Ruth Ann Ross, "Gainsharing: Sharing Improved Performance," in Rock and Berge, *The Compensation Handbook*, p. 105; Roy, "Pricing and the Development of Salary Structures," p. 108.

87 Risher, "Can Gainsharing," p. 148.

88 Ibid.

89 Ibid., p. 146.

90 Ibid.

91 Ross and Ross, "Gainsharing," p. 181; Risher "Can Gainsharing," p. 147.

92 Risher, "Can Gainsharing," p. 149.

93 Ross and Ross, "Gainsharing," p. 182.

CHAPTER 10

Benefits

This chapter explores the area of employment benefits, once considered a relatively minor aspect of HRM but increasingly seen as a major dimension of workforce management. As the diversity of jobs, skills, services, and persons employed in the public service and nonprofit agencies has grown, so too has the range of benefits developed to attract, motivate, and retain the workforce needed to meet the changing challenges of contemporary public life. This chapter explores some of the newer developments in benefits administration and sets forth how benefit management plays a large role in contemporary HRM practice.

INTRODUCTION TO READING

The reading for this chapter by Dennis Daley is subtitled "Not on the Fringes Anymore." This play on words points to the increasingly important role that benefits play in an organization's total compensation package. As Daley notes, benefits are now falling in the range of 20 to 40 percent of the cost of compensation. This cost is likely to increase since the price of health care, a critical part of most benefits packages, continues to rise at a rate higher than other consumer items. Furthermore, the presence or absence of certain fringe benefits may be a deciding factor in recruiting and retaining good employees in a competitive employment market. Benefits are indeed no longer "fringe." They are a significant cost to the organization and represent an important management tool for public administration.

Many benefit programs, such as social security and workers' compensation, were established by government mandate. Social security is a federal program that is uniformly administered across all states, while workers' compensation programs vary considerably by state.

Other benefit programs have been added as employers realized the importance of supporting healthy, motivated employees and recognized the substantial role that benefits packages played in keeping them that way. Daley notes that keeping today's "knowledge professional" healthy and able to work is critical because of the difficulty of replacing these employees quickly or cheaply.

The changing nature of benefits packages and their criticality is also a reflection of our changing workforce. Demographic changes such as the increased entry of women with children and employees with aging parents they need to care for have led to the development of programs generally referred to as **work-life programs** such as child care options, family-friendly scheduling of leaves, and flexible workdays.

Finally, Daley points to the importance of educating a public sector workforce about the benefits package options available to them in "cafeteria" systems wherein employees are allowed to select benefits from a list of options. Finding a way to communicate effectively about complicated benefits options is a continuing challenge for human resource management professionals.

As you read the selection, keep the following questions in mind:

- How do changes in the demographic makeup of the workforce affect employee interest in benefits and their administration?

- In what ways are work-life programs management tools?
- Why does Daley say that benefits are not "on the fringe" anymore?

READING

An Overview of Benefits for the Public Sector: Not on the Fringes Anymore

DENNIS M. DALEY

Benefits compose a major portion of the total compensation package. Along with wages and salaries, benefits serve to recruit, motivate, and retain employees. This article provides a descriptive overview of the myriad of benefits (and their sub-options) available for public sector use. Health care (medical, dental, vision, and wellness) and pension (social security, government retirement, and deferred compensation) systems are reviewed. Finally, special pay options (overtime, moonlighting, business expenses, and paid time off) and employee development are detailed.

Benefits are a major component in compensation. They can compose from 20 to 40 percent of the total compensation package. Yet, benefits are still a hodgepodge. Mainly composed of health care and retirement pension programs, benefits also include a vast array of miscellaneous services. Further complicating matters is the fact that not all benefits are tangible; many offer intrinsic incentives upon which it is difficult to place a dollar value. Furthermore, the value of benefits, even those with clear price tags, actually will vary from individual to individual. However, benefits still serve the same set of purposes that pay does—to attract, retain, and motivate employees.

Benefits distort the market-based approach found in Frederick Taylor's simple notion of paying workers and letting them choose how to use their money. As an organizational matter, benefits arise from the vagaries of governmental tax laws and market economies of scale. The organization can

tap into these more economically than an individual can. In essence, the organization pays wholesale while the individual must purchase at retail prices. Hence, the organization can provide benefits that are highly valued by individuals at reduced costs.

However, these cost differentials also distort the market. Individuals who receive a subsidized or discounted benefit will prefer it over one that is not. Hence, two "benefits" or consumer needs of equal use will not be treated equally in their preference calculations. This situation can lead to the overpurchase of subsidized benefits and the underutilization of those not subsidized. The introduction of cafeteria benefit plans is meant to partially adjust for this problem.

Because benefits compose a growing proportion of the total compensation package, it is necessary to treat benefits with the same strategic pay considerations to which wage and salary decisions are subjected. While benefits are more likely to satisfy attraction and retention needs than to be motivational, this latter role should not be overlooked. Hence, organizationally specific information on benefits desired by employees, whether public [or] private,

Source: Dennis M. Daley, "An Overview of Benefits for the Public Sector: Not on the Fringes Anymore," *Review of Public Personnel Administration* 28:3 (Summer 1998): 5–22. Reprinted by permission of the publisher, Sage Publications.

is important (Moore 1991; Bergmann, Bergmann, & Grahn, 1994; Davis & Ward, 1995; Streib, 1996).

Because benefits are paid for in pre-tax dollars, the employee obtains them for less than it would cost if taxable wages and salaries were used. The organization also derives tax savings. Tax deductions are allowed for those in the private sector. Yet, even public sector organizations receive tax breaks; the salary upon which social security and other employment taxes is calculated is often lower, thereby reducing the payments due from the organization.

Because of the size of their workforces, organizations can also negotiate favorable rates under group plans. In most cases, a single individual would be required to pay substantially more. The organization, thereby, satisfies workers' needs at a bargain rate. This can occur even when the organization is not paying for the benefit itself, but merely serving as a conduit for employees to purchase optional services.

These "savings" need not all be passed on to the individual consumer. It should be noted that public sector organizations have often suffered from this problem. Benefits contracts have been awarded on the basis of patronage. Vendors may be political players who make campaign contributions or underwrite the organization by providing it with professional equipment and services. To cover the costs of obtaining this patronage, the plans may not be as generous as those found in similar, private sector organizations or may require higher deductibles and copayments. These problems can exist even when only optional benefits entirely paid for by the employee are being provided.

Since the major benefits that organizations provide deal with health and retirement, employees are forced to take care of these long-term requirements. A healthy worker might see no urgent need for health insurance, and retirement is a lifetime away. If individuals are allowed to make their own choices in these matters, they are likely to prefer present pressing needs and discount future uncertainties. Will society be content to sit idly by when the negative consequences of poor choices occur? From the organizational perspective, will its workforce "blame" it and judge it harshly for allowing these poor choices? Will employees themselves be more worried and less motivated? Forcing employees to make decisions that adequately take into account the long-term may be authoritarian or paternalistic, but it is also insurance for the organization's future well-being.

HEALTH CARE

One of the two primary benefits sought by employees is health insurance (Perry & Cayer, 1997). With the growing importance of professionalism (i.e., the knowledge worker) as the key organizational asset, maintaining a healthy workforce takes on an added importance. Skilled, knowledge workers are not interchangeable parts that can be easily replaced. Their loss or even reduced attention (Napoleon suffered illnesses in his last few, active years, including on the day of Waterloo; Franklin D. Roosevelt was seriously ill during the latter years of World War II) can be critical to an organization's performance (Buchmueller & Valletta, 1996).

Modern medical costs for hospital care will run into the thousands of dollars in a matter of a few days for even a minor illness. Something which requires intensive care indeed truly merits the name catastrophic, not only in terms of its life-threatening nature but in respect to its enormous costs. Fears of illness and the subsequent devastating financial burdens that they can impose are quite disquieting.

Health Insurance

Health insurance is the means by which these fears can be, to some extent, allayed. In addition to major medical expenses, health insurance can also inexpensively aid in alleviating other health-related threats to motivation and productivity. Health insurance plans may include additional provisions for prescription drug, mental health, dental, and eye care benefits. What is included and the extent of that coverage varies substantially from plan to plan.

Deductible ($200 per individually annually with a $500 family cap) and copayment (20 percent of charges) cost containment provisions also alter the real value and costs of these benefits (Cayer, 1997). These plans may also limit exposure through a total out-of-pocket provision ($1500 per individual with a $3000 family cap). It is because of this extensive variability among plans that it is extremely difficult to do cost comparisons on health benefits.

The basic health care covered under insurance plans is likely to be separated into segments requiring different levels of copayments. Preventive care such as is found in an annual physical examination and periodic eye and dental checkups is often fully reimbursed (directly paid by the insurance company to reduce paperwork and delays) and exempt from any deductible provisions. Relatively common, minor medical procedures may be reimbursed at a 90 percent level. More serious or long-term (but not catastrophic or life threatening in nature) illnesses may require a 50/50 match. Catastrophic care (e.g., cancer and heart disease), whether as part of the general policy or as an additional or optional benefit, again provides something on the order of 80 or 90 percent reimbursement. Since the cost of catastrophic care quickly escalates into the hundreds of thousands of dollars, even at these reimbursement levels the copayment requirements are substantial.

Employer-provided health plans usually provide options for family coverage (paid in full or part by the organization, or entirely at the employee's expense). Concerns about the health of family members can adversely affect an employee's productivity. Hence, the extension of health benefits to family members is essential.

Family coverage is a two-part phenomenon. It provides health insurance for the spouse and for the children; spouse coverage is actually the more expensive part. Since it is coverage for an adult, it has an adult risk exposure profile. Importantly, it extends insurance coverage for pregnancy (which is one of the major insurance costs). A spouse is also at risk for other adult illnesses, including the costly cancer and heart disease risks. Proposals for domestic partners' benefits address the same concern (Gossett, 1994; Hostetler & Pynes, 1995).

Child coverage is a relatively less costly component. After the first few years, children are surprisingly healthy and resilient. Most efforts are devoted to preventive medicine. Some plans, in fact, authorize employee-parent and children coverage, excluding the spouse. These options assume that the spouse is covered under another organization's health plan. This saves the organization and employee from paying for unneeded, duplicate insurance.

With dual-income families being more and more the norm, another concern arises vis-á-vis children's health coverage. When dual-income parents are given the choice of two health plans, they will gravitate to the better plan. Providing better child care benefits can lead to increased insurance costs for the organization. Of course, such a family-friendly policy is also going to be a major attraction for many desirable job candidates (Osterman, 1995).

To pay for uncovered aspects of the health plans, tax laws allow for employees to establish medical

and dependent care (a legal option is also available) accounts. Pre-tax dollars from their salaries are deposited into these accounts by the employees according to a salary reduction agreement. These "trust funds" are then used to pay the medical, dependent, or legal expenses incurred. Unfortunately, unexpended funds revert to the federal government at the end of the year. However, it is quite easy to budget for anticipated, on-going expenses or to plan some less serious operations.

Organizations can facilitate medical, dental, and eye care by arranging for on-site or nearby services. To avoid liability, these are set up as independent businesses. The organization often provides space and equips an office that is leased or sold on favorable terms. They also informally guarantee employee use of these services. This not only insures readily available medical facilities for employees, but often reduces time lost from work. Instead of waiting at a doctor's office, the employee can remain at work until actually seen by the physician, dentist, or optometrist.

While health insurance covers the costs of obtaining medical care, it does not itself address the loss of income that also occurs due to illness. Workmen's compensation legally covers employees for job-related accidents. Sick leave also serves to continue an employee's income for short periods of illness (Garcia, 1987; Kroesser, Meckley, & Ransom, 1991).

While part of the social security program covers long-term disability, the amounts may not be enough to fully or adequately replace lost wages and salaries. Disability insurance for replacing the lost income (enabling one to continue paying for the ongoing expenses which that level of income was financing) is often provided. Short-term disability policies can often provide 100 percent of pay replacement for up to a month, and replace 50 percent of pay over the next 6 months. Long-term disability (often integrated with, i.e., reduced by, Social Security) can replace two-thirds of pay until the disabled employee reaches age 65. In case of permanent disability, long-term medical care insurance for home health care and nursing homes may be necessary (albeit this is quite expensive and seldom provided as an organization-paid benefit).

The Family Medical Leave Act (FMLA) mandates up to three months unpaid leave for employees who desire to take care of or assist sick relatives, and for maternity and paternity leave (Alfred, 1995; Crampton & Mishra, 1995). Dependent care accounts (for elders and children) can be used to help pay for these costs (Kossek, DeMarr, Backman, & Kollar, 1993). While the FMLA guarantees an employee job security, it does place a burden on organizations for finding qualified temporary replacements. The Consolidated Omnibus Reconciliation Act of 1986 (COBRA) mandates the continuation of group-rate employee benefits for up to 18 months for leaving (up to three years for families of divorced or dead employees).

Sick leave which can be accumulated at a rate of four to eight hours per month provides an employee with pay during short-term illness. This encourages employees to take care of themselves when necessary, instead of attempting to "gut it out" only to lapse into a more long-term illness. It also removes potentially infectious individuals from the workplace. In addition, sick leave can be used for medical appointments and caring for ill family members.

Sick leave tends to be used, and thereby costs an organization. Patterns of use should be examined with the thought for the introduction of cost-effective preventive action. Unfortunately, sick leave abuse also does occur. This needs to be treated. However, it must first be established that there is indeed a case of abuse. Anti-abuse policies where there is no abuse or only a few cases can undermine employee morale and trust.

In order to prevent sick leave abuse, programs allow for sick leave to be accumulated and applied towards service requirements in calculating retirement benefits. Alternatively, employees may be paid for unused sick leave. While meant as a protection against loss of income due to illness, it is often treated as just another form of paid leave. The incidence of Monday and Friday illnesses can be somewhat staggering. Monthly or quarterly incentives are often provided employees for not using their sick leave. Unused sick leave is a liability redeemed at the time of separation or retirement. Leave banks have been introduced to help solve this problem.

Annual, paid leave or vacation time (one to four weeks per year, depending on seniority) is another health benefit. It benefits the individual to step back from the day-to-day stresses in an organization. Vacations refresh and renew. As is the case with sick leave, this time can often be accumulated and applied towards retirement. Since this can create substantial liability, the amount of leave that can be accumulated may be capped.

Concerns on health policies lead to mandating the annual usage of some leave. Since the purpose of leave is to refresh and renew the individual employee, it does no one any good if it is not used. Leave also benefits an individual's family relationships. While one-day leaves (a Friday or Monday added to a weekend) are conveniently permitted, a required one week block (five vacation days) is considered minimal. Short mini-vacations as enjoyable as they can be are intensive. An individual needs one to two days of leisured leave to "decompress" from the job and begin shedding stress; the days added beneficially enhance this.

All types of leave—vacation, sick, and paid holidays (secular and religious)—may be lumped together in a leave bank. A leave bank eliminates concerns about sick leave abuse. This reduces the organization's accounting and monitoring requirements. It also avoids the political questions that can arise regarding which holidays are observed and which are not.

Wellness programs focus on preventative health care. They undertake to encourage behaviors that lead to good health and ease stress. They encourage individuals to exercise, eat healthfully, and give up hazardous habits. Many of these activities are geared to behaviors that are associated with the risk of cancer and heart disease—two of the costliest insured illnesses (Erfurt, Foote, & Heirich, 1992).

As part of such efforts, organizations may actually establish gyms or health spas for their employees (or subsidize memberships). Many large organizations construct walking trails around and build their parking lots at the edge of their "campuses." As a social activity, employee sports teams may be encouraged.

Cafeterias help insure that employees eat a proper diet. They also insure that employees are readily available for lunch time emergencies. Vending machines can be stocked with fruits and other acceptable snacks. Nutritional information is made available to employees. Since obesity is a major problem among Americans (and contributes to heart disease and stroke), weight loss programs are also often sponsored.

Stress reduction is also the focus of many wellness efforts. Psychological stress can adversely affect productivity and lead to job burnout (Golembiewski, 1988; Cordes & Dougherty, 1993). Stress can also contribute to physical illnesses, including stroke and heart disease.

Uncertainty and a sense of helplessness are two

conditions that contribute to job stress that are readily dealt with through communication and participation. The simple policy of keeping employees informed of what is occurring in an organization reduces stress. Goalsetting and related TQM [total quality management] and MBO [management by objectives] approaches also provide the employees with information on what is expected of or from them, thereby reducing job stress. Since America is a highly individualistic society, control over the basic aspects of the job is highly desired. Hence, a lack of autonomy will tend to place an employee under stress. This will even occur in team environments. Depending on others (which is really what organizations are all about) is perceived as a stressful loss of control. The more extensive employee participation is, the more individuals will feel that they are in control of their jobs.

In addition to communication and participation, wellness programs focus on a number of stress reduction techniques. Stress is an individual phenomenon. It affects people differently. The same event can trigger different responses. In fact, these responses can be both good and bad. For example, approaching project deadlines may turn one individual into a babbling basket case while another is turned on by the challenge. One individual meticulously plans and works on projects so they are completed well before they are due; the other only starts the "night before."

Stress reduction techniques are often surprisingly simple. Because of this, it is first necessary that stress and the body's physical, emotional, and behavioral reactions to it be described. This helps establish the importance of stress reduction for the employee and the organization. Stress can originate on the job or from events in an individual's life. Awareness of the sources of stress in an individual's life can be used in preparing to cope with it.

Relaxation techniques—deep breathing, muscle relaxation, breaks, massage, and imagery—are simple coping mechanisms. They temporarily break the stressors' grip on the individual; pleasant experiences or thoughts can be introduced to assist in this. More complex techniques—personality profiles, conflict resolution, diet and exercise regimes, and time management—can be employed in developing long-term stress strategies.

Health concerns may also lead to the organization becoming more intrusive. Lifestyle behaviors which increase health risks (and potential costs) may be targeted for modification—"lose the habit or the organization loses you." The exercise, diet, and stress reduction options may become required.

Growing concerns are also evident in regard to the use of medical records and genetic testing. Illness is not neutral; health conditions tend to be viewed as "deserving" and "undeserving." Individuals attach social stigmas to illnesses that are the consequences of lifestyle choices and, therefore, perceived as preventable. Whether the dissemination and use of such information is deemed to be relevant and job-related is still a subject of debate. Clearly, information regarding these stigmatized illnesses can exert a negative effect on careers.

A more sinister concern adheres to the use of genetic testing. Advances in medical science (the discovery of DNA markers) are allowing us to identify and monitor individuals who may possess a propensity for developing certain hereditary diseases and illnesses. In many cases this can lead to early intervention and treatment. Minimally, it aids in the further study of these diseases. However, this information can also exert a negative effect on careers. Organizations may choose not to hire, develop, or promote individuals who may develop costly illnesses at some future date. Of course, this is a matter over which the individual has no control; socially, however, the disease is "undeserved." In fact, the genetic test may represent only a probability and not a certainty.

Employee Assistance Programs

For individual employees the availability of counseling, drug and alcohol treatment, and other aspects of employee assistance programs (EAP) can be quite encouraging (Johnson, 1986; Johnson & O'Neill, 1989; Mani, 1991; Perry & Cayer, 1992). Employee assistance programs represent the personnel function in its most positive, humanistic mode. The initial success with alcohol treatment led to the expansion of EAPs. Today, they not only deal with other serious illnesses such as drug dependency and psychological disorders but with family and financial problems as well. In addition, some EAPs include career counseling, weight control, and related wellness activities.

Employee assistance programs treat the whole person. Organizations are cognizant that nonwork behaviors and personal problems can adversely affect an employee's work. They also recognize that their individual employees are valuable resources. Each employee represents a substantial human investment in job training and organizational socialization. While termination and replacement are options, they are often the least preferred and last resorts. Hence, efforts spent in helping employees solve their problems are usually worthwhile for the organization.

Employee assistance programs are usually contracted for from other groups and organizations in the community. A nonprofit, umbrella organization may serve as an overall contact agency and coordinator. The independent EAP can provide excellent services due to its communitywide economy of scale. Its independence also assures employees of confidentiality in what are still personal problems. This allows the employee's organization to make the EAP available and, in some instances due to job-related concerns, to make referrals. Yet, the organization stops short of actually meddling in an individual's private life (and the potential liability problems associated with that).

Employee assistance programs have also been the source of economical personnel functions. Family and marriage counseling services have formed the nucleus for alternate dispute resolution and mediation processes. Their very independence and confidentiality have helped in resolving conflicts. Family finances and budget planning have opened the door to financial planning for retirement (and other major life goals).

Cost Containment

Cost containment is also an organizational concept (Moore, 1989). Without some effort at managing care, health insurance itself would cease to be affordable, even under group rates. In most cases, the employee is subject only to a small, preliminary deductible payment. This discourages frivolous benefit abuse while not endangering its serious application. Cost shifting also takes place through varying partial copayments that are often required depending on the nature of the procedure. With the importance of wellness issues most health insurance plans also include fully reimbursable preventive physical (as well as dental and eye) examinations as a standard feature.

Cost containment has led to the creation of various managed care options as alternatives to the traditional fee-for-services physician. The *preferred provider organization* (PPO) lists doctors who accept patients under a set payment schedule (analogous to Medicare provisions). The *health maintenance organization* (HMO) is a business that provides full medical care for a pre-set fee. Each of these options, more or less, introduces financial incentives in balance to the provision of medical services.

Under HMO plans, doctors are usually on salary rather than "commission" as is the case under fee-for-service arrangements. In addition, there is usually some form of gainsharing or bonus incentive included as an added inducement against over-medication. It is assumed that the doctor's intrinsic desire to professionally serve their patients will counterbalance these financial incentives to insure adequate patient health care.

A utilization review is conducted prior to authorizing a procedure. The purpose is to assure that necessary medical services are provided while "what if" and "wouldn't it be nice" questions are discouraged. These utilization review procedures often raise the spectre of an individual's being denied needed services for the sake of corporate profits. Without a doubt, some of this occurs, especially where reviewers lack the relevant professional expertise of either physicians or registered nurses. Even so, the traditional fee-for-service approach often profited by ordering unneeded tests. Since there is an added danger in over medication and from unnecessary procedures, utilization review is also likely to protect an individual's health and well-being.

A major danger inherent in cost containment efforts is the shifting of costs to the employee-patient. As a safeguard against such financial concerns coming at the expense of patient care, HMOs and PPOs are, albeit on a voluntarily basis, subject to accreditation by the nonprofit National Committee for Quality Assurance (NCQA). Many organizations and employees will only do business with accredited plans. While cost remains the most important factor in the determination of health care providers, quality is rapidly becoming a close second consideration. This is especially true for large organizations and for those considered as innovative leaders in their field.

While traditional indemnity plans are still the most prevalent form of health insurance offered employees, the use of HMOs and PPOs is rapidly growing. This is especially true in regard to health maintenance organizations, which tend to offer a wider array of medical services and generate fewer customer complaints. Interestingly, in the public sector HMO and PPO cost savings are apparently "reinvested" into added services. While preferred provider organizations are a bit more inexpensive, the amounts spent on traditional indemnity plans hardly differ from the costs incurred by HMOs (Perry & Cayer, 1997). Given the importance of health care to employees, this may indeed be wise use of cost containment's savings (Lust & Danehower, 1990).

RETIREMENT AND PENSIONS

Modern medicine has for the first time created a world in which there are truly substantial numbers of older people. This is actually a relatively new phenomenon. Until the 20th century, old age was a rarity and an exceedingly short affair. Today, there are not only more people living into their 60s and 70s, but one in which life expectancies well into the 80s and 90s are not at all uncommon. In fact, the baby boom generation (those born between 1946 and 1964) is actually creating a permanent age shift in the nation's population demographics.

This is far different from when social security was established in the 1930s; at that time five-year payout periods were envisioned as the maximum that would be required. Individuals can no longer be expected to "die at their desks" or go into the hereafter shortly thereafter. Hence, the dilemma for contemporary retirement fund management.

While psychological perceptions are slowly adjusting (over 50 is still seen as old), today's healthier individuals are quite capable of productive work for far longer than those of a generation or so ago. The magic age of 65 established by Bismarckian Prussia over a century ago (so, workers could retire after 50 years employment) is, with today's health standards and life expectancies, now somewhere between 75 and 80 years.

However, many individuals will not want to work that long. If they can afford to, they will want to seek new challenges and experiences. These may be in the pursuit of "leisure" activities or in other jobs. In addition, military and paramilitary organizations (e.g., police and firefighters) which require a physically fit workforce for the demanding tasks they may be called upon to perform will still require retirement at an earlier age.

Not to provide the individual with some form of post-employment financial security would cause the same worries and resultant adverse effects on productivity as failing to provide for health insurance. To insure employees' current commitment and attention on productivity, future security must be guaranteed.

Retirement Income

Retirement from employment need not mean that an individual ceases to work. While many individuals need to continue working to supplement their "retirement" income, many also undertake new employment for the enjoyment or activity it affords them. Voluntary and nonprofit organizations become the focus of attention for many of the still active elderly. Dynamic public service activities are often the result. However, to engage in such pursuits requires financial security.

While it is assumed that prior major expenses (e.g., home mortgages and children's education) reduce future needs, retirement income is still a substantial requirement. While all projections are subject to the vagaries of individual preferences and inflationary changes, general estimates suggest that a minimum figure from 80 to 85 percent of pre-retirement income is necessary to maintain one's life-style during retirement.

The money to provide this future stream of income during retirement is derived from social security, pensions, and individual savings. It is highly unlikely that any individual will be able to enjoy a financially secure retirement without contributions from all three sources.

The social security system provides a foundation for retirement. Social security guarantees a basic pension to virtually every American worker. Social security is a defined benefit plan with redistributive provisions for poorer workers. While social security was not designed to be the sole source of retirement income, it is for some individuals. On average social security replaces 40 percent of pre-retirement income. This will vary from 50 percent of pre-retirement income for salaries under $20,000 to 25 percent of pre-retirement income for salaries over $50,000. Under social security's redistributive formula, those who are financially better off (as are most professional workers) can see this proportion (but not the actual amount of the benefit) "erode."

Payroll taxes (combining employee and employer contributions) are used to fund fictitious individual accounts within the social security "trust fund." In actuality, current taxes from employees and employers are used to pay benefits to current retirees.

Perhaps more importantly, the related Medicare (along with private Medicare supplemental insurance) program offers some degree of insurance against the remaining major life expense that individuals face: health care. Medicaid, a program for providing medical care for the poor, is extensively used for nursing home care by the elderly. This is not limited to just the elderly poor, but includes many who are not-so-poor. Many elderly engage in activities designed to pass on their assets to their children (and grandchildren) rather than see them eaten-up in paying for long-term care.

Government retirement benefits may also include added health care provisions for the retired employees. While these benefits will be coordinated with those under Medicare, they can provide added financial and psychological security. Long-term care provisions alleviate the fears associated with losing the legacy of a "lifetime's work" or your independence.

Contrary to its trust fund language, social security and Medicare are pay-as-you-go programs. The taxes dedicated to these programs are not really invested in trust funds, but are instead used to pay for current expenses. Any surplus is used to cover other governmental expenses (albeit the funds receive Treasury bond IOUs). Unfortunately, the tax rates funding social security and Medicare are inadequate for the growing demand being placed on them. Escalating retirement (due to increased life expectancy) and health care (due to better but more expensive services) costs, on the one hand, and low tax rates and fewer taxpayers, on the other, are rapidly undermining the financial solvency of both these programs. This is a long-term problem. The current payroll tax will cover expenses until after 2010. The trust fund "surplus" won't be exhausted until sometime after 2030. Since this surplus is actually made up of Treasury bills, it can only be drawn on by imposing new taxes.

Somewhat unfortunately (but understandable in a pluralist society), the self-interest of elderly recipients and their role as active voters have hindered necessary reforms. However, ultimately adjustments will be made. Taxes supporting both social security and Medicare will be raised. The retirement age for receiving social security benefits will also be raised. Medicare will be modified to include more managed care, including added deductibles and copayments.

Both programs may be subjected to means testing that reduces benefits or eligibility for those financially well-off.

This makes the pension and savings components of the retirement equation all the more important. These will be expected to assume an even greater role in underwriting future retirement benefits.

Pensions provide the structure built upon the social security foundation. While social security sustains life, it is the pension that will make that life worth sustaining. Social security alone can only provide an individual with a retirement of "genteel poverty" at best (at worst, it can be quite a miserable existence).

Pensions are categorized either as defined-benefit or defined-contribution plans. Pensions are funded through salary reduction contributions from the employee and matching payments from the employer. The Employee Retirement Income Security Act of 1974 (ERISA) establishes a ten-year vesting requirement for private sector organizations (five years is more common); in general, its procedures have been voluntarily adopted among public organizations.

Employees are entitled to a refund on their contributions upon leaving employment prior to vesting, but forfeit the employer match. However, upon being vested the employer's match is legally theirs, and they are entitled to retirement benefits. Most plans require that the employee obtain the age of 65 (earlier retirement beginning at age 55 or 62 at a reduced benefit level may be available) before receiving benefits. Police and firefighters are commonly required to retire at 55 due to the physical (and psychological) demands involved in their jobs. The Tax Reform Act of 1976 requires that pensions begin paying-out by age 70 and a half (even if the employee is not formally retired).

Early retirement (prior to age 65) may be encouraged when organizations are trying to downsize. In such instances, added "bridge" benefits, including part-time employment or consultant work, are often provided that compensate the individual for any reduced social security or pension effects. Early retirement may also appeal to individuals for various personal reasons (Feldman, 1994).

Traditionally, pensions were defined-benefit plans. Under a defined-benefit plan individuals are guaranteed from 50 to 75 percent of their highest salary upon retirement. Alternatively, their retirement benefit may be calculated on the basis of 2 to 3 percent of the highest salary multiplied by the number of years of service. Most systems also define "highest salary" in terms of a three- to five-year average.

Defined-benefit plans are not readily portable from one employer to another. Hence, they can somewhat discourage job changes that might otherwise be beneficial to both the individual and the organization. Under a uniform system that provided pensions calculated on 2 percent of highest salary multiplied by years of service, two individuals who shared identical salary histories would receive different pensions if one had changed jobs. Assume two individuals were paid $20,000 at the end of ten years, $40,000 after 20 years, and $60,000 on the completion of 30 years. An individual who had been employed for the entire 30 years by one organization would be eligible for a pension of $36,000. An individual who changed jobs every ten years, on the other hand, would qualify for three separate pensions of $4,000, $8,000, and $12,000—a total pension of only $24,000 (Hegji, 1993).

The defined-contribution plan does not suffer from a portability problem. It is based entirely on each year's employee and employer contribution. These funds are invested, and their growth and accumulation are the basis for future retirement income. The defined contribution plans are less generous to long term employees as they dispense with the multiplier effect found in the defined contribution plans.

The impact of inflation on retirement income is serious. Even at low two or three percent rates, inflation will erode the purchasing power of a pension rather quickly. Defined-contribution plans contain no provisions for dealing with inflation other than the aggressive investment strategies that individuals pursue. Defined-benefit plans may benefit from legislative enactment of cost-of-living adjustments (similar to those in social security).

If social security and pensions provide the "retirement home," it is individual savings that "furnishes" it. For most individuals, individual savings may, in fact, be their home. While this is an asset, it is not readily available for use in meeting retirement expenses. The introduction of "reverse mortgages" which allow individuals to borrow against their home's equity does meet some of these needs.

Yet, these homes may not be [a] sufficient source of savings. The immense appreciation in the real es-

tate market makes the value of these houses appear large. Adjusting the value of a house for inflation provides perspective on its real worth. Retirement needs additional savings sources. The major retirement arena for individual savings is the 401k and 403b tax-sheltered, supplemental retirement accounts. The tax code (from whence the 401k and 403b terminology is derived) encourages this form of retirement savings. In addition to employee-employer funded retirement pensions, individuals may also make tax-deferred contributions to a retirement account. Income tax on the principal (and the interest it earns) is deferred until it is withdrawn from the account during retirement (when the individual is usually in a lower tax bracket). At age 70 and a half the distribution of retirement benefits must begin.

Defined-benefit plans primarily relied upon the taxing power of government as their guarantee. They often create an unfunded liability because these retirement systems operate on a pay-as-you-go approach. On the other hand, defined-contribution plans are totally dependent upon the investment of their funds. This has moved pension management to the forefront. Whereas in the past state treasurers placed pension funds (i.e., the employee contributions) into government securities and other very safe investments merely to protect the principal, more aggressive strategies are called for today. The growth and interest that totally safe investments can earn seldom meet the projections as to what the employee will need in retirement (Cayer, 1995).

Investment risk has changed the way in which pension funds are managed. Since a defined-contribution plan doesn't protect the individual from loss in the way that a defined-benefit plan does, the fiduciary responsibility of pension administrators becomes quite important (Ferris, 1987).

The political management of these pension funds has come under intense scrutiny. Proposals to use pensions as funding sources for socially desirable projects or to encourage local venture capital activities raise serious questions (Cayer, Martin & Ifflander, 1986). Public pensions have (through loans to their own governments) also been diverted to pay for on-going budgetary expenses.

In fact, this is what happens with the social security trust fund. By law it is invested in Treasury bonds. Since these bonds must eventually be redeemed by the federal government, the purpose of a fiscally responsible investment fund is subverted into pay-as-you-go burden. By law, these transactions are also off-budget so as to disguise the real size of the deficit.

More and more, the trend is to allow employees to choose how to manage their retirement funds. Unfortunately, public sector agencies lag behind those in the private sector (which really isn't doing all that well itself) on providing employees with proper pre-retirement planning services. Employee productivity can suffer when employees are plagued by nagging questions and uncertainties over their future (Siegal & Rees, 1992; Siegal, 1994). Even where employees have full control over their pension investments, the provision of financial planning services is becoming an essential employee benefit. If employees are to make decisions regarding the investment of their retirement funds, they need to receive expert advice from a certified financial planner (CFP) or a CPA who is a personal financial specialist (PFS) to assist and guide them.

Funds for retirement are invested in a combination of fixed assets (bonds, certificates of deposit, and other money market accounts) and stocks. Stocks, because of their equity in a company, are the dynamic part of these investment portfolios. Risk is involved—for great gains and large losses. Stock investments may range from the relatively safe blue chips to bets on emerging growth companies. Even more risky are international ventures (the U.S. stock market is the most regulated and consumer-friendly in the world). While the developed nations are safer investments than the developing, all such investments must not only contend with currency fluctuations, but with political risk as well.

Health and Family Considerations

Providing income for the individual employee in retirement is not the sole concern of pensions. With retirement projected to last from ten to twenty years, health care is also a concern. Many individuals see Medicare as a basic, minimum level of service. Supplemental health insurance and long-term care insurance (home health care and nursing home coverage) may be included in ongoing employee benefits packages.

Family concerns prior to and during retirement are also important matters. Many organizations provide employees with life insurance (in multiples of their salary, usually about 1 1/2 times earnings). Optional group life insurance policies may also be avail-

able for purchase (with a benefit of from 1 to 3 times earnings). In the event of their early death, the life insurance will provide for their families. While the family would receive some benefits from the accumulated pension fund, these might not yet amount to much (or become available only later). Hence, life insurance serves as a financial bridge. Terminally ill employees may also be provided with the option for a "living benefit." A living benefit allows the employee to borrow against (or sell the right to) the policy's death benefit to cover expenses during a terminal illness. Such options assume that the surviving family, if any, is not denied support.

Adequate retirement income is not usually the concern of just one person; in many cases there is a spouse and perhaps dependent children involved. While many spouses will have pension rights of their own, others will not. Benefits to take care of the survivor in their retirement are also an issue (Nielson & Beehr, 1994). Under the Retirement Equity Act of 1984 pensions must include provisions for a joint-and-survivor annuity within the plan itself, or through an insurance option.

OTHER REWARDS

Organizations may use a wide array of other benefits—special pay, employee development, business expenses, living expenses, and social activities—to induce employees to affiliate, remain, and stay motivated.

Special pay options can be used. Most organizations operate on the basis of a 40-hour work week. When employees are needed for longer periods, they will be offered overtime (one-and-a-half to double) or compensatory time (allowing for longer vacation periods). On-call pay can be used to reduce overtime. As long as the individual is not prevented from beneficially using their own time, the more costly expenses associated with overtime can be avoided. One should also note here the flextime programs that partially adjust work hours for the convenience of the employee (McGuire & Liro, 1986, 1987; Harrick, Vanek & Michlitsch, 1986; Buckley, Kicza & Crane, 1987; Vega & Gilbert, 1997).

Moonlighting or second job opportunities may also be tolerated or encouraged. This is especially true with regard to public sector jobs. Unfortunately, this practice stems more from an inability or unwillingness to pay employees adequately than from a purposive policy. Hence, individuals are allowed to supplement their income with outside, secondary jobs. While this somewhat eases the financial pressure on both employee and employer, it raises a number of other, potentially serious questions.

Moonlighting at a second job draws upon both an individual's physical and mental energies. A second job may reduce one's capacity or willingness to fully perform in a first job. For some reason the public sector job is always thought of as being the first or primary job; it may not be. The public job may become secondary and be treated as such.

More seriously, second jobs may give rise to concerns about or perceptions of conflict of interests. Police and regulatory officials must clearly be prohibited or separated from employment by the people and organizations over which they enforce rules. Even ordinary administrations need to be separated from organizations with which their governmental entities do business. If moonlighting is allowed, an organization needs to monitor this activity carefully.

There are organizational advantages to moonlighting beyond the financial. When employees such as police officers or research consultants are legitimately employed by private firms, this lessens the demand for free public services. This also helps to build support for the public sector. Private businesses not only appreciate the special services that they can receive (because of the governmental economy of scale), but also come to know those who work for government as people rather than "bureaucrats."

Organizations pay people for time not worked. Paid leave (vacations and holidays) is the most well known, but they may also pay for "coffee" breaks and travel time. Unemployment compensation, advanced termination notice, transition, and severance packages are another form of pay for time not worked. These, again, are benefits designed to take an employee's mind away from future fears (by providing a financial bridge between jobs or assistance in securing alternative employment) and concentrate it on current productivity (Woska, 1988; Ting, 1996).

While clearly designed to make the organization better able to cope with its environment, employee development is also a major individual benefit. The knowledge-based organization must invest in its people if it is to exist. Yet, that very investment in people improves and adds value to those people. Education, training, and professional conferences are all means of enhancing organizational produc-

tivity. Since it's more economical to hold conferences in major locations, they also serve the social benefit of providing the employee with a "paid vacation."

Employee development has the added advantage of not only enhancing technical skills, but of psychologically motivating the individuals involved. The organizational investment is a recognition of the employee's worth. The added skills, while paid for by the organization, belong to the individual. For the organization to fully obtain the benefits of its education and training programs, it must keep the individual. This implies a long-term relationship and fosters organizational commitment and loyalty.

Tuition reimbursement and educational leave are two means of encouraging employees to add to their knowledge and skills. Prior approval of course work is typically required in tuition reimbursement programs. They also usually stipulate that courses [be] job-related and that the minimum of a "B" letter grade (or equivalent) be earned. Educational leave may vary from a flextime arrangement (with work hours made up) to granting paid time-off for courses. A few public organizations (such as the military) even send employees to school as their duty assignment.

Business expenses are also paid for or provided by the organization. Employee equipment, parking, transportation, and vehicles can be furnished or subsidized. Uniform or clothing allowances can be included. On-site child care (including sick baby care) facilities may be available (Suntrup, 1989; Kossek, Ernst & Nichol, 1992). All of these items help defray the direct costs of going to work.

Indirectly, organizations can subsidize living expenses. They can provide housing allowances and underwrite mortgages. They may actually provide the housing itself (in locations convenient to the organizations' offices). Commissaries and cafeterias can reduce food costs. Other retail services may also be made available to employees at discounted rates. In recruitment relocation and temporary housing expenses are often paid. In some cases, the organization may even assist in the sale (including buying) of an existing house.

Social activities designed to build teamwork and a sense of "family" loyalty can also be undertaken. The organization can create clubs (and even build or help the community build various sport facilities); it can organize parties and outings. Even a newsletter can be used to allow employees to place short ads.

Family-friendly benefits recognize the demographic changes that have made women a permanent part of the modern workforce. Since women in the workforce still bear the major brunt of family responsibilities, organizations are finding that they must make adjustments to accommodate these requirements. Flextime schedules (geared to school hours) and daycare are only two of the most well known benefits. Educational assistance (tutoring, scholarships, school matching, etc.) for dependents may be offered. Trailing spouse programs are used in recruitment ranging from assisting in job searches to actually creating a job for the spouse ("spousal accommodation").

Motivation can be further enhanced through cafeteria benefit plans. These attempt to fine-tune the benefits offered by allowing the individual to allocate their benefit dollars among those options that they themselves deem most useful. Some benefit programs are obviously mandatory for all employees; however, many others are merely in the desirable category. While many employees may desire them, for others they are clearly inappropriate. To provide these benefits to all employees is a waste of resources both in terms of the money spent and in the motivation they fail to elicit; in fact, they may result in a Herzbergian dissatisfier (Barber, Dunham, & Formisano, 1992).

The motivational value of extrinsic rewards can be enhanced by incorporating intrinsic recognition and growth aspects into these awards. By turning a tangible reward into a special prize, it takes on added trophy value. As a trophy, a clock or television set constantly reminds the individual and others of the recipient's accomplishments.

COMMUNICATION

Benefits are part of the total compensation package. Their worth needs to be communicated to the employee. Benefits compose a large portion of the compensation package. For an organization to leave them out of the picture is to grossly undervalue what it is willing to pay for an employee's productivity. The inclusion of benefits information states the true wage and effort bargain.

Employees need to be clearly informed of what benefits are provided. This is especially important in the recruitment of new employees. Understanding is improved if generic descriptions are replaced by individualized reports. This can readily and inexpensively be done with available computer technology. These computer programs also incorporate spreadsheet "what if" analysis provisions that can project the implications of different choices.

The complexity of benefits makes training all the more important. Mistakes in providing benefits information and counseling are not only costly, but often tragic. Since these mistakes only come to light when a "crisis" calls for their use, they quickly can undermine employee confidence and trust in the organization. While benefits liability insurance can cover the organization for the financial risks involved, only the adequate training of the benefits specialists can offer "insurance" against an erosion in trust.

Benefit statements must be provided annually and provide a good opportunity for highlighting this area. Employees are presented with the value of the benefits they receive. Organizations can magnify the value of the benefit package by calculating their cost not in terms of the actual dollars spent (at group rates), but as what the equivalent individual benefit would have cost. When benefit use results in costs even greater than this, these real savings to the individual can be pointed out. Finally, the intangible benefits can be listed.

NOTES

Allred, S. (1995). An overview of the Family and Medical Leave Act of 1993. *Public Personnel Management, 24* (1), 67–73.

Barber, A. E., Dunham, R. B. & Formisano, R. A. (1992). The impact of flexible benefits on employee satisfaction: A field study. *Personnel Psychology, 45* (1), 55–75.

Bergmann, T. J., Bergmann, M. A. & Grahn, J. L. (1994). How important are employee benefits to public sector employees? *Public Personnel Management, 23* (3), 397–406.

Buchmueller, T. C. & Valletta, R. G. (1996). The effects of employee provided health insurance on worker-mobility. *Industrial and Labor Relations Review, 49* (3), 439–455.

Buckley, M. R., Kicza, D. C. & Crane, N. (1987). A note on the effectiveness of flextime as an organizational intervention. *Public Personnel Management, 16* (3), 259–267.

Cayer, N. J. (1995). Pension fund management. In J. Rabin, T. Vocino, W. B. Hildeth & G. Miller (Eds.), *Handbook of public personnel administration* (pp. 377–389). New York, NY: Marcel Dekker.

Cayer, N. J. (1997). Issues in compensation and benefits. In C. Ban & N. M. Riccucci (Eds.), *Public personnel management: Current concerns, future challenges* (pp. 221–236). New York, NY: Longman.

Cayer, N. J., Martin, L. J. & Ifflander, A. J. (1986). Public pension plans and social investing. *Public Personnel Management, 15* (1), 75–78.

Cordes, C. L. & Dougherty, T. W. (1993). A review and integration of research on job burnout. *Academy of Management Review, 18* (4), 621–656.

Crampton, S. M. & Mishra, J. M. (1995). Family and medical leave legislation: Organizational policies and strategies. *Public Personnel Management, 24* (3), 271–289.

Davis, E. & Ward, E. (1995). Health benefit satisfaction in the public and private sectors: The role of distributive and procedural justice. *Public Personnel Management, 24* (3), 255–270.

Erfurt, J. C., Foote, A. & Heirich, M. (1992). The cost-effectiveness of worksite wellness programs for hypertension control, weight loss, smoking cessation, and exercise. *Personnel Psychology, 45* (1), 5–27.

Feldman, D. C. (1994). The decision to retire early: A review and conceptualization. *Academy of Management Review, 19* (2), 285–311.

Garcia, R. L. (1987). Sick-time usage by management and professional employees in the public sector. *Review of Public Personnel Administration, 7* (3), 45–59.

Golembiewski, R. T. (1988) *Phases of burnout: Developing concepts and applications.* New York, NY: Praeger.

Gossett, C. W. (1994). Domestic partnership benefits. *Review of Public Personnel Administration, 14* (1), 64–84.

Harrick, E. J., Vanek, G. R. & Michlitsch, J. E. (1986). Alternate work schedules, productivity, leave usage, and employee attitudes: A field study. *Public Personnel Management, 15* (2), 159–169.

Hegji, C. E. (1993). A note on job transfer, pension portability, and compensating salary differentials. *Review of Public Personnel Administration, 13* (1), 76–86.

Hostetler, D. & Pynes, J. E. (1995). Domestic partnership benefits: Dispelling the myths. *Review of Public Personnel Administration, 15* (1), 41–59.

Johnson, A. (1986). A comparison of employee assistance programs in corporate and government organizational contexts. *Review of Public Personnel Administration, 6* (2), 28–42.

Johnson, A. & O'Neill, N. (1989). Employee assistance programs and the troubled employee in the public sector workplace. *Review of Public Personnel Administration, 9* (3), 66–80.

Kossek, E., DeMarr, B. J., Backman, K. & Kollar, M. (1993). Assessing employees' emerging elder care needs and reactions to dependent care benefits. *Public Personnel Management, 22* (4), 617–638.

Kossek, E. & Nichol, V. (1992). The effect of on-site child care on employee attitudes and performance. *Personnel Psychology, 45* (3), 485–509.

Kroesser, H. L., Meckley, R. F. & Ranson, J. T. (1991). Selected factors affecting employees' sick leave use. *Public Personnel Management, 20* (2), 171–180.

Lust, J. A. & Danehower, C. (1990). Models of satisfaction with benefits. *Journal of Business Pyschology, 5,* 213–221.

McGuire, J. B. & Liro, J. R. (1986). Flexible work schedules, work attitudes, and perceptions of productivity. *Public Personnel Management, 15* (1), 65–73.

McGuire, J. B. & Liro, J. R. (1987). Absenteeism and flexible work schedules. *Public Personnel Management, 16* (1), 47–59.

Moore, P. (1989). Health care cost containment in large American cities. *Public Personnel Management, 18* (1), 87–100.

Moore, P. (1991). Comparison of state and local employee benefits and private employee benefits. *Public Personnel Management, 20* (4), 429–440.

Nielson, N. L. & Beehr, T. A. (1994). Retirement income for surviving spouses. *Public Personnel Management, 23* (3), 407–428.

Osterman, P. (1995). Work/family program and the employment relationship. *Administrative Science Quarterly, 40* (4), 681–700.

Perry, R. W. & Cayer, N. J. (1992). Evaluating employee assistance programs: Concerns and strategies for public employees. *Public Personnel Management, 21* (3), 323–333.

Perry, R. W. & Cayer, N. J. (1997). Factors affecting municipal satisfaction with health care plans. *Review of Personnel Administration, 17* (2), 5–19.

Siegal, S. R. (1994). A comparative study of pre-retirement programs in the public sector. *Public Personnel Management, 23* (4), 631–647.

Siegal, S. R. & Rees, B. Y. (1992). Preparing the public employee for retirement. *Public Personnel Management, 21* (1), 89–100.

Streib, G. (1996). Specialty health care services in municipal government. *Review of Public Personnel Administration, 16* (2), 57–72.

Suntrup, E. L. (1989). Child-care delivery systems in the government sector. *Review of Public Personnel Administration, 10* (1), 48–59.

Ting, Y. (1996). Workforce reductions and termination benefits in governments: The case of advance notice. *Public Personnel Management, 25* (2), 183–198.

Vega, A. & Gilbert, M. J. (1997). Longer days, shorter weeks: Compressed work weeks in policing. *Public Personnel Management, 26* (3), 391–402.

Woska, W. J. (1988). Pay for time not worked: A public-sector budget dilemma. *Public Administration Review, 48* (1), 551–556.

OVERVIEW

The reading for this chapter described benefits by their function—that is, those related to health care, pensions, special pay options, and employee development. Another way to examine the myriad of benefits available to employees and identify their role in compensation is to assess their taxation status and consider those that are voluntary versus those that are required by statute. Table 10.1 displays selected benefits by both their mandatory or voluntary status and by their function.

All public and private sector employers must participate in the mandatory benefit programs listed in Table 10.1; the rest of the benefits vary from jurisdiction to jurisdiction. As we discussed in Chapter 9, compensation policies differ among public, for-profit, and nonprofit organizations for a variety of reasons. Smaller organizations may not have the resources (or the legal requirements) to offer benefits. Unfortunately, it is not unusual to find small for-profit or nonprofit organizations without formal benefits packages, although a variety of nonmonetary, informal benefits (e.g., flexible working hours) may be available.[1] Nevertheless, in spite of the cost, it is to the advantage of an organization recruiting in a competitive marketplace to provide a wide array of employee benefits.

This chapter looks at the advantages of providing a wide array of employee benefits, reviews the relative use of benefits in state and local governments, discusses some of the difficulties in implementing benefit programs, and examines benefits as they are generally implemented in the private and public sectors.

KEY DIFFERENCES BETWEEN PUBLIC AND PRIVATE BENEFITS

The Employee Benefit Research Institute (EBRI) points to four key differences between public and private sector benefit programs.[2] First, public employee benefit plans are products of the political process, and the plans' features, including eligibility, contributions, and types of benefits, are laid out in statutes and ordinances. Major changes to public sector benefits packages have to be made within the political decision-making process. Many interest groups will be attentive to these changes, including taxpayer groups interested in limiting public spending and collective bargaining units representing public employees. Because tax monies largely pay for public employee benefits, spending on benefits is a public, political issue.

A second key difference between the public and private sectors is the role that federalism plays. State and local governments do not pay taxes; therefore, tax incentives to offer certain benefits are not equally persuasive to them as they would be to private sector corporations. Federalism also allows states considerable flexibility in the type and level of benefits provided in some benefit programs.

A third difference between public and private sector benefit systems is that for public employees, "the immediate employing entity is not the sponsor or the administrator of the benefit plans under which they are covered."[3] In some cases, for example, the state may administer a health care plan in which a city or county participates. In the private sector, on the other hand, the employing company tends to administer its own benefits package.

A fourth key difference between benefits in the public and private sector is that the public sector often provides different benefits packages to different occupational groups. The most common examples are law enforcement and firefighting employees, who generally have their own retirement systems. Another example can be found in the benefit plans designed specifically for public school teachers. Finally, while private sector companies often provide separate benefits for executives, this is much more rare in the public sector.

The EBRI notes that in spite of these differences, the public and private sectors share a strong common interest in recruiting and retaining good employees. Benefits are an increasingly important part of the compensation package, used as important incentives to recruit and retain key personnel.

Table 10.1   Selected Benefits

Types of Benefits by Tax Treatment	Types of Benefits by Function
Mandatory	*Retirement Income Benefits*

<ul><li>Social Security retirement (OASI)</li><li>Social Security disability (DI)</li><li>Medicare Part A (Social Security HI)</li><li>Workers' compensation</li><li>Unemployment insurance</li><li>Medicaid</li><li>Supplemental Security Income (SSI)[a]</li><li>Public assistance[a]</li></ul>	<ul><li>Social Security retirement (OASI)</li><li>Supplemental Security Income (SSI)[a]</li><li>Keogh plans</li><li>Defined benefit pension plans</li><li>Defined contribution pension plans
	money purchase pension plans
	deferred profit-sharing plans
	savings and thrift plans
	employee stock ownership plans
	stock bonus plans
	simplified employee pension plans
	individual retirement account plans
	cash or deferred arrangements
	    401(k)
	    403(b)</li></ul>

Voluntary	*Health Care*
Fully Taxable<ul><li>Vacations</li><li>Paid lunch</li><li>Rest periods</li><li>Severance pay</li><li>Cash bonuses and awards</li></ul>	<ul><li>Employee and dependent health insurance</li><li>Retiree health insurance</li><li>Dental insurance</li><li>Vision insurance</li><li>Medicare (Social Security, HI, SMI)</li><li>Medicaid[a]</li></ul>
Tax Exempt[b]<ul><li>Employee and dependent health insurance</li><li>Retiree health insurance</li><li>Dental insurance</li><li>Vision insurance</li><li>Medicare Part B (Social Security SMI)</li><li>Educational assistance[c]</li><li>Legal assistance</li><li>Child care</li><li>Discounts</li><li>Flexible spending accounts</li><li>Parking</li><li>Cafeteria facility</li><li>Meals</li></ul>	*Other Benefits*

Tax Deferred[b]<ul><li>Keogh plans</li><li>Defined benefit pension plans</li><li>Defined contribution pension plans
money purchase pension plans
deferred profit-sharing plans
savings and thrift plans
employee stock ownership plans
stock bonus plans
simplified employee pension plans
individual retirement account plans
cash or deferred arrangements
    401(k)
    403(b)</li></ul>
	<ul><li>Social Security disability (DI)</li><li>Long-term disability insurance</li><li>Life insurance</li><li>Workers' compensation</li><li>Unemployment insurance</li><li>Public assistance[a]</li><li>Severance pay</li><li>Child care</li><li>Vacations</li><li>Sick leave or sickness and accident insurance</li><li>Other leave (maternity, funeral, jury, etc.)</li><li>Paid lunch</li><li>Rest periods</li><li>Legal assistance</li><li>Education</li><li>Flexible spending accounts</li><li>Bonuses and awards</li><li>Parking</li><li>Cafeteria facility</li><li>Meals</li><li>Discounts</li></ul>

Other Tax Preferred[b,d]<ul><li>Life insurance</li><li>Long-term disability insurance</li><li>Sick leave or sickness and accident insurance</li><li>Other leave (maternity, funeral, jury, etc.)</li></ul>	

Source: Employee Benefit Research Institute (EBRI), *Fundamentals of Employee Benefit Programs,* 5th ed. (Washington, D.C.: Employee Benefit Research Institute, 1997), p. 6.

[a] Eligibility based on need. Financed from general government revenues.
[b] Subject to conditions and limitations.
[c] Expired December 31, 1994, and has not yet been reinstated retroactively by Congress.
[d] Value of insurance and leave availability are not taxed; insurance benefits and leave pay generally are taxed when paid.

MAJOR BENEFIT PROGRAMS

Mandatory Programs

Social Security Retirement—Old Age and Survivors Insurance (OASI): Provides retirement income for workers age sixty-two and older, their spouses, surviving spouses, and dependents. Established in 1935, this program is funded with payroll taxes.

Social Security Disability Insurance (DI): Provides payments to workers meeting the definition of disability: "the inability to engage in any substantial gainful activity by reason of any medically determinable physical or mental impairment which can be expected to result in death or which has lasted or can be expected to last for a continuous period of not less than 12 months."[4] This program was established in 1956. A recipient's monthly benefits depend on annual earnings.

Supplemental Security Income (SSI): Provides assistance to the aged, blind, and disabled on a means-tested basis. The federal treasury funds this program. States can add on to benefits if they choose.

Unemployment insurance: This is actually a network of state and federal laws. Funded as a payroll tax, it provides payments based on a percentage of pay as long as the recipient is actually looking for work. The maximum length of this benefit is twenty-six weeks. Benefit levels vary from state to state.

Workers' compensation: This is a combination of state and federal programs. All states but New Jersey and Texas have a state-level employer-funded program that awards "cash and/or medical benefits to workers or beneficiaries of workers who are injured, become ill, or die while performing their job."[5] Thirty states and the federal government provide full coverage to all public sector workers. The other states cover some groups of workers, such as those working in hazardous occupations.

Voluntary Programs

Pensions

Defined benefit plans: A pension plan that pays a specified amount at retirement. The amount is usually based on an average highest salary and years of service.[6]

Defined contribution programs: A pension plan in which the contributions are a specified amount and the benefits at retirement are contingent on the accumulated value of the contributions. Defined contributions may include various plans used in conjunction with defined benefit plans.[7]

Health Care Plans

Fee for service: A traditional way of providing medical benefits in which individuals choose their medical provider and facility, and the plan reimburses either the individual or the provider for some or all of the cost.[8]

Preferred provider organizations: A type of fee for service that offers individuals "a higher benefit for services provided by a network of selected health care providers . . . although participants may choose any provider."[9]

Health maintenance organizations (HMOs): Prepaid services from a selected group of doctors and facilities.[10]

Selected Work-Life Programs

Family and Medical Leave Act of 1993 (FMLA): "Federal mandate to employers to provide up to 12 weeks of unpaid leave for the birth or adoption of a child and for family illness (employee, spouse, child or parent). Generally applies to employees with 1 year of service who work 1250 hours during the year and are employed by establishments with 50 or more workers."[11] The leave provided is unpaid. Paid family leave is much rarer, with only 4 percent of all state and local government employees having this type of benefit (see Table 10.2).

Table 10.2   Participation in Benefits Provided by State and Local Governments as Employers— Percentage of Full-Time Employees Participating[a] in Employee Benefit Programs: State and Local Governments,[b] 1994

Employee Benefit Program	All Employees	White Collar Employees[c]	Teachers	Blue Collar and Service Employees
Paid Leave				
Holidays	73%	86%	33%	91%
Vacations	66	84	9	91
Personal leave	38	30	58	31
Funeral leave	62	59	58	70
Jury duty leave	94	94	94	93
Military leave	75	80	61	82
Family leave	4	4	3	6
Unpaid Leave				
Family leave	93	93	96	90
Disability Benefits				
Short-term disability	95	94	97	96
paid sick leave	94	93	96	94
sickness and accident insurance	21	24	11	26
Long-term disability insurance	30	31	37	23
Survivor Benefits				
Life insurance	87	87	85	87
Accidental death and dismemberment	56	55	53	59
Survivor income benefits	2	1	3	2
Health Care Benefits				
Medical care	87	89	84	86
Dental care	62	62	59	66
Vision care	35	36	30	37
Outpatient prescription drug coverage	86	89	84	84
Retirement Income Benefits[d]				
All retirement[e]	96	96	97	95
defined benefit pension	91	90	93	91
defined contribution	9	10	7	9
types of plans				
savings and thrift	2	3	1	2
money purchase pension	7	7	5	7
cash or deferred arrangements				
with employer contributions	7	8	5	8
salary reduction	2	3	1	2
savings and thrift	2	3	1	2
money purchase pension	f	f	f	f
other[g]	5	5	3	6
no employer contributions	17	18	18	16
Other Benefits				
Flexible benefits plans[h]	5	5	7	3
Reimbursement accounts[h]	64	68	59	61

Source: U.S. Department of Labor, Bureau of Labor Statistics, *Employee Benefits in State and Local Governments, 1994* (Washington, DC: U.S. Government Printing Office, 1996).

[a] Includes workers covered but not yet participating due to minimum service requirements. Does not include workers offered but not electing contributory benefits.

[b] These tabulations provide representative data for full-time employees in state and local governments in all U.S. states and the District of Columbia. The estimate number of full-time workers employed by state and local governments was 12.9 million.

[c] Excludes teachers.

[d] Includes defined benefit pension plans and defined contribution retirement plans. Many employees participated in both types of plans.

[e] The total is less than the sum of the individual items because some employees participated in more than one type of plan.

[f] Less than 0.5 percent.

[g] Includes required contributions made to money purchase pension plans on a pretax basis.

[h] For flexible plans and reimbursement accounts, data represent percentage of eligible employees.

Flextime: Allows employees to set their own work hours while working a five-day work-week. Certain core hours are usually required.[12]

Compressed workweeks: A system in which employees work eighty hours in two weeks but in different formats from the usual eight-hour day; for example, four ten-hour days is a commonly administered program.[13]

Employee assistance programs: Offer counseling and referral services for various problems, including substance abuse, indebtedness, and emotional problems. These services are typically outsourced to protect the privacy of employees.[14]

Wellness programs: Offer first aid and emergency assessment, immunization screenings, smoking suppression, and health counseling.[15]

Fitness programs: Can consist of various options for physical fitness opportunities, including providing a room at the workplace for exercise or subsidizing gym membership.

Caregiver assistance programs: Include both child and elder care assistance and "can range from posting referral information to on-site care centers."[16]

Telecommuting: Workplace arrangements that allow an employee to work away from the traditional work site.

Flexible spending accounts: Allow employees to set aside a portion of their pre-tax income for dependent care or health care premiums.

Domestic partner benefits: Allow nonmarried partners of employees to qualify for certain health benefits. Many organizations require certification that the partners have cohabitated for a certain period of time and share living expenses.

Job sharing: Two or more employees split the responsibility for one job.[17]

WORK-LIFE PROGRAMS AS A MANAGEMENT TOOL

Many work-life programs began in response to the rapidly increasing number of women in the workforce. Employers recognized that increased flexibility in hours and opportunities to access and pay for child care were critical to attracting and retaining working women with children. These programs were generally referred to as being "family friendly." Eventually, however, employers saw that all types of employees, not just those with child care responsibilities, appreciated the benefits targeted as "family friendly." In fact, some childless employees began to demand access to the same workplace flexibility that those with children had been given.[18] This has led to the renaming of these programs as work-life programs because, as the National Academy of Public Administration put it, "everyone has a nonwork life but not everyone has family issues."[19]

The importance of the "nonwork life" aspect of personal existance relative to the work life aspect has been changing. A *U.S. News and World Report* study noted that nearly half of Americans had taken various steps such as cutting back hours spent at work and turning down or not seeking a promotion in order to protect their quality of life.[20] And a study of IBM workers reported that "work life programs [were] more important than any other employment consideration including compensation and salary."[21]

Employers have turned increasingly to providing work-life programs as they recognize the improved productivity that results.[22] There is also some evidence that flexibility in hours and benefits may be critical in the retention of good employees. For example, one study found that attrition rates for employees working under alternative work schedules (AWS) were half of those engaged in similar work without AWS.[23] Furthermore, employees working under AWS were found to be twice as productive as those on non-AWS schedules.[24] One business professor was quoted as saying, "Some [companies] are reporting that they get better applicants just because they offer good day care nearby or on site."[25]

Diversity and Benefits: Domestic Partnership Benefits

A contentious issue in benefits administration has been the debate over whether to extend various benefits such as health and life insurance to the partners of unmarried employees. This is often framed as a gay and lesbian rights issue; however, many corporations and jurisdictions allow "domestic partners" to include unmarried heterosexual couples.

Several states and as many as 165 cities and counties have passed laws or established policies allowing domestic partner benefits.[26] Most jurisdictions pose requirements to qualify for domestic partner benefits. They include such conditions as the stipulation that domestic partners not be related, that neither person is married to anyone else, and that the couple attest that they are living in a committed relationship. Some ordinances and policies require evidence of financial interdependence as well.[27]

The practical impact of domestic partner benefits policies on cities and states appears to be slight. A recent study of cities and counties offering domestic partner benefits found that only three of forty indicated that there had been an increase in the cost of insurance premiums for the jurisdiction.[28] Other studies show that the cost of domestic partner benefits is no greater than other spousal benefits, and that only 1 to 2 percent of employees take advantage of the plans when they are made available.[29]

Focus on Flexibility

One type of work-life program that has gained in popularity is the use of flexible work schedules. These schedules include allowing employees to arrive and depart from work at alternate times (earlier or later than traditionally) or may refer to compressed workweeks, in which employees work a regular forty-hour week over fewer days (for example, four ten-hour days). A 1994 survey of U.S. employers found that 66 percent offered some form of flexible work scheduling.[30] Of those

companies, 71 percent offered flextime, 65 percent offered part-time opportunities, 34 percent used job sharing, 21 percent used compressed workweeks, 14 percent had summer hours, and 5 percent reported some other form of flexible work hours arrangement.[31] An increasing number of employees are using flexible work arrangements. In 1997, 27.6 percent of U.S. workers were on flexible schedules, up from 15.1 percent in 1991.[32] Private sector employees are more likely to be on flexible schedules (28.8 percent) than public sector employees (21.7 percent).[33] Among levels of government, the federal government has more workers on flexible schedules (34.5 percent) than state (29.4 percent) or local governments (13.1 percent).[34]

Employers are using flexible work schedules as they realize that they can help retain and recruit valuable employees who need or want flexibility. Studies have indicated that flexible work schedules can increase productivity, decrease turnover, and reduce employee stress.[35] In addition, varying the hours that employees are in the office may allow the organization to offer more business hours of access to customers without paying overtime.[36]

Not every job or employee, however, is well suited to flexible work scheduling. Some jobs, for example, require intensive in-person contact and would therefore be less suitable for a compressed workweek schedule where the employee was present only four days a week. There are also limits to flexibility, since nearly every public sector organization and nonprofit agency will have core hours during which all or nearly all employees need to be present. Some employees—for example, those with small children in day care or those who become too exhausted from an extended workday—are not good candidates for a compressed workweek with ten-hour days.[37] A further concern for the organization in regard to compressed workweeks is to pay attention to how weeks with holidays will be handled, so that workers with compressed schedules continue to get the same amount of vacation and holiday time as those not on compressed schedules.[38]

All organizations should keep in mind some

practical concerns when considering adopting flexible scheduling: [39]*

- State and federal laws
- Length of company workday and workweek
- Core time
- Allowable starting and quitting times
- Eligibility
- Degree of individual flexibility
- Lunch hour
- Personal time off
- Carry-over hours
- Overtime
- Coverage and work flow
- Accountability (supervisory or supervisors to whom the employee reports)
- Enrollment process (how one applies for flexible scheduling)
- Evaluation process (how one's performance is evaluated)

A study of how to make flexible scheduling work recommended the following goals:[40]

- Ensure that flexible scheduling has the support of senior management and that this support is communicated throughout the organization.
- Build organizational support by defining and explaining the link between flexible scheduling and the goals of the organization.
- Develop pilot programs, and ensure middle management supports them sufficiently to permit a true assessment of their costs and benefits.
- Support managers and users of flextime by providing the tools they need to understand and use the program.
- Evaluate the effectiveness of the program while facilitating the sharing of case studies and models. If necessary, revise the system.
- Internalize the practice by incorporating

*The following list was reprinted from *Creating a Flexible Workplace*, 2/e by Barney Olmsted and Suzanne Smith. Copyright © 1994 *Amacom*, a division of American Management Association International. Reprinted by permission of the publisher, *Amacom* Books, a division of American Management Association International.

flextime into other organizational initiatives, expanding and refining HRM's role and assessing the acceptance and perceptions of these alternative arrangements.
- Sustain the commitment by continually communicating internally about issues relating to flextime.
- Implement accountability measures for the flextime system, evaluate the work environment, and make modifications accordingly.

Technology and Benefits: Telecommuting

One of the greatest advantages to come from the development of the personal computer, the modem, and wireless communication is the ability to allow workers to work from home or some other location away from the workplace. This flexibility can be invaluable to workers who, for a personal reason such as child care or injury, need to work from home. There are added advantages to metropolitan areas that are trying to encourage a reduction in commuting trips to reduce traffic congestion, improve air quality, and reduce energy use.[41]

The use of telecommuting has increased rapidly. The number of U.S. workers using technology to work from home rose to 15.7 million in 1998 according to a recent study.[42] This number includes contract and part-time workers, as well as full-time employees who telecommute.

While employees may enjoy the added flexibility provided by telecommuting options, successful implementation requires that organizations develop thoughtful policies regarding telecommuting. Because the employee's home becomes a remote work site, and therefore is subject to many of the same laws that govern safety in the main work area, one expert recommends "spelling out remote work policies and procedures."[43] The policy should include the following components:

- A policy statement spelling out the basic principles of the program
- Selection criteria for remote work candidates

- Limits on work time, required core hours and/or response times
- Who pays for what—equipment costs and insurance
- Designated work area for workers' compensation
- Timekeeping or reporting requirements
- Employer's right to inspect workplace upon reasonable advance notice (OSHA [Organizational Safety and Health Administration] requires a safe workplace)
- Monitoring rights of employer
- Protection of employer intellectual property
- Applicability of all existing employer policies and procedures to telecommuters
- Indemnification of employer
- Childcare arrangements
- Work expectations
- Performance measurement

As with other flexible benefits options, experts in this area stress the need to make it clear to employees that the benefit accorded to telecommute is indeed a benefit granted and not something to which they are entitled. Telecommuting should be offered to employees when it helps the organization achieve its performance goals.

CHALLENGES TO THE ADMINISTRATION OF BENEFITS

Cost

Employee benefits are among the fastest growing portions of the cost of compensation. In 1996, benefits were approximately 28 percent of compensation costs.[44] To compare, in 1929, fringe benefits were only 3 percent of the cost of compensation.[45] The cost of benefits is estimated to add two dollars per hour to the wage of service workers and eight dollars per hour to the wage of managers.[46]

Benefits packages are generally more costly in the public sector than in the private sector. For example, a private sector worker retiring after thirty years of service can expect to receive benefits equal to 30 percent of his or her ending income. A public sector worker with thirty years of service, in contrast, can expect to collect benefits equal to 50 percent of his or her income.[47] The rate of growth in the cost of benefits has been highest recently for state and local governments as opposed to the federal government or the private sector.[48] Although public sector employees have tried to compensate for less than competitive salaries by increasing benefit packages, the reluctance of Congress, state legislatures, and city councils to increase taxes may be a limitation to staying ahead of private sector benefit packages.[49]

Government forecasts indicate that spending on health care could double by the end of 2001 to $2.1 trillion overall.[50] The cost of health care continues to far outpace the cost of living. Health care costs were 6.6 percent of the cost of compensation in 1994, up from 2.0 percent in 1970.[51] The rising cost of health care benefits presents a challenge to employers that want to provide competitive benefits packages. This is especially important given that many applicants decide between accepting or declining a job offer depending on the content of the benefits package.[52] How can an organization continue to offer an attractive benefits package while controlling costs?

Many organizations focus on health care, since it represents a fast-growing portion of benefits costs. The increasing use of HMOs in the public sector is one way in which public sector employers are attempting to control health care costs. The Bureau of Labor Statistics reports that in 1994, 62 percent of full-time state and local government employees were covered by HMOs or preferred provider health plans, compared with 57 percent in 1992.[53] There are other methods as well to controlling health costs:

- Indexing financial incentives (e.g., copayments) to salaries
- Tying premiums to family size
- Encouraging changes to employees' high-risk behavior; (e.g., incentives for smoking cessation, regular exercise, etc.)

- Letting employees choose their benefits
- Establishing medical savings accounts[54]

Another way that organizations attempt to control the cost of benefits while continuing to offer the competitive levels and variety of benefits that employees have come to expect is through flexible benefits plans. A common version of a flexible benefits plan is known as a **cafeteria plan,** which allows participating employees to choose among a number of benefits and pay for them with pretax dollars.[55] Items included for employees to choose from are typically "group term life insurance, medical expense reimbursement, child care expenses and dental care expenses."[56] Some organizations include the education-related benefits (e.g., tuition reimbursement) that Daley discussed as part of their flexible benefits plan choices.[57] Cost is controlled by the establishment of a monetary limit to how much an employee may earn in benefits, but the choice among benefits allows employees to design a benefits package that best suits their personal situation—for example, child care for those with families and deferred tax annuities for those nearing retirement.

Bruzzese suggests that there are five key ingredients to implementing a flexible benefits plan successfully:[58]

1. *Organizational buy-in.* Employees will resist change, especially if change is away from 100 percent employer-paid coverage. Getting elected officials and unions behind the plan is critical.
2. *Plan design.* First, be consistent with organizational vision statements, values, and principles. Second, look at budget constraints and what the organization can afford, and, third, make sure that the existing payroll and HR systems can manage the plan design selected since it will include many new options.
3. *Pricing.* The organization must establish a fiscal framework of the flexible benefits plan that fits within its overall benefits budget.
4. *Administration.* Pay attention to enrollment processes, confirmation statements,

payroll, ongoing qualified family status changes, and flexible spending accounts administration.
5. *Communication.* Keep workers informed. One city that switched to a flexible benefits plan reported that it held employee information sessions up to thirty-five times the first year.[59]

Educating Employees and Managers About Benefits

In the chapter reading, Dennis Daley highlights the importance of communicating with employees about the worth of their benefits packages.[60] He points out that employees need to understand the value of their benefits package and recommends that organizations supply individualized reports outlining this information for each employee.[61] The importance of ongoing efforts to educate employees about their benefits packages is noted by one study of employees' perceptions of their benefits packages that found that many thought they had benefits to which they did not actually have access.[62]

Educating employees about benefits is especially important if the organization has recently made substantial changes in its benefits offerings. The change to flexible benefits is a good example of a major change. Fort Collins, Colorado, took several steps to make sure that the city's new flexible benefits plan was implemented successfully.[63] First, managers made sure that employee input was gathered about the plan by having a benefits committee, comprising people from different departments, help design the plan and facilitate its implementation. Second, a representative from each department took responsibility for educating the employees in that department and making sure that the correct forms were available and turned in on schedule. Third, many information sessions were held so employees could learn about the new benefits available to them. Finally, easy access to the information was a key part of their efforts. This included voice mail updates on plan changes. Other ways to educate employees include newsletters, e-mail updates, and "enrollment kits that have 'how to' workbook forms and other information about open enrollment dates, meetings, etc."[64]

Employees are not the only workers who need to be educated about the organization's benefits package. Managers who must implement scheduling with alternative work schedules or determine whether an employee's absence qualifies under the Family and Medical Leave Act (FMLA) need training and education about the organization's benefits also. One study found that 88 percent of New York State personnel administrators found that record keeping after the FMLA was implemented to be "very difficult" or "somewhat difficult."[65] These personnelists found that communication between supervisors and employees about the FMLA policy was critical.[66] Given the importance the benefits can have in recruitment, it is also important that managers have a working understanding of the benefits packages to which new employees will have access.

Ethics and Benefits: Managing Paid Leave

As Table 10.2 on page 273 illustrates, there are many forms of paid leave: holidays, vacation, personal leave, funeral leave, jury duty leave, military leave, and family leave. Some forms are quite common; for example, 94 percent of state and local government employees receive jury duty leave. Others, like paid family leave, are quite rare, with only 4 percent of state and local government receiving that particular benefit in 1994 (see Table 10.2).

Unscheduled absences can be quite costly for organizations since employee salaries must still be paid and there is often a need for additional salary for coverage of the absent employee and/or a loss in productivity. A 1998 survey of public and private organizations found that the "rate of unscheduled absences had increased by 25% from the previous year and that dollars lost to absenteeism had increased by 32% since last year."[67] Absenteeism among government employees in-

creased 14 percent from 1997.[68] The chief reason given by employees for taking unscheduled absences in that 1998 survey were family issues (26 percent), personal illness (22 percent), personal needs (20 percent), stress (16 percent), and entitlement—the belief that they should get to take all sick days allotted whether or not they are ill (16 percent).[69]

One form of paid leave that can be the cause of controversy in an organization is paid sick leave. Although nearly all public sector employees have access to sick leave, potential problems arise when sick leave is the only form of paid leave available. Unscheduled needs to be absent from work—for example, for a medical appointment or to care for a sick child—must then be taken as sick leave, even though the employee is not actually ill. This not only encourages dishonesty in reporting, but results in more time taken off than is really necessary. Abuse of sick leave can be lessened by first developing a clear policy that "specifies the organization's standards and employee requirements."[70] Smith recommends the following steps for dealing with sick leave abuse:

(1) Recognize the problem and intervene early; (2) Find out why the employee is abusing leave. If there is a personal problem refer them to the organization's EAP (Employee Assistance Program); (3) Learn to say no to requests for leave when they are inappropriate; (4) Document everything; and, (5) Learn from past mistakes.[71]

The addition of a category of personal leave, which can be used for any purpose, or the combination of personal leave and sick leave gives the employee more flexibility over the use of unscheduled paid leave and tends to have a positive impact on employee morale.[72] Incentives to encourage employees not to use more personal or sick leave than they need can also help hold down the costs of benefits. These incentives may include cash payments for unused sick leave or cash for unused sick leave available at retirement or paid time off given in another form.[73] These incentive programs should be checked to make sure they do not violate the Americans with Disabilities Act. In addition, the organization should be mindful that these types of incentive programs may unintentionally punish parents with small children who must use more sick leave for family issues than employees without children.[74]

▩ CONCLUSION

Benefits will continue to be an important and costly part of the total compensation package. As health care costs continue to escalate, organizations will look for ways to provide access to health care yet control its proportion of the cost of benefits. The need to care for increasing numbers of aging parents and the presence of working parents all point to the importance of giving employees a variety of benefits from which to choose that will best fit their life situation. Benefits have been shown to have positive impacts on productivity, retention, and morale. They are a critical part of the compensation package, not just on the fringe anymore.

▩ MANAGER'S VOCABULARY

work-life programs
Social Security Retirement—Old Age and Survivors Insurance (OASI)
Social Security Disability Insurance (DI)
Supplemental Security Income (SSI)
unemployment insurance
workers' compensation
defined benefit plans
defined contribution programs
fee for service
preferred provider organizations
health maintenance organizations (HMOs)
Family and Medical Leave Act of 1993 (FMLA)
flextime
compressed workweeks
employee assistance program
wellness programs
fitness programs
caregiver assistance programs
telecommuting
flexible spending accounts
domestic partner benefits
job sharing
cafeteria plan

▩ STUDY QUESTIONS

1. About what portion of the total compensation package is devoted to benefits?

2. Why are benefits different between the public and private sectors?

3. How can an organization use benefits as part of its recruitment and retention efforts?

4. What are some of the ways that managers can cut down on abuse of sick leave?

▩ EXPERIENTIAL EXERCISES

1. You are the Director of the licensing division of the County Department of Motor Vehicles, which employs fifteen clerks and a shift supervisor. The work is highly stressful, with constant direct contact with the public. In general, your crew is highly efficient and handles customer relations well. You have found that it takes considerable time to train a new employee. When compiling time sheets for a monthly report, you notice that one of your most valuable employees has been submitting sick leave reports every Friday for the past several months. When you inquire about this, she admits that she has not actually been ill, but has had to miss work every Friday in order to attend a series of meetings with her attorney con-

PINAL COUNTY EMPLOYEE BENEFITS WORKSHEET FOR PLAN YEAR 2000

BENEFIT OPTIONS   ANNUAL PREMIUM

LIFE INSURANCE (Required)
$10,000 Basic Life, AD&D, and Basic Dependent Life $ ____40.00____

MEDICAL PLAN
Pinal County Medical (BCBS of AZ Network)

Employee Only	$ 2,420	Employee and Children	$ 3,750
Employee and Spouse	$ 4,430	Employee and Family	$ 5,500

$ _____

DENTAL PLANS
Extended Dental   **Basic Dental**

Employee Only	$ 276	Employee Only	$ 89
Employee and Family	$ 732	Employee and Family	$ 191

$ _____

VISION PLAN
Pinal County Vision

Employee Only	$ 60
Employee and Family	$ 120

$ _____

EMPLOYEE ASSISTANCE PROGRAM
Employee and Family $ 0 $ ___NO CHARGE___

EMPLOYEE SUPPLEMENTAL LIFE INSURANCE
Coverage in addition to the Basic Life Insurance—up to $350,000—in $5,000 increments.
Complete the following steps to calculate the annual premium.
  1. Determine the Annual Cost Factor from the chart below based on your age as of January 1 of the Plan Year.
  2. Divide the additional coverage amount by $1,000.
  3. Multiply the Annual Cost Factor in Step 1 and the Additional Coverage in Step 2 to determine the premium.

Age	Annual Cost Factor	Age	Annual Cost Factor
Under 30	.48	55–59	6.36
30–39	.72	60–64	7.20
40–44	1.32	65–69	12.24
45–49	2.16	70–74	21.48
50–54	4.08	75–85	33.48

_____ X $_____ = $_____
Annual Cost Factor   Coverage Amount ÷ $1,000

SHORT TERM DISABILITY
Complete the following steps to calculate the annual premium.
  1. Determine the Annual Cost Factor for the chart below based on your age as of January 1 of the Plan Year.
  2. Indicate your Annual Salary.
  3. Multiply the Annual Cost Factor and Annual Salary to determine your Annual Premium.
  Example: Joe, age 24, has an annual salary of $15,000 (Multiply .0056 and $15,000 = $84.00 Annual Premium)

Age	Annual Cost Factor
Under 40	.0056
40–49	.0086
50 and over	.0150

_____ X $_____ = $_____
Annual Cost Factor   Annual Salary

FLEXIBLE SPENDING ACCOUNT
*Combined Maximum County Benefit Contribution for Flex is $2,000.00
HEALTH CARE FLEXIBLE SPENDING ACCOUNT (see Benefits Booklet)
*Maximum Benefit Contribution is $2,000. $ _____
DAY CARE FLEXIBLE SPENDING ACCOUNT (see Benefits Booklet)
*Maximum Contribution is $5,000 per family. $ _____

- -

1. **Total Employee Premiums** (Total of ALL preceding benefits selected) $ _____
2. **Minus Pinal County Employee Benefit Allowance** $ __−2,640.00__
3. **Employee Annual Premium Deduction and Contribution**   = $ _____ **

Dependent Supplemental Life (This benefit may not be purchased with the County Benefit Allowance.)
All Eligible Dependents–Spouse $5,000 and Children $1,000 each. $25.00 $ _____
                                                                              .96 Per Payroll

Total Bi-Weekly Payroll Deduction (Divide the Annual Premium** by 26) $ _____
                                                                              Per Payroll
Your Plan Year is 1/1/2000 thru 12/31/2000

Source: This information was graciously provided by Mike Arnold, Pinal County human resource director, July 3, 2000.

cerning a custody battle over her young child. She reports that sick leave was her only option under county personnel rules and that her supervisor, who is a stickler for procedure, will not allow her to leave early because "it wouldn't be fair to the other girls." You are concerned about several issues. First, you are worried that using sick leave when not actually ill is unethical. Second, you are worried that you may lose a valuable employee. At the same time, you know that being shorthanded every Friday is a hardship on other employees. You ask your department head for a meeting about this issue, and she tells you to have several suggestions ready when you meet next week. What solutions might you suggest to resolve this dilemma?

2. You are a new employee of Pinal County in Arizona, which offers its employees a cafeteria-style benefit plan. The benefits worksheet on page 281 is a part of the county's plan. The county will contribute $2,640 per year to spend on your total package. Any additional costs will be deducted from your paycheck.

   a. Which benefits will you select as part of your coverage?

   b. How would your choices differ if you were fifty-five years old as opposed to twenty-five years old?

   c. What sort of educational program would you want the city to provide to you to help you make these selections?

■ CASES APPLICABLE TO THIS CHAPTER

"Flextime" and "A Family and Medical Leave Act Puzzler."

■ NOTES

1. Patricia J. Fredericksen, "Benefit Packaging and Employee Retention: The Constraints of Job Sector" (paper presented at the annual meeting of the Western Political Science Association, Seattle, Washington, March 25–27, 1999).

2. Employee Benefit Research Institute (EBRI), *Fundamentals of Employee Benefit Programs,* 5th ed. (Washington, D.C.: Employee Benefit Research Institute, 1997), pp. 363–366.

3. Ibid., p.365.

4. Ibid., p. 437.

5. Ibid., p. 421.

6. Sally A. Zinno, "Employee Related Benefits," in Tracy Daniel Connor, ed., *Nonprofit Management Handbook,* 2nd ed. (New York: Wiley, 1997).

7. Ibid.

8. Bureau of Labor Statistics Reports, 1994.

9. Ibid.

10. Ibid.

11. Ibid.

12. National Academy for Public Administration (NAPA),

Work/Life Programs: Helping Managers, Helping Employees (Washington, D.C.: NAPA, 1998), p. 24.

13. Ibid., p. 22.

14. Ibid., p. 24.

15. Ibid.

16. Ibid., p. 25

17. Genevieve Capowski, "The Joy of Flex," *Management Review* (March 1996): 14.

18. Gillian Flynn, "Backlash," *Personnel Journal* (September 1996): 59–69.

19. NAPA, *Work/Life Programs,* p. 9.

20. Quoted in ibid., p. 17.

21. Quoted in ibid., p. 19.

22. Charles Marner Solomon, "Flexibility Comes Out of Flux," *Personnel Journal* (June 1996): 34–43.

23. Quoted in ibid., p. 23.

24. Quoted in ibid.

25. Gail Dutton, "Warming the Cold Heart of Business," *Management Review* (June 1997): 18.

26. Stephanie L. Witt and W. David Patton, "Gay Rights and the City: Initiatives, Ordinances and Personnel Policies" (paper presented at the Annual Meeting of the Western Political Science Association, Los Angeles, March 1998).

27. For an excellent review of the qualifications for domestic partner benefits, see Charles W. Gossett, "Domestic Partnership Benefits," *Review of Public Personnel Administration* 14 (Winter 1994).

28. Witt and Patton, "Gay Rights," p. 3.

29 Dawn Anfuso, "Consider Cost, Controls and Reasons for Implementing Domestic Partner Benefits," *Personnel Journal* (February 1997): 97.

30 Solomon, "Flexibility Comes out of Flux," p. 36.

31 Ibid.

32 USDL-BLS 98–119 Workers on Flexible and Shift Schedules in 1997 Summary, available at: **http://stats.bls.gov/newsrels.htm.**

33 Ibid.

34 Ibid.

35 Solomon, "Flexibility Comes out of Flux," p. 35.

36 Maureen Smith, "Compressed Workweeks: A Working Solution?" *IPMA News* (June 1999): 16.

37 Ibid.

38 Ibid.

39 Capowski, "Joy of Flex," p. 18.

40 Solomon, "Flexibility Comes out of Flux," p. 42.

41 NAPA, *Work/Life Programs,* p. 28.

42 Working Moms Refuge "Telecommuting Boosted in 1998 by Internet and Economy," available at: **http://www.momsrefuge.com/telecommute/survey.html.**

43 The following information is drawn from June Langhoff "Telecommuting and the Law," International Telework Association and Council, available at: **http://www.telecommute.org/Publications/tclaw.htm.**

44 Patricia J. Frederickson and Dennis L. Soden, "Employee Attitudes Toward Benefit Packaging," *Review of Public Personnel Administration* 18 (Summer 1998): 24.

45 Chester Levine, "Employee Benefits: Growing in Diversity and Cost," *Occupational Outlook Quarterly* 37 (Winter 1993–1994): 38–42.

46 Ibid., p. 42.

47 Kenneth Silverstein, "Public Private Benefits: Is Less More?" *American City and County* 110:13 (1995): 12.

48 Ibid.

49 Frederickson and Soden, "Employee Attitudes," p. 24.

50 "Cost of Health Care Could Double by 2001," *IPMA News* (March 1999): 3.

51 EBRI, *Fundamentals,* p. 251.

52 Levine, "Employee Benfits," pp. 38–42.

53 Bureau of Labor Statistics, *BLS Reports on Employee Benefits in State and Local Governments, 1994* (Washington, D.C.: U.S. Department of Labor, Bureau of Labor Statistics, 1995), p. 1.

54 Richard E. McDermott and Joan Ogden, "Five Ways to Improve Your Health Benefits," *HR Magazine* 40 (August 1995): 44–48.

55 Anita Bruzzese, "Be Flexible," *Public HR,* February 26, 1999, p. 46.

56 Ibid.

57 Dennis M. Daley, "An Overview of Benefits for the Public Sector: Not on the Fringes Anymore," *Review of Public Personnel Administration* 18 (Summer 1998): 19.

58 This section draws heavily on Bruzzese, "Be Flexible," pp. 48, 53.

59 Ibid., p. 48.

60 Daly, "Overview of Benefits," p. 20.

61 Ibid., p. 21.

62 Frederickson and Soden, "Employee Attitudes," p. 37.

63 Fort Collins's experience is detailed in Bruzzese, "Be Flexible," pp. 48, 53.

64 Ibid., p. 53.

65 Soon Hee Kim, "Administering Family Leave Benefits and New Challenges for Public Personnel Management," *Review of Public Personnel Administration* 18 (Summer 1998): 48.

66 Ibid.

67 "1998 Unscheduled Absence Survey," *IPMA News* (June 1999): 18.

68 Ibid., p. 20.

69 Ibid., p. 19.

70 Maureen Smith, "Sick Leave Policies: When Does Use Become Abuse?" *IPMA News* (June 1999): 17.

71 Ibid., p. 18.

72 Dawn Anfuso, "Offering Personal Time Rather Than Sick Leave Raises Morale," *Personnel Journal* (May 1995): 126.

73 Rolf E. Rogers and Stephen R. Herting, "Patterns of Absenteeism Among Government Employees," *Public Personnel Management* 22 (Summer 1993): 223.

74 Smith, "Sick Leave Policies," p. 17.

CHAPTER 11

Performance Management

A principal theme that runs throughout this book is the need to integrate human resource management and line management activities in organizations; the task of assessing **performance** is one area where this need stands out particularly clearly. Continuing calls for public sector reform typically highlight private sector approaches to managing productivity. Monitoring performance within organizations through the performance appraisal process represents "a conscientious effort at formally, rationally and objectively organizing our assessment of others."[1] The traditional supervisor-subordinate **performance appraisal** activity is being scrutinized in terms of its utility for contemporary public administration. Increasingly a more comprehensive, systemic approach to performance is lauded as the best means to leverage individual and group achievement toward organizational purposes. While there is general agreement on the value of a systemic approach, there is no clear consensus as to which appraisal techniques and processes are the most effective or what the most appropriate protocol for merging performance assessment with other human resource activities might look like.

As with most of what we know about the dynamic nature of human resource management, we sometimes face more questions than answers about philosophy, structure, technique, and purpose. Performance assessment is no exception to this general problem. Should we consider performance appraisal as a special set of activities managed by a human resource department to maintain a uniform appraisal system for the whole organization?

Should performance assessment instead be limited to a dyadic process occurring between employees and their supervisors? Should performance assessment retain a focus on documenting past efforts to reward or punish, or should it be viewed as a means of enhancing future productivity? Should performance assessment be limited to what is accomplished by individuals, or should we consider work groups, departments, or entire organizations as the proper unit of analysis? Should performance assessment be a distinct activity, or should it occur as a component of an entire system of assessing, managing, and improving individual and group performance to contribute to organizational productivity? Should we even assess performance, or should we focus only on dealing with employees who have recognized deficiencies? Can we even agree on what is commendable performance?

In this chapter, we review the techniques in common use for the traditional **supervisor-subordinate performance appraisal.** This review describes the different instruments in common use and discusses the methods and logic employed in these dyadic appraisals. The importance of the appraiser in this process is a necessary part of this discussion, and many of the problems that can ensue are addressed here, along with recommendations for reducing error in the appraisal process. We move beyond traditional dyadic appraisals and consider less traditional approaches such as 360-degree evaluation. In addition, we discuss performance from a broader perspective and consider productivity paradigms, reform efforts, and organizationwide performance issues.

With the reading later in this chapter, the larger questions about performance present in the public and nonprofit sectors emerge. The improvement of performance in public organizations and the contracting of nonprofit organizations requires the consideration of several questions. What is an appropriate level of performance to aim for over time? Who will appraise the performance achieved? Who will be appraised? For what purpose will we assess performance?

PERFORMANCE APPRAISAL TECHNIQUES

The methods used to assess the character and contributions of an employee vary greatly, so identifying a typical performance appraisal process is impossible. These many approaches to performance appraisal can best be discussed in the context of what in particular is being assessed about the employee: his or her traits, achievements, or bank of competencies. The assessment of traits, achievements, and competencies is predicated on the assumption that these factors are in some manner indicative of the person's execution of work tasks, activities, and responsibilities. Performance levels are usually differentiated according to whether performance in a position is proficient, sufficient, or insufficient when compared to a set standard. Unfortunately, in many settings performance assessment may be neither constructive in outcome nor reliable in its content. The standard against which employees are judged may be ambiguous. The rationale for assessment may be inconsistent with the mission, goals, and objectives of the organization. The commitment of appraisers to do a good job of appraisal may vary in strength.

Performance Appraisal Approaches

Trait-based appraisal Although the phrases *employee evaluation* and *performance appraisal* are often used interchangeably, traditional employee evaluation implies an assessment of an employee's personal traits and characteristics rather than the quality of execution of job responsibilities.

Unfortunately, many performance appraisals focus less on performance than on traits (e.g., personality traits and other psychological indicators), which may be only loosely linked to performance. In essence, it is not unusual to find that organizations assess the employee rather than this person's effort, skill level, or contribution to the organization. Although it is often criticized in the professional literature, **trait-based appraisal** remains quite common in all job sectors. Indeed, trait-based employee assessments are often rooted in trait-based predictors used in the recruitment and selection process.[2] Assessment of personal characteristics has been used to discern among applicants for positions, so employee assessment based on personal traits is a somewhat logical progression. If we can consider personal traits and characteristics to be predictive of later employee performance, then the logic follows that we could later somehow assess traits to segregate out the relative value of employee contributions to the organization.

Trait-based assessment suggests that we can identify general traits that are associated with proficient performance in a particular position and identify traits associated with insufficient performance. The sample trait assessment format set out in Figure 11.1 on page 286 features a list of traits commonly used to assess police patrol officer performance. These traits are then assessed in terms of a range of descriptors.

Achievement-based appraisal **Achievement-based appraisal** considers performance in terms of the level of achievement of duties, with some position-based criteria used to differentiate among several levels of achievement. The employee's position description serves as the foundational document for these assessments. The activities necessary to discharge the obligations of a particular position (or class of positions) are detailed. The appraisal hinges on the responsibilities of the position and a scale of achievement in terms of levels of proficiency, sufficiency, and insufficiency. In Figure 11.2 on page 287, the sample appraisal instrument for a patrol officer still identifies per-

Figure 11.1 Sample Trait-Based Appraisal Instrument for a Patrol Officer

For each officer, the supervisor must indicate the appropriate assessment using the scale below.

Trait	Always Outstanding	Excellent	Good/Acceptable	Not Acceptable	Fails to Demonstrate
Dependability					
Attendance					
Cooperation					
Initiative					
Health					
Appearance					
Courage					
Supervisor Comments:					
Employee Comments:					

sonal traits or characteristics such as initiative and appearance, but these are now linked to certain behaviors that serve to demonstrate expected performance. Many achievement-based performance assessments offer the advantage of shifting evaluation from a person to the person's performance. The intent remains to examine (and either reward or punish) past behavior.

In recent years performance appraisal techniques have shifted primary focus to the management of performance. Although prior accomplishments are still examined, these efforts are considered in the context of performance goals established at the beginning of the performance appraisal period. Ideally, the employee and his or her supervisor (or other appropriate parties) would develop these performance goals in consideration of the organization's goals and mission and the activities of others. The instrument displayed in Figure 11.3 extends the assessment to specific goals for performance.

Competency-based appraisal The attention of many personnelists and managers has moved to the demonstration of skill or competence as a means to assess the contributions being made by employees. The guiding presumption is that the more varied and sophisticated the employee's skill set is, the

greater is his or her capacity for leveraging those skills toward achieving the organization's goals. An employee's **competency-based appraisal** could vary according to the amount of knowledge the person holds about a particular function (**depth of skill**) or the expanse of knowledge he or she holds about related responsibilities and activities (**breadth of skill**).[3] In addition, employees could be assessed in terms of the potential managerial applications of their skills (**vertical skills**).[4] Skill sets and competencies offer a useful base for allocating resources and rewards in organizations, but require some reliable instruments and processes for assessing the relative competency levels of employees.[5] Greater attention to the importance of measuring and managing employee skills affirms both the importance of employee skill sets as a means to improve organization performance and the utility of training investments.[6]

Performance Appraisal Instruments

Appraisal instruments may employ a combination of trait, achievement, and competency assessments and a variety of methods to identify, measure, and assess employees relative to some standard. Here we look at the most common methods.

Figure 11.2   Sample Achievement-Based Appraisal Instrument for a Patrol Officer

For each officer, the supervisor must indicate the appropriate assessment using the scale below.

	Outstanding	Acceptable	Needs Improvement	Unsatisfactory
Initiative	Seeks and sets additional tasks; shows ingenuity; excellent at problem solving	Resourceful; completed suggested and supplemental work	Routine response; waits for calls; may not follow up	Needs direction and prodding to complete assigned tasks
Attitude toward citizens	Courteous and respectful; takes direction; considerate; demonstrates collaborative approach to problem solving	Respectful and courteous	Shows little respect; addresses community concerns grudgingly	Poor attitude; impatient with citizen concerns
Appearance	Takes pride in shoeshine; equipment is maintained and properly worn; uniform is pressed	Favorable appearance; generally tidy, with appropriate equipment and uniform	Neglectful of appearance; uniform may be unpressed; improper uniform for tasks	Unkempt; slovenly; stained uniform; equipment missing
Ability to take direction	Readily completes assignments; questions are appropriate to address clarity and comprehension	Requires additional information only to complete orders	Can carry out simple orders but needs direction for complex tasks	Clueless
Written communication skills	Excellent reports that are well written, completed on time, and understandable; demonstrates mastery of grammar, spelling, and structure; no errors	Satisfactory; few errors; generally literate	Incomplete reports; demonstrates a lack of understanding of basic writing	Fundamentally illiterate; cannot communicate in a written form

Figure 11.3   Sample Achievement-Based Appraisal Instrument for a Patrol Office Extended to Specific Goals for Performance

For each officer, the supervisor must indicate the appropriate assessment using the previously established goals listed below.

Performance Goal	Goal Weight	Achieved Goal	Exceeded Goal	Did Not Achieve Goal	Comments
Achieve a 20 percent reduction in calls for service response time for Area I					
Reduce reported incidents of school-related vandalism by 10 percent					
Attend 12 public meetings to address citizen concerns and suggest problem-solving strategies					

Graphic rating A **graphic rating performance assessment instrument** employs a scale of assessment responses, similar to the formats used in survey research dealing with attitudes. This is a fairly simple and speedy method. The appraiser completes a scale that represents the qualitative or quantitative degree to which the employee displays a particular trait, masters a specific skill, or discharges a given duty. These rating methods are often used with trait-based assessments, as depicted in Figure 11.1. They are the most useful when the points along the scale are defined in terms of what the different scale scores mean.

Ranking In the **ranking performance assessment instrument,** employees are assessed in terms of their merits relative to those of other employees. Are the employees in the top quartile of all employees with regard to a particular trait, achievement, or competency, or do they belong in the bottom quartile? An assessor using ranking would look at all police officers in a unit using the sample form displayed in Figure 11.1 and then rank each officer in comparison to the others according to how well he or she rates on each trait. There may be a decision that only 10 percent of officers can receive "Outstanding" and 10 percent should receive "Failure."

This exercise looks a lot like the normal curve discussion that may occur in grading models for some college and university courses. One rationale for ranking is that this method forces the appraiser to differentiate among employees rather than assign all subordinates similar (and usually high) ratings.

Forced choice As with the ranking instrument, the **forced-choice performance assessment instrument** requires the appraiser to choose between employee pairings, selecting the employee in the pairing whose traits, competencies, or performance of duties is superior. Forced-choice methods are intended to avoid generic descriptions of employees by requiring raters to make some relative assessment of what each employee does in comparison to others. Potentially one could then assess areas in which the employee

may need counseling or require additional training, or deserve to be rewarded or recognized. In the forced-choice model in Figure 11.4, the appraiser is asked to designate the most common actions and least common actions evidenced by a particular teacher relative to other teachers. This method of performance appraisal can be used with trait, achievement, or competency-based appraisals.

Behaviorally anchored rating scales Similar to the graphic rating scales, **behaviorally anchored rating scales** (BARS) aid the appraiser by offering degrees of achievement that can be used to assess an employee. However, instead of a focus on personal traits, BARS processes direct attention to overt indicators of performance derived from a particular position description. The appraisal sample displayed in Figure 11.2 provides some guidance as to the range of behaviors that may be associated with a particular trait or skill.

BARS instruments are complex and time-consuming to develop for each type of position in an organization. They are so closely linked to an employee's position description that if that description changes, so must the appraisal instrument. For example, as police organizations have embraced the philosophy of community-oriented policing, officers' responsibilities have been broadened from crime control to encompass crime prevention as well. This police services philosophy results in a fairly dramatic change in an officer's position description (or would if it were updated), and the BARS performance appraisal instrument would change accordingly.

Essay Attempts to address the limitations of graphic scales and overcome some of the rigidity of the ranking method have led to either the inclusion of essay sections in many appraisal instruments or the complete replacement of graphic scales with a narrative essay. Thus, in **essay performance assessment instruments,** appraisers have the opportunity to outline achievements, point out extraordinary conditions or events affecting the person being rated, and suggest the importance of particular skills or traits that an employee can leverage to accomplish organizational goals. If

Figure 11.4   Forced-Choice Performance Assessment Instrument for a Teacher

Performance Categories	Select the strategy MOST COMMONLY used by the educator for each performance category:	Select the strategy LEAST COMMONLY used by the educator for each performance category:
Instructional strategies	Provides opportunities for students to participate actively and successfully: • Varies activities appropriately • Interacts with groups appropriately • Solicits student participation • Extends responses and contributions • Provides time for response and consideration • Implements at appropriate level Evaluates and provides feedback on student progress during instruction: • Communicates learning expectations • Monitors student performance • Solicits responses and demonstrations for assessment • Reinforces correct response and performances • Provides corrective feedback and clarifies • Repetitive review or none needed	Provides opportunities for students to participate actively and successfully: • Varies activities appropriately • Interacts with groups appropriately • Solicits student participation • Extends responses and contributions • Provides time for response and consideration • Implements at appropriate level Evaluates and provides feedback on student progress during instruction: • Communicates learning expectations • Monitors student performance • Solicits responses and demonstrations for assessment • Reinforces correct response and performances • Provides corrective feedback and clarifies • Repetitive review or none needed

the appraiser is skilled in written communication, essay instruments serve to individualize an appraisal, reflecting considerations about an employee that might not be conveyed in uniform formats such as a rating scale or forced-choice instrument. Appraisal instruments often include narrative sections as a direct reflection of the need for context and situational factors affecting quantitative ratings. Examples include sections to justify a rating, provide an overall assessment of the employee, or include employee comments regarding the assessment made of his or her performance.

Objective/goal In the case of the **objective/goal performance assessment instrument,** the appraiser focuses on some previously established goals or objectives for which the employee is responsible. The appraisal then examines the extent to which the employee was able to meet these goals. Although these appraisals are often achievement-based, the goals may be directly re-

lated to the acquisition of a skill or development of a trait. For example, an employee might have developed a set of performance goals for the coming year. Some of these goals could relate to a particular set of achievements (e.g., developing a web page to communicate crime statistics to a community or presenting research to a fixed number of civic groups). Other goals may be linked to the acquisition or enhancement of certain skills (e.g., training in computer software). It may be that other goals are linked to traits (e.g., improved clarity in verbal communication or an improved physical fitness rating). The method assumes that there is some benchmark for an employee and that successful employees will improve their personal characteristics, exceed previous accomplishments, or enhance their skills.

Critical incident In the case of the **critical incident** method, the appraiser is asked to develop a sample of activities, events, and incidents from a certain period of time for an employee. Using this sample, the appraiser considers these vignettes as evidence of whether the employee meets some identified performance standard. The BARS approach is often based on a critical incident study for various groups of employees doing similar work. The performance standards used to assess employee performance are derived from focus group sessions and survey analysis among employees doing substantially equivalent work.

Ethical Issues in Performance Management

In search of the best approach to performance management, it may be too easily forgotten that ultimately performance management is all about people and their relationships with each other in the context of their work. Two examples serve to illustrate the danger of excessively objectifying employees in this complex and subtle process.

First, can employees simply become objects to be manipulated through performance management systems? The premise behind the **management by objectives** (MBO) performance model is that managers, in collaboration with their employees, can establish objectives for employees that will serve as a baseline for assessing performance at the end of a given time period (usually six months or a year). This model assumes that the objectives decided on are both achievable and challenging. Can the same concerns about rater bias be applied to the establishment of the performance objectives? Is there anything wrong with methodically establishing high performance standards to weed out "low performers"? Are long-term organizational goals necessarily enhanced by the constant raising of the bar for employees?

Second, software applications have been developed that are designed to streamline the appraisal process, particularly for large organizations. With the best intentions of the programmers, it appears that although the computerization of performance management can offer some advantages in terms of the elaborate data collection possible, it may sacrifice the critical interpersonal dynamics aspect of an effective performance management system. Reliance on performance assessments through computers may limit the communication and careful individualized assessment of a person's work effort. Sayre's caution that human resource management could result in a "triumph of technique over purpose" could easily have been written in response to the boom in computer-based human resource management.

Appraising the Performance of Appraisers

All performance appraisal methods depend on the skills and training of the appraiser. In general, the appraiser's written and verbal communication skills contribute to the utility of the appraisal. In addition, the knowledge that the appraiser has of the employee's position, responsibilities, background, and abilities can contribute to whether the appraisal is general and vague or whether it is specific and directly relevant to the demands of a particular job. Certainly, the object of the appraisal—traits, competencies, or achievements—will drive the composition of the instrument and ultimately determine how closely it might be linked to some organizational definition of higher versus lower performance. Finally, in the ideal situation, appraisers are able to consider objectively the contributions that different employees make to the organization. Unfortunately, appraisers are seldom perfectly objective or innately skilled and may not be able to assess performance accurately. Personal bias, selective memory, and unreliable assessment measures can limit the utility of many assessment programs. Here we look at the most common problems encountered in appraisal.

Personal bias **Personal bias** may occur when an appraiser holds a negative view of the employee that is not related to job performance. The source of disdain (e.g., racism, sexism, or personality conflict) can vary, but in these situations, employees are assessed in an unfavorable light regardless of their actual achievements, personal characteristics, or skills. The reverse may be true as well. Some appraisers may try to compensate for their feelings toward an employee by offering an unrealistically positive assessment of the employee's contributions. Although we often use the term *bias* to suggest malicious differentiation, the appraiser may be unaware that he or she is assigning more positive assessments of employee performance than might be warranted.

Halos and horns The "**halo effect**" occurs when the employee can do no wrong in the eyes of the appraiser.[7] In this case, the appraiser will assess everything that an employee does positively. This may be due to the kindness and compassion of the rater, but could also be linked to whether the appraiser likes the employee or seeks to address past inequities. This bias is quite common because appraisers are generally reluctant to record a negative assessment of performance.[8] Conversely, the "**horns effect**" occurs when an employee is always assessed more stringently, either out of dislike or from a desire to appear tough or demanding to employees and/or supervisors.

Constant error In some cases, appraisals conducted by a particular individual are generally considered to be either too harsh or too lenient; this is referred to as **constant error.** The accuracy of an employee's appraisal is evaluated in terms of the appraiser rather than the employee. We may see this in academic settings when one instructor is considered to be especially demanding and critical and another is considered to be an "easy A." Either way, there is an assumption that the employee (or the student) did not merit the appraisal (or grade) received.

Recency effect The **recency effect** could occur using most methods, but may be especially problematic on instruments using the more open formats found in the essay and critical incident methods. With the recency effect, the appraiser may be biased by actions or events (positive or negative) occurring closer to the appraisal point, while other relevant events would have receded from consideration.

Central tendency Rating employees to the average, often called **central tendency,** is a response

to several factors. Appraisers may have difficulty ranking employees according to the assessment criteria, may be pressed for time, or may have a predilection for equity in all such interpersonal judgment situations. Regardless of the rationale, central tendency occurs when employees are all rated the same (or close to it) according to some achievement, competency, or trait norm prevailing in that unit or organization.

Performance Management and Implications for Diversity

Assessing the performance of unique individual employees according to some common yardstick is a task fraught with problems. Several commonly experienced problems come immediately to mind. First, concerns arise from very real cultural differences that may exist in the assessment of concepts such as time, quality, and effectiveness—critical components of performance. People from differing cultures do not necessarily have the same vision of what a deadline may mean or what appropriate customer service requires. Diversity is not limited to issues of ethnicity or gender. Differences in professions and disciplinary socialization can have significant effects on performance assessment for a work group. If a work group transcends functional lines (e.g., a group encompassing marketing specialists, financial managers, and engineers as members), then the differences in professional focus have implications for how these different disciplines view what it is they are supposed to accomplish.

Assume a group was assembled from across departments in a local government to develop a new transit system. For the marketing people, a job well done might have a great deal to do with the saturation of the community with educational materials and much less to do with the cost of the project. However, for the financial person, project cost could signal success or failure regardless of how well it is received by the community. For the engineers, neither cost nor popular approval may be as important as the engineering integrity of the design itself.

Most obvious, there may be instances of bias

drawn from personal prejudice. It is entirely possible (and offensive) that individuals in organizations employ negative stereotypes to weigh the relative contributions of others. This potential for bias is of particular concern when activities related to the achievement of performance goals are not easily measured, as in the case of communication and relationship building. Certainly the potential for appraiser bias is of grave concern when organizations use performance assessment as a means to distribute rewards and punishment within the organization. Although any distribution of resources (e.g., compensation, training time, equipment, or opportunities) should occur in an equitable fashion, policymakers often cannot agree on the best way to define equity,[9] and performance assessment for nonroutine tasks may be little more than an educated guess.

Reducing Appraiser Error

Rating error can be reduced through several mechanisms. The design of the appraisal instrument can help reduce rater error. If the traits, competencies, and achievement categories are well defined and instructions are clearly outlined, error can be minimized. The more closely measures can be linked with performance goals, the less margin for error may be present. Appraisal systems that rely on easily identified and documented indicators for which objective standards can be ascertained will certainly be less suspect than systems with a great deal of subjectivity and appraiser latitude in defining objectives and deriving obscure measures. Alternatives to the traditional dyadic appraisal models discussed thus far, such as the 360-degree evaluation process discussed later in this chapter, could offer the advantage of multiple appraisers to control for rater bias.

Ideally, the timing of the appraisal should be linked to the purpose of the performance assessment; however, poor timing can contribute to appraiser bias. If all appraisals are due during the busiest time of the year or are required before an employee has really had an opportunity to perform (e.g., immediately after hire or soon after

taking on a new project), then a legitimate assessment is unlikely.

Appraiser training is an important countermeasure for reducing assessment error. To address problems with rater bias, some researchers recommend training coupled with the use of performance diaries in which the appraiser documents employee performance with entries in the diary over the course of the entire appraisal period.[10] In addition to the rather obvious need to train appraisers on how to use a particular performance appraisal instrument, organizations would like to have confidence that their appraisers have a clear understanding of the purpose of the appraisal process and its applications in human resource management. Furthermore, appraisers may need training in how to work with employees to assess performance. Appraisers may even require basic interpersonal education in how to discuss uncomfortable topics. Some sensitivity training may be necessary to address the demands of an increasingly diverse workforce in terms of communication styles, value differences, or unconventional cultural norms regarding such matters as time urgency, physical space, or social roles.

Influences on Individual Performance

Exactly what contributes to performance—is it an employee's individual traits, or is performance related to behaviors? Should we carefully assess individual character traits, or pay closer attention to activities over established time periods? Is performance best assessed through specific and memorable events that seem to encapsulate a particular employee's performance? Do we consider the performance of an employee as an independent judgment, or should we compare each worker with each other? Figure 11.5 illustrates the range of hypothesized influences on individual performance.

Factors outside the direct control of the individual could include a range of technical and policy constraints on performance. For example, vague organizational goals, an inappropriately heavy workload, and responsibility incommensurate with authority would hamper the most com-

Figure 11.5   Influences on Individual Performance

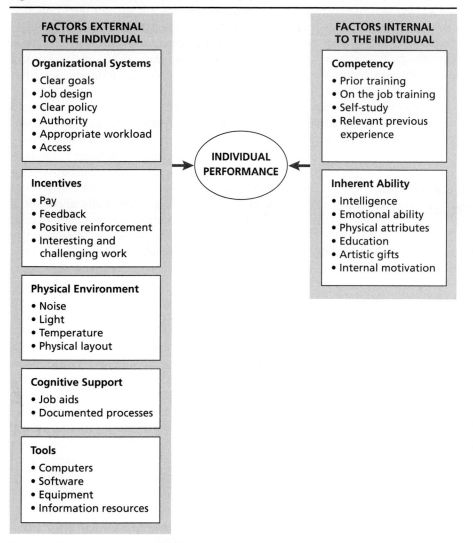

Source: From Figure 6-1, "Performance Model," in National Academy of Public Administration, "Measuring Results: Successful Human Resources Management," *HRM Series* 3 August 1997, p. 50. Copyright © 1997. Reprinted by permission of the National Academy of Public Administration.

petent of employees. Certainly employees need to have sufficient resources and tools to do their job. An employee responsible for a web site who does not have access to a computer and Internet connection with an adequate modem certainly cannot attain high (or even expected) performance. If a staff member is expected to complete detailed

complex tasks while also serving as department receptionist, then the physical environment could detract from that employee's ability to perform.

There are internal factors to be considered as well. Does the employee have sufficient training and skills to perform a particular task? Are there other abilities or personal characteristics that may limit or impede performance? Suppose a graduate student is charged with a heavy load of data entry and is locked in a small room with no window and only a computer for company. This scenario may be appealing to a person who prefers quiet, autonomy, and limited social interaction; for such persons this type of arrangement of workspace may contribute to their performance. An employee who tolerates noise well and craves social interaction may achieve only poor performance in the same physical environment.

Beyond the Boss-Employee Assessment: Groups, Directions, and Practice

Hays and Kearney suggest that the performance management systems of the future will likely reflect increased sensitivity to the structure of the organization and will be more closely linked to planning and an assessment of the formal and informal environment of the organization.[11] In addition, variations on the traditional supervisor-subordinate model of performance appraisal will become common, with the use of peer and client evaluations and team-based approaches to performance management increasingly coming to the fore.

A model of performance assessment that incorporates multiple raters—commonly peers, supervisors, clients, and even subordinates—is called **360-degree evaluation.** The premise behind 360-degree models is that multiple raters, each familiar with different views of an employee's work, can accurately assess performance using a standard instrument. In application, 360-degree evaluation is intended to help employees improve their overall performance by developing skills or addressing communication problems.

Walter Tornow correctly notes that 360-degree models presume that employees can improve their performance, particularly in leadership venues, if they learn how their efforts affect others.[12] Although 360-degree models were initially used to enhance employee development and assist supervisors in improving their relationships with subordinates, this performance assessment method has been used more recently in merit pay applica-

tions for local government.[13] However, these multi-appraiser models are not without their critics. If done properly, the 360-degree models should be ongoing, with formal assessment at least twice per year, and employees, clients, and supervisors may not be willing to devote sufficient time to this form of assessment.[14]

In the future, greater emphasis will be placed on collaborative processes to address performance issues. Reflecting widespread demands for reinvention and organizational reform, performance targeting includes collaboration between supervisors and employees.[15] For such systems to work as intended, it is strategically important to engage the supervisor and this person's superior in setting goals, with the employee being an active participant in goal development.[16]

Discussions about collaboration, strategic management, and systemic approaches to performance suggest a need to move from considering performance at the individual level to an organizationwide perspective. In this regard, discussions about public sector productivity echo many of the issues discussed to this point. The different economic sectors—public, private, and nonprofit—face different environments and political and legal constraints. However, as we will see in the next section, the assumptions about strengthening performance and the best means to accomplish this task are closely linked to a variety of human resource activities, especially performance assessment.

REFLECTIONS ON PERFORMANCE AND PRODUCTIVITY

Efforts to raise the efficiency and effectiveness of public action are a constant fixture of government, directly reflecting our cultural preoccupation with improvement, growth, and progress. Since 1882, when President Chester Arthur vetoed a bill that included almost five hundred unnecessary public projects, there have been eleven reform commissions appointed by Congress or the President to find ways to improve federal government performance.[17] More recent efforts at government reform have considered a number of approaches to improving the performance of public agencies. A careful study of the prescriptions for change found in the reinventing-government literature and other more recent performance measurement discussions offer important considerations for managers and their human resource administrators. Some performance improvement paradigms advocate a dramatic decentralization of authority as an effective catalyst for bringing about outcome-based accountability. Others address customer satisfaction as the key indicator of an effective public agency—and argue that their goal can be achieved through improved processes and enhanced product or service quality. Prescriptions for improving the performance of public sector organizations have serious implications for efforts to monitor and manage performance within organizations—for individuals, work groups, and departments alike.

In the **decentralization/accountability paradigm,** individual accountability rests with employees, who are made responsible for results.[18] The rationale follows that decentralized authority allows employees to be individually accountable for decisions at the customer service level, reducing the frustrations that a customer or client may feel in acquiring products or services. Performance is then measurable by the output of individual employees. Incentives for improved performance in the form of rewards can then be distributed based on measurable indicators of productivity that can be closely monitored and documented. Conversely, poor performance can be monitored, and either disciplinary action or additional training can be directed in a swift and targeted manner to where it is required.

A second major influence on public sector management was W. Edwards Deming's advocacy of **total quality management (TQM).**[19] Although TQM has spawned a number of variants, the basic tenet is improved quality of the resultant service or product, with quality being defined by the customer or client. Improved quality is dependent on the quality and commitment of employees and a streamlined production process. Deming advocated a statistical approach to quality, maintaining that productivity improves as

variability in the quality of a product or service decreases. This statistical approach competes with a traditional focus on output indicators such as production quotas.[20]

The purist approach to TQM manifests a quasi-religious cast and includes strict adherence to the fourteen points illustrated in Box 11.1. TQM themes include a call for constant improvement of quality, with a derivative distaste for both waste and production quotas. To this end, TQM proponents emphasize process and craftsmanship to improve outcomes. Commitment is critical—by the organization to customers, by supervisors to their employees, and by employees to their work. In this regard, training is of paramount importance. In the TQM framework, supervisors should ensure that their employees have appropriate training, direction, and the materials to do their work—and then get out of their way. James Bowman suggests that TQM may even supplant traditional supervisor-subordinate models of performance appraisal.[21]

Often the difficulties of neatly transferring management trends such as TQM or the decentralization/accountability paradigm to the assessment of performance and productivity in government reflect some major differences between the public and private sectors. TQM adherents considered private sector organizations exclusively as they developed the principles of TQM. In particular, TQM appears to work best with manufacturing or production processes, where production activities are relatively routine and predictable. Most of the activities of government are not production oriented, however, and many public sector service delivery processes are difficult to define clearly and even more difficult to measure with any degree of confidence. A focus on customer-driven operations, along with an emphasis on collaborative efforts to improve quality, might require that people other than a supervisor appraise efforts or that workplace efforts be considered in the aggregate rather than at the individual level. A deemphasis on control and the documentation of mistakes might shift the purpose of appraisal to problem solving rather than problem seeking. It is clear that reinventing-government efforts often add to rather than eliminate the

---

Box 11.1   The Deming Management Method

---

1. "Create constancy of purpose for improvement of product and service." Organizations should redefine their objective from a short-term program-specific view to a long-term vision of customer satisfaction and programmatic improvement and innovation.

2. "Adopt a new philosophy." "Mistakes and negativism are unacceptable."

3. "Cease dependence on mass inspection." It is more efficient and effective to do it right than to correct mistakes.

4. "End the practice of awarding business on price tag alone." Organizations should seek relationships with those who can provide high quality goods and services.

5. "Improve constantly and forever the system of production and service." Waste reduction and quality enhancement are constant and ongoing.

6. "Institute training." Workers need to be properly trained.

7. "Institute leadership." Supervisors need to lead, helping employees do a better job and providing assistance to those who need it.

8. "Drive out fear." Employees need to feel secure in their work situation. Fear limits innovation.

9. "Break down barriers between staff areas." Unfortunately, separate departments often compete instead of cooperate to reach organizational goals.

10. "Eliminate slogans, exhortations, and targets for the workforce." Commitment is demonstrated by actions and results, not platitudes.

11. "Eliminate numerical quotas." Numbers do not necessarily reflect quality in outcome, process or method.

12. "Remove barrier to pride of workmanship." Supervisors need to identify and remove the obstacles in the way of workers performing their jobs.

13. "Institute a vigorous program of education and retraining." The entire organization—management and workforce—needs to learn that quality comes first.

14. "Take action to accomplish the transformation." Management at all levels must be committed to the philosophy of quality and workers must be prepared and willing.

Source: From W. Edwards Deming. *Out of the Crisis,* pp. 23–24. Published by and reprinted by permission of the MIT Press.

---

important performance-related questions facing public sector administrators.

INTRODUCTION TO READING

In the following selection, Berman, West, and Wang consider performance assessment practices in common use in county government. In this study, performance is being assessed for a department (human resources) rather than a person. However, some of the challenges in measurement, process, and the perceived utility of that process echo issues raised in the traditional supervisor-subordinate model of performance assessment.

As you read the selection, keep the following questions in mind:

- In the reading, the focus is on aggregate measures of performance for human resource management. Can the same lessons be applied at the microlevel for individuals and groups?
- How do the authors assess the application of performance measurement systems? What other methods could be used to assess effectiveness?
- What major challenges may face local governments as they develop effective systems to appraise and manage performance for in-

dividuals, departments, and government as a whole?

- The authors gathered data from counties with populations greater than 50,000 persons. Why? What might this suggest to performance and productivity champions?

- Gary Roberts states, "If there is an inherent belief in the utility of performance appraisal, a mediocre system is superior to no system at all."[22] What do you think? What would Berman, West, and Wang say about this statement?

READING

Using Performance Measurement in Human Resource Management: A Survey of U.S. Counties

EVAN BERMAN, JONATHAN WEST, AND XIAOHU WANG

This article examines the use of performance measurement in human resource management. Based on a survey of counties with populations over 50,000, it finds that performance measurement is widely used. Many measures reflect traditional concerns with compliance, but measures are also used to assess human resource management reforms in recruitment and compensation. This study also finds that mission-orientation and broad support affect the use of performance measurement in human resource management, as well as technical ability to gather such data. Many efforts are relatively recent, and thus it is too early to tell whether these measures will find enduring use.

In recent years, performance measurement has received much attention in public administration (Ammons, 1995, 1996; Behn, 1996; Center for Accountability and Performance, 1998; Gianakis & McCue, 1997; Fisher, 1994). Performance measurement is defined as measuring levels of achievement through a range of indicators. Traditionally, performance measurement has been used in human resource management to monitor compliance such as meeting affirmative action requirements (Mushkin & Sandifer, 1980; Stutz & Massengale, 1997), but it is also used increasingly to assess organizational effectiveness and the human resource efforts that con-

tribute to it (such as recruitment, compensation and training) (Hornestay, 1999; Fitzenz, 1995; Fitzenz & Phillips, 1998; Phillips, 1996). Although no prescribed or even recommended measurement matrix exists for public personnel activities, organizations have long used a broad range of human resource measures (many of which are examined in this study), and organizations are continuously developing new ones as they seek to improve their accountability and performance (Mushkin & Sandifer, 1980; Stutz & Massengale, 1997; Tigue & Strachota, 1994).

Recent systematic studies show that performance measurement is widely used in many cities and agencies, but these studies do not discuss specific uses in public personnel management (Berman & West, 1998; Brudney, Hebert & Wright, 1999). This national study examines the use of performance measurement in personnel functions in counties

Source: Evan Berman, Jonathan West, and XiaoHu Wang, "Using Performance Measurement in Human Resource Management," *Review of Public Personnel Administration* 29:2 (1999): 5–17. Reprinted by permission of the publisher, Sage Publications.

with populations over 50,000. It focuses on the different kinds of measures that are used, as well as conditions that influence use.

FRAMEWORK

Definitions of performance measurement frequently distinguish among activities (or workloads), outputs, outcomes, and efficiency measures. Outputs are the immediate results of activities (e.g., the number of completed personnel transactions), whereas outcomes (or effectiveness) measure the extent to which an activity has achieved its goals or objectives, including measures of quality and client satisfaction. Efficiency is a measure of the cost per outcome or output. The number of employees who participate, for example, in training is an activity measure, whereas the percentage of employees with certain skills, the proportion of clients satisfied with human resource services, or the ability to attract and retain employees might be viewed as human resource management outcome measures.[1] The cost per recruited employee is an efficiency measure. Although, in theory, a broad range of measures might be constructed for all human resource activities, concerns about data availability, and the need to focus on the purpose of performance measurement (e.g., increased accountability) make overly comprehensive efforts impractical. Rather, measures are constructed which are practiced, based on existing data, and that reflect the priorities of managers. As the saying goes, "what gets measured gets done."

In this regard, considerable interest exists in developing performance measures that reflect new human resource reforms such as better and faster recruitment (Barzelay & Armajani, 1997; Human Resources, 1999; ICMA, 1999). Another area of interest involves monitoring the competitiveness of compensation and benefits (City of Virginia Beach, 1998), including continuing education and child care benefits (National Academy of Public Administration, 1998). Workforce development is an increasing concern, and some HR departments now monitor participation in job skill courses or skill development over time (Epstein, 1992; Ludeman, 1991; Paddock, 1997). For example, performance measurement is used to monitor the number of employees participating in productivity improvement and customer service efforts, two strategic issues which have been raised in many jurisdictions (Hatry, Gerhart & Marshall, 1996; Leithe, 1996).

It might be noted that a certain skepticism exists about the use of performance measurement in government. Concern exists that performance measurement, like other productivity improvement efforts, is a fleeting fad to which many organizations only give lip service (Halachmi, 1999). The concern is not limited to human resource management (Loffler, 1999). It is difficult to assess this claim, as many productivity improvement efforts begin in small ways, with most managers sitting on the sidelines, waiting for new efforts to prove themselves. When such efforts are shown to be successful they are promptly replicated and diffused. When they fail to live up to their promise, they lose momentum. Performance measurement has now entered the phase in which ineffective applications are being identified and weeded out (Theurer, 1998).

Three research questions guide this study. First, what kinds of performance measures are used in county personnel functions? No prescribed or best metric for performance measurement exists, but most jurisdictions have comparable human resource management activities. For example, all jurisdictions recruit personnel, and thus may be concerned with the outcome of their advertising efforts or test scores of new employees. The number of new employees promoted within 12 months is often used as a measure to attract quality employees. To determine the range (or "breadth") of performance measures, this study includes human resource management measures that have been repeatedly suggested in the literature, and focuses on the areas of recruitment, compensation, skill development and employee relations, all of which have received much attention lately. To determine the nature (or "depth") of human resource management performance measures, we ask counties to characterize the extent that, overall, their measures reflect workload, effectiveness, quality and client satisfaction. This provides an indication of the relative emphasis that counties put on developing their human resource performance measures.

Second, who assumes leadership for development of human resource performance measures? The development of performance measurement in human resource management does not occur in isolation from other organizational initiatives (Few & Vogt, 1997; Jones, 1997; Leithe, 1996; Nyhan & Marlowe, 1995; West, 1995). In recent years, many performance measurement efforts were led by either county administrators or budget directors who required all departments, including human resource management, to develop performance measures. The presence of jurisdiction-wide performance measurement efforts may spur the use of performance measurement in human resource management. In some instances human resource managers lead jurisdiction-wide efforts, or they are otherwise pro-active in developing modern human resource performance measures. We examine whether human resources–led efforts lead to different emphases in the depth of human resource performance measurement. Specifically, we surmise that human resources–led efforts are more likely to emphasize quality measures which help the HR director provide accountability to their internal customers (such as budget and other offices).

Third, which county conditions, if any, affect the use of performance measurement? Performance measurement requires technical abilities that often transcend the ability of individual departments (Berman, 1998; Holzer, 1992). Many performance measurement efforts require employee and client surveys; yet, few managers are trained in gathering and analyzing such data in scientifically valid ways. Performance measurement also requires the ability to conceptualize outcome and output measures that are relevant and feasible. This study examines whether mission-orientation also increases the use of performance measurement. Such efforts are associated with increased customer-orientation and use of client-feedback to assess services (Griefel, 1994; Wray & Hauer, 1996).

In addition to technical abilities, performance measurement also requires broad support among users of performance measurement data. As an accountability strategy, performance measurement presumes interest among users of these data. These users include elected officials, citizen advisory boards, county administrators and even department heads and supervisors who benefit from accountability. Some concern exists that, thus far, elected officials have not been much interested in performance measurement (Tigue, 1994), even though a few chief executives have championed the use of such measures (Leithe, 1996; Loffler, 1999). Nonetheless, elected officials often prefer traditional forms of accountability based on testimony and citizen complaints. Yet, the use of performance measurement is contingent on the willingness of county managers and elected officials to be persuaded by information that includes performance measurement data.

METHODS

A survey was administered in 1998 regarding the use of performance measurement in counties. The survey was pre-tested on a group of fifty managers and, following minor changes, mailed to all 856 counties with populations over 50,000, identified through *Counties USA,* 1997. After three waves of mailing, 209 responses were received from counties which use performance measurement. Of these, 162 respondents provided in-depth information about the use of specific performance measures in human resource management. Most of the remaining respondents (43 of 47) indicated that they use performance measures in their human resource management and they, like the other 162 respondents, also provided broad characterizations about this use. To determine the extent that the 162 respondents represent all counties that use performance measurement,[2] a telephone survey was conducted among a random sample of counties that did not respond. Of the 106 non-responding counties that were contacted, only 13 counties indicated that they use performance measurement in some way. Thus, it follows that (856−209) * 13/10=79 counties did not respond to the survey and use performance measurement. Consequently, the survey *response rate* of counties using performance measurement in human resource management is (162/162 + 43 + 79=) 57.0%. One caveat is that this study does not examine counties which do not use performance measurement.

To ensure valid survey data, we also conducted follow-up telephone calls with respondents who indicated the use of a wide range of measures. Respondents were asked for specific examples, and their survey responses were verified. Very few changes were made as a result of these telephone interviews. The telephone survey also included some randomly selected survey items. Comparison of these responses with those of the mail survey respondents does not indicate problems of non-response bias. To determine the extent that performance measurement is used, this study uses a broad range of indicators, reflecting both breadth (different aspects of human resource management that are measured) as well as depth (the nature of performance measures, that is, whether they measure workload as well [as] quality, effectiveness and client satisfaction). Organizations that report a broader and deeper use of performance measurement in human resource management are said to have a

Table 1   Type of HR Performance Measures in County Governments

HR Performance Measures	All Counties
Employee Relations	
Job turnover rates	75.3%
Accident rates	71.9
Absenteeism	66.3
Job satisfaction	41.8
Substance abuse	49.4
Workplace violence	37.1
Aggregate Measure (alpha = .75)	45.5
Career and Skill Development	
Use of educational benefit programs	54.9
Employees taking job skill courses	51.7
Number of promotions	48.4
Career progression by job class	43.0
Employees eligible for training programs	32.6
Complaints about career progression	30.4
Aggregate Measure (alpha = .82)	45.1
Recruitment	
Test scores of new employees	49.7
Percentage of vacancies	49.7
Outcome of advertising and recruitment efforts	43.5
Employees who fail probation	34.9
Number of internships	30.6
Employees who exceed minimum job qualifications	29.5
New employees promoted within 12 months	20.1
Aggregate Measure (alpha = .79)	25.9
Compensation and Benefits	
Comparing salaries for technical jobs	81.8
Comparing salaries for managerial jobs	81.8
Comparison of fringe benefits	69.5
Comparing sick leave practices	61.9
Comparing performance incentives	42.0
Comparing continuing education benefits	34.9
Comparing child/elder care practices	17.8
Aggregate Measure (alpha = .85)	25.1
All Measures (alpha = .86)	37.2
N = 162	

greater commitment to it, and organizations that report a high use are re-contacted by interview[er]s to ensure the validity of their responses. These measures are discussed in the text and tables below.

FINDINGS

Performance measurement is common in human resource management. Table 1 shows the use (breadth) of performance measurement in employee relations, career and skills development, recruitment, and compensation and benefit functions. Among the most frequent measures are comparisons of salary (81.8%), fringe benefits (69.5%) and sick leave practices (61.9%), as well as job turnover rates (75.3%), accident rates (71.9%) and absenteeism (66.3%). In addition, many organizations also measure the use of educational benefit programs (54.9%), employees who participate in skill courses (51.7%), vacancies (49.7%) and test scores of new employees (49.7%).

Other measures are less often used, such as comparing child and elder care practices in other jurisdictions (17.8%), new employees who are promoted within 12 months (20.1%), employees who exceed minimum job qualifications (29.5%), the number of internships (30.6%), complaints about career progression (30.4%), employees who are eligible for training programs (32.6%), comparing continuing education benefits (34.9%), the number of employees who fail probation (34.9%), and workplace violence (37.1%). Many of these measures concern training and the development of employees, both of which reflect matters of workforce effectiveness.

Table 2 characterizes the nature (depth) of human resource management performance measures that are used. About two-thirds of respondents characterized their measures as emphasizing workload (66.5%), about half as effectiveness (47.2%), and fewer as including quality (40.8%) and client satisfaction measures (28.4%). Although these characterizations are not exclusive, very few organizations that do *not* use workload measures use quality (15.3%) or client satisfaction measures (9.7%), reflecting that the latter are more challenging to develop.

A composite measure was constructed to assess commitment to performance measurement in the human resource management function. This measure is based on the breadth and depth of human resource performance measurement, as reported in Tables 1 and 2. Defining strong commitment as using performance measurement in at least half of each area of the human resource management areas shown in Table 1, and using workload as well as effectiveness or quality or client satisfaction measures, shows that 16.0% of respondents can be said to have strong commitment to using performance measurement in human resource. If low commitment is defined as using less than six performance measures shown in Table 1 (that is, less than one-quarter shown), then 30.4% of respondents fall in this category. About 53.6% of respondents can be said to have moderate commitment to using performance measurement in human resources.[3]

Commitment to using performance measurement in human resource management does not vary by county size or form of government. More

Table 2   Nature of HR Performance Measurements by Responsibility

HR Performance Measures	% Used	Responsibility[1]	
		OMB	HRM
Workload	66.5	.167**	
Effectiveness	47.2	.189**	
Service Quality	40.8	.134*	.191**
Client Satisfaction	28.4		.138**

[1]Relationship with implementation responsibility.
Measures are tau-c. **1% significance *5% significance *N* = 205.

counties in the West have a high commitment to using performance measurement in human resource management than other counties: 39.1% versus 10.9% ($t = 2.59$, $p < .01$). The disparity is, in part, caused by the near absence of counties in the South (3.8%) with a high commitment: these counties are more likely to have only moderate commitment (64.4% versus 43.8%). There are no statistically significant regional differences concerning low commitment. Commitment increases over time, too: 20.4% of counties that have used performance measurement longer than four years have a high commitment to using it in human resource management, as compared to only 11.1% of counties that have used performance measurement less than four years.

Many of the interviewees noted the use of performance measurement in recruitment. In Lewis County, Washington, performance measurement is used to document the number of recruitment efforts and the steps that are involved in each. This involves tracking the number of applications, the type of service provided such as basic screening, testing, designing and grading testing instruments, and the development of interview questions. Performance measurement is also used to track the speed at which new openings are posted. These measures are used for both productivity improvement and accountability: the human resource department evaluates the cost per recruitment, and these data are provided to the county commissioners on a monthly basis.

Table 2 also shows how the nature of human resource performance measurement is affected by the office which takes the lead responsibility for developing it. When the County Office of Management and Budget leads in developing performance measurement throughout the county, human resource departments are more likely to emphasize workloads and effectiveness measures. For example, 81.8% of counties in which the Office of Management and Budget leads in developing performance measurement county-wide use workload measures in human resource management, compared to 62.5% of counties in which the Office of Management and Budget does not lead (tau-c = $.167$, $p < .01$). By contrast, when human resource departments have a lead responsibility, human resource measures will more strongly emphasize service quality and client satisfaction; twice the number of human resource performance measurement efforts involve client satisfaction when human resource has a lead role (51.5% versus 25.4%, tau-c = $.138$, $p < .01$). These differences re-

flect different purposes; budget offices are often interested in workloads for purposes of budget preparation, whereas human resource departments are necessarily interested in measures of their clients' satisfaction with human resource services.

Table 3 examines various conditions, mentioned above, that may affect the use of performance measurement in human resource management. About sixty percent of counties have staff (63.4%) and information systems (55.3%) to gather data that are necessary for performance measurement. In many instances, this involves capacity to develop and implement client feedback questionnaires; this capacity often is jurisdiction-wide, as few departments, including human resource management, have adequate resources to develop and maintain such expertise by themselves. Computerization also facilitates the collection of some traditional measures, such as those involving vacancies and absenteeism. Table 3 shows that having adequate infrastructure and resources is positively associated with breadth (more human resource performance measures) as well as depth (use in workload, effectiveness, quality, client satisfaction). For example, whereas 44.0% of counties that have adequate management information systems for performance measurement use effectiveness, service quality and client satisfaction measures, only 18.0% of those who report not having such capacity do so (tau-c = $.297$, $p < .01$). Having staff capable of analyzing performance data also increases the use of such measures by a ratio of 40.2% versus 25.0% (tau-c = 189, $p < .05$).

Support for human resource performance measurement can come from many different sources. Most common is support from the county administrator (79.8%). Interviewees frequently noted that the administrator strongly supports performance measurement county-wide, and that this support bolsters the use of human resource performance measures. Often, elected officials are said to be supportive of performance measurement efforts, though they seldom act as instigators or catalysts. Broad support for performance measurement does not affect the breadth of performance measurement, but it does affect the type of measures that are used. Many of the listed actors are internal customers of human resource management, and thus it is not surprising that when they advocate performance measurement for their own units they also indicate expectations for measuring the effectiveness

Table 3 General County Conditions and HR Performance Measurement

General Conditions	% Present	HR Performance Measures Type (breadth)	Nature (depth)
Mission-orientation			
We have written customer comments	65.5	.172*	.228**
Performance measures are used to evaluate goals and missions	64.5	.208**	.432**
Goals and missions are frequently discussed	62.5	.271**	.406**
We survey the satisfaction of program clients	58.6	.260**	.441**
Aggregate (alpha = .78)	62.7	.241**	.407**
Technical Ability			
Can develop outcome measures	73.3	.150*	.229**
Have staff capable of analyzing performance measurement data	63.4	.191*	.227**
Have management information systems to collect performance measurement data	55.3	.249**	.272**
Can determine the validity of performance measures	54.7	.309**	.207**
Aggregate (alpha = .83)	61.7	.188*	.327**
Support for Performance Measurement			
County manager supports performance measurement	79.8	.003	.153**
Most department heads support performance measurement	40.8	.076	.287**
Elected officials support performance measurement	34.6	.079	.330**
Most supervisors support performance measurement	21.2	.091	.218**
Citizen advisory boards support performance measurement	19.9	.101	.173**
Aggregate (alpha = .78)	39.2	.072	.305**
Entrepreneurship			
Increased privatization	58.0	.092	.128
Private contracting has increased	53.8	.195*	.107
Entrepreneurial activities have increased	53.3	.116	.223**
Franchises are awarded to private organizations	39.9	.184*	.087
Aggregate (alpha = .69)	50.2	.233**	.221**

Measures are tau-c; **1% significance; *5% significance. $N = 191$.
$N = 196$ (except for column "breadth," $N = 131$).

of human resource management. Indeed, when department heads are perceived as advocates for performance measurement, 51.3% of human resource departments have a broad range of quality and satisfaction measures compared to 29.3% when advocacy is lacking (tau-c = .185, $p < .01$).

Mission-orientation and entrepreneurship are associated with the use of performance measurement in human resource management. Both may increase awareness about the quality of human resources and their effectiveness. The items in Table 3 include many that have been advocated in recent years. Overall, it

Table 4   Determinants of HR Performance Measurement

Independent Variables	Dependent Variable Nature of HR Performance Measurement ("depth of use")		
	Regression Coefficient	Beta Coefficient	Standard Error
Constant	−.138		.164
Mission-Orientation	.241	.234	.081**
Technical Ability	.114	.105	.084
Support	.066	.155	.033*
Entrepreneurship	.036	.035	.072
Size	.051	.103	.037
Northeast	−.084	−.071	.094
South	−.052	−.066	.072
West	.004	.004	.086
OMB[1]	.094	.113	.062
HRM[1]	.085	.079	.073

$R = .482$; R^2 adj = .189
[1]Implementation responsibility
**1 % significance; *5 % significance; $N = 185$

Independent Variables	Type of HR Performance Measurement ("breadth of use")		
	Regression Coefficient	Beta Coefficient	Standard Error
Constant	.226		.145
Mission-Orientation	.230	.289	.080**
Technical Ability	.212	.270	.080**
Support	−.020	−.068	.029
Entrepreneurship	.096	.132	.068
Size	−.028	−.079	.034
Northeast	.035	.048	.076
South	.025	.045	.065
West	.167	.222	.079*
OMB[1]	−.019	−.032	.055
HRM[1]	.012	.018	.060

$R = .529$; R^2 adj = .210
[1]Implementation responsibility
**1 % significance; *5 % significance; $N = 114$

is found that mission-orientation and, to a lesser extent entrepreneurship, increase the breadth and depth of human resource performance measurement. These orientations show especially strong associations with career development and recruitment human resource activities; quality-oriented organizations require talented employees and managers who often are impatient with prolonged recruitment efforts which, too often, fail to attract top candidates. Among organizations with mission-orientation, 65.2% measure recruitment outcomes and 76.0% track the number of employees who take job skill courses. By contrast, the respective percentages of organizations that have a weak mission orientation are 32.8% and 39.8% (resp. $t = 3.52$ and $t - 4.17$, both $p < .01$). Interestingly, mission orientation is not associated with tracking promotion rates, perhaps, reflecting the fact that many mission-oriented organizations have become increasingly flat structures with fewer promotion opportunities.

Table 4 examines the effect of the conditions mentioned in Table 3 on the index variable of the breadth and depth of human resource performance measurement.[4] The model shows that mission-orientation is associated with both the depth and breadth of using performance measurement in human resource management. This suggests that such efforts as customer-orientation have broad effects in the organization, including the use of performance measurement in human resource management.[5] In addition, technical abilities such as information technology and capable staff result in using performance measurement in a broader range of areas, whereas broad support (such as from elected officials and senior managers) causes performance measures to focus more on outcomes, which may be consistent with these stakeholders' interests. The results also show that the locus of responsibility (the personnel department or Office of Management and Budget) does not affect the depth or breadth of human resource performance measurement when the above county conditions are controlled for. One interpretation may be that these four conditions are themselves affected by leadership. For example, in the Office of Management and Budget leadership may result in counties investing in performance measurement training and information on technology.

Interviews were also conducted to determine the outcome or impact of using performance measure-

ment in human resource management. In many instances respondents report that performance measurement is useful to monitor trends and to control costs and improve productivity. Several respondents indicated the importance of recruitment measures. Rather than only collecting data about the number of recruitment efforts (which indicate human resource management activity), survey interviewees also recorded data about the way they do business, such as the number of job applications they obtain at job fairs, the time to post job advertisements or fill positions, and the cost of filling positions. Such information has strategic importance for decisions about improving human resource management operations.

However, in many settings, performance measurement is seen as a recent development. One respondent noted that performance measurement is itself useful to help justify doing it, but also that "I would like to have ammunition to persuade more of us here to do more in this area (of performance measurement)." The data suggest that human resource performance measurement is associated with some improved outcomes. According to respondents, performance measurement helps organizations to better determine their long-term budget needs: 95.0% of respondents whose jurisdiction has a high level of commitment to using performance measurement in human resource management agree with this aspect, compared to 46.0% of jurisdiction[s] with a low or medium commitment (tau-c = .284, $p < .01$). Similarly, human resource management performance measurement is associated with improving the effective use of resources (85.0% versus 58.4%, tau-c = .187, $p < .05$).

CONCLUSION

A national survey of all U.S. counties with populations over 50,000 finds that performance measurement is widely used. Many measures reflect traditional concerns with compliance rather than recent interest in performance improvement. However, measures are also used to assess human resource management reforms in such areas as recruitment and compensation. This study also finds that mission-orientation and stakeholder support increase the use of performance measurement in human resource management. Support and mission-orientation are also associated with having adequate technical ability for gathering performance measurement data. Many efforts are relatively recent, and thus it is too early to tell whether these measures will find enduring use.

Human resource managers have been under pressure for some time to justify their operations. A recent report by the General Accounting Office (1998) notes the reduction of human resource management staff at federal agencies, as personnel operations such as hiring and benefits management are streamlined and automated. In many local governments, human resource departments face similar pressures. Line managers look for new ways to increase value and productivity from human resources. As a competitive resource, training is used for improving worker effectiveness and furthering productivity improvement efforts, not merely to compensate for skill deficiencies. Performance measurement, then, is not only used for documenting performance improvement in traditional activities, but also for demonstrating accountability that new human resource approaches are working.

As with all new productivity improvement efforts, in time the good is separated from the bad. As many human resource managers are trying new ways to increase their performance and provide accountability, new performance measures must be proposed, implemented and evaluated. Processes for designing performance measures include input from stakeholders and feedback from those using pre-existing measures. Future studies should track the way in which performance measures evolve over time. They should also examine whether these measures add value to the human resource function: do they adequately inform managers? Do stakeholders believe that they provide human resource accountability? Are they used for determining the cost-effectiveness of services? Are measures comparable across organizations? In short, how effective is the use of performance measurement in human resource management?

NOTES

1. These different purposes affect how performance measurement is used: for example, educational benefits are sometimes reported to show that a jurisdiction is comparable to others. However, when the purpose is workforce effectiveness, these measures are often accompanied by employee surveys and focus groups to identify factors that affect the willingness of employees to increase skills.

2. In this study, we examine counties that use performance measurement; thus, our purpose here is to examine the extent to which our sample represents all counties that use performance measurements. We do not claim that our sample represents all counties, hence, there is no 'creaming' involved in this methodology.

3. These results vary, of course, according to the standards that are used: if low commitment is defined as using fewer than one-third of measures shown in Table 1, then the percentage of counties with a low commitment to HR performance measurement increases to 40.8%.

4. This measure also includes a measure of reporting performance measurement to the county manager's office.

5. The four conditions add considerable explanation to the models. The increase in the adjusted-R^2 as a result of adding these four conditions (given the control variables and leadership variables) is, respectively, .101 for the "breadth" model and .126 for the "depth" model.

REFERENCES

Ammons, D. (1996). *Municipal benchmarks: Assessing local performance and establishing community standards.* Thousand Oaks, CA: Sage.

Ammons, D. (1995). *Accountability for performance measuring and monitoring in local government.* Washington, D.C.: International City/County Management Association.

Barzelay, M. & Armajani, B. (1997). Innovation in the concept of government operations: A new paradigm for staff agencies. In A. Altshuler & R. Behn (Eds.), *Innovation in American government* (pp. 119–145). Washington D.C.: Brookings.

Behn, R. (1996, July 8). Performance measures: To punish, or to motivate? *Governing.*

Berman, E. (1998). *Productivity in public and nonprofit organizations.* Thousand Oaks, CA: Sage.

Berman, E. & West, J. (1998). Productivity enhancement efforts in public and nonprofit organizations. *Public Productivity & Management Review 22*(2), 207–219.

Brudney, J., Herbert, T. & Wright D. (1999). Reinventing government in the American states: Measuring and explaining administrative reform. *Public Administration Review 59* (1), 19–30.

Center for Accountability and Performance (1998). *Performance measurement: Concepts and techniques.* Washington, D.C.: American Society for Public Administration.

City of Virginia Beach, Virginia. (1998). *Public Personnel Administration 27* (3), 415–422.

Epstein, P. (1992). Managing and analyzing the productivity of professionals and managers. In M. Holzer (Ed.), *Public productivity handbook* (pp. 335–368). NY: Marcel Dekker.

Few, P. & Vogt, A. (1997). Measuring the performance of local government in North Carolina. *Government Finance Review 13* (4), 29–34.

Fisher, R. (1994). An overview of performance measurement. *Public Management 76* (9), S2–S8.

Fitzenz, J. (1995). *How to measure human resource management.* New York: McGraw-Hill.

Firzenz, J. & Phillips J. (1998). *A new vision for human resources.* Crisp Publishing.

General Accounting Office. (1998). *Management reform: Agencies' initial efforts to restructure personnel operations.* Washington, D.C.: U.S. Government Printing Office.

Gianakis, G. & McCue, C. (1997). Local government capacity building through performance measurement. In J. Gargan (Ed.), *Handbook of local government administration* (pp. 239–261). NY: Marcel Dekker.

Grifel, S. (1994). Organizational culture: Its importance in performance measurement. *Public Management 76* (9), S19–S21.

Halachmi, A. (1999). *Performance and quality measurement in government.* Burke, VT: Charelaine Press

Hatry, H., Gerhart, C. & Marshall M. (1996). Eleven ways to make performance measurement more useful to public managers. *Public Management 76* (9), S15–S20.

Holzer, M. (1992). *Public Productivity Handbook.* NY: Marcel Dekker.

Hornestay, D. (1999). The human factor. *Government Executive* (February). (http://www.govexec.com/gpp/0299hr.htm)

Human Resources (1999, February). *Governing,* 23–25.

International City Managers Association (1999). Performance indicators/support services/human resources. *ICMA Comparative Performance Measurement Program.* http://www.icma.org/performance/PI-support.cfm

Jones, A. (1997). Winston-Salem's participation in the North Carolina performance measurement project. *Government Finance Review 13* (3), 40–42.

Loffler, E. (1999). Service quality measurement of innovative public organizations. In A. Halachmi (Ed.). *Performance and quality measurement in government* (pp. 129–144). Burke, VT: Chatelaine Press.

Ludeman, K. (1991). Measuring skills and behavior. *Training and Development 45* (11), 61–66.

Mushkin, S. & Sandifer F. (1980). Personnel management. In G. Washnis (Ed.), *Productivity improvement handbook for state & local government* (pp. 530–584). NY: J. Wiley & Sons.

NAPA. (1998). *Work/life programs: Helping managers, helping employees.* Washington, D.C.: National Academy of Public Administration.

Nyhan, R. & Marlowe, H. (1995). Performance measurement in the public sector: Challenges and opportunities. *Public Productivity and Management Review 18* (4), 333–348.

Paddock, S. (1997). Benchmarks in management training. *Public Personnel Management 26* (4), 441–460.

Phillips, J. (1996). *Accountability in human resource management.* Houston, TX: Gulf Publishing.

Stutz, J. & Massengale, R. (1997). Measuring diversity initiatives. *HR Magazine 42* (12), 85–88.

Theurer, J. (1998). Seven pitfalls to avoid when establishing performance measures. *Public Management, 80* (7), 21–24.

Tigue, P. (1994). Use of performance measures by GFOA members. *Government Finance Review 10* (6), 42–44.

Tigue, P. & D. Strachota (1994). *The use of performance measures in city and county budgets.* Chicago, Illinois: Government Finance Officers Association.

West, J. (1995). *Quality management today: What local government managers need to know.* Washington, D.C.: International City/County Management Association.

Wray, L. & Hauer, J. (1996). Best practices reviews by local government. *Public Management 78* (1), 7–11.

PERFORMANCE MANAGEMENT SYSTEMS

Performance management systems incorporate a holistic approach to improving performance and productivity in organizations. They are premised on the assumption that the employees in an organization, regardless of rank or decision-making level, can come to understand how they contribute to organizational goals and that many activities within organizations can be analyzed to determine how they either contribute to or detract from the achievement of organizational ends. Performance appraisal of an individual, work group, or depart-

ment would serve as separate components of a performance management system.[23] The design of the job or the identification of specific knowledge, skills, or abilities associated with a particular position would all be linked in a system approach to performance management. Assessment could not be considered without attention to all other facets of human resource management. In fact, performance management systems are an integral part of strategic planning and should be viewed as a key feature of implementation efforts for organizations.[24]

The performance matrix shown in Figure 11.6 indicates how varying organizational factors, such

Figure 11.6 Performance Matrix

Performance Matrix			
		Stages	
Levels	**Accomplishment Models**	**Measures of Opportunity**	**Methods of Improvement**
Policy institutional systems	**Organization models** • Cultural goals of the organization • Major missions • Requirements and units • Exemplary standards	**Stakes analysis** • Performance measures • Potential for improving performance • Stakes • Critical roles	**Programs and policies** • Environmental programs (data, tools, incentives) • People programs (knowledge, selection, or recruiting incentives) • Management programs (organization, resources, standards)
Strategy job systems	**Job models** • Mission of job • Major responsibilities • Requirements and units • Exemplary standards	**Job assessment** • Performance measures • Potential for improving performance • Critical responsibilities	**Job strategies** • Data systems • Training designs • Incentive schedules • Human factors • Selection systems • Recruitment systems
Tactics task systems	**Task models** • Responsibilities of tasks • Major duties • Requirements and units • Exemplary standards	**Task analysis** • Performance measures or observations • Potential for improving performance • Specific deficiencies • Cost of programs	**Tactical instruments** • Feedback • Guidance • Training • Reinforcement

Source: From National Academy of Public Administration, "Theory and Practice," *Human Performance Improvement Series Focus,* September 1998, p. 5. Copyright © 1998. Reprinted by permission of the National Academy of Public Administration.

as resource constraints and opportunities for performance management, converge on three planes of decision making and action: policy, strategic, and tactical levels. This matrix echoes the logic of strategic planning: mission, goals and objectives, and action planning. At the *policy* level, we are concerned with maintaining an organization's fit to its environment, which for both public and non-profit organizations means accommodating the interests of political actors, interest groups, and agency clientele. The challenge for managers is to mesh the culture of the organization with its mission, the expectations of stakeholders, and the development of the resources, technology, and workforce skills to meet the organization's mission-defined challenges.[25] *Strategy* entails the specification of the goals and objectives that give life to the mission; it requires the development of evaluative criteria to assess whether the goals and objectives are being met. *Tactics* pertain to the specific actions to be taken to accomplish organizational goals and objectives. This is the area of organizational life that entails learning from experience on the part of "street-level" personnel and requires that the learning gained from active contact with customers (internal and external) feeds back on the strategic and policymaking levels.

The public and nonprofit sectors may face somewhat different challenges as they attempt to assess performance for an organization, workplace groups, and individual employees. The often ambiguous nature of public goals and the limitations of technology and resources that can be used for public action complicate and inhibit efforts to manage performance. Three central questions guide public organizations as they attempt to develop performance management systems: (1) How do we define and assess performance? (2) Who appraises whom? and (3) For what purpose do we assess performance?

How Do We Define and Assess Performance?

Some government activities involve well-established processes with clearly defined outputs and beneficiaries. These activities can be measured, and improvements can be made to the processes involved in each system. For example, some local government functions are rather easily measured; among them are park and recreation department program attendance, solid waste collection on fixed schedules, and water quality. State governments process insurance forms and pension checks, route child support payments, and authorize road construction projects, activities that lend themselves to outcome measurement. Increasingly we may even see these routinized activities provided by nongovernmental actors through contracting arrangements precisely because they are more easily designed as delivery units and measured.

Unfortunately, in many other instances of public service delivery performance levels may not be readily measured. Considering the quality or effectiveness of many public programs is difficult because the objectives used as yardsticks are often vague or too simplistic. Identifying performance goals at an organizational level may not tidily devolve to an assessment of individual performance. Can we assess the performance of the public employees charged with implementing a particular program or developing a service when we are unable to assess organizational performance clearly? For example, how do we assess the quality of education? If the quality of education is reflected in a student's preparation for a career, then it is easy to measure the number of graduates who successfully land jobs. However, this goal and measure would not accurately reflect the education effort because variables outside the control of the educator and the student play a role in the number of graduates who find work and the type of work they find. If we ask students (as clients) to assess the quality of their education, the criteria used for that assessment could differ widely: how quickly the class passes, how funny the instructor is, or how often they refer to course materials at work. Are any of these assessments more or less valid than the others? Do any of these assessment questions accurately reflect the quality of education? Even if we could clearly identify the indicators of performance, for individuals or organizations, we are still faced with the appropriate mesh of performance appraisal technique and process.[26]

To Appraise or Be Appraised?

The constraints and opportunities posed by organizational structure, as well as the formal and informal distribution of power and authority, are important factors to consider in assessing performance. For example, using a group-based structure and rewarding group effort would work at cross-purposes with a performance appraisal system relying on the conventional dyadic supervisor-subordinate performance appraisal process. The assessment of group-based performance requires consideration of collective achievement by individuals in the group and judgements about their ability to contribute to the group effort. Group-based assessment requires consideration of the ability of individual members to work with others to ensure that their knowledge, insights, and skills are shared within the work group. If we rely on supervisors of the work group to assess performance without considering the key perceptions held by an employee's peers, then we are receiving only a partial picture of performance. For project-based systems, a performance assessment frame linked to the project cycle may be more useful than assessing performance during set blocks of time. Conversely, if we opt for the TQM characterization of supervisors as the enablers of high performance, then we must incorporate employee evaluations of their supervisor.

Can we hold public servants accountable in their performance assessment for the actions of individuals over whom they have no direct control? As may be common with the implementation of public goods provisions through nonprofit or private sector organizations, a public employee could be entirely dependent on the activities of people outside the organization to implement a particular program. In these cases, their ability to manage the work of others over whom they may have no direct supervisory influence is crucial yet extremely difficult to measure and assess uniformly. Failure to consider the structure of the organization and to understand key agency processes leads to disappointing results with respect to performance improvement efforts.

For What Purpose Do We Assess Performance?

Decisions about what purposes are served by performance appraisal should comport with the organization's mission in general and with the job-specific elements of work for which the employee or group of employees are held responsible. Performance appraisal can be delineated in terms of whether it is used to judge (or grade) employees or to develop their capacity to perform.[27] Certainly appraisal systems are founded on basic assumptions about people and their motivation,

the links to performance that various benefits and incentives may have, and even whether employees can be trusted to do the job or must be controlled. For example, an organization that employs the logic behind TQM assumes that high performance is a natural outgrowth of a well-trained workforce given sufficient autonomy, adequate resources, and the essential tools or equipment to do the job.[28] A performance appraisal system would then serve as a means to identify training needs or certain skills and competencies associated with different performance levels. In this way, performance appraisal would be used as a mechanism to develop employees.

In other applications, employee assessment may be a means to punish detrimental behaviors or warn about the consequences of poor performance; conversely, the same process can be used to reward favored activities or reinforce positive behaviors such as the acquisition of competencies needed in the workplace. As noted in Chapter 9 on salary and wage management, organizations often link performance assessment with compensation and merit pay.[29] Performance appraisal may also serve to help management identify employees for promotion or to select individuals for either reassignment or dismissal if their performance is subpar. In these applications, appraisal serves as a means to judge the relative importance of individual contributions to the organization.

What managers may seek in terms of performance outcomes also drives decisions about the subject of assessment (groups or individuals). The direction of that assessment may also be linked to what we expect to discover. For example, if we want to know about employee-client relations, then we should probably use some assessment method that includes a survey of client opinions. Conversely, if we would like to assess a work group or other collaborative efforts within an organization, we would expect both peers and supervisors to appraise performance and work groups to assess other work groups.

The intent and focus of assessment will affect the performance management system adopted for an organization. It is important to note that production activities would require a different assessment approach than would service activities. Measurement may be entirely quantitative, or it may address performance appraisal through the use of qualitative indicators. Finally, the anticipated application of the performance information should be tied to the performance management system.

DOING IT RIGHT: EFFECTIVE PERFORMANCE APPRAISAL

Employees are interested in an objective assessment of their performance.[30] Not surprisingly, favorable performance appraisals tend to enhance an employee's perception about the accuracy of performance appraisal.[31] However, the employee's perception about the accuracy of his or her own performance appraisal does not translate to a positive perception about the utility of the overall performance management system for the organization.[32] The appraisal process may not be a useful approach to improving organizational performance.[33] Some research indicates that managers and subordinates do not necessarily share the same perception of the performance appraisal.[34] For performance appraisal to be useful, employees and managers have to believe that it is a legitimate and useful process.[35] Even if organizational members develop a technically ideal system merging into a single process all of the latest innovations, not everyone may consider the appraisal process and results to be effective.[36] Increasing participation by employees in the appraisal process is positively associated with an enhanced perception of the effectiveness of the appraisal, the utility of the process, the legitimacy of the performance goals, and the relationship between employees and supervisors.[37] Participation by employees in the performance appraisal process enhances perceptions of system effectiveness.[38]

No single template appraisal format is appropriate for all organizations. The most useful performance management system is one in which the format establishes linkages to organizational goals.[39] Although most prescriptions for effective performance appraisal focus on developing instruments and procedures to support the traditional supervisor-employee models of assessment, the general suggestions offered by Longenecker and Nykodym can be applied across dimensions: individual, group, and organizational.[40] First, the performance management system should be developed with specific intent rather than result from casual loading of faddish technical applications on an existing system. For example, the role that supervisors may play versus peers versus clients in evaluating the performance of a particular employee will change with the intent of the assessment. If we want to discover how to improve customer service, then we have different expectations about who will appraise an employee's efforts than we might if we were using the performance management system solely to distribute internal rewards.

Second, we have to assume that the performance appraisal system will be job related, but that it may be used as well to address performance concerns at multiple levels: the organization, the work group or service units, and individual employees. To that end, if employees participate in establishing performance goals, their interests and concerns can be made an integral part of the performance management system. Under normal circumstances, employee feedback is limited to a response in the "employee comments" section of a "one size fits all" appraisal instrument.

Third, to be effective, the performance management system must be linked to the manner in which positions and activities are identified and assigned—whether this is done through a traditional job analysis and classification model or reflects a work classification model. If performance assessment is not integrated into the manner in which work is structured—individual versus group or perhaps task versus project—then the assessment instrument cannot begin to discern relative levels of performance. For example, if all positions are carefully identified in terms of an individual employee's holding a particular set of responsibilities relating to a clearly defined set of tasks, then assessment in terms of group-based effort in a project-driven environment would be most inappropriate.

Berman, West, and Wang join other public administration scholars in cautioning decision makers against quickly adding the latest fad or computer gadget to the performance management system. They note:

> As with all new productivity improvement efforts, in time the good is separated from the bad. As many human resource managers are trying new ways to increase their performance and provide accountability, new performance measures must be proposed, implemented and evaluated. Studies . . . should . . . examine whether these measures add value to the human resource function.[41]

TECHNOLOGY AND PERFORMANCE MANAGEMENT

Performance appraisal has not escaped the explosion of computer software application. In a recent segment in the International Personnel Management Association's *IPMA News,* Elizabeth Fried reviewed five vendors of software for 360-degree evaluation systems.[42] These software packages vary in cost (from $99, plus $50 per employee, to a base package of $50,000) and include general training and support through implementation.[43] The cost of the package does not include any infrastructure commitment that must be made by the organization to be certain that anyone doing the appraisal can gain access to the appropriate computers and servers. The most interesting aspects of the software appraisal packages are what they promise. The software will prompt the appraiser to respond to questions that are available from a common database of questions, as well as some queries that can be customized. Some allow the appraiser to customize the appraisal to a particular job title and to assign weights to different items.

These software programs even provide the option for an appraiser to comment after rating a performance item. Open summary comments are also available. All five of the software packages that Fried evaluated provided elaborate scaling options. In fact, the potential for scoring and using multiple scales and customizing the scale weights and ranges appeared to be the heftiest portion of the software packages. The packages also have elaborate reporting functions, giving appraisers the option of generating bar graphs and defining the reporting groups either according to demographic data or work units. These software packages even had an "on-line goal setting" feature, by which the computer program would "automatically identify areas for development and provide specific actions to take."[44]

Some computer programs monitor the appraiser's comments to be certain that they are consistent with legal guidelines.[45] Some provide generic position descriptions and provide performance criteria; the appraiser clicks on the position description and locates performance criteria associated with the job in question.[46] An appraiser who cannot think of anything to write can select from the sample text provided in the programs and even receive on-line coaching tips for improving the employee's performance![47] Obviously, these programs are intended to have time-saving benefits for the appraiser. However, template appraisal using computer-generated assessment seems to tarnish what could be a constructive opportunity to discuss employee performance and development.

■ CONCLUSION

Performance assessment is a complex activity. Aside from the technical nature of identifying performance levels, we see enormous challenges in linking individual performance to organization-wide goals and productivity. Intuitively, a systemic approach to performance management is appealing, but much of the structure in organizations (established through analysis, classification, and compensation systems) must be integrated with performance management. In addition, it is difficult to dispense wholly with familiar practices such as supervisor-subordinate appraisal, which may suggest control and accountability but often do not realistically reflect the changing work environment. As will be seen in later chapters, performance assessment serves to bridge initial human resource activities such as job analysis, classification, recruitment, and selection with subsequent concerns: the development, training, and, if necessary, discipline of employees.

■ MANAGER'S VOCABULARY

performance
performance appraisal
supervisor-subordinate performance appraisal
trait-based appraisal
achievement-based appraisal
competency-based appraisal
depth of skill
breadth of skill
vertical skills
graphic rating performance assessment instrument
ranking performance assessment instrument
forced-choice performance assessment instrument
behaviorally anchored rating scale
essay performance assessment instrument
objective/goal performance assessment instrument
critical incident
management by objectives

personal bias
halo effect
horns effect
constant error
recency effect
central tendency
360-degree evaluation
decentralization/accountability paradigm
total quality management (TQM)

■ STUDY QUESTIONS

1. How should performance be assessed for individuals?

2. How should performance be assessed for departments or work groups?

3. How should performance be assessed for the organization?

4. What performance assessment instrument might be appropriate for different jobs or organizations? How might the performance instrument for a clerk be different from that for a manager?

5. How can dyadic performance assessment be translated to organizationwide or departmental assessments, such as described by Berman, West, and Wang?

■ EXPERIENTIAL EXERCISES

1. You are the director of the Department of Public Performance and Productivity for Blue Berg City. In response to citizen perceptions of waste and mismanagement for many units in Blue Berg's municipal government, the City Manager has asked you to recommend appropriate reforms to the Mayor and City Council. Luckily, you are enrolled in an M.P.A. program and are taking a class on human resource management. You recognize the importance of a performance management system that complements the direction set through Blue Berg's strategic plan, a document that calls for a citizen-driven government and features an emphasis on active collaboration of public, nonprofit, and private sector organizations to address "the demands of the millennium." Because these decision makers

are faced with severe time constraints, you must identify critical reforms and provide the appropriate rationale in a one-page memorandum. The City Manager cautions you that this memo could "make or break your career in Blue Berg." Draw on the concepts presented in various chapters in this book to draft this memo.

2. Consider Table 11.1. Can you draw any conclusions about the instruments used to assess the performance of employees? For what purpose might assessment occur? What errors may result? Why?

3. Obtain three different performance appraisal forms from a public sector organization. Indicate whether the forms are trait, achievement, or competency based, or some type of hybrid. What methods are used in the appraisal instrument?

	Appraisal 1	**Appraisal 2**	**Appraisal 3**
Trait	_____	_____	_____
Achievement	_____	_____	_____
Competency	_____	_____	_____
Hybrid	_____	_____	_____
Methods			
Graphic rating	_____	_____	_____
Ranking	_____	_____	_____
Forced choice	_____	_____	_____
BARS	_____	_____	_____
Essay	_____	_____	_____
Objective/goal	_____	_____	_____
Critical incident	_____	_____	_____

Consider the following questions after you have examined the position appraisal forms:

a. How well does each of the appraisal instruments capture performance?

b. Are the various levels of performance well articulated?

c. Which would you prefer? Why?

d. Could these performance appraisal instruments be used easily for different jobs? What modifications might be necessary?

e. How well do the methods used for each appraisal instrument reflect the performance levels that we wish to assess in each position?

Table 11.1 Percentage Distributions of Performance Ratings, Fiscal Years 1990–1995

Fiscal Year (FY)	Unacceptable	Minimally Successful	Fully Successful	Exceeds Fully Successful	Outstanding	Average Rating	Number of Ratings Reported
General Schedule 13–15 (Supervisors and Management Officials)[a]							
FY 1990	0.06	0.16	19.52	49.73	30.54	4.11	143,219
FY 1991	0.06	0.14	17.85	47.25	34.70	4.16	148,983
FY 1992	0.06	0.14	16.62	46.41	36.77	4.20	149,810
FY 1993	0.07	0.14	13.98	44.69	41.12	4.27	151,728
FY 1994	0.04 (r)	0.13	12.11 (r)	41.92 (r)	45.79 (r)	4.33 (r)	147,041 (r)
FY 1995	0.03	0.15	9.47	37.52	52.83	4.43	132,444
General Schedule 13–15 (Other)							
FY 1990	0.18	0.26	26.11	45.30	28.15	4.01	93,192
FY 1991	0.09	0.21	22.71	45.27	31.72	4.08	85,973
FY 1992	0.04	0.13	22.66	45.26	31.91	4.09	91,484
FY 1993	0.06	0.14	20.61	45.71	33.48	4.12	103,342
FY 1994	0.05	0.19 (r)	17.87 (r)	40.22 (r)	41.66 (r)	4.23 (r)	120,917 (r)
FY 1995	0.04	0.17	15.33	38.57	45.88	4.30	135,736
General Schedule 1–12							
FY 1990	0.13	0.45	35.75	39.07	24.61	3.88	1,147,505
FY 1991	0.12	0.37	31.16	41.17	27.19	3.95	1,126,784
FY 1992	0.13	0.36	29.55	41.32	28.64	3.98	1,174,895
FY 1993	0.13	0.34	26.52	41.96	31.05	4.03	1,145,962
FY 1994	0.14	0.31	24.20	41.63	33.72	4.08	1.096,553
FY 1995	0.16	0.42	22.78	39.87	36.77	4.13	1,053,375
Federal Wage System							
FY 1990	0.08	0.34	39.10	40.80	19.68	3.80	332,601
FY 1991	0.05	0.26	33.71	43.78	22.20	3.88	310,381
FY 1992	0.04	0.23	30.46	44.66	24.61	3.94	308,661
FY 1993	0.05	0.19	26.13	45.11	28.53	4.02	283,381
FY 1994	0.03	0.15	23.92	44.61	31.29	4.07	263,182
FY 1995	0.03	0.26	21.57	41.99	36.16	4.14	243,334

[a]Prior to FY 1994, these employees were covered by the Performance Management and Recognition System (PMRS), which terminated November 1, 1993.

(r) = revised

Note: Percentages may not add to 100 due to rounding.

Source: Performance Management Information System (PERMIS) Data File, Office of Compensation Policy. (202) 606-2720 DMCARBAL@OPM.GOV

■ CASES APPLICABLE TO THIS CHAPTER

"Liberty Police Department" and "Helping Hands" (Task 3).

■ NOTES

1 Dennis M. Daley, *Performance Appraisal in the Public Sector* (Westport, CT: Quorum Books, 1992), p. 14.

2 See, for example, Robert P. Tett, Douglas N. Jackson, Mitchell Rothstein, and John R. Reddon, "Meta-Analysis of Personality-Job Performance Relations: A Reply to Ones, Mount, Barrick, and Hunter," *Personnel Psychology* 47 (1994): 157–170; or Miguel Quinones, J. Keven Ford, and Mark S. Teachout, "The Relationship Between Work Experience and Job Performance: A Conceptual and Meta-Analytic Review," *Personnel Psychology* 48 (1995): 887–909.

3 The skill depth and breadth concepts originate in G. Ledford, *The Design of Skill-Based Pay Plans* (Los Angeles: University of Southern California, Center for Effective Organizations, 1989), pp. 1–2. For the purpose of this chapter, these definitions are drawn from Reginald Shareef, "Skill-Based Pay in the Public Sector," *Review of Public Personnel Administration* 24:3 (1994): 61.

4 Shareef, "Skill-Based Pay," p. 62.

5 Ibid., p. 67.

6 Maureen Smith, "Competency-Based Performance Appraisal Systems," *IPMA News* (August 1999): 16.

7 Kevin R. Murphy and Jeanette N. Cleveland, *Performance Appraisal: An Organizational Perspective* (Needham Heights, MA: Allyn and Bacon, 1991), pp. 219–223.

8 Peter W. Dorfman, Walter G. Stephan, and John Loveland, "Performance Appraisal Behaviors: Supervisor Perceptions and Subordinate Reactions," *Personnel Psychology* 39 (1986): 579–596.

9 Deborah Stone offers eight definitions of equity, noting that they differ in terms of how the recipients are identified, how the resources to be distributed are defined, and the process used to distribute those resources to the selected recipients. Deborah Stone, *Policy Paradox: The Art of Political Decision Making* (New York: Norton, 1997), p. 43.

10 See, for example, H. J. Bernardin and Richard W. Beatty, *Performance Appraisal: Assessing Human Behavior at Work* (Boston: Kent Publishing, 1986); or Bernard P. Maroney and M. Ronald Buckeley, "Does Research in Performance Appraisal Influence the Practice of Performance Appraisal? Regretfully Not!" *Public Personnel Management* 21:2 (1992): 193–194.

11 Steven W. Hays and Richard C. Kearney, "Anticipated Changes in Human Resource Management: Surveying the Field" (paper presented at the National Conference of the American Society for Public Administration, Orlando, FL, April 10-14, 1999), pp. 11–12, 15–16; cited with permission.

12 Walter W. Tornow, "Introduction to Special Issue on 360-Degree Feedback," *Human Resource Management* 32:2–3 (1993): 211.

13 James Fox and Charles Klein, "The 360-Degree Evaluation," *Public Management* 78:11 (1996): 20–22.

14 Steven Ginsberg "In a New Approach to Evaluations, Everyone's a Critic," *Washington Post*, July 27, 1997, p. H4.

15 Arie Halachmi, "From Performance Appraisal to Performance Targeting," *Public Personnel Management* 22:2 (1993): 323–344.

16 Ibid., pp. 338–339

17 Patricia Ingraham, "Commissions, Cycles and Changes: The Role of Blue Ribbon Commissions in Executive Branch Change," in Patricia Ingraham and Don Kettl, eds., *Agenda for Excellence* (Chatham, NJ: Chatham House, 1992), pp. 187–207.

18 See, for example, Thomas J. Peters and Robert H. Waterman, Jr., *In Search of Excellence: Lessons from America's Best-Run Companies* (New York: Warner Books, 1982). David Osborne and Peter Plastrik, *Banishing Bureaucracy: The Five Strategies for Reinventing Government* (Reading, MA: Addison-Wesley, 1997).

19 W. Edwards Deming, *Out of the Crisis* (Cambridge, MA: MIT Center for Advanced Engineering Study, 1986).

20 Mary Walton, *The Deming Management Method* (New York: Perigee, 1986), pp. 96–118.

21 James S. Bowman, "At Last, an Alternative to Performance Appraisal: Total Quality Management," *Public Administration Review* 54:2 (1994): 129–136.

22 Gary E. Roberts, "Municipal Government Performance Appraisal System Practices: Is the Whole Less Than the Sum of Its Parts," *Public Personnel Management* 24:2 (1995): 221.

23 Sally Coleman Selden, Pat Ingraham, and Willow Jacobson, "Human Resource Practices in State Governments: Findings from a National Survey" (paper presented at the National Conference of the American Society for Public Administration, Orlando, FL, April 10–14, 1999); cited with permission.

24 Ibid., pp. 21–22.

25 Lloyd Baird and Ilan Meshoulam, "Managing Two Fits of Strategic Human Resource Management," *Academy of Management Review* 13:1 (1988): 122.

26 L. O. Olsen and A. C. Bennett, "Performance Appraisal: Management Technique of Social Process? Part I—Management Technique," *Management Review* 64 (December 1975): 18–23; L. O. Olsen and A. C. Bennett, "Performance Appraisal: Management Technique or Social Process? Part II—Social Process," *Management Review* 65 (1976): 22–28.

27 Larry L. Cummings and Donald P. Schwab, *Performance in Organizations: Determinants and Appraisal* (Glenview, IL: Scott, Foresman, 1973), p. 5.

28 Steven Cohen and Ronald Brand, *Total Quality Management in Government* (San Francisco: Jossey-Bass, 1993), pp. 6–8.

29 Selden, Ingraham, and Jacobson, "Human Resource Practices," p. 22

30 Nicholas P. Lovrich, Jr., Paul L. Shaffer, Ronald H. Hopkins, and Donald A. Yale, "Do Public Servants Welcome or Fear Merit Evaluation of Their Performance," *Public Administration Review* 40:3 (1980).

31 Eugene F. Stone and Dianna L. Stone, "The Effects of Multiple Sources of Performance Feedback and Feedback Favorability on Self-Perceived Task Competence and Perceived Feedback Accuracy," *Journal of Management* 10:3 (1984): 371–378.

32 Joan L. Pearce and Lyman W. Porter, "Employee Responses to Formal Performance Appraisal Feedback," *Journal of Applied Psychology* 71:2 (1986): 211–218.

33 Gary E. Roberts, "Barriers to Municipal Government Performance Appraisal Systems: Evidence from a Survey of Municipal Personnel Administrators," *Public Personnel Management* 23:2 (1994): 225–236.

34 Clinton O. Longenecker, D. A. Gioa, and H. P. Sims, "Behind the Mask: The Politics of Employee Appraisal," *Academy of Management Executives* 1:3 (1978): 183–193.

35 Maroney and Buckeley, "Does Research in Performance Appraisal," pp. 185–196; Adiba Ash "Participants' Reaction to Subordinate Appraisal of Managers: Results of a Pilot," *Public Personnel Management* 23:2 (1994): 237–256.

36 Roberts, "Barriers to Municipal Government"; D. T. Wright, "The Split Role of Performance Appraisal," *Personnel Administrator* 30:5 (1985): 83–87.

37 Stanley B. Silverman and Kenneth N. Wexley, "Reactions of Employees to Performance Appraisal Interviewers as a Function of Their Participation in Rating Scale Development," *Personnel Psychology* 37:4 (1984): 703–710.

38 Lovrich et al., "Do Public Servants Welcome or Fear Merit Evaluation of Their Performance."

39 Jerald Greenburg, "Determinants of Perceived Fairness of Performance Evaluation," *Journal of Applied Psychology* 71:2 (1986): 340–342.

40 Clinton O. Longenecker and Nick Nykodym, "Public Sector Performance Appraisal Effectiveness: A Case Study," *Public Personnel Management* 25:2 (1996): 151–164.

41 Evan M. Berman, Jonathan P. West, and XiaoHu Wang, "Using Performance Measurement in Human Resource Management," *Review of Public Personnel Administration* 29:2 (1999): 15–16.

42 N. Elizabeth Fried, "360-Degree Feedback Software—Vendor Feature Comparison," *IPMA News* (August 1999): 21.

43 Ibid., p. 23

44 Ibid., p. 22.

45 Jenny C. McCune, "Employee Appraisals, the Electronic Way," *Management Review* (October 1997): 44–46.

46 Ibid., p. 45

47 Ibid.

CHAPTER 12

Human Resource Training and Development

Human resource development (HRD) is the application of strategies and interventions designed to enhance the knowledge and skills of individuals to improve their capacity to contribute to their organizations, promote their careers, and improve their quality of life. The Academy of Human Resource Development defines HRD as a profession "that focuses on improving individual and organizational performance through learning."[1]

The foundation of HRD is continual learning through the use of individual learning strategies, formal training programs, or group and team learning approaches. The conventional strategy used for HRD has been the provision of formal training programs focusing on specific job skills for employees on the line and the development of supervisory and managerial skills among administrative personnel. Conventional training is still an important function of HRD, and classroom instruction remains the most common HRD method of teaching. However, the sizable cost of training and the paucity of evidence documenting training benefits are being carefully scrutinized. New methods of HRD are being introduced to help individuals gain control over their own learning strategies and to help organizations effectively target their resources for specific learning objectives.

INTRODUCTION TO READING

The following selection is the executive summary of a report prepared by the U.S. Merit System Protection Board from a study to see if the federal HRD system was able to prepare employees for the demographic and technological changes experienced by the federal government. The report notes that most federal employees receive some training every year and that the HRD system does a relatively good job of training in current job areas. But it also notes that HRD budgets are significantly underfunded and that HRD staffs are too few in number and unprepared for the kind of training and employee development needed most. The report recommends that HRD offices be given more adequate funding and staffing priority and that HRD professionals be more closely integrated into the strategic planning and program evaluation activities of agency managers. HRD experts who are involved in planning and evaluation can offer their professional advice for individual and organizational learning programs to improve the capacity of employees to contribute to the goals and objectives of government agencies.

As you read the selection, keep the following questions in mind:

- Why are training budgets and staffs often underfunded?
- What facets of training and development most likely would be sacrificed to adjust for low budgets?
- What are the long-term consequences of making these sacrifices?
- Do you agree with the recommendations made in the report regarding funding and involvement in organizational strategic planning?
- What implications would these recommendations have for improving the productivity of the public workforce?

▬▬▬▬▬ **READING**

Executive Summary of *Leadership for Change*

BEN L. ERDREICH AND ANTONIO C. AMADOR

The next decade promises to be a time of great change for Federal workers. The reinvention of Government means that the ways of doing business will have to change dramatically in many organizations. Missions will change and organizations will be expected to streamline their operations. In order to provide the services that will be expected from them, organizations will need workforces that are prepared to make these changes. Moreover, since one of the changes that can also be expected is a downsizing of the Federal workforce, members of the workforce who remain will have to learn to work in new ways. Accomplishment of these sorts of changes rests on training and retraining current employees. The primary issue addressed in this report is whether the systems and processes for supporting human resource development (HRD) in the Federal Government are prepared to handle the daunting task ahead.

As discussed in this report, there are a number of problems with the way HRD is practiced in many Federal organizations. People are sent to training for a variety of reasons and limited training dollars are not always spent wisely. Since there will also certainly be severe budget limitations in most organizations in the near future, it is critical that organizations get the most out of their training investments. Unfortunately, unless they learn to manage in new ways, many organizations may have a difficult time ensuring that their workforces are prepared to work more efficiently. To be successful in facilitating the changes that will be needed in the capabilities of Federal employees, HRD staffs will need to become integral participants in organizational strategic planning and agencies will need to make a long-term commitment to evaluating the operation of their programs.

Federal Government operations are undergoing more scrutiny today than at any time in the last 100 years. In many cases organizations are being asked to change fundamentally the way they do business. This change cannot be successfully accomplished unless Federal workers are prepared for it, and the HRD function is the mechanism through which they will receive this preparation. It is this critical function that is the subject of this study by the U.S. Merit Systems Protection Board (MSPB or the Board). Among the Board's statutory responsibilities is the requirement to provide the President and Congress with periodic reports on the health of the Federal civil service and to review the significant actions of the U.S. Office of Personnel Management (OPM). The purpose of these reviews is to enhance the efficiency and effectiveness of the Federal Government by providing for a well-qualified and motivated workforce. The role played by the HRD function at this time is critical. The Board initiated this study to determine whether the system for meeting the training and development needs of federal employees is up to the challenges it now faces. The information reported in this study was obtained in a variety of ways. We held discussions with the people responsible for developing HRD policy for the entire Federal Government and individual agencies. We conducted a telephone survey of employees working in HRD in the field whose job it was to see that workers actually got the training they needed. We also asked agencies to answer a set of questions about the HRD activities in their subordinate

Source: Ben L. Erdreich and Antonio C. Amador, *Leadership for Change: Human Resources Development in the Federal Government* (Washington, D.C.: U.S. Merit System Protection Board, July 1995).

organizations. Finally, we used data from a 1992 MSPB survey to find out what Federal employees thought about the training and development they were or were not getting.

FINDINGS

More than three-quarters of the Federal workforce spent some time in training during the most recent year for which data are available. According to OPM, during fiscal year 1991 over $1.4 billion was spent in over 2 million separate incidents of training. The average amount spent per training event was $643, with each training event lasting an average of just over 3 days. About one in every six employees received training in new technologies.

Respondents to our 1992 Merit Principles Survey (MPS), for the most part (75 percent) believed that their most recent training experience was effective in improving their ability to perform their current jobs. Similarly, most employees (58 percent) said that the training they received as a Federal employee had effectively prepared them to perform their jobs well.

Despite the fact that most employees had received some type of training and most thought that the training was useful, about one-third of the MPS respondents said they needed more training to perform their jobs effectively. A similar proportion of employees (31 percent) did not believe that they had received the training they needed to keep pace as the requirements of their jobs have changed.

The one area that all of our study participants agreed was not a problem at this time was in training in basic skills. MPS respondents, HRD specialists in the field, and agency offices in charge of HRD policy all said that, except in a few isolated locations, they did not see any great need for such remedial kinds of training among Federal workers.

Employees responding to our 1992 survey cited the lack of adequate funds (45 percent) as the primary reason they did not receive the training they believed they needed. Our telephone survey produced a similar response, with 56 percent of the HRD specialists telling us that their budgets for training were not sufficient to meet the needs of their organizations. Agencies also held this

opinion, with less than half of those responding to our inquiries saying that sufficient funds were available to meet their training needs.

Agencies that thought their training budgets were sufficient to meet their needs shared a common vision as to why they were successful. Training budgets were more likely to be seen as adequate when training was not identified as a stand-alone or line item in either headquarters or field-level budgets. Training was more likely to be supported when its costs were included in program funding. In essence, programs are justified, but training is not, except as an associated cost of running a program.

In addition to inadequate training budgets, another reason employees may not receive the training they need is because many organizations do not always do a good job of identifying and prioritizing their training needs. Rather than basing their selections on a determination of need, agencies sometimes send employees to training as a reward for performance or because they can be spared from their duties.

Less than half of the respondents to our telephone survey thought that their office did a good job of assessing their organization's training needs. Only 47 percent of the HRD specialists we surveyed said that the procedures they used to identify training needs provided them with a realistic picture of their organization's current training needs. Even less, 33 percent, thought that their assessment procedures led to an accurate picture of their needs in the immediate future.

Almost half the agencies that responded to our written questions were concerned that the HRD function itself may not be up to its role in assisting managers in the task of meeting the Federal Government's training and development needs. HRD staffs in most organizations tend to be small; in many cases only one person is devoted to HRD. Unfortunately, these small staffs frequently are responsible for providing support for large numbers of employees. The limited number of people assigned to HRD results in little or no time being devoted to such critical activities as assessing needs and evaluating training. Perhaps more importantly, HRD staff members rarely assisted agency managers in strategic planning for their organizations.

CONCLUSIONS

Our study revealed that there were a number of reasons that Federal organizations in the future may have trouble ensuring that all of their training needs are met. The HRD staffs in many organizations primarily perform administrative duties and management frequently has little confidence that the funds devoted to training are wisely spent. This has profound implications for attempts to successfully restructure the Federal bureaucracy. Unless organizations change the way they do business and place a greater emphasis on effective program evaluation and strategic planning, they will have difficulty prioritizing the use of the limited resources that are likely to be available for training. And unless they include their HRD staffs in program evaluation efforts and strategic planning the transition to an optimally efficient Government will be difficult to achieve.

RECOMMENDATIONS

1. Agencies and organizations throughout the Government need to commit themselves to evaluating their current performance. This effort should include a greater emphasis on both strategic planning and continual and effective program evaluation.
2. HRD staffs need to become integral participants in their organizations' strategic planning and program evaluation processes. In many organizations this will represent a fundamental change in the way they have been doing business. For this change to occur management will need to see their HRD staffs in a new light. To encourage managers to include their HRD offices as they attempt to evaluate and improve their operations, the people working in HRD will need to market their skills to managers. Rather than focusing on getting people into courses, HRD offices need to convince management that their first concern is the business of the organization.
3. Agencies should work to ensure that their HRD staffs have the skills needed to meet the demands of the new roles discussed in this report.
4. OPM should use its position as the agency in charge of human resources management for the entire Government to make a case for improving the quality of HRD activities. This includes working to educate the administration, Congress, and agency heads about the value of training as an investment in a better performing Government. Rather than accepting the view of some organizations that training budgets are a place to save money, OPM should be making agencies aware that spending money on training can be a way of improving performance and solving organizational problems.
5. OPM should continue to lead the effort to define the proper roles for HRD specialists and facilitate their professional development. This should include the development of model career pathways, a comprehensive development program for HRD specialists, and training in the skills required to fill the new roles HRD staff members must assume.
6. OPM should continue to emphasize the importance of accurate assessments of training needs and encourage the development of formal assessment procedures that highlight both current performance problems and future changes in mission objectives.

THE NEED FOR HUMAN RESOURCE DEVELOPMENT

Members of the modern public workforce must possess much more knowledge and skills than the stereotypical bureaucrat of the past was expected to command. Public employees and their administrators must now be a resource to the public and other coworkers by being well informed on a wide range of topics and being adaptable to rapidly changing demands. Government workers facilitate discussions between disparate groups and make difficult decisions with scarce resources while ensuring equal access and public accountability. All of this knowledge and skill must be applied to public problems and issues efficiently and effectively, even though in most situations there is little hope for significant pay incentives or surplus funds dedicated to keeping employees up-to-date on current information. Knowledge will be in great demand, but resources to obtain that knowledge will likely continue to be rather limited. Because of these predictable constraints, the need to find cost-effective ways of developing employees will be important to public organizations seeking the best ways of serving their citizens.

In some ways, HRD is related to the field of organizational development; an important aspect of organizational development is developing methods for organizations to promote employee and organizational learning. According to Peter Senge and others,[2] a culture of learning is increasingly important in organizations—not only for individuals who want to increase their knowledge and skills, but for the organizations themselves as their members share insights, make use of institutional knowledge, and benefit from experience. Organizations can learn through the process of collectively solving important management and operational problems, or through active participation in planning for the future. Organizations can further develop their learning capacity through collaboration and cooperation with external organizations such as universities and other public agencies. By comparing operations and practices with those of similar jurisdictions, organizations can learn valuable lessons from the experiences of others. By teaming up with university researchers, organizations can often learn about the lessons of public administration research conducted around the country and even in other countries.

HRD strategies focus on the needs of the individual as they arise in the context of the needs of the organization. While the focus of HRD is often on the individual or on small work groups, the objective of HRD practices overall is to facilitate the accomplishment of the mission of the organiza-

tion. Training, **mentoring,** job rotation, apprenticeships, and other HRD strategies should be directed toward the improvement of the ability of individuals to help the organization provide public goods and services more effectively.

Public and nonprofit sector managers and HRD professionals need to develop and pursue new strategies to accommodate change. It is widely believed that a comprehensive strategy of continuous employee development is more effective than isolated training sessions or periodic workshops. As a supplement to the overall employee development effort, a sort of "just-in-time" employee development program is often developed so that employees acquire specific knowledge and skills as they are needed for time-sensitive requirements of the organizations.

One of the most important needs for employee development derives from the practice of promoting individuals who have never had any supervisory training or experience to supervisory positions. This is particularly true in the public sector, where an employee is often promoted to a supervisory position because he or she has performed well in an operational position. The practice of promoting from within is commendable as a general rule, but the employee may be completely unable to function as a supervisor without additional training. Employee development initiatives such as mentoring, internships, and training can be useful ways of improving supervision in many of the public organizations that routinely promote employees in this way.

Another important reason for emphasizing employee development stems from the fact that a significant portion of the contemporary workforce is functionally illiterate in terms of verbal or mathematical knowledge. A study of the problems of illiteracy in the public workforce found that some aspect of illiteracy in their workforce affects 61 percent of local governments.[3] Job applicants, and some current employees too, are sometimes deficient in language and math skills. Some local governments identified employees who were unable to write clear reports or read and understand instructions adequately. Research indicates that those who are functionally illiterate also tend to be absent from work more often than other employees and that they tend to be involved in more accidents on the job.[4]

PUBLIC AND NONPROFIT BUDGETS AND HRD

Despite the demonstrated need for employee development in public organizations, HRD is often neglected as a budget priority and indeed is typically the first budget item to be slashed when organizations are required to trim their costs.

There are a number of reasons for the relatively low status of HRD in budgetary contests for resources. Training and employee development are usually not viewed as the central function of most public agencies. The responsibility of public works departments, for example, is to provide clean and safe roads, water, and sewer systems. Health and welfare departments are focused on social services and public health. Training and other development programs can be viewed as taking employees away from these central functions and adversely affecting the already stretched resources of the agency. HRD programs are considered desirable, but unfortunately they tend to be viewed as unnecessary to the central purpose of most public agencies. When cost-cutting becomes necessary, it is easier to cut training programs than to eliminate jobs in the labor-intensive services of most public agencies. Because of limited budget resources and the lack of clear linkages between many training programs and the manifest needs of public organizations, managers may have to consider new ways of developing the capabilities of their employees.[5]

Another reason for the low status given to HRD is the difficulty of seeing immediate benefits from such practices as training, job rotation, educational incentives, internships, and mentoring. Most people feel there is some benefit to these practices, but placing a dollar amount on the benefits can be difficult. The benefits of learning are often intangible, so its value is difficult to estimate and its effects are difficult to see. This transferability problem leads many managers to doubt the efficacy of employee development programs. Frequently the benefits of employee development are realized only after several years, while the up-front costs are immediate.

The costs of these development programs are much easier to determine than the benefits. The relatively high estimated cost-to-benefit ratio makes employee development programs easy targets for budget cuts and elimination. Public and nonprofit sector managers and their HRD professionals are under pressure to find ways of more accurately measuring the benefits of development programs, and they are expected to be able to target training and development initiatives directly to meet the needs of managers.

In a number of public agencies, training and development are viewed as essential to the operation of the organization. Police, fire, and emergency medical service agencies, for example, spend large amounts of time and money on employee development programs. In these agencies, training is viewed as essential because of the liabilities to the organization if employees make mistakes in high-risk situations. They understand that they can provide the best service possible (often in life-and-death situations) only when training on all expected situations is available. Other public agencies are not as immediately concerned with life-and-death problems, but are nonetheless faced with public service situations that pose financial liabilities and situations where poor performance can adversely affect the lives of the public.

Wise managers see the need to keep employees up-to-date on the information and skills needed to perform at their best. The first requirement of a successful employee development strategy is commitment at the top of the organization. When top management is convinced of the benefits of HRD programs and commit the necessary resources, employees can use these programs to their full potential.

HUMAN RESOURCE DEVELOPMENT STRATEGIES

The most common forms of employee development are often not considered part of HRD. In one sense, the nation's largest HRD program is composed of its system of public schools and its colleges and universities. For the most part, these institutions prepare individuals for professions and vocations. Most organizations—public, nonprofit, and private—look to the education system for new recruits. Except for knowledge and skills that are unique to each organization, students learn the fundamental skills and information they need to perform at an entry level in almost any profession. In addition to classroom instruction, many educational programs are instituting internships and apprenticeships to help students make the transition from school to work and to help them learn the skills they can obtain only in on-the-job settings.

HRD strategies draw on a wide variety of methods designed to help employees learn for the purpose of improving capabilities and performance and adapting to a rapidly changing environment. Training is the most common method of structured learning. Many training techniques are instructor-oriented, meaning they are designed and delivered by an instructor who assumes much of the responsibility for ensuring that learning occurs. Most HRD professionals believe that learning will become more important on the job in the future, but the learning taking place will be less formal, more oriented to the individual learner, and structured within the parameters of the organization's mission. One author has observed, "There is indeed a growing emphasis on learning in the workplace—but not necessarily on training."[6] Individual learning strategies are intended to assist individuals in becoming more responsible for their own learning (see Box 12.1).

Organizations can facilitate learning by providing opportunities for employees to progress in their careers while accomplishing organizational objectives (see Box 12.2 on page 326). Learning is an essential characteristic of successful organizations that are required to respond to change. Successful organizations adapt to changing demands through their ability to learn.[7]

There are many methods used to advance individual and organizational learning, and as technology advances, more methods are added to this list every day. The Internet is a major resource for learning. Satellite, cable, microwave, radio, and video transmission technologies are just beginning to provide new opportunities for employees and organizations to work together. Whatever the technique, the objective is to facilitate continuous learning to keep pace with the increasing demands placed on public and nonprofit organizations and their employees.

EMPLOYEE TRAINING

Training is the most common HRD intervention in organizations. Indeed, many employees travel great distances to conferences and workshops to receive training in their fields. Despite the prevalence of training in the work environment, much of what is conducted under the name of training is ineffective or unproductive. Training must be targeted to meet the needs of the organization and the employee, designed appropriately, and evaluated carefully to improve its effectiveness.

Public sector training entails instruction in a large number of topics, including training for job skills, customer service, supervisory and interpersonal skills, team building, policy development and analysis, and organization culture. The variety of topics covered in training programs can be divided into types according to the designated recipient of the training: orientation for new employees, followed by development programs for rank-in-file employees, supervisors, managers, and executives.[8]

Orientation Training

Orientation training is designed to give new employees an understanding of the mission of the organization and the specific duties to be performed to give maximum expression to organizational goals and objectives. The first training an employee should experience on entering an organization is an orientation to the organization, the job, and the employee's place in the organization. Besides the benefit of having new employees understand their way around the organization, employee orientation benefits both the organization and the employee in a number of important ways. Orientation helps reduce start-up costs by allowing the employee to perform immediately upon starting the job and cuts down on employee turnover because employees experience less stress by knowing what to expect on the job.[9]

Box 12.1   Individual Learning Strategies

Job rotation	Temporary appointments to new positions are intended to stretch the experience and challenge employees. Job rotation gives an individual on-the-job training in a variety of settings to learn all the skills of a work group or to prepare that person for future career changes.
Special assignments	Specific tasks or projects are intended to present new opportunities for employees to experience new situations or learn new skills. They are often used with promising employees to prepare them for promotion into positions of higher responsibility.
Internship	Employees may be temporarily assigned to another work unit or management position, where they apply prior or concurrent learning to a real job setting. After the completion of the assignment, employees apply their internship experience to their learning program.
Reflecting on experience	Employees formally analyze the results of a special work assignment to consider lessons learned and apply new principles to their assignments. Reflection is often done in small groups of employees who have each accepted new assignments.
Learning teams	Small teams meet together to work on learning and being more effective, often in specific areas such as new technology or management development.
Coaching and counseling	Managers, team leaders, or senior colleagues assist employees through listening, observing, and providing feedback, often using critical incidents to teach employees about important aspects of performance.
Manager as teacher	Managers use everyday opportunities to teach employees or provide opportunities to assist them in learning.
Mentoring	A senior employee outside the chain of command oversees an employee's career development. A mentor helps the employee deal with the inner workings of the organization and offers counsel to the employee about professional development and career choices. The word *mentor* comes from Greek mythology: Odysseus entrusted his son's education and upbringing to Mentor, his loyal friend.
Individual development plan	The employee and manager work together to develop a plan that outlines specific goals and objectives, including education, training, and other learning strategies for individual development that satisfy both the employee and the organization's needs.
Self-development	An individual works independently to develop learning opportunities. These can include getting involved in professional organizations or computer networks, enrolling in university courses, and undertaking self-study courses.

Source: Federal Human Resource Development Council, *Getting Results Through Learning,* 1997, pp. 6–7, available at: **http://www.amsc.belvoir.army.mil/hrdc/handbook/foreword.htm**.

In orientation training, employees should:

- Become acquainted with the purpose, mission, and services of the organization
- Learn about the key people and culture of the organization and the location of important physical facilities
- Become familiar with the compensation and benefit programs of the organization

- Understand all safety rules and regulations
- Learn about the structure and functions of their assigned department, who their supervisors and coworkers are, and what duties, responsibilities, and behaviors are expected of them on their specific job.[10]

An orientation training checklist would include the following items on the facing page:

Box 12.2 Organizational Learning Strategies

Meetings	Meetings provide one of the best opportunities for organizational learning. Presentations, team-building activities, and reports from employees on individual learning assignments can be given time for the benefit of those attending.
Action learning	A subgroup is assigned to work on a work problem, then report back to managers or a larger group of employees.
Cross-functional teams	Teams comprising members with different knowledge, skills, and abilities work together on a problem or a project. Learning is gained through collaboration and cooperation among team members.
Work-outs	Groups of employees from all backgrounds, excluding managers, meet to discuss answers to organizational problems in a town-hall style of meeting. Alternatives are presented to management in similar meetings where decisions are made whether to accept or reject proposals at the meeting.
Strategic planning	Groups of employees meet to develop an organizational mission statement, goals, specific action plans, and critical success indicators. Organizations learn about their own strengths and weaknesses, as well as identify threats and opportunities in their environment.
Organization scorecard	Performance indicators are selected and tracked to show all levels of employees how the organization is meeting its objectives. The scorecard is regularly updated to give emphasis to important objectives and show the organization's progress.
Benchmarking	The best practices in similar organizations are sought out to help an organization improve its own operations. This method of organizational learning involves self-assessment of problem areas, finding model practices in other organizations, analyzing why these practices work in other organizations, and adapting these practices for use.
Groupware	In this computer-aided method of gathering input from all members of the group simultaneously, each member has a computer networked to the system that displays ideas and comments in the order they are input onto the master screen. Group members can brainstorm, comment, respond, and prioritize—either anonymously or by self-identification.
Computer conferencing	Video and fiber-optic technology allows individuals in remote or distant locations to interact in real time in the same way as if they were in the same room. Conferences, training seminars, meetings, discussions, and classes can be conducted across distant locations.

Source: Federal Human Resource Development Council, *Getting Results Through Learning*, pp. 7–9.

- New employee orientation checklist (covering the objectives listed above)
- Names, titles, and telephone and office numbers of key personnel
- Map of the property and physical facilities
- Directory of sources of information
- Employee handbook and personnel policies and procedures
- Copy of operational policy and procedure manual
- Description of compensation and benefits
- Copies of performance evaluation forms and procedures
- List of on-the-job training opportunities
- Organizational chart
- Copy of the applicable job description with duties and responsibilities
- Detailed outline of emergency and accident prevention and reporting procedures[11]

Employee Development Training

Training for employee development is typically focused on improving the performance of continuing employees in their particular job knowledge and skills. On-the-job training is frequently used to demonstrate job functions, and classroom sessions are used to convey general information. Supervisory development involves new and continuing front-line managers and develops skills such as delegation, the building of employee motivation, interpersonal communications, and how to work with small groups. Supervisors are often taught by a "tell-show-do" method: supervisory practices are discussed and demonstrated, and then the trainees practice each of the skills. A debriefing session is often conducted after practicing the skill to answer any questions and clarify supervisory practices.

Management and Executive Training

Management and executive development is targeted at upper-level managers and focuses on management theory as well as discussions about how to perform management practices such as coaching, mentoring, team building, and oversight of personnel functions. Managers often receive training through methods such as role playing, simulations, case studies, active learning, and applied projects. Executive development includes broader conceptual and organizational issues such as policy development and analysis, politics, strategic planning, negotiation, media relations and image management, intergovernmental networking, leadership, and organizational culture.

Executive development programs are often done in small groups or are self-directed, limited only by time constraints and costs. Public sector management and executive development programs have been developed in almost every state. Thirty-six university-based public sector management and executive development programs have been identified, and these are located throughout the United States.[12]

TRAINING PHASES

The provision of effective training for managers and employees is a much more complicated undertaking than simply sending someone to a conference or arranging for a motivational speaker. These can be useful steps to take, but they may not be what people really need to perform their job duties better. To be effective, training should address the actual needs of individuals and the organization and should be designed to teach individuals in ways they are most able to transfer the information taught to their work. Training designed to accomplish learning objectives should go through three **training phases**: assessment, design and delivery, and eventually evaluation (see Table 12.1 on page 328).[13]

The first phase is to assess the need for training. There are many reasons training may be needed; some are for the benefit of the organization, others for the department, and others are based on what the individual needs to learn to do the job assigned.

Phase 2, design and delivery, involves conceptualizing a plan of how the training will take

Table 12.1   Training Phases

Phase 1: Assessment	Phase 2: Design and Delivery	Phase 3: Evaluation
Organizational Assessment	**Training Design**	**Measuring Against Training Objectives and Evaluation Criteria**
Organization policies	Training objectives	Reaction
Stakeholder attitudes	Learning principles	Learning
Performance record	Training strategy	Behavior
Job Assessment	**Delivery Methods**	Results
Job analysis	Participative	
Performance audit	Learning focus	
Individual Assessment		
Performance appraisal		
Employee development plan		
Professional requirements		
Legal requirements		
Individual deficiencies		

place, what methods will be used, as well as the time required and the specific teaching aids needed. In the third and final phase, a systematic evaluation is conducted of the learning that took place as a result of the training.

Phase 1: Assessment

Often training is conducted without first determining which employees need the training in question. This approach can result in a great deal of wasted time for employees and a bad reputation for those providing the training. Instead, training should be designed to meet the needs of the organization and those who work there. Management fads are frequently the subject matter for training, but these training topics can be counterproductive if employees have more pressing training needs they are missing.

In order to target training efforts properly, a **needs assessment** should be conducted to learn what people need to know in order to perform more effectively in their assigned jobs. Assess-

ments are intended to determine the difference (or gap) between what employees need to know and should be doing and what they currently know and actually are doing. Training needs assessments typically investigate three particular domains—organizational climate, job demands, and individuals' capacity to perform and expand their range of activity.

Organizational climate assessments generally analyze the organization's mission, goals, and culture. Do employees understand the stated mission and goals of the organization? Do they share the values of the organization and understand what is accepted as ethical behavior? An organizational assessment could also analyze the familiarity of employees with agency policies, such as personnel practices and equal employment guidelines. Stakeholder assessments of customers, citizens, and employees can show how these groups view the organization and identify what the organization can do to serve their needs appropriately. The organization may also want to assess its overall performance in relation to its own standards or the performance of similar types, a practice known as **benchmarking**. Each of these organizational assessments can provide management and trainers with valuable information about the needs of the organization, which can then be applied to the design of the training program and the structure of its evaluation.

Job demands assessments analyze the duties, responsibilities, skills, and knowledge that make up a job and determine which areas should be the subject of training. Some aspect of a job may involve new technology or the following of new regulatory guidelines (e.g., workplace safety provisions), and these developments should be presented to employees who need the new information. In some cases, there may be a general problem of performance among those responsible for a specific task. Training may be needed to improve performance for all employees in a particular job classification. For example, if it is found that law enforcement officers are "profiling" minority youth in traffic stops—i.e., disproportionately detaining minority drivers—a department-wide training program would be indicated.

Job demands assessment is probably the most common form of training needs assessment. It can be used to identify job duties and responsibilities and the associated knowledge and skills needed to perform job tasks. Subject matter experts can be used to make certain that the essential duties and responsibilities are identified. The objective of the job demands assessment is to determine what type of training is needed to either help employees learn a new task or improve performance on existing work. Employees can be asked by survey or interview whether they see a need for additional training in any of their job duties and responsibilities. In addition, a performance audit can be conducted of work groups or individual employees to determine whether there are common deficiencies in the knowledge or skill required to perform specific jobs.

Individual assessments are done to help individuals improve their work performance. This assessment can help managers and trainers identify which individuals need to be trained and what type and level of training they need. In some cases, remedial training is required to bring employees up to their job level. Employees may also be trained in the jobs of coworkers so work team members are familiar with the jobs of other members, or they may learn to perform at the next job level in preparation for a promotion. Supervisors can provide valuable input as to which employees should receive training as identified from performance appraisals and employee development plans. Employees can also identify any legally mandated or professional training needs, as well as any self-identified deficiencies that they are willing to address through training.

Phase 2: Design and Delivery

Once the training needs and participants are identified, a training program can be designed to meet the needs of employees and the organization. It begins by identifying the training objectives and then designing the best approach to achieve these objectives. In the development of the design, the trainer should consider the type of individual receiving the training, the type of task to be trained, the principles of learning that apply for optimum learning, cost controls, the most appropriate method to be used to achieve learning by the participants, and technology.

Learning objectives Training programs can fail if they are not directly related to the problems existing in the organization in question. Therefore, the first step in training design is to establish the objectives of the training program. Administrative problems typically exist at three levels: context, process, and behavior. Context problems arise when the organization's mission is insufficiently understood and employers are concentrating efforts on inappropriate goals; process problems arise when needed procedures for deciding action are either nonexistent or are being circumvented; and behavioral problems arise when organization members either cannot or will not do the things required of them in their work. For training to be effective, it needs to be directed appropriately to the context, process, or behavior problems clearly identified at the outset.

Training objectives should be measurable and have training evaluation clearly in mind.[14] Evaluations are made on the reaction of participants: what is learned, how behavior is affected, and the actual improved performance results attributable to the training intervention.[15] Objectives might relate to the reaction of participants to the training; for example, participants should perceive the training as interesting and useful. An objective emphasizing learning would identify the learning expected, and this could be measured by a test of relevant skills or knowledge at the conclusion of the training and again after some period of time to assess retention of learning.

Because the purpose of training frequently is to change the behavior of employees on the job, behavioral training objectives may be the most important ones. Behavioral objectives identify what an employee will be able to do and often how well they are able to do specific tasks—for example: "In the first five minutes of questioning a witness, police officers will be able to inform the citizen of his or her rights when investigating a crime." Training objectives also can be related to the changes in performance that are anticipated as a result of training—for example, a reduction in the number of complaints, completion of cases or forms, or any measurable performance indicator related to the subject of the training.

Considering the learner Adult learners have a significant body of knowledge they have gained by life experience.[16] This knowledge can be a valuable resource for the instructor in helping participants understand related learning objectives. For example, when the topic is how the hiring process should work in a personnel office, there is no substitute for the experience participants have had when they have applied for jobs to show the appropriate ways and inappropriate ways to hire.

Adults are usually willing to take responsibility for their own learning. They can see the relationship of learning to their lives and understand the value of learning to their own well-being. Adult learners tend to be problem centered, tend to take training to resolve a current problem or need, and want the training to be relevant to their needs. Consequently, it is important for training to be focused and for the instructor to help participants apply the concepts they learn to their situation. Finally, adults generally want to be actively involved in the learning process; they want to discuss how ideas apply to themselves and their own circumstances, and they want to practice the techniques or skills that are presented.

Competency-based training Training should be targeted to meet the needs of individuals to perform better in their jobs. The training design should include strategies for teaching specific knowledge, skills, and abilities required in each job. A large amount of training has been devoted to supervisory and managerial functions, but managers perform a variety of functions and often find their time wasted when training is directed to tasks they do not perform. Management must be competent in many different areas, but different levels of management tend to have differing responsibilities. Paul Sandwith has identified six groups (domains) of management competencies and matched these with six levels of management.[17] All managers must have knowledge, skills, and abilities in the conceptual, leadership, interpersonal, administrative, and technical domains. Depending on their level of management, managers must possess a different level of knowledge and practice different skills in each of these domains. Sandwith advocates designing specific training options to address one or more of the learning domains for each level of management. Table 12.2 simplifies the competency domain model to three levels of management.

Principles of learning Our understanding of how people learn has changed from the traditional teacher-oriented model toward an appreciation of how participants perceive and process information. Learning is a process whereby individuals make sense of the world around them. Typically

Table 12.2   Sandwith's Competency Domain

	Technical Domain	Administrative Domain	Interpersonal Domain	Leadership Domain	Conceptual Domain
Supervisor	• Knowledge of work group job duties • Scheduling • Problem solving • Productivity monitoring • Maintenance	• Personnel policies and procedures • Health and safety • Contract management • Performance appraisal • Discipline • Budget management	• Job training • Delegation • Goal setting • Performance management • Complaint management • Presentations • Leading meetings • Conflict management • Selection interviews • Dealing with upper management • Writing reports	• Personal role model • Encouraging and developing employees • Managing individual performance • Developing and managing the work team • Professional ethics	• Understanding the job role • Understanding the relationship of the job with other job roles • Adaptation of innovations • Work section planning
Management	• Knowledge of functional unit roles and responsibilities • Knowledge of procedures for facilitating operations	• Personnel policies and procedures: recruitment, performance, promotion, discipline, union relations • Financial management: budget development, cost-benefit analysis, cost control, productivity, purchasing • Delegation, assignment, and reporting	• Interaction with union representatives, customers, suppliers, and contractors • Verbal and written presentation • Conflict management • Leading staff meetings and participating in management meetings • Counseling with reporting supervisors	• Personal role model • Representing reporting units to management • Representing the organization to the community • Developing the supervisory team and subordinate managers • Professional ethics • Developing unit plans	• Understanding the role of reporting units • Implementing organization mission
Executive	• Knowledge of the operations and roles of the organization • Knowledge of decision-making and policymaking methods	• Development of personnel policies • Budget guidelines and approval	• Representing the organization to key stakeholders • Verbal and written communications and presentations • Leading management meetings • Negotiation, persuasion, compassion	• Organization mission, culture, planning • Inspiring and guiding managers and employees • Developing resources for organizational success	• Professional ethics • Providing the vision and direction of the organization • Understanding internal and external organizational relationships

learning is the result of perceiving a problem, clarifying the nature of the problem, and developing possible solutions.[18] This process of problem solving through hypothesis testing is known as the scientific method, and it is used formally by scientists to learn about their disciplines. But all of us use this process informally as we seek to understand our world and solve our own problems. We encounter a problem, think of what the cause might be, and try out possible solutions. The knowledge gained from these problem-solving experiences is transformed into learning as individuals think about their experiences and apply the principles to other problems.[19] Ronald Sims explains that learning is "more than a stimulus-response process. Thinking and analysis occur during reflection and generalization, as well as in the testing of hypotheses."[20]

Montgomery Van Wart has identified seven fundamental **training principles** from the literature on learning theory that can help participants gain the most from their training experiences:[21]

1. Foster participant goal setting.
2. Increase the similarity of training to the work environment.
3. Use underlying principles.
4. Increase the organization of the material.
5. Actively involve the learner.
6. Give feedback.
7. Use a variety of techniques and stimuli.

Participant goal setting also begins with an accurate needs assessment. Training participants should see a need for the training they are to receive, and they should be able to make the connection between the training offered and their ability to perform better at their jobs. This is one reason that training objectives should align directly with the needs and goals of participants. Training participants should also be ready to receive the training that is prepared for them.[22] They may need prerequisite experience, skills, or knowledge to understand the material presented. Goal setting can be enhanced by involving the learners in the needs assessment phase and discussing with them early in the training session how the training will benefit them. Participants should also receive confirming experiences early in the training program to demonstrate to themselves that the training is useful.

Training is of no value unless participants are able to transfer what is taught and learned in the training session to their work. One of the best ways to improve training transferability is to help participants relate what is being discussed in the training to their work situations. Training can be more realistic through the use of participative teaching methods. Case studies, real work examples, role playing, simulations, and site visits can be used to make the concepts authentic and applicable to training participants. To retain the information learned, participants should have the opportunity to apply the concepts and tasks taught in the training session to their job. A review session several weeks after the initial training will also help participants review the materials learned and report on how they have applied them. Unless trainees use knowledge gained in training, they are likely to rely on old patterns of action.

Learning theory suggests that people are better able to apply concepts and techniques that they are taught when they understand the reasons why the instruction provides a better way to act. When participants understand underlying principles behind the specific application taught, they are able to apply these principles to new situations.

The organization of training materials has a major impact on the ability of participants to learn. A clear, logical format helps trainees follow the presentation and apply the material to familiar situations. The training should have written objectives and an outline of how concepts or methods will be presented. Visual aids such as graphs, tables, pictures, and videos are also useful to help participants understand what is being presented. A common training format is to "tell-show-do." For example, if a training concept is mission statements, the instructor may open the segment by defining what mission statements are, setting forth the need for mission statements, listing the reasons for their use, and giving examples. The full group then divides up into smaller ones, with each given the task of developing a mission statement, and then the full group reconvenes and settles on one statement. The last step in the process would be to discuss the principles involved in the light of the exercise they just completed.

People are also more likely to learn if they are actively engaged in the learning process instead of merely listening to someone talk. The objective should be to help participants become actively engaged so they apply the new concepts to their situations. One of the oldest methods of involving participants is the Socratic method: the instructor asks questions to help students come to desired conclusions themselves and to generate discussion. Active engagement can also be accomplished through structured debates and the use of small and large group discussions. A concluding segment or debriefing session can result in useful discussion following a case study, a simulation, or self-assessment exercises. Trainees may also be given assignments for homework, case studies, or practice exercises. They can be assigned to go to a work setting to observe or practice the material discussed in the training session. Discussion of the results of these assignments can also contribute to the active involvement of training participants.

Individuals are able to learn more efficiently when the instructor provides regular feedback to them regarding their progress and opportunities for exploring new ideas. Many people are motivated by achievement and need a goal to help them focus their learning. Periodic feedback helps training participants know if they are working in the direction intended by the instructor. Feedback also helps trainees know if they are doing well in the opinion of the instructor at learning what they are supposed to learn and whether they are applying the principles in ways that were intended. Another valuable quality of feedback is that it provides an opportunity for participants to discuss the implications of the principles presented and explore ways these principles will apply to their work situations.

Presenting information in a variety of ways helps participants understand the concepts under consideration and makes the training more interesting and enjoyable. For years, the lecture was pretty much the exclusive method of presenting information, and this method remains effective for some subjects and may be useful in introducing topics. However, most people want to be more actively involved in learning than just listening to a teacher talk. As they use more of their senses, learning is enhanced. The use of a variety of people to give expert information or discuss their experience helps participants relate the information being discussed to their own situations. Many new and old media technologies—for example, films, videos, overhead transparencies, and computer-generated slide shows—can be used to improve the quality and diversity of presentations.

Sometimes it is useful to have participants go through the process they are learning about, such as demonstrating how to answer a telephone effectively. Participants can learn by remembering the touch, the sound, and the experience of performing a task.

A word of caution regarding the use of training techniques and multimedia: it is easy to fall into the trap of substituting gimmicks for substance. A video by itself does not teach effectively; its relevance to the learning objective must be made clear to participants. Exercises, simulations, overheads, computer displays, and other training techniques are very useful methods, *but they are just tools.* Training must be designed to help participants achieve learning objectives. Effective trainers use a variety of tools to tie together a conceptual theme or to illustrate a point that needs to be made. Training should not degenerate to the point of being unfocused in its learning objectives or just offering entertainment; the limited time available for training is too valuable to be wasted.

Incorporating cost controls Now more than ever before, training must be cost-effective, and managers must perceive it as having value if they are to devote scarce resources to continuing HRD programs. Because of the limited organizational resources devoted to training and other HRD practices, managers must be able to see the return on investment: measurable changes in performance are the bottom line. Training must be competency driven, transformational, quantifiable, and technology based.[23] Training must improve the ability of employees to perform their jobs, alter unproductive behavior, and add skills so that trainees become more valuable organizational assets.

The costs and benefits of training should be measurable using a variety of methods. All costs should be identified to give management a clear picture of the resources that are going into training. Most organizations measure the effectiveness of training with an after-session evaluation. This method has some value, but does not really measure learning. A better method is to ask a variety of affected people—participants, their managers, peers, and subordinates—about training outcomes. Before-and-after measurements of productivity and control group comparisons can also be used to quantify the benefits of training.

Appropriate training methods The use of a variety of training methods makes training more interesting and can help participants to learn (see Table 12.3). Lectures are useful for disseminating a large amount of information or introducing a new idea. When they are combined with discussion and participative methods, participants can analyze and practice the information and ideas imparted.

Frequently trainers depend on one or two training techniques. This is a mistake, because people learn in several different ways, and the use of a variety of methods can help more people learn the material presented. In addition, each method has advantages and disadvantages, addresses different learning principles, and is more or less appropriate for different subjects or participant needs. For

example, group discussion is useful for experienced professionals who can add the lessons of their experience to the subject under discussion. Role playing and simulation may be appropriate for those who have not yet had significant or relevant on-the-job experience. And some training methods can be used to support another method. For example, an instructor may ask trainees to read a case study before coming to the classroom. After a brief lecture, the group may break into small discussion groups to prepare for a debate on the issues presented in the case study.

A common method of training employees involves the use of videotapes.[24] Employees can review videotapes at their own pace, see demonstrations of the skills required by the job, and take tests to determine their level of knowledge, abilities, and skills. Videotapes can provide an overview of the organization and introduce new employees to key personnel without taking the

Table 12.3   Training Methods

Self-Study Methods	Classroom Methods (Passive Learning Methods)	Classroom Methods (Active/ Participative Learning Methods)	Experiment and Practice Methods	On-the-Job Learning Methods
Videotape	Lecture	Student presentations	Self-assessments	Apprenticeships
Assigned readings	Guest speakers	Instructor-guided questions and answers	Workbook exercises	Coaching[c]
Training manuals	Panel presentation	Large group discussions	Demonstrations	Mentoring
Computer-based	Films/videotape	Small group training	Role playing discussions	Job rotation
Vestibule training[a]		Case studies Debate Teleconferencing	Simulation Written tests Behavior modeling[b]	**Action learning**[d]

a. Vestibule training allows employees to practice all of the job duties required in a controlled setting resembling the workplace with a trainer present to provide feedback.
b. Behavior modeling involves observing a model's behavior of "good" or "bad" practices and applying the appropriate behavior in a controlled setting (such as role playing) and eventually to the job.
c. In coaching, experienced employees observe and offer advice to new employees in much the same way as a coach guides an athletic team.
d. Action learning involves classroom instruction in a specific subject, followed by an assignment on a real-world project that applies the principles discussed in the classroom. Action learning usually involves extensive training and an involved, complex problem to be solved by the learning participants.

time out of managers' schedules to meet every new employee. The next most common methods used are lectures, on-the-job training, role playing, simulation, and case studies.

The analogy of the toolbox fits for designing training programs. There are many methods, each with particular applications. The right tool for the right job can result in a valuable learning experience for participants. The wrong tool can be clumsy and awkward, and training participants will be left wondering what the trainer was trying to accomplish. Effective training design and delivery requires matching the appropriate training method to the subject matter and learning objectives. Skillful application of methods is the means to learning, not the end. Training methods can be divided into self-study, classroom-passive, classroom-participative, classroom-practice, and on-the-job methods or techniques.

Technological considerations in human resource development One of the most exciting developments in human resource development are the emerging technologies for delivering information to employees. Technology provides access to learning anytime and anywhere. Developments in video, CD-ROM, computer software, the Internet, and two-way interactive transmission all have tremendous potential for maintaining the continued development of employees. There appears to be a rush to exploit these technologies for a variety of reasons: with rapid change comes the need for continual upgrading of information, organizations are more decentralized and their employees more widely distributed, many needed skills (particularly in technology) are deficient in the workforce,[25] and (reflective of the bottom line) employers believe there is significant potential for cost savings. Before we jump headlong onto the information technology bandwagon, there are a few considerations that deserve careful attention.

The delivery of education beyond the classroom has a long history of partial successes and unfulfilled potential.[26] Successful uses of distance learning can be cited in the areas of rural school access to special instruction (e.g., satellite instruction in foreign language, advanced math, and so forth) and rural medical practitioner access to diagnostic and treatment information via the Internet. The Agricultural Extension Act of 1914 has been somewhat successful as well for farmers, but the performance demonstrated has been nothing like the promises made at its inception. Many universities offer correspondence courses that many feared would replace classroom professors. Thomas Edison believed film would replace books in the classroom.[27] Perhaps the greatest disappointment has been the unachieved potential of television. Educators believed television could disseminate information to vast audiences. Although to some degree (particularly with the development of cable television) this vision has come true, for the most part television has succumbed to the attraction of the highly profitable delivery of base entertainment and crass commercialism. Today the educators' vision is set on the potential of computers and the Internet for the coming *renaissance* in learning. In reality, the oldest of learning technologies provides the advantages of modern technological delivery methods: "When compared to the average online courses available today, books are no less accessible or interactive. Learners can control how much of a book to read, when to read it, and who to read it with."[28]

A great deal of experimentation has gone into learning technologies sponsored by federal grant money in the hope of achieving enhanced productivity and cost savings. Online schools such as the University of Phoenix and the New School for Social Research offer degrees through their distance-learning programs. One of the most ambitious efforts at distance learning has been the Western Governors' University and associated organizations that seek to coordinate the efforts of several western states. Participation by the states has been intermittent, however, and enrollment numbers have been disappointing. This result is consistent with efforts of private companies that enthusiastically developed expensive "intranets" for distance learning, only to see them underused.[29]

The learning technology literature gives the

new technologies mixed reviews when it comes to learning outcomes, concluding that, as a general rule, newer forms of instructional media have not proven to be superior to traditional delivery methods.[30] Regardless of the delivery method, students can learn equally well with different technologies. What is broadly known is that student engagement is closely related to learning, and that engagement can be significantly enhanced with the use of a range of learning technologies.[31] The reason for the unfulfilled expectations evidenced thus far in the use of new instrumental technologies may be that these new learning modalities are not yet fully developed.

Many of the new technologies have been used as enhancements for the delivery of information for learning. The method of teaching has not changed significantly, but the enhancements, or the availability of supporting information, have improved markedly.[32] The potential for enhancing training on terms with the new learning technologies lies in relating them more closely to the content, context, and methodology of learning. The standard "teaching by telling" or "sage on a stage" method can now be replaced by experiential and customized learning. The literature discusses four key developments in learning technologies that promise to revolutionize the delivery, content, and context of training:[33]

- *Internet-based training (IBT).* The use of the Internet for training rests on its capacity to serve as an economic distribution mechanism for computer-based training and a medium for electronic correspondence courses. It also provides a platform for interactive multimedia IBT, and presents the potential for live, real-time videoconferencing, collaboration, and networking over the Internet.
- *Intelligent tutoring system (ITS).* This is a self-paced interactive learning environment with artificial intelligence and voice recognition technologies that allow for customized training to meet specific individual needs. ITS generates instructions based on the learner's performance, interprets and responds to

the learner's interactions, assesses the level of the learner's knowledge, and makes pedagogical inferences and decisions based on the learner's interactions. ITS will be able to monitor, evaluate, and improve its own teaching performance based on its own experience in teaching. ITS is being developed by a variety of organizations, including the Defense Department and US West.

- *Learning objectives software.* Some of the most intense work in training software is evidenced in the development of independent, reusable, pre-programmed components of learning called learning objectives software. Trainers are able to combine learning objectives in diverse applications by configuring training components in different ways. Eventually, learning libraries will be filled with learning objective components made available to trainers who will be able to link these objectives into meaningful content.
- *Voice recognition.* Possibly the most conspicuous change in learning technology will be the development of natural, real-time voice recognition. Keyboards and mouse controllers may become a thing of the past as we simply talk to our computers. This technology promises to be essential to language training and applications where the computer user's hands are not free to use a keyboard.

Phase 3: Evaluation

Evaluation of training indicates how effective the training has been and what changes are necessary to make training more helpful to future participants. Evaluation begins with the learning objectives established before the training program was designed. Evaluation should measure how well the training achieved these specific learning objectives. Since training is conducted with the objective of imparting information, learning a skill, or realizing some tangible result, the evaluation of training should determine whether these purposes were realized.

Most training involves some kind of feedback instrument such as an evaluation form that tells the trainer how participants enjoyed the training experience or if they thought it was useful. Although measuring the reaction of participants to the training can be helpful for some purposes, it does not really tell us whether the trainee actually learned anything. A good evaluation measures participant reaction as well as actual learning, whether behavior changed, and whether real results were realized as a result of the training.[34] An effective evaluation addresses all four levels of evaluation if each is appropriate to the training's learning objectives:

Reaction, measured by evaluation surveys administered at the end of a training session or program

Learning, measured by testing the participant after the training

Behavior, usually measured by observation by qualified evaluators such as a supervisor or others who know how a job should be performed

Results, measured in quantitative terms such as number of errors, complaints, cases completed, and other measures of productivity

Useful training evaluation requires an **evaluation design** that measures actual change in learning, behavior, or results that are related to the training experience. The evaluation may also be used to determine if training participants were able to reach a specified level of performance or competence.

The simplest method of evaluation is to measure knowledge, skill, behavior, or results after training is completed. While this post-test assessment design cannot measure change because there was no measurement before training occurred, but it can be useful for determining whether a standard of performance or level of knowledge has been achieved. For example, you may want to know if training resulted in all firefighters being able to identify critical equipment for use on the scene of a meth lab incident. Even in this case, it could be possible that the training had no effect on the learning of firefighters. They may have learned about this equipment on another job or in school.

More useful evaluations measure a group that has received the training and one that has not received the training. This can be done in any one of three ways. The first is for a group that will receive training to be measured before and again after training to see if a change took place as a result of training. This pre-test and post-test design is frequently used but requires advanced planning to test the group before training. This design has the drawback of assuming that any change recorded was the result of training; in fact, many factors could have influenced change during the time period between the pre-test and the post-test.

The second method is to measure the group that has received training and compare results against a control group that has not received training; the difference should be the result of training. The problem with this method is more serious than the first because no two groups are exactly alike, and many factors could account for differences between groups besides a training intervention.

The third method, which combines these two evaluation techniques, resolves most of these concerns. A pre-test and post-test is conducted both on the group that receives training and on a control group that does not receive training (see Figure 12.1). If the training is effective, there should

Figure 12.1 Evaluation Design Using a Control Group with Pre-test and Post-test

Training Group	Measure	→	Train	→	Measure
Control Group	Measure	→	No Training	→	Measure

be improvement registered in the test group post-test and no comparable improvement noted in the control group post-test.

Whatever method is used to evaluate training, the important thing is to measure results that can be directly attributable to the training received.

HRD PRACTICES IN GOVERNMENT

Effective HRD practices are becoming increasingly important to the survival of public, private, and nonprofit organizations. This significance is reflected in the amount of money spent annually on employee training, management training, and organizational development. It has been estimated that in 1995, $200 billion was spent on HRD activities in all sectors of the U.S. economy.[35] In 1991, state governments spent more than $12 billion for training activities, the federal government spent about $1 billion, and local governments probably spent several times more than the states. This compares to about $45 billion spent by the private sector.[36] Research indicates that the public sector is lagging behind private organizations in the way training is conducted. In the first phase of training, for example, 38 percent of private organizations report they use needs assessment studies to plan for appropriate training.[37] Only 13 percent of state government agencies consistently use needs assessments to address their training needs.[38] It is difficult to imagine how state agencies are meeting the real needs of their employees if they are not systematically assessing their training needs.

Some differences were found in the training methods used in state agencies compared to private organizations.[39] Both used the lecture method most heavily (91 percent for state agencies and 93 percent for private organizations). Role playing, the second most common method used in the private sector (63 percent), was used by only 7 percent of state agencies. Simulations were also used more in the private sector than in state agencies. Both groups used computer-assisted learning and case studies almost equally.

The weakest area of training for state agencies was found in the evaluation of their training programs. Almost half (47 percent) of the state agencies surveyed said they did not assess employee performance after the completion of training. Another 29 percent measured performance immediately after the completion of training—and these were often only measures of reaction.[40] There appears to be significant room for improvement in the areas of needs assessment and evaluation for training in public agencies to be effective.

The training situation might be better for nonprofit organizations, probably because of the rapid change in role of these organizations and the need to operate on very limited budgets.[41] One example of how management training has evolved in the nonprofit sector is the United Way's National Academy for Voluntarism (NAV).[42] The NAV program was designed to use academics and consultants from outside the local United Way network to take advantage of experts in various fields of study and bring in new ideas to the voluntary sector. The designers also wanted the training to have application beyond the United Way system and attract customers from outside the system. The training was to be designed with United Way values in mind, not using canned presentations and encouraging active participation. The training program featured four one-week modules on the following topics:

Management skills (communication, personnel, management by objectives, performance)

Leadership and team excellence (productivity, team building, conflict, motivation, leadership)

Organization change (change, culture, organizational assessment)

Strategic planning (strategy, direction, plans, control)

A growing trend in public management and development training programs is the certification movement. There are over 2.2 million managerial positions in the U.S. public sector; it is coming to pass that public administration is maturing into a recognized profession.[43] This maturation is reflected in the large number of graduate programs in public administration and the accreditation efforts of the National Association of Schools of Public Affairs and Administration (NASPAA).[44] A number of professions have historically certified those who have met the educational and practical requirements of the profession. Associations for public accountants, attorneys, and engineers certify that qualified individuals have met their requirements for official certification. Now an increasing number of public sector professionals have developed certification programs.[45] Local government clerks are certified by the International Institute for Municipal Clerks and city treasurers by the Municipal Treasurers Association of the United States and Canada. Twenty states have developed Certified Public Manager programs in their states, consisting of 300 hours of management training for state managers.[46]

The most compelling reason for certification is to improve the abilities of public managers who have been routinely criticized as being unprofessional "rank amateurs."[47] There are other benefits too:[48]

- Giving public management a professional identity, an enhanced image, consistent values, and norms of conduct
- Standardizing the body of knowledge practitioners should know to be competent in a profession
- Providing clients or customers some assurance (although no guarantee) of professional competence
- Promoting continued learning and updating of professional knowledge and skills
- Allowing for the free interaction of others within the profession to share ideas and experiences
- Encouraging the public and elected officials to take the public management profession more seriously[49]

- Increasing the salable skills possessed by public managers and providing a rationale for better pay (of course, this can be a substantial advantage in some situations—but turn into a disadvantage for public managers in others)

Those who speak against certification programs note the following negatives:

- There is no relationship between certification and performance on the job. An individual can go through extensive training programs and still not be able (or be unwilling) to perform essential job functions.
- There is no standard test of the practices and experience of most professions.
- Certification may diminish the responsibility of professionals to maintain high standards of practice if the certification is awarded on a minimum set of standards.
- Certification may lock in the scope of knowledge and skills of a profession, limiting its ability to grow and develop.[50]
- Many professions have not yet reached agreement on what are the essential characteristics of the profession or on what constitutes competency in the performance of job duties and responsibilities.[51]
- Many professions have not yet agreed on a single organization to administer the certification.[52]

Finally, there is one more reason heard often against certification programs—namely, that certified professionals will use their certification to demand higher compensation. This is a poor reason to limit the development of employees and managers, and can sometimes be countered by not awarding a certification but encouraging ongoing learning through continuing education credits or certificates of completion of professional training programs.

EXAMPLES OF TRAINING TOPICS

Diversity Training

An increasing demand for employee development has been in part the result of the increased diversity of the public workforce. As the demography of the workforce continues to change, diversity will become increasingly important to organizations as they adjust their personnel functions to accommodate newly recognized needs of their current and potential employees.

When discussing diversity, we include individuals from many different backgrounds who have different experiences, characteristics, and heritage who can offer unique perspectives for the benefit of the group or organization as a whole. These differences may include differences in culture, race, ethnicity, age, sex, religion, disability, nationality, region, or other distinctions. Everyone is included in a diverse workforce, and the unique needs of all individuals are viewed as deserving of equal acknowledgment. The focus is less on differences than on the contribution of each perspective to the implementation of the goals of the agency and its service delivery to internal and external communities.

Many public organizations have decided that it is wise for them to encourage and appreciate diversity as they endeavor to serve the needs of their citizens. As is the case during any time of transition, some people will have difficulty adjusting or understanding the changes going on around them. In response to the needs of a diverse workforce and multicultural citizenry, public organizations around the country have implemented diversity training programs. The International Personnel Management Association has noted that diversity management programs are designed to "facilitate the exchange of new perspectives, improve problem solving by inviting different ideas, and create a respectful, accepting work environment, all of which make good business sense."[53] Diversity management programs include the following objectives:

- Building an institutional culture that incorporates differences
- Developing multicultural teams
- Recruiting and retaining a diverse workforce
- Resolving conflict between employers and employees
- Reducing employee turnover
- Promoting employee productivity

The topics of diversity training can vary according to the specific needs of every organization, but some common themes include the following topics:

- Understanding differences in the meanings ascribed to cultural symbols and language
- Communicating across cultures
- Gaining skills in removing cultural barriers
- Appreciating and valuing differences of perspective
- Establishing alliances for effective team building[54]

Ethics Training

Many public organizations are requiring ethics training for all employees. Federal government employees and their counterparts in state and local government increasingly are under public scrutiny for suspected misconduct. Even the appearance of unethical behavior can lead to negative media exposure and criticism by the public and elected officials. In order to promote the observation of standards of ethical conduct, professional organizations have established codes of ethical conduct,[55] and in some cases the specification of ethical behavior has been established by law.

The Ethics in Government Act of 1978 represents an early effort to establish a code of conduct for federal employees. The act established the Office of Government Ethics (OGE) to prevent and resolve conflicts of interest and promote high ethical standards for federal government employees. The OGE provides reference publications, booklets, pamphlets, and an ethics newsgram for executive agencies that offer ethics training for their employees. It also provides training programs and computer- and web-based training for distance learning. The OGE's training programs are designed around Executive Order 12674 (1989) and Executive Order 12731 (1990), which outline fourteen "principles of ethical conduct for government officers and employees" to "ensure that every citizen can have complete confidence in the integrity of the Federal government."[56] (See Box 12.3.)

The OGE identifies "Agency Best Practices" to highlight commendable efforts at promoting ethical conduct in government. One of the best practices is found in the Bureau of Public Debt (BPD) in the Department of Treasury, which developed an interactive ethics training program on CD-ROM. The training program was developed completely in-house using available computer equipment. The program provides general ethics information and updates and, combined with a

---

Box 12.3   Office of Government Ethics Fourteen Principles of Ethical Conduct

(a) Public service is a public trust, requiring employees to place loyalty to the Constitution, the laws, and ethical principles above private gain.

(b) Employees shall not hold financial interests that conflict with the conscientious performance of duty.

(c) Employees shall not engage in financial transactions using nonpublic Government information or allow the improper use of such information to further any private interest.

(d) An employee shall not, except pursuant to such reasonable exceptions as are provided by regulation, solicit or accept any gift or other item of monetary value from any person or entity seeking official action from, doing business with, or conducting activities regulated by the employee's agency, or whose interests may be substantially affected by the performance or nonperformance of the employee's duties.

(e) Employees shall put forth honest effort in the performance of their duties.

(f) Employees shall make no unauthorized commitments or promises of any kind purporting to bind the Government.

(g) Employees shall not use public office for private gain.

(h) Employees shall act impartially and not give preferential treatment to any private organization or individual.

(i) Employees shall protect and conserve Federal property and shall not use it for other than authorized activities.

(j) Employees shall not engage in outside employment or activities, including seeking or negotiating for employment, that conflict with official Government duties and responsibilities.

(k) Employees shall disclose waste, fraud, abuse, and corruption to appropriate authorities.

(l) Employees shall satisfy in good faith their obligations as citizens, including all just financial obligations, especially those—such as Federal, State, or local taxes—that are imposed by law.

(m) Employees shall adhere to all laws and regulations that provide equal opportunity for all Americans regardless of race, color, religion, sex, national origin, age, or handicap.

(n) Employees shall endeavor to avoid any actions creating the appearance that they are violating the law or the ethical standards promulgated pursuant to this order.

Source: Executive Order 12731, October 17, 1990.

computer training program, offers BPD employees all the ethics training required each year.[57]

In addition to OGE, most federal government agencies have ethics officers who assist management in developing ethics policies and providing training opportunities. For example, the National Institutes of Health requires any employee who files a financial disclosure report to complete an ethics training program. State and local governments frequently provide ethics training through formal training programs such as the Certified Public Manager programs or professional training programs such as those offered through the International Institute for Municipal Clerks. The State of California provides an ethics orientation program that examines the following topics:

- Common law doctrine
- Conflict of interest
- Statutes, rules, and regulations
- Legal opinions and advice
- Political Reform Act
- Making a contract, making a decision
- Incompatible activities
- Revolving door and post-government employment
- Limitations on gifts
- Statement of economic interests
- Bureau of state audit reports[58]

■ CONCLUSION

The HRD function is often performed by the human resource management department in public and nonprofit organizations. Some of the important responsibilities of human resource management are to make certain the organization is staffed with employees possessing appropriate knowledge and skills to carry out the organization's mission, and developing and advancing employees to satisfy both their professional needs and the needs of the organization. Employees are usually hired with the fundamental professional knowledge and experience required to perform on the job, but they need to learn the unique components of a specific job and the special circum-

stances of the organization. It is becoming increasingly common for organizations to hire people who can adjust quickly to the particular responsibilities and culture of an organization and adapt well to the changes that occur in the work or profession. HRD professionals become the central figures in helping employees and the organization find ways to learn and adapt to change.[59]

Human resource development professionals are no longer simply the people who do training. The HRD manager serves as the link between employee and organizational learning and the goals of the organization. Today HRD professionals act as consultants to functional managers, managers of HRD programs, and facilitators of learning.[60] They need to keep up with changes occurring within and outside the organization, and they must help managers adjust to change by acquiring the knowledge and skills needed to perform in a dynamic environment. HRD professionals must be learning specialists skilled in the use of instructional technologies and the application of adult learning principles, consultants to management on learning needs and strategies, and managers of HRD programs. HRD professionals should be aware of trends and new ideas and be able to anticipate change to provide learning opportunities so that employees can perform in a dynamic environment.

Some of the trends anticipated for the near future involve the ability of employees and organizations to learn:[61]

- It will become increasingly important to learn ways to receive direct feedback from citizen-customers on past performance and future needs.
- Employees will increasingly challenge assumptions, values, and how work gets done as information and comparisons with other organizations become more available.
- People will be more interested in learning how to learn than in receiving "information dumps" and other passive learning methods.
- Career paths will become more horizontal than vertical as opportunities for upward

mobility decrease due to the flattening organizational structures.

- The most important training will be "just-in-time" training, designed to give employees the information they need when they need it.

Peter Block wrote, "Learning and performing will become one and the same thing. Everything you say about learning will be about performance. People will get the point that learning is everything."[62]

■ MANAGER'S VOCABULARY

mentoring
training phases
needs assessment
benchmarking
training principles
evaluation design
action learning
cross-functional teams

■ STUDY QUESTIONS

1. What are the greatest needs for training in the organization where you work or with which you are familiar?

2. Is it necessary for other areas of government to budget as much for training and development as public safety departments budget for training?

3. What could government do to help high school students prepare for meaningful work in government?

4. Which individual learning strategies and organizational learning strategies are the most effective or least effective in your experience?

5. Which of the principles of training are most neglected? How does this affect the effectiveness of training programs?

6. Which of the phases of training are most neglected? How does this shortcoming affect the effectiveness of training programs?

■ EXPERIENTIAL EXERCISES

1. *Human Resource Development Methods*
In the last legislative session, the governor was successful in creating a new Department of Juvenile Corrections to handle youth offenders. You are a manager on the staff of the new department and are given the task of helping the department's employees learn how to adjust to the differences between juvenile corrections and adult corrections. Describe how you would use at least five of the following development methods to fulfill your responsibilities:

Individual Learning Strategies	Organizational Learning Strategies
Job rotation	Meetings
Special assignments	**Action learning**
Internship	**Cross-functional teams**
Reflecting on experience	Work-outs
Learning teams	Strategic planning
Coaching and counseling	Organization scorecard
Manager as teacher	Benchmarking
Mentoring	Groupware
Individual development plan	Computer conferencing
Self-development	

2. *Needs Assessment*

You have been asked by the administrator of your graduate program to recommend changes to the program for teaching public administration. She has requested that you provide her with the topics you believe should be included in the new program, categorized by major course headings. Develop a plan for assessing the educational needs of a modern public administration curriculum, prepare a survey of an important group knowledgeable about the needs of public administration professionals, and survey at least ten people using your instrument. Analyze the data, and make recommendations to the administrator.

2. *Training Design*

A small community in your area has just called and asked you to come tomorrow to work with city department managers to help them learn how to conduct performance appraisals among their employees. Design a training module that would take about one hour to introduce city officials to the issues and procedures involved in conducting performance appraisals. Use the information in the chapter, particularly the training principles repeated below. If time permits, take 15 minutes to try out your training module on your class.

Seven Fundamental Training Principles

1. Foster participant goal setting.
2. Increase the similarity of training to the work environment.
3. Use underlying principles.
4. Organize the material thoughtfully.
5. Actively involve the learner.
6. Give feedback.
7. Use a variety of techniques and stimuli.

4. *Training Evaluation*

Your training program for performance appraisal went beautifully in the City of Sunshine; you received several compliments after the session, and the participants kept you there forty-five minutes beyond your ending time asking you questions. The evaluation form you passed out at the end of the session showed high scores (9s and 10s on a scale of 10) for being "satisfied" with the training. Some written comments were a little confusing, however: "Entertaining, but I'm not sure how I'm going to use this on the job." "I don't know if I will really be able to sit down with my employees and tell them what I really think." Design an evaluation of your training program assuming you had as much time as you need before and after your assignment to train the managers of the neighboring City of Snowville.

■ NOTES

1 J. Schmitz, *Information about the Human Resource Development Profession,* Academy of Human Resource Development, February 11, 1999, available at: **http://www.ahrd. org/profession.htm.**

2 Peter Senge, T*he Fifth Discipline: The Art and Practice of the Learning Organization* (New York: Doubleday/ Currency, 1990).

3 Claire J. Anderson and Betty Roper Ricks, "Illiteracy— The Neglected Enemy in Public Service," *Public Personnel Management* 22:1 (1993): 137–152.

4 Ibid., p. 145.

5 Federal Human Resource Development Council, *Getting Results Through Learning,* 1997, p. 3, available at: **http://www. amsc.belvoir.army.mil/hrdc/handbook/foreword.htm.**

6 Chris Argyris et al., "The Future of Workplace Learning and Performance," *Training and Development* (May 1994): S41.

7 Richard A. Cosier and Dan R. Dalton, "Management Training and Development in a Nonprofit Organization," *Public Personnel Management* 22:1 (1993): 38.

8 Montgomery Van Wart, "Providing a Base for Executive Development at the State Level," *Public Personnel Management* 22:2 (1993): 269–282.

9 James A. Buford, Jr., *Personnel Management and Human Resources in Local Government: Concepts and Applications for Students and Practitioners* (Auburn, AL: Center for Government Services, 1991), p. 200.

10 Cheryl Beeler, "Roll Out the Welcome Wagon," *Public Management* 76:8 (1994): 13–17.

11 Ibid., p. 17.

12 Montgomery Van Wart, "Providing a Base for Executive Development at the State Level," *Public Personnel Management* 22:2 (1993): 272.

13 Cynthia D. Fisher, Lyle F. Schoenfeldt, and James B. Shaw, *Human Resource Management,* 3rd ed. (Boston: Houghton Mifflin, 1996), pp. 356–398; Montgomery Van Wart, "Organizational Investment in Employee Development," in Stephen E. Condrey, ed., *Handbook of Human Resource Management in Government* (San Francisco: Jossey-Bass, 1998), pp. 276–297.

14 Buford, *Personnel Management,* p. 201

15 Donald L. Kirkpatrick, "Four Steps to Measuring Training Effectiveness," *Personnel Administrator* (November 1983): 19–25.

16 Malcolm Knowles, *The Adult Learner: A Neglected Species* (Houston, TX: Gulf Publishing, 1978).

17 Paul Sandwith, "A Hierarchy of Management Training Requirements: The Competency Domain Model," *Public Personnel Management* 22:1 (1993): 52–55.

18 John Dewey, *Democracy and Education* (New York: Macmillan, 1938).

19 David A. Kolb, *Experiential Learning: Experience as a Source of Learning and Development* (Englewood Cliffs, NJ: Prentice Hall, 1984).

20 Ronald Sims, "The Enhancement of Learning in Public Sector Training Programs," *Public Personnel Management* 22:2 (1993): 249.

21 Montgomery Van Wart, N. Joseph Cayer, and S. Cook, *Handbook of Training and Development for the Public Sector* (San Francisco: Jossey-Bass, 1993).

22 Raymond A. Noe, "Trainees' Attributes and Attitudes: Neglected Influences on Training Effectiveness," *Academy of Management Review* (October 1986): 736–749.

23 Martha H. Peak, "Training: No Longer for the Fainthearted," *Management Review* (February 1997): 23–27.

24 Industry Report, "Who's Learning What?" *Training* (October 1994): 53.

25 Laurie J. Bassi, *Are Employers' Recruitment Strategies Changing: Competence over Credentials?* (Washington, D.C.: National Institute on Postsecondary Education, Libraries, and Lifelong Learning, U.S. Department of Education, "Competence Without Credentials," March 1999), available at: **http://www.ed.gov/pubs/Competence/section3.html.**

26 Stephen R. Barley, *Competence Without Credentials: The Promise and Potential Problems of Computer-Based Distance Education* (Washington, D.C.: National Institute on Postsecondary Education, Libraries, and Lifelong Learning, U.S. Department of Education, Competence Without Credentials, March 1999), available at: **http://www.ed.gov/ pubs/Competence/section2.html.**

27 Kenneth C. Green, *High Tech vs. High Touch: The Potential Promise and Probable Limits of Technology-Based Education and Training on Campuses* (Washington, D.C.: National Institute on Postsecondary Education, Libraries, and Lifelong Learning, U.S. Department of Education, Competence Without Credentials, March 1999), available at: **http://www.ed.gov/pubs/Competence/section4.html.**

28 American Society for Training and Development, *1998 Learning Technology Research Report* (1998), available at: **http://www.astd.org/virtual_communicationresearch/ 1998_learning_technologies.html.**

29 Barley, *Potential Problems,* p. 2.

30 Gerald Van Dusen, *The Virtual Campus: Technology and Reform in Higher Education,* ASHE-ERIC Higher Education Report 25, no. 5 (Washington, D.C.: George Washington University, 1997), p. 38.

31 Kelly McCullum, "In Test, Students Taught On-Line Outdo Those Taught in Class," *Chronicle of Higher Education,* February 12, 1997, p. A-23.

32 Green, *High Tech,* p. 1.

33 American Society for Training and Development, 2000 *The 1998 Learning Technology Research Report,* available at: **http://www.astd.org/virtual_community/research/1998_ learning_technologies.htm.**

34 Kirkpatrick, "Four Steps," pp. 19–25.

35 J. Schmitz, *Information about the Human Resource Devel-*

opment Profession, 2000 available at: **http://www.ahrd. org/profession.htm.**

36 George R. Gray, McKenzie E. Hall, Marianne Miller, and Charles Shasky, "Training Practices in State Government Agencies," *Public Personnel Management* 26:2 (1997): 187.

37 Ron Zemke, "The Systems Approach: A Nice Theory But . . . ," *Training October* (1985): 103–108.

38 Gray et al., *Training Practices,* p. 190.

39 Ibid., p. 195.

40 Ibid., p. 197.

41 John A. Byrne, "Profiting from the Nonprofits," *Business Week,* March 26, 1990, pp. 66–72.

42 Richard A. Cosier and Dan R. Dalton, "Management Training and Development in a Nonprofit Organization," *Public Personnel Management* 22:1 (1993): 37–42.

43 Arthur Finkle, "CPM—Professionalizing Professionalism," *Public Administration Quarterly* 9 (Spring 1985): 47–54.

44 Steven W. Hays and Bruce Duke, "Professional Certification in Public Management: A Status Report and Proposal," *Public Administration Review* 56:5 (1996): 425–432.

45 Homer S. Black and Kenneth E. Everand, "The Academy of Administrative Management: Path to the Professional Management Certification," *Management World* 20:1 (1992): 6–7.

46 Hays and Duke, "Professional Certification," p. 427.

47 Peter Drucker, "The Deadly Sins of Public Administration," *Public Administration Review* 40:2 (1980): 103–106.

48 Carolyn Wiley, "Reexamining Professional Certification in Human Resource Management," *Human Resource Management* 34:2 (1995): 269–289.

49 Wallace Swan, "Professionalism and Testing: Integrating Professional Testing Requirements into State Law and Civil Service Regulations," *Public Administration Quarterly* 8 (1985): 496–508.

50 Robert A Levit, "Response to *Reexamining Professional Certification in Human Resource Management* by Carolyn Wiley," *Human Resource Management* 34:2 (1995): 291–293.

51 Warren R. Wilhelm, "Response to Reexamining Professional Certification in Human Resource Management by Carolyn Wiley," *Human Resource Management,* 34:2 (1995): 295–297.

52 James Gazell and Darrell Pugh, "The Future of Professionalization and Professionalism in Public Administration: Advancements, Barriers, and Prospects," *International Journal of Public Administration* 16:12 (1993): 1933–1964.

53 International Personnel Management Association, 2000 *IPMA/NASPE HR Benchmarking Project, Diversity Best Practices,* available at: **http://www.ipma-hr.org/tests/ bpdiversity.html.**

54 National MultiCultural Institute, *Diversity Training and Consulting,* available at: **http://www.nmci.org/training. htm.**

55 American Society for Public Administration National Council, *ASPA Code of Conduct,* September 20, 2000, available at: **http://www.aspanet.org/member/coe.htm.**

56 Executive Order 12674, April 12, 1989.

57 U.S. Office of Government Ethics, *Agency Best Practices, Technology Saves Time and Money in Ethics Training Program,* available at: **http://www.usoge.gov/bestprac.html.**

58 California Department of General Services, Legal Services, *Ethics Orientation for the State of California,* available at: **http://www.ols.dgs.ca.gov/TRAINING/Ethics.asp.**

59 Federal Human Resource Development Council, *Getting Results Through Learning,* pp. 17–18.

60 Leonard Nadler and Zeace Nadler, *Developing Human Resources,* 3rd ed. (San Francisco: Jossey-Bass, 1989).

61 Federal Human Resource Development Council, *Getting Results Through Learning,* p. 24.

62 Ibid.

CHAPTER 13

Discipline and Termination of Public Employees

Two of the most important and most challenging functions of management are the exercise of discipline and the dismissal of employees. **Discipline** can mean a positive or negative action imposed by another, as in the "instruction designed to train to proper conduct or action" or "the punishment inflicted by way of correction."

Alternatively, discipline can imply autonomous change in the sense of personal self-control and sense of purpose, as in "the training effect of experience."[1] The difference between these definitions appears to be drawn from the locus of control—that is, who opts for or imposes the change or correction. **Dismissal** simply means "to discharge."[2] However, the euphemisms we tend to employ to discuss these concepts suggest the discomfort and concerns we share about the notion of disciplinary action generally, and about employee dismissal in particular. Box 13.1 lists several phrases used to denote dismissal. Note that each has a slightly different connotation, but each one tends to suggest action that none of us would relish enduring.

When employee actions are not consistent with the goals of the organization, either the goals or the actions of the employees must change. As we learned in Chapter 6, organizational goals must be

---

Box 13.1   Let me count the ways to say . . .

A person being removed from his or her position of employment is:	An employee's behavior or performance can be modified through:
Dismissed	Discipline
Canned	Punishment
Fired	Corrective discipline
Terminated	Corrective training
Getting the boot	Corrective action
Getting the bounce	Involuntary behavioral
Sacked	Corrective education
Experiencing an involuntary separation from the organization	Preemptive education
Experiencing involuntary organizational exit	Counseling
Getting the pink slip	Preterminative action
Told to clean out his or her desk	Contemplative leave
	Temporary special assignments

revisited periodically through strategic planning efforts to ensure that operational goals appropriately address the mission of the organization. If organizational goals can be assumed to be appropriate reflections of the organizational mission, then performance concerns or workplace disputes may necessitate behavior change on the part of employees or a restricted portion of the workforce. This line of reasoning seems simple and sequential in the abstract, but disciplinary action and, in the extreme, dismissal or discharge are complicated areas of personnel management in practice. We need to concern ourselves with the tension between proper consideration for the welfare of an individual employee and legitimate concerns about the achievement of organizational objectives.

This tension is somewhat heightened in public sector organizations for several reasons. Public sector employees are citizens who hold employment rights and protections—by statute and under the U.S. Constitution—that neither nonprofit nor for-profit employees have. Public employees are concerned with delivering often essential public goods and services for citizens and their communities. An inability to perform in this context may be harmful to others beyond a simple decline in service or production in a for-profit organization. However, nonprofit and for-profit organizations that deliver public goods through contract and grant arrangements share this concern. In the broader context of environmental conditions for public agencies, we cannot forget that public sector employees are held strictly accountable for their actions as agents of the people. Public employees are expected to be productive and professional and to be subject to public scrutiny in all of their public business. They are also attempting to balance their professional and personal lives, define their responsibilities and performance levels within reasonable limits, and manage changing conceptions about their roles within organizations. They do this in public organizations that are mandated to do more with less while staying current with technological change. The tensions that

erupt into conflict between individuals within organizations, and between organizations and their employees, are not surprising considering all of these factors.

INTRODUCTION TO READING

In the following reading, Edward Seidler discusses the implications for disciplinary action in an organization using total quality management (TQM) principles. Recall from Chapter 11 that several of the important tenets of TQM include an emphasis on work teams to improve work processes, an intolerance for mistakes or negativity, and supervisors acting as facilitators rather than overseers.

As you read the selection, keep the following questions in mind:

- Seidler characterizes TQM advocates as having an unrealistically positive view of employees. What do you think? Can employees be self-directed, or must they be closely monitored and controlled?
- Should work teams be responsible for monitoring and guiding the performance of their members? What advantages may result from this approach? What disadvantages might result?
- If we cannot trust employees to take their cues from the situation as they improve performance, can we trust work teams to implement corrective and disciplinary actions appropriately?
- Seidler discusses three models of the disciplinary process using work teams: team as recommender, team as decision maker, and a hybrid of the two. What problems may exist with each? How might the type of employee problem—behavioral or performance related—influence the utility of each of the three models?

READING

Discipline and Deselection in the TQM Environment

EDWARD SEIDLER

"If men were angels, no government would be necessary. If angels were to govern men, neither external nor internal controls on government would be necessary."[1] This statement about the human condition from Federalist 51 posits a view of people which most authors of Total Quality Management have chosen to ignore. When reviewing the literature on quality management, one is struck by the absence of any mention of individuals who have problems in the work place, and the reader is left with the conclusion that "men are angels." There is an assumption that all employees with the right type of training and the proper coaching will fit into the TQM organization. Johnston, in summarizing various authors on the attitudes toward workers, stated that "under TQM, the workers are viewed as the greatest source of improvements."[2] Workers who are managed correctly will take responsibility for their work, be committed to the organization, and have ownership of the service or product. "Absenteeism and sick leave abuse are not a problem when workers feel like they are an important part of the business."[3] While this deduction is derived from MacGregor's Theory Y view of employees, work and management, it fails to provide for the prospect that some employees' behavior may not be modified by coaching and training, and that other measures, such as termination, may have to be utilized to correct the situation.

The literature assumes that the employees involved in a TQM organization manifest a love for their work and are interested in doing their best for the organization. The purpose of this article is not to engage in a lengthy debate about the merits of Theory Y, but to recognize that in most organizations,

the universality of these assumptions has its limits. In many organizations, some people were initially selected who did not fully subscribe to the organization's culture nor to the work ethic. Some persons lacked basic qualities such as trust, which, as one author noted, for an organization to manage without managers, one must assume that "employees are trustworthy adults."[4] Most organizations, particularly public ones, are not created anew when they start the total quality experience. TQM is being implemented in on-going organizations that contain some individuals who lack some of the basic attributes to perform efficiently and effectively, and the organizations have failed to either correct or remove the problem employee. Without a significant modification in behavior or a severance from the organization, these individuals imperil an organization's implementation of TQM.

To fully develop the plan for discipline and how it would be conducted in a TQM organization, it is necessary to review some of the basic concepts of TQM.

CONCEPTS OF TQM

Total Quality Management, as many authors have noted, is a total philosophy for running an organization. It has as its main objective the meeting of both internal and external customer's expectations through continuously improving all processes and products. It uses basic statistical tools to measure and refine work processes. Since quality is a top-level management responsibility, they must provide the work environment and organizational conditions to allow this to occur. The refinement, measurement and improvement comes from the workers closest to the daily processes. These workers have the knowledge and experience to make these improvements.

However, unlike other processes which solicit

Source: Edward Seidler, "Discipline and Deselection in the TQM Environment," *Public Personnel Management* 25:4 (1996): 529–537.

employee input such as suggestion systems or quality circles, the quality management system takes the next logical step. Workers are organized into teams and given the power to modify and adapt the process as the team feels necessary. TQM writers argue that for the process to be successful, work groups must be "empowered" to function as a self-directed team.[5]

This theoretical prospective has been translated into practice when one reviews the standards for the Baldridge Award, the Deming Prize (two major awards for total quality organizations), or the ISO 9000 certification. The ISO is the International Organization for Standardization in Geneva, Switzerland. ISO 9000 is a series of five standards for quality management. As an organization moves from the traditional work group to the empowered team, the organization is rated higher.[6]

While Table 1 clarifies the distinction between a work group and a work team, further refinements have been suggested by literature as to the degree of autonomy that a team will enjoy. Three types of teams have been suggested:

a. Semi-autonomous teams—led by supervisor;
b. Semi-managing teams—led by elective leader;
c. Semi-designing teams—have authority to determine their own composition and external relations.[7]

There also needs to be a division in the processes which are under the control of the team. First, there is the issue of the production process. Questions need to be answered as to how much autonomy the team would have in terms of work processes, such as task design, machinery, allocation of tasks among workers, needed training, etc. Second, there is the issue of personnel decisions. Traditional hierarchical organization theory establishes the primary responsibility for basic personnel decisions to the supervisory role. Since supervisors have the responsibility for ensuring that the work is completed, the supervisor has the intimate knowledge of the work place to determine the degree to which various workers are contributing to or hindering the work process. Consequently, the supervisor is in the best position to recommend disciplinary action, merit increases, and to conduct performance appraisals. The supervisor, having extensive knowledge of the requirements of the work process, also should have a primary role in choosing the employees who will be able to perform the tasks.[8] The role of the supervisor has been codified in the *National Labor Relations Act* and similar state and local statutes which govern the collective bargaining process. For example, the *Educational Employment Relations Act* of the State of California offers a typical definition.

(m) "Supervisory employee" means any employee, regardless of job description, having authority in the

Table 1   Comparison Between the Working Group and the Team

Working Group	Team
Strong, clearly focused leader	Shared leadership roles
Individual accountability	Individual & mutual accountability
The group's purpose is the same as the broader organizational mission	Specific team purpose that the team itself delivers
Individual work-products	Collective work-products
Runs efficient meetings	Encourages open-minded discussion & active problem solving meetings
Measures its effectiveness indirectly by its influence on others, e.g., financial performance of the business	Measures performance directly by assessing collective work-products
Discusses, decides & delegates	Discusses, decides & does real work together

interest of the employer to hire, transfer, suspend, lay off, recall, promote, discharge, assign, reward or discipline other employees, or the responsibility to assign work to and direct them, or to adjust their grievances, or effectively recommend such action, if, in connection with the foregoing functions, the exercise of that authority is not of a merely routine or clerical nature, but requires the use of independent judgment.[9]

The logic of empowering work teams to control production leads to the extension that the employees themselves would be just as knowledgeable, or more knowledgeable than supervisors about who would be best for the job, or how individual employees are performing. It should be noted that just because a team has control over work processes, it does not necessarily follow that the team must also have control over personnel issues. However, for the concept of team self-direction and empowerment to be meaningful, a strong, compelling argument can be made for the team to have control over personnel issues.

Some authors have raised the concern that team members would not be objective in their evaluations of employees; either they would treat the person as a friend and not be willing to confront the employee if there were problems, or, possibly, they would want to drive an employee out who did not conform to the group's non-work related norms.[10] However, the same criticism can be made regarding the objectivity of the supervisor. Comparative research is lacking to indicate whether personnel decisions made by a supervisor are better or worse than those made by a team. As was noted earlier, there is a dearth of any empirical studies regarding the conduct of discipline by a team.

Although one can argue that teams can make as objective personnel decisions as supervisors, two conditions need to be present in order for the system to properly function. First, the team must have developed good interactive skills, have worked as a cohesive team, and have mastered controlling work processes. Team self-direction is a developmental process. In making the transition to a work team, employees need to learn how to function as a group and begin working on production processes with which they have a high degree of familiarity. The success or failure of the team to be able to modify work processes is an indicator as to whether the team is able to be empowered with the personnel

decision process. If a team has been judged mature enough to handle personnel decisions, then the team must receive extensive training in the personnel process as the second condition. (This poses an interesting problem. Who determines if a team is mature enough? Management, the team itself, other teams automatic if certain conditions are present?)

Training in the personnel process is another one of the components of training in which quality management mandates. The team has already received task and work improvement training, e.g., statistics, quality control methodology, and training in group processes. Training in personnel procedures requires that the team understand the basic requirements of equal employment law. Selection requires that the team understands the process both from an organizational and legal perspective. Discipline also requires training. This training component would cover the interpersonal aspects of confrontation, problem definition, and clarification, progressive discipline, employee legal rights, and the concept of just cause, or whatever the organization uses as the basis for discipline.

In summary, personnel decision making is a logical extension of the team empowerment process. For the team to function, it must be experienced and mature in group processes and it must receive training in both the legal aspects of personnel selection as well as the organizational policies which govern personnel.

DISCIPLINE PROCESS MODELS FOR TEAMS

Although there are many variations on organizational structures for disciplinary processing, there would appear to be three major models that can be constructed around the degree of autonomy that the organization will allow. The first model is the team as recommender. The team makes what it feels are appropriate recommendations for discipline to management and then management may accept, modify or reflect the recommendations as necessary. This model safeguards the organization from legal or technical problems that might arise in a disciplinary hearing. If the organization was serious about optimizing empowerment, this model could provide a developmental step in the process of full team self-direction.

The second model is at the opposite end of the

spectrum. In this model the team is completely autonomous in making personnel decisions. Team members are completely responsible for selection and disciplinary decisions. This model can only be implemented when the team has developed sufficient maturity and has been trained in personnel procedures. Barkman has suggested that one of the team members might receive advance human resources training and serve as a resource to the team.[11]

The third model falls between the extremes of the first two models. The team proposes the disciplinary plan, but instead of being reviewed by management, the plan is reviewed by members of other work teams who may make modifications accordingly. This model allows for peer review, which should prevent any inappropriate extreme action from occurring.

It is important to note that any of the above three models or their variations are considered to be the last, extreme step. For all three models, quality theorists posit that an important preliminary step must occur: there must be informal intervention by team members to work with an employee who is having problems. Every effort has to be made to counsel and assist an employee. If additional training is necessary, it must be provided. The employee must receive every opportunity to improve before any formal mechanism of discipline is implemented.

The human resources department could serve as an expert to the team as the team develops its disciplinary plan and could assist the team to avoid any legal problems. Although the above would suggest that with maturity and training, a team should be able to be empowered to handle discipline, there are some serious issues and problems that need to be addressed before empowerment in this area can be fully implemented.

ISSUES AND PROBLEMS

The disciplinary process, more than the selection process, is a minefield of procedural dictates. In the public sector the employee's employment has been viewed by the courts as a property right. As a consequence, the courts have developed procedural safeguards to ensure that the employee's due process rights are not violated. The safeguards have been developed based on the experience of the traditional hierarchical organizations and would re-

quire some adaptation in a system that utilized empowered teams for discipline.

Another question in the public sector is that the law often reserves the authority for personnel actions to the agency head or manager responsible for the jurisdiction, e.g., the appointing authority; or, it reserves the right to the governing board, e.g., Board of Education. If a team has been empowered, then the personnel authority would have to act as ratifiers and should not change the recommendation. Whether courts would allow the appointing authority or governing board to abrogate their responsibility in this area is questionable unless the basic authorizing statutes were revised. This problem reinforces the need for management and the governing body to be committed to the tenants of quality management and the consequences of empowerment. At the present time some managers or boards will overrule recommendations for discipline, not because of flaws in the disciplinary procedure, but for political reasons. It is unlikely that the political pressures will disappear just because a jurisdiction has implemented quality management.

Last, an underlying assumption of this paper that if the organization has a union, that union has been a significant force in the development of the quality management process. As the Electromation decision of the NLRB points out, work place teams should be carefully constructed to avoid violating the NLRA.[12] State public employment relations boards will probably rule in much the same way if unions challenge a work team experiment. The involvement of employee organizations is a necessary and sufficient condition for the implementation of any quality management program.

FURTHER RESEARCH

As noted at the beginning of this article, there is a paucity of research on discipline in a team setting. One author noted that research on selection out is scarce, although firings, layoffs, and retirements are a part of organizational life. "Researchers spend virtually no time studying selection out."[13] In a recently published book on human resources and quality management, the author noted that since only the most sophisticated organizations have empowered teams with personnel decision, "there are few stories to tell."[14]

The research agenda in this area covers subjects

that concern a variety of disciplines. Legal scholars need to review the impact of the team approach on the property rights issue. Group theorists need to research the issues of group dynamics in the discipline process. What types of conditions must be present for a team to function effectively? Does the potential for excluding a colleague from a work team prevent a team from acting on a problem, i.e., does an avoidance syndrome occur? This process causes significant role modification for managers and supervisors. They move from controllers and directors to coaches and resource personnel. What mechanisms are needed to alleviate the fears and anxieties that such a role shift causes?

If team empowerment in this area increases, then practitioners need to have solid, empirically based research for making design and implementation decisions rather than limited anecdotal evidence. If Total Quality Management is truly more than a fad, and is going to serve as a basis of organizational structuring in the next century, these decisions must be based on good research to avoid costly and damaging decisions.

CONCLUSION

This paper has been a preliminary exploration into the issue of discipline in a total quality environment. Proponents of quality management have argued that employees need to work in teams and be empowered to make decisions regarding production processes. Logically, the empowered team should also be able to handle the personnel decisions so that the team controls both the process and the persons who carry out the process. Three separate models for team organization were proposed: recommender; autonomous decider; and a synthesis of the two, using other teams as reviewers. Mature teams and training appear to be necessary conditions for success. The public sector organization is faced with problems in implementing this process, due to procedural safeguards that are present in the disciplinary process, and the surrender of authority by appointing authorities and governing boards. All organizations need to involve employee organizations extensively in the planning and design of empowered teams.

At this time, it is impossible to predict whether quality management will be just a fad or have a significant impact on the governance of private and public organizations in the next century.

NOTES

1. Madison, J., Jay, J. and Hamilton, A., *The Federalist Papers.* (New York: New American Library, 1961) p. 322.
2. Johnston, L. The TQM Coordinator as Change Agent in Implementing Total Quality Management. Unpublished Master's thesis (Monterey: Naval Postgraduate School, 1989) p. 52.
3. Pascarelli as cited by Johnson, 52.
4. Lee, C., *Training Beyond Teamwork* (1990), p. 25–32.
5. Bowen, D. E., and Lawler, E. Total Quality-Oriented Human Resources Management. *Business Week,* Carr, General Dynamics, Lareau, Schmidt and Finnigan, Carter. (Organizational Dynamic, 1990) p. 29–41.
6. Mahoney, F. and Thor, C. *The TQM Trilogy (New York, 1994)* AMACOM.
7. Katzenbach, J. and Smith, D. The Discipline of Teams (*Harvard Business Review,* March–April) p. 111–120.
8. Cotton, J., Employee Involvement (*Newbury Park:* Sage, 1993) p. 191.
9. California.
10. Cotton, J., Employee Involvement (*Newbury Park:* Sage, 1993) p. 197.
11. Barkman, D. F., Team Discipline: Put Performance on the Line (*Personnel Journal,* 66(3), 1987) p. 60.
12. Liss, W., Labor Law for Supervisors (*Supervision* 54(6), August 1993) p. 20–21.
13. Howard as quoted in Schmidt, et al., 341.
14. Carter, C., *Human Resource Management and the Total Quality Imperative* (New York: AMACOM, 1994). p. 157.

REFERENCES

Barkman, D. F., (1987), "Team Discipline: Put Performance on the Line" *Personnel Journal,* 66(3), 58–63.

Barry, D., (1991). Managing the bossless team: lessons in distributed leadership. *Organizational Dynamics,* 20(1), 31–47.

Bowen, D. E., Lawler, E. (1990). "Total Quality-Oriented Human Resources Management" *Organizational Dynamic,* 20 (Spring), 29–41.

Bowman, James S., (1994). "At Last, an Alternative to Performance Appraisal: Total Quality Management" *Public Administration Review,* 54(2), 129–136.

Business Week (1991). Special Edition. The Quality Imperative 25(October).

Carr, C. "Self-Managed Workers" *Training and Development,* 45(September), 37–42.

Carter, C., *Human Resource Management and the Total Quality Imperative.* AMACOM, New York, 1994.

Cotton, J. (1993). *Employee Involvement.* Sage, Newbury Park.

General Dynamics (1992). America's Advantage–Seminar for Aerospace & Defense on TQM. (April).

Jain, H. C. (1990). "Human Resource Management in Selected Japanese firms, their foreign subsidiaries and locally owned counterparts" *International Labor Review,* 129(1), 73–89.

Johnston, L. (1989). The TQM Coordinator as Change Agent in Implementing Total Quality Management. Unpublished Master's thesis, Naval Postgraduate School, Monterey.

Katzenbach, J., Smith, D., (1993). "The Discipline of Teams" *Harvard Business Review,* March–April, 111–120.

Lareau, W. (1991). *American Samurai.* Clinton, New Jersey, New Win.

Lawler, E. E. (1990). "The New Plant Revolution Revisited" *Organizational Dynamics,* 19(2), 5–14.

Lee, C. (1990). "Beyond Teamwork", *Training.* (June), 25–32.

Liss, W., "Labor Law for Supervisors" *Supervision,* 54(6), August 1993, 20–21.

Madison, J., Jay, J. and Hamilton, A., *The Federalist Papers.* New American Library, New York, 1961.

Mahoney, F., Thor, C. (1994). *The TQM Trilogy.* AMACOM, New York.

Schmidt, N., Borman, W. and Associates. (1993). *Personnel Selection in Organizations.* Jossey-Bass Publishers, San Francisco.

Schmidt, W., Finnigan, J. (1992). *The Race without a Finish Line.* Jossey-Bass Publishers, San Francisco (1994). *TQM Manager.* Jossey-Bass Publishers, San Francisco.

PERFORMANCE MANAGEMENT OR DISCIPLINE?

Managing employees is a complex activity, and the difficulty is heightened as we recognize that the workplace also serves to reflect social trends. In addition to the challenge of managing performance when the nature of work and workplace technology are changing, we must also consider a broad range of human behavior in organizations. Changing social norms lead to differences in how people believe they should or can act toward others in the workplace and how they should be treated in that environment. What we may define as inappropriate behavior today may have been condoned with a wink or a shrug a decade or so ago. Violence and other forms of dysfunction in private lives often spill into the workplace. Harassment of others because of difference—in gender, sexuality, ethnicity, age, or ability—is not a relic of the past but a far too common contemporary occurrence. Harassment, violence, and other behaviors that demean others and detract from the delivery of public services must be severely sanctioned in the workplace.

When an employee's performance is insufficient or an employee's behavior threatens individual or organizational effort, organizations are duty bound to address these problems. They must consider the costs to the organization if employees are not disciplined for failure to meet organizational standards or to observe organizational rules.[3] Inappropriate, inconsistent, and inadequate discipline to address problems with employee behavior and performance have serious implications for public sector organizations in terms of perceptions about government performance, employee motivation and morale, and degraded organizational capacity.

"The cumulative effect on society of poor public sector discipline practice is to increase public cynicism about government."[4] Much of the lore surrounding government incompetence comes from accounts about how incompetent public employees cannot be fired. The perception that management is impeded because of civil service protections (Chapter 3), union advocacy (Chapter 5), and employment rights (Chapter 4) leads to calls for government downsizing. A major recommendation from the National Performance Review dealt with the ability of federal government supervisors to terminate unproductive employees:[5]

> The Gore report stressed the need to reduce the time required to terminate managers and employees for poor performance. . . . Although it was possible to fire inept workers in the federal management when the Gore report was written, the time it took to accomplish this task undermined good management. . . . To halve the

time required for terminating employees for cause, it called for legislation to be drafted lowering the requirement for advance notice of termination from 30 to 15 days.[6]

Recall from Chapter 11 two of the more common theories of human motivation in the workplace: expectancy theory and equity theory. When productive and diligent employees observe that others are not held to the same standard or receive rewards (or at least receive no punishment) for low performance, absenteeism, insubordination, or a variety of other offenses, they may negatively assess the organization and their own role within it. In addition, employers have a certain responsibility to ensure that the workplace is free of unnecessary physical and emotional risk. If the behavior of one or two employees detracts from the performance of others, then the organization must act. If the activities of an employee cause discomfort and a deterioration in the collegiality of the unit, then the supervisor may have an ethical, if not legal, imperative to act.

Discipline

Discipline implies corrective action through education or punishment to modify employee behavior or performance so that the employee's actions are compatible with organizational goals and norms. Often disciplinary action is called an **adverse action**. Adverse actions are decisions made by an organization that disadvantage an employee in some way; in the public service, such decisions must be for **just cause**—that is, based on specific and job-related factors (see Box 13.2).[7] Adverse action taken in response to behavioral problems requires that an employee have a clear understanding of what constitutes appropriate behavior in a particular situation. In addition, adverse action, taken in response to unacceptable performance, implies that performance must be assessed and documented. Discipline, like performance appraisal or job analysis, should not be personal but rather a response to an action, performance, or job requirement and should be consistent for all employees in similar situations in terms of penalty and progression.[8]

Disciplinary action in contemporary public sector work settings requires considering the scope of responsibilities as well as the authority structure within the organization:

- What does an employee do?
- During what time frame does that person have authority to engage in different behaviors?

Box 13.2   Tests for Just Cause

- Did the organization give the employee forewarning or foreknowledge of the possible or probable disciplinary consequences of the employee's conduct?
- Was the organization's rule or managerial order reasonably related to (a) the orderly, efficient, and safe operation of the organization's activities and (b) the performance that the organization might reasonably expect of the employee?
- Did the organization, before administering discipline to an employee, make an effort to discover whether the employee did in fact violate or disobey a rule or order of management?
- Was the organization's investigation conducted fairly and objectively?
- At the investigation did the "judge" obtain substantial evidence or proof that the employee was guilty as charged?
- Has the organization applied its rules, orders, and penalties evenhandedly and without discrimination to all employees?
- Was the degree of discipline administered by the organization in a particular case reasonably related to (a) the seriousness of the offense and (b) the service record of the employee with the organization?

Source: Slightly revised from Steven E. Aufrecht, "Toward a Model for Determining Appropriate Corrective Action in Public Employee Discipline," *Journal of Collective Negotiations,* 25:3 (1996): 192. These tests for just cause originate with C. R. Daugherty, 50, LA 83, 1968.

- How is his or her conduct assessed compared to similar behaviors by nonpublic employees?
- Are there different standards in place to assess public versus nonpublic employees?
- Who supervises the employee?
- Are the employee's responsibilities contingent on the efforts of a work group or more autonomous?
- What is the effect of this person's decisions on others?
- Does the employee exercise authority over others within the organization or significant decision-making authority over constituents outside the organization?

Aufrecht argues that discipline is a means to ensure that employee effort is coordinated toward the attainment of the organization's mission.[9] The policies, procedures, and rules of behavior that an organization establishes should, in theory, facilitate this effort.[10] If an employee does not comply with established policies or codes, then Aufrecht holds that a supervisor can respond in two general ways: work to modify employee behavior or remove the employee from the position.[11] Unfortunately, no textbook can provide a disciplinary process template that is universally appropriate. Aufrecht thus cautions us: "There is no formula available for determining the proper corrective action in an organizational discipline case. There are too many competing values and variables. Human beings ultimately must make judgments."[12] The following sections address these management options in greater detail and summarize prevailing thought about proper organizational guidelines for discipline and, when necessary, discharge.[13]

Disciplinary Action

Disciplinary action varies along fundamental dimensions: according to the degree of formality employed, according to the punitive versus corrective intent held by the organization, the intent of the employee, and the locus of control in terms of centralization or decentralization of disciplinary policy.[14] (See Figure 13.1.) Proportion-

ality dictates that disciplinary action should be commensurate with the severity of the consequences of the behavior or the magnitude of the performance gap.

Formality Disciplinary responses vary according to the degree to which discipline is recorded, documented, and retained within the organizational memory. Highly informal episodes of discipline are likely to be unwritten and are generally intended to be corrective without presumption of a pattern of inappropriate behavior or performance on the part of the employee. Formality in disciplinary actions increases with a written record of the action by the employee and the organizational response to that action. In addition to the record, formality will increase with the number of procedures in place orchestrating the process and potential outcomes for disciplinary action.

Intent Consideration of intent requires two perspectives—namely, the employee's view and that held by the organization. Disciplinary efforts differ according to whether the goal is to strengthen an employee's performance (e.g., by offering training or adapting a work structure) or remove some privilege as an incentive to change behavior (suspend, loss of a perk). From an employee's perspective, we may also need to consider the intent of the discipline. Stone suggests that Americans are preoccupied with causality.[15] If something is considered to be a problem, then we must root out its cause. If we find the cause we eliminate it, and in doing so we eliminate the problem.

To this end, Stone characterizes dimensions of intentionality. Did we intend our actions, and did we know what the outcome might be? In terms of public sector workplace discipline, we need to consider whether employees intend a behavior or performance level and whether they understand the negative ramifications of their action or behavior. If there is no intent and no understanding of the ramifications, then efforts to improve the employee's understanding or skills through training or perhaps a restructuring of a position or work schedule are appropriate corrective actions.

Figure 13.1   Disciplinary Action

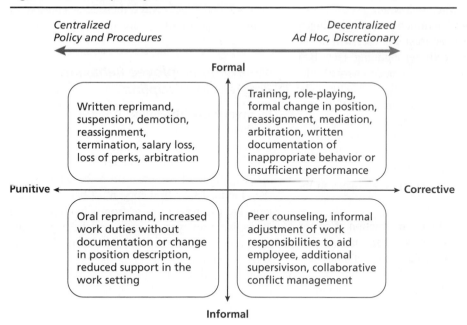

If the employee demonstrates intent and a lack of concern about the outcomes, then punitive rather than corrective actions may be necessary. The problem in carrying out this line of thinking lies in demonstrating intent and understanding.

Locus of control Ideally the difficulty in assessing intent and managing performance means that consistency and objectivity are critical components of a disciplinary policy. However, individuals are unique and situations vary. Supervisors may need to exercise greater discretion and informality in managing performance or responding to employee behaviors than a formal policy may allow. Locus of control issues entail this question: should control rest with the supervisor, as in a decentralized system, or be consolidated in a centralized system through standardized procedures and "one size fits all" responses to discipline? This is a difficult question because, in the ideal situation, we would have a maximum of both local discretion and centrally enforced consistency in disciplinary actions.

Ethical Considerations

In the reading for this chapter, Seidler considers the implications for disciplinary action in a team-based environment such as TQM. Graham Sewell offers a different perspective in his assessment of **peer surveillance** in team-based employment settings.[16] Sewell suggests that two forms of surveillance—**vertical surveillance** (e.g., electronic monitoring) and **horizontal surveillance** (e.g., peer surveillance)—can serve to maintain control and enforce disciplinary norms in group-based work settings.[17] Group-based work arrangements may offer a useful means of maintaining discipline in organizations as the team members impose informal discipline to ensure compliance with team and organizational goals.[18] However, with a reliance on informal means to manage disciplinary issues, there is a potential for abuse of authority and violation of employee rights. Certainly informal norms have served to encourage (and discourage) a variety of workplace behaviors that are now inappropriate and heavily sanctioned by law, including sexual harassment and retaliatory action against whistleblowers.

Trust is an important dimension of disciplinary action. Employees must trust that they will not be arbitrarily charged with wrongdoing (see Box 13.3). An employee who has been charged with inappropriate behavior must believe that he or she will be sanctioned only if evidence is sufficient to warrant punishment or correction. Employees must believe that they will have the opportunity to challenge false accusations. Unfortunately, it has been necessary to codify these commonsense-based approaches to managing employees in the workplace:

> Trust is influenced by the interaction of power, politics, and conflict in organizations. . . . The mere presence of these factors is not unusual or predictive of low trust. . . . What counts is what kinds of power, politics, and conflict organizations experience and how they choose to deal

with these challenges. If they are managed in moral and ethical ways, these issues present as much opportunity as threat.[19]

Modifying Employee Behavior: Progressive Discipline

In **progressive discipline** systems, supervisors combine corrective and punitive actions and vary the remedy for misconduct in accord with an assessment of intent, the frequency of violations, and the magnitude of the problem being addressed.[20] (See Figure 13.2.) In theory, most behavior problems are assumed to arise from situations where corrective employee assistance is the appropriate response; however, if a behavior or performance problem continues or even increases, then the punitive actions will escalate in response. Developmental discipline is intended to correct inappropriate behavior by taking a rehabilitative outlook

---

Box 13.3   Managing Conflict through Trust

Ethical, High-trust Actions

- Forming coalitions
- Avoiding petty disputes
- Keeping promises
- Appealing to ideals and values
- Telling the truth
- Being civil
- Willingness to accommodate, compromise, and collaborate
- Keeping conflict functional
- Not personalizing disputes
- Allowing people to save face

Unethical, Low-trust Actions

- Machiavellian behavior
- Concealing intentions
- Insincerity
- Blaming others
- Personalizing conflict
- Spreading rumors about people
- Harboring grudges
- Promoting zero-sum legitimacy
- Engaging in character assassination
- Lying

Source: David G. Carnevale, *Trustworthy Government: Leading and Management Strategies for Building Trust and High Performance.* Copyright © 1995 by Jossey-Bass. Reprinted by permission of Jossey-Bass Inc., a subsidiary of John Wiley & Sons, Inc.

Figure 13.2 Progressive Discipline

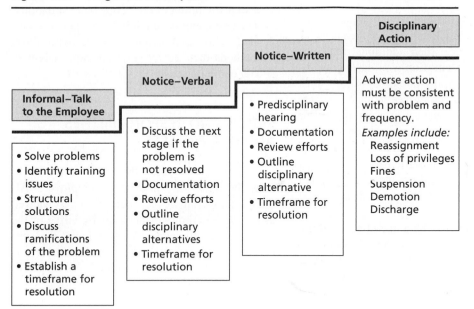

on problem situations and precludes the use of punishment for past actions by employees—be it misconduct or insufficient performance—until it is clear that the employee is unwilling or unable to benefit from the rehabilitative effort.[21]

In most cases, the first step in the progressive discipline model is to talk to the employee about the problem.[22] A useful approach to progressive discipline is to begin as a problem solver. At this point the supervisor can discuss the expectations for performance or behavior and to determine whether training deficiencies are contributing to insufficient performance or whether personal issues are prompting inappropriate behaviors at work. (A discussion of the factors that can contribute to employee performance is included in Chapter 11.) Personal role demands, including child or elder care, often affect employee performance and behavior. If an employee is experiencing violence or harassment in the workplace or has insufficient training or experience to perform as the demands of a position have changed, then a supervisor could employ a number of strategies to

address performance problems, including a counseling referral, disciplinary action for the harassing employees, or targeted training.

If the problems in question continue, the supervisor must then discuss the problem with the employee again, notifying the person that the next stage will be a written notice about unacceptable behavior or performance with guidelines for remedy attached.[23] Documentation is critical at this stage. Before any adverse action occurs, the employee should have the opportunity to respond in a predisciplinary hearing, which is a formal meeting in which the employee, supervisor, and other appropriate individuals consider the action in question and the employee's defense of that action.[24] Necessary disciplinary action that may ensue after **due process** hearings could include suspension with or without compensation, fines or pay reductions, or removal from the position or work setting through demotion, reassignment to another position away from the work unit where problems are present, or discharge from the organization.

Demotions and Reassignment

If counseling or less dramatic sanctions are not effective in addressing inappropriate behavior or deficient performance, then additional remedies may be employed. **Demotion** would be an appropriate response, assuming due process guidelines have been met, if the employee is unable to perform in the position because of a gap in skill or competency. If performance levels do not improve after adequate training has been provided or if the employee is unwilling to participate in additional training, then a reduction in grade, class, or position may be the best action for both the employee and the organization.

A **reassignment** may be a useful action if the problem lies with the work setting, the demands of a particular position, or interpersonal disputes. If, for example, the employee is late to work because of personal obligations coupled with the location of the work site, creative performance solutions could entail a transfer to a site better situated for the employee (if this is feasible) or even flexible scheduling or telecommuting. Transfers are not necessarily punitive, but rather may reflect an accommodation to retain an employee.

Discharge

Sometimes the most viable option is to discharge the employee. Discharge in the public sector requires just cause. However, even if cause is found, managers may be unwilling to discharge employees. Klaas and Dell'omo found that managers may be unwilling to pursue the necessary actions to discharge an employee when they perceive that the effort involved would be great, and just cause was not indisputably established.[25] In addition, a supervisor may be unwilling to pursue discharge without clearly established cause if the employee is likely to file a grievance:[26]

> While an employer's best defense against a wrongful discharge claim often is established through careful employee selection and consistent application of disciplinary procedures, the

manner in which the employee is terminated also is important in protecting against liability. The best methods of minimizing claims associated with termination coincide with those methods dictated by good business judgment and common sense.[27]

RIGHTS AND RESPONSIBILITIES AND DUE PROCESS

Chapter 4 examined how the courts have come to view the rights of public sector employees. Although public employees were originally viewed as having no employment rights by virtue of the doctrines of privilege and sovereignty, the contemporary interpretation by American courts is that public employees are entitled to strong protection against arbitrary treatment by local, state, or federal government agencies by virtue of the constitutional protections available to all citizens against unwarranted government action. Among the most important of these protections with respect to public employment are due process rights, which constrain government from taking a citizen's property (or job) without due process of law. Public sector employees are viewed as having a bona fide property right in their jobs once they have passed their period of probationary service. Any adverse action taken by government against an employee requires careful consideration of due process considerations. Although private and nonprofit sector employees are not generally viewed as holding a property right, due process procedures are still recommended in the case of adverse action. Bohlander notes that the right to challenge an adverse action is a generally accepted foundation of workplace democracy.[28] As a general rule, the **appeal** or **grievance process** should be commensurate in formality to the consequence facing the employee.[29]

Procedures vary somewhat across jurisdictions and agencies, but most public organizations and government jurisdictions have formal, written guidelines.[30] In a unionized setting, the procedures are established through contract language for specific groups of employees. Usually these procedures include notifying the appropriate supervisor that a challenge was filed by an employee. Next, the union representatives or liaisons in the personnel office receive an oral notice. Written notices of challenge are a necessary step in most processes, and the same individuals will be likely to receive these. The process continues until resolution is reached. A final arbitration hearing is a common end point.

Some organizations have established independent mechanisms to manage disputes or **ombudsman offices** as places for employees to take issues for a neutral hearing and informal resolution of issues. These activities vary according to the level of formality and the specific steps involved. Usually organizational policies identify the contact chain and specify the oral or written nature of the challenge. In addition, policies usually outline appropriate forms of documentation and identify the expectations of due process.

Although most union contracts specify grievance procedures, many organizations establish independent grievance systems. These systems, typically established collaboratively by employees and management, offer important advantages to public sector organizations. First, it is possible to streamline independent systems to manage disputes to offer "timely workplace justice."[31] Second, employee disputes may not be bound by contract language in an independent system but could reflect an open forum for concerns.[32] Certainly, independent grievance systems could improve conflict management practices by reducing the adversarial nature of the process.[33] Finally, independent grievance systems can be a means to enhance individual performance by identifying problems in policy and practice that impede an employee's ability to do their work.[34]

The term **at-will employment** is drawn from a court decision in which it was held that in the private marketplace an employer does not have to provide cause to discharge an employee.[35] Employment at will can be used to prevent employees from asserting a property right.[36] There are some limitations to employer action despite the strength of the at-will employment doctrine. Civil rights legislation intercedes in the employment relationship to protect certain groups of people (e.g., minorities, women, persons over forty) from discriminatory action. Formal collective bargaining contracts can serve to constrain and proscribe employer action against an employee through procedural agreements regarding disciplinary procedures, grievance and appeal structures, and scope-of-work agreements. The at-will employment doctrine does not have universal application and is limited when the employer action violates the public interest (e.g., involves retribution for whistle-blowing),[37] there is a presumption of a contract between the employer and employee,[38] the employer acts with malicious intent,[39] or the employer wrongfully denies an employee compensation or benefit due.[40] Although at-will employment is usually associated with the private sector, some states are experimenting with at-will employment for public employees. In Georgia, new employees are hired as unclassified personnel and considered at will by the Georgia State Personnel Board. This designation means that they do not have the same formal protections exercised by other state employees.[41]

The Americans with Disabilities Act (ADA) offers additional legal protections to ensure that employees, public or private, are given sufficient opportunity to perform. However, ADA protections do not extend to disciplinary actions in the case of violence-free workplace policies when a previously protected employee threatens another.[42]

In addition, employees are protected from adverse action in retaliation for reports of wrongdoing. **Whistleblowing** protections were provided at the federal level in the Civil Service Reform Act of 1978 and expanded in the Whistleblower Protection Act of 1989.[43] According to a study conducted by the U.S. Merit Systems Protection Board, federal employees appear to be willing to report illegal or wasteful activities such as waste due to poor management, practices that impose danger on employees or constituents, or overt bribery and theft.[44] Unfortunately, more than one-third of the employees who had made such reports have experienced retaliatory acts ranging from informal harassment or denial of some organizational benefit to demotion, unrequested reassignment, or suspension.[45]

Disciplinary Investigations

Procedural due process is an important underlying principle in **disciplinary investigations**. Employers must have sufficient evidence prior to taking adverse action. That evidence should demonstrate the magnitude of the problem, thereby guiding the approach to discipline. Disciplinary investigations are not bound by the "probable cause" standard used in criminal proceedings in the judicial system. Employers enjoy a right to maintain supervision over their employees. However, employers do need to prevent bias in the investigations they do carry out (they should not single out individuals who receive closer supervision than other employees), and they need to acquire evidence systematically as documentation for any formal disciplinary action. The common

mistakes made in disciplinary investigations listed in Box 13.4 offer some guidance as to appropriate action to be taken and effort at documentation required in disciplinary investigations. It is not always necessary to "catch employees red-handed," but employers must recognize that there will be certain expectations that the organization has established appropriate procedures to prevent wrongdoing and has in effect clear policies that identify appropriate versus inappropriate behavior.

Managing Discipline and Dismissal

Disrespect—whether shown by an employee to a supervisor or client or demonstrated by a supervisor toward a subordinate—is never acceptable behavior. A positive, respectful approach to communicating with others during a dispute of any type can defuse emotional and threatening situations. Clearly, calmly, and respectfully stating a view can contribute to a positive hearing by another person. Allowing another person to retain dignity during a trying situation is important. Table 13.1 sets out ways to improve communication.

Box 13.4   Common Mistakes in Disciplinary Investigations

- Delaying the investigation, which can result in loss of evidence and deterioration in witness memory.
- Failing to obtain sworn statements or depositions of witnesses, which may limit the range of evidence available for decision if these individuals are not able to testify at a hearing.
- Losing evidence (e.g., documents or physical evidence of wrong-doing) or failing to control access to evidence raises the potential for charges of tampering.
- Failing to obtain all perspectives on the story.
- Failing to interview witnesses singly and in privacy, thus raising the potential of influence and collusion.
- Developing the investigation with the intent to support or challenge an outcome. Investigations should simply be a means to gather evidence rather than to advocate or prosecute during the investigatory phase.
- Failing to be logical in assessing evidence. Analysis of "facts" should suggest sources of additional evidence that could serve to substantiate or challenge those "facts."

Source: David G. Carnevale, *Trustworthy Government: Leadership and Management Strategies for Building Trust and High Performance.* Copyright © 1995 by Jossey-Bass. Reprinted by permission of Jossey-Bass Inc., a subsidiary of John Wiley & Sons, Inc.

Table 13.1   Communication Skills Can Diffuse Difficult Situations

Improve communication by:	This technique will serve to:	Rationale:
Offering the other person face-saving comments	Allow the other person to retain some pride. The person will be more likely to listen or accommodate the change as a concession of his or her own.	Criticism is hard to take even for the most secure person. Is it really necessary to emphasize a mistake, or is the goal to avoid error in the future?
Letting the other person exercise options	Support the self-esteem of the other person by giving him or her some control. Demonstrates trust in the other person and confidence in his or her abilities to make good decisions.	People want to maintain a sense of power. Also, there are few situations that have only one right way to respond. A person who contributes to decisions in a project retains ownership and commitment.
Avoiding sarcasm	Demonstrate respect for the other person and keep the focus of a dispute or disagreement on the issue rather than the person.	Sarcasm humiliates people and sets the stage for personal attacks rather than professional disagreements about work-related activities.
Avoiding exaggeration	Maintain the focus of the dispute on the professional or work-related issue rather than on exaggeration.	Exaggeration exacerbates a dispute. People will become defensive even when they know a charge is outrageous.
Leaving drama in the theater	Maintain focus on the disputed issue rather than the parties involved.	Acting incredulous or shocked as a means to drive home the enormity of another's action mocks and demeans him or her. Even a facial expression, when it is meant to disparage or humiliate, serves to personalize a dispute rather than address a legitimate professional concern.
Not dismissing people	Maintain open communication and suggest respect for others.	A discussion that closes with a remark or gesture meant to dismiss the other person forces a conflict "underground."

Source: The recommendations are drawn, with some revision, from Dianna Booher, "When the Problem is not the Problem," *IPMA News* 64:5 (1999) 17.

Rollinson and associates found that managers had different approaches to dealing with disciplinary actions depending on the employee's length of service or the supervisor's perception about the amount of time and effort that the disciplinary action would entail.[46] There are few absolutes in personnel management; however, we can state rather unequivocally that the excerpt in Box 13.5 on page 364 does indeed represent the WRONG way to approach employee dismissal. Such dismissal actions do occur, as the successful cases of wrongful termination lawsuits prove. After reviewing this text and considering your own experiences in the workplace, you can probably identify some of the problems with the approach set forth in the *Malek Manual.*

Box 13.5 Please, please, please don't do this

The *Malek Manual* was written by staff in the White House Personnel Office in 1969 in response to President Richard Nixon's concerns about controlling federal agency employees and responding to perceived political threats:

> Frontal assault. You simply call an individual in and tell him he is no longer wanted, that you'll assist him in finding another job and will keep him around until such time as he finds other employment. But you do expect him to immediately relinquish his duties, accept reassignment to a make-shift position at his current grade and then quietly resign for the good of the service. Of course, you promise him that he will leave with honor and with the finest recommendations, a farewell luncheon, and perhaps even a Departmental award. You, naturally, point out that should he not accept such an offer, and he later is forced to resign or retire through the regular process or on his own volition, his employment references from the Department and his permanent personnel record may not look the same as if he accepted your offer. There should be no witnesses in the room at the time. Caution: this technique should only be used for the timid at heart with a giant ego. This is an extremely dangerous technique and the very fact of your conversation can be used against the Department in any subsequent adverse action proceedings. It should never be used with that fervent, zealous employee committed to Democratic policies and programs, or to the bureaucracy, who might relish the opportunity to be martyred on the cross of his cause.

Source: White House Personnel Office, "The Malek Manual," in Frank J. Thompson, ed., *Classics of Public Personnel Policy,* 2nd ed. (Pacific Grove, CA: Brooks/Cole, 1991), pp. 76–77.

EMERGING CONCERNS AND CONSIDERATIONS

Work Arrangements

As the nature of work changes, so too will expectations about employee performance and behavior in the workplace change. As flexible work arrangements such as telecommuting and flexible scheduling become more common, different expectations will emerge about how employees will communicate with their supervisors and with one another. In addition, as Seidler indicates in the chapter reading, changing arrangements in work groups mean that we are certain to see the same kind of shifts in reporting and monitoring relationship that we have already observed in performance management systems.

Violence

We lament the decline of civility in public settings, but incivility is not as simple as occasioning

wounded feelings in the workplace.[47] It probably is not necessary to offer a list of incidents of workplace violence to illustrate that a problem exists in their area. Unfortunately, each of us can list events in schools, public organizations, and private organizations in which people have been subject to indignity, injuries, and even death. It is not endemic to any single government level or agency, nor is it a problem associated with exclusively urban areas.

Violence in the workplace may directly affect large numbers of people, or it can arise from an incident between two employees. In some situations, domestic violence can spill over into the workplace through diminished performance, behavioral problems, or incidents of physical or emotional abuse played out at work.[48] Public, private, and nonprofit sector organizations now find that in addition to managing workplace interactions among employees, they have to develop structural and procedural remedies to protect their employees and constituents from incivilities.[49] Many organizations are setting out explicit policies and procedures for a violence-free workplace and providing corrective alternatives such as training and constructive conflict management mechanisms to manage employee disputes.[50]

Technology

Just as technology has increased the speed of activity in the workplace, so too it has influenced discipline. The seduction of electronic communication has tempted some employees to believe that their workplace communications are entirely private. But as you discovered in Chapter 4, there are few privacy protections in place for public sector employees. Nevertheless, employers must establish properly framed policies on e-mail, the use of computer equipment, and communication norms. Under most circumstances, employees can be held accountable for the types of material that they access through the Internet.[51]

Employers increasingly are using high-tech approaches to monitoring employee behaviors.[52] Surveillance cameras, recording equipment, and software to monitor Internet usage and e-mail may mean that most of these actions are recorded in some archival record for later retrieval. This will mean that one's stellar performance in working with citizens will be recorded for one's supervisor to use in the next performance appraisal. It may also mean that Jack's habit of borrowing office supplies or the fact that Megan was playing video games at her desk will be on permanent record.

Technology has also expanded the scope of investigation of employee wrongdoing in more serious matters. For example, it is employed to address incidents of workplace violence. Electronic surveillance equipment can be used effectively to monitor performance levels and employee behavior that could be considered threatening to others in the workplace.

Other forms of technology may include metal detectors or security badges that control entry into the workplace, and cellular phones and pagers for field-based personnel so that contact with supervisors can be maintained even at a distance from an office setting.

Diversity

In the 1993 Winter Commission report on state and local public service, academics, and practitioners alike noted a clear disparity between the demographic composition of people in public service and that of the general citizenry.[53] The Commission called for "aggressive recruitment" of underrepresented groups, an undertaking that will necessarily serve to deepen the diversity of values present in the public workforce.[54] Jewell Scott calls for greater recognition of the content of contemporary and future workforce diversity, a condition of operation that requires the presence of effective methods of handling conflict between employees who possess differing values:[55]

> Similarity leads to feeling good . . . and to interpersonal attraction. . . . The greater the perceived similarity and the opportunity for contact, the more rewards are experienced, which results in more interaction as well as in more positive intergroup attitudes. . . . Positive intergroup attitudes can be eliminated or seriously reduced if there is much intergroup anxiety. . . . Cultural distance increases intergroup anxiety. . . . Any factor that increases uncertainty about how to behave in social situations, or in the individual's sense of control over the outcomes of the social interaction, increases anxiety.[56]

Public managers need skills for managing various forms of conflict now, and in the future they will need these skills to manage the demographically diverse workforce of this century. Managers who choose to address disputes between employees or between an employee and some organizational norm can opt for decidedly compassionate methods. Table 13.2 on page 366 offers some suggestions for management actions in working with employees in disciplinary scenarios. If the overall goal is to achieve the organizational mission, which in the public sector requires action for the public interest, then common ground should be both possible and productive.

Table 13.2   Managing Conflict and Diversity

What managers can do . . .

Emphasize shared goals	Ownership in project outcomes or continuing focus on organizational goals rather than personal objectives may result in a decrease in the competitive nature of a work group or a decline in conflict between agencies or departments.
Offer ways for similarity	Even dissimilar people share a great deal. Physical indications of similarity include common dress or uniforms. Intellectual indications of similarity could include professional standards or socialization. Emotional indications of similarity could emerge from shared dedication to an institution or community. Interpersonal indications of similarity could be drawn from historical incidents of cooperation.
Define the significance of dissimilarity	Celebrate difference! Characterize diversity as a desirable means to increase creativity. Use problems that may have resulted as learning opportunities rather than as evidence that "it just won't work." It has to: our society is diverse.
Learn about other cultures	Cross-cultural training is very useful. Remember that diversity is not only ethnic or gender difference. Simply learning about another's language (e.g., engineers learning about what marketing types are really saying) can help.
Praise effort and ability	Is ability emphasized over effort? "People can learn to do very complex tasks even if they have modest abilities, provided they persist and work hard. . . . Effort is something that people can do something about."

Source: Harry C. Triandis, "A Theoretical Framework for the Study of Diversity," in Martin M. Chemers, Stuart Oskamp, and Mark A. Costanzo, eds., *Diversity in Organizations,* pp. 32–34, copyright © 1995 by Sage Publications, Inc. Reprinted by permission of Sage Publications, Inc.

Organizations can continue to pursue the zero-sum politics of yore, in which what I win you lose, but if they do, achievement will be impaired. Americans especially—with our ideas of competing individually and in groups (often ruthlessly) for position, resources, and dominance—must acquiesce to nonzero-sum politics in which all gain in pursuit of a common vision. That approach is a tool that fits very well because the essence of the high-performing organization is precisely that the sum is greater than its parts.[57]

■ CONCLUSION

Discipline does not need to be an unpleasant task to be avoided. It is important to treat employees with dignity and compassion, but also in a consistent and predictable manner. For this reason, managing disciplinary action is necessary and should focus on discipline to achieve organizational goals rather than discipline born of vindictiveness. In addition, we need to understand that the differences that will arise, and the disputes they occasion, may not be deliberate efforts to subvert organizational goals or countermand a supervisor's direction. Conflict in the workplace may be a result of personal factors, cultural differences, unclear standards, or some aspects of work structure. Clear workplace standards that outline appropriate and inappropriate behavior are critical to protect the interests of employees and employers alike. Discipline is a critical function in organizations that brings together managers and human resource specialists.

▓ MANAGER'S VOCABULARY

discipline
dismissal
adverse action
just cause
peer surveillance
vertical surveillance
horizontal surveillance
progressive discipline
predisciplinary hearing
due process
demotion
reassignment
appeal/grievance process
ombudsman offices
at-will employment
whistleblowing
disciplinary investigation

▓ STUDY QUESTIONS

1. What is the disciplinary process?

2. Why is due process important?

3. How should disciplinary problems be handled? Explain your answer.

4. What role does formality play in the protection of employee rights? Recall the discussion of employee rights in Chapter 4. What did Rosenbloom say about due process protections and the at-will employment doctrine?

5. What are the implications of at-will employment for public sector employees?

6. How might changing work arrangements such as the use of temporary versus permanent employees affect employment protections?

7. What is progressive discipline?

8. What are the problems with informality in discipline?

9. What procedures should be in place for employee appeal?

▓ EXPERIENTIAL EXERCISES

1. You are the director of the State Commission on Diversity. As an intelligent and discerning manager, you recognize that there are some workplace frictions as a result of the evolving diversity of public sector agencies. You hire a well-known consultant in matters of diversity, who counsels you as follows:

   When there is a history of conflict, much cultural distance, little knowledge of the other culture, no knowledge of the other language, no network overlap, differences in status, and no superordinate goals, there is a maximum of perceived dissimilarity. If there is an opportunity for interaction, this results in a punishing experience, which will lead to avoidance or aggression. Such hostile interactions will lead to no network overlap and to high probabilities of ethnic affirmation (e.g., my group is the best), [and] to invalid stereotypes. . . . Under these circumstances, the most effective way to establish control is to kill the other. If the other is dead, one has total control over the situation.[58]

Although the consultant's explanation of human behavior may be clinically accurate, you are a bit overwhelmed by this dire warning. You recall a newspaper article about a violent incident in a large private firm in which an employee from the marketing department physically attacked an employee in the finance department over frustration on a project. If this level of hostility could evolve between these professionals, what might occur in other departments where differences go beyond training and the organizational structure? Draft a memo explaining your concerns to the governor, and outline a program that could be employed in state agencies to serve as an intervention or resolution vehicle for these kinds of situations. (Hint: A review of employee assistance benefits or consideration of ombudsman programs may be useful.)

2. Professor Drake has just begun grading student papers from her M.P.A. seminar when she discovers that two of the students did not cite sources appropriately. In one case, it appears that the student lifted large portions from an article without any quotation marks or other indications of any type that this work was not the original analysis of the student. The other student also lifted several sentences directly from a textbook. However, in the second case, the student did note that the material was drawn from the textbook. But because the student did not use quotation marks to denote directly quoted material, it was difficult to differentiate between the student's analysis and that of the textbook author.

   According to university policy, both cases are plagiarism. The guidelines established by the faculty senate grant course professors the authority to handle the matter as they see fit (failing grade for the assignment or course, grade reduction for the assignment or course, additional course work, or resubmission of the assignment). In addition, faculty may also refer the student to the Academic Standards Committee for possible expulsion from the university. Students can appeal the initial course-related decision through the standard appeal process for grade disputes. This system is essentially decentralized, though faculty have the option of referring a student to the Academic Standards Committee, a university-wide, formal disciplinary body.

   What should Professor Drake do? Should both cases of plagiarism be handled in the same manner? What level of formality should be employed? How should Professor Drake ascertain intent? Was it a simple error, or sloppiness, or a deliberate attempt to represent another's work as their own?

3. Several faculty have presented concerns to the faculty senate about an epidemic of plagiarism that appears to be sweeping the university community. In fact, they indicate that it is difficult even to gain a sense of the problem because plagiarism is often managed by a professor in the classroom and that professors are reluctant to refer cases to the university's Academic Standards Committee. The faculty senate also discovers that faculty vary greatly in their response to plagiarism. Some professors tend to ignore academic dishonesty because of the effort involved in doc-

umentation, while others spend enormous amounts of time perusing student papers and documenting cases. Corrective measures vary as well. Some faculty have the student rewrite the assignment, others sternly lecture about scholastic integrity, and others fail the student for the assignment or the course. In response to these concerns, the faculty senate wants to crack down on academic dishonesty and develop a uniform approach to the problem. It proposes mandatory reporting and documentation of all suspected cases of plagiarism to the Student Affairs Division. The Academic Standards Committee would then review these cases and recommend the appropriate action. Faculty would no longer have the authority to manage plagiarism through grades or assignment revisions, but would be required to report the student and refer all documentation to the centralized body.

What are the advantages or disadvantages of this new centralized approach to disciplining academic dishonesty? Is this policy reasonable? Is it fair or unfair? Why or why not?

■ CASE APPLICABLE TO THIS CHAPTER

"Conflicting Perceptions" (Task 1).

■ NOTES

[1] *The Random House Dictionary* (New York: Random Hose, 1980), p. 249.

[2] Ibid., p. 252.

[3] Steven E. Aufrecht, "Toward a Model for Determining Appropriate Corrective Action in Public Employee Discipline," *Journal of Collective Negotiations in the Public Sector* 25:3 (1996): 180–183.

[4] Ibid., p. 172.

[5] National Performance Review, *From Red Tape to Results: Creating a Government That Works Better and Costs Less* (Washington, D.C.: U.S. Government Printing Office, 1993).

[6] Frank J. Thompson and Beryl A. Radin, *Reinventing Public Personnel Management: The Winter and Gore Initiatives* (Albany, NY: National Commission on the State and Local Public Service, 1997), p. 10.

[7] Steven W. Hays, "Employee Discipline and Removal: Coping with Job Security," in Steven W. Hays and Richard C. Kearney, eds., *Public Personnel Administration: Problems and Prospects,* 3rd ed. (Englewood Cliffs, NJ: Prentice-Hall, 1995), pp. 150–153.

[8] Ibid., pp. 152–154.

[9] Aufrecht, "Toward a Model," p. 178.

[10] Ibid.

[11] Ibid.

[12] Ibid., pp. 185–186.

[13] Much of what we use as a guideline for adverse action is drawn from court interpretation; case law, however, tends to shift frequently. Managers are encouraged to consult with organizational specialists in this regard.

[14] The logic of formality and informality in administrative action is developed in Lief H. Carter and Christine B. Harrington, *Administrative Law and Politics,* 2nd ed. (New York: HarperCollins, 1991), pp. 201–207, 545.

[15] Deborah Stone, *Policy Paradox: The Art of Political Decision Making* (New York: Norton, 1997), pp. 188–195.

[16] Graham Sewell "The Discipline of Teams: The Control of Team-Based Industrial Work Through Electronic and Peer Surveillance," *Administrative Science Quarterly* 43:2 (June 1998): 397–420.

[17] Ibid., p. 14.

[18] James R. Barker "Tightening the Iron Cage: Concertive Control in Self-Managing Teams," *Administrative Science Quarterly* 38:3 (1993): 408–437.

[19] David G. Carnevale, *Trustworthy Government: Leadership and Management Strategies for Building Trust and High Performance* (San Francisco: Jossey-Bass, 1995), p. 145.

[20] Hays, "Employee Discipline and Removal," p. 154.

[21] Ibid., p. 156.

[22] Maureen Smith "Progressive Discipline in the Workplace," *IMPA News* 64:11 (1998): 18.

[23] Ibid.

[24] Ibid., p. 10.

[25] Brian S. Klaas and Gregory G. Dell'omo, "Managerial Use of Dismissal: Organizational-Level Determinants," *Personnel Psychology* 50:4 (1997): 927–954.

[26] Ibid., p. 934.

[27] Bettye Springer, "Terminating Problem Employees," *Public Management* 78:4 (1996): 16.

[28] George W. Bohlander, "Public Sector Independent Grievance Systems: Methods and Procedures," *Public Personnel Management* 18:3 (1989): 339.

[29] *Board of Regents v. Roth,* 408 U.S. 564 (1972).

[30] Dennis M. Daley, "Formal Disciplinary Procedures and Conflict Resolution Remedies: Availability and the Effects of Size and City Manager Among North Carolina Municipalities," *Public Personnel Management* 22:1 (1993): 158.

[31] Bohlander, "Public Sector Independent Grievance System," p. 339.

[32] Ibid., p. 340.

[33] Ibid.

[34] Ibid.

[35] *Payne v. Western and Atlantic RA Company*, 82 Tenn. 597 (1884).

[36] Hays, "Employee Discipline and Removal," p. 151.

[37] *Palmateer v. International Harvester,* 85 Ill.2d 124, 421 N.E.2d 876 (1981).

[38] *Touissant v. Blue Cross and Blue Shield of Michigan*, 408 Mich. 579, 292 N.W.2d 880 (1980).

[39] *Monge v. Beebe Rubber Company,* 114 N.H. 130, 316, A.2d 549 (1974).

[40] 373 Mass. 96, 36 N.W. 2d 1251 (1977).

[41] "Georgia's At-Will Employees," *Public HR* 1:1 (1998): 8.

[42] *Palmer v. Circuit Court of Cook County Illinois,* 95-3659 U.S. Cir. 7th (1997).

[43] Whistleblower Protection Act of 1989; Civil Service Reform Act of 1978.

[44] U.S. Merit Systems Protection Board, *Whistleblowing in the Federal Government: An Update* (Washington, D.C.: U.S. Government Printing Office, 1993), pp. 4, 9.

[45] Ibid., pp. 19–22.

[46] Derek Rollinson, and Caroline Hook, "Supervisor and Manager Styles in Handling Discipline and Grievance," *Personnel Review* 25:4 (1996): 38–56.

[47] Charles Mahtesian, "The Politics of Ugliness," *Governing* 10:9 (1997): 18–22.

[48] "Violence at Home Can Mean Violence at Work," *IPMA News* 65:4 (1999): 10.

[49] Mitchell Schnurman, "Companies Plan Against Violence," *Idaho Statesman,* August 2, 1999, p. 6B.

[50] Michelle Dalton Liberatore, "Killer Jobs," *Public HR* 1:1 (1998): 32.

[51] Urofsky et al. v. Gilmore, 98-1481 WL 61952 U.S. Cir. 4th (1999).

[52] William Bogard, *The Simulation of Surveillance: Hypercontrol in Telematic Societies* (Cambridge: Cambridge University Press, 1996); David Lyon, "An Electronic Panopticon? A Sociological Critique of Surveillance Theory," *Sociological Review* 41:4 (1993): 653–678.

[53] National Commission on the State and Local Public Service, *Hard Truths/Tough Choices: An Agenda for State and Local Reform* (Albany, N.Y.: Nelson Rockefeller Institute of Government, 1993), p. 31.

[54] Ibid.

[55] Jewell D. Scott, "Morality as an Organizational Problem: Past Success, Future Challenges," *Public Administration Review* 52 (1992): 105–107.

[56] Harry C. Triandis, "A Theoretical Framework for the Study of Diversity," in Martin M. Chemers, Stuart Oskamp, and Mark A. Costanzo, eds., *Diversity in Organizations* (Thousand Oaks, CA: Sage, 1995), p. 29.

[57] Ibid., p. 130.

[58] Triandis, "A Theoretical Framework," p. 30.

CHAPTER 14

Developing a Policy and Procedure Manual

References abound throughout this book to the importance of policies and procedures in human resource management. Unfortunately, although it is a common habit to refer in passing to the critical role of policies and procedures, textbooks in public administration and human resource management as a rule do not consider in any detail the issues that managers must consider when drafting policy documents. For example, when disciplinary action is being contemplated, it is vital that there is a clearly articulated policy that differentiates between appropriate and inappropriate workplace behavior. What should be included in such a policy? How should the content of such policies be derived? How should disciplinary action documents be worded? What are the ramifications of having no policy at all?

Policies in the context of human resource management suggest general guidelines or principles that reflect prudent and practical considerations in the achievement of the organization's mission. **Procedures** are generally considered to be the step-by-step detail of the best method to accomplish a desired goal. A policy may represent a general overview or framework, such as setting out in policy statements general expectations about the manner in which recruiting and selection activities will be conducted (through open process, for example, or systematic contact with references). A procedure could entail the specific tasks and recommendations for the manner of their completion, as in the case of specific steps a manager must take to announce a position opening and initiate a job search.

Unfortunately, it is commonplace to have policies in effect that were written to control behavior in reaction to past problems rather than reflecting the more proactive orientation of facilitating high levels of performance. Policies are often considered to be a means of preempting problems or offering general tried-and-true approaches to handling repeatedly initiated activities in the organization. In this way, policies and procedures constitute an important form of risk management. The term **risk management** refers to the efforts of organizations to manage their exposure to potential loss or hazard, including exposure to lawsuits. Risk managers deal with problems that organizations have with parties external to the organization (e.g., managing the effects of a policy decision adversely affecting community members). In many cases risk management has also been the responsibility that a public organization has to provide protection for a community in the case of a natural disaster. Risk managers also address some problems drawn from internal operations such as production processes or management programs, wherein employees are owed due consideration for workplace safety provisions. Of course, these several types of problems can have implications for others outside the organization, but for our purposes let us isolate the human resource arena as the issue for our discussion.

INTRODUCTION TO READING

In the following reading, Richard Zeckhauser and Kip Viscusi discuss the role that government should play to manage risk. Managers can draw parallels between the dilemmas that may face government in assessing and managing risk and the challenges facing managers in deciding how much risk-management-directed policy is too much policy.

As you read the selection, keep the following questions in mind:

- How can managers balance the cost of poor disciplinary decisions with the cost of too many rules, whose existence might impede performance?
- Should policies be used to referee disputes such as those among employees or between employees and their respective supervisors?

- Should policies be used as a safety net or insurance for the organization to prevent improper actions or decisions?
- How can an organization combine latitude and accountability into workplace policies and procedures? How much detail should be included in policies and procedures?
- How does a manager assign an acceptable level of risk?

Zeckhauser and Viscusi caution that government policy should not mirror citizens' irrationalities but, rather, should "promote the decisions people would make if they understood risks correctly and made sound decisions based on this understanding."[1] How could this be accomplished at the organizational level with employees?

READING

The Risk Management Dilemma

RICHARD J. ZECKHAUSER AND W. KIP VISCUSI

Market processes play a central and constructive role in allocating risks, but impediments such as inaccurately perceived risks and externalities create a potential role for government intervention. Individuals overestimate small risks, are averse to imprecisely understood risks, and give excessive weight to errors of commission over errors of omission. The challenge for the government is to strike an appropriate balance in its risk regulation efforts and to avoid institutionalizing common irrational responses to risk. Excessive expenditures on risk reduction, often undertaken by or required by government, not only squander resources but also may increase risks to us all; they can divert expenditures that could have been used to enhance our standard of living and, directly or indirectly, our health. Risk equity concerns often prove problematic: they may direct excessive attention to unimportant risks and hinder efforts to deploy resources to produce the greatest gains in societal health status.

Source: Richard J. Zeckhauser and W. Kip Viscusi, "The Risk Management Dilemma," *Annals of the American Academy of Political and Social Science* 545 (1996): 144–156.

When society allocates resources, three questions must be answered: who should decide; whose values count; and who should pay? In a democratic, capitalist society, the answer is straightforward: individuals and corporate decision makers should decide and pay for themselves, making their own values the basis for decision. The government establishes property rights and enforces contracts but otherwise sits on the sidelines.

The government often participates actively, however, in decisions affecting physical risks, frequently by overriding individual choices. When bad outcomes do occur, payment is often made by insurance companies and government, whose actions may have played no role in the bad outcomes. This approach is understandable because of three common characteristics of physical risks: surrounding uncertainty, significant consequences, and externalities. Even perfectly rational individuals have difficulty making consequential decisions under conditions of uncertainty. Moreover, if adverse consequences are significant, transfer of payment responsibility (risk spreading) is desirable. Finally, in many risk-taking decisions, such as a factory choosing an emissions level, one actor may impose significant adverse effects on others (that is, externalities).

Risk management thus presents a dilemma: challenging circumstances undermine many of the justifications for self-interested decentralized choice, but when we depart from this norm, both legitimacy and efficiency are undermined. We examine this dilemma here, looking first at the sources of risk and then at challenges to decision making.

SOURCES OF RISK

Nature is the source of many risks, such as earthquakes and hurricanes. But human action—the only avenue for affecting risk costs—usually amplifies (or ameliorates) the consequences. For example, houses built near major faults or coastlines are more likely to be damaged than houses built elsewhere.

Three primary sources of risk are generated by human action: lifestyle choices, contractual arrangements, and externalities from choices by others. Lifestyle choices—drinking to excess, smoking, and failing to eat a nutritious diet or take sufficient exercise—create many of the most important risks to human health.[1] Governments try to influence these choices; for example, they provide nutrition information, punish public intoxication, and require warning labels on cigarette packages.

Other risks are contracted for voluntarily with some other economic agent; for example, people buy potentially risky products and decide to work in hazardous jobs. In return, they expect some offset: higher wages for risky jobs or lower prices for the product. Such trade-offs, and their role in promoting efficiency, have been part of economic thought since Adam Smith. Nevertheless, the rationality of trading risk for resources is often called into question, frequently by the government. For example, the government intervenes to protect the well-being of those exposed to the risk through mechanisms such as product and job safety regulations, workers' compensation, and tort liability compensation for damages.

Contracts on risk acceptance often have significant legitimacy and strength. Indeed, even when risks escalate, individuals in high-risk jobs often carry out their obligations; for example, fire fighters and police officers rarely renege on their obligations when confronting an extraordinary risk. However, individuals often attempt to exploit the risk terms in a contract. For example, housing prices near toxic waste dumps are substantially depressed, but a purchaser who knows the risk and receives a discounted house price may well lobby or sue government agencies to expedite the cleanup.

In the third group of risks, externalities, actions by one party create risks or costs for others. These are the most obvious candidates for government intervention. In such situations, the firms or individuals imposing the risk have no incentive to care about the adverse external effects of their actions. Water and air pollution by firms, and drunk driving, are classic examples of externally imposed risks. The rationale for regulating externalities is clear-cut, but the optimal degree of regulation rarely is. Externality-regulating efforts can substantially redistribute resources; thus efforts to reduce pollution may benefit the politically influential rather than those who suffer the greatest harm or whose health could be saved most cheaply.

Our perception of the seriousness of a risk often depends on the risk's specific source; as a society, we tend to take some types of risks far more seriously than others. Consider now some important risks that we tend to respond to less than rationally.

Ordinary Versus Catastrophic Risks

From the standpoint of an individual citizen, a reasonable objective would be to target risk regulation efforts to maximize the expected number of lives saved for the resources spent. Such an approach would treat equally two situations: one where one person faces a risk of 1/1000, the other where 100 people together confront a risk of 1/100,000. Yet, while the expected number of lives lost is the same in each instance, the death of 100 people in an airplane crash or natural catastrophe typically receives much more publicity than the separate deaths of 100 individuals. That is, society is especially concerned with large-scale catastrophes.

Except in wars—and recent terrorist attacks—large numbers of people rarely die at the same time in contemporary developed nations. Early in the twentieth century, a natural disaster would frequently account for hundreds of deaths in the United States, but society has adapted to these threats through design improvements, through fire-protection devices, and by locating populations away from the riskiest areas. At least as judged by insurance claims, in many of the most recent catastrophes, such as those related to hurricanes, there are greater losses from property damage than from personal injury.[2] Largely because of the high value society attaches to a life—our most fundamental source of value—we have successfully developed substantial expenditures to preserve lives.

Extensive media coverage also leads people to overestimate certain risks and give undue importance to catastrophic events.[3] Do not the lives that are lost in unheralded highway accidents merit the same preventive efforts as those that will be lost due to a highly visible catastrophe, such as a hurricane or earthquake? It is noteworthy that we have responded to the isolated automobile accident case by making various kinds of insurance mandatory, whereas our principal response to natural catastrophes has been to offer subsidized federal insurance coverage and massive ex post bailouts once the catastrophes have hit. Interestingly, for both autos and hurricanes, those who impose the greatest risks often get subsidized; many states impose regulations to temper auto insurance rate differentials, and beach front dwellers pay a fraction of the fair actuarial charges for flood insurance.

Lurking Risks

Lurking risks are major long-term risks of particularly catastrophic consequences that we have never experienced but fear greatly. They include nuclear war, major climate change, the chance that Earth will be hit by an asteroid, and new viruses that may emerge from shrinking rain forests. There may be considerable time before these risks are resolved, and by the nature of these risks, past happenings provide little guidance to gauge their likelihood or consequences.

In lurking risks, catastrophic consequences—in some cases, possibly the end of civilization itself—are coupled with small probabilities, so that risk judgments may differ widely. In the 1960s, for example, much of the U.S. public believed that the chance of a nuclear war within a decade was about 1/3, whereas many experts estimated the annual risk to be from 10^3 to 10^5.[4] Such differences in risk perception often cannot be resolved, yet perceived risks must largely determine the size of major national and international risk-reducing expenditures, such as efforts to cut or build nuclear stockpiles or to curb global warming. Assessing magnitudes of loss is often no easier. For example, if a potent new virus emerges, how likely is it to be more damaging than the acquired immune deficiency syndrome (AIDS) or more than ten times as widespread, or only a tenth? We simply do not know.

What is the source of our fears of lurking risks? One possibility is that society needs a major fear. As the threat of nuclear war has faded, fear about climate change and AIDS has taken hold. Despite increases in most measures of our well-being, we fear for survival of the planet. (Witness the "Save the Planet" motto of the pop culture Hard Rock Café chain.)

Yet the scientific community is substantially more worried about climate change than the public is. Its risks are linked with the pollution dangers associated with fossil fuels. And our energy mix is a Hobson's choice: significant reductions in fossil fuel can be achieved only by incurring the dangers of nuclear power. Interestingly, the lower the real risk, the relatively more important is its perception in determining its effect on welfare, for that perception will stir anxiety, which in turn creates a very real loss in utility.

Special Status of Health Risks

Risks of property damage receive far less attention than risks to health. Indeed, this health-over-resources bias is a general phenomenon. For example, society's redistributional efforts focus on health care—Medicaid expenditures significantly exceed welfare expenditures in virtually all cities—although the same dollars might offer substantially greater benefits if spent on transport or appliances. Indeed, controlling for pertinent factors such as age, poor people visit the physician more often than do the affluent.

A desire to control externalities may explain subsidized vaccinations and certainly explains why we pay some individuals for undergoing tuberculosis treatments. It cannot, however, explain our pro-health bias. Rather, we suspect that health status plays an important signaling role: worse health or risk outcomes for the poor are visible and stir the compassion of those who determine *political* outcomes. Relying on willingness-to-pay to place a toxic waste dump in an impoverished community would be widely perceived as unfair, even if the associated risks were negligible. By contrast, high homicide rates among young black males are treated with relative complacency

The Costs of Risks and Risk Avoidance

As a society, we are doing extremely well in reducing per capita risk costs. Overall death and injury rates, particularly from accidents and natural catastrophes, have fallen dramatically and fairly consistently this century, presumably due to technological advances. Nonetheless, our risk avoidance activities are woefully inefficient. Had the same resources been put where they addressed the greatest reduction, these rates would now be far lower.[5]

The costs imposed by risks are the sum of the value of the losses incurred and the resource costs of reducing risks. We throw away value whenever the same expenditures would produce greater risk reduction elsewhere. Still greater waste, indeed profligacy, is achieved if the expenditures entail such large reductions in income that lives are lost on net. Studies of the relationship between societal income and mortality suggest that a reduction of income in the range of $12 million may cost one statistical life. In addition to better housing, food, and sanitation, higher incomes are also associated with better diets and exercise habits and less of both smoking and excess drinking. Assessing merely the associated increase in risky health habits alone, the life-costing income loss is on the order of $15 million to $18

million.[6] These numbers are below the regulatory expenditures per statistical life saved for many programs, suggesting that beyond wasting dollars, such programs discard lives.

THE CHALLENGE TO RATIONAL DECISIONS

Economists argue that individuals' preferences are to be relied on and taken as given, while paternalistic critics assert that individuals do not know what they want or are easily manipulated. Yet economists, and their decision analyst fellow travelers, are the first to question the underlying rationality of individuals' choices about risks and to suggest that informed expert opinion offers a superior guide to policy.

Individuals systematically overassess small risks and underassess a range of truly consequential larger risks such as those posed by a poor diet. Increases in risk are much more salient than decreases. Ambiguous risks—ones whose probabilities are hard to estimate—are often the cause for alarm. Moreover, researchers have documented many anomalous behaviors regarding choices involving uncertainty.[7]

Yet the rational decision framework remains the appropriate normative reference point: policies should not institutionalize the errors people make but, rather, should promote the outcomes they would choose if they understood the risks accurately and could make sound decisions that reflected their values. (Individuals who are well equipped to choose between apples and oranges may have difficulty when the oranges are received only probabilistically and there is a small probability that one of the apples is poisoned.)

Omission and Commission

Actions often generate risks, but sometimes inaction leads to greater risks. In theory, errors of omission and commission should be treated similarly; in practice, the latter count far more heavily. This is partly because they are framed as losses incurred rather than as gains forgone. When a treatment creates a significant risk, it may be rejected, however great the risks avoided. Estrogen-replacement therapy decreases a woman's heart attack risk, but increases her breast cancer risk. A woman should consider the relative utility costs of the two diseases, and the changes in probability entailed by the therapy, and then calculate her expected utility. (The cover story on this issue in *Time* magazine[8] omitted any risk numbers that could facilitate such a calculation, suggesting that such numbers were hardly relevant.)

The Food and Drug Administration (FDA), which regulates prescription drugs and medical devices, should balance the risks of placing potentially hazardous products on the market and the risks that sick people will suffer if these innovative technologies are not available. The consensus of outside analysts is that the agency has erred on the side of excessive caution, suggesting that society's net risk has been increased by delays in approving beneficial new drugs, such as beta blockers for heart disease.[9]

Concepts of Fairness

Human health is a special commodity. It is an ultimate source of value, and its primary production comes from nature, not people. Given these features, fairness plays a major role when risks to health are discussed. Yet what fairness in risk means is rarely clear. Differences in risk levels are perceived as unfair. For example, if the downwind town of Eastside has a greater risk than Westside, that is unfair. Yet risk increases that might balance matters—locating a toxic waste dump in Westside—are unfair as well.[10] Fairness issues are made still more intractable because money (or other compensation), however efficient an arrangement it may offer, is often regarded as inappropriate compensation for bearing risk.

Risk equity has also been a concern for trade policy. Should we prohibit imports from less developed countries that do not adhere to U.S. safety standards and environmental objectives? While this may appear to be in the best interest of these nations' citizens, it would actually decrease their employment and income, which are the main contributors to economic and physical well-being. Allowing such imports is likely to benefit even their health. Japan's enormous growth in per capita income from 1935 to 1975 was accompanied by age-specific reductions in mortality of over 35 percent for individuals under 65.[11]

Should companies in the United States be permitted to export products that are considered too hazardous for use in this country to other countries that may welcome them, as with many products? For example, pharmaceutical companies may not manufacture drugs in the United States for sale overseas unless they have been approved by the FDA for U.S. usage. Since the FDA drug approval process is lengthy, however, many drugs are first approved in Europe. The result is that U.S. companies have been forced to move operations abroad to supply these markets.

On an even more touchy issue, a less developed country might seek to expand its revenues by becoming a depository for nuclear wastes, as poverty-stricken but geologically blessed Equatorial Guinea was offered—and under pressure refused—just a few years ago. Should it have this privilege, or should more affluent nations interfere with its decision? Although intervention to provide information regarding risks certainly seems well founded, interfering with the actual decision appears to be a much more problematic role for a foreign government or international authority.

The role of entitlements often affects the zeal with which we undertake risk reduction efforts. If we must pay for the reduction ourselves, there may be substantial reluctance to make the expenditures. For example, many people do not remove lead paint from their houses or asbestos insulation from their basements. However, these same individuals might insist that their children's day-care centers meet the highest safety standards; their insistence might be particularly intense if a large party such as the city or a corporation ran the center.

THE CHALLENGE TO GOVERNMENT

Ideally, society, and the government acting as its agent, should undertake the risk reduction efforts that would best promote the welfare of its citizens.

Balancing Risks and Costs

The benefit-cost approach, which seeks to quantify the pertinent consequences of alternative policies, can be adjusted to allow for uncertain outcomes and such factors as risk aversion. Appropriately conducted analyses must also seek valuations for such hard-to-assess outputs as damage to a unique ecological resource.

The reality of government policy-making strays far from any careful process of weighing costs and benefits. The legislative mandates of risk regulation efforts almost invariably articulate risk-based objectives and sometimes exclude the consideration of costs altogether.

Executive branch efforts to balance the competing concerns of risk and cost have had limited success. Since the Carter administration, risk regulations must meet a cost-effectiveness test that gives preference to regulations that could achieve the same objective for less money. This requirement eliminates some of the least efficient options, but it does not ensure that an appropriate balance is struck between cost and risk. Since the Reagan administration imposed a benefit-cost test requirement, agencies have undertaken more comprehensive regulatory analyses.

However, these tests are not binding; they are typically inconsistent with the more narrowly written mandates of regulatory agencies, which impose legal constraints. As a result, the U.S. Office of Management and Budget, which oversees the risk regulation agencies, has never rejected a regulation with a cost per life saved of under $100 million.[12] Most risk and environmental regulations that are adopted have costs far in excess of any established estimate for the value of life, indeed above the amounts (discussed earlier) whose expenditure leads to the loss of statistical life. This suggests that many programs that are supposed to reduce risk actually cost lives.

As chronicled here and elsewhere in this volume, individuals have difficulty responding to risk appropriately, particularly to low-probability risks. If government responds to individuals' fears and irrationalities rather than the actual risks, we increase the probability of adopting policies that achieve few risk reduction benefits in return for the expenditures made. The gains in health will be as illusory as the fears that generated the policies.

PROCESS

The risk debate parallels the debate over the federal budget. We all want lower taxes, but we do not want to sacrifice the government programs that taxes pay for. Similarly, we all want less risk and demand a lot of improvement in all risk measures, but we do not want to spend the money to achieve these gains. Government proposals to promote energy conservation and decreased air pollution through a nickel-a-gallon gas tax, for example, created a public uproar, suggesting that the public's expressions of unbounded commitment to the environment may in fact have quite narrow financial limits.

The government also reassures the public about risk levels. The FDA, for example, does not state that our food is so safe that only 1 in 10 million Americans will be killed by bacteria contamination. Rather, it declares that our food is safe and makes unqualified commitments to maintaining this safety. In some cases such ceremonial commitments to public safety run counter to the best interests of the citizens exposed to the risk.

GOVERNMENT AS INSURER

The government also plays an important role in insuring many classes of risks. For example, the major risks of old age—lack of health and wealth—are covered by Medicare and Social Security. In addition, the government often provides humanitarian relief after major national catastrophes, such as hurricanes and tornadoes. The government also runs subsidized insurance programs for such adverse events. If the government is going to compensate people ex post for disaster-related losses, then it is in the government's interest to promote the purchase of insurance to reduce the cost of the humanitarian ex post bailout. For massive catastrophes, the government has a risk-spreading advantage over insurers; it has an enormous asset base that it can tax into the future.

GOVERNMENT AS REFEREE

In debates on risk issues, all affected parties have standing, making compromises and trade-offs difficult. Individuals' current endowments have legitimacy, as do claimed rights such as the right to a safe environment. Even physical entities may have rights. For example, advocates of stringent hazardous waste cleanup claim that contaminated raw land that does not undergo remediation will simply be "dead zones." That may be true, but it also may be an economically efficient outcome that gets overridden by a rights philosophy. If even undeveloped acreage has standing in the *political* debate, wholly apart from the potential uses of the land, then it will be difficult to forge the types of *political* compromises that are necessary for sound risk regulation policies.

Politics is likely to exacerbate inefficiencies. The HAZWRAP Program, which is to clean up the Department of Energy's nuclear material and weapon sites, is estimated to cost between $100 billion and $300 billion. Cleanup efforts have been recognized as public works (that is, pork barrel concerns have been legitimized), and expenditures have been spread across states rather than spent where they provide the greatest risk reduction. Significant expenditures will have no effects on human health, often providing cleaned-up land at more than ten times the local price of never-contaminated land.[13] Risk reduction policies often have their genesis in legal actions between private parties. Many of the most significant hazards, such as those posed by asbestos, first rose to prominence in the courts. Information about these risks was not available when most individuals were exposed. As a result, thousands of people suffered from asbestos exposure. Their illnesses first became well known to legislators and regulators through the workers' compensation and tort liability claims that they filed. This litigation explosion focused public attention on asbestos and led to government regulations that dramatically curtailed exposure.

Compensation through the courts serves three functions. First, it transfers income to those in need, to meet both their medical expenses and their income losses. Second, these income transfers are funded by the parties responsible for the accident or illness, thus creating financial incentives for safety. Third, such ex post payments highlight the existence of risks not adequately handled at present through risk regulation.

REGULATORY COSTS

In the past, most government regulations consisted of restrictions on telephone rates, restrictions on interstate commerce, and similar kinds of economic regulation. Over the past two decades, health, safety, and environmental regulation has increased in importance and now accounts for the majority of regulatory costs.[14] By 1991, total regulatory costs to the U.S. economy were estimated to be $542 billion. Of this amount, $115 billion was accounted for by environmental regulations and $36 billion by other *social* regulations, chiefly for health and safety. Only $73 billion was attributed to traditional economic regulations. Moreover, much of the regulatory burden consists of paperwork costs of $189 billion; a significant portion of these costs are related to compliance with risk regulations.

IMPROVING WELFARE

Singly and collectively, we have trouble responding to risks. We over-respond to many that are minuscule and ignore some hazards that have significant consequences for our lives. Public attention shifts quickly to the latest publicized hazard, and government policy often follows: witness our ready sacrifice of civil liberties in response to the terrorist threat suggested by the Oklahoma City bombing. Government policy should not mirror citizens' irrationalities but, rather, should promote the decisions people would make if they understood risks correctly and made sound decisions based on this understanding.

Making such policy is a challenge. To begin, scientific information is not always precise. Many important risks are not known with the same precision as are, for example, the familiar risks of automobiles. Scientific debates continue over the risks posed by substances ranging from cellular phones to animal fats to nuclear power.

When the magnitude of the risk is unclear, what should the government do? The current procedure is to focus on the worst-case scenario.[15] Unfortunately, this leads to policies that pay the greatest attention to the risks about which least is known. If chemical A poses a lifetime fatality risk that is known to be .00002, whereas equally widely used chemical B poses a risk that might be .00003 but probably is zero, current practice would first address the risks from chemical B, though we could save a greater expected number of lives if we focused on A. Since our imprecision is often greatest with respect to risks of new technologies, this conservatism often leads us to accept old risks and has impeded the technological and economic progress that have dramatically reduced risk in our society.

For these reasons, a flurry of congressional legislation passed in 1995 but not yet, as of this writing, signed by the president requires that federal agencies follow best-estimate risk assessment procedures. Such procedures will have the agencies assess the mean level of the risk and use assumptions regarding best estimates of the likely scenarios that will prevail, rather than focusing on worst-case outcomes.[16]

Unfortunately, the role of policy analysis within government policy-making is peripheral to much actual decision making. Whether analysis is to be done at all has become a *political* battle between those who would choose to promote more balanced risk regulation policies and those who wish to pursue the more absolutist approach of maximal risk reduction independent of cost.

If we are to achieve all that is possible with risk regulation efforts, we must understand how these policies will perform, and design them—based on an accurate assessment of the risks—to achieve the greatest expected health gains for the dollars spent.

NOTES

1. See Willard Manning et al., *The Cost of Poor Health Habits* (Cambridge, MA: Harvard University Press, 1991).
2. The largest losses of life from disasters in the United States, for each major category apart from terrorism, occurred long ago. The largest flood disaster was the Galveston tidal wave of 1900. The most devastating hurricane occurred in Florida in 1928. The most deadly tornado was in Illinois in 1925; the most deadly earthquake occurred in San Francisco in 1906; and the most catastrophic fire was in Wisconsin in 1871. See National Safety Council, *Accident Facts* (Chicago: National Safety Council, 1993), p. 15. By contrast, the largest financial losses associated with disasters have occurred more recently. Other than the Great Chicago Fire of 1871, the most costly fire was the Oakland wildfire of 1991. The most costly insured hurricane was in 1992, and the most costly U.S. earthquake was in 1989. For data on these and other financial losses and catastrophes, see Insurance Information Institute, *Property/Casualty Fact Book* (New York: Insurance Information Institute, 1994), pp. 77–85.
3. For a discussion of the role of publicity, see Paul Slovic, "Perception of Risk," *Science,* 236:280–86 (1987).
4. Thomas Schelling, personal communication, 1995.
5. See Richard J. Zeckhauser and W. Kip Viscusi, "Risk Within Reason," *Science,* 248(4955):559–64 (1990).
6. For an introduction to these issues, see Ralph Keeney, "Mortality Risks Induced by the Costs of Regulations," *Risk Analysis,* 10(1): 147–59 (1994). The health-habit study is presented in Randall Lutter, John F. Morrall III, and W. Kip Viscusi, "Risky Behavior and the Income-Mortality Relationship" (Working paper, Duke University, 1995). The rationale for lower-income people to choose riskier lifestyles is examined in John Pratt and Richard Zeckhauser, "Willingness to Pay and the Distribution of Risk and Wealth" (Working paper, Harvard University, 1995).
7. The framing of risk problems has a considerable effect on how risks are viewed and what preferences are expressed. See Daniel Kahneman and Amos Tversky, "Prospect Theory: An Analysis of Decision Under Risk," *Econometrica, 47:263–91* (1979). For example, car accident rates per trip appear negligible, but when expressed as annual or lifetime fatality rates, they seem considerable.
8. *Time,* 26 June 1995.
9. Asymmetric incentives help explain this. There is little penalty for not approving a drug that would have saved statistical lives, but allowing a drug that has identifiable adverse effects, such as thalidomide, would impose enormous *political* costs. For further analysis of the excessive conservatism of the FDA, see Henry G. Grabowski and John M. Vernon, *The Regulation of Pharmaceuticals: Balancing the Benefits and Risks* (Washington, DC: *American* Enterprise Institute, 1983).
10. Advocates of environmental equity in Chapel Hill, NC, which has traditionally sited landfills in rural areas, have proposed balancing risks by siting a new one near heavily populated residential areas. Severely increased risk will be the inefficient outcome.
11. See Richard J. Zeckhauser, Ryuzo Sato, and John Rizzo, "Health Intervention and Population Heterogeneity: Evidence from Japan and the United States" (Monograph, National Institute for Research Advancement, Dec. 1985), p. 29.
12. See W. Kip Viscusi, *Fatal Tradeoffs: Public and Private Responsibilities for Risk* (New York: Oxford University Press, 1992).
13. Martin Marietta Energy Systems, "An Application of an Interim Version of the Formal Priority System to Fiscal Year 1992 Environmental Restoration Planning" (Report to the U.S. Department of Energy, Nov. 1990).
14. For a review of these trends in regulatory expenditures, see W. Kip Viscusi, John Vernon, and Joseph Harrington, Jr., *The Economics of Regulation and Antitrust* (Cambridge: MIT Press, 1996).
15. See Albert L. Nichols and Richard J. Zeckhauser, "The Dangers of Caution: Conservatism in Assessment and the Mismanagement of Risk," in *Advances in Applied MicroEconomics,* vol. 4, ed. Kerry Smith (Greenwich, CT: JAI Press, 1986), pp. 55–82.
16. A number of pieces of legislation proposed or passed by Congress in 1995 would address both the mean risk and benefit-cost issues. These include Senate bill no. 333 and House bills nos. 1022, 690, 228, and 1923.

WHY DO WE NEED RULES?

Max Weber offers a quite contemporary-sounding depiction of the importance of written policies and procedures in public administration. As he points out, policies are established to address legal issues and are developed from the perspective of managers to develop uniform practice within the organization by employees:

> The management of the office follows general rules, which are more or less stable, more or less exhaustive, and which can be learned by all relevant personnel. Knowledge of these rules represents a special technical learning which the official[s] in a bureaucracy possess. It involves organizational jurisprudence and entails the system of administrative and business management practices that give life to the mission and goals of an organization. The reduction of modern office management to a complex web of operational rules is deeply embedded in its very nature.[2]

Generally policy and procedures manuals are used to communicate expectations about performance and conduct in the workplace, and they may describe as well employee benefits and protections.[3] In the contemporary setting, policy manuals often provide a means to codify the organization's vision, mission, and goals as developed through the strategic planning process. This document may or may not be considered an **employee handbook**, but often employee handbooks are used to communicate the policies and procedures of the organization and to explain the terms of employment fully.[4] Formal policies and procedures and related employment guidelines that are published in employee handbooks are often used as a reference in judicial and quasi-judicial proceedings to resolve personnel disputes. For this reason, the precise language used in the manual is important, and experienced personnelists recommend that certain specific policy statements and topics be included in such employment documents to protect the interests of the organization and its supervisory and administrative cadre.

Language

Recall the discussion about at-will employment from earlier chapters. The written and oral statements made in an organization can suggest contractual intent in some states.[5] If appropriate disclaimers are not included in the employee handbook of policies and procedures, then the substance of the handbook could lead to an **implied contract.** In this case, and if state law provides remedy, employees may be able to sue the employer for breach of contract if policy claims are not implemented in practice or if substantive policies change without sufficient notice to employees.[6]

Recommended Statements and Topics

The potential for implied contract in the case of at-will employees or the potential for additional employment guarantees for others protected by civil service tenure demands that government employee handbooks include pertinent disclaimer statements and a form on which the employees can acknowledge receipt and comprehension of the handbook.[7] In addition, DiNome and associates suggest including sections on topics where litigation has been frequent enough to indicate the predisposition of courts, such as political patronage, equal employment opportunity, sexual harassment and discrimination, the Family and Medical Leave Act, workplace violence, whistleblower protection, and grievance procedures.[8]

POLICIES: A MEANS TO CONTROL OR FACILITATE?

The contending purposes of policies and procedures echo a tension that we have seen in a variety of topics in this book. For example, consider the implications of policies and procedures in terms of a performance management system (see Chapter 11). Do we look to policies as a means to control behavior so that we can achieve organizational goals, as specified in the decentralization-accountability model? Entrepreneurial public management is considered to be a risk-taking enterprise, where management decisions are streamlined, authority is decentralized, and accountability to customer-citizen satisfaction dominates.[9] "Innovative public managers are entrepreneurial. They take risks . . . with an opportunistic bias toward action and a conscious underestimation of bureaucratic and political obstacles their innovations face."[10] In the contemporary setting of governments' reinventing themselves, there is indeed a tension between risk management (minimized exposure) and risk taking to promote learning and innovation in achieving customer service and service delivery improvement.

Policies may enhance productivity by limiting behaviors that had previously impeded performance. For example, David Katz reports that a zero-tolerance policy on violence in a school district had measurable benefits for productivity. Before the application of the policy, the Calcasiu Public School system in Lake Charles, Louisiana, had lost more than 240 teacher workdays in anti-violence-related activity; after the policy was adopted, only six hours in teacher time was lost from the classroom for this purpose.[11] Policies also may serve to facilitate performance by clearly defining latitude and discretion, as in the case of the total quality management (TQM) model. Zeckhauser and Viscusi advocate policies that offer critical parameters, but at the same time provide the latitude necessary for the exercise of some discretion in policy implementation: "Policies should not institutionalize the errors people make but, rather, should promote the outcomes they would choose if they understood the risks accurately and could make sound decisions that reflected their values."[12] Policies may serve to guide people to manage the foreseeable disputes that will occur in their organizational interactions. The rules of engagement to be followed during situations of workplace conflict can be established through policies such as those specified in grievance policies (see Chapter 13).

Policies are also used as a means to communicate about the distribution of resources and sanctions in an organization. Employees can read the manual to learn about how to request training opportunities or about benefits that might accrue from certain performance levels, or to inquire about the benefits accruing to longevity with the organization. Policies can detail the sanctions that may be imposed for certain behaviors and identify the types of behaviors that will be rewarded or sanctioned. Policies may articulate what is meant by sick leave versus other forms of excused absence (e.g., compensated jury duty, personal days off, bereavement period). Employees can discover what is meant by a standard workweek or what the expected times may be for arrival and departure from work. Expectations about licensure or examinations or about accreditation may be detailed with pertinent time lines and provisions for seniority.

Most public sector organizations or their political jurisdictions develop their own broad policies and workplace guidelines, or they receive some portion of these policies through statute. The topics covered in policy vary considerably by jurisdiction. Most sets of policies include general provisions that by and large follow the chapter titles in this book. Additional provisions reflect the expectations and historical experiences of specific jurisdictions and agencies. Individual agencies and departments may have some latitude in developing their own policies and procedures, though in most cases some guidance will be provided through a central human resource office for a state, county, or municipality. At the federal level, the Office of Personnel Management has the responsibility for most federal departments and bureaus. Box 14.1 on page 382 offers some suggestions about useful policies to address.

NEW POLICIES FOR AN EVOLVING WORKPLACE

Throughout this book, we have discussed the ways in which the work environment is changing and the new demands these changes pose for both human resource specialists and line managers. Some policy areas are particularly critical for public and nonprofit managers.

Box 14.1   Sample Policy Manual Topics

Staffing

Job announcements
Hiring and selection procedures
Nepotism policy
Minimum age of employees
Reemployment and reinstatement policy
Reference checks
Driving policy
Employment processing
Classification policy
Volunteer or intern policy

Salary and Benefits

Salary warrants
Health insurance benefits
Retirement benefits
Deductions: Withholding tax, retirement, insurance, bonds, deferred compensation
Salary adjustments: Regular increases, longevity pay, merit increases, promotion, demotion, salary decreases
Garnishment: Internal Revenue Service, child support

Attendance and Leave

Work hours
Overtime (Fair Labor Standards Act, exempt and nonexempt)
Holidays
Leave: Annual vacation, sick, compensatory, emergency, extended sick, sick leave pool, military, volunteer fireman's, seeing eye dog training, jury duty, judicial witness, educational, short or extended leave without pay

Employee Relations

Performance evaluations
Employee recognition program
Employee assistance program
Safety policy
Smoking policy
Temporary reassignment or removal from workplace
Suspension with pay for investigative purposes
Reprimands: Verbal, written
Probation
Disciplinary suspension
Salary decrease or demotions
Participation in employee organizations and associations
Drug-free workplace policy

Ethics

Ethics policy
Political activities
Outside or dual employment with the state
Prohibited activities
Conflict of interest and standards of conduct

General Management

Conferences
Workers' compensation
Emergency evacuation procedures

Complaints and Grievances

Complaint policy
Grievance policy
Personnel files (access and confidentiality)
Agency rules, work rules, ability to perform duties, quality and quantity of work, management-directed transfers, reassignments, reorganizations, facilities use, witness fees

Equal Employment and Affirmative Action

Equal employment opportunity employer
Prohibition against discrimination on basis of age, sex, race, color, religion, national origin, or disability
Disabled, reasonable accommodation
Sexual harassment
Equal employment opportunity complaint procedures
Affirmative action
Workforce diversity

Job Separations

Resignations, transfers
Retirement
Reduction in force
Death
Dismissal

Source: The list is drawn from recommended policy topics for the State of Texas, available at: **www.sorm.state.tx.us/VolumeFour/422.htm.**

Considering Diversity

Samuel Krislov articulated the importance of a diverse workplace in the public sector as follows:

> The diffusion of social responsibility not only legitimizes individual policies in the regime generally, but also brings to the representative members of all segments of the society who occupy public positions a broader social point of view than they would otherwise have had; they in turn transmit this socialization experience to others in their social groups.[13]

Diversity offers the means to socialize others to consider alternatives to stereotypical roles and behaviors. In addition to formal policies designed to establish the organization's position on diversity in the workplace, the stereotypes that are held about the relative skills, strengths, capacities, or aptitudes of women versus men may result in policy dilemmas. For example, policies that exclude people from work because of gender are usually found to be discriminatory if challenged unless the agency can establish a bona fide occupational qualification (BFOQ).[14] Diversity policy that is included in employee handbooks can serve as a critical mechanism to communicate expectations about tolerance and appreciation for difference in the workplace. Clearly communicated policy in this regard is related to other workplace policies pertaining to workplace violence, sexual harassment, privacy, and disciplinary action. Policies in these areas should offer clear and consistent standards of behavior and provide helpful guidelines for the reporting of wrongful conduct for those who are victimized in the workplace. At the same time, policies must advise employees of the rights of due process in force for those who are accused of having engaged in unacceptable behaviors.

Violence

A number of shocking incidents of mass violence in the public schools and in work settings have prompted public and private organizations to develop violence-free policies.[15] Dennis Davis identifies four **components for an effective violence policy:**[16]

1. There must be a clear statement about a violence-free workplace.
2. Behavior that is inconsistent with the policy must be defined (e.g., the nature and scope of violence).
3. Agency expectations about employee compliance to this policy must be clearly established in the policy.
4. The repercussions for violent behavior, including any and all potential disciplinary actions, should be identified.

Harassment

Although there are laws and policies against sexual harassment and the courts have sought to clarify their interpretation of these statutes and agency rules, it still appears that a great deal more guidance in this area may be necessary in the contemporary workplace. In 1967 Samuel Krislov wrote about racial and ethnic discrimination and suggested that we may have social patterns of behavior that support discriminatory practices despite appropriate laws and the best efforts of managers. The "early pattern of discrimination had itself created social patterns that remained to reinforce unequal employment practices even when a more positive attitude on the part of the administrators in power was evident."[17] The same general observation would seem to apply to sexual harassment and other negative, discourteous, and inappropriate behaviors to others in the workplace.

Sexual harassment has been defined by a series of court decisions. Employers are liable for a hostile environment that results in some detriment to an employee's work. Although sexual harassment has received increasing attention, malicious and debilitating treatment of others may not be limited solely to sexual behavior. Perceived differences also occasion mistreatment in the workplace. In some areas, agency policies can address potential problems even though current court interpretation is lacking, unclear, or inconsistent.

Safety

Aside from concerns about violent behavior in the workplace, agencies must abide by state and federal statutes affording protections to employees and specifying appropriate safety measures. In addition, the agency may be faced with the dilemma of how paternalistic it can or should be in the assignment of safety-related policies. Consider the case of employees who work with chemicals that have been associated with fetal abnormality and death. Recall that the only exemption for sex discrimination is for a BFOQ. Although agencies cannot exclude people from certain work or work areas because of gender, they may still face liability if a fetus is harmed. More than 40 states currently allow children born alive to recover in tort for prenatal injuries caused by third parties. Employer warnings may preclude claims by injured employees, but these warnings will not preclude claims by injured children. The general rule is that parents cannot waive causes of action on behalf of their children and the parents' negligence will not be imputed to the children.

Privacy

Supervisors must balance a valid concern about monitoring employee behavior in the workplace with due respect for their privacy. Intrusions on an employee's privacy could lead to problems with morale and under some circumstances even provoke legal challenge.[18] Although employers may record their employees using video cameras and microphones, this could be subject to legal challenge in certain states and under certain conditions at the federal level.[19] Desks and lockers can be inspected under certain circumstances, but the scope of this inspection could be subject to whether employees could enjoy a **reasonable expectation of privacy**.[20] Certainly the policy language used can provide notice to employees about what may be subject to review by supervisors. However, this area is under frequent review by the courts, and the emerging technology—voice mail, e-mail, and Internet use—remains largely unexplored territory; application of Fourth Amendment protection is emerging slowly.[21]

Personal Relationships

That employees may develop friendships in the workplace should not be surprising given the amount of time we spend at work and the logic that people who have something in common, even if it is their office, may tend to develop friendships. Generally platonic friendships that tend to occur in the workplace are treated as a positive outgrowth of work, although there are generally some cautions against demonstrating favoritism. However, relationships that extend beyond friendship tend to cause quite a stir. Sexual harassment addresses behavior that is unwelcome and creates a hostile environment, but how should organizations respond when the relationship is, at least initially, welcomed by both parties?

Workplace disruption may occur not because of problems between the involved parties but because of concerns held by other employees. Perceptions of favoritism, eroded privacy, or the social implications when one party is married to another person can create discomfort and discord in the workplace. Recent accounts of adultery and fraternization in the military certainly have heightened the profile of these relationships in the public sector, but their occurrence throughout the public sector is not a novelty. Meyer notes that "although firms probably can't and shouldn't try to stop love in the workplace, they should take steps to protect themselves and ensure that the work environment is healthy, professional and productive."[22]

Location and Structure of Work

As employees consider alternative work arrangements such as formal telecommuting and flexdesign, it may be necessary to revise existing policies. Timeframes will differ, as will expectations about arrival and departure times. Policy artifacts such as language about an 8:00 A.M. work-day start could be subject to equity challenges.

Technology

With respect to Internet policy,[23] some specific suggestions are available. It is wise to identify clearly that computers and related equipment and software should be used in a way that relates directly to the organization's mission. It is important to note that other policies (e.g., intellectual property, privacy, sexual harassment) still apply in conjunction with Internet policy. Policies should be explicit about the conditions under which employees have the authority to speak on behalf of the organization. Authority to communicate would link with employee use of e-mail, listservs, news groups, and chatrooms. Policies related to the distribution or acquisition of technology may also be useful as access to communication technology may be viewed by some as a reward or benefit.

PRACTICAL APPROACHES TO POLICY DEVELOPMENT

Richard Rudolph addressed the importance of managing risk for elected and appointed public officials in response to decisions that could give rise to civil rights, privacy, or access challenges.[24] The suggestions that he offers to public officials to manage risk can be easily adapted to human resource management efforts (see Box 14.2). All employees should have copies of, or at least access to, department and agency policies. In addition, they should be asked to sign statements indicating that they understand the policies and are willing to abide by them. The policies in question should be in writing. Workplace conduct expectations should be documented, and this extends to retaining minutes of meetings even if they are not open to the public. Although it may be difficult for small jurisdictions, it would probably be prudent for any policies or procedures to be reviewed by counsel to ensure that legal expectations for due process and statutory guidelines established in different states are properly observed. Providing access to the general position descriptions and the classification system would be useful. Much of this can be accomplished through web sites. Many of the references to state policies and procedures used in this book were obtained from web sites maintained by the central human resource department for the states.

The general approach to developing policies should probably consider basic standards of courtesy and common sense, though Rosenbloom cautions that common sense and constitutional

---

Box 14.2   Checklist for Risk Management and Employee Relations

- Are policies and procedures guiding personnel actions placed in writing?
- Are policies and procedures guiding workplace behaviors placed in writing?
- Are accurate and complete minutes of all meetings, both open and closed sessions, properly recorded and maintained?
- Have all ordinances and administrative policies been reviewed by legal counsel prior to their implementation?
- Are the principal duties to be performed by employees documented in writing?
- Are the duties to be performed by employees legitimately related to the scope of the agency's responsibility?
- Have all policies and procedures been developed in accordance with state and local due process requirements?

Source: Richard Rudolph, "Public Officials Liability," *CPCU Journal* 51:3 (1998): 166. Course authors made minor revisions for consistency in format.

Box 14.3   Suggestions for Developing Employment Policies

Avoid gratuitous references to gender, age, or race in policies and procedures.

Develop employee handbooks with job descriptions and personnel policies.

Establish a procedure for documenting all evaluations in writing.

Establish a procedure to document all reprimands or other disciplinary measures in writing.

Establish a procedure to notify all eligible employees about promotion opportunities.

Establish specific guidelines for recruitment and selection of employees.

Establish specific guidelines for performance management activities, including goal setting, appraisal, and performance management strategies.

Establish specific policies and procedures addressing all disciplinary activities.

Source: These suggestions are drawn from multiple sources, including Rudolph, "Public Officials' Liability," p. 167.

---

interpretation on occasion may not go hand in hand.[25] (See Box 14.3.) Just as we need to have a legitimate rationale in the workplace for considering personal characteristics such as age or race in assessing the ability of an employee to perform, so must we have a legitimate rationale for references to gender, age, or race in policies and procedures. The employee handbook and general workplace policies and procedures can be used to establish uniform procedures to improve productivity and communicate the scope of employee rights and responsibilities.

Box 14.4   Checklist for Improving Documentation

How is documentation managed for different policy considerations?

- Is the process for gathering and maintaining documentation clearly communicated for each policy or procedural area?
- Who controls documentation?
- Where is documentation maintained?
- Who manages and maintains documentation?
- Is the documentation keeper unrelated to or disinterested in the outcome of any disputes?
- How long are records maintained?
- Are documents backed up?
- How long are the documents stored, and which portions are retained?
- What priority is set on the documentation process and its quality control?
- Are time constraints imposed by rules documented?

What are the implications of documentation for employees?

- Does the documentation process itself adversely affect individuals or select groups in the workplace?
- Is management or agency action required to provide notice to employees of action?
- If so, how is such notice given?
- Are employees required to acknowledge notification or instruction on grievance procedures?
- What is the means of acknowledgment (e.g., signature, statement)?
- Is a copy of such documentation provided to those employees?
- Do notices clearly set forth the options available to the employee?

Source: Rudolph, "Public Officials' Liability," p. 167.

An important consideration in developing a policy is to consider how the policy itself will be established. Will employees have the opportunity to participate in its development, or will they simply receive some dictate? It is highly advisable that employees be involved in the periodic updating of policies and procedures and that an employee involvement process be in place for policy review efforts. Throughout the course of this book, we have emphasized the importance of documentation. The policy and procedure manual can offer guidelines for gathering documentation about actions related to employment, including simple procedures on retention, collection, and scope. (See Box 14.4 on page 386.)

ETHICAL CONSIDERATIONS IN POLICY DEVELOPMENT AND APPLICATION

The ethics of policy development begin with the consideration of the following questions. What are the intended outcomes of the policy? Who develops the policy, and to whom does it apply? One of the most pressing concerns in the development of policies and procedures rests with the intention of the document. If we look to policies and procedures to manage risk and anticipate that risk management must be a means to control behavior, then this suggests a particular approach to be taken in developing policies and procedures. If we instead consider that policies are a means to manage risk in order to give employees the latitude to perform and to self-manage their behavior and activities, then we are considering a very different outcome.

Hersey and Blanchard suggest that managers guided by a control-oriented approach tend to view employees as passive and dependent.[26] In contrast, managers who perceive the importance of self-direction for employees tend to focus on the importance of affiliation in the work setting, creativity in performing even routine functions, and promoting employee participation and decision making. The control approach contributes to a pessimistic and condemnatory public view of the public organization and its employees, encourag-

ing organizational members to adopt a mentality perpetuating this negative view.[27] Public organizations may seriously compromise their contribution to effective governance with practices that overly emphasize control over performance.

■ CONCLUSION

Clear guidelines must be established to offer decision makers the ability to identify and assess candidates in appropriate and uniform ways. Should managers have policies in addition to those legally required for affirmative action? If so, what should these policies include? In Chapter 7, the logic of the analysis and classification system underscores policies and procedures that will be in place to identify the steps to be taken in developing new positions, evaluating current jobs, and establishing a framework for their evaluation and classification. Should we establish guidelines about when and how a manager might ask that a position be analyzed or evaluated? Do we need to specify the format for position descriptions or simply leave this up to each manager? The discussion presented in Chapters 9 and 10 makes it clear that guidelines are necessary to ensure equitable and appropriate compensation and benefit packaging. What types of concerns might we want to address in policies? How would we handle issues relevant to when someone does and does not qualify for a benefit? How do we define benefits and the qualifications of recipients? Can someone use sick leave to care for an elderly parent? Policies are an important means to address these questions, engage employees in discussions about their workplace, and ensure that employees have the opportunity to understand their rights and responsibilities in the workplace.

■ MANAGER'S VOCABULARY

policy
procedures
risk management

employee handbook
implied contract
components for an effective violence policy
reasonable expectation of privacy

■ STUDY QUESTIONS

1. How can managers balance employee self-direction with legitimate needs for accountability and control?

2. How should an organization go about developing a policy and procedure manual or employee handbook?

3. Why are policies and procedures important?

4. How can managers address problems with implied contract in a policy manual?

5. What types of workplace policies are the most important for you?

6. What types of policies might be necessary in a regulatory agency, such as a police agency, versus one that distributes social benefits to others, such as a social service agency?

7. How important is the location or the mission of the organization to the content of the policy and procedure manual?

■ EXPERIENTIAL EXERCISES

1. You are thirty minutes late to the regular Monday management meeting because your car stalled *again* on the way to work. As you race into the meeting room, throwing your notebook on the table and flinging your coat across the back of the chair, you offer a rambling set of apologies to the assembly. "I am very sorry to miss the opening points to the meeting. It is my car—I really need to give it up." As you look up, you notice that your colleagues are smiling at you in a very odd way. Devon Shire, your supervisor, says, "Oh, don't worry about it. It is lucky that you came in when you did. We were just discussing how much we need to revamp our policies and procedures manual." Inwardly you groan as you begin to realize that your colleagues' smiles reflect a combination of personal relief and wicked glee at your predicament. Your supervisor continues: "Would you draft revisions to the policy and procedures manual? We'll need them for review next week. Well, ladies and gentlemen, that's it for now: same time, same place on Monday. Have a good week!" Later at your desk, you begin reviewing the first page of the 153-page document, noting that the date of the last revision was 1973. It begins:

> Section I: Supervisor's Responsibilities to the Agency[28]
> *Policy Statement:* In simple and brief terms, the task of a supervisor is to produce through the combined use of people and machines. Probably the most complicated of these two tools are the people. Therefore, this factor demands the greatest ingenuity of the supervisor. In your effort to produce in an efficient manner, you will encounter many obstacles. Some of these obstacles will be created unconsciously by ourselves. Others will be created by outsiders, or by some employees for selfish reasons. You should anticipate the obstacles and make the atmosphere of our organization unfertile for their creation. Some of these obstacles can be a lack of incentive by the employees, union organization

attempts, conflict between employees and management, conflict among the employees themselves, poor employee attitudes, lack of concern for the welfare of our jobs, etc.

(a) It is always dangerous to become involved in other people's private affairs. This is also true in regard to the private lives of your employees. Although you should be sincerely interested in the welfare and personal lives of your employees, be wise enough not to involve yourself to the extent it interferes with your primary responsibility. Be helpful, but not a "busy-body." If a problem is affecting their work, then it may be best to direct them to professional assistance, or you may ask for guidance from the manpower office.

(b) Having both male and female employees creates potential problems that can destroy your departmental morale. You should speak and act in only the best moral manner so as to provide the best influence for your people. A supervisor should not be involved in any dirty-story telling or other activities while on the job so as to downgrade his reputation with his people or improperly influence the moral conduct of this people.

Draft a memo to your supervisor outlining what actions will be necessary to revise this section of the manual.

2. Examine the policy excerpt from the preceding exercise in the context of Boxes 14.2 and 14.3. Rewrite the policy statements in the preceding exercise in the context of the recommendations made in this chapter. If you are charged with revising this policy, in what section would you place this type of policy statement?

3. Bring to class a copy of a policy from a public organization that discusses a particular topic, such as leave or privacy. Each student should bring a different policy. Break into small groups to compare the policy in terms of the following factors:

a. What substantive provisions are identified?

b. How is specific content of the different policies similar in intent?

c. How does the intent of the several policies differ?

d. What assumptions about the role of the worker are communicated in each of the policies?

e. What is missing in the policy statements that ought to be there?

■ CASES APPLICABLE TO THIS CHAPTER

"Helping Hands" (Task 4) and "Conflicting Perceptions" (Task 2).

■ NOTES

[1] Richard J. Zeckhauser and W. Kip Viscusi, "The Risk Management Dilemma," *Annals of the American Academy of Political and Social Science* 545 (1996): 121–144.

[2] Max Weber, "Bureaucracy," in Jay M. Shafritz and J. Steven Ott, eds., *Classics of Organization Theory,* 4th ed. (Orlando, FL: Harcourt Brace, 1996), p. 81.

[3] John A. DiNome, Saundra M. Yaklin, and David H. Rosenbloom, "Employee Rights: Avoiding Legal Liability," in Siegrun Fox Freyss, ed., *Human Resource Management in Local Government: An Essential Guide* (Washington, D.C.: International City/County Management Association, 1999), p. 93.

[4] Walter Bithell, "Employee Handbook Can Open Communication," *Idaho Statesman,* August 1, 1999, p. 3d.

[5] DiNome, Yaklin, and Rosenbloom, "Employee Rights," pp. 93–94; Bithell, "Employee Handbook," p. 3d.

[6] Bithell, "Employee Handbook," p. 3d; DiNome, Yaklin, and Rosenbloom, "Employee Rights," p. 94.

[7] Bithell, "Employee Handbook," p. 3d; DiNome, Yaklin, and Rosenbloom, "Employee Rights," p. 94.

[8] DiNome, Yaklin, and Rosenbloom, "Employee Rights," pp. 94–121.

[9] Myuing Jae Moon, "The Pursuit of Managerial Entrepreneurship: Does Organization Matter," *Public Administration Review* 59:1 (1999): 32.

[10] Mary B. Sanger and Martin A. Levin, "Using Old Stuff in New Ways: Innovation as a Case of Evolutionary Tinkering," *Journal of Policy Analysis and Management* 11:1 (1992): 88.

[11] David M. Katz, "School Violence Spurs Copycats, Prevention," *National Underwriting/Property and Casualty Risk and Benefits* 103:24 (1999): 8–9.

[12] Zeckhauser and Viscusi, "The Risk Management Dilemma."

[13] Samuel Krislov, "The Negro and the Federal Service in an Era of Change," in Frank J. Thompson, ed., *Classics of Public Personnel Policy*, 2nd ed. (Pacific Grove, CA: Brooks/Cole, 1991), p. 247.

[14] James H. Thompson and James S. Worthington, "Risk Management: Identifying a Company's Vulnerability," *National Public Accountant* 38:12 (1993): 18.

[15] Katz, "School Violence," pp. 8–9; Mark Hoffman, "Acts of Violence Cast Spotlight on School Risk Management," *Business Insurance*, June 8, 1998, pp. 3–6.

[16] Dennis Davis as referenced in Michelle Dalton Liberatore, "Killer Jobs," *Public HR* 1:1 (1998): 32.

[17] Krislov, "The Negro and Federal Service," p. 240.

[18] Patrick F. Kilker, "Employee Privacy," *IPMA News* 65:5 (1999): 21.

[19] Ibid.

[20] Ibid.; DiNome, Yaklin, and Rosenbloom, "Employee Rights," p. 126.

[21] DiNome, Yaklin, and Rosenbloom, "Employee Rights," p. 126.

[22] Harvey R. Meyer, "When Cupid Aims at the Workplace," *Nation's Business* (July 1998): 57.

[23] "Be Clear on Expectations About Internet Use," *Public Employment Law Report* 6:2 (1999): 6.

[24] Richard Rudolph, "Public Officials' Liability," *CPCU Journal* 51:3 (1998): 164–170.

[25] DiNome, Yaklin, and Rosenbloom, "Employee Rights," p. 123.

[26] Paul Hersey and Kenneth Blanchard, *Management of Organizational Behavior: Utilizing Human Resources,* 5th ed. (Englewood Cliffs, NJ: Prentice Hall, 1988), pp. 51–83.

[27] Charles T. Goodsell, *The Case for Bureaucracy* (Chatham, NJ: Chatham House, 1985), pp. 9–11; Michael Lipsky, *Street-Level Bureaucracy* (Thousand Oaks, CA: Sage, 1980), pp. 479–483; Ralph P. Hummel, *The Bureaucratic Experience,* 3rd ed. (New York: St. Martin's Press, 1987), pp. 25–39.

[28] The policy sample has been changed only slightly for readability. Most of the provisions are drawn verbatim from J. W. Lawson II, *How to Develop a Company Personnel Policy Manual* (Chicago: Dartnell Corporation, 1973), pp. 31–32.

CHAPTER 15

New Roles and Competencies for Human Resource Management

In the preceding chapters we have described a wide range of knowledge, skills, and abilities (KSAs) required of public human resources managers or line managers concerned with human resources issues. In this final chapter, we perform a job analysis of the HR professional, summarizing the competencies of the HR profession, including the roles the HR manager must perform and the KSAs needed to be an effective HR manager in the modern public service environment.

No longer are HR managers confined to performing only the traditional techniques of personnel management, such as conducting salary surveys and performing job audits. To be an effective contributor to organizational goals, HR managers must understand and perform a wide variety of tasks, ranging from expansive strategic thinking to the most minute of details in employee job descriptions.

Our purpose in this book has been to describe an emergent kind of human resource manager, one who operates in a changing organizational environment and a very different world from that of the past. These changes require new professional outlooks and competencies for human resource administrators as they fulfill increasingly challenging roles. A competency is defined as "a cluster of related knowledge, attitudes and skills that affects a major part of one's job."[1] Professional competencies encompass the traditional KSAs of a job and also include the attitudes, motives, and temperament that distinguish excellent performers from others sharing similar responsibilities.[2] Competencies for specific types of positions have

been developed by locating persons commonly regarded as high-performing individuals in that type of work and identifying the shared characteristics that distinguish these highly regarded individuals from their peers.[3]

INTRODUCTION TO READING

New roles and professional competencies require human resource professionals to rewrite their old job descriptions. The old list of KSAs would have been focused on technical abilities and knowledge of employment laws. While these are still important, they now are only part of the required knowledge and abilities needed by the modern HR professional.

In the chapter reading, W. Warner Burke describes many of the new KSAs necessary for success in the HR profession. His list reflects changes in the workplace as a result of an emphasis on performance, the trauma of restructuring, the rise of work through groups and teams, and the interconnectedness of work in the information age.

As you read the selection, keep the following questions in mind:

- How are performance improvement, restructuring, and organizational change different from each other? Is knowledge of these processes an important set of competencies for public managers?
- Burke's discussion of globalization implies operations overseas, which does not apply to

most governments. How should public managers apply the "six key skills for developing a global mindset" to the public and nonprofit sector HRM professional setting?

- Burke ranks the nine "need-to-knows" in order of how obvious they are. How would you rank these nine competencies in order of *importance* for public or nonprofit managers?

- Burke says these nine "need-to-knows" are not exhaustive, and he lists organizational design, leadership, and the relationship between employer and employee as other areas he could have covered. What are some other subjects public and nonprofit HR practitioners need to know today?

▓▓▓▓▓ READING

What Human Resource Practitioners Need to Know for the Twenty-First Century

W. WARNER BURKE

INTRODUCTION

It may be that *learning* is now in the process of replacing *leadership* as the organizational management term of the day. If so, look for a spate of books in the near future on organizational learning, lifelong learning, adult learning, nontraditional learning, unlearning, learning dissemination, etc. But *what* do we need to learn, to know? The purpose of this paper is to provide a brief list of "need to knows" for the human resource (HR) practitioner over the remainder of the decade and into the next century. The list of definitions and explanations are by necessity brief, but for more depth numerous references are included for further perusal, if not *learning*. Beyond piquing your interest with this list, it is my hope that you will find the references a valuable addition.

It should be noted at the outset that this list of "need to knows" is *in addition* to the basics of HR practice—employee relations, compensation and benefits, selection and placement, training and development, succession planning, etc.

Source: "What Human Resource Practitioners Need to Know for the Twenty-First Century," by W. Warner Burke, *Human Resource Management,* Spring 1997, Vol. 36, No. 1, pp. 71–79. Copyright © 1997 by John Wiley & Sons, Inc. Reprinted by permission of John Wiley & Sons, Inc.

The nine need-to-knows are presented in an approximate order moving from the more obvious to perhaps the not so obvious. We begin, therefore, with performance improvement, an obvious need-to-know, and conclude with power shifts, a more subtle and complex need-to-know, that is not so obvious.

Note that whenever the term "employees" is used, I mean any and all organizational members, nonmanagement and management.

Each of the nine sections concludes with an implications statement for the HR practitioner.

1. Performance Improvement

Improving performance is a lot like the weather. We do a lot of talking about it. Two kinds of actions are needed. First, we need to understand more about and expand our measurements of performance; and second, we need to learn more about the critical antecedents of performance, that is, what are the direct and indirect enhancers and inhibitors of high performance?

Measurement

For too long we have been driven by the bottom line—narrowly defined. There is far more to performance than profit and loss. Again, we talk a great deal about such important matters as customer service, but if we do not measure it, incorporate customer service into our definition of performance, and do not reward people accordingly, then it is merely talk. Kaplan and Norton (1996, 1993, 1992) have provided significant help. Their "balanced scorecard" of performance includes "as expected" financial measures, but they include three additional perspectives that balance what may ultimately be defined as organizational performance—customer satisfaction, internal business competencies, and innovation and learning, which means essentially continuous improvement and creating value. Kaplan and Norton further provide ways of quantitatively measuring these softer, more qualitative domains, and they give numerous corporate examples.

Antecedents

Does pay, for example, enhance performance? Rarely, if ever, and at best only temporarily. There are many other important enhancers, especially those associated with intrinsic motivation, the work itself that in turn contribute to high performance. It seems clear that high congruence between job requirements and an individual's skills and abilities directly enhances motivation and, in turn, performance. It also seems clear that individual commitment to the mission of the organization enhances motivation and, in turn, performance, but probably more indirectly. These are examples of what we need to learn more about to understand as thoroughly as possible the complexities of performance improvement. Key sources for recent findings on performance enhancers include Huselid (1995); Kleiner, Block, Roomkin, and Salsberg (1987); and Lawler, Mohrman, and Ledford (1995).

Implications

The prudent HR practitioner will be deeply involved in matters of individual and organizational performance. Besides, how much closer can one get to the core of a business than to be involved in performance measurement and enhancement? Thus, it behooves the HR practitioner to learn as much as possible about (1) broader ways of defining and measuring performance and (2) what in the human equation contributes to high performance.

2. RESTRUCTURING

It is obvious that the restructuring of corporations in America continues to take the country by storm.

Such activities as downsizing, reengineering, and business process redesign proceed unabated. Unbelievable as it may seem, restructuring has even reached the university. We at Teachers College are in the midst of a significant restructuring. What is not so obvious is the effect, the long-term impact and consequences of these activities. There is widespread reporting that downsizing, for example, continues in spite of considerable uncertainty regarding its effects on the bottom line (McKinley, Sanchez, & Schick, 1995) and the negative impact on people (*New York Times,* 1996). Harder evidence confirms much of what has been cited in the popular press, see, for example, Cameron, Freeman, and Mishra (1991).

Yet there is some indication that the way downsizing is implemented can make a difference. If it is systemic and part of a larger strategic effort, negative effects can be minimized (Cameron et al., 1991).

Although minimal at this stage, what documentation (beyond anecdotes) of reengineering that does exist shows negative to mixed results (Cameron, 1996). The point about restructuring is that much of what is known shows more negative than positive outcomes.

Implications

The HR practitioner must go beyond the popular press to understand the consequences of restructuring. These are early days, thus the evidence is only beginning to accumulate. There is help, nevertheless. Brockner's (1992) work provides guidance, particularly regarding those who remain at the organization after downsizing; a recent article by Feldman (1996) is also quite useful; and for an up-to-date assessment of the effectiveness of TQM, downsizing, and reengineering, see Cameron (1996).

3. ORGANIZATION CHANGE

Based on a huge data set, Ulrich, Brockbank, Yeung, and Lake (1995) have highlighted the importance of understanding and being competent in the practice of managing organizational change for HR practitioners. In fact the competence category in their study, management of change, resulted in the highest proportion (41.2%) of the critical competencies for HR practitioners to be effective in their jobs. The other two critical competence categories, but less proportionally, were HR functional expertise (23.3%) and knowledge of business (18.8%). As Ulrich et al.

stage, "The high [proportion] in managing change suggests that this competence is the most important predictor for overall competence of HR professionals" (pp. 482–483).

Implications

With change now being equated with death and taxes, the HR practitioner must establish a reasonable base of understanding of and competence in organization change and the management thereof. It is only natural that organizational executives and manageers should turn to their HR person for help in change management: if not to the HR practitioner, then to whom? If not to the HR practitioner, then executives and manageers must look externally. For us external consultants this mode of seeking help is fine, but the growing expectation is that the organization's HR practitioner *should be* a main resource.

In addition to a few basic books on organization development (Block, 1981; Burke, 1994; French & Bell, 1995) some current useful sources for learning more about change management include Berger and Sikora (1994); Carr, Hard, and Trahant (1996); Howard and Associates (1994); Hurst (1995); Litwin, Bray, and Brooke (1996); Nadler, Shaw, Walton, and Associates (1995); Nevis, Lancourt, and Vassallo (1996); Nolan and Croson (1995); Tichy and Sherman (1994); and the annual series by Pasmore and Woodman

4. GLOBALIZATION

Not every corporation in America is "going global"; it just seems that way with all the hype and admonitions about being expansive in thinking and being other-culture sensitive. We should bear in mind that 90% or more of businesses in America are family-owned, employing a small number of people. Many of these small businesses, however, serve big ones as suppliers and service providers, and the big corporations are indeed being pressed to go global. Thus even many smaller businesses are being influenced by the globalization movement. Moreover, as Henry Wendt, former Chairman of a large global corporation, put it:

> Indeed, it is fair to say that through the remainder of this century and well into the next, [global corporations] are likely to be decisive not only for the way individuals live and work, but for the way in which the politics and economics are bound together (Wendt, 1993, p. 3).

Wendt is not the only one sending this message. Globalization is with us now and is likely to progress geometrically into the 21st century.

Implications

A leading expert on globalization, particularly from the corporate perspective, is Stephen Rhinesmith. In addition to emphasizing the importance of understanding change management (see above), he stresses that "It is impossible to develop a free-flowing, competitive global organization with structured, inhibited people. So globalization is largely the business of mindset and behavior change" (Rhinesmith, 1996). In other words, it is the human factor, and therefore the HR practitioner is central to any organization's "going global." Rhinesmith's book is helpful to the HR practitioner in that he focuses on six key skills for developing the global mindset—managing competitiveness, complexity, organizational alignment, change, multicultural teams, and learning. The book edited by Pucik, Tichy, and Barnett (1992) is also useful.

5. GROUPS AND TEAMS

At the present time there are at least three clear and definite trends concerning group dynamics. *First* is the distinguishing of group from team. Previously we tended to use group and team interchangeably, much as we did with leader and manager. Today, however, we are at least more cognizant that a group may be nothing much more than an assemblage, whereas a team is a group with a common and challenging goal, and members behave interdependently. Two recent sources have provided clarity, one from the world of practice (Katzenbach & Smith, 1993) and the other from academia (Guzzo, Salas, & Associates, 1995). As Katzenbach and Smith point out, a real team is derived predominantly from a group of people with a highly challenging goal, not from the designation "team" or from team building activities. The Guzzo et al. book provides useful knowledge regarding team research, especially the chapter by McIntrye and Salas (1995).

Second, self-directed groups are becoming more prevalent. This trend is a result of organizational structures becoming flatter with the consequent outcome of wider spans of control and therefore greater reliance on at least semiautonomous work groups. Downsizing is also contributing to more reliance on groups. Another contributor is at least some managers' attempts to empower their direct reports by providing more autonomy to them as a group. There are, no doubt, other reasons for this trend; in any case, the movement toward self-directed groups is here to stay and will accelerate. Arguably the best source for understanding this form of group dynamics is the work of Hackman (1992).

Third is the trend toward the use of large group interventions. This kind of organizational intervention involves the meeting of an entire system, or relatively autonomous subsystem, in a singular space usually for one to three days to tackle a significant issue or problem(s) facing the organization. The limit of the size of the group, which may range from 50 to 500 people (and sometimes even larger), is often a function of available and appropriate space. Reasons for this trend include management's desire for widespread participation and involvement, the potential for speed of decision making and action, and the attraction of having the entire organization in one space together, face-to-face, in so-called "real time" to solve big problems.

Bunker and Alban have assembled a useful array (1992) and an in depth discussion (in press) of different approaches to large group interventions.

Implications

Even though culturally it is not exactly the American way, organizational leaders and managers are relying more and more on groups and not as much on individuals, at least when compared with the past. The astute HR practitioner will become an expert on group dynamics and teamwork. Learning more about how to (a) select people for group- and teamwork, (b) use groups for specific purposes, and (c) reward people in a more collective sense should be the goal of every HR practitioner today.

6. ACTION LEARNING

As argued earlier (Burke, 1995). I believe we are in the early stages of a third wave of innovation in the domain of training and development. The first wave was the T Group, beginning in the late 1940s. The second wave was "structured feedback" beginning in the late 1950s, becoming stronger in the 1970s and particularly now. Accomplishing many of the same objectives as the T Group, feedback on one's behavior (especially interpersonally, structured feedback) today takes the so-called 360° form, yet differs from the first wave in that the structured process, typically, is not face-to-face. In the early stages of use and not yet fully understood, the third wave of innovation is action learning. A working definition:

> In essence, action learning is combining the solving of actual problems in real time in the organization with learning about how to work together better, how to solve problems more effectively, and how to improve the learning process in general—that is, learning about learning (Burke, 1995, p. 166).

For additional explanation, see Froiland (1994) and for applications toward organization change, see Tichy and Sherman (1994).

Implications

The HR practitioner needs to learn about this third wave because action learning:

- reduces significantly the time between learning and application.
- is based on sound knowledge about and experience with group beheavior and experiential learning.
- concentrates both on results or outcomes and process.
- can reduce costs.
- provides useful feedback to organizational members on their behavior and performance,
- can deliver innovative solutions to tough if not heretofore irresolvable problems,
- can increase organiational commitment, and
- can enhance organizational learning (Burke, 1995).

7. INTER-

The cryptic title for this section means that this need-to-know domain covers a number of "inters"—interpersonal, intergroup, and interorganizational. Despite the fact of so many people staring at computer terminals much of their working days, there appears to be as strong, or perhaps even stronger, a need as ever (maybe in part *because* of the isolation of sitting before a screen) to interact with others both for work and social reasons. Furthermore, rather than growing more adept (perhaps it is my narrow viewpoint), people today seem to be *less* skillful than ever in interpersonal skills. For some pessimistic evidence supporting this view, see Goleman (1995).

In any case, with fewer people having *the* answer, with greater reliance on gropus and teams, with more emphasis on cross-group activities (i.e., attempts to attenuate the problems of "silos" that result from hierarchy as well as functional and business center territoriality in most organizational structures), and with the burgeoning of interorganizational relations (e.g., mergers and acquisitions), there is a strong trend toward interaction of all kinds in the workplace. If enrollment in our courses and workshops at the University are indicative, people are expressing an ever greater interest in gaining knowledge and skill in conflict management and resolution, in cooperation, and in negotiation in the workplace.

So, it is a matter of *relationships,* relating with others to get work done, to get complicated problems solved, and with the increasingly chaotic conditions of work these days, to check periodically with colleagues to see if we are relatively sane.

Implications

To use the term that Argyris (1970) wrote about, HR practitioners need to see themselves as interventionists, to be *in between* people, groups, and organizations to facilitate relationships. There is a great need. For example, when it comes to making a strategic alliance or merger (read acquisition) work, the due diligence that managers conduct prior to the eventual relationship typically goes well. Evidence shows, however, that most of these interorganizational relationships rarely reach the potential that is touted by both parties beforehand. The devil is in the details of the relationships and corporate culture. For a current summary and evaluation of interorganizational relationships, see Burke and Biggart (1996). For some new thinking on interpersonal relations, see Senge (1990) on the concept and skill of dialogue, and Barrett (1995) and Cooperrider and Srivastva (1987) on appreciative inquiry. For more learning about conflict, cooperation, and distributive justice and intergroup relationships, see Deutsch (1985) and Bunker, Rubin, and Associates (1995).

8. TIMESHIFT

More than ever, employees talk these days about how much harder and longer they work. It also seems that people try to cram more activity into the time they have. Another related trend is the blurring of time on the job and off the job—people work more at home, on airplanes, and trains, etc.—as well as the mixing of personal activities, for example, mailing a gift in time for Mother's day, with regular work activities (Crispell, 1996). We are a nation of very busy people (Burns, 1993), and seemingly we complain more about being tired. Yet a recent study showed that "employed Americans are no more likely than they were 20 years ago to say that work wears them out . . ."—24% in 1975 compared with 23% in 1995 (Robinson & Godbey, 1996, p. 48). We obviously have a conundrum here.

One explanation is the point made above about the blurring of the boundary between work and personal life, although we as individual workers may be getting slightly better at this balance (Robinson & Godbey, 1996). The fact that many today are taking care of certain personal needs during work hours and that more take work home (since we have at our disposal laptops, E-mail, voice mail, and fax machines), we stretch our work day and our personal time. It appears that fewer of us leave our work at the office, thus with the blurred stretching of our day in both work and personal life, we perhaps are able to take care of both more adequately.

Another explanation is that many of us who report that we are very busy seek recognition for our hard work. As Robison and Godbey (1996) point out, "Stress is prestigious."

Implications

First, supervisors and HR practitioners need to be tolerant of the blurring of work and personal life. Provided productivity and quality of performance do not suffer, we should have little if any problem with this blurry boundary situation.

Second, while we as employees like to be recognized for the results we achieve, we have an even stronger need to be recognized for our *efforts* (not to mention our unique talents) in achieving the results. See, for example, Chen and Church (1993), Deutsch (1985), and Kanfer (1990). Supervisors and HR practitioners would be wise to emphasize effort in their recognition processes. Stronger motivation and subsequent performance are likely to follow.

9. POWERSHIFTS

We can consider the shifts of power at two broad levels—*micro* or organizational, and *macro*, meaning multiorganizational, societal, and global.

Micro

I remember Chris Argyris during a National Training Laboratories summer session at Bethel, Maine in 1967 saying that the computer would force more openness in organizations because so many employees would have access to information about the organization and its performance. Almost 30 years later in a meeting I attended recently, Stan Davis stated that the Internet represented a significant shift of power to the people. Technology is obviously making a difference regarding shifts of power; so are changes in organizational structure to flatter hierarchies as well as trends toward the virtual (Davidow & Malone, 1992) and the knowledge-based organization (Davis & Botkin, 1994). Moreover, even though there are strong needs for job security in the present, it is nevertheless unlikely, when compared with past behavior, that people will be as patient and tolerant of abusive bosses (Hornstein, 1996).

Macro

At a much broader level power is gradually but clearly shifting from the nation state to global corporations (Korten, 1995). One (if not *the*) issue in this regard is that as the economy in developed and in developing countries grows, so does the divide between rich and poor. While there is no conspiracy involved, it does seem, as Estes (1996) dramatically highlights, that "the tyranny of the bottom line" has uncontrolled and unconcerned power over the public. He argues that corporate power has gone awry. And as Korten (1995) points out, corporations, particularly those operating globally, do not have the checks and balances of government organizations.

Implications

At the micro level it is essential that the HR practitioner be discerning about the use of power and its consequences, such as, distinguishing between mere compliance on the part of employees and intrinsic motivation and commitment. Understanding this distinction has implications for job placement and the reward process. In addition to being aware of abusive bosses and taking appropriate action, being clear about the differences between leadership and management helps in the understanding of the different forms, bases, and uses of power.

At the macro level, the HR practitioner may feel rather powerless. Yet being sensitive to the issues touched on above can encourage the HR practitioner to speak out on matters such as downsizing in the exclusive service of the bottom line, of potential harm to the environment merely to save costs, and other matters related to corporate responsibilitiy.

By way of an overall summary, refer to Table 1.

Table 1   Summary of Nine "Need to Knows"

The Nine	What HR Practitioners Need to Know
Performance Improvement	Broadened measurement; determine key performance enhancers
Restructuring	What are the long-term consequences?
Organization Change	How to manage change; HR practitioner's role
Globalization	Understanding the impact cross-culturally and on small and medium size business
Groups and Teams	Differentiation: self-directed groups, teams, large group interventions
Action Learning	"Third Wave" of training and development
Inter	Relationships at multiple levels
Timeshift	Blurring of work and personal time: "stress is prestigious"
Powershifts	More dispersion individually and organizationally, yet more toward the global corporation

CONCLUSION

These nine need-to-knows are not by any means exhaustive. Space does not allow for further coverage. We could have covered much more on the changing nature of organizational design and structure. We could have covered leadership in more depth, the kind likely to be required in the 21st century. We could have covered the changing nature of the psychological contract between employer and employee. And even for the nine need-to-knows that were covered, we barely skimmed the surface. But if you, the reader, and especially if you are an HR practitioner, agree in large measure with these nine and see a need to learn more, then your plate is quite full for the time being. Nine is quite enough for now.

So you learn more about these "need to knows"—then what? Are these just nice to know? There are at least three primary and overlapping benefits: (1) a broadened repertoire and therefore an avoidance of overspecialization, (2) the advantage of anticipation and (3) the power of diagnosis. First, organizational executives are *not* looking for their HR practitioners to know more and more about less and less. The HR generalist inside the organization is more valuable: continuing to broaden one's repertoire is therefore critical. Second, executives need HR practitioners who can tell them what to expect in the future and then to help them plan and take action. Continuing to expand one's need-to-know list puts the HR practitioner in an anticipatory and therefore preventive position. Finally, learning these need-to-knows, especially in more depth than this paper provides, helps the HR practitioner to *understand* and diagnose organizational issues and problems both more accurately and comprehensively. This enhanced understanding increases the HR practitioner's value as an adviser and as a staff executive in the organization.

REFERENCES

Argyris, C. (1970). *Intervention theory and method.* Reading, MA: Addison-Wesley.

Barrett, F.J. (1995). Creating appreciative learning cultures. *Organziational Dynamics, 24*(2), 36–49.

Berger, L.A., & Sikora, M.J. (eds.) (1994). *The change management handbook: A roadmap to corporate transformation.* Burr Ridge, IL: Irwin.

Block, P. (1981). *Flawless consulting.* Erlanger, KY: Pfeiffer & Co.

Brockner, J. (1992). Managing the effects of layoffs on survivors. *California Management Review, 34*(2), 9–28.

Bunker, B.B., & Alban, B.T. (1992). Large group interventions. Special issue. *Journal of Applied Behavioral Science, 28*(4), 473–591.

Bunker, B.B., & Alban, B.T. (in press). *The new way to change organizations: Large group interventions* (working title). San Francisco: Jossey-Bass.

Bunker, B.B., Rubin, J.Z., & Associates (1995). *Conflict, cooperation, and justice.* San Francisco: Jossey-Bass.

Burke, W.W. (1995). Organization change: What we know, what we need to know. *Journal of Management Inquiry, 4,* 158–171.

Burke, W.W. (1994). *Organization development: A process of learning and changing,* 2nd ed. Reading, MA: Addison-Wesley.

Burke, W.W., & Biggart, N.W. (1996). Interorganizational relations. In Druckman, D., Singer, J.E., & Van Cott, H. (Eds.) *Enhancing organizational performance.* Washington, DC: National Academy Press.

Burns, L.S. (1993). *Busy bodies.* New York: W. W. Norton & Co.

Cameron, K.S. (1996). Techniques for making organizations effective: Some popular approaches. In Druckman, D., Singer, J.E., & Van Cott, H. (Eds.) *Enhancing organizational performance,* Washington, DC: National Academy Press.

Cameron, K.S., Freeman, S.J., & Mishra, A.K. (1991). Best practices in white-collar downsizing: Managing contradictions. *Academy of Management Executive, 5*(3), 57–73.

Carr, D.K., Hard, K.J., & Trahant, W.J. (1996). *Managing the change process: A field book for change agents, consultants, team leaders, and reengineering managers.* New York: McGraw-Hill.

Chen, Y.R., & Church, A.H. (1993). Reward allocation preferences in groups and organizations. *International Journal of Conflict Management, 4,* 25–49.

Cooperrider, D.L., & Srivastva, S. (1987). Appreciative inquiry into organizational life. In Woodman, R.W., & Pasmore, W.A. (Eds.), *Research in organization change and development, 1,* (pp. 129–169). Greenwich, CT: JAI Press.

Crispell, D. (1996). Chaotic workplace. *American Demographics, 18*(6), 50–52.

Deutsch, M. (1985). *Distributive justice, a social-psychological perspective.* New Haven, CT: Yale University Press.

Davidow, W.H., & Malone, M.S. (1992). *The virtual corporation.* New York: Harper Business.

Davis, S., & Botkin, J. (1994). *The monster under the bed: How business is mastering the opportunity of knowledge for profit.* New York: Simon & Schuster.

Estes, R. (1996). *Tyranny of the bottom line: Why corpora-

tions make good people do bad things. San Francisco: Berrett-Kohler Publishing, Inc.

Feldman, D.C. (1996). Managing careers in downsizing firms. *Human Resource Management, 35,* 145–161.

French, W.L., & Bell, C.H. Jr. (1995). *Organization development: Behavioral science interventions for organization improvement,* 5th ed. Englewood Cliffs, NJ: Prentice-Hall.

Froiland, P. (1994). Action learning: Taming real problems in real time. *Training.* January 27.

Goleman, D. (1995). *Emotional intelligence.* New York: Bantam.

Guzzo, R.A., Salas, E., & Associates (1995). *Team effectiveness and decision making in organizations.* San Francisco: Jossey-Bass

Hackman, J.R. (1992). The psychology of self-management in organizations. In Glaser, R. (Ed.), *Classic readings in self-management teamwork* (pp. 142–193). King of Prussia, PA: Organization Design and Development.

Hornstein, H.A. (1996). *Brutal bosses and their prey.* New York: Riverhead Books.

Howard, A., & Associates (1994). *Diagnosis for organizational change: Methods and models.* New York: Guilford.

Huselid, M.A. (1995). The impact of human resource management practices on turnover, productivity, and corporate financial planning. *Academy of Management Journal, 38,* 635–672.

Hurst, D.K. (1995). *Crisis and renewal: Meeting the challenge of organizational change.* Boston: Harvard Business School Press.

Kanfer, R. (1990). Motivation theory and industrial and organizational psychology. In Dunnette, M.D., & Hough, L.M. (Eds.), *Handbook of industrial and organizational psychology* (2nd ed. 1, pp.75–170). Palo Alto, CA: Consulting Psychologists Press.

Kaplan, R.S., & Norton, D.P. (1996). Using the balanced scorecard as a strategic management system. *Harvard Business Review, 74*(1), 75–85.

Kaplan R.S., & Norton, D.P. (1993). Putting the balanced scorecard to work. *Harvard Business Review, 71*(5), 134–147.

Kaplan, R.S., & Norton, D.P. (1992). The balanced scorecard—measures that drive performance. *Harvard Business Review, 70*(1), 71–79.

Katzenbach, J.R., & Smith, D.K. (1993). *The wisdom of teams: Creating the high-performance organization.* Boston: Harvard Business School Press.

Kleiner, M.M., Block, R.N., Roomkin, M., & Salsberg, S.W. (Eds.) (1987). *Human resources and the performance of the firm.* Washington, DC: BNA Press.

Korten, D.C. (1995). *When corporations rule the world.* West Hartford, CT: Kumarian Press: San Francisco: Berrett-Koehler.

Lawler, E.E. III, Mohrman, S.A., & Ledford, G.E. Jr. (1995). *Creating high performance organizations: Survey of practices and results of employee involvement and TQM in Fortune 1000 companies.* San Francisco: Jossey-Bass.

Litwin, G.H., Bray, J., & Brooke, K.L. (1996). *Mobilizing the organization: Bringing strategy to life.* London: Prentice-Hill.

McIntyre, R.M., & Salas, E. (1995). Measuring and managing team performance: Lessons from complex environments. In Guzzo, R.A., Salas, E., & Associates, *Team effectiveness and decision making in organizations* (pp. 9–15). San Francisco: Jossey-Bass.

McKinley, W., Sanchez, C.M., & Schick, A.G. (1995). Organizational downsizing: Constraining, cloning, learning. *Academy of Management Executive, 9*(3), 32–41.

Nadler, D.A., Shaw, R.B., Walton, A.E., & Associates (1995). *Discontinuous change: Leading organizational transformation.* San Francisco: Jossey-Bass.

Nevis, E.C., Lancourt, J. & Vassallo, H.G. (1996). *Intentional revolutions: A seven-point strategy for transforming organizations.* San Francisco: Jossey-Bass.

New York Times (1996). *The downsizing of America.* New York: Time Books.

Nolan, R.L., & Croson, D.C. (1995). *Creative destruction: A Six-stage process for transforming the organization.* Boston: Harvard Business School Press.

Pasmore, W.A., & Woodman, R.W. (Annual series beginning in 1988). *Research in organizational change and development.* Greenwich, CT: JAI Press.

Pucik, V., Tichy, N.M., & Barnett, C.K. (Eds.), (1992). *Globalizing management: Creating and leading the competitive organization.* New York: Wiley.

Rhinesmith, S.H. (1996). *A manager's guide to globalization: Six skills for success in a changing world,* 2nd ed. Alexandria, VA: American Society for Training and Development and Chicago: Irwin.

Robinson, J.P., & Godbey, G. (1996). The great American slowdown. *American Demographics, 18*(6), 42–48.

Senge, P. (1990). *The fifth discipline: The art and practice of the learning corporation.* New York: Doubleday Currency.

Tichy, N.M., & Sherman, S. (1994). *Control your destiny or someone else will.* New York: Harper Business.

Ulrich, D., Brockbank, W., Yeung, A.K., & Lake, D.G. (1995), Human resource competencies: An empirical assessment. *Human Resource Management, 34,* 473–495.

Wendt, H. (1993). *Global embrace: Corporate challenges in a transnational world.* New York: Harper Business.

NEW ROLES AND COMPETENCIES

Three types of competencies have been identified: **core competencies,** which are required of everyone in an organization; **leadership competencies,** which are behaviors that differentiate level of performance; and **functional competencies,** required in specific jobs or professions.[4] Certainly the new human resource professional must be technically competent in core HR practices—such as recruitment and selection, compensation and benefits administration, training and development, and performance management—because these techniques are necessary to accomplish the basic purpose of HR management. As HR professionals adapt to new roles, they must continue to provide the organization with basic HR services, including finding qualified candidates to fill positions within the organization, developing and maintaining an equitable compensation and benefit system, providing programs to teach employees at all levels their legal and functional responsibilities, and working with other leaders to determine how the organization will operate (policies and procedures).

The new roles expected of HRM professionals are more strategic in character, requiring a "corporate" perspective with consultative and regulatory capacities. Another role will be to act as a facilitator of organizational change, working with several agencies or departments to achieve broad goals and agency missions. The National Academy of Public Administration (NAPA) undertook a major study of the emerging roles of HR managers and identified thirty-one critical core competencies necessary for success in HRM leadership roles. The NAPA study of HRM administrative roles involved the use of sample surveys and focus group sessions composed of federal HR managers and case analysis of agencies using competency-based systems. The academy produced a report of its results, listing in a **competency model** the five HR roles and thirty-one core competencies necessary to accomplish these roles successfully (see Box 15.1).[5]

EMERGING ROLES

Several of the emerging roles that federal HR managers have identified may be uncomfortable for some contemporary HR professionals in state and local government or in nonprofit sector agencies. They are often quite accustomed to acting as the HR expert, providing technical expertise across the spectrum of HR practices and cautioning against potential infringement of personnel rules and employment laws. The new roles discussed here are less familiar than the old roles that characterized the field in the past, but they are increasingly required of HR professionals.

Public and nonprofit organizations are tapping more deeply into their human resources as they adopt a more strategic approach to conducting the business of government and nonprofit operations and are including HR managers as a key part of their administrative team. HR managers are being asked to help agency and department administrators make structural and cultural changes in their organizations. The tendency appears to be that organizations depend on HR professionals for expertise in organizational dynamics as well as human resources. These new roles may require HR professionals to adopt a more comprehensive orientation toward the organizations they work in if they are to develop their full potential for contributing to effective organizational leadership.

Human Resources Expert (and Advocate)

HR professionals are being asked to change their focus from being the watchdog of restrictive personnel policies to providing a wide range of services to their customers. HR customers exist at several layers:

- Employees, who receive needed information on conditions of employment and employee development services
- Managers, who need consulting services for the full range of human resource processes, from hiring to performance management

Box 15.1   NAPA Human Resource Competency Model Matrix

New Roles	Necessary Competencies
Business partner	Develops effective solutions to mission requirements using principles and programs
	Understands clients and organizational culture
	Knows mission
	Able to assess and balance competing values and priorities
	Understands individual and team behavior
	Understands public service environment
HR expert	Knows, applies, and manages best practices for maximizing human potential
	Knows HR laws and policies
	Customer service orientation
	Understands business process
	Able to manage resources effectively
	Able to design and use surveys to obtain feedback from customers
	Promotes work-life issues and integrates with results-oriented organizational planning process
Change agent	Has analytical skills
	Uses consultation and negotiation skills
	Able to be innovative and creative
	Uses consensus-building skills
	Able to influence others to act
Leader	Applies mentoring, coaching, and counseling skills to develop talent
	Able to build trust relationships
	Exhibits ethical behavior
	Able to make decisions
	Practices and promotes integrity
	Knows staff and line roles
Advocate	Values, promotes, and manages diversity
	Communicates well
	Manages conflict
Cross-cutting	Applies organizational development principles
	Knows business systems thinking and information technology
	Able to work in teams
	Has marketing skills

Source: New Times, New Competencies, New Professionals: A Guide for Implementing a Competency Model for HR Professionals: A Strategy for Becoming a High Performance Organization (Washington, D.C: National Academy of Public Administration, 1997), tables 1–1 and 1–2.

- The organization itself, which requires HR services in planning for its needs for human resources and organizing itself to create an environment for the maximum productivity of its employees
- The public, as the advocate of the democratic values of fairness and equality and organizational values of efficiency and effectiveness

Since the passage of reform statutes such as the Pendleton Act in 1883, personnel systems have striven for impartiality and objectivity with the *prime directive* to uphold merit principles. Decisions that had been made on the basis of political affiliation or social advantage were no longer acceptable. Job applicants and employees should be treated equally and equitably, with exclusive consideration of an individual's qualifications for job actions such as hiring or promotion. Over time, many personnel offices took this to the extreme of viewing organizational goals and department needs as "someone else's problem" and the enforcement of civil service rules as the exclusive focus of personnel administration. A strict numeric rating could be applied to the number of candidates who could qualify for an interview list or who should receive a performance (or merit) raise. Personnel rules were viewed as rather absolute and binding in virtually all circumstances, and dutiful managers began to find ways around the formal HRM system.[6]

Although equity and equal treatment remain paramount as the foundational values of merit principles, other important values must also receive consideration in making human resource decisions. The accomplishment of democratically determined organizational work goals is the very reason for public and nonprofit agencies to exist. The HR professional should certainly keep the values of effectiveness and efficiency in the operation of the agency as a top priority. Public officials should always bear in mind and maintain the integrity of democratic principles and honor the concept of the public good. HR professionals are encouraged: to assess and balance competing values and conflicting priorities; to understand the public service environment; to mentor, coach, and counsel with employees and agencies; to provide customer service; to apply best practices; and to promote social equity oriented work-life issues such as diversity and mutual respect in the workplace.

Strategic (Business) Partner

Some HR offices have been viewed by line managers as closed shops, where the technical work of developing lists of qualified candidates for interviewing or evaluating jobs according to an internal job classification system was done in virtual secrecy. The intention was probably to eliminate undue influence from departmental managers from the "science" of human resource management techniques. More often than not, however, the result was suspicion of the motivations of personnel officers and alienation from the organization that personnel professionals were supposed to serve. The new roles and competencies of HR management demonstrate the problems associated with reclusive personnel units and reflect the wisdom of Wallace Sayre's warning against the "triumph of technique over purpose."[7] The NAPA study advises HR professionals to work in teams, build consensus, understand their customers and the **organizational culture,** consult and negotiate, and build trust as widely as possible. As organizations move increasingly toward using teams to accomplish their missions, managers will need to learn new competencies required to make teams productive, including generating and refining ideas on how to address problems, organizing and integrating collaborative work, sustaining group *esprit* over time, and managing the boundaries of group responsibilities.[8]

Organizational Dynamics Expert (Change Agent)

Administrators are depending on HR professionals to provide needed knowledge and skills as organizations change the direction and the focus of their attention. Public and nonprofit organizations experience frequent reorganization as new leaders enter office and policy priorities change. The HR professional is increasingly looked to as the expert in organizational dynamics, or the **change agent,** to advise administrators on agency restructuring and planned change. HR professionals are asked to contribute through their knowledge of organizational development principles and their understanding of the various business systems, including information technology systems that typify the contemporary public and nonprofit work environment.

The HR professional may be asked to facilitate desired change within specific subunits of the organization. An understanding of group dynamics and organizational skills—including consensus building, problem solving, negotiating, and marketing—is important in facilitating change in organizations. Because of the rapid rate of change in contemporary organizations, a number of strategic competencies have been identified for managers as they cope with change:[9]

- Stay flexible.[10]
- Keep trying things out.
- Gain a thorough understanding of your core competencies.
- Keep monitoring the environment around the globe (find and use best practices).
- Keep introducing insights from outside.

Leadership

Many personnel managers would not have considered themselves leaders just a few years ago. Personnel management was, by established tradition, a support function. The personnel office provided the gateway into the organization by screening applicants and developing qualified lists of candidates. It developed and maintained classification and compensation systems and sometimes provided training programs for employees either directly or by the brokering of training provided by consultants. If personnel offices ventured into consulting with agency managers (welcome or not), it was generally to give legal advice,

usually in cases of employee discipline or termination. Agency leadership was left to elected and appointed officials bearing formal responsibility for organizational mission and performance.

The HR manager in modern public and nonprofit organizations must command a number of leadership competencies to perform in the new organizational roles identified here. HR professionals must be innovative and creative in finding new ways to accomplish organizational goals while promoting adherence to laws, policies, and ethical practices. They should work with others by consulting, counseling, influencing, negotiating, and collaborating. They must promote integrity and trust.

Leadership in today's environment includes developing an organizational culture for a learning organization[11] and building intellectual capital within the organization.[12] A learning organization is composed of individuals who capitalize on their successes, retain the lessons of their mistakes, and have managers who seek out other comparable organizations that are successfully addressing the needs of their customers and the general public. Leaders in these organizations know how to learn and know how to teach the importance of learning in the organization through example and through the organizational priorities they establish.[13] The leaders of a learning organization must be viewed as credible, and employees need to be cognizant of their leader's values and vision for the organizational culture to be broadly shared and manifested in the behavior of employees.[14] High-performance agencies build the capacity to learn and invest in the intellectual capital within their organizations to achieve high levels of performance over the long run.[15] The competencies needed to build intellectual capital include disseminating information throughout the organization, encouraging innovation, recognizing and rewarding creative problem solving, and exercising integrity.[16]

Warren Bennis believes that leaders in today's knowledge-intensive world must release the brain power of their people and energize the know-how and creativity of their workforce. Leadership, according to Bennis, "is the main instrument for leveraging intellectual capital."[17] Those emerging leaders who can build the intellectual capital of their organizations share five competencies with all exemplary leaders:

- *Possess passion and purpose.* Leaders possess a strong determination to achieve a goal.
- *Generate and sustain trust.* Exemplary leaders demonstrate competence, constancy, caring, candor, and congruity.
- *Exhibit hope and optimism.* All successful leaders believe they can achieve what they set out to do.
- *Manifest a bias for action.* Convert purpose and vision into action, such that they articulate "a dream with a deadline."
- *Learn and grow.* Create an environment for learning, thinking, and talking with new people from within and outside the organization.[18]

EXECUTIVE CORE QUALIFICATIONS

The emerging roles and competencies that have been identified for HR professionals are similar to other competencies identified for success in public administration, for "high performance HR professionals, line managers, and leaders share many of the same competencies."[19] Indeed, most management competencies apply to managers in business, government, or the nonprofit sector, and for managers in various departments in organizations.[20] As an example, the six **executive core qualifications** that the United Nations High Commissioner for Refugees expects of its workforce are: (1) organizational commitment; (2) flexibility and adaptability; (3) teamwork; (4) performance orientation; (5) communication; and (6) professional and ethical personal behavior.[21]

The Federal **Senior Executive Service** (SES) requires that each new appointee meet qualifications that emphasize leadership skills needed to succeed in the SES.[22] The U.S. Office of Personnel Management (OPM) uses five executive core

qualifications (ECQ) to assess experience and potential for determining whether candidates have the broad executive skills needed to succeed in executive-level public service. OPM has developed a list of leadership competencies from research into the experience of public and private sector executives that support each ECQ.[23] Box 15.2 lists the ECQs and corresponding leadership competencies.

USING THE COMPETENCY MODEL

The most common reasons for integrating competency models in organizations are the following:[24]

- *Improve overall performance.* Competencies are the basis of a performance management plan. Job competencies are determined through a review of the requirements and qualifications of the job and are compared to the abilities of the person performing the job. Specific objectives can be developed to help the incumbent focus attention on developing needed competencies.[25]
- *Initiate a cultural change program.* Leaders create the appropriate environment (or organizational culture) for achieving organizational goals. These goals include developing a set of competencies that will facilitate the achievement of operational objectives.[26]
- *Increase the effectiveness of training and development.* Studies have shown that excellence at executive levels of government is "largely serendipitous" and that more needs to be done to develop leadership competencies among the senior career service employees in government.[27] One of the reasons for developing core competencies for positions in government and not-for-profit organizations is to identify specific areas for training and development (see Chapter 12). Using the list of SES Executive Core Qualifications, the Federal Executive Institute and Graduate School of the U.S. Department of Agriculture have developed a training curriculum

Box 15.2   SES Executive Core Qualifications

Executive Core Qualifications (ECQ)	Leadership Competencies
Leading change	Creativity and innovation
	Continual learning
	External awareness
	Flexibility
	Resilience
	Service motivation
	Strategic thinking
	Vision
Leading people	Conflict management
	Cultural awareness
	Integrity and honesty
	Team building
Results driven	Accountability
	Customer service
	Decisiveness
	Entrepreneurship
	Problem solving
	Technical credibility
Business acumen	Financial management
	Human resource management
	Technology management
Building coalitions and communication	Influencing and negotiating
	Interpersonal skills
	Oral communication
	Partnering
	Political savvy
	Written communication

defining each leadership competency and identifying several learning objectives for each ECQ.[28]

- *Improve recruitment and selection processes and reduce turnover.* When competencies have been identified for specific jobs, candidates can be tested for their KSAs in these competencies in the selection process. Employees can be trained in new competencies as old ones become obsolete, thereby reduc-

ing turnover and offering security to employees.

- *Clarify managerial and specialist roles, and increase the focus on organizational objectives.* An understanding of the core competencies needed in an organization helps managers and employees maintain a focus on their most critical long-term needs.[29] As the work environment and organizations change over time, it is helpful to reassess what is being done compared to the mission and stated focus of the organization. Some organizations may need to alter their direction, while others will require more thorough reevaluation and renewal.[30] Many public and private organizations are finding they need to form strategic alliances with others in order to accomplish their mission.[31]

- *Assist in career and succession planning.* There are employee and organizational benefits to assisting employees with career planning. Employees can use the competency model to identify the competencies needed for their future careers. The knowledge and skills needed to be successful change rapidly. Employees can make career choices when they have a clear idea of the competencies for future work. Organizations benefit as employees become more capable and flexible. New competencies can be applied to changing needs and demands.

A very important use of the competency model is seen in **succession planning** for organizations. With the aging of the workforce, there is a looming crisis regarding who will be prepared to succeed managers who are expected to retire in the next decade. A realistic succession plan would include an analysis of the competencies needed in upper-level managerial positions for the recruitment and development of their replacements.[32]

■ CONCLUSION

There is some evidence that we are not doing a very good job of preparing prospective human resource professionals to perform within the new roles of HR management.[33] The full spectrum of expanding roles and the lengthening list of competencies required for success in contemporary HRM assignments needs to be presented and learned to prepare public and nonprofit sector HR professionals and managers adequately. As important as the technical components of HR are, the competencies related to interpersonal skills,

problem solving, and integrating HR with the organizational mission deserve great attention in the training of HRM professionals.[34] To ensure that HR professionals are fully competent in all applicable roles, some public organizations are requiring certification in core competencies. The Senior Executive Service (SES), for example, requires candidates to pass a series of competency examinations.[35] The National Institutes of Health requires its HR professionals to be certified in the competencies to act as partners and consultants. They "must have the ability to listen to a customer, understand what the customer is trying to achieve, and offer creative solutions."[36]

In some ways, it is difficult to describe the competencies of the HR professional in a book such as this because the knowledge and skills of HR management are not static, sequential, or linear; rather, the competencies of the HR manager are interconnected and complex. Some functions such as strategic HRM and performance management cross over all aspects of HRM. Other subjects such as compensation depend on several other factors, including the external market, classification, labor contracts, and internal policies. The environment of the public workplace is continuously changing as legislators write new laws and the courts interpret these statutes against the U.S. and state constitutions. The contemporary public service environment is dynamic and somewhat unpredictable, and the political aspects of public sector human resource management make the profession a challenging one. While the challenge of operating in the volatile public environment is somewhat daunting, the genuine and deep satisfaction of serving the public interest along with employees dedicated to public service is profoundly rewarding for those who seek a meaningful and enriching profession.

■ MANAGER'S VOCABULARY

core competencies
leadership competencies
functional competencies

competency model
organizational culture
change agent
executive core qualifications
Senior Executive Service (SES)
succession planning

■ STUDY QUESTIONS

1. How have the roles performed by HR professionals changed in recent years?

2. What new knowledge, skills, and abilities are required of HR professionals in these new roles?

3. What values are important for HR professionals to consider when performing their various roles in public or nonprofit organizations?

4. Why should human resources be a major consideration in the strategic direction of public and nonprofit organizations?

5. Should HR managers be leaders?

6. What core competencies do HR professionals, line managers, and organizational leaders share?

7. How should an analysis of organizational competencies and individual job competencies be used in public and nonprofit organizations?

8. How could core competencies be used as a basis for compensation for any public or nonprofit employee?

■ EXPERIENTIAL EXERCISES

1. Consider an organization with which you are familiar. Develop a list of core competencies that could be used in planning for leadership succession in this organization, and answer the following:

    a. Who will be leaving the organization?

    b. What competencies will be lost?

    c. What additional competencies are needed for this organization?

    d. Who should be recruited?

    e. What should be tested for in the selection process?

    f. What topics should be provided in training programs?

    g. What other programs could be implemented to prepare the next generation of leaders?

2. Using your current job, a past job, or a job you would someday like to have, list the core competencies, leadership competencies, and functional competencies that have become obsolete in this job over the past decade and the ones you anticipate will be needed to perform this job in the future.

3. Individually, or in a small group, identify the core competencies of successful teachers and successful students. Describe what you and your student colleagues could do to develop these competencies.

■ NOTES

1. Scott B. Parry, "Just What Is a Competency? (And Why Should You Care?)." *Training* 35:6 (1998): 59.

2. Eric Raimy, "HR's New Leader," *Public HR* 2:2 (1999): 31.

3. Ron Zemke and Susan Zemke, "Putting Competencies to Work," *Training* 36:1 (1999): 70.

4. Raimy, "HR's New Leader," p. 31.

5. *New Times, New Competencies, New Professionals: A Guide for Implementing a Competency Model for HR Professionals: A Strategy for Becoming a High Performance Organization* (Washington, D.C: National Academy of Public Administration, 1997).

6. Lorna Jorgensen, Kelli Fairless, and W. David Patton, "Underground Merit Systems and the Balance Between Service and Compliance," *Review of Public Personnel Administration* 16 (Spring 1996): 5–20.

7. Wallace S. Sayre, "The Triumph of Technique over Purpose," *Public Administration Review* 8:1 (1948).

8. Caela Farren, "Smart Teams," *Executive Excellence* 16:7 (1999): 15.

9. Robert Baldock, "5 Futures," *Management Review* 88:9 (1999): 53–54.

10. David A. Nadler and Michael L. Tushman, "The Organization of the Future: Strategic Imperatives and Core Competencies for the 21st Century," *Organizational Dynamics* 28:1 (1999): 8–14.

11. Roy Harrison, "Intellectual Assets," *People Management* 4:7 (1998): 33.

12. William Miller, "Building the Ultimate Resource," *Management Review* 88:1 (1999): 42.

13. Jon P. Briscoe and Douglas T. Hall, "Grooming and Picking Leaders Using Competency Frameworks: Do They Work? An Alternative Approach and New Guidelines for Practice," *Organizational Dynamics* 28:2 (1999): 46–49.

14. Rick L. Edgeman and Jens J. Dahlgaard, "A Paradigm for Leadership Excellence," *Total Quality Management* 9:4/5 (1998): S75.

15. Timothy R. Athey and Michael S. Orth, "Emerging Competency Methods for the Future," *Human Resource Management* 38:3 (1999): 220–222.

16. Miller, "Building the Ultimate Resource," pp. 43–45.

17. Warren Bennis, "Five Competencies of New Leaders," *Executive Excellence* 16:7 (1999):4–5.

18. Ibid.

19. *New Times,* p. xv.

20. Parry, "Just What Is a Competency?" p. 60.

21. 22 Rebecca Johnson, "Humanitarian Resources," *People Management* 5:14 (1999): 34.

22. U.S. Office of Personnel Management, *Executive Core Qualifications*, n.d., available at: **http://www.opm.gov/ses/html/ecq4.htm.**

23. Ibid., p. 1.

24. Les Pickett, "Competencies and Managerial Effectiveness: Putting Competencies to Work," *Public Personnel Management* 27:1 (1998): 105–106.

25. Ibid., p. 107.

26. Briscoe and Hall, "Grooming and Picking Leaders," p. 47.

27. Mark W. Huddleston, *Profiles in Excellence: Conversations with the Best of America's Career Executive Service* (Arlington, VA: Price Waterhouse Coopers Endowment for the Business of Government, 1999), p. 14.

28. Leadership Effectiveness Framework, Graduate School, U.S. Department of Agriculture, July 1999.

29. Harry Scarbrough, "Path(ological) Dependency? Core Competencies from an Organizational Perspective," *British Journal of Management* 9:3 (1998): 219.

30. Pierre-Xavier Meschi, "Competence Building and Corporate Renewal," *Business Strategy Review* 10:2 (1999): 48–49.

31. Eric Rule, "Competencies of High-Performing Strategic Alliances," *Strategy and Leadership* 26:4 (1998): 36.

32. U.S. Office of Personnel Management, *Executive Succession Planning Tool Kit* (Washington, D.C.: U.S. Government Printing Office, 1995), pp. 2–3.

33. Mitchell Langbert, "Professors, Managers, and Human Resource Education," *Human Resource Management* 39:1 (1999): 65.

34. Ibid., p. 77.

35. U.S. Office of Personnel Management, *Executive Core Qualifications,* p. 1.

36. Raimy, "HR's New Leader," p. 31.

Case Appendix

TABLE OF CASES AND RELEVANT CHAPTERS

Case	Relevant Chapter	1	2	3	4	5	6	7	8	9	10	11	12	13	14	15
1. City of Franklin versus AFME						P										
2. Conflicting Perceptions														P	S	
3. Downsizing at the ACHD			P													
4. A Family and Medical Leave Act Puzzler											P					
5. Flextime											P					
6. Governor Pat Ronage's Hiring Freeze				S	S	P										
7. Helping Hands							S	S				S			S	
8. Liberty Police Department							P					S				
9. Negotiator's Dilemma						P				S						
10. A Quandary over Accepting the Job										P						
11. Radicals in the Rank-and-File								P								
12. Salary Compression at State University										P						
13. The Scheduling Software Case		P														
14. Three Strikes and You're Out!						S										

P = primary chapter, S = secondary chapters

1. CITY OF FRANKLIN VERSUS AFME

The City of Franklin is a small, conservative community located in the mountains of the Pacific Northwest. It has a mayor-council form of government and instructs the human resource manager to handle labor negotiations each year. There are three unions in the city: the International Association of Fire Fighters (IAFF), the International Brotherhood of Police Officers (IBPO), and the American Federation of Municipal Employees (AFME).

Nearby ski resorts have enjoyed considerable growth and prosperity, but Franklin and similar communities in the area have not been able to share in the economic boom. Franklin's economy is dependent on natural resource production, which has been doing moderately well, but city revenues have remained flat. The community is not heavily taxed, but citizens recently voted out most of the previous city council who proposed a modest property tax increase. In the same election, citizens voted down a school construction bond and voted for term limits.

During the last negotiation session, the AFME local agreed to accept less-than-satisfactory wage increases because of the city's financial situation. Their leadership promised the members that they would be able to make up for the lost wages this time, and even got the city to include language in the contract to reflect this promise.

The city's financial situation is not much better this time around, however, and city officials have been anxious to open their books to the union leadership and encourage more cooperation at the bargaining table. City officials are debating whether to lay off ten of the seventy-five members of the AFME bargaining unit to allow for expected wage increases for all city employees.

The seventy-five members of the AFME bargaining unit have an average compensation (wages and benefits) of $37,000. The IAFF unit has fifty-three members with an average compensation of $48,000, and the IBPO has sixty-three members with an average compensation of $51,000. There are thirty-three management employees who are not members of any union, and

their average compensation is $52,000. The personnel budget is: $2,775,000 (AFME), $2,544,000 (IAFF), $3,213,000 (IBPO), and $1,716,000 (management). The total personnel budget for the past year is $10,248,000. The total projected city budget for the coming year is $19,889,000, which represents a 2 percent increase over the previous year.

The AFME union has called for the beginning of negotiations. The class is divided into two groups, one representing the City of Franklin negotiating team and the other representing the AFME bargaining unit. You may assign anyone to your negotiation team. Typically, someone is chosen to work on financial issues, personnel issues, legal issues, and specific departmental issues. A chief spokesperson is selected to participate in negotiation sessions. You may or may not wish to have the mayor or a city council member attend negotiation sessions; the same range of choices on participation also applies to the union president or someone from the union's national headquarters. Last year's contract has been distributed to all team members. A list of issues to be considered for the negotiation table follows the contract.

Last Year's Contract:
Article I. Preamble

Whereas, pursuant to the provisions of the Franklin Municipal Code, Chapter 15, Title 34, the City of Franklin (City) and the American Federation of Municipal Employees (Union) agree to the terms and conditions of employment herein stated with respect to wages, rates of pay, working conditions in relation to employees in the city-wide Technical/Clerical bargaining unit.

Whereas the City and the Union agree that a spirit of labor-management cooperation, trust, efficiency, and service are in the best interest of the community and that effective resolution of problems is important to a cooperative relationship, the City and Union are committed to fair and cooperative settlement of their differences.

Whereas representatives of the City and the Union have met and negotiated in good faith regarding wages, rates of pay, working conditions, and all terms and conditions of employment, the City and Union now desire to enter into a Collective Labor Agreement for the period [2 years ago] to [last year].

Now, therefore, the City and Union hereby agree as follows:

Article II. General Provisions

Exclusive Representative. The City hereby recognizes the Union as the sole and exclusive bargaining agent for all members of the Technical/Clerical bargaining unit. These members include all paid members of City departments not in public safety (police and fire) departments and not in supervisory, administrative, or confidential positions.

Union Business. No more than five (5) members of the Union's contract negotiation committee shall be allowed time off for the purpose of negotiation meetings with the City. Other time off for attendance at conventions, seminars, and other meetings for Union business will be permitted at the discretion of the respective department head if it is determined to be in the interest of the City.

Strikes. No employee of the City (including specifically members of the Technical/Clerical bargaining unit) shall strike against the City or recognize a picket line of any labor organization.

Management Rights. The City shall retain the exclusive right to exercise the regular and customary functions of management, including but not limited to directing the activities of the City, determining levels of service and methods of operation (including contracting out services to other entities), use of equipment, hiring, layoffs, transfers, promotions, discipline and discharge, work schedules, work assignments, and staffing levels.

Prevailing Union Rights. All rights, benefits, and privileges enjoyed by the Union which may or may not be included in this agreement shall remain in force.

Article III. Wages and Benefits

Wages. Wages of employees represented by the Union for the term of the agreement shall include an across-the-board increase of 2.25 percent, recognizing the financial situation of the City and in anticipation of future wage increases to make up for increases representing less than parity with comparable cities.

Overtime. Overtime shall be distributed at the discretion of City officials, with due consideration given to the seniority of employees represented by the Union.

Vacation. Employees represented by the Union shall be entitled to vacation according to years of service in their department: Probationary employees accrue no vacation leave. Less than five years, monthly accrual of 8 hours; five to fourteen years, 12 hours; fifteen years or more, 20 hours.

Holidays. Employees represented by the Union shall receive eight (8) holidays—specifically, New Year's Day, President's Day, Memorial Day, Independence Day, Labor Day, Thanksgiving Day, Christmas Eve Day, and Christmas Day.

Sick Leave. Employees represented by the Union shall be eligible for sick leave with full pay. Employees shall accumulate four (4) hours eligibility per month after completion of a six (6) month probationary period. Sick leave use must be approved by the employee's supervisor prior to taking leave. City and Union agree that sick leave shall be utilized only for sickness or injury of the employee or immediate family member. Verification of illness from a certified medical doctor will be required at the discretion of the City. Sick leave may be converted to cash at the end of the budget year at a rate of four days sick leave to one day's wages, or two days sick leave to one day of annual leave.

Medical Insurance. The City will provide a bona fide medical insurance program for City employees and contribute eighty (80) percent of the program's premium costs.

Life Insurance. The City will provide a bona fide life insurance program at one times the employee's salary for City employees and contribute one hundred (100) percent of the program's premium costs.

Disability Insurance. The City will provide a bona fide disability insurance program for City employees who shall be allowed to participate voluntarily at their own expense.

Dental Insurance. The City will provide a bona fide dental insurance program for City employees and contribute fifty (50) percent of the program's premium costs.

Flexible Work Schedules. The City and Union agree to discuss the use of flextime and other flexible work schedules. City employees shall be eligible to arrive and leave work during the range from 7:30 A.M. to 5:30 P.M. so long as they are in compliance with state and federal laws and notwithstanding shift schedules.

Article IV. Grievance Provisions

Definition. Grievances are defined as a complaint involving the interpretation, or application of this agreement, City policy or involving disciplinary or other adverse actions.

Procedures. The steps of the grievance procedure are as follows:

1. Grievances shall be verbally made to the immediate supervisor within five (5) working days after the incident provoking the grievance.
2. If the response from the supervisor is unsatisfactory, the grievance shall be made in writing to the Union Grievance Committee stating the specific provision of this agreement, policy or adverse action, the dates of any perceived violation, and the specific remedy desired. Such written notice shall be made within five (5) working days of the response from the supervisor.
3. If the Union Grievance Committee finds the grievance meritorious it shall attempt to resolve the grievance informally for up to ten

(10) working days, and if still unresolved, it shall submit the grievance to the department head of the department where the provoking incident occurred. The department head may assign a deputy department head to address the concerns of the grievant.
4. The decision of the department head is the final response of the City. Grievance decisions made by the department head may be appealed to the Mayor who may, at his or her discretion, form a Grievance Board made of one member selected by the Union (a City employee not represented by the Union), one member selected by the City (a City employee not in the affected department), and a third member selected by the first two members of the Board. The decision of this Board shall be final and adhered to by the Union and City.

Article V. Bargaining Procedures

Timing. The Union shall notify the City of its intent to commence negotiations. Negotiations may proceed for a period of three (3) months, after which time an impasse is declared and the City and Union agree to engage in defined impasse resolution processes. An extension may be granted upon appeal to the Mayor if both parties agree to an extension.

Article VI. Impasse Resolution

Arbitration. In the event agreement in subsequent negotiations cannot be reached within the designated time period, the City and Union will submit their record of negotiations to an arbitrator agreed upon by the City and Union. If no arbitrator can be agreed upon, the City may unilaterally implement its final offer. The arbitrator may hear arguments from the City and Union in a manner he or she desires, or may request that the City and Union present their final best offers. If the latter method of arbitration is selected, the arbitrator will select either the City offer in total or the Union offer in total.

Following is a list of issues to consider in the negotiations; it is not exhaustive and not listed in any order of preference. It is the task of the negotiating team to refine and prioritize this list in preparation for negotiations.

Union membership (confidential employees?).

Union business (time for regular union meetings?).

Strikes (should all city employees be included in contract language?)

Contracting out (should the union be included in contracting out discussions?)

Wages (catch up from last year and additional increase according to surrounding cities?)

Career ladder

Overtime (distributed by seniority?)

Vacation leave (are we low?)

Holidays (should Martin Luther King, Jr., and Veterans Day be honored?)

Sick leave (time before verification)

Sick leave (conversion rate)

Medical and dental insurance (premiums)

Medical insurance for dependents

Medical insurance for retirees

Disability insurance, premiums

Grievance procedures, management response time

Impasse (try mediation?)

Following are the management issues; again, this list is not exhaustive and not listed in any order of preference. It is the task of the City negotiating team to refine and prioritize this list.

Union membership (technical specialists?)

Strikes (any demonstration, including sick-outs?)

Management rights (concern over erosion of management rights)

Wages (limited by budget and citizen mood)

Merit pay (pay for performance)

Vacation leave (formula to combine vacation and sick leave to make personal leave)

Sick leave (eliminate conversion)

Insurance (reduce premium costs)

Grievance procedure (streamline the process, fewer steps)

Layoffs (best procedures?)

2. CONFLICTING PERCEPTIONS: "I'M AFRAID TO WORK WITH HIM"

On Monday morning at 8:00 A.M., Ana arrives in the office to find an e-mail from George requesting a meeting to discuss some problems with his working relationships with another staff member. At approximately 8:15 A.M., Betty arrives in Ana's office with Friday's interoffice mail and a request to discuss a personal issue with her. She does not give Ana a great deal of information but does indicate that it is a grave matter and it affects her ability to work in the unit. Betty will be meeting with Ana at 10:00 A.M., and George will meet with Ana at 11:00 A.M.

Betty

Betty is considered to be an outstanding employee. A senior secretary with twenty-five years of service to the Department of Transportation, she has an unblemished service record with outstanding performance evaluations. She has an exceptional institutional memory and is unfailingly professional and pleasant. Ana relies on Betty quite heavily.

During her interview with Ana, Betty shares her concerns about working with George. Since he joined the training unit approximately six months ago, transferring from Human Resource Services, Betty observed that she has learned a great deal about George. She has decided, based on her observations and interpretations of his work habits, that he is homosexual and may have AIDS. She is concerned about doing work for him and the close proximity within which they work because of fears of infection. Betty knows very little about the virus, but she is very afraid. She will be retiring in five years and fears "catching that homosexual disease." She wants Ana to know that it is important for her to work hard and do well, as she has done in the past, but that she simply is not able to do the work necessary for George. She believes that he is getting very angry with her. But Betty is really not comfortable about talking to George about this and, moreover, does not know how to avoid touching his work or working near him in this office.

George

George is the trainer responsible for organization development within the training unit of the Department of Transportation. He has two years of service in the department and a solid record, with good evaluations from training sessions and past employment with the department.

George notes during his interview with Ana that he feels very confident in his abilities, having received a master's in public administration. He does, however, recognize that he is a bit impatient when personally stressed. To address this issue, George tends to use a quirky sense of humor and a touch of the dramatic in his actions. He has been ill but has not discussed the symptoms or source of his illness with any coworkers because of a strong sense of privacy. Since it has not affected his job, he does not believe that it is relevant.

George wishes to discuss concerns he has about Betty's attitude toward him. She appears to be hesitant and evasive when he asks her to perform even the simplest of tasks, yet he is dependent on her for both clerical support and general information about the unit's workings. George has asked her if there are any problems or confusion, but he has not received any tangible feedback. She has not been rude, but he does notice a drawing back from him in her behavior toward

him, which she does not demonstrate with others. However, he does not feel he has the time or the authority to address this matter with her.

Ana

Ana, Betty's direct supervisor, is the director of the training unit within the Department of Transportation. She has ten years of service with the department. Ana prides herself on maintaining a pleasant and open working environment. She relies heavily on Betty, an outstanding employee, to handle details in the office, as Ana is responsible for external relations.

Ana is pleased with the evaluations of training done by George and believes that he has a great deal of potential. Ana does want to foster George's career and has identified some areas in which he could improve, allowing him to realize his potential.

Task 1

Consider the evolution of employee rights, motivation, diversity in the workplace, the changing workforce, values of public service, staff development and promotion, and discipline. Then answer the following questions:

1. What are the central issues from a human resource management perspective?
2. What issues are not relevant from a human resource management perspective?
3. What should Ana do?
4. Is disciplinary action warranted?

Task 2

Answer the following questions:

1. What policies may Ana consider developing as a result of this dispute?
2. Why might it be advantageous to have no policy in place?

3. DOWNSIZING AT THE ADA COUNTY HIGHWAY DISTRICT

Ada County Highway District is a separate unit of local government responsible for all roads, streets, and public rights of way within the county, except for those designated as part of the state or federal highway system. Under the district's jurisdiction are 1,723 centerline miles of roadway and 413 bridges. The district operates on a fiscal year basis beginning on October 1, and is governed by a five-member board elected to rotating terms.

The Adams and Cloverdale Divisions perform roadway maintenance activities and equipment services from operational centers located at 3730 Adams Street and 440 North Cloverdale Road, respectively. The department's roadway maintenance responsibilities include pothole patching, seal coating, snow removal, sanding, drainage facility installation and repair (within the public right-of-way), guardrails, fencing, street sweeping, crack sealing, bridge repairs, concrete repairs, grading of gravel roads, weed control, and maintaining district buildings and grounds. The department is also responsible for the repair, service, and maintenance of all equipment operated by the district for its maintenance.

You are the superintendent of the Adams Division of the Ada County Highway District. Due to an unusually heavy winter and several flash floods that destroyed two bridges, the district has experienced an unexpected shortfall in revenues. You have been asked to prepare a 5 percent holdback in your current budget. It is mid-September now, so your plan should include a 5 percent holdback for the entire new fiscal year budget set to begin on October 1.

Civil service rules for your jurisdiction require that downsizing take into account rank and seniority. Points for seniority are assigned according

to years of service, with 1 point awarded for each year. Downsizing should begin with the employees with the least number of points and proceed upward until the cost savings has been achieved. Points are assigned for rank according to the following scale: crew chief, 5 points; leadworker, 4 points; mechanic/welder, 3 points; general equipment operator 2, 3 points; general equipment operator 1, 2 points; motor grader operator, 1 point; mechanic, 1 point. The district assumes that fringe benefits are equal to 25 percent of the cost of salary.

Questions

All of the information you need to answer the questions that follow is contained in Figure A3.

1. How would you rank employees for possible reduction-in-force proceedings?
2. How many positions would you have to cut in order to achieve a 5 percent holdback in personnel expenditures?
3. Assuming that the remaining employees wish to remain with the organization, what reorganizations could the bumping process create? How could these changes affect the Highway District and its ability to accomplish its mission?
4. What other approaches could you take to achieve the 5 percent holdback besides a reduction in permanent employees (e.g., hiring part-time, temporary, or contract workers)? What are the implications for human resources of pursuing any of these options?
5. What are the human resources impacts of privatizing the Maintenance and Operations Division?

Source: The description of the Ada County Highway District and the Maintenance and Operations Divisions is taken from *FY 1999 Ada County Highway District Budget* (Boise, ID: Ada County Highway District, 1999), pp. 14–15, 45–47. The salaries, seniority, and rankings of these positions have been fictionalized.

Figure A3   Maintenance and Operations, Adams Division

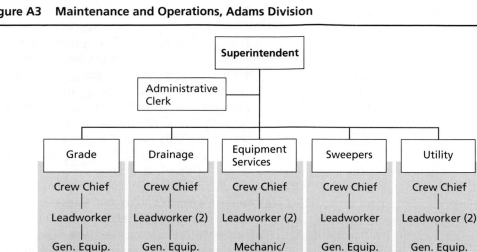

Salaries and Seniority of Personnel in Adams
Division, Maintenance and Operations, ACHD
Crew Chiefs: $40,000
 Grade crew: 20 years seniority
 Drainage crew: 15 years seniority
 Equipment services: 14 years seniority
 Brooms: 11 years seniority
 Utility: 10 years seniority
Leadworkers (LW): $30,000
 LW1: 10 years seniority
 LW2: 10 years seniority
 LW3: 7 years seniority
 LW4: 8 years seniority
 LW5: 6 years seniority
 LW6: 10 years seniority
 LW7: 5 years seniority
 LW8: 6 years seniority
General Equipment Operators
 GEO1: $20,000 (five with 1 year senority; five
 with 2 years seniority; five with 3 years seniority)
 GEO2: $25,000 (five with 4 years seniority; five with 5 years
 seniority; five with 6 years seniority)
Motor Grader Operator: $23,000
 MGO1: 5 years seniority
 MGO2: 3 years seniority
 MGO3: 2 years seniority
Mechanics/Welders: $24,000
 MW1: 10 years seniority
 MW2: 6 years seniority
 MW3: 5 years seniority
 MW4: 3 years seniority
 MW5: 2 years seniority

Total Wages, Adams Division Maintenance
and Operations: $1,429,000
2 percent holdback = $28,580
5 percent holdback = $71,450

Expenditures Budget, Adams Division, Maintenance
and Operations
Wages $1,429,000
FICA $130,000
State Retirement $166,000
Health Insurance $47,000
Workers' Compensation $47,000
Temporaries $80,000
Overtime $65,000
Printing $8,000
Utitlies $13,00
Books/Dues/Subscriptions $1,000
Supplies $39,500
Leases/Rentals $25,000
Equipment rental $35,000
Travel/Meetings $8,000
Liability Payments $5,000
Miscellaneous $2,000
Maintenance/Equipment $2,000
Maintenance/Buildings/Grounds $122,000
Discretionary Fund for Managers $20,000
Materials(asphalt, gravel,etc.) $1,109,000
Professional Services $58,000
Contractual Services $340,000

4. A FAMILY AND MEDICAL LEAVE ACT PUZZLER

John and Candy Smith are both employees of Oceanview City. John is a captain with the city police force, and Candy works as a clerk for the Department of Public Works. They have just had their first child, Benjamin.

The pregnancy entailed many complications, and Candy missed twenty days of work in her eighth month of pregnancy, drawing on her accumulated sick leave. Her supervisor, Bob White, had become increasingly concerned over her absences because he relied heavily on her in his understaffed department. Bob felt that her absences affected her overall performance on the job, and her annual performance evaluation, given in her sixth month of pregnancy, was significantly lower than last year's.

When Candy was in her eighth month of pregnancy, her doctor ordered constant bed rest for her. Candy submitted the medical certification forms and took four weeks of leave under the Family and Medical Leave Act (FMLA). Her recovery from the birth has taken an additional four weeks. John has now requested leave under the FMLA to care for Benjamin while Candy recovers.

Questions

1. Was Candy's supervisor correct in lowering her performance appraisal because of her numerous absences during her pregnancy?
2. How much FMLA leave is John entitled to? What are the qualifications for taking leave under the FMLA?
3. When Candy returns to work, her original job is no longer available, and she is placed on a different shift in a similar job with the same salary and benefits as before. Candy challenges this decision as a failure to meet the job restoration requirements of FMLA. Is she correct?

5. FLEXTIME

The State Department of Transportation (DOT) is a large agency with fifteen hundred employees. It has experienced consistent growth over the past ten years as it responds to the numerous new mandates given to it by the state legislature. With the exception of its clerical and secretarial employees, the DOT featured a predominantly male workforce. The agency's growth has resulted in the hiring of many new female engineers. All fifteen hundred employees traditionally have worked a Monday through Friday workweek, from 8:00 A.M. to 5:00 P.M.

Recently the agency has found it increasingly challenging to fill its open positions with qualified employees. Equally troubling has been the persistent loss of employees to higher-paying private sector firms, a problem that has been especially pronounced in high-technology positions. A governor's task force on recruitment and retention of high-tech employees has just published a report recommending that retention of high-tech employees become a critical priority for state agencies. As a result, the DOT director has issued a memorandum directing managers to implement several new initiatives aimed at retaining employees, including flexible scheduling and an educational incentive program to allow employees to pursue further education in high technology. The memo directs managers to allow flexible scheduling if it would further the agency's goals of retaining quality employees. Because of staff shortages in the HRM department, the agency's personnel manual does not yet reflect these several policy changes.

Mike, the manager of the Division of Information Technology in the DOT, is trained as a software engineer but has been in his management position for two years. Other than several workshops sponsored by the agency, though, he has received no formal management training. His group of eight employees has primary responsibility for developing and maintaining software applications used throughout the agency and across the state at DOT field offices. Turnover has been high in his division, as several employees have left for higher-paying jobs with private software companies. The group is currently comprised of four software engineers and four programmers. The engineers all have B.S. degrees in engineering, and the four programmers are each working on a second bachelor's degree in computer information systems under the state's educational incentive program.

Three of the four programmers have requested flexible scheduling for the upcoming fall semester in order to attend a required course at the local university. Mike has approved a 6 A.M. to 3 P.M. schedule for Tuesdays and Thursdays to accommodate their course work. Last week, two of the four software engineers also submitted requests for flextime. Bill, who has joint custody of his two children, would like to work four ten-hour days in order to spend Fridays with his sons. Sally would like to work 6 A.M. to 3 P.M. Monday through Friday in order to meet her young child at the school bus each day.

Yesterday Mike received an e-mail from Bill voicing his concern that if the programmers received flextime and he did not, he would be penalized for already having the appropriate degree in hand. Bill made it clear that if Mike did not grant his flextime request, he would go over his head to the assistant director of the agency. The e-mail ended by reminding Mike that one of the recently departed employees had cited the need to work closer to her children as a reason for taking a job at a private company. As he deleted Bill's e-mail, Mike remembered that he had to meet with his own boss next week to give an update on his efforts to retain high-tech employees.

Questions

1. Mike allowed the programmers to have flexible scheduling because their course work seemed job-related to him. He knows that most of the employees have children. Should he grant flextime to the two parents who have requested it on this basis alone?

2. How should Mike weigh out the need to cover the core customer service hours of 8 A.M. to 5 P.M. with employee requests for flexible scheduling?

3. What will Mike say to his boss next week about his retention efforts?

4. What recommendations would you make for the development of the personnel manual's treatment of flexible scheduling?

6. GOVERNOR PAT RONAGE'S HIRING FREEZE

As the state personnel director, you have been invited to a cabinet meeting with the governor and all department heads. Governor Pat Ronage was recently elected to her first term in a bitter political campaign. You have heard rumors that she is out for revenge on her political enemies and is not particularly concerned that it could affect the state's merit system. Protections against political patronage were implemented several years ago, and the current workforce has been hired, promoted, and disciplined generally on their merits, not on the basis of political affiliation.

Just after entering the meeting room, Governor Ronage warmly greets you and asks you to sit next to her as she begins the meeting. "My thanks to all of you for coming on short notice. As you are all aware, the state is undergoing some difficult economic times that will require us to tighten our belts and be especially careful with the taxpayers' money. As a result of the hard times, I am proposing several steps to address the situation. First, I want each of the department heads to submit budgets reflecting four levels of budget allocation: 1 percent increase, no increase, 1 percent decrease, and 3 percent decrease. Second, I want to move additional funds into the Department of Economic Development, and finally, by executive order I am implementing a hiring freeze. I have asked the attorney general to prepare the executive order. I want your advice, suggestions, and

Source: This case is based on *Rutan v. Republican Party of Illinois*, 497 U.S. 62, 110 S. Ct. 2729, 111 L. Ed. 2d 52 (1990).

proposals on implementing these three steps in writing within thirty days. Thank you."

Governor Ronage then gives you a copy of the executive order and says, "I would like to hear your comments on this within the hour in my office. I want to go public with it by this afternoon." The executive order says:

> State employees with relevant authority are hereby prohibited from hiring any employee, filling any vacancy, creating any new position, or taking any similar action until specifically authorized in writing by the Governor. No exceptions to this order are permitted without the Governor's express permission after submission of appropriate requests to the Office of the Governor. This Order applies to every state agency, bureau, board, or commission subject to the control of the Governor.

On the way back to your office, Joe Merritt, the state education superintendent (and a political rival of Governor Ronage), stops you and says, "You're not going along with this are you? Ronage just wants to use this as an excuse to hire and promote her political cronies. This isn't budget cutting. This is the victor going after the spoils."

After returning to your office, several questions occur to you. Prepare a memorandum to the Governor that addresses each issue.

Questions

1. Could this executive order be used to circumvent the state merit system by allowing the Governor to hire and promote her political friends? How?
2. If the Governor does use this situation to hire and promote her political friends, is that a problem? Does it violate any constitutional protections?
3. Are there legitimate government interests served in allowing the Governor to select the employees she wants hired or promoted? Would this make government more effective or efficient?

4. Should all employees be affected by political employment decisions or just a certain few? Which ones?

7. HELPING HANDS

Helping Hands is a nonprofit organization established to respond to the needs of the Green Valley neighborhood in the south central area of Newburg. In 1971, Helping Hands began as a small collection of volunteers who organized to provide weekly meals to housebound senior citizens in the neighborhood. Over the course of several years, with hundreds of volunteers and thousands of benefiting residents, Helping Hands has grown to a full-time staff of 7, a seasonal part-time staff of 70 or so, and a cadre of more than 150 volunteers. An 11-member directing board oversees Helping Hands community programs, which range from an expanded version of the original meals program to activities for youth.

Helping Hands has initiated several short-term programs over the years, dabbling with literacy, community corrections, parenting classes, a medical and dental clinic, and even a mobile kindergarten class. Nevertheless, the board, staff, and volunteers consider three programs to be the core of Helping Hands, reflective of community need and the organization's central mission: Meals for Seniors, KidsCare, and NewStart. All three are fairly stable in terms of funding and community support. Funding sources range from federal and state grants and contracts to local initiatives for contract support in Newburg. An overview of the Helping Hands programs is detailed below.

Meals for Seniors provides between 67 and 153 meals daily (participants vary seasonally) to seniors in the neighborhood service area of Green Valley. No one is turned away. Qualifying criteria vary, but generally service is provided to elderly, low-income residents in the community. Although the program was designed for senior citizens, a number of nonseniors who are housebound for medical reasons also participate in the program.

The annual budget, excluding personnel costs, was $21,900 last year. The de facto project director, Janie Martin, anticipates a 13 percent increase in participants this year. Funding sources range from federal and state grants to a line item in Newburg's municipal budget. There is substantial community support as well with individual and corporate donations.

KidsCare provides after-school and summer programming for two elementary schools (P.S. 104 and St. James Charter). At peak, in the summer term, 857 children participated daily in the program. During the school year, an average of 253 children attend the after-school program each day. The annual budget for last year, excluding personnel costs, was $255,000. The de facto project director, Jack Libby, anticipates a 17 percent increase in participants at P.S. 104 and St. James Charter this year. The project director also reports that St. Andrew's School for Boys has approached Helping Hands about adding a site there within eighteen months. Revenue is generated by a sliding-fee scale for families and contracts with Children's Protective Services in Newburg. In addition, the University of Newburg works closely with Helping Hands through an in-service practicum opportunity for students majoring in elementary education and early childhood development.

NewStart provides victims of domestic violence (women and children) shelter and support in a holistic program designed to help these individuals and families emotionally, economically, and physically. Services encompass personal counseling, job skill assessment and training, housing, and human service referrals. Program capacity is limited to thirty women (with up to five children each) for a ninety-day transitional program and a six-month follow-up. The current waiting list has 147 applicants. The annual budget, excluding personnel, is $1,095,000. This program is supported through several contracts with the Department of Health and Human Services. Additional support is generated through corporate and individual donations (services, cash, and goods), and foundation grants. Beth Small and Marie Zaragiosa share leadership for this program.

Jesse Dexter, the new Executive Director, is preparing for his first Helping Hands board meeting. He joined the organization after the retirement of Sasha Kiser, one of the several founding volunteers who became the Executive Director in 1975. She is a charismatic, tenacious, and forthright person who single-handedly focused public attention on community issues in the Green Valley neighborhood. Her retirement has been a shock to the organization.

Much of the growth and reported success of Helping Hands was reportedly due to her long-standing relationships with administrators in state and local human service agencies and her friendships with board members of several foundations. Ms. Kiser personally selected the staff, many of whom had first volunteered with Helping Hands over the years. Jesse is no exception. He met Ms. Kiser when she made a presentation at one of his M.P.A. classes. In 1988, Jesse held an internship with Helping Hands and continued to keep in touch with Ms. Kiser after he completed his M.P.A. While working in various public sector and nonprofit organizations over the next ten years, Jesse developed an impressive reputation for program development and management. When Ms. Kiser decided to retire, she called Jesse and offered him the job. As usual, the board approved her decision with little discussion at the next meeting. Announcing that everything was in good hands, Ms. Kiser left two weeks later for her first vacation in twenty-five years—a three-month tour of the Mediterranean.

In the short time that he has been Executive Director, Jesse has discovered a great deal about Helping Hands. For example, much of the administration is quite inconsistent with good management practice in nonprofit organizations. This is disturbing for a nonprofit that administers five state contracts and fourteen different state, federal, and foundation grants. As he prepares for the board meeting, Jesse quickly glances over the list that he has developed:

- No formal strategic plan exists, although one is referenced in three of the grant applications submitted the previous year.
- No centralized, written policies and procedures exist to guide budgeting, hiring, discipline, volunteer management, or employee leave. Guidelines have been given in memoranda from Ms. Kiser to address specific situations. These memoranda are in the possession of individual employees and supervisors and do not appear to reflect general practice; rather, they are merely instructions for particular circumstances.
- There is no formal compensation system. Salary and wage decisions have been made on an individual basis for all employees. Generally, employees do not have health or dental insurance, but they do receive a variety of nonmonetary benefits awarded by Ms. Kiser through memos according to merit or need (e.g., computer access or leave). Currently, Dexter is the only employee of Helping Hands with medical and dental insurance.
- There are no position descriptions.
- There is no organizational chart. The authority structure appears to be based on seniority with very little daily supervision. For the most part, everyone just does what they believe they are supposed to do. Apparently Ms. Kiser would occasionally adjust activities or responsibilities, but this was fluid and handled informally. Management of volunteers was left to the staff handling a particular program.
- No records were kept to document training and certification for staff or volunteers. This includes the first aid certification required for the KidsCare program and the nutritional and diabetes management training in the Meals for Seniors program.
- No centralized personnel records exist covering such matters as certification, education levels, training, resumés, or salary history.
- There is no formal risk management program or liability insurance for the board, staff, or volunteers.

Dexter sighs, wishing that this was simply a rather nasty case study from an M.P.A. seminar. Unfortunately, he knows that these problems are symptoms of a nonprofit organization that has expanded rapidly in partnership with public agencies. Nonprofit organizations with some success in addressing community needs can often leverage this success to acquire additional contracts and increase their resource base.

Despite the internal chaos, Helping Hands continues to receive many opportunities. Reputations matter in the funding world, and Helping Hands is well respected. Dexter has recently been approached by the local police department and the director of the policy center at Newburg University to partner on a community outreach grant for at-risk youth. In the meantime, reports are due on two of the federal grants, and it does not appear that anyone has been collecting the necessary data on the programs involved. In fact, it is pretty difficult to figure out who has responsibilities for many of the administrative tasks that require attention. Ms. Kiser did not believe in job titles or position descriptions, which she thought might "limit a person's potential." Dexter smiles ruefully, remembering her favorite saying: "People who care always know what needs doing." Grabbing his notepad, Dexter begins to make notes for his board presentation.

Task 1

Divide the class into two groups. One group will consider themselves to be the Board of Directors and will elect the appropriate leadership (board chair, treasurer, secretary). The other group will be the staff (with one student designated as the Executive Director). (Descriptions of the Board of Directors and staff are contained in the boxes.) Each group independently will decide how to address the problem of succession planning in the future with and without a strategic plan. Both groups must then (using a formal board meeting as the setting) convince the other of the best course of action.

Full-Time Helping Hands Staff

Dexter Jesse. M.P.A. Interned with Helping Hands in 1988 and recently rejoined Helping Hands as the Executive Director. Annual salary: $63,000 plus health and dental insurance, five-week annual vacation, a personal laptop computer, and professional association memberships paid by the organization.

Janie Martin. B.A. in literature. Began with Helping Hands as a volunteer in 1973. Now leads the Meals for Seniors program; works with no other staff members; supervises approximately twenty-three volunteers. Annual salary: $24,000 plus vacation, leave at her discretion, a personal laptop computer, and an automobile for her exclusive use.

Jack Libby. Ed.D. in early childhood development. Hired at the inception of KidsCare. Works with Elisa and Pat and supervises approximately 111 volunteers and 65 part-time and temporary staff. Annual salary: $38,000 plus two weeks of annual vacation, a personal laptop computer, and professional association memberships.

Beth Small. High school diploma. Began with Helping Hands as a volunteer after a brief stay at NewStart. Works with Elisa and Pat and, with Marie, jointly supervises approximately sixteen volunteers and five part-time or temporary staff. Annual salary: $20,000 plus leave at her discretion and free child care through KidsCare.

Marie Zaragiosa. B.S. in finance and some graduate work in accounting. Hired three years ago in response to concerns about the status of financial statements. Works with Elisa and Pat and jointly supervises with Beth approximately sixteen volunteers and five part-time and temporary staff. Annual salary: $25,000 plus leave at her discretion, with expenses for graduate coursework reimbursed by Helping Hands.

Elisa Gandiaga. M.A. in communication. Began with Helping Hands during an internship in 1995. Divides her time between KidsCare and NewStart as needed. Annual salary: $28,000, two weeks of annual vacation, a personal laptop computer, and professional association memberships.

Pat Nucoliso. M.A. in political science. Began with Helping Hands as a volunteer in 1989. Divides her time between KidsCare and NewStart as needed. Annual salary: $33,000 plus leave at her discretion.

Helping Hands Board of Directors

Steven Dubin, Chair; attorney, member since 1974

Daniel Roboiselli, Vice-Chair; business owner, member since 1980

Angela Gandiaga, Secretary; realtor, member since 1993

John Wrightman, Treasurer; banker, member since 1976

Erin Kinley; doctor, member since 1993

Sara Denise; teacher, member since 1997

Bo Ellison; counselor, member since 1988

Devon Maischefko; attorney, member since 1991

Andrew Guiterrez; assistant to the mayor, member since 1999

Tom Sullivan; attorney, member since 1978

Ethan Webb; social activist, member since 1971

Task 2

Answer the following questions:

1. If you were charged with developing position descriptions and a classification system, how would you proceed?
2. Outline a rudimentary classification system using the information provided in the case about the general job responsibilities and skills of the staff. What problems can you identify as you begin?

Task 3

Assume that you are a board member for Helping Hands. After the Executive Director reviews the current state of the organization, he asks for board members to volunteer to chair different committees to address some of the deficiencies in Helping Hands. You volunteer to consider performance. Develop a system to assess organizational and individual performance. How would you proceed? What other types of information might you require? Who else should be involved?

Task 4

Answer the following questions.

1. What policies should the Executive Director consider developing for Helping Hands?
2. What are the implications of having no policies in place in terms of (a) liability and (b) employee performance?

8. LIBERTY POLICE DEPARTMENT

Liberty is a small city located in a scenic and temperate valley in the Midwest. For decades, the community was relatively stable in terms of population influx and economic indicators. Historically, the city's economy was based on agriculture, supporting service industries, and some light manufacturing. Education levels were fairly high, and the community favored a rather conservative approach to the role of government in most policy arenas. There appeared to be a high degree of civic engagement, evidenced by comparatively high voter turnouts, relatively high levels of participation in organized religion, and active participation in community activities and associations. Social and physical disorder was minimal. Neighborhoods were generally well maintained across the city. Social scientists indicated that this community evidenced a high degree of respect for law enforcement and demonstrated consensus about community priorities. Liberty was ethnically homogeneous. Most of the residents were born in either Liberty or the region. Police department personnel were quite representative of the community, and policing practices were consistent with community expectations. Crime was low compared to cities across the United States.

In the late 1970s, however, Liberty began to experience some dramatic population and economic growth. Demands on the public infrastructure (roads, utilities, schools, parks) grew in response to the increase in population and economic boom. More and more people moved to Liberty to participate in a growing economy and to enjoy the many amenities available in the region. The economic base expanded to include a variety of facilities devoted to technology development and production. Variation in ethnicity, education levels, and income levels grew along with the population explosion. As the demand for housing grew, the traditionally rural character of the community began to change. Subdivisions covered farmland throughout the county. The city's perimeter began to expand with annexation. New issues surfaced in municipal elections, reflecting a changing political context for the region. Political decision making demonstrated a shift in emphasis from rural to urban concerns. Letters to the editor in the local newspaper began to contain references to the erosion of Liberty values because of the arrival of so many newcomers.

The police department tried to respond to this changing community within the constraints placed on them by a limited budget and existing personnel. Crime rates did not change dramatically, but public safety experts indicated that the type of crime occurring was changing. The police department was responding to increasingly threatening situations. The newspaper published a series of stories suggesting heightened gang activity and criminal activity related to drug commerce. The city council authorized an expansion in force from 132 to 150 officers and a demand for some version of community-oriented policing. As one council member put it, "Buy some bikes and horses. It works in Chicago."

Stories charging police officers with bigotry and abuse began to filter through coffee shops and office hallways. Citizen groups called for more access to information about the police department. Within a two-month period, three critical incidents—two officer-involved shootings and a car accident during a pursuit—divided an already panicky community. The local newspaper, *Liberty Times,* began a series of editorials noting the growing demands on the department's limited resources and public perceptions that the department no longer represented its community.

As you put the newspaper down after reading the latest diatribe, a former classmate from your M.P.A. program pokes his head into your office and asks, "Do you have a minute . . . or an hour?" You welcome the police chief into your office. As director of human resources, you have seen less of your old friend since many of the recruitment, selection, and disciplinary responsibilities were decentralized to city departments.

The chief wastes no time: "Did you see the paper? Well—wait until tomorrow! I was just notified that four female recruits filed an appeal at the Police Training Academy alleging improper treatment based on gender. I am not sure how best to proceed." Before you can comment on the policies and procedures that have been established to address this situation, the chief continues in a resigned monotone:

We have not yet hired the additional eighteen officers that the council authorized last month. It takes approximately eighteen months from the announcement to bring someone on board. According to city guidelines, the advertisement must run for thirty days. Then we have to do a preliminary review of the applications through your office for affirmative action and minimum qualifications like the new requirement for a bachelor's degree or evidence of progress toward that degree—assume three weeks for that check. Background checks of the remaining applicant pool will take another four months because I'm understaffed and can't pull any more detectives to run the checks. By this time, of the 150 or so initial applications, we may have 80 applicants left to screen; after five months, they may have found other positions and so are no longer interested. Callbacks and interview scheduling require another two weeks, and if we are lucky, we will have interviews with 40 or so candidates to select for the eighteen positions. Interviews and testing will take another two to three weeks or so. In the last contract the fraternal order negotiated selection representation for sworn staff. Selection may take another two weeks. After that, if they don't have three years of law enforcement experience, they will need to attend the police academy for sixteen weeks. Remember also that policy requires a six-month probationary period in which new officers must be partnered with a senior patrol officer.

Furthermore, we aren't even talking about the council's decision not to authorize additional support personnel for research, administration, and technology. I may have more sworn officers, but the demands for data management, network and web support, reporting, the new administrative requirements from the human resource decentralization last year, and basic clerical and administrative support continue to grow.

Worse, I may be losing one of my best technology people. He lives outside town and just notified me that he will need to take care of his parents and will not be able to handle the commute and his personal responsibilities. My other tech expert just received an offer from the private sector at twice her present salary.

As you sit there taking all of this in, the police chief continues to unload his problems:

We have the diversity goals, but I still have a department with some very lopsided demographics. Eighty percent of my civilian staff are women, and they are concentrated in the clerical positions rather than in the technical or research slots. Only 10 percent of my patrol personnel are female, and less than 3 percent of investigative positions are held by women.

I'm seeing some of the same representation problems when I consider ethnicity and race. Unfortunately, because of past practices in hiring—they were legal but highly discriminatory if you ask me—most of these employees are fairly recent hires, which places them at the lowest end of the salary scale. Many of these officers and detectives have been hired within the past three years. Although they tend to have proportionally higher educational levels, with graduate and bachelor's degrees, they are easily the lowest-paid sworn personnel because of our classification and compensation system.

We are facing a real crunch in staffing. I have approximately 130 civilian staff in addition to sworn personnel. Almost 17 percent of the department's personnel will be eligible for retirement within the next five years. We also are seeing some problems with retention. Many of our newer officers are leaving after two or three years to better-paying jobs in larger cities or are moving to the state and federal level. Jobs are plentiful, and we are even losing clerical civilian personnel to the private sector.

In addition, we have a severe skills gap for personnel. Many of our employees are simply not comfortable using the paperless system that was initiated last year. Although some of the concern stems from a general deficit in computer and network skills, other problems are drawn from the new on-line financial management system. Also, we are not able to obtain the same reporting for response time and calls for service from the computer-aided dispatch system operated by the county.

You open your mouth to start to respond, but he is not finished yet:

The city planner just warned me that we have another subdivision on the horizon. They knew this was coming a year ago, and I am just now hearing about a new 250-home development in a multiple use zone. Our impact statement is due tomorrow, and I do not have the personnel or the time to assess the effects of this new development on our jurisdiction properly.

Three of the grants that we wrote last year were awarded, which will result in the addition of five new community-oriented policing programs. We have these little programs scattered all over the city, and the personnel associated with them are project-specific, so the reporting relationship with my captains and lieutenants is very confusing. In most cases, we receive word that the grant was funded and then have to put the program together immediately. In some cases, we were simply going after the grant money because of a new request for proposal but really hadn't considered what we would do to implement the grant-funded programs within our existing structure and facilities.

We will have to contract with two of the neighborhood nonprofit organizations, the Neighborhood Alliance and Citizens Against Drugs, on the mayor's new domestic violence initiative. I don't have any personnel with the skills to write or administer these contracts. And . . .

Before the chief can continue, you finally get a word in: "I get the picture! It is a good thing that we have M.P.A. degrees. Now, let's see. Where should we start?"

Task

1. Perform a SWOT (strengths, weaknesses, opportunities, and threats) analysis.
   a. Review the process for strategic planning outlined in Chapter 6. Determine who or what would comprise the internal environment facing the Liberty Police

Department. Briefly outline this environment using the categories of strengths, weaknesses, opportunities, and threats.

b. Determine who or what would comprise the external environment facing the Liberty Police Department. Briefly outline this environment using the SWOT categories.

2. Identify participants and stakeholders
   a. Who should participate in the planning process? Why?
   b. What role should the human resource department play? Why?
   c. How might citizen demands shape the planning process?

3. Evaluate the big picture:
   a. How can pivotal events catalyze or control planning in this case?
   b. What might occur if the Liberty Police Department does not plan strategically?

9. NEGOTIATOR'S DILEMMA

Negotiations with the police and firefighters' unions have been tough this year. The city is taking a hard line, insisting that there is no extra money in the budget and in fact can barely squeak out enough to cover the cost-of-living increase. The city's negotiator says the city respects the firefighters and wants to help them but is having trouble finding a way to do it.

Union elections for the firefighters are coming up next month, and the person running against you for union president, a position you have held for one term, is a hard-line radical who wants to "bash" management. If he is elected, he will destroy everything you have worked for over the past four years. Better relations with management, open information, inclusion in all the meetings with department brass, and monthly meetings with the Mayor and City Council President to discuss the needs of union members are among your accomplishments. You have got a lot done, but what the firefighters' union members really want is the big raise they came to expect

from the prenegotiation meetings held in every fire station across the city.

The city negotiator just telephoned you and wants to meet with your team in half an hour. She said that simultaneous contract negotiations with the police have been going badly, and the mayor says he wants to "stick it to them." If you would agree to a 2 percent raise instead of holding out for 5 percent, she could settle with the police union for 2 percent. In return, she would guarantee an additional 2 percent be placed in deferred compensation for firefighters (but you have to keep this quiet because he would not do the same for police), and she would help you get reelected as union president. But if you continue to hold out for 4 percent, along with the police, she will continue her hard line, and the best you could hope for would be 2.5 to 3.0 percent.

You like the city's negotiator, but you're not sure you can trust her completely; she may have offered the same deal to the police union. If the police make a deal before you, you will have to settle for 2 percent and not get anything more. You decide to talk it over with your team, then meet with the city's negotiation team to work out some sort of a deal.

Question

1. What would you do? Why?

10. A QUANDARY OVER ACCEPTING THE JOB

Finding a job in city management has been more difficult than Dan Jacobsen thought it would be. As one of the top graduates in his M.P.A. class, it did not seem that finding a job as an assistant city manager or possibly a deputy department head would be so difficult. Dan has been scouring the country but would like to find something relatively close to home.

After submitting over a dozen applications, he received calls for five interviews. He just missed getting the first three jobs: an assistant city manager, a personnel director, and a public information officer for a state agency. (Those hiring for the first two positions were hoping for someone with more experience, and the last one wanted someone from that state.) Dan's next interview is for a city administrator job in Wheatly, a small town just a couple of hours from home. He had not expected to find a city administrator job so soon after graduate school, so the idea sounds exciting. Dan put off the fifth interview for a sanitation supervisor in a large city (where Dan's uncle works in personnel) until he sees how the interview in Wheatly goes.

The interview began well. He met briefly with the mayor, John Carpenter, a warm and friendly man. Dan thought that the mayor liked him. Then they both went to meet with city council members for the main interview. Time passed quickly as two of the council members asked questions, and the others, including the mayor, listened quietly. One of the questioning council members, Glen Farr, was a large man who identified himself as "just a farm boy." The other questioner, Kammie Hunter, said she had gone to the same university from which Dan had just graduated.

Oddly, no one asked Dan much about his education or the little experience he had. Hunter tried to ask some serious questions, but Farr kept talking. Early on, Farr said, "Your football team has done really well this year. I think that's a real good university. I'm sure you'll do well here." Dan noted the angry glances Hunter made at Farr when he said things like that.

Near the end of the interview, Farr asked Dan if he was married. Dan looked at the mayor and Hunter, who just rolled her eyes and shook her head. Before he could answer, Farr plowed ahead: "That's okay. We've got a lot of good Christian girls around here." Then he laughed loudly, and the mayor could not contain a chuckle. With that, Hunter interrupted and apologized for Farr's remarks, then ended the interview, saying they would get back to Dan in a few days.

As he drove home, Dan thought about the interview and wondered whether he should have

said something about the questions being asked. He was sure he had done well, but he did not really know since there had not been many questions he could use to demonstrate his knowledge or set out what he could do for the town. Most of all, he was concerned about the remark about marriage and "good Christian girls." Dan was not particularly active in his synagogue, but he nevertheless thought the comments were insensitive. He decided to call the mayor in the morning and discuss his thoughts.

Questions

1. What would you say to the mayor if you were Dan?
2. What went wrong with Dan's interview in Wheatly?
3. How could this situation have been prevented?
4. If you were the human resource manager, how would you advise the mayor and council to conduct an interview for a city administrator position?

11. RADICALS IN THE RANK-AND-FILE

You have just walked into the office to begin your first day as the director of human resource management in Bestview. During your interview, Mayor Sienkowicz, council members Cloran and Nickers, and the city manager, Dirk Liu, had cautioned you about the "radical element" in the "rank-and-file." They told you that "everything runs pretty smoothly around here. It's a good group of employees except for a couple of rabble-rousers who are trying to stir things up. That Lori-Ann Wyman is always raising something." At that time, you smiled politely and murmured a neutral, "Thanks. I'll keep that in mind."

Now you reflect on your conversation. Wyman's name seems familiar, but you can't quite place it. Then just as you recall the LoriAnn Wyman with whom you took a few classes during your M.P.A. program, the door to your office bangs open. Mayor Sienkowicz bursts into the room holding the local newspaper: "You better read this. She is at it again!" Your assistant chooses that moment to step in with the announcement that "Davis Smith, a reporter with the *Tribune,* is on line 1. He wants written comment on the union's study, but you may want to read this first." Your assistant holds out a memorandum neatly addressed to you from that "radical element": LoriAnn Wyman, president of the police union.

> Recent studies commissioned by the police union suggest that existing job analysis and classification schemes are fraught with the values and biases of the managers and human resource specialists who developed them. Because many consider certain conditions to be "the way things are here," there is no opportunity to challenge assumptions that would be considered archaic and obsolete in an objective assessment of a particular organization's classification structure. Position analysis and job evaluation in many organizations are simply mechanisms that contribute to inequities in compensation and promotional opportunity.
>
> According to the latest human resource statistics for the Bestview Police Department (enclosed), workforce demographics suggest a distressing pattern of gender and ethnic mar-

ginalization in the police department. This is unfortunate since the City of Bestview prides itself on the diversification of the workforce to reflect city demographics. Although overall demographic percentages for the department appear to be consistent with municipal goals, a more detailed analysis that considers the division between sworn and civilian personnel as well as the assignment of supervisory responsibilities suggests a more troubling picture.

In preparation for future efforts to address conditions faced by the employees in the Bestview Police Department and other municipal departments, we are joining with other municipal unions to request your action. In conjunction with our colleagues in the Clerical Workers Association, the Recreation Specialists Association, and the Educational Professionals Association, we request a formal review of the human resource management system in the City of Bestview.

Police Dispatch

The position provides public safety and operational radio communications by performing a variety of duties requiring operation of telecommunications equipment. Incumbents either operate or supervise employees who operate multifrequency/channel radio systems, law enforcement telecommunications terminals, computer terminals, and associated equipment; respond to telephone hot-line circuits; dispatch mobile law enforcement and emergency response units to specified points as required; identify locations where assistance is required, determine the availability and location of departmental units, and dispatch units by radio; request emergency services as requested or required by field personnel; respond to other law enforcement and emergency response agencies, dispatching departmental units for response as necessary; act as incident coordinators, tracking and responding to emergency response calls; access data related to

Source: With very minor revision to fit the material to this case study, the position descriptions were drawn from the California State Personnel Board on June 9, 2000, at 10:33 A.M. The salary ranges are artificial, generated for the purpose of discussion. The dispatch position description is from California State Personnel Board Series Specification for Communications Operator, April 1, 1995. The basic text used for the sample position of dispatcher was drawn from **http://www.dpa.ca.gov/textdocs/specs/s1/s1670.txt.** The police officer position description is from California State Personnel Board Series Specification for California Police, established July 13, 1972. The basic text used for the sample position of police officer was drawn from **www.dpa.ca.gov/textdocs/specs/s1/s1945.txt** on June 9, 2000, at 10:33 A.M. The position description for a secretary is from California State Personnel Board Series Specification for Secretary, June 8, 1977. The basic text used for the sample position of secretary was drawn from **http://www.dpa.ca.gov/textdocs/specs/s1/s1176.txt.**

Bestview Police Department Demographic Summary

	Sworn and Civilian Overall Demographic	Sworn and Civilian Management Responsibility	
		Supervisory	Nonsupervisory
Gender			
Female	56	4	52
Male	97	30	67
Ethnicity			
African American	14	1	13
Anglo/Caucasian	99	28	71
Asian American	2	0	2
Hispanic/Latino	32	4	28
Native American	6	1	5

Department personnel totals 153 employees.

Percentage distribute by demographic category:

36.6 percent female

63.4 percent male

9.2 percent African American; 64.7 percent Anglo/Caucasian

1.3 percent Asian American; 20.9 percent Hispanic/Latino

3.9 percent Native American

Bestview Police Department Sworn Demographic Summary

	Sworn by Divisions		Sworn by Management Responsibility	
	Patrol	Investigations	Supervisory	Nonsupervisory
Gender				
Female	11	1	0	12
Male	73	22	28	67
Ethnicity				
African American	11	0	1	10
Anglo/Caucasian	63	19	23	59
Asian American	2	0	0	2
Hispanic/Latino	8	3	3	8
Native American	0	1	1	0
Total (107 sworn employees)	84	23	28	79

Supervisory sworn personnel include the chief, three captains, six lieutenants, six sergeants, and twelve corporals.
Nine of the twelve female sworn personnel are designated as community policing officers, bike patrol, or school resource officers. The female investigator is assigned exclusively to child abuse.

Bestview Police Department Civilian Demographic Summary

	Civilian by Classification Status		Civilian by Management Responsibility	
	Clerical	Professional	Supervisory	Nonsupervisory
Gender				
Female	44	0	4	40
Male	0	2	2	0
Ethnicity				
African American	3	0	0	3
Anglo/Caucasian	15	2	5	12
Asian American	0	0	0	0
Hispanic/Latino	21	0	1	20
Native American	5	0	0	5
Total (46 civilian employees)	44	2	6	40

All but one of the civilian supervisory personnel are located in dispatch.
Computer support is contracted with the city; these personnel are not considered employees of the police department.
All but four of the civilian employees use either the dispatch position description or the secretary/assistant descriptions. The remaining four employees are grant funded, and the chief has decided that temporary positions do not require a position description.
The average salary for all civilian staff is $22,332. The salary for one of the men is $41,811 and for the other is $39,779.

warrants, driver licenses, vehicle and vessel registrations, hazardous materials, weapons, stolen property, and criminal history information through the State Law Enforcement Telecommunications System; access data on other law enforcement records' databases; maintain required logs; answer telephone inquiries and provide information; and perform other related duties.

This is the entry, working, and journey level for this series. Employees work under general supervision in a Communications Center following established policies and procedures in order to perform a variety of duties. Duties include operating multifrequency/channel radio telephone systems and computer-aided transmitting and receiving equipment to receive calls from field units, telephones, or other sources; filling out dispatch logs or typing entries into computer terminals; receiving and transmitting reports of incidents and requests for assistance; answering telephone requests

for information; relaying calls for emergency services vehicles, other law enforcement agencies, or other assistance requested by field units. At the full journey level, employees work under direction and perform all of the above and select receivers and transmitters and adjust volume controls; dispatch units or other equipment to specific points as required; provide information as requested or required by officers in the field; and act as a lead person.

Factors Affecting Position Allocation
None.

Knowledge and Abilities
Knowledge of alphanumeric sequences. Ability to work under stress and maintain composure; follow instructions precisely; listen and translate what is heard into the appropriate action; speak English over the telephone quickly and be easily understood; adapt quickly to a variety of situations; act in an emergency situ-

ation; write rapidly and legibly; perform several functions simultaneously; hear in the presence of significant background noise; read and comprehend at the level required for the job; determine officer's welfare from voice inflection; establish priorities and take appropriate action; extract critical information from incoming calls; recall a variety of situations and retain information; anticipate the officer's need for assistance; type; operate and monitor a wide range of frequencies and a variety of highly technical communication systems and equipment.

Special Personal Characteristics/ Physical Requirements/Experience or Education

Consistently report to work with a minimum of absences; willingness to work on Saturdays, Sundays, and holidays at odd or irregular hours and night shifts; voice well modulated for radio transmission and clear enunciation; emotional stability; hearing necessary to perform the duties of the position; and a satisfactory record as a law-abiding citizen. Existing law requires that a thorough background investigation shall be conducted to verify the absence of past behavior indicative of unsuitability to perform public safety dispatcher duties. The background investigation shall include a check of Department of Motor Vehicles' records, and a search of local, State, and national criminal history files to disclose any criminal record. Persons unsuccessful in the investigation cannot be appointed as Dispatcher. Existing law requires that a medical examination shall be conducted to verify the absence of any medical condition that would preclude the safe and efficient performance of dispatcher duties. Persons unsuccessful in the medical exam cannot be appointed Dispatcher. Penal Code Section 13510(c) requires that agencies participating in the P.O.S.T. [Peace Officer Standards and Testing] program shall evaluate oral communication skills to ensure skill levels commen-

surate with the satisfactory performance of dispatch duties. Penal Code Section 13510(c) requires that agencies participating in the P.O.S.T. program shall require that the P.O.S.T. Public Safety Dispatcher's Basic Course be the minimum basic training for all public safety dispatchers in the State. The course shall be completed within 12 months of hire or assignment to dispatcher duties. Failure to successfully complete the course shall be cause for termination based on failure to meet the required conditions of employment. Education equivalent to completion of the twelfth grade and either six months of experience in the state service performing the duties of a Dispatcher-Clerk or one year of experience in dispatching work involving the operation of radio communications equipment/systems, or two years of experience involving a substantial amount of direct and telephone contact with the public and the responsibility to perform numerous tasks simultaneously.
Salary Range: $24,078–43,002

Police Officer

Police officers are primarily concerned with maintaining law and order; providing general law enforcement services and a high level of police service to city property, employees, officials, and the public. Incumbents have peace officer powers for all purposes and provide assistance under the State Emergency Services Act when acting under mutual assistance agreements with other local police or sheriff's departments. Incumbents work in one of three settings: (1) in a line enforcement assignment; (2) in a staff assignment; (3) in the Division of Investigation.

In a line enforcement assignment, incumbents supervise, or provide full law enforcement police services in marked police emergency vehicles, on foot patrol, or mounted patrol of city property under a variety of environmental and climatic conditions; enforce general laws, regulations, and court rulings; maintain public order; make arrests; serve court-issued warrants; recover evidence and provide for its safekeeping; conduct preliminary investigations and prepare written reports on law violations, burglaries, homicides, accidental deaths, thefts, accidents, bomb threats, property damage, fires, and similar matters; testify in court as required; take charge of situations in the event of emergencies or accidents; arrest law violators for felony and misdemeanor offenses; control crowds during disturbances and other assemblies; direct and control traffic; enforce parking regulations; issue traffic and misdemeanor citations; direct and give information to the public; administer first aid and cardiopulmonary resuscitation.

In a staff capacity, incumbents supervise or perform special studies; develop law enforcement and police protection plans for city officers, employees, and properties; develop and administer crime prevention, employee protection, first aid, cardiopulmonary resuscitation training; develop and administer crime prevention and employee safety inspection programs; and develop workload and budgetary information.

In the Division of Investigation, incumbents conduct criminal and specialized investigation of criminal acts occurring within their jurisdiction; gather information and evidence leading to the identity and apprehension of perpetrators of crimes; interview victims, witnesses, informants, and suspects for information to support criminal complaints; prepare affidavits in support of search and arrest warrants; prepare investigative reports, crime information, and wanted person bulletins; conduct in-depth investigations relating to the protection of the mayor; perform special studies and intelligence-gathering activities regarding public officials; analyze threats and risks to public officials; provide for the detection, removal, and disposal of explosive devices; provide special weapons and tactics support for line en-

forcement operations; provide training in specialized areas of law enforcement.

Factors Affecting Position Allocation
The difficulty and complexity of the work assignment as indicated by the scope and variety of the work performed, the problems encountered and the decisions made, control exercised over the work of others, and inherent responsibilities of the position. For supervisory positions, allocation level depends on numbers of subordinate staff and location in the organization structure. Size of required subordinate staff may be counterbalanced by remoteness of assignment and inherent requirement for independent action, or program and/or policy-setting responsibilities. Under general supervision, incumbents provide full law enforcement police protective services to officials, employees, the public, and State property. Under direction, incumbents may be assigned staff support duties performing less complex work related to training or background investigations. Incumbents shall receive P.O.S.T. Patrol initial orientation and transition training.

Knowledge and Abilities
Ability to write legibly, present ideas and information effectively, both orally and in writing; stand and walk for long periods of time; think clearly and logically and take effective action in emergencies or while under physical or mental stress; function effectively in a paramilitary setting; conduct investigations; handle firearms safely; enforce the law courteously and without unnecessary force; maintain personal composure; engage in riot control tactics; exercise self-restraint; maintain physical conditioning appropriate to the effective performance of the work; maintain cooperative relations with representatives of other law enforcement agencies; operate two- and four-wheel patrol vehicles. Apply the knowledge required for law enforcement work such as laws of arrest, the Penal Code, rules of evidence,

rights of citizens, and policies and procedures of the Bestview Police Department.

Special Personal Characteristics/ Physical Requirements/Experience or Education

Interest in law enforcement work; willingness to work all hours of the day or at night and to report for duty at any time when emergencies arise; satisfactory record as a law-abiding citizen; alertness; keenness of observation; firmness; and tact. Good health, sound physical condition, strength, endurance, agility, and hearing necessary to perform the duties of the position. Experience in police or law enforcement work and education beyond twelfth grade.

Felony Disqualification

Existing law provides that persons convicted of a felony are disqualified from employment as peace officers. Such persons are not eligible to be appointed to positions in this class.

Salary Range: $26,078–58,002

Secretary/Assistant

Incumbents screen incoming correspondence, refer to appropriate staff member for reply, and follow up to ensure that deadlines are met; arrange correspondence for administrator's personal reply in order of priority with appropriate background material attached for reference; independently or in accordance with general instructions, compose correspondence on a wide range of subjects requiring a thorough knowledge of the procedures and policies of the office; review outgoing correspondence prepared by other staff members for administrator's signature for consistency with administrative policy as well as for format, grammatical construction, and clerical error; gather and summarize data; brief reports and correspondence; attend meetings and conferences, take and/or summarize notes into minutes and distribute minutes; screen a variety of visitors and telephone calls, and where appro-

priate, refer to other staff members or personally provide authoritative information on established agency programs and policies; arrange meetings for administrator, prepare agenda, and make adjustments as necessary in scheduled meeting times; relieve the administrator of routine office details; maintain confidential and administrative files. Incumbents in a secretarial capacity receive and screen telephone calls and visitors, use considerable judgment in providing factual information in response to numerous inquiries, establish and maintain confidential and administrative files, and prepare summaries of data pertinent to the work of the supervisor or the office. The work typically requires a detailed knowledge of the programs, policies, and activities of the employing unit.

Factors Affecting Position Allocation

Relative level of difficulty, variety, complexity of duties, independence of action and decision, the degree of supervision received, and the level of the administrator to whom the secretary reports are factors used in differentiating among levels. Other factors affecting the scope of the secretary's responsibility are the willingness of the supervisor to delegate to his or her secretary, the secretary's willingness to assume delegated responsibilities, the presence of other positions that tend to dilute the secretary's responsibilities, and the limitations of clerical and administrative tasks that may be delegated to the secretary due to the technical nature of the supervisor's function.

Knowledge and Abilities

Knowledge of modern office methods, supplies, and equipment; business English and correspondence; procedures with particular reference to the work involved in public safety. Ability to read and write English at a level required for successful job performance; type at 40 words per minute; perform difficult clerical work; make clear and comprehensive reports and keep difficult records; prepare correspondence independently; communicate effectively; meet and deal tactfully with the public; direct the work of others; perform minor administrative assignments independently; handle with courtesy and tact a wide variety of public contacts both on the telephone and in person; communicate effectively; understand and carry out directions following a minimum of explanation; analyze situations accurately and take effective action.

Special Personal Characteristics/ Physical Requirements/Experience or Education

Incumbents should demonstrate two years of experience in clerical work. However, academic education above the twelfth grade may be substituted for one year of the required general experience on the basis of either (a) one year of general education being equivalent to three months of experience; or (b) one year of education of a business or commercial nature being equivalent to six months of experience. Students who are enrolled in the last semester or its equivalent of course work, which upon completion will fulfill these requirements, will be admitted to the examination, but they must submit evidence of completion before they can be considered for appointment. A demonstrated interest in assuming increasing responsibility; mature judgment; loyalty; poise; tact; and discretion. Education equivalent to completion of the twelfth grade; ability to take dictation at 110 words per minute.

Salary Range: $18,012–26,008

Questions

Consider the position descriptions for patrol officer, secretary, and dispatcher and the information attached to the memo from Officer Wyman. Given what you know about job analysis, job evaluation, and position classification, respond to the following questions.

1. Can you identify any patterns associated with gender or ethnicity?

2. What might account for disparities between genders or ethnic groups?
3. If you were the director of human resource management in Bestview, what actions should you take? What actions should be taken from a line-manager's point of view? What actions should be taken by city administrators? Why?
4. What political issues should be considered? Would your recommendations change if you had to consider the political issues?

12. SALARY COMPRESSION AT STATE UNIVERSITY

You are the department chair of a medium-sized public administration program at State University, which is located in a pleasant southwestern city known for its good quality of life. Last month the senior member of your eight-person faculty, Professor Mack, announced his retirement effective at the end of this academic year. Professor Mack is earning $50,000 at the end of his thirty years of service. During several phone conversations with colleagues at other universities, you realize that the starting salary for new assistant professors in your field is approximately $43,000. You recognize that offering a salary at that level would compress the salaries of several junior faculty members below that of the new hire. The dean has asked for your recommendation about what the starting salary should be for the new professor. She has made it clear that you should hire a new Ph.D. who is just starting out in academia.

You review the existing salary structure for your department:

Professor Ortiz	1 year experience	$35,000
Professor Oles	4 years experience	$38,000
Professor O'Leary	6 years experience	$39,000
Professor Miller	10 years experience	$42,000
Professor Gore	15 years experience	$45,000
Professor Marcell	20 years experience	$45,500
Professor Levine	20 years experience	$48,000

As the search process begins, you are visited by several members of the faculty concerned about what the salary of Professor Mack's replacement will be. Professors Oles and O'Leary are particularly concerned about a newly hired Ph.D.'s earning more than they do after several years of experience. On the other hand, you are worried that without a competitive salary, you will be unable to attract a highly qualified candidate. You consult with the former department chair, who tells you that the quality of life in State University's city makes up for low salaries and that the damage to the morale of the department would be too great to consider compressing the junior faculty's salaries. Your department is known for its faculty's ability to get along with each other, and you hesitate to harm a good working environment.

Questions

1. How does this case illustrate the tension between internal and external equity?
2. What are the possible ramifications of hiring at or below the competitive market salary?
3. How should you determine what the appropriate salary offer should be relative to the external labor market?
4. What steps would you take to determine the correct salary offer?
5. What should you tell the dean with regard to the recommended salary?

13. THE SCHEDULING SOFTWARE CASE

The Procurement Division of the Department of the Military is responsible for securing all the material goods for the state's ten military reserve divisions. Every day the procurement division's 500 employees process several thousand orders for material. This processing includes operating the division's packaging and shipping machinery as well as the initial intake processing using specially developed agency software.

Five years ago, as part of a total quality management initiative pushed by upper management, the division developed certification standards for all machine operators. An analysis of the division's work processes revealed that individual machine operators were often not qualified to operate their particular piece of equipment and concluded that the higher-than-usual accident rate in the division was due in part to this lack of appropriate training and certification. Over the next year, the HR department established a certification program that called for employees to be recertified annually, and personnel within the HR department developed a rather cumbersome software program designed to track recertification dates of employees.

The HR department of the state military department consisted of twenty-five employees at the time of this case. A series of downsizing moves had reduced the number of employees from a high of forty-two to the current twenty-five. The HR department consistently had trouble with regard to its responsibility for the recertification program. A chief problem was the high rates of turnover among its own information technology (IT) staff. Tight budget conditions made it impossible for the agency to compete with local private corporations for good IT personnel. The HR department had hired several IT recent graduates, only to have them leave for higher-paying jobs in the private sector within a few months. The remaining twenty-five employees' time was focused on legally mandated HR activities such as pension processing and equal employment opportunity (EEO) compliance. Data input and maintenance and training on the recertification program fell as a departmental priority. The most recent downsizing had resulted in the unexpected departure of the last programmer familiar with HR's tracking program for its recertification software. Within months the HR department stopped issuing reminders of recertification deadlines.

Line managers were relieved when attention to

the recertification software was eliminated, as they tended to perceive it as a hindrance to their attempts to "get the job done." They also felt strongly that they knew their workers and their abilities and resented attempts to control which workers would operate which machine.

Several HR directors had come and left the agency in the past few years. Most left after finding that line management at the procurement agency resented HR's attempts to increase their influence over the day-to-day management of employees. A series of unfavorable EEO decisions had left the HR department in the position of monitoring compliance with consent decrees ordering the increased use of minorities in management. This resulted in a lingering impression among line managers of HR as "the police."

A recent audit had revealed that many of the procurement division's machine operators were not current on their certifications. Jim Roberts, head of the procurement division's operations section, met with the agency's IT department and requested the development of scheduling software that would allow managers to view the certifications of everyone scheduled to work on their shift. The software development job was assigned to Linda James, a programmer who had been with the agency for eight years. She had begun her career with the agency in production but had moved to the IT division after completing her degree in computer information systems at the local university. In the development meetings, line managers and Roberts made it clear that they considered the program a tool to help meet the operational goals of the production side of the agency. HR was not included in the development process.

After several months of work, the IT division team that Linda James headed released the new scheduling software. When John Smith, the new director of HR came on board, he was shocked to learn that this new major software application had been developed without HR input. Smith was aware of the collapse of the recertification software originally maintained by HR and saw an opportunity to regain valuable human resource

tracking data with the scheduling software. Smith called a meeting with Roberts, James, and the IT development team to request additional features for the software to allow HR to track compliance with certification standards and form a new database to assist in HR planning. Roberts was opposed to the changes from the beginning. In his mind, the scheduling software was a valuable tool for his shift managers. Adding all the information and variables that Smith wanted would make the program needlessly complicated and take valuable time away from his shift supervisors.

James listened to this argument as it bounced back and forth between line management and HR. She was torn because her experience in production had taught her that HR requests usually meant more work on tasks that did not help them meet their production goals. She also felt that using the scheduling software for HR tracking data would make the program into something different than she had designed. When Smith asked her to come up with a set of estimates on the feasibility of making his requested changes to the scheduling software, she knew that she would have to figure out a way to balance these competing needs.

Questions

1. If you were the head of the procurement division, how would you resolve this conflict between Smith and Roberts? How would you better integrate HR into the larger processes of the organization?
2. Should James agree to the changes in the scheduling software that Smith requested?
3. How can HR departments meet their own needs for IT expertise, especially in a competitive marketplace?

14. THREE STRIKES AND YOU'RE OUT!

In the thirteen years that Maria Hernandez has worked for the county, she has worked her way up from an entry-level secretary in the Flood Control

Division to an administrative assistant in the Streets Division of the Public Works Department. Maria has received average to above-average performance evaluations during her time in the Flood Control Division and was transferred to Streets about two years ago. She has worked for four different supervisors during the past two years, taking a transfer to the West Section about six months ago under Larry Jorgensen, a manager with a reputation for being able to "get rid of dead wood."

When Maria transferred into the section, she had used up all of her sick leave following an extended illness. Since coming into the section, she has taken vacation and sick leave every time she becomes eligible, often absent on a Monday or Friday. She took off three weeks recently under the Family Medical Leave Act but says she can no longer afford the time off without pay. About three months ago, Maria informed Jorgensen that she was pregnant, and it was then that he began documenting the number of times she was taking off work and the inordinate amount of time she was on the telephone on personal business. He asked Maria for verification of her condition, and she became agitated and stormed out of the office. The next day she produced a prescription bottle for sedatives. Two weeks ago, Jorgensen filled out an annual performance evaluation on Hernandez, giving her an unsatisfactory rating and placing her on probation.

Maria Hernandez has appealed the evaluation and demanded that her union represent her on three claims: (1) racial discrimination, because she was born in Nicaragua; (2) unfair treatment because she has never received an unsatisfactory rating before in her thirteen years with the county; and (3) discrimination based on a disability because she is "obviously" pregnant, demanding that the county accommodate her disability.

The hearing is set for today. Present at the hearing will be the union team (including Maria Hernandez), the management team (including Larry Jorgensen), and a panel of three arbitrators (one selected by the union, one by management, and one by the two selected arbitrators), who will hear and decide on the case.

The union team will go first, followed by the management team. Both sides will present their arguments, produce and cross-examine witnesses, and conclude.

Set out the arguments of the management team to be used by the city's representative to the arbitration. Feel free to be creative and innovative, but you must stay within the facts presented here. The arbitrators will render a decision.

Index

Credits

Chapter 2: Reading 1: Reprinted with permission of *Public Personnel Management,* published by the International Personnel Management Association (IPMA), Alexandria, VA, 703-549-7100, www.ipma-hr.org.

Chapter 3: Reading: From Paul P. Van Riper, Ch. 5 in *History of the United States Civil Service.* Copyright © 1958 by Harper & Row, Inc.; Freyss's three distinct cultural systems: From Siegrun Fox Freyss, "Municipal Government Personnel Systems: A Test of Two Archetypical Models," *Review of Public Personnel Administration 15,* Fall 1995, pp. 69–93. Reprinted by permission of the publisher, Institute of Public Affairs, University of South Carolina.

Chapter 4: Box 4.4: From Anthony R. Pratkanis and Marlene E. Turner, "The Proactive Removal of Discriminatory Barriers: Affirmative Action as Effective Help," *Journal of Social Issues, 52,* no. 4, p. 113. Copyright © 1996 by Plenum Publishing Company. Reprinted by permission of Plenum Publishing Company.; Box 4.5: From Scott Plous, "Ten Myths About Affirmative Action," *Journal of Social Issues, 52,* no. 4, 1996, pp. 25–31. Copyright © 1996 The Society for the Psychological Study of Social Issues. Reprinted by permission of Blackwell Publishers, Journals Department, UK.; Reading: David H. Rosenbloom, "What Every Public Personnel Manager Should Know About the Constitution," *Public Personnel Administration: Problems and Prospects,* 4/e, pp. 39–55. Copyright © 1990. Reprinted by permission of the author.

Chapter 7: Figure 7.5: From Ernest McCormick, Paul Jeannerer, and Robert C. Meeham, "AQ Study of Job Characteristics and Job Dimensions as Based on the Position Analysis Questionnaire (PAQ)," *Journal of Applied Psychology 56,* no. 4, 1972, p. 249. Copyright © 1972 by the American Psychological Association. Reprinted with permission.

Chapter 9: Reading: Reprinted with permission of *Public Personnel Management,* published by the International Personnel Management Association (IPMA), Alexandria, VA, (703) 549-7100, www.ipma-hr.org.

Chapter 12: Table 12.2: From "A Hierarchy of Management Training Requirements: The Competency Domain Model," by Paul Sandwith, *Public Personnel Management 22,* no. 1, 1993, pp. 52–55. Reprinted with permission of Public Personnel Management Association (IPMA), 1617 Duke St., Alexandria, VA 22314, 703-549-7100, www.ipma-hr.org.

Chapter 13: Reading: "Discipline and Deselection in the TQM Environment," by Edward Seidler, *Public Personnel Management* 25:4, 1996, pp. 529–537. Reprinted with permission of Public Personnel Management, published by the International Personnel Management Association (IPMA), 1617 Duke St., Alexandria, VA 22314, 703-549-7100, www.ipma-hr.org.; Box 13.2: Slightly revised from Steven E. Aufrecht, "Toward a Model for Determining Appropriate Corrective Action in Public Employee Discipline," *Journal of Collective Negotiations,* 25:3, p. 192. Copyright © 1996. Reprinted by permission of Baywood Publishing Company, Inc.

Chapter 14: Box 14.2: Drawn from Richard Rudolph, "Public Officials Liability," CPCU Journal 51, no. 3, Fall 1998, p. 166 by permission of CPCU Society.; Figure 14.4: Drawn from Richard Rudolph, "Public Officials Liability," CPCU Journal 51, no. 3, Fall 1998, p. 167 by permission of CPCU Society,; Reading: Richard J. Zeckhauser and W. Kip Viscusi, *Annals of the American Academy of Political & Social Science,* May 1996, Vol. 545, p. 144, copyright © 1996 by Sage Publications, Inc. Reprinted by permission of Sage Publications, Inc.

Chapter 15: Box 15.1: From *New Times, New Competencies, New Professionals: A Guide for Implementing a Competency Model for HR Professionals: A Strategy for Becoming a High Performance Organization.* Copyright © 1997. Reprinted by permission of National Academy of Public Administration.